Business Law Today

Text & Summarized Cases, Volume 2

Eleventh Edition

Roger LeRoy Miller

CENGAGE
Learning

Australia • Brazil • Japan • Korea • Mexico • Singapore • Spain • United Kingdom • United States

Business Law Today: Volume 2, Eleventh Edition

Business Law Today, Standard: Text & Summarized Cases, 11th Edition
Roger LeRoy Miller

© 2017, 2014, 2011, 2008 Cengage Learning. All rights reserved.

This book contains select works from existing Cengage Learning resources and was produced by Cengage Learning Custom Solutions for collegiate use. As such, those adopting and/or contributing to this work are responsible for editorial content accuracy, continuity and completeness.

Compilation © 2016 Cengage Learning

ISBN: 978-1-337-03541-5

Cengage Learning
20 Channel Center Street
Boston, MA 02210
USA

Cengage Learning is a leading provider of customized learning solutions with office locations around the globe, including Singapore, the United Kingdom, Australia, Mexico, Brazil, and Japan. Locate your local office at:
www.international.cengage.com/region.

Cengage Learning products are represented in Canada by Nelson Education, Ltd.

For your lifelong learning solutions, visit **www.cengage.com/custom.**

Visit our corporate website at **www.cengage.com.**

Printed at CLDPC, USA, 07-18

LANDMARK IN THE LAW

The Uniform Commercial Code

Of all the attempts to produce a uniform body of laws relating to commercial transactions in the United States, none has been as successful or comprehensive as the Uniform Commercial Code (UCC).

THE ORIGINS OF THE UCC The UCC was the brainchild of William A. Schnader, president of the National Conference of Commissioners on Uniform State Laws (NCCUSL). The drafting of the UCC began in 1945. The most significant individual involved in the project was its chief editor, Karl N. Llewellyn of the Columbia University Law School. Llewellyn's intellect, continuous efforts, and ability to compromise made the first version of the UCC—completed in 1949—a legal landmark. Over the next several years, the UCC was substantially accepted by almost every state in the nation.

COMPREHENSIVE COVERAGE The UCC attempts to provide a consistent, integrated framework of rules to deal with all phases ordinarily arising in a commercial sales or lease transaction. For example, consider the following events, all of which may occur during a single transaction:

1. *A contract for the sale or lease of goods is formed and executed.* Article 2 and Article 2A of the UCC provide rules governing all aspects of this transaction.

2. *The transaction may involve a payment—by check, electronic fund transfer, or other means.* Article 3 (on negotiable instruments), Article 4 (on bank deposits and collections), Article 4A (on fund transfers), and Article 5 (on letters of credit) cover this part of the transaction.

3. *The transaction may involve a bill of lading or a warehouse receipt that covers goods when they are shipped or stored.* Article 7 (on documents of title) deals with this subject.

4. *The transaction may involve a demand by the seller or lender for some form of security for the remaining balance owed.* Article 9 (on secured transactions) covers this part of the transaction.

PERIODIC CHANGES AND UPDATES Various articles and sections of the UCC are periodically changed or supplemented to clarify certain rules or to establish new rules when changes in business customs render the existing UCC provisions inapplicable.

For instance, when leases of goods in the commercial context became important, Article 2A governing leases was added to the UCC. To clarify the rights of parties to commercial fund transfers, particularly electronic fund transfers, Article 4A was issued. Articles 3 and 4, on negotiable instruments and banking relationships, have undergone significant revisions. Because of other changes in business and in the law, the NCCUSL recommended the repeal of Article 6 (on bulk transfers) and offered a revised Article 6 to those states that preferred not to repeal it. The NCCUSL also substantially revised Article 9 on secured transactions, and the revised Article 9 has been adopted by all of the states.

APPLICATION TO TODAY'S WORLD *By periodically revising the UCC's articles, the NCCUSL has been able to adapt its provisions to changing business customs and practices. UCC provisions governing sales and lease contracts have also been extended to contracts formed in the online environment.*

17-1 The Scope of Articles 2 and 2A

Article 2 of the UCC sets forth the requirements for *sales contracts,* as well as the duties and obligations of the parties involved in the sales contract. Article 2A covers similar issues for *lease contracts.* Bear in mind, however, that the parties to sales or lease contracts are free to agree to terms different from those stated in the UCC.

17-1a Article 2—Sales

Article 2 of the UCC governs **sales contracts,** or contracts for the sale of goods. To facilitate commercial transactions, Article 2 modifies some of the common law contract requirements that were discussed in previous chapters.

To the extent that it has not been modified by the UCC, however, the common law of contracts also applies to sales contracts. In other words, the common law requirements for a valid contract—agreement, consideration, capacity, and legality—are also applicable to sales contracts.

In general, the rule is that when a UCC provision addresses a certain issue, the UCC governs, but when the UCC is silent, the common law governs. The relationship between general contract law and the law governing sales of goods is illustrated in Exhibit 17–1.

Sales Contract A contract for the sale of goods.

Exhibit 17–1 The Law Governing Contracts

This exhibit graphically illustrates the relationship between general contract law and statutory law (UCC Articles 2 and 2A) governing contracts for the sale and lease of goods. Sales contracts are not governed exclusively by Article 2 of the UCC but are also governed by general contract law whenever it is relevant and has not been modified by the UCC.

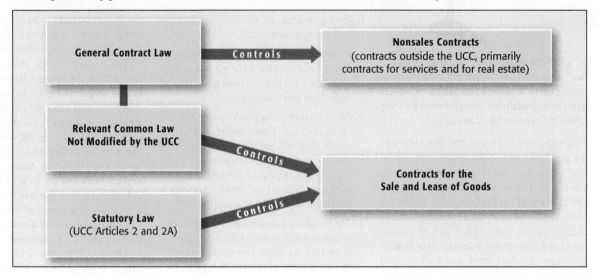

In regard to Article 2, keep two points in mind.

1. Article 2 deals with the sale of *goods*. It does not deal with real property (real estate), services, or intangible property such as stocks and bonds. Thus, if the subject matter of a dispute is goods, the UCC governs. If it is real estate or services, the common law applies.

2. In some situations, the rules can vary depending on whether the buyer or the seller is a *merchant*.

Sale The passing of title to property from the seller to the buyer for a price.

What Is a Sale?   The UCC defines a **sale** as "the passing of title [evidence of ownership rights] from the seller to the buyer for a price" [UCC 2–106(1)]. The price may be payable in cash (or its equivalent) or in other goods or services. (For a discussion of whether states can impose taxes on online sales, see this chapter's *Adapting the Law to the Online Environment* feature.)

In the following case, the court was asked to determine who owned the "personal property" damaged in a fire. How did the UCC's definition of a sale affect the answer to that question?

CASE 17.1

Nautilus Insurance Co. v. Cheran Investments LLC

Court of Appeals of Nebraska, 2014 WL 292809 (2014).

FACTS Under a contract with Cheran Investments, LLC, Blasini, Inc., agreed to buy the business assets of the Attic Bar & Grill in Omaha, Nebraska. The contract required Blasini to make a down payment and monthly payments until the price was fully paid. Blasini obtained insurance on the property from Nautilus Insurance Co. Less than three years later, a fire damaged the "personal property" (the business assets, such as furniture and equipment) in the Attic. Because

Who carries the risk of loss and personal property at a bar?

the purchase price had not yet been fully paid, Nautilus filed an action in a Nebraska state court against several defendants, including Cheran, to determine who was entitled to the insurance proceeds for the damage. The court concluded that Blasini had "failed to consummate the purchase agreement" and declared Cheran the owner of the personal property. Blasini appealed, arguing that title to the Attic's assets had passed at the time of the sale.

ISSUE Did the sale of the Attic's assets pass title to those goods to Blasini?

DECISION Yes. A state intermediate appellate court reversed the lower court's ruling. When the contract for the sale of the Attic's assets was formed, title to the assets passed to Blasini, which became the owner. The appellate court remanded the case to the lower court, however, to determine whether Blasini had breached the contract.

REASON The sale of the personal property in the Attic involved "goods," and thus the agreement for their sale was subject to the UCC. All of the items designated in the agreement were movable, and no real estate, intellectual property, or goodwill was transferred under the agreement. Blasini entered into a contract to buy the assets of the bar and grill and agreed to assume its operation. Under UCC 2–401, title to the goods passed to Blasini at the time the agreement was made. No physical delivery was necessary because Blasini was to assume the operation of the Attic, which is where the goods were located. "Therefore, irrespective of whether Blasini paid the purchase price . . . , Blasini became the owner of the property in the purchase agreement."

WHAT IF THE FACTS WERE DIFFERENT? *Suppose that Blasini had made no payments under the contract for the sale of the Attic's assets. How should that circumstance affect the distribution of the insurance proceeds?*

What Are Goods?

To be characterized as a *good,* the item of property must be *tangible,* and it must be *movable.* **Tangible property** has physical existence—it can be touched or seen. **Intangible property**—such as corporate stocks and bonds, patents and copyrights, and ordinary contract rights—has only conceptual existence and thus does not come under Article 2. A *movable* item can be carried from place to place.

Goods Associated with Real Estate.

Because real estate cannot be carried from place to place, it is excluded from Article 2. Goods *associated* with real estate often fall within the scope of Article 2, however [UCC 2–107]. For instance, a contract for the sale of minerals, oil, or natural gas is a contract for the sale of goods if *severance, or separation, is to be made by the seller.* In contrast, a contract for the sale of growing crops or timber to be cut is a contract for the sale of goods *regardless of who severs them from the land.*

Goods and Services Combined.

When contracts involve a combination of goods and services, courts generally use the **predominant-factor test** to determine whether a contract is primarily for the sale of goods or for the sale of services. If a court decides that a mixed contract is primarily a goods contract, *any* dispute, even a dispute over the services portion, will be decided under the UCC.

CASE EXAMPLE 17.1 Gene and Martha Jannusch agreed to sell Festival Foods, a concessions business, to Lindsey and Louann Naffziger for a price of $150,000. The deal included a truck, a trailer, freezers, roasters, chairs, tables, a fountain service, signs, and lighting. The Naffzigers paid $10,000 down with the balance to come from a bank loan. They took possession of the equipment and began to use it immediately in Festival Foods operations at various events.

After six events, the Naffzigers returned the truck and all the equipment and wanted out of the deal because the business did not generate as much income as they expected. The Jannusches sued the Naffzigers for the balance due on the purchase price, claiming that the Naffzigers could no longer reject the goods under the UCC. The Naffzigers claimed that the UCC did not apply because the deal primarily involved the sale of a business rather than the sale of goods.

The court found that the UCC governed under the predominant-factor test. The primary value of the contract was in the goods, not the value of the business. The parties had agreed on the essential terms of the contract (such as the price). Thus, a contract had been formed, and the Naffzigers had breached it. The Naffzigers had taken possession of the business and had no right to return it.[2] ▪

Tangible Property Property that has physical existence and can be distinguished by the senses of touch and sight.

Intangible Property Property that cannot be seen or touched but exists only conceptually, such as corporate stocks. Such property is not governed by Article 2 of the UCC.

LEARNING OBJECTIVE 1
If a contract involves both goods and services, does the UCC apply?

Predominant-Factor Test A test courts use to determine whether a contract is primarily for the sale of goods or for the sale of services.

If a couple buys a concessions business that includes a truck, trailer, and tables and chairs, would this purchase be a sale of goods or services?

---

2. *Jannusch v. Naffziger,* 379 Ill.App.3d 381, 883 N.E.2d 711 (2008).

ADAPTING THE LAW TO THE **ONLINE** ENVIRONMENT
Taxing Web Purchases

In 1992, the United States Supreme Court ruled that an individual state cannot compel an out-of-state business that lacks a substantial physical presence within that state to collect and remit state taxes.[a] Although Congress has the power to pass legislation requiring out-of-state corporations to collect and remit state sales taxes, it has not yet done so. Thus, only online retailers that also have a physical presence within a state must collect state taxes on any Web sales made to residents of that state. (State residents are supposed to self-report their purchases and pay use taxes to the state, which they rarely do.)

Redefining Physical Presence
Several states have found a way to collect taxes on Internet sales made to state residents by out-of-state corporations. These states have simply redefined *physical presence*. In 2008, New York changed its tax laws in this manner. Now, an online retailer that pays any party within New York to solicit business for its products is considered to have a physical presence in the state and must collect state taxes. Since then, at least seventeen other states have made similar changes in an effort to increase their revenues by collecting sales tax from online retailers.

These new laws are often called "Amazon tax" laws because they are aimed largely at Amazon.com. Nevertheless, they affect all online sellers, especially those that pay affiliates to direct traffic to their Web sites. The laws allow states to tax online commerce even though, to date, Congress has explicitly chosen not to tax Internet sales.

Local Governments Sue Online Travel Companies
Travelocity, Priceline.com, Hotels.com, and Orbitz.com are online travel companies (OTCs) that offer, among other things, hotel booking services. By 2016, more than twenty-five cities, including Atlanta, Charleston, Philadelphia, and San Antonio, had filed suits claiming that the OTCs owed taxes on hotel reservations that they had booked. All of the cities involved in the suits impose a hotel occupancy tax, which is essentially a sales tax.

Initially, some cities won their cases, but more recently, cities have been losing in court.[b] As of 2016, the OTCs had prevailed in eighteen of twenty-five cases nationwide. An exception is a 2014 case in Wyoming in which the state supreme court held that Travelocity, Priceline, Hotwire, Expedia, and Trip Network had to collect and remit sales tax.[c]

The Market Place Fairness Act
By the time you read this, online sales taxes may have become a reality for every online business that has annual revenues of more than $1 million. For several years now, legislation called the Market Place Fairness Act has been under consideration in the U.S. Senate. The act, if passed, would allow states to collect sales taxes from online retailers for in-state transactions.

A significant problem with such legislation is the complexity of collecting taxes for multiple jurisdictions. The current tax system involves 9,600 taxing jurisdictions. Even one zip code may cover multiple taxing entities, such as different cities and counties. Consider that the Dallas–Fort Worth airport includes six separate taxing jurisdictions. Current software enables retailers to collect and remit sales taxes for different jurisdictions, but the software is extremely costly to install and operate. Overstock.com, for example, spent $1.3 million to add just one state to its sales tax collection system.

CRITICAL THINKING

- Some argue that if online retailers are required to collect and pay sales taxes in jurisdictions in which they have no physical presence, they have no democratic way to fight high taxes in those places. Is this an instance of taxation without representation? Discuss.

a. *Quill Corp. v. North Dakota,* 504 U.S. 298, 112 S.Ct. 1904, 119 L.Ed.2d 91 (1992).

b. *Travelscape, LLC v. South Carolina Department of Revenue,* 391 S.C. 89, 705 S.E.2d 28 (2011).

c. *Travelocity.com, LP v. Wyoming Dept. of Revenue,* 329 P.3d 131 (2014).

Who Is a Merchant?   Article 2 governs the sale of goods in general. It applies to sales transactions between all buyers and sellers. In a limited number of instances, though, the UCC presumes that certain special business standards ought to be imposed because of merchants' relatively high degree of commercial expertise.[3] Such standards do not apply to the casual or inexperienced seller or buyer (consumer).

3. The provisions that apply only to merchants deal principally with the Statute of Frauds, firm offers, confirmatory memoranda, warranties, and contract modifications. These special rules reflect expedient business practices commonly known to merchants in the commercial setting. They will be discussed later in this chapter.

Section 2–104 sets out three ways in which merchant status can arise:

1. A merchant is a person who *deals in goods of the kind* involved in the sales contract. Thus, a retailer, a wholesaler, or a manufacturer is a merchant of those goods sold in the business. A merchant for one type of goods is not necessarily a merchant for another type. For instance, a sporting equipment retailer is a merchant when selling tennis rackets but not when selling a used iPad.

2. A merchant is a person who, by occupation, *holds himself or herself out as having special knowledge and skill* related to the practices or goods involved in the transaction. This broad definition may include banks or universities as merchants.

3. A person who *employs a merchant as a broker, agent, or other intermediary* has the status of merchant in that transaction. Hence, if an art collector hires a broker to purchase or sell art for her, the collector is considered a merchant in the transaction.

In summary, a person is a **merchant** when she or he, acting in a mercantile (commercial) capacity, possesses or uses an expertise specifically related to the goods being sold. This basic distinction is not always clear-cut. For instance, state courts appear to be split on whether farmers should be considered merchants.

Should merchants be allowed to use buying patterns to learn personal information about their customers? Whether you shop on the Internet or in stores, most major retailers compile information about you based on what, when, and how you buy. Sometimes, based on your purchases, you will instantly be given printed coupons at the cash register. These customized coupons reflect your preferences based on past behavior. If you regularly use Amazon .com, for instance, you receive customized offers every time you visit that site.

Target Brands, Inc., uses a very sophisticated data collection process that assigns each shopper a unique guest identification code. Over time, a shopper's habits become the source of predictions for future consumer behavior. For example, Target can accurately predict which female shoppers are pregnant based on their recent purchases of vitamin and mineral supplements. When Target's system detects a buying pattern suggesting that a customer is pregnant, it starts offering coupons for baby-related products and services.

A father in Minneapolis, Minnesota, complained to a Target manager that his daughter was receiving such coupons for no reason. In reality, Target's system had accurately discovered his daughter's pregnancy. The father was even more furious when he learned that his daughter had lied to him. Was Target's action legal? Probably, it was. Target had complied with the relevant federal and state privacy laws. Current laws even allow retailers to share their customer data with affiliate companies.

17-1b Article 2A—Leases

Leases of personal property (goods such as automobiles and industrial equipment) have become increasingly common. In this context, a **lease** is a transfer of the right to possess and use goods for a period of time in exchange for payment. Article 2A of the UCC was created to fill the need for uniform guidelines in this area.

Article 2A covers any transaction that creates a lease of goods, as well as subleases of goods [UCC 2A–102, 2A–103(1)(k)]. Article 2A is essentially a repetition of Article 2, except that it applies to leases of goods rather than sales of goods and thus varies to reflect differences between sales and lease transactions. (Note that Article 2A does not apply to leases of real property, such as land or buildings.)

Definition of a Lease Agreement
Article 2A defines a **lease agreement** as the bargain between a lessor and a lessee with respect to the lease of goods, as found in their language and

Merchant Under the UCC, a person who deals in goods of the kind involved in the sales contract or who holds herself or himself out as having skill or knowledge peculiar to the practices or goods being purchased or sold.

ETHICAL ISSUE

Is it ethical for Target Brands to data mine information about what its customers have purchased?

Lease Under Article 2A of the UCC, a transfer of the right to possess and use goods for a period of time in exchange for payment.

Lease Agreement An agreement in which one person (the lessor) agrees to transfer the right to the possession and use of property to another person (the lessee) in exchange for rental payments.

Lessor A person who transfers the right to the possession and use of goods to another in exchange for rental payments.

Lessee A person who acquires the right to the possession and use of another's goods in exchange for rental payments.

as implied by other circumstances, including course of dealing and usage of trade or course of performance [UCC 2A–103(1)(k)]. A **lessor** is one who transfers the right to the possession and use of goods under a lease [UCC 2A–103(1)(p)]. A **lessee** is one who acquires the right to the temporary possession and use of goods under a lease [UCC 2A–103(1)(o)]. In other words, the lessee is the party who is leasing the goods from the lessor.

Article 2A applies to all types of leases of goods, including commercial leases and consumer leases. Special rules apply to certain types of leases, however, including consumer leases.

Consumer Leases   Under UCC 2A–103(1)(e), a *consumer lease* involves three elements:

1. A lessor who regularly engages in the business of leasing or selling.
2. A lessee (except an organization) who leases the goods "primarily for a personal, family, or household purpose."
3. Total lease payments that are less than a dollar amount set by state statute.

To ensure special protection for consumers, certain provisions of Article 2A apply only to consumer leases. For instance, one provision states that a consumer may recover attorneys' fees if a court finds that a term in a consumer lease contract is unconscionable [UCC 2A–108(4)(a)].

17-2 The Formation of Sales and Lease Contracts

As mentioned, Article 2 and Article 2A of the UCC modify common law contract rules in several ways. Remember, though, that parties to sales contracts are normally free to establish whatever terms they wish. The UCC comes into play only when the parties have failed to provide in their contract for a contingency that later gives rise to a dispute. The UCC makes this clear time and again by using such phrases as "unless the parties otherwise agree" or "absent a contrary agreement by the parties."

17-2a Offer

In general contract law, the moment a definite offer is met by an unqualified acceptance, a binding contract is formed. In commercial sales transactions, the verbal exchanges, correspondence, and actions of the parties may not reveal exactly when a binding contractual obligation arises. The UCC states that an agreement sufficient to constitute a contract can exist even if the moment of its making is undetermined [UCC 2–204(2), 2A–204(2)].

Open Terms   Remember that under the common law of contracts, an offer must be definite enough for the parties (and the courts) to ascertain its essential terms when it is accepted. In contrast, the UCC states that a sales or lease contract will not fail for indefiniteness even if one or more terms are left open as long as *both* of the following are true:

1. The parties intended to make a contract.
2. There is a reasonably certain basis for the court to grant an appropriate remedy [UCC 2–204(3), 2A–204(3)].

The UCC provides numerous *open-term* provisions (discussed next) that can be used to fill the gaps in a contract. Thus, if a dispute occurs, all that is necessary to prove the existence of a contract is an indication (such as a purchase order) that there is a contract. Missing terms can be proved by evidence, or a court can presume that the parties intended whatever is reasonable under the circumstances.

Keep in mind, though, that if too many terms are left open, a court may find that the parties did not intend to form a contract. In addition, the *quantity* of goods involved must be

KNOW THIS
Under the UCC, it is the actions of the parties that determine whether they intended to form a contract.

expressly stated in the contract. If the quantity term is left open, the courts will have no basis for determining a remedy.

Open Price Term. If the parties have not agreed on a price, the court will determine a "reasonable price at the time for delivery" [UCC 2–305(1)]. If either the buyer or the seller is to determine the price, the price is to be fixed (set) in good faith [UCC 2–305(2)]. Under the UCC, *good faith* means honesty in fact and the observance of reasonable commercial standards of fair dealing in the trade [UCC 2–103(1)(b)]. The concepts of *good faith* and *commercial reasonableness* permeate the UCC.

Sometimes, the price fails to be fixed through the fault of one of the parties. In that situation, the other party can treat the contract as canceled or fix a reasonable price. **EXAMPLE 17.2** Perez and Merrick enter into a contract for the sale of unfinished doors and agree that Perez will determine the price. Perez refuses to specify the price. Merrick can either treat the contract as canceled or set a reasonable price [UCC 2–305(3)]. ■

Open Payment Term. When parties do not specify payment terms, payment is due at the time and place at which the buyer is to receive the goods [UCC 2–310(a)]. The buyer can tender payment using any commercially normal or acceptable means, such as a check or credit card. If the seller demands payment in cash, the buyer must be given a reasonable time to obtain it [UCC 2–511(2)].

EXAMPLE 17.3 Max Angel agrees to purchase hay from Wagner's farm. Angel leaves his truck and trailer at the farm for the seller to load the hay. Nothing is said about when payment is due, and the parties are unaware of the UCC's rules. Nevertheless, because the parties did not specify when payment was due, UCC 2–310(a) controls, and payment is due at the time Angel picks up the hay. Therefore, Wagner can refuse to release the hay (or the vehicles on which the hay is loaded) to Angel until he pays for it. ■

Open Delivery Term. When no delivery terms are specified, the buyer normally takes delivery at the seller's place of business [UCC 2–308(a)]. If the seller has no place of business, the seller's residence is used. When goods are located in some other place and both parties know it, delivery is made there. If the time for shipment or delivery is not clearly specified in the sales contract, the court will infer a "reasonable" time for performance [UCC 2–309(1)].

Duration of an Ongoing Contract. A single contract might specify successive performances but not indicate how long the parties are required to deal with each other. In this situation, either party may terminate the ongoing contractual relationship. Principles of good faith and sound commercial practice call for reasonable notification before termination, however, to give the other party time to make substitute arrangements [UCC 2–309(2), (3)].

Options and Cooperation Regarding Performance. When the contract contemplates shipment of the goods but does not specify the shipping arrangements, the *seller* has the right to make these arrangements in good faith, using commercial reasonableness in the situation [UCC 2–311].

When a sales contract omits terms relating to the assortment of goods, the *buyer* can specify the assortment. **EXAMPLE 17.4** Petry Drugs, Inc., enters an e-contract to purchase one thousand toothbrushes from Marconi's Dental Supply. The toothbrushes come in a variety of colors, but the contract does not specify color. Petry, the buyer, has the right to take six hundred blue toothbrushes and four hundred green ones if it wishes. Petry, however, must exercise good faith and commercial reasonableness in making its selection [UCC 2–311]. ■

Open Quantity Terms. Normally, if the parties do not specify a quantity, there is no contract, because a court will have no basis for determining a remedy.

KNOW THIS
The common law requires that the parties make their terms definite before they have a contract. The UCC applies general commercial standards to make the terms of a contract definite.

"Business, more than any other occupation, is a continual dealing with the future. It is a continual calculation, an instinctive exercise in foresight."

HENRY R. LUCE
1898–1967
(U.S. EDITOR AND PUBLISHER)

If no time for payment for hay is specified in a sales contract, when is payment due?

There is almost no way for a court to determine objectively what is a reasonable quantity of goods for someone to buy (whereas a court can objectively determine a reasonable price for particular goods by looking at the market). Nevertheless, the UCC recognizes two exceptions involving *requirements* and *output contracts* [UCC 2–306(1)].

Requirements Contract
An agreement in which a buyer agrees to purchase and the seller agrees to sell all or up to a stated amount of what the buyer needs or requires.

1. *Requirements Contracts.* In a **requirements contract,** the buyer agrees to purchase and the seller agrees to sell all or up to a stated amount of what the buyer *needs* or *requires.* **EXAMPLE 17.5** Umpqua Cannery forms a contract with Al Garcia. The cannery agrees to purchase from Garcia, and Garcia agrees to sell to the cannery, all of the green beans that the cannery needs or requires during the following summer. There is implicit consideration in this contract because the buyer (the cannery) gives up the right to buy goods (green beans) from any other seller. This forfeited right creates a legal *detriment*—that is, consideration. ■

   Requirements contracts are common in the business world and normally are enforceable. In contrast, if the buyer promises to purchase only if the buyer *wishes* to do so, or if the buyer reserves the right to buy the goods from someone other than the seller, the promise is illusory (without consideration) and unenforceable by either party.

Output Contract An agreement in which a seller agrees to sell and a buyer agrees to buy all or up to a stated amount of what the seller produces.

2. *Output Contracts.* In an **output contract,** the seller agrees to sell and the buyer agrees to buy all or up to a stated amount of what the seller *produces.* **EXAMPLE 17.6** Ruth Sewell has planted two acres of organic tomatoes. Bella Union, a local restaurant, agrees to buy all of the tomatoes that Sewell produces that year to use at the restaurant. ■ Again, because the seller essentially forfeits the right to sell goods to another buyer, there is implicit consideration in an output contract.

The UCC imposes a *good faith limitation* on requirements and output contracts. The quantity under such contracts is the amount of requirements or the amount of output that occurs during a *normal* production year. The actual quantity purchased or sold cannot be unreasonably disproportionate to normal or comparable prior requirements or output [UCC 2–306(1)].

PREVENTING LEGAL DISPUTES

If a business owner leaves certain terms of a sales or lease contract open, the UCC allows a court to supply the missing terms. Although this rule can sometimes be advantageous (to establish that a contract existed, for instance), it can also be a major disadvantage. If a party fails to state a price in the contract offer, for example, a court will impose a reasonable price by looking at the market price of similar goods *at the time of delivery.* Thus, instead of receiving the usual price for the goods, a business will receive what a court considers a reasonable price when the goods are delivered. Therefore, when drafting contracts for the sale or lease of goods, make sure that the contract clearly states any terms that are essential to the bargain, particularly the price. It is generally better to establish the terms of a contract than to leave it up to a court to determine what terms are reasonable after a dispute has arisen.

Merchant's Firm Offer Under regular contract principles, an offer can be revoked at any time before acceptance. The major common law exception is an *option contract,* in which the offeree pays consideration for the offeror's irrevocable promise to keep the offer open for a stated period. The UCC creates a second exception for firm offers made by a merchant to sell, buy, or lease goods.

Firm Offer An offer (by a merchant) that is irrevocable without the necessity of consideration for a stated period of time or, if no definite period is stated, for a reasonable time (neither period to exceed three months).

A **firm offer** arises when a merchant-offeror gives *assurances* in a *signed writing* that the offer will remain open. The offer must be both *written* and *signed* by the offeror.[4] A merchant's firm offer is irrevocable without the necessity of consideration[5] for the stated period or, if no

---

4. *Signed* includes any symbol executed or adopted by a party with a present intention to authenticate a writing [UCC 1–201(39)]. A complete signature is not required. Therefore, initials, a thumbprint, a trade name, or any mark used in lieu of a written signature will suffice, regardless of its location on the document.
5. If the offeree pays consideration, then an option contract (not a merchant's firm offer) is formed.

definite period is stated, a reasonable period (neither period to exceed three months) [UCC 2–205, 2A–205].

EXAMPLE 17.7 Osaka, a used-car dealer, e-mails Saucedo on January 1 stating, "I have a used 2016 Toyota RAV4 on the lot that I'll sell you for $26,000 any time between now and January 31." This e-mail creates a firm offer, and Osaka will be liable for breach if he sells that Toyota RAV4 to someone other than Saucedo before January 31. ■

17–2b Acceptance

Acceptance of an offer to buy, sell, or lease goods generally may be made in any reasonable manner and by any reasonable means. The UCC permits acceptance of an offer to buy goods "either by a prompt *promise* to ship or by the prompt or current shipment of conforming or nonconforming goods" [UCC 2–206(1)(b)]. *Conforming goods* accord with the contract's terms, whereas *nonconforming goods* do not.

Shipment of Nonconforming Goods The prompt shipment of nonconforming goods constitutes both an acceptance, which creates a contract, and a breach of that contract. This rule does not apply if the seller **seasonably** (within a reasonable amount of time) notifies the buyer that the nonconforming shipment is offered only as an *accommodation,* or a favor. The notice of accommodation must clearly indicate to the buyer that the shipment does not constitute an acceptance and that, therefore, no contract has been formed.

EXAMPLE 17.8 McFarrell Pharmacy orders five cases of Johnson & Johnson 3-by-5-inch gauze pads from H.T. Medical Supply, Inc. If H.T. ships five cases of Xeroform 3-by-5-inch gauze pads instead, the shipment acts as both an acceptance of McFarrell's offer and a *breach* of the resulting contract. McFarrell may sue H.T. for any appropriate damages.

If, however, H.T. notifies McFarrell that the Xeroform gauze pads are being shipped *as an accommodation*—because H.T. has only Xeroform pads in stock—the shipment will constitute a counteroffer, not an acceptance. A contract will be formed only if McFarrell accepts the Xeroform gauze pads. ■

Communication of Acceptance Required Under the common law, because a unilateral offer invites acceptance by performance, the offeree need not notify the offeror of performance unless the offeror would not otherwise know about it. In other words, a unilateral offer can be accepted by beginning performance.

The UCC is more stringent than the common law in this regard because it requires notification. Under the UCC, if the offeror is not notified within a reasonable time that the offeree has accepted the contract by beginning performance, then the offeror can treat the offer as having lapsed before acceptance [UCC 2–206(2), 2A–206(2)].

Additional Terms Recall that under the common law, the *mirror image rule* requires that the terms of the acceptance exactly match those of the offer. **EXAMPLE 17.9** Aldrich e-mails an offer to sell twenty Samsung Galaxy Tab S 8.4 tablets to Beale. If Beale accepts the offer but changes it to require Tab S 10.5 tablets, then there is no contract. ■

To avoid these problems, the UCC dispenses with the mirror image rule. Under the UCC, a contract is formed if the offeree's response indicates a *definite* acceptance of the offer, *even if the acceptance includes terms additional to or different from those contained in the offer* [UCC 2–207(1)]. Whether the additional terms become part of the contract depends, in part, on whether the parties are nonmerchants or merchants.

Rules When One Party or Both Parties Are Nonmerchants. If one (or both) of the parties is a *nonmerchant,* the contract is formed according to the terms of the original offer submitted by the original offeror and not according to the additional terms of the acceptance [UCC 2–207(2)].

KNOW THIS
The UCC provides that acceptance can be made by any means that is reasonable under the circumstances—including prompt shipment of the goods.

Seasonably Within a specified time period or, if no period is specified, within a reasonable time.

If a pharmacy orders 3" x 5" gauze pads, but is shipped 2" x 2" pads, is this an acceptance of the pharmacy's order?

LEARNING OBJECTIVE 2

In a sales contract, if an offeree includes additional or different terms in an acceptance, will a contract result? If so, what happens to these terms?

CASE EXAMPLE 17.10 OfficeSupplyStore.com sells office supplies on the Web. Employees of the Kansas City School District in Missouri ordered $17,642.54 worth of office supplies—without the authority or approval of their employer—from the Web site. The invoices accompanying the goods contained a forum-selection clause that required all disputes to be resolved in California.

When the goods were not paid for, Office Supply filed suit in California. The Kansas City School District objected, arguing that the forum-selection clause was not binding. The court held that the forum-selection clause was not part of the parties' contract. The clause was an additional term included in the invoices delivered to a nonmerchant buyer (the school district) with the purchased goods. Therefore, the clause would have become part of the contract only if the buyer expressly agreed, which did not happen in this case.[6] ▪

Rules When Both Parties Are Merchants. The drafters of the UCC created a special rule for merchants to avoid the "battle of the forms," which occurs when two merchants exchange separate standard forms containing different contract terms. Under UCC 2–207(2), in contracts *between merchants,* the additional terms *automatically* become part of the contract unless one of the following conditions exists:

1. The original offer expressly limited acceptance to its terms.

2. The new or changed terms materially alter the contract.

3. The offeror objects to the new or changed terms within a reasonable period of time.

When determining whether an alteration is material, courts consider several factors. Generally, if the modification does not involve an unreasonable element of surprise or hardship for the offeror, the court will hold that the modification did not materially alter the contract. As shown in the following case, however, what constitutes a material alteration is frequently a question of fact that only a court can decide.

---

6. *OfficeSupplyStore.com v. Kansas City School Board,* 334 S.W.3d 574 (Kan. 2011).

CASE 17.2

C. Mahendra (N.Y.), LLC v. National Gold & Diamond Center, Inc.

New York Supreme Court, Appellate Division, First Department, 125 A.D.3d 454, 3 N.Y.S.3d 27 (2015).

FACTS C. Mahendra (N.Y.), LLC, is a New York wholesaler of loose diamonds. National Gold & Diamond Center, Inc., is a California seller of jewelry. Over a ten-year period, National placed orders, totaling millions of dollars, with Mahendra by phoning and negotiating the terms. Mahendra shipped diamonds "on memorandum" for National to examine. Mahendra then sent invoices for the diamonds that National chose to keep. Both the memoranda and the invoices stated, "You consent to the exclusive jurisdiction of the . . . courts situated in New York County." When two orders totaling $64,000 went unpaid, Mahendra filed a suit in a New York state court against National, alleging breach of contract. National filed a motion to dismiss the complaint for lack of personal jurisdiction, contending that

What happens if one party to an ongoing contract inserts a forum-selection clause without approval?

the forum-selection clause was not binding. The court granted the motion. Mahendra appealed.

ISSUE Did the forum-selection clause materially alter the parties' contracts?

DECISION Yes. A state intermediate appellate court agreed that the forum-selection clause was an additional term that materially altered the parties' contracts and was therefore not binding.

REASON The court explained that UCC 2–207 deals with situations in which parties do business through an exchange of forms, such as purchase orders and invoices. In such forms, a merchant often includes terms that were not negotiated with, or even mentioned to, the other party. Under UCC 2–207(2) "the additional terms are to be construed as proposals for addition to the contract. Between merchants such terms become part of the contract unless . . . they materially alter it."

In this case, through phone calls, the parties negotiated the essential terms to form contracts for purchases of diamonds. The memoranda and invoices that Mahendra sent to National were "merely confirmatory." The forum-selection clause in those documents was not a subject of negotiation or discussion, and National did not sign the forms or otherwise consent to the clause. The court thus ruled that the forum-selection clause was not binding. The court reversed the dismissal of Mahendra's complaint on another ground, however. It found that National's phone calls with Mahendra were sufficient contacts to subject the defendant to personal jurisdiction in New York under the state's long-arm statute.

CRITICAL THINKING—Legal Consideration *What is Mahendra's best argument that the forum-selection clause was, in fact, binding on National? Discuss.*

Prior Dealings Between Merchants. Courts also consider the parties' prior dealings in contracts between merchants. **CASE EXAMPLE 17.11** WPS, Inc., submitted a proposal to manufacture equipment for Expro Americas, LLC, and Surface Production Systems, Inc. (SPS). Expro and SPS then submitted two purchase orders. WPS accepted the first purchase order in part and the second order conditionally. Among other things, WPS's acceptance required that Expro and SPS give their "full release to proceed" and agree to "pay all valid costs associated with any order cancellation." The parties' negotiations continued, and Expro and SPS eventually submitted a third purchase order.

Although the third purchase order did not comply with all of WPS's requirements, it did give WPS full permission to proceed and agreed that Expro and SPS would pay all cancellation costs. With Expro and SPS's knowledge, WPS then began working on that order. Expro and SPS later canceled the order and refused to pay the cancellation costs. When the dispute ended up in court, Expro and SPS claimed that the parties' contract was not enforceable because the additional terms in WPS's acceptance had materially altered the contract. The court found in favor of WPS. Expro and SPS had given a release to proceed that authorized WPS to go forward with manufacturing the equipment. Because "the parties operated as if they had additional time to resolve the outstanding differences," the court reasoned that Expro and SPS were contractually obligated to pay the cancellation costs.[7]

Conditioned on Offeror's Assent. Regardless of merchant status, the UCC provides that the offeree's expression cannot be construed as an acceptance if it contains additional or different terms that are explicitly conditioned on the offeror's assent to those terms [UCC 2–207(1)]. **EXAMPLE 17.12** Philips offers to sell Hundert 650 pounds of turkey thighs at a specified price and with specified delivery terms. Hundert responds, "I accept your offer for 650 pounds of turkey thighs *on the condition that you give me ninety days to pay for them.*" Hundert's response will be construed not as an acceptance but as a counteroffer, which Philips may or may not accept.

Additional Terms May Be Stricken. The UCC provides yet another option for dealing with conflicting terms in the parties' writings. Section 2–207(3) states that conduct by both parties that recognizes the existence of a contract is sufficient to establish a contract for the sale of goods even though the writings of the parties do not otherwise establish a contract. In this situation, "the terms of the particular contract will consist of those terms on which the writings of the parties agree, together with any supplementary terms incorporated under any other provisions of this Act."

In a dispute over contract terms, this provision allows a court simply to strike from the contract those terms on which the parties do not agree. **EXAMPLE 17.13** SMT Marketing orders

iStockPhoto.com/mphillips007

If a supplier offers to sell 100 pounds of turkey thighs at a specific price and delivery date, can the buyer accept on the condition that it pay ninety days after delivery?

---

7. *WPS, Inc. v. Expro Americas, LLC,* 369 S.W.3d 384 (Tex.App. 2012).

goods over the phone from Brigg Sales, Inc., which ships the goods with an acknowledgment form (confirming the order) to SMT. SMT accepts and pays for the goods. The parties' writings do not establish a contract, but there is no question that a contract exists. If a dispute arises over the terms, such as the extent of any warranties, UCC 2–207(3) provides the governing rule. ■

As noted previously, the fact that a merchant's acceptance frequently contains terms that add to or even conflict with those of the offer is often referred to as the "battle of the forms." Although the UCC tries to eliminate this battle, the problem of differing contract terms still arises in commercial settings, particularly when standard forms for placing and confirming orders are used.

17–2c Consideration

The common law rule that a contract requires consideration also applies to sales and lease contracts. Unlike the common law, however, the UCC does not require a contract modification to be supported by new consideration. An agreement modifying a contract for the sale or lease of goods "needs no consideration to be binding" [UCC 2–209(1), 2A–208(1)]. Of course, a contract modification must be sought in good faith [UCC 1–304].

In some situations, an agreement to modify a sales or lease contract without consideration must be in writing to be enforceable. If the contract itself prohibits any changes to the contract unless they are in a signed writing, for instance, then only those changes agreed to in a signed writing are enforceable.

If a consumer (nonmerchant buyer) is dealing with a merchant and the merchant supplies the form that contains a clause prohibiting oral modification, the consumer must sign a separate acknowledgment of the clause [UCC 2–209(2), 2A–208(2)]. Also, any modification that brings a sales contract under Article 2's Statute of Frauds provision usually must be in writing to be enforceable.

17–2d The Statute of Frauds

The UCC contains Statute of Frauds provisions covering sales and lease contracts. Under these provisions, sales contracts for goods priced at $500 or more and lease contracts requiring payments of $1,000 or more must be in writing to be enforceable [UCC 2–201(1), 2A–201(1)]. (These low threshold amounts may eventually be raised.)

Sufficiency of the Writing   A writing, including an e-mail or other electronic record, will be sufficient to satisfy the UCC's Statute of Frauds as long as it meets the following requirements:

1. It indicates that the parties intended to form a contract.
2. It is signed by the party (or agent of the party) against whom enforcement is sought.
(Remember that a typed name can qualify as a signature.)

The contract normally will not be enforceable beyond the quantity of goods shown in the writing, however. All other terms can be proved in court by oral testimony. For leases, the writing or record must reasonably identify and describe the goods leased and the lease term.

Special Rules for Contracts between Merchants   Once again, the UCC provides a special rule for merchants in sales transactions. (There is no corresponding rule that applies to leases under Article 2A.) Merchants can satisfy the Statute of Frauds if, after the parties have agreed orally, one of the merchants sends a signed written confirmation to the other merchant within a reasonable time.

The communication must indicate the terms of the agreement, and the merchant receiving the confirmation must have reason to know of its contents. Unless the merchant who receives the confirmation gives written notice of objection to its contents within ten days after receipt, the writing or record is sufficient, even though she or he has not signed anything [UCC 2–201(2)].

EXAMPLE 17.14 Alfonso is a merchant-buyer in Cleveland. He contracts over the telephone to purchase $6,000 worth of spare aircraft parts from Goldstein, a merchant-seller in New York City. Two days later, Goldstein e-mails a signed confirmation detailing the terms of the oral contract, and Alfonso receives it. Alfonso does not notify Goldstein in writing of any objection to the contents of the confirmation within ten days of receipt. Therefore, Alfonso cannot raise the Statute of Frauds as a defense against the enforcement of the oral contract. ■

Exceptions In addition to the special rules for merchants, the UCC defines three exceptions to the writing requirements of the Statute of Frauds. An oral contract for the sale of goods priced at $500 or more—or the lease of goods involving total payments of $1,000 or more—will be enforceable despite the absence of a writing in the circumstances described next [UCC 2–201(3), 2A–201(4)].

Specially Manufactured Goods. An oral contract for the sale or lease of custom-made goods will be enforceable if the following conditions exist:

1. The goods are *specially manufactured* for a particular buyer or specially manufactured or obtained for a particular lessee.

2. The goods are *not suitable for resale or lease* to others in the ordinary course of the seller's or lessor's business.

3. The seller or lessor has *substantially started to manufacture* the goods or has made commitments for the manufacture or procurement of the goods.

Under these conditions, once the seller or lessor has taken action, the buyer or lessee cannot repudiate the agreement claiming the Statute of Frauds as a defense. **EXAMPLE 17.15** Womach orders custom window treatments from Hunter Douglas to use at her day spa business. The contract is oral, and the price is $6,000. When Hunter Douglas manufactures the window coverings and tenders delivery to Womach, she refuses to pay for them, even though the job is completed on time. Womach claims that she is not liable because the contract is oral. If the unique style, size, and color of the window treatments make it improbable that Hunter Douglas can find another buyer, Womach is liable to Hunter Douglas. ■

Admissions. An oral contract for the sale or lease of goods is enforceable if the party against whom enforcement of the contract is sought admits in pleadings, testimony, or other court proceedings that a contract for sale or lease was made. In this situation, the contract will be enforceable even though it was oral, but enforceability will be limited to the quantity of goods admitted.

CASE EXAMPLE 17.16 Gerald Lindgren, a farmer, agreed by phone to sell his crops to Glacial Plains Cooperative. The parties reached four oral agreements: two for the delivery of soybeans and two for the delivery of corn. Lindgren made the soybean deliveries and part of the first corn delivery, but he sold the rest of his corn to another dealer. Glacial Plains bought corn elsewhere, paying a higher price, and then sued Lindgren for breach of contract. In papers filed with the court, Lindgren acknowledged his oral agreements with Glacial Plains and admitted that he did not fully perform. The court applied the admissions exception and held that the four agreements were enforceable.[8] ■

LEARNING OBJECTIVE 3
What exceptions to the writing requirements of the Statute of Frauds are provided in Article 2 and Article 2A of the UCC?

Can oral agreements for delivery of corn be enforced if the seller admits that the agreements occurred?

Under what conditions will an oral agreement for renting chairs be enforceable?

Partial Performance. An oral contract for the sale or lease of goods is enforceable if payment has been made and accepted or goods have been received and accepted. This is the "partial performance" exception. The oral contract will be enforced at least to the extent that performance *actually* took place.

EXAMPLE 17.17 Jamal orally contracts to lease to Opus Enterprises a thousand chairs at $2 each to be used during a one-day concert. Before delivery, Opus sends Jamal a check for $1,000, which Jamal cashes. Later, when Jamal attempts to deliver the chairs, Opus refuses delivery, claiming the Statute of Frauds as a defense, and demands the return of its $1,000. Under the UCC's partial performance rule, Jamal can enforce the oral contract by tender of delivery of five hundred chairs for the $1,000 accepted. Similarly, if Opus had made no payment but had accepted the delivery of five hundred chairs from Jamal, the oral contract would have been enforceable against Opus for $1,000, the lease payment due for the five hundred chairs delivered. ■

These exceptions and other ways in which sales law differs from general contract law are summarized in Exhibit 17–2.

17–2e Parol Evidence

Recall that *parol evidence* consists of evidence outside the contract, such as evidence of the parties' prior negotiations, prior agreements, or oral agreements made at the time of contract formation. When a contract completely sets forth all the terms and conditions agreed to by the parties and is intended as a final statement of their agreement, it is considered *fully integrated*. The *parol evidence rule* applies. The terms of a fully integrated contract cannot be contradicted by evidence outside the contract.

If, however, the writing (or record) contains some of the terms the parties agreed on but not others, the contract is *not fully integrated*. In this situation, a court may allow evidence of

Exhibit 17–2 Major Differences between Contract Law and Sales Law

TOPIC	CONTRACT LAW	SALES LAW
Contract Terms	Contract must contain all material terms.	Open terms are acceptable, if parties intended to form a contract, but quantity term normally must be specified, and contract is not enforceable beyond quantity term.
Acceptance	Mirror image rule applies. If additional terms are added in acceptance, counteroffer is created.	Additional terms will not negate acceptance unless acceptance is made expressly conditional on assent to the additional terms.
Contract Modification	Modification requires consideration.	Modification does not require consideration.
Irrevocable Offers	Option contracts (with consideration) are irrevocable.	Merchants' firm offers (without consideration) are irrevocable.
Statute of Frauds Requirements	All material terms must be included in the writing.	Writing is required only for the sale of goods priced at $500 or more, but contract is not enforceable beyond quantity specified. Merchants can satisfy the requirement by a confirmatory memorandum evidencing agreement. *Exceptions:* 1. Specially manufactured goods. 2. Admissions by party against whom enforcement is sought. 3. Partial performance.

iStockPhoto.com/abzee

consistent additional terms to explain or supplement the terms stated in the contract. The court may also allow the parties to submit evidence of *course of dealing, usage of trade,* or *course of performance* [UCC 2–202, 2A–202]. A court will not under any circumstances allow the parties to submit evidence that contradicts the contract's stated terms, however. (This is also the rule under the common law.)

Course of Dealing and Usage of Trade
Under the UCC, the meaning of any agreement, evidenced by the language of the parties and by their actions, must be interpreted in light of commercial practices and other surrounding circumstances. In interpreting a commercial agreement, the court will assume that the course of prior dealing between the parties and the usage of trade were taken into account when the agreement was phrased.

Course of Dealing. A **course of dealing** is a sequence of actions and communications between the parties to a particular transaction that establishes a common basis for their understanding [UCC 1–303(b)]. A course of dealing is restricted to the sequence of conduct between the parties in their transactions prior to the agreement.

Under the UCC, a course of dealing between the parties is relevant in ascertaining the meaning of the parties' agreement. It "may give particular meaning to specific terms of the agreement, and may supplement or qualify the terms of the agreement" [UCC 1–303(d)].

Course of Dealing
Prior conduct between the parties to a contract that establishes a common basis for their understanding.

Usage of Trade. Any practice or method of dealing that is so regularly observed in a place, vocation, or trade as to justify an expectation by the parties that it will be observed in their transaction is a **usage of trade** [UCC 1–303(c)].

EXAMPLE 17.18 United Loans, Inc., hires Fleet Title Review to search the public records for prior claims on potential borrrowers' assets. Fleet's invoice states, "Liability limited to amount of fee." In the search industry, liability limits are common. After conducting many searches for United, Fleet reports that there are no claims with respect to Main Street Autos. United loans $100,000 to Main, with payment guaranteed by Main's assets.

When Main defaults on the loan, United learns that another lender has priority to Main's assets under a previous claim. If United sues Fleet Title for breach of contract, Fleet's liability will normally be limited to the amount of its fee. The statement in the invoice was part of the contract between United and Title, according to the usage of trade in the industry and the parties' course of dealing. ∎

Usage of Trade Any practice or method of dealing that is so regularly observed in a place, vocation, or trade that parties justifiably expect it will be observed in their transaction.

Course of Performance
A **course of performance** is the conduct that occurs under the terms of a particular agreement [UCC 1–303(a)]. Presumably, the parties themselves know best what they meant by their words. Thus, the course of performance actually carried out under their agreement is the best indication of what they meant [UCC 2–208(1), 2A–207(1)].

EXAMPLE 17.19 Janson's Lumber Company contracts with Lopez to sell Lopez a specified number of two-by-fours. The lumber in fact does not measure exactly 2 inches by 4 inches but rather $1\frac{7}{8}$ inches by $3\frac{3}{4}$ inches. Janson's agrees to deliver the lumber in five deliveries, and Lopez, without objection, accepts the lumber in the first three deliveries. On the fourth delivery, however, Lopez objects that the two-by-fours do not measure 2 inches by 4 inches.

The course of performance in this transaction—that is, Lopez's acceptance of three deliveries without objection under the agreement—is relevant in determining that here the term *two-by-four* actually means "$1\frac{7}{8}$ by $3\frac{3}{4}$." Janson's can also prove that two-by-fours need not be exactly 2 inches by 4 inches by applying course of prior dealing, usage of trade, or both. Janson's can, for example, show that in previous transactions, Lopez took $1\frac{7}{8}$-by-$3\frac{3}{4}$-inch lumber without objection. In addition, Janson's can show that in the lumber trade, two-by-fours are commonly $1\frac{7}{8}$ inches by $3\frac{3}{4}$ inches. ∎

Course of Performance
The conduct that occurs under the terms of a particular agreement, which indicates what the parties to that agreement intended the agreement to mean.

Do two-by-fours actually measure 2 inches by 4 inches?

Rules of Construction
The UCC provides *rules of construction* for interpreting contracts. Express terms, course of performance, course of dealing, and usage of trade are to be construed

to be consistent with each other whenever reasonable. When such a construction is unreasonable, however, the UCC establishes the following order of priority [UCC 1–303(e), 2–208(2), 2A–207(2)]:

1. Express terms.

2. Course of performance.

3. Course of dealing.

4. Usage of trade.

17–2f Unconscionability

As previously discussed, an unconscionable contract is one that is so unfair and one sided that it would be unreasonable to enforce it. The UCC allows the courts to evaluate unconscionability. If a court deems a contract or a clause in a contract to have been unconscionable at the time it was made, the court can do any of the following [UCC 2–302, 2A–108]:

1. Refuse to enforce the contract.

2. Enforce the remainder of the contract without the unconscionable part.

3. Limit the application of the unconscionable term to avoid an unconscionable result.

The following *Classic Case* illustrates an early application of the UCC's unconscionability provisions.

★★★ CLASSIC CASE 17.3 ★★★

Jones v. Star Credit Corp.

Supreme Court of New York, Nassau County, 59 Misc.2d 189, 298 N.Y.S.2d 264 (1969).

FACTS The Joneses, the plaintiffs, agreed to purchase a freezer for $900 as the result of a salesperson's visit to their home. Tax and financing charges raised the total price to $1,234.80. After making payments totaling $619.88, the plaintiffs brought a suit in a New York state court to have the purchase contract declared unconscionable under the UCC. At trial, the freezer was found to have a maximum retail value of approximately $300.

ISSUE Could this contract be denied enforcement on the ground of unconscionability?

DECISION Yes. The court held that the contract was not enforceable as it stood, and the contract was reformed so that no further payments were required.

REASON The court relied on UCC 2–302(1), which states that if "the court as a matter of law finds the contract or any clause of the contract to have been unconscionable at the time it was made,

Can a retailer sell a freezer at four times its wholesale price?

iStockPhoto.com/JazzIRT

the court may . . . so limit the application of any unconscionable clause as to avoid any unconscionable result." The court then considered the disparity between the $900 purchase price and the $300 retail value, as well as the fact that the credit charges alone exceeded the retail value. These excessive charges were exacted despite the seller's knowledge of the plaintiffs' limited resources. The court reformed the contract so that the plaintiffs' payments, amounting to more than $600, were regarded as payment in full.

CRITICAL THINKING—Legal Consideration *Why would the seller's knowledge of the buyers' limited resources support a finding of unconscionability?*

IMPACT OF THIS CASE ON TODAY'S LAW *This early case illustrates the approach that many courts today take when deciding whether a sales contract is unconscionable—an approach that focuses on excessive price and unequal bargaining power.*

17-3 Title and Risk of Loss

Before the creation of the UCC, *title*—the right of ownership—was the central concept in sales law and controlled all issues of rights and remedies of the parties to a sales contract. In some situations, title is still relevant under the UCC, and the UCC has special rules for determining who has title. (These rules do not apply to leased goods, obviously, because title remains with the lessor, or owner, of the goods.) In most situations, however, the UCC focuses less on title than on the concepts of *identification, risk of loss,* and *insurable interest.*

17-3a Identification

Before any interest in specific goods can pass from the seller or lessor to the buyer or lessee, the goods must exist and must be identified as the specific goods designated in the contract. **Identification** takes place when specific goods are designated as the subject matter of a sales or lease contract.

Identification allows title to pass from the seller to the buyer. (Remember that title to leased goods does not pass to the lessee.) In addition, it allows risk of loss to pass from the seller or lessor to the buyer or lessee. This is important because it gives the buyer or lessee the right to insure the goods and the right to recover from third parties who damage the goods.

For goods already in existence, the parties can agree in their contract on when identification will take place. If the parties do not so specify, the UCC provisions discussed here determine when identification takes place [UCC 2–501(1), 2A–217].

Identification In a sale of goods, the express designation of the goods provided for in the contract.

Existing Goods If the contract calls for the sale or lease of specific goods that are already in existence, identification takes place at the time the contract is made. **EXAMPLE 17.20** Litco Company contracts to lease a fleet of five cars designated by their vehicle identification numbers (VINs). Because the cars are identified by their VINs, identification has taken place, and Litco acquires an insurable interest in the cars at the time of contracting. ■

Future Goods Any goods that are not in existence at the time of contracting are known as *future goods.* Various rules apply to identification of future goods, depending on the goods.

- If a sale or lease involves unborn animals to be born within twelve months after contracting, identification takes place when the animals are conceived.
- If a sale involves crops that are to be harvested within twelve months (or the next harvest season occurring after contracting, whichever is longer), identification takes place when the crops are planted. Otherwise, identification takes place when the crops begin to grow.
- In a sale or lease of any other future goods, identification occurs when the goods are shipped, marked, or otherwise designated by the seller or lessor as the goods to which the contract refers.

Can identification take place for automobiles by using vehicle identification numbers?

Goods That Are Part of a Larger Mass As a general rule, goods that are part of a larger mass are identified when the goods are marked, shipped, or somehow designated by the seller or lessor as the particular goods that are the subject of the contract. **EXAMPLE 17.21** Carlos orders 10,000 pairs of men's jeans from a lot that contains 90,000 articles of clothing for men, women, and children. Until the seller separates the 10,000 pairs of men's jeans from the other items, title and risk of loss remain with the seller. ■

A common exception to this rule involves fungible goods. **Fungible goods** are goods that are alike naturally, by agreement, or by trade usage. Typical examples include specific grades or types of wheat, petroleum, and cooking oil, which usually are stored in large containers. If

Fungible Goods Goods that are alike by physical nature, agreement, or trade usage.

the owners of these goods hold title as *tenants in common* (owners with undivided shares of the whole), a seller-owner can pass title and risk of loss to the buyer without actually separating the goods. The buyer replaces the seller as an owner in common [UCC 2–105(4)].

17–3b Passage of Title

Once goods are identified, the provisions of UCC 2–401 apply to the passage of title. Parties can expressly agree when and how title will pass. Throughout UCC 2–401, the words "unless otherwise explicitly agreed" appear, meaning that any explicit understanding between the buyer and the seller determines when title passes.

Without an explicit agreement to the contrary, *title passes to the buyer at the time and the place the seller performs by delivering the goods* [UCC 2–401(2)]. For instance, if a person buys cattle at a livestock auction, title will pass to the buyer when the cattle are physically delivered to him or her (unless, of course, the parties agree otherwise).

CASE EXAMPLE 17.22 Timothy Allen contracted with Indy Route 66 Cycles, Inc., to have a motorcycle custom built for him. Indy built the motorcycle and issued a "Certificate of Origin." Two years later, federal law enforcement officers arrested Allen on drug charges and seized his home and other property. The officers also seized the Indy-made motorcycle from the garage of the home of Allen's sister, Tena. Indy filed a claim against the government, arguing that it owned the motorcycle because it still possessed the "Certificate of Origin." The court applied UCC Section 2–401(2) and ruled in favor of the government. Testimony by Indy's former vice president was "inconclusive" but implied that Indy had delivered the motorcycle to Allen. Because Indy had given up possession of the cycle to Allen, this was sufficient to pass title even though Indy had kept a "Certificate of Origin."[9]

(In the future, the delivery of goods may sometimes be accomplished by drones. This chapter's *Managerial Strategy* feature discusses the use of drones in commerce.)

Shipment and Destination Contracts Unless otherwise agreed, delivery arrangements can determine when title passes from the seller to the buyer. In a **shipment contract,** the seller is required or authorized to ship goods by carrier, such as a trucking company. Under a shipment contract, the seller is required only to deliver conforming goods into the hands of a carrier, and title passes to the buyer at the time and place of shipment [UCC 2–401(2)(a)]. Generally, *all contracts are assumed to be shipment contracts if nothing to the contrary is stated in the contract.*

In a **destination contract,** the seller is required to deliver the goods to a particular destination, usually directly to the buyer, but sometimes to another party designated by the buyer. Title passes to the buyer when the goods are *tendered* at that destination [UCC 2–401(2)(b)]. *Tender of delivery* occurs when the seller places or holds conforming goods at the buyer's disposal (with any necessary notice), enabling the buyer to take possession [UCC 2–503(1)].

Delivery without Movement of the Goods When the sales contract does not call for the seller to ship or deliver the goods (when the buyer is to pick up the goods), the passage of title depends on whether the seller must deliver a **document of title,** such as a bill of lading or a warehouse receipt, to the buyer. A *bill of lading* is a receipt for goods that is signed by a carrier and serves as a contract for the transport of the goods. A *warehouse receipt* is a receipt issued by a warehouser for goods stored in a warehouse.

When a document of title is required, title passes to the buyer *when and where the document is delivered.* Thus, if the goods are stored in a warehouse, title passes to the buyer when the

Shipment Contract A contract for the sale of goods in which the seller is required or authorized to ship the goods by carrier. The seller assumes liability for any losses or damage to the goods until they are delivered to the carrier.

When does title pass to the buyer of a motorcycle?

iStockPhoto.com/Hirkophoto

Destination Contract A contract for the sale of goods in which the seller is required or authorized to ship the goods by carrier and tender delivery of the goods at a particular destination. The seller assumes liability for any losses or damage to the goods until they are tendered at the destination specified in the contract.

Document of Title A paper exchanged in the regular course of business that evidences the right to possession of goods (for example, a bill of lading or a warehouse receipt).

---

9. *United States v. 2007 Custom Motorcycle,* 2011 WL 232331 (D.Ariz. 2011).

MANAGERIAL STRATEGY — Commercial Use of Drones

Management Faces a Legal Issue

The commercial use of drones—small, pilotless aerial vehicles—has, until recently, been on hold in the United States. Possible commercial uses of drones are numerous—railroad track inspection, oil and gas pipeline review, real estate videos for use by brokers, discovery for land boundary disputes, and many others. In addition, businesses have begun making plans to use drones for delivery of goods. Amazon is developing Amazon Prime Air, a drone-based delivery service. Google Project Wing is another drone-based service that is under development.

The problem has been the Federal Aviation Agency (FAA). The FAA claims authority to regulate *all* unmanned aircraft systems (UASs). In 2012, Congress mandated the FAA "to establish a roadmap for getting UASs integrated into the national air space." Not until 2015, however, did the FAA issue its proposed rules on commercial drone use. The rules require operators to apply for a license to use drones commercially. Drone flights are expected to be limited to daylight hours, and drones will not be allowed to go above five hundred feet or faster than one hundred miles per hour. The proposed rules also require that licensed drone operators maintain a continuous visual line of sight with the drones during operation.

The proposed FAA rules are now in a public comment period, and it is expected that final rules will be issued in 2016 or 2017. Thus, it is not yet clear how soon your packages from Amazon.com will be delivered by a commercial drone.

What the Courts Say

In the past, the FAA has attempted to fine other-than-recreational users of drones. One case involved Texas EquuSearch, a group that searches for missing persons. The organization requested an emergency injunction after receiving an e-mail from an FAA employee indicating that its drone use was illegal. The U.S. Court of Appeals for the District of Columbia Circuit refused to act on the suit. The court stated that the e-mail from the FAA did not have legal effect and therefore was not subject to judicial review.[a]

In a case involving an administrative hearing, the FAA assessed a civil penalty against Raphael Pirker for careless and reckless operation of an unmanned aircraft. Pirker flew a drone over the University of Virginia in 2011 while filming a video advertisement for the medical school. Pirker appealed to the National Transportation Safety Board Office of Administrative Law Judges. He prevailed in early 2014.[b] The FAA has appealed the ruling.

MANAGERIAL IMPLICATIONS

In other countries, the commercial drone business is flourishing. In the United States, whether it is worthwhile to create such a business will depend on how strict the final FAA rules on drones are. Delivery by drones via Amazon Prime Air or Google Project Wing may be in jeopardy.

a. *Texas EquuSearch Mounted Search and Recovery Team, RP Search Services, Inc., v. Federal Aviation Administration,* 2014 WL 2860332 (C.A.D.C. 2014).
b. *Huerta v. Pirker,* Decisional Order of National Transportation Safety Board Office of Administrative Judges, Docket CP-217, March 6, 2014.

---

appropriate documents are delivered to the buyer. The goods never move. In fact, the buyer can choose to leave the goods at the same warehouse for a period of time, and the buyer's title to those goods will be unaffected.

When no documents of title are required and delivery is made without moving the goods, title passes at the time and place the sales contract is made, if the goods have already been identified. If the goods have not been identified, title does not pass until identification occurs [UCC 2–401(3)].

EXAMPLE 17.23 Greg sells lumber to Bodan. They agree that Bodan will pick up the lumber at the lumberyard. If the lumber has been identified (segregated, marked, or in any other way distinguished from all other lumber), title passes to Bodan when the contract is signed. If the lumber is still in large storage bins at the lumberyard, title does not pass to Bodan until the particular pieces of lumber to be sold under this contract are identified. ■

Sales or Leases by Nonowners

Problems occur when a person who acquires goods with *imperfect* title attempts to sell or lease them. Sections 2–402 and 2–403 of the UCC deal with the rights of two parties who lay claim to the same goods, sold with imperfect title. Generally, a buyer acquires at least whatever title the seller has to the goods sold.

Void Title. A buyer may unknowingly purchase goods from a seller who is not the owner of the goods. If the seller is a thief, the seller's title is *void*—legally, no title exists. Thus, the buyer

LEARNING OBJECTIVE 4

Risk of loss does not necessarily pass with title. If the parties to a contract do not expressly agree when risk passes and the goods are to be delivered without movement by the seller, when does risk pass?

acquires no title, and the real owner can reclaim the goods from the buyer. If the goods were leased, the same result would occur, because the lessor has no leasehold interest to transfer.

EXAMPLE 17.24 If Saki steals diamonds owned by Bruce, Saki has a *void title* to those diamonds. If Saki sells the diamonds to Shannon, Bruce can reclaim them from Shannon even though Shannon acted in good faith and honestly was not aware that the goods were stolen. ■ Article 2A contains similar provisions for leases.

Voidable Title. A seller has *voidable title* if the goods that she or he is selling were (1) obtained by fraud, (2) paid for with a check that is later *dishonored* (returned for insufficient funds), or (3) purchased on credit when the seller was **insolvent.** Under the UCC, insolvency occurs when a person ceases to pay his or her debts in the ordinary course of business, cannot pay debts as they become due, or is insolvent under federal bankruptcy law [UCC 1–201(23)].

In contrast to a seller with *void title,* a seller with *voidable title* has the power to transfer good title to a good faith purchaser for value. A **good faith purchaser** is one who buys without knowledge of circumstances that would make a person of ordinary prudence inquire about the validity of the seller's title to the goods. One who purchases *for value* gives legally sufficient consideration (value) for the goods purchased. The real, or original, owner cannot recover goods from a good faith purchaser for value [UCC 2–403(1)].[10]

If the buyer of the goods is not a good faith purchaser for value, then the actual owner of the goods can reclaim them from the buyer (or from the seller, if the goods are still in the seller's possession). Exhibit 17–3 illustrates these concepts.

The Entrustment Rule. According to Section 2–403(2), when goods are entrusted to a merchant *who deals in goods of that kind,* the merchant has the power to transfer all rights to *a buyer in the ordinary course of business.* This is known as the **entrustment rule.** Entrusted goods include both goods that are turned over to the merchant and purchased goods left with the

---

10. The real owner could, of course, sue the person who initially obtained voidable title to the goods.

Insolvent A condition in which a person cannot pay his or her debts as they become due or ceases to pay debts in the ordinary course of business.

Good Faith Purchaser A purchaser who buys without notice of any circumstance that would cause a person of ordinary prudence to inquire as to whether the seller has valid title to the goods being sold.

Entrustment Rule The rule that entrusting goods to a merchant who deals in goods of that kind gives that merchant the power to transfer those goods and all rights to them to a buyer in the ordinary course of business.

Exhibit 17–3 Void and Voidable Titles

If goods are transferred from their owner to another by theft, the thief acquires no ownership rights. Because the thief's title is *void,* a later buyer can acquire no title, and the owner can recover the goods. If the transfer occurs by fraud, for instance, the transferee acquires a *voidable* title, as shown in this exhibit. A later good faith purchaser for value can acquire good title, and the original owner cannot recover the goods.

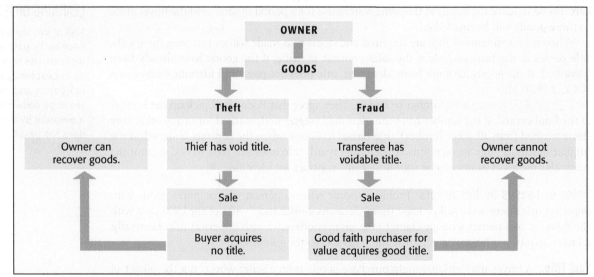

merchant for later delivery or pickup [UCC 2–403(3)]. Article 2A provides a similar rule for leased goods [UCC 2A–305(2)].

Under the UCC, a person is a **buyer in the ordinary course of business** in the following circumstances:

1. She or he buys goods in good faith (honestly).
2. The goods are purchased without knowledge that the sale violates the rights of another person in the goods.
3. The goods are purchased in the ordinary course from a merchant (other than a pawnbroker) in the business of selling goods of that kind.
4. The sale to that person is consistent with the usual or customary practices in the kind of business in which the seller is engaged [UCC 1–201(9)].

The entrustment rule basically allows innocent buyers to obtain legitimate title to goods purchased from merchants even if the merchants do not have good title. **EXAMPLE 17.25** Jan leaves her watch with a jeweler to be repaired. The jeweler sells both new and used watches. The jeweler sells Jan's watch to Kim, a customer, who is unaware that the jeweler has no right to sell it. Kim, as a good faith buyer, gets good title against Jan's claim of ownership.[11] Kim, however, obtains only those rights held by the person entrusting the goods (here, Jan).

Now suppose that Jan stole the watch from Greg and left it with the jeweler to be repaired. The jeweler then sells it to Kim. In this situation, Kim gets good title against Jan, who entrusted the watch to the jeweler, but not against Greg (the real owner), who neither entrusted the watch to Jan nor authorized Jan to entrust it. ■

17-3c Risk of Loss

Under the UCC, risk of loss does not necessarily pass with title. When risk of loss passes from a seller or lessor to a buyer or lessee is generally determined by the contract between the parties. Sometimes, the contract states expressly when the risk of loss passes. At other times, it does not, and a court must interpret the performance and delivery terms of the contract to determine whether the risk has passed.

Like risk of loss, the risk of liability that arises from the goods does not necessarily require the passage of title. In addition, as with risk of loss, when this risk passes from a seller to a buyer is generally determined by the contract between the parties. **CASE EXAMPLE 17.26** Tammy Herring contracted to buy a horse named Toby from Stacy and Gregory Bowman, who owned Summit Stables in Washington. The contract required Herring to make monthly payments until she paid $2,200 in total for Toby. Additionally, Herring agreed to pay Toby's monthly boarding fee at Summit Stables until the purchase price balance was paid. The Bowmans were to provide Toby's registration papers to Herring only when she had paid in full.

One day, another stable boarder, Diana Person, was injured when she was thrown from a buggy drawn by Toby and driven by Herring's daughter. Person sued the Bowmans to recover for her injuries, but the court held that Herring (not the Bowmans) owned Toby at the time of the accident. Herring argued that she did not own the horse because she did not yet have its registration papers, but the court found that the contract clearly showed that Herring owned Toby. Therefore, the Bowmans were not liable for the injuries that Toby caused.[12] ■

Delivery with Movement of the Goods—Carrier Cases

When the contract involves movement of the goods through a common carrier but does not specify when risk of loss passes, the courts first look for specific delivery terms in the contract.

Buyer in the Ordinary Course of Business A buyer who, in good faith and without knowledge that the sale violates the ownership rights or security interest of a third party in the goods, purchases goods in the ordinary course of business from a person in the business of selling goods of that kind.

KNOW THIS
The purpose of holding most goods in inventory is to turn those goods into revenues by selling them. That is one of the reasons for the entrustment rule.

---

11. Jan, of course, can sue the jeweler for the tort of trespass to personalty or conversion for the equivalent cash value of the watch.
12. *Person v. Bowman*, 173 Wash.App. 1024 (2013).

When does the risk of loss pass to the buyer in the sale of a horse?

The terms that have traditionally been used in contracts within the United States are listed and defined in Exhibit 17–4. These terms determine which party will pay the costs of delivering the goods and who bears the risk of loss. If the contract does not include these terms, then the courts must decide whether the contract is a shipment or a destination contract.

Shipment Contracts. In a shipment contract, the seller or lessor is required or authorized to ship goods by carrier, but is not required to deliver them to a particular final destination. The risk of loss in a shipment contract passes to the buyer or lessee when the goods are delivered to the carrier [UCC 2–319(1)(a), 2–509(1)(a), 2A–219(2)(a)].

EXAMPLE 17.27 Pitman, a seller in Texas, sells five hundred cases of grapefruit to a buyer in New York, F.O.B. Houston (free on board in Houston—see Exhibit 17–4). The contract authorizes shipment by carrier. It does not require that the seller tender the grapefruit in New York. Risk passes to the buyer when conforming goods are properly placed in the possession of the carrier in Houston. If the goods are damaged in transit, the loss is the buyer's. (Actually, buyers have recourse against carriers, subject to certain limitations, and buyers usually insure the goods from the time the goods leave the seller.) ∎

Destination Contracts. In a destination contract, the risk of loss passes to the buyer or lessee when the goods are tendered to the buyer or lessee at the specified destination [UCC 2–319(1)(b), 2–509(1)(b), 2A–219(2)(b)]. In *Example 17.27,* if the contract had been F.O.B. New York, the risk of loss during transit to New York would have been the seller's. Risk of loss would not have passed to the buyer until the carrier tendered the grapefruit to the buyer in New York.

Delivery without Movement of the Goods The UCC also addresses situations in which the contract does not require the goods to be shipped or moved. Frequently, the buyer or lessee is to pick up the goods from the seller or lessor, or the goods are held by a bailee.

A **bailment** is a temporary delivery of personal property, without passage of title, into the care of another, called a *bailee*. Under the UCC, a *bailee* is a party who, by a bill of lading, warehouse receipt, or other document of title, acknowledges possession of goods and/or contracts to deliver them. For instance, a warehousing company or a trucking company may be a bailee.

Goods Held by the Seller. When the seller keeps the goods for pickup, a document of title usually is not used. If the seller is a merchant, risk of loss to goods held by the seller passes to the buyer when the buyer *actually takes physical possession of the goods* [UCC 2–509(3)]. In

Bailment A situation in which the personal property of one person (a bailor) is entrusted to another (a bailee), who is obligated to return the bailed property to the bailor or dispose of it as directed.

Exhibit 17–4 Contract Terms—Definitions

The contract terms listed and defined in this exhibit help to determine which party will bear the costs of delivery and when risk of loss will pass from the seller to the buyer.

F.O.B. (free on board)—Indicates that the selling price of goods includes transportation costs to the specific F.O.B. place named in the contract. The seller pays the expenses and carries the risk of loss to the F.O.B. place named [UCC 2–319(1)]. If the named place is the place from which the goods are shipped (for example, the seller's city or place of business), the contract is a shipment contract. If the named place is the place to which the goods are to be shipped (for example, the buyer's city or place of business), the contract is a destination contract.

F.A.S. (free alongside ship)—Requires that the seller, at his or her own expense and risk, deliver the goods alongside the carrier before risk passes to the buyer [UCC 2–319(2)]. An F.A.S. contract is essentially an F.O.B. contract for ships.

C.I.F. or **C.&F.** (cost, insurance, and freight, or just cost and freight)—Requires, among other things, that the seller "put the goods in the possession of a carrier" before risk passes to the buyer [UCC 2–320(2)]. (These are basically pricing terms, and the contracts remain shipment contracts, not destination contracts.)

Delivery ex-ship (delivery from the carrying vessel)—Means that risk of loss does not pass to the buyer until the goods are properly unloaded from the ship or other carrier [UCC 2–322].

other words, the merchant bears the risk of loss between the time the contract is formed and the time the buyer picks up the goods.

CASE EXAMPLE 17.28 Henry Ganno purchased a twelve-foot beam at a lumberyard. The lumberyard loaded the beam onto Ganno's truck, but did not tie it down (it was policy not to secure loads for customers). After he drove onto the highway, the beam fell out of Ganno's truck, and he was injured while trying to retrieve it. Ganno sued the lumberyard for negligence, but the court held that Ganno—not the lumberyard—bore the risk of loss and injury after he left the lumberyard's premises. Once the truck was loaded, the risk of loss passed to Ganno under the UCC because he had taken physical possession of the goods.[13] ▪

If the seller is not a merchant, the risk of loss to goods held by the seller passes to the buyer on *tender of delivery* [UCC 2–509(3)]. This means that the seller bears the risk of loss until he or she makes the goods available to the buyer and notifies the buyer that the goods are ready to be picked up.

With respect to leases, similar rules apply. The risk of loss passes to the lessee on the lessee's receipt of the goods if the lessor is a merchant. Otherwise, the risk passes to the lessee on tender of delivery [UCC 2A–219(2)(c)].

Goods Held by a Bailee. When a bailee is holding goods for a person who has contracted to sell them and the goods are to be delivered without being moved, the goods are usually represented by a document of title. The title document may be written, such as a bill of lading or a warehouse receipt, or evidenced by an electronic record.

When goods are held by a bailee, risk of loss passes to the buyer when one of the following occurs:

1. The buyer receives a negotiable document of title for the goods.

2. The bailee acknowledges the buyer's right to possess the goods.

3. The buyer receives a nonnegotiable document of title, *and* the buyer has a *reasonable time* to present the document to the bailee and demand the goods. If the bailee refuses to honor the document, the risk of loss remains with the seller [UCC 2–503(4)(b), 2–509(2)].

With respect to leases, if goods held by a bailee are to be delivered without being moved, the risk of loss passes to the lessee on acknowledgment by the bailee of the lessee's right to possession of the goods [UCC 2A–219(2)(b)].

Risk of Loss When the Contract Is Breached When a sales or lease contract is breached, the transfer of risk operates differently depending on which party breaches. Generally, the party in breach bears the risk of loss.

When the Seller or Lessor Breaches. If the seller or lessor breaches by supplying goods that are so nonconforming that the buyer has the right to reject them, the risk of loss does not pass to the buyer. **EXAMPLE 17.29** A buyer orders ten stainless steel refrigerators from a seller, F.O.B. the seller's plant. The seller ships white refrigerators instead. The white refrigerators (nonconforming goods) are damaged in transit. The risk of loss falls on the seller. Had the seller shipped stainless steel refrigerators (conforming goods) instead, the risk would have fallen on the buyer [UCC 2–510(1)]. ▪

With nonconforming goods, the risk of loss does not pass to the buyer until one of the following occurs:

1. The defects are **cured** (that is, the goods are repaired, replaced, or discounted in price by the seller).

2. The buyer accepts the goods in spite of their defects (thus waiving the right to reject).

Cure The right of a party who tenders nonconforming performance to correct his or her performance within the contract period.

---

13. *Ganno v. Lanoga Corp.*, 119 Wash.App. 310, 80 P.3d 180 (2003).

When a seller ships nonconforming refrigerators that are damaged in shipment, who incurs the risk of loss?

If a buyer accepts a shipment of goods and later discovers a defect, acceptance can be revoked. Revocation allows the buyer to pass the risk of loss back to the seller, at least to the extent that the buyer's insurance does not cover the loss [UCC 2–510(2)]. Article 2A provides similar rules for leases.

When the Buyer or Lessee Breaches. The general rule is that when a buyer or lessee breaches a contract, the risk of loss immediately shifts to the buyer or lessee. This rule has three important limitations:

1. The seller or lessor must already have identified the contract goods.

2. The buyer or lessee bears the risk for only a commercially reasonable time after the seller or lessor has learned of the breach.

3. The buyer or lessee is liable only to the extent of any deficiency in the seller's insurance coverage [UCC 2–510(3), 2A–220(2)].

17–3d Insurable Interest

Parties to sales and lease contracts often obtain insurance coverage to protect against damage, loss, or destruction of goods. Any party purchasing insurance must have a sufficient interest in the insured item to obtain a valid policy. Insurance laws—not the UCC—determine sufficiency. The UCC is helpful, however, because it contains certain rules regarding insurable interests in goods.

Insurable Interest A property interest in goods being sold or leased that is sufficiently substantial to permit a party to insure against damage to the goods.

Insurable Interest of the Buyer or Lessee   A buyer or lessee has an **insurable interest** in *identified* goods. The moment the contract goods are identified by the seller or lessor, the buyer or lessee has a property interest in them. That allows the buyer or lessee to obtain necessary insurance coverage for those goods even before the risk of loss has passed [UCC 2–501(1), 2A–218(1)]. When the parties do not explicitly agree on identification in their contract, then the UCC provisions on identification discussed earlier in this chapter apply.

Insurable Interest of the Seller or Lessor   A seller has an insurable interest in goods as long as she or he retains title to the goods. Even after title passes to the buyer, a seller who has a *security interest* in the goods (a right to secure payment) still has an insurable interest [UCC 2–501(2)]. Thus, both a buyer and a seller can have an insurable interest in the same goods at the same time. Of course, the buyer or seller must sustain an actual loss to recover from an insurance company. In regard to leases, the lessor retains an insurable interest in leased goods until the lessee exercises an option to buy and the risk of loss has passed to the lessee [UCC 2A–218(3)].

See the *Business Application* feature at the end of this chapter for a discussion of insurance coverage and other measures that buyers and sellers can take to protect against losses.

17–4 Contracts for the International Sale of Goods

LEARNING OBJECTIVE 5

What law governs contracts for the international sale of goods?

International sales contracts between firms or individuals located in different countries are governed by the 1980 United Nations Convention on Contracts for the International Sale of Goods (CISG). The CISG governs international contracts only if the countries of the parties to the contract have ratified the CISG and if the parties have not agreed that some other law will govern their contract. As of 2015, the CISG had been adopted by seventy-eight countries, including the United States, Canada, some Central and South American countries, China, most European nations, Japan, and Mexico. That means that the CISG is the uniform international sales law of countries that account for more than two-thirds of all global trade.

17–4a Applicability of the CISG

Essentially, the CISG is to international sales contracts what Article 2 of the UCC is to domestic sales contracts. As discussed earlier, in domestic transactions the UCC applies when the parties to a contract for a sale of goods have failed to specify in writing some important term concerning price, delivery, or the like. Similarly, whenever the parties subject to the CISG have failed to specify in writing the precise terms of a contract for the international sale of goods, the CISG will be applied.

Unlike the UCC, *the CISG does not apply to consumer sales.* Neither the UCC nor the CISG applies to contracts for services.

17–4b A Comparison of CISG and UCC Provisions

The provisions of the CISG, although similar for the most part to those of the UCC, differ from them in certain respects. If the CISG and the UCC conflict, the CISG applies (because it is a treaty of the U.S. national government and therefore takes precedence over state laws under the U.S. Constitution). We look here at some differences with respect to contract formation.

The appendix at the end of this chapter—which shows an actual international sales contract used by Starbucks Coffee Company—illustrates many of the special terms and clauses that are typically contained in international contracts for the sale of goods. Annotations in the appendix explain the meaning and significance of specific contract clauses.

Statute of Frauds Unlike the UCC, the CISG does not include any Statute of Frauds provisions. Under Article 11 of the CISG, an international sales contract does not need to be evidenced by a writing or to be in any particular form.

Offers UCC 2–205 provides that a merchant's firm offer is irrevocable, even without consideration, if the merchant gives assurances in a signed writing or record. In contrast, under the CISG, an offer can become irrevocable without a signed writing or record. Article 16(2) of the CISG provides that an offer will be irrevocable in either of the following circumstances:

1. The offeror states orally that the offer is irrevocable.

2. The offeree reasonably relies on the offer as being irrevocable.

In both of these situations, the offer will be irrevocable without a writing or record and without consideration.

Another difference is that, under the UCC, if the price term is left open, the court will determine "a reasonable price at the time for delivery" [UCC 2–305(1)]. Under the CISG, however, the price term must be specified, or at least provisions for its specification must be included in the agreement. Otherwise, normally no contract will exist.

Acceptances Under the UCC, a definite expression of acceptance that contains additional terms can still result in the formation of a contract, unless the additional terms are conditioned on the assent of the offeror. In other words, the UCC does away with the mirror image rule in domestic sales contracts.

Article 19 of the CISG provides that a contract can be formed even though the acceptance contains additional terms, unless the additional terms materially alter the contract. Under the CISG, however, a "material alteration" includes almost any change in the terms. If an additional term relates to payment, quality, quantity, price, time and place of delivery, extent of one party's liability to the other, or the settlement of disputes, the CISG considers the added term a material alteration. In effect, then, the CISG requires that the terms of the acceptance mirror those of the offer.

Additionally, under the UCC, an acceptance is effective on dispatch, so a contract is created when the acceptance is transmitted. Under the CISG, in contrast, a contract is created not at the time the acceptance is transmitted but only on its *receipt* by the offeror. (The offer becomes *irrevocable,* however, when the acceptance is sent.)

Also, in contrast to the UCC, the CISG provides that acceptance by performance does not require that the offeror be notified of the performance.

Reviewing . . . The Formation of Sales and Lease Contracts

Guy Holcomb owns and operates Oasis Goodtime Emporium, an adult entertainment establishment. Holcomb wanted to create an adult Internet system for Oasis that would offer customers adult theme videos and live chat room programs using performers at the club. On May 10, Holcomb signed a work order authorizing Thomas Consulting Group (TCG) "to deliver a working prototype of a customer chat system, demonstrating the integration of live video and chatting in a Web browser." In exchange for creating the prototype, Holcomb agreed to pay TCG $64,697. On May 20, Holcomb signed an additional work order in the amount of $12,943 for TCG to install a customized firewall system. The work orders stated that Holcomb would make monthly installment payments to TCG, and both parties expected the work would be finished by September.

Due to unforeseen problems largely attributable to system configuration and software incompatibility, the project required more time than anticipated. By the end of the summer, the Web site was still not ready, and Holcomb had fallen behind in the payments to TCG. TCG was threatening to cease work and file suit for breach of contract unless the bill was paid. Rather than make further payments, Holcomb wanted to abandon the Web site project. Using the information presented in the chapter, answer the following questions.

1. Would a court be likely to decide that the transaction between Holcomb and TCG was covered by the Uniform Commercial Code (UCC)? Why or why not?

2. Would a court be likely to consider Holcomb a merchant under the UCC? Why or why not?

3. Did the parties have a valid contract under the UCC? Explain.

4. Suppose that Holcomb and TCG meet in October in an attempt to resolve their problems. At that time, the parties reach an oral agreement that TCG will continue to work without demanding full payment of the past-due amounts and Holcomb will pay CCG $5,000 per week. Assuming that the contract falls under the UCC, is the oral agreement enforceable? Why or why not?

DEBATE THIS

■ The UCC should require the same degree of definiteness of terms, especially with respect to price and quantity, as general contract law does.

BUSINESS APPLICATION

Who Bears the Risk of Loss— the Seller or the Buyer?*

The shipment of goods is a major aspect of commercial transactions. Many issues arise when an unforeseen event, such as fire or theft, causes damage to goods in transit. At the time of contract negotiation, both the seller and the buyer should determine the importance of the risk of loss. In some circumstances, risk is relatively unimportant (such as when ten boxes of copier paper are being sold), and the delivery terms should simply reflect costs and price. In other circumstances, risk is extremely important (such as when a fragile piece of pharmaceutical testing equipment is being sold), and the parties will need an express agreement as to the moment risk is to pass so that they can insure the goods accordingly. Risk should always be considered before a loss occurs, not after.

A major consideration relating to risk is when to insure goods against possible losses. Buyers and sellers should determine the point at which risk passes so that they can obtain insurance coverage to protect themselves against loss when they have an insurable interest in the goods.

* This *Business Application* is not meant to substitute for the services of an attorney who is licensed to practice law in your state.

Checklist to Determine Risk of Loss

The UCC uses a three-part checklist to determine risk of loss:

1. If the contract includes terms allocating the risk of loss, those terms are binding and must be applied.

2. If the contract is silent as to risk and either party breaches the contract, the breaching party is liable for the risk of loss.

3. If the contract makes no reference to risk and the goods are to be shipped or delivered, the risk of loss is borne by the party having control over the goods (delivery terms) if neither party breaches.

If You Are the Seller

If you are a seller of goods to be shipped, realize that as long as you have control over the goods, you are liable for any loss unless the buyer is in breach or the contract contains an explicit agreement to the contrary. When there is no explicit agreement, the delivery terms in your contract can serve as a basis for determining control. Thus, if goods are shipped "F.O.B. buyer's business," risk of loss does not pass to the buyer until there is a tender of delivery at the destination—the buyer's business. Any loss or damage in transit falls on the seller because the seller has control until proper tender has been made.

If You Are the Buyer

If you are a buyer of goods, it is important to remember that most sellers prefer "F.O.B. seller's business" as a delivery term. Under this term, once the goods are delivered to the carrier, the buyer bears the risk of loss. Thus, if conforming goods are completely destroyed or lost in transit, the buyer not only suffers the loss but is obligated to pay the seller the contract price.

CHECKLIST for the Seller or the Buyer:

1. Before entering into a contract, determine the importance of the risk of loss for a given sale.

2. If risk is extremely important, the contract should expressly state the moment the risk of loss will pass from the seller to the buyer. This clause could even provide that risk will not pass until the goods are "delivered, installed, inspected, and tested (or in running order for a period of time)."

3. If an express clause is not included, delivery terms determine the passage of risk of loss.

4. When appropriate, either party or both parties should consider procuring insurance.

Key Terms

bailment 420	fungible goods 415	merchant 403
buyer in the ordinary course of business 419	good faith purchaser 418	output contract 406
course of dealing 413	identification 415	predominant-factor test 401
course of performance 413	insolvent 418	requirements contract 406
cure 421	insurable interest 422	sale 400
destination contract 416	intangible property 401	sales contract 399
document of title 416	lease 403	seasonably 407
entrustment rule 418	lease agreement 403	shipment contract 416
firm offer 406	lessee 404	tangible property 401
	lessor 404	usage of trade 413

Chapter Summary: The Formation of Sales and Lease Contracts

The Scope of Articles 2 and 2A	1. *The UCC*—The UCC attempts to provide a consistent, uniform, and integrated framework of rules to deal with all phases ordinarily arising in a commercial sales or lease transaction, including contract formation, passage of title and risk of loss, performance, remedies, payment for goods, warehoused goods, and secured transactions.
	2. *Article 2 (sales)*—Article 2 governs contracts for the sale of goods (tangible, movable personal property). The common law of contracts also applies to sales contracts to the extent that the common law has not been modified by the UCC. If there is a conflict between a common law rule and the UCC, the UCC controls.
	3. *Article 2A (leases)*—Article 2A governs contracts for the lease of goods. Except that it applies to leases, instead of sales, of goods, Article 2A is essentially a repetition of Article 2 and varies only to reflect differences between sales and lease transactions.

Continues

The Formation of Sales and Lease Contracts	**1.** *Offer—*
	   a. Not all terms have to be included for a contract to be formed (only the subject matter and quantity term must be specified).
	   b. The price does not have to be included for a contract to be formed.
	   c. Particulars of performance can be left open.
	   d. A written and signed offer by a *merchant,* covering a period of three months or less, is irrevocable without payment of consideration.
	2. *Acceptance—*
	   a. Acceptance may be made by any reasonable means of communication. It is effective when dispatched.
	   b. An offer can be accepted by a promise to ship or by prompt shipment of conforming goods, or by prompt shipment of nonconforming goods if not accompanied by a notice of accommodation.
	   c. Acceptance by performance requires notice within a reasonable time. Otherwise, the offer can be treated as lapsed.
	   d. A definite expression of acceptance creates a contract even if the terms of the acceptance differ from those of the offer, unless the additional or different terms in the acceptance are expressly conditioned on the offeror's assent to those terms.
	3. *Consideration—*A modification of a contract for the sale of goods does not require consideration.
	4. *The Statute of Frauds—*
	   a. All contracts for the sale of goods priced at $500 or more must be in writing. A writing is sufficient as long as it indicates a contract between the parties and is signed by the party against whom enforcement is sought. A contract is not enforceable beyond the quantity shown in the writing.
	   b. When written confirmation of an oral contract *between merchants* is not objected to in writing by the receiver within ten days, the contract is enforceable.
	   c. For exceptions to the Statute of Frauds, see Exhibit 17–2.
	5. *Parol evidence rule—*
	   a. The terms of a clear and complete written contract cannot be contradicted by evidence of prior agreements or contemporaneous oral agreements.
	   b. Evidence is admissible to clarify the terms of a writing if the contract terms are ambiguous or if evidence of course of dealing, usage of trade, or course of performance is necessary to learn or to clarify the parties' intentions.
	6. *Unconscionability—*An unconscionable contract is one that is so unfair and one sided that it would be unreasonable to enforce it. If the court deems a sales contract to have been unconscionable at the time it was made, the court can (a) refuse to enforce the contract, (b) refuse to enforce the unconscionable clause, or (c) limit the application of any unconscionable clauses to avoid an unconscionable result.

Title and Risk of Loss	**1.** *Shipment contract—*In the absence of an agreement, title and risk pass on the seller's or lessor's delivery of conforming goods to the carrier [UCC 2–319(1)(a), 2–401(2)(a), 2–509(1)(a), 2A–219(2)(a)].
	2. *Destination contract—*In the absence of an agreement, title and risk pass on the seller's or lessor's *tender* of delivery of conforming goods to the buyer or lessee at the point of destination [UCC 2–319(1)(b), 2–401(2)(b), 2–509(1)(b), 2A–219(2)(b)].
	3. *Delivery without movement of the goods—*In the absence of an agreement, if the goods are not represented by a document of title, title passes on the formation of the contract, and risk passes on the buyer's or lessee's receipt of the goods if the seller or lessor is a merchant or on the tender of delivery if the seller or lessor is a nonmerchant.
	4. *Sales or leases by nonowners—*Between the owner and a good faith purchaser:
	   a. Void title—Owner prevails [UCC 2–403(1)].
	   b. Voidable title—Buyer prevails [UCC 2–403(1)].
	   c. Entrusted to a merchant—Buyer prevails [UCC 2–403(2), (3); 2A–305(2)].
	5. *Risk of loss when the contract is breached—*
	   a. If the seller or lessor breaches by tendering nonconforming goods that are rejected by the buyer or lessee, the risk of loss does not pass to the buyer or lessee until the defects are cured (unless the buyer or lessee accepts the goods in spite of their defects, thus waiving the right to reject) [UCC 2–510(1), 2A–220(1)].
	   b. If the buyer or lessee breaches the contract, the risk of loss immediately shifts to the buyer or lessee for goods that are identified to the contract. The buyer or lessee bears the risk for only a commercially reasonable time after the seller or lessor has learned of the breach [UCC 2–510(3), 2A–220(2)].

Contracts for the International Sale of Goods	International sales contracts are governed by the United Nations Convention on Contracts for the International Sale of Goods (CISG) if the countries of the parties to the contract have ratified the CISG and if the parties have not agreed that some other law will govern their contract. Essentially, the CISG is to international sales contracts what Article 2 of the UCC is to domestic sales contracts. Whenever parties who are subject to the CISG have failed to specify in writing the precise terms of a contract for the international sale of goods, the CISG will be applied.

Issue Spotters

1. E-Design, Inc., orders 150 computer desks. Fav-O-Rite Supplies, Inc., ships 150 printer stands. Is this an acceptance of the offer or a counteroffer? If it is an acceptance, is it a breach of the contract? What if Fav-O-Rite told E-Design it was sending the printer stands as "an accommodation"? (See *The Formation of Sales and Lease Contracts*.)

2. Truck Parts, Inc. (TPI), often sells supplies to United Fix-It Company (UFC), which services trucks. Over the phone, they negotiate for the sale of eighty-four sets of tires. TPI sends a letter to UFC detailing the terms and two weeks later ships the tires. Is there an enforceable contract between them? Why or why not? (See *The Formation of Sales and Lease Contracts*.)

—**Check your answers to the *Issue Spotters* against the answers provided in Appendix D at the end of this text.**

Learning Objectives Check

1. If a contract involves both goods and services, does the UCC apply?

2. In a sales contract, if an offeree includes additional or different terms in an acceptance, will a contract result? If so, what happens to these terms?

3. What exceptions to the writing requirements of the Statute of Frauds are provided in Article 2 and Article 2A of the UCC?

4. Risk of loss does not necessarily pass with title. If the parties to a contract do not expressly agree when risk passes and the goods are to be delivered without movement by the seller, when does risk pass?

5. What law governs contracts for the international sale of goods?

—**Answers to the even-numbered *Learning Objectives Check* questions can be found in Appendix E at the end of this text.**

Business Scenarios and Case Problems

17–1. Additional Terms. Strike offers to sell Bailey one thousand shirts for a stated price. The offer declares that shipment will be made by Dependable Truck Line. Bailey replies, "I accept your offer for one thousand shirts at the price quoted. Delivery to be by Yellow Express Truck Line." Both Strike and Bailey are merchants. Three weeks later, Strike ships the shirts by Dependable Truck Line, and Bailey refuses to accept delivery. Strike sues for breach of contract. Bailey claims that there never was a contract because his reply, which included a modification of carriers, did not constitute an acceptance. Bailey further claims that even if there had been a contract, Strike would have been in breach because Strike shipped the shirts by Dependable, contrary to the contract terms. Discuss fully Bailey's claims. (See *The Formation of Sales and Lease Contracts*.)

17–2. Spotlight on Goods and Services—The Statute of Frauds. Fallsview Glatt Kosher Caterers ran a business that provided travel packages, including food, entertainment, and lectures on religious subjects, to customers during the Passover holiday at a New York resort. Willie Rosenfeld verbally agreed to pay Fallsview $24,050 for the Passover package for himself and his family. Rosenfeld did not appear at the resort and never paid the money owed. Fallsview sued Rosenfeld for breach of contract. Rosenfeld claimed that the contract was unenforceable because it was not in writing and violated the UCC's Statute of Frauds. Is the contract valid? Explain. [*Fallsview Glatt Kosher Caterers, Inc. v. Rosenfeld,* 794 N.Y.S.2d 790 (N.Y. Super. 2005)] (See *The Formation of Sales and Lease Contracts*.)

17–3. Business Case Problem with Sample Answer— Passage of Title. Kenzie Godfrey was a passenger in a taxi when it collided with a car driven by Dawn Altieri. Altieri had originally leased the car from G.E. Capital Auto Lease, Inc. By the time of the accident, she had bought it, but she had not fully paid for it or completed the transfer-of-title paperwork. Godfrey suffered a brain injury and sought to recover damages from the owner of the car that Altieri was driving. Who had title to the car at the time of the accident? Explain. [*Godfrey v. G.E. Capital Auto Lease, Inc.,* 89 A.D.3d 471, 933 N.Y.S.2d 208 (1 Dept. 2011)] (See *Title and Risk of Loss.*)

—**For a sample answer to Problem 17–3, go to Appendix F at the end of this text.**

17–4. Additional Terms. B.S. International, Ltd. (BSI), makes costume jewelry. JMAM, LLC, is a wholesaler of costume jewelry. JMAM sent BSI a letter with the terms for orders, including the necessary procedure for obtaining credit for items that customers rejected. The letter stated, "By signing below, you agree to the terms." Steven Baracsi, BSI's owner, signed the letter and returned it. For six years, BSI made jewelry for JMAM, which resold it. Items rejected by customers were sent back to JMAM, but were never returned to BSI. BSI filed a suit against JMAM, claiming $41,294.21 for the unreturned items. BSI showed the court a copy of JMAM's terms. Across the bottom had been typed a "PS" requiring the return of rejected merchandise. Was this "PS" part of the contract? Discuss. [*B.S. International, Ltd. v. JMAM, LLC,* 13 A.3d 1057 (R.I. 2011)] (See *Formation of Sales and Lease Contracts*.)

17–5. Goods Held by the Seller or Lessor. Douglas Singletary bought a manufactured home from Andy's Mobile Home and Land Sales. The contract stated that the buyer accepted the home "as is where is." Singletary paid the full price, and his crew began to ready the home to relocate it to his property. The night before the home was to be moved, however, it was destroyed by fire. Who suffered the loss? Explain. [*Singletary, III v. P&A Investments, Inc.,* 712 S.E.2d 681 (N.C.App. 2011)] (See *Title and Risk of Loss.*)

17–6. The Statute of Frauds. Kendall Gardner agreed to buy a specially built shaving mill from B&C Shavings. He planned to use the mill to produce wood shavings for poultry processors. B&C faxed an invoice to Gardner reflecting a purchase price of $86,200, with a 30 percent down payment and the "balance due before shipment." Gardner paid the down payment. B&C finished the mill and wrote Gardner a letter telling him to "pay the balance due or you will lose the down payment." By then, Gardner had lost his customers for the wood shavings, could not pay the balance due, and asked for the return of his down payment. Did these parties have an enforceable contract under the Statute of Frauds? Explain. [*Bowen v. Gardner,* 2013 Ark.App. 52, 425 S.W.3d 875 (2013)] (See *The Formation of Sales and Lease Contracts.*)

17–7. Risk of Loss. Ethicon, Inc., a pharmaceutical company, entered into an agreement with UPS Supply Chain Solutions, Inc., to transport pharmaceuticals. The drivers were provided by International Management Services Co. under a contract with a UPS subsidiary, Worldwide Dedicated Services, Inc. During the transport of a shipment from Ethicon's facility in Texas to buyers "F.O.B. Tennessee," one of the trucks collided with a concrete barrier near Little Rock, Arkansas, and caught fire, damaging the goods. Who was liable for the loss? Why? [*Royal & Sun Alliance Insurance, PLC v. International Management Services Co.,* 703 F.3d 604 (2d Cir. 2013)] (See *Title and Risk of Loss.*)

17–8. Goods and Services Combined. Allied Shelving and Equipment, Inc., sells and installs shelving systems. National Deli, LLC, contracted with Allied to provide and install a parallel rack system (a series of large shelves) in National's warehouse. Both parties were dissatisfied with the result. National filed a suit in a Florida state court against Allied, which filed a counterclaim. Each contended that the other had materially breached the contract. The court applied common law contract principles to rule in National's favor on both claims. Allied appealed, arguing that the court should have applied the UCC. When does a court apply common law principles to a contract that involves both goods and services? In this case, why might an appellate court rule that the UCC should be applied instead? Explain. [*Allied Shelving and Equipment, Inc. v. National Deli, LLC,* 40 Fla. L. Weekly D145, 154 So.3d 482 (Dist.App. 2015)] (See *The Scope of Articles 2 and 2A.*)

17–9. A Question of Ethics—Statute of Frauds. Daniel Fox owned Fox & Lamberth Enterprises, Inc., a kitchen remodeling business. Fox leased a building from Carl Hussong. When Fox planned to close his business, Craftsmen Home Improvement, Inc., expressed an interest in buying his assets. Fox set a price of $50,000. Craftsmen's owners agreed and gave Fox a list of the desired items and a "Bill of Sale" that set the terms for payment. Craftsmen expected to negotiate a new lease with Hussong and modified the premises, including removal of some of the displays. When Hussong and Craftsmen could not agree on new terms, Craftsmen told Fox that the deal was off. [*Fox & Lamberth Enterprises, Inc. v. Craftsmen Home Improvement, Inc.,* __ N.E.2d __ (2 Dist. 2006)]

1. In Fox's suit for breach of contract, Craftsmen raised the Statute of Frauds as a defense. What are the requirements of the Statute of Frauds? Did the deal between Fox and Craftsmen meet these requirements? Did it fall under one of the exceptions? Explain. (See *The Formation and of Sales and Lease Contracts.*)

2. Craftsmen also claimed that the "predominant factor" of its agreement with Fox was a lease for Hussong's building. What is the predominant-factor test? Does it apply here? In any event, is it fair to hold a party to a contract to buy a business's assets when the buyer is unable to negotiate a favorable lease of the premises on which the assets are located? Discuss. (See *The Scope of Articles 2 and 2A.*)

Critical Thinking and Writing Assignments

17–10. Business Law Critical Thinking Group Assignment. Mountain Stream Trout Co. agreed to buy "market size" trout from trout grower Lake Farms, LLC. Their five-year contract did not define *market size*. At the time, in the trade, *market size* referred to fish of one-pound live weight. After three years, Mountain Stream began taking fewer, smaller deliveries of larger fish, claiming that *market size* varied according to whatever its customers demanded and that its customers now demanded larger fish. Lake Farms filed a suit for breach of contract. (See *The Formation and of Sales and Lease Contracts.*)

1. The first group will decide whether parol evidence is admissible to explain the terms of this contract. Are there any exceptions that could apply?

2. A second group will determine the impact of course of dealing and usage of trade on the interpretation of contract terms.

3. A third group will discuss how parties to a commercial contract can avoid the possibility that a court will interpret the contract terms in accordance with trade usage.

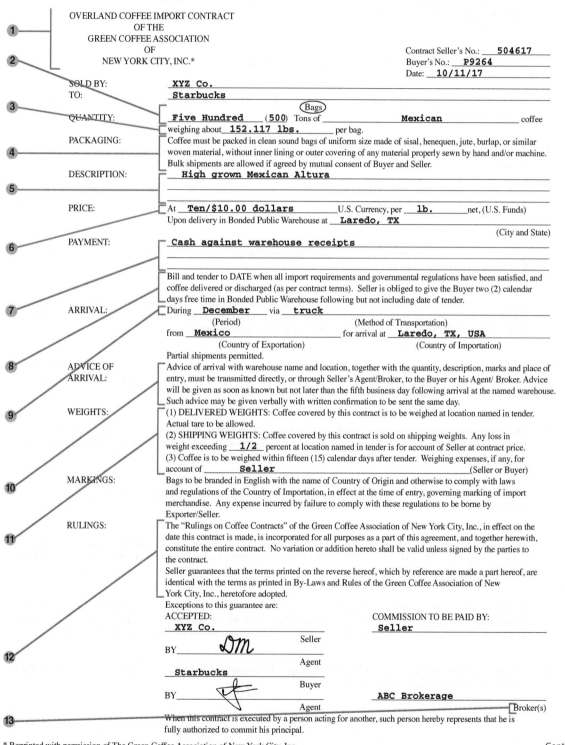

OVERLAND COFFEE IMPORT CONTRACT
OF THE
GREEN COFFEE ASSOCIATION
OF
NEW YORK CITY, INC.*

Contract Seller's No.: __504617__
Buyer's No.: __P9264__
Date: __10/11/17__

① ②

SOLD BY: __XYZ Co.__
TO: __Starbucks__

③ QUANTITY: __Five Hundred__ (__500__) Tons of __Mexican__ (Bags) coffee
weighing about __152.117 lbs.__ per bag.

PACKAGING: Coffee must be packed in clean sound bags of uniform size made of sisal, henequen, jute, burlap, or similar
woven material, without inner lining or outer covering of any material properly sewn by hand and/or machine.
Bulk shipments are allowed if agreed by mutual consent of Buyer and Seller.

④

DESCRIPTION: __High grown Mexican Altura__

⑤

PRICE: At __Ten/$10.00 dollars__ U.S. Currency, per __1b.__ net, (U.S. Funds)
Upon delivery in Bonded Public Warehouse at __Laredo, TX__
(City and State)

⑥ PAYMENT: __Cash against warehouse receipts__

Bill and tender to DATE when all import requirements and governmental regulations have been satisfied, and
coffee delivered or discharged (as per contract terms). Seller is obliged to give the Buyer two (2) calendar
days free time in Bonded Public Warehouse following but not including date of tender.

⑦ ARRIVAL: During __December__ via __truck__
(Period)   (Method of Transportation)
from __Mexico__ for arrival at __Laredo, TX, USA__
(Country of Exportation)   (Country of Importation)
Partial shipments permitted.

⑧ ADVICE OF ARRIVAL: Advice of arrival with warehouse name and location, together with the quantity, description, marks and place of
entry, must be transmitted directly, or through Seller's Agent/Broker, to the Buyer or his Agent/ Broker. Advice
will be given as soon as known but not later than the fifth business day following arrival at the named warehouse.
Such advice may be given verbally with written confirmation to be sent the same day.

⑨ WEIGHTS: (1) DELIVERED WEIGHTS: Coffee covered by this contract is to be weighed at location named in tender.
Actual tare to be allowed.
(2) SHIPPING WEIGHTS: Coffee covered by this contract is sold on shipping weights. Any loss in
weight exceeding __1/2__ percent at location named in tender is for account of Seller at contract price.
(3) Coffee is to be weighed within fifteen (15) calendar days after tender. Weighing expenses, if any, for
account of __Seller__ (Seller or Buyer)

⑩ MARKINGS: Bags to be branded in English with the name of Country of Origin and otherwise to comply with laws
and regulations of the Country of Importation, in effect at the time of entry, governing marking of import
merchandise. Any expense incurred by failure to comply with these regulations to be borne by
Exporter/Seller.

⑪ RULINGS: The "Rulings on Coffee Contracts" of the Green Coffee Association of New York City, Inc., in effect on the
date this contract is made, is incorporated for all purposes as a part of this agreement, and together herewith,
constitute the entire contract. No variation or addition hereto shall be valid unless signed by the parties to
the contract.
Seller guarantees that the terms printed on the reverse hereof, which by reference are made a part hereof, are
identical with the terms as printed in By-Laws and Rules of the Green Coffee Association of New
York City, Inc., heretofore adopted.
Exceptions to this guarantee are:

ACCEPTED: COMMISSION TO BE PAID BY:
__XYZ Co.__   __Seller__
BY ___*Dm*___ Seller
Agent
__Starbucks__
BY _____ Buyer
Agent   __ABC Brokerage__ Broker(s)

⑫

⑬ When this contract is executed by a person acting for another, such person hereby represents that he is
fully authorized to commit his principal.

* Reprinted with permission of The Green Coffee Association of New York City, Inc.

Continues

1 This is a contract for a sale of coffee to be *imported* internationally. If the parties have their principal places of business located in different countries, the contract may be subject to the United Nations Convention on Contracts for the International Sale of Goods (CISG). If the parties' principal places of business are located in the United States, the contract may be subject to the Uniform Commercial Code (UCC).

2 Quantity is one of the most important terms to include in a contract. Without it, a court may not be able to enforce the contract.

3 Weight per unit (bag) can be exactly stated or approximately stated. If it is not so stated, usage of trade in international contracts determines standards of weight.

4 Packaging requirements can be conditions for acceptance and payment. Bulk shipments are not permitted without the consent of the buyer.

5 A description of the coffee and the "Markings" constitute express warranties. International contracts rely more heavily on descriptions and models or samples.

6 Under the UCC, parties may enter into a valid contract even though the price is not set. Under the CISG, a contract must provide for an exact determination of the price.

7 The terms of payment may take one of two forms: credit or cash. Credit terms can be complicated. A cash term can be simple, and payment can be made by any means acceptable in the ordinary course of business (for example, a personal check or a letter of credit). If the seller insists on actual cash, the buyer must be given a reasonable time to get it.

8 *Tender* means the seller has placed goods that conform to the contract at the buyer's disposition. This contract requires that the coffee meet all import regulations and that it be ready for pickup by the buyer at a "Bonded Public Warehouse." (A *bonded warehouse* is a place in which goods can be stored without payment of taxes until the goods are removed.)

9 The delivery date is significant because, if it is not met, the buyer may hold the seller in breach of the contract. Under this contract, the seller is given a "period" within which to deliver the goods, instead of a specific day. The seller is also given some time to rectify goods that do not pass inspection (see the "Guarantee" clause on the second page of the contract).

10 As part of a proper tender, the seller (or its agent) must inform the buyer (or its agent) when the goods have arrived at their destination.

11 In some contracts, delivered and shipping weights can be important. During shipping, some loss can be attributed to the type of goods (spoilage of fresh produce, for example) or to the transportation itself. A seller and buyer can agree on the extent to which either of them will bear such losses.

12 Documents are often incorporated in a contract by reference, because including them word for word can make a contract difficult to read. If the document is later revised, the entire contract might have to be reworked. Documents that are typically incorporated by reference include detailed payment and delivery terms, special provisions, and sets of rules, codes, and standards.

13 In international sales transactions, and for domestic deals involving certain products, brokers are used to form the contracts. When so used, the brokers are entitled to a commission.

TERMS AND CONDITIONS

14 ARBITRATION: All controversies relating to, in connection with, or arising out of this contract, its modification, making or the authority or obligations of the signatories hereto, and whether involving the principals, agents, brokers, or others who actually subscribe hereto, shall be settled by arbitration in accordance with the "Rules of Arbitration" of the Green Coffee Association of New York City, Inc., as they exist at the time of the arbitration (including provisions as to payment of fees and expenses). Arbitration is the sole remedy hereunder, and it shall be held in accordance with the law of New York State, and judgment of any award may be entered in the courts of that State, or in any other court of competent jurisdiction. All notices or judicial service in reference to arbitration or enforcement shall be deemed given if transmitted as required by the aforesaid rules.

15 GUARANTEE: (a) If all or any of the coffee is refused admission into the country of importation by reason of any violation of governmental laws or acts, which violation existed at the time the coffee arrived at Bonded Public Warehouse, seller is required, as to the amount not admitted and as soon as possible, to deliver replacement coffee in conformity to all terms and conditions of this contract, excepting only the Arrival terms, but not later than thirty (30) days after the date of the violation notice. Any payment made and expenses incurred for any coffee denied entry shall be refunded within ten (10) calendar days of denial of entry, and payment shall be made for the replacement delivery in accordance with the terms of this contract. Consequently, if Buyer removes the coffee from the Bonded Public Warehouse, Seller's responsibility as to such portion hereunder ceases.
(b) Contracts containing the overstamp "No Pass-No Sale" on the face of the contract shall be interpreted to mean: If any or all of the coffee is not admitted into the country of Importation in its original condition by reason of failure to meet requirements of the government's laws or Acts, the contract shall be deemed null and void as to that portion of the coffee which is not admitted in its original condition. Any payment made and expenses incurred for any coffee denied entry shall be refunded within ten (10) calendar days of denial of entry.

16 CONTINGENCY: This contract is not contingent upon any other contract.

CLAIMS: Coffee shall be considered accepted as to quality unless within *fifteen* (15) calendar days after delivery at Bonded Public Warehouse or within *fifteen* (15) calendar days after all Government clearances have been received, whichever is later, either:
(a) Claims are settled by the parties hereto, or,
17 (b) Arbitration proceedings have been filed by one of the parties in accordance with the provisions hereof.
(c) If neither (a) nor (b) has been done in the stated period or if any portion of the coffee has been removed from the Bonded Public Warehouse before representative sealed samples have been drawn by the Green Coffee Association of New York City, Inc., in accordance with its rules, Seller's responsibility for quality claims ceases for that portion so removed.
(d) Any question of quality submitted to arbitration shall be a matter of allowance only, unless otherwise provided in the contract.

18 DELIVERY: (a) No more than three (3) chops may be tendered for each lot of 250 bags.
(b) Each chop of coffee tendered is to be uniform in grade and appearance. All expense necessary to make coffee uniform shall be for account of seller.
(c) Notice of arrival and/or sampling order constitutes a tender, and must be given not later than the fifth business day following arrival at Bonded Public Warehouse stated on the contract.

INSURANCE: Seller is responsible for any loss or damage, or both, until Delivery and Discharge of coffee at the Bonded Public Warehouse in the Country of Importation.

All Insurance Risks, costs and responsibility are for Seller's Account until Delivery and Discharge of coffee at the Bonded Public Warehouse in the Country of Importation.

Buyer's insurance responsibility begins from the day of importation or from the day of tender, whichever is later.

19 FREIGHT: Seller to provide and pay for all transportation and related expenses to the Bonded Public Warehouse in the Country of Importation.

20 EXPORT DUTIES/TAXES: Exporter is to pay all Export taxes, duties or other fees or charges, if any, levied because of exportation.

IMPORT DUTIES/TAXES: Any Duty or Tax whatsoever, imposed by the government or any authority of the Country of Importation, shall be borne by the Importer/Buyer.

21 INSOLVENCY OR FINANCIAL FAILURE OF BUYER OR SELLER: If, at any time before the contract is fully executed, either party hereto shall meet with creditors because of inability generally to make payment of obligations when due, or shall suspend such payments, fail to meet his general trade obligations in the regular course of business, shall file a petition in bankruptcy or, for an arrangement, shall become insolvent, or commit an act of bankruptcy, then the other party may at his option, expressed in writing, declare the aforesaid to constitute a breach and default of this contract, and may, in addition to other remedies, decline to deliver further or make payment or may sell or purchase for the defaulter's account, and may collect damage for any injury or loss, or shall account for the profit, if any, occasioned by such sale or purchase.

This clause is subject to the provisions of (11 USC 365 (e) 1) if invoked.

22 BREACH OR DEFAULT OF CONTRACT: In the event either party hereto fails to perform, or breaches or repudiates this agreement, the other party shall subject to the specific provisions of this contract be entitled to the remedies and relief provided for by the Uniform Commercial Code of the State of New York. The computation and ascertainment of damages, or the determination of any other dispute as to relief, shall be made by the arbitrators in accordance with the Arbitration Clause herein.

23 Consequential damages shall not, however, be allowed.

Continues

14 Arbitration is the settling of a dispute by submitting it to a disinterested party (other than a court), which renders a decision. The procedures and costs can be provided for in an arbitration clause or incorporated through other documents. To enforce an award rendered in an arbitration, the winning party can "enter" (submit) the award in a court "of competent jurisdiction."

15 When goods are imported internationally, they must meet certain import requirements before being released to the buyer. Because of this, buyers frequently want a guaranty clause that covers the goods not admitted into the country and that either requires the seller to replace the goods within a stated time or allows the contract for those goods not admitted to be void.

16 In the "Claims" clause, the parties agree that the buyer has a certain time within which to reject the goods. The right to reject is a right by law and does not need to be stated in a contract. If the buyer does not exercise the right within the time specified in the contract, the goods will be considered accepted.

17 Many international contracts include definitions of terms so that the parties understand what they mean. Some terms are used in a particular industry in a specific way. Here, the word *chop* refers to a unit of like-grade coffee beans. The buyer has a right to inspect ("sample") the coffee. If the coffee does not conform to the contract, the seller must correct the nonconformity.

18 The "Delivery," "Insurance," and "Freight" clauses, with the "Arrival" clause on the first page of the contract, indicate that this is a destination contract. The seller has the obligation to deliver the goods to the destination, not simply deliver them into the hands of a carrier. Under this contract, the destination is a "Bonded Public Warehouse" in a specific location. The seller bears the risk of loss until the goods are delivered at their destination. Typically, the seller will have bought insurance to cover the risk.

19 Delivery terms are commonly placed in all sales contracts. Such terms determine who pays freight and other costs and, in the absence of an agreement specifying otherwise, who bears the risk of loss. International contracts may use these delivery terms, or they may use INCOTERMS, which are published by the International Chamber of Commerce. For example, the INCOTERM DDP (delivered duty paid) requires the seller to arrange shipment, obtain and pay for import or export permits, and get the goods through customs to a named destination.

20 Exported and imported goods are subject to duties, taxes, and other charges imposed by the governments of the countries involved. International contracts spell out who is responsible for these charges.

21 This clause protects a party if the other party should become financially unable to fulfill the obligations under the contract. Thus, if the seller cannot afford to deliver, or the buyer cannot afford to pay, for the stated reasons, the other party can consider the contract breached. This right is subject to "11 USC 365(e)(1)," which refers to a specific provision of the U.S. Bankruptcy Code dealing with executory contracts.

22 In the "Breach or Default of Contract" clause, the parties agree that the remedies under this contract are the remedies (except for consequential damages) provided by the UCC, as in effect in the state of New York. The amount and "ascertainment" of damages, as well as other disputes about relief, are to be determined by arbitration.

23 Three clauses frequently included in international contracts are *omitted* here. There is no choice-of-language clause designating the official language to be used in interpreting the contract terms. There is no choice-of-forum clause designating the place in which disputes will be litigated, except for arbitration (law of New York State). Finally, there is no *force majeure* clause relieving the sellers or buyers from nonperformance due to events beyond their control.

18

CHAPTER OUTLINE
- Performance Obligations
- Anticipatory Repudiation
- Remedies for Breach
- Warranties

Performance and Breach of Sales and Lease Contracts

"Gratitude is as the good faith of merchants: it holds commerce together."

FRANÇOIS DE LA ROCHEFOUCAULD
1613–1680
(FRENCH AUTHOR)

The performance required of the parties under a sales or lease contract consists of the duties and obligations each party has under the terms of the contract. The basic obligation of the seller or lessor is to transfer and deliver the goods as stated in the contract, and the basic duty of the buyer or lessee is to accept and pay for the goods.

Keep in mind that "duties and obligations" under the terms of the contract include those specified by the agreement, by custom, and by the Uniform Commercial Code (UCC). Thus, parties to a sales or lease contract may be bound not only by terms they expressly agreed on, but also by terms implied by custom, such as a customary method of weighing or measuring particular goods. Because, as the chapter-opening quotation indicates, good faith "holds commerce together," the UCC also imposes a duty of good faith on the parties involved in commercial contracts. This duty basically requires honesty and fair dealing.

Sometimes, circumstances make it difficult for a person to carry out the promised performance, and the contract is breached. When breach occurs, the aggrieved (wronged) party looks for remedies—which we discuss later in this chapter. We also examine the various types of warranties that arise in sales and lease contracts.

LEARNING OBJECTIVES

The five Learning Objectives *below are designed to help improve your understanding of the chapter. After reading this chapter, you should be able to answer the following questions:*

1. What are the respective obligations of the parties under a contract for the sale or lease of goods?

2. What is the perfect tender rule? What are some important exceptions to this rule that apply to sales and lease contracts?

3. What options are available to the nonbreaching party when the other party to a sales or lease contract repudiates the contract prior to the time for performance?

4. What remedies are available to a seller or lessor when the buyer or lessee breaches the contract?

5. What implied warranties arise under the UCC?

433

18-1 Performance Obligations

As noted in this chapter's introduction, in the performance of a sales or lease contract, the basic obligation of the seller or lessor is to *transfer and deliver conforming goods*. The basic obligation of the buyer or lessee is to *accept and pay for conforming goods* in accordance with the contract [UCC 2–301, 2A–516(1)].

Overall performance of a sales or lease contract is controlled by the agreement between the parties. When the contract is unclear and disputes arise, the courts look to the UCC and impose standards of good faith and commercial reasonableness.

18-1a The UCC's Good Faith Provision

The obligations of good faith and commercial reasonableness underlie every sales and lease contract. The UCC's good faith provision, which can never be disclaimed, reads as follows: "Every contract or duty within this Act imposes an obligation of good faith in its performance or enforcement" [UCC 1–304].

Good faith means honesty in fact. For a merchant, it means honesty in fact and the observance of reasonable commercial standards of fair dealing in the trade [UCC 2–103(1)(b)]. In other words, merchants are held to a higher standard of performance or duty than are nonmerchants.

The principle of good faith applies to both parties to a sales contract and provides a framework for the entire agreement. If a sales contract leaves open some details of performance, for instance, the parties must exercise good faith and commercial reasonableness when later specifying the details.

Conforming Goods Goods that conform to contract specifications.

Tender of Delivery A seller's or lessor's act of placing conforming goods at the disposal of the buyer or lessee and providing whatever notification is reasonably necessary to enable the buyer or lessee to take delivery.

18-1b Obligations of the Seller or Lessor

The major obligation of the seller or lessor under a sales or lease contract is to deliver or tender delivery of conforming goods to the buyer or lessee. **Conforming goods** are goods that conform to the contract description in every way. **Tender of delivery** occurs when the seller or lessor makes conforming goods available to the buyer or lessee and provides whatever notification is reasonably necessary to enable the buyer or lessee to take delivery [UCC 2–503(1), 2A–508(1)].

Tender must occur at a *reasonable hour* and in a *reasonable manner*. In other words, a seller cannot call the buyer at 2:00 A.M. and say, "The goods are ready. I'll give you twenty minutes to get them." Unless the parties have agreed otherwise, the goods must be tendered for delivery at a reasonable hour and kept available for a reasonable period of time to enable the buyer to take possession of them [UCC 2–503(1)(a)].

Normally, all goods called for by a contract must be tendered in a single delivery, unless the parties have agreed that the goods may be delivered in several lots or *installments* [UCC 2–307, 2–612, 2A–510]. **EXAMPLE 18.1** An order for 1,000 Under Armour men's shirts cannot be delivered two shirts at a time. If, however, the parties agree that the shirts will be delivered in four orders of 250 each as they are produced (for summer, fall, winter, and spring inventory), then tender of delivery may occur in this manner. ■

In the following case, the seller of a log-cabin kit gave the buyers two days' notice to arrange for their final payment on the contract and take delivery. Did this notice comply with UCC 2–503?

Why can't a wholesale supplier of men's sweaters deliver 200 of them two at a time?

iStockPhoto.com/ronen

CASE 18.1

Garziano v. Louisiana Log Home Co.

United States Court of Appeals, Fifth Circuit, __ F.3d __, 569 Fed.Appx. 292 (2014).

FACTS Richard and Nancy Garziano contracted with Louisiana Log Home Co. (LLH) for a log-cabin kit to be delivered to them in Pass Christian, Mississippi. The contract required three installment payments. The final payment, due at delivery, was to include the cost of transportation. Two days before delivery, LLH told the buyers that the final payment would be $7,686.43, plus the transportation cost of $2,625.60. The Garzianos replied that they thought they had paid off the balance for the cabin and that they expected the shipping costs to be lower. They refused to pay more, and LLH did not deliver the kit. The Garzianos filed a claim in a federal district court against LLH, alleging that LLH had breached the contract by failing to inform them of the price of delivery in a timely manner. The court issued a judgment in LLH's favor and allowed the seller to keep the Garzianos' first two installment payments and the log-cabin kit without determining the actual amount of damages suffered. The Garzianos appealed.

Can a purchaser of a log cabin kit refuse to pay because the delivery charges seem excessive?

iStockPhoto.com/crtaylor_photography

ISSUE Was LLH's notice in compliance with UCC 2–503?

DECISION Yes. The U.S. Court of Appeals for the Fifth Circuit affirmed the lower court's judgment. Because the lower court had not determined the actual amount of LLH's damages, however, the appellate court remanded the case to the lower court to make that finding and to remit to the Garzianos any funds paid on the contract that were in excess of LLH's actual damages.

REASON UCC 2–503(1) imposes a duty to "hold conforming goods at the buyer's disposition and give the buyer any notification reasonably necessary" to enable the buyer to take delivery. The contract between LLH and the Garzianos provided that "all costs of transportation shall be borne by the purchaser" and that "shipping charges are paid directly to the trucking company at the time of delivery by cash or personal check." The contract also specified an "F.O.B. Factory Price" without shipping costs of $43,656.43 for the log-cabin kit. These terms put the Garzianos on notice that they had not yet paid the full price for the kit and that they were responsible for the shipping costs. When LLH gave two days' notice in an attempt to deliver the goods, the Garzianos breached the contract by refusing to pay the balance due and the shipping costs. "While the Garzianos may have been surprised at the size of the delivery fee, the notice provided to the Garzianos was not so deficient as to prevent them from effectively taking delivery so that their refusal to pay would be excused."

CRITICAL THINKING—Legal Consideration *How might the parties have avoided the dispute in this case?*

Place of Delivery

The UCC provides for the place of delivery under a contract only if the contract does not indicate the place where the buyer or lessee will take possession. If the contract does not indicate where the goods will be delivered, then the place for delivery will be one of the following:

1. The *seller's place of business.*
2. The *seller's residence,* if the seller has no business location [UCC 2–308(a)].
3. The *location of the goods,* if both parties know at the time of contracting that the goods are located somewhere other than the seller's business [UCC 2–308(b)].

   EXAMPLE 18.2 Li Wan and Jo Boyd both live in San Francisco. In San Francisco, Wan contracts to sell Boyd five used trucks, which both parties know are located in a Chicago warehouse. If nothing more is specified in the contract, the place of delivery for the trucks is Chicago. Wan may tender delivery either by giving Boyd a negotiable or nonnegotiable document of title or by obtaining the bailee's (warehouser's) acknowledgment that the buyer is entitled to possession.[1] ■

---

1. If the seller delivers a nonnegotiable document of title or merely instructs the bailee in a writing (or electronic record) to release the goods to the buyer without the bailee's *acknowledgment* of the buyer's rights, this is also a sufficient tender, unless the buyer objects [UCC 2–503(4)]. Risk of loss, however, does not pass until the buyer has a reasonable amount of time in which to present the document or to give the bailee instructions for delivery.

These used trucks are located in Chicago. If nothing is specified in the sales contract, where is their place of delivery?

iStockPhoto.com/Hasenonkel

KNOW THIS

Documents of title include bills of lading, warehouse receipts, and any other documents that, in the regular course of business, entitle a person holding these documents to obtain possession of, and title to, the goods covered.

LEARNING OBJECTIVE 2

What is the perfect tender rule? What are some important exceptions to this rule that apply to sales and lease contracts?

"Resolve to perform what you ought. Perform without fail what you resolve."

BENJAMIN FRANKLIN
1706–1790
(AMERICAN POLITICIAN AND INVENTOR)

Delivery via Carrier In many instances, circumstances or delivery terms in the contract (such as F.O.B. or F.A.S. terms, which were shown in Exhibit 17–4) make it apparent that the parties intended the goods to be moved by a carrier. In carrier contracts, the seller fulfills the obligation to deliver the goods through either a shipment contract or a destination contract.

Shipment Contracts. Recall that a *shipment contract* requires or authorizes the seller to ship goods by a carrier, rather than to deliver them at a particular destination [UCC 2–319, 2–509(1)(a)]. Under a shipment contract, unless otherwise agreed, the seller must do the following:

1. Put the goods into the hands of the carrier.

2. Make a contract for their transportation that is reasonable according to the nature of the goods and their value. (For instance, certain types of goods require refrigeration in transit.)

3. Obtain and promptly deliver or tender to the buyer any documents necessary to enable the buyer to obtain possession of the goods from the carrier.

4. Promptly notify the buyer that shipment has been made [UCC 2–504].

If the seller fails to notify the buyer that shipment has been made or fails to make a proper contract for transportation, the buyer may be able to consider the contract breached and reject the shipment. The buyer can reject the shipment only if a *material loss* of the goods or a *significant delay* results. Of course, the parties can agree in their contract that a lesser amount of loss or delay will be grounds for rejection.

Destination Contracts. In a *destination contract*, the seller agrees to deliver conforming goods to the buyer at a particular destination. The seller must give the buyer appropriate notice about the delivery and hold the goods at the buyer's disposal for a reasonable length of time. The seller must also provide the buyer with any documents of title necessary to enable the buyer to obtain delivery from the carrier [UCC 2–503].

The Perfect Tender Rule As previously noted, the seller or lessor has an obligation to ship or tender *conforming goods,* and the buyer or lessee is required to accept and pay for the goods according to the terms of the contract. Under the common law, the seller was obligated to deliver goods that conformed to the terms of the contract in every detail. This was called the *perfect tender* doctrine.

The UCC preserves the perfect tender doctrine by stating that if the goods or tender of delivery fail *in any respect* to conform to the contract, the buyer or lessee has the right to accept the goods, reject the entire shipment, or accept part and reject part [UCC 2–601, 2A–509].

The corollary to this rule is that if the goods conform in every respect, the buyer or lessee does *not* have a right to reject the goods. **CASE EXAMPLE 18.3** U.S. Golf & Tennis Centers, Inc., agreed to buy 96,000 golf balls from Wilson Sporting Goods Company for a total price of $20,000. Wilson represented that U.S. Golf was receiving its lowest price ($5 per two-dozen unit). Wilson shipped golf balls to U.S. Golf that conformed to the contract in quantity and quality, but it did not receive payment.

U.S. Golf claimed that it had learned that Wilson had sold the product for $2 per unit to another buyer and asked Wilson to reduce the contract price of the balls to $4 per unit (for a total of $16,000). Wilson refused and filed a suit. The court ruled in favor of Wilson. Because it was undisputed that the shipment of golf balls conformed in quantity and quality to the contract specifications, U.S. Golf was obligated to accept the goods and pay the agreed-on price.[2] ■

---

2. *Wilson Sporting Goods Co. v. U.S. Golf & Tennis Centers, Inc.,* 2012 WL 601804 (Tenn.App. 2012).

Exceptions to the Perfect Tender Rule Because of the rigidity of the perfect tender rule, several exceptions to the rule have been created, some of which are discussed here.

Agreement of the Parties. Exceptions to the perfect tender rule may be established by agreement. If the parties have agreed, for instance, that defective goods or parts will not be rejected if the seller or lessor is able to repair or replace them within a reasonable period of time, the perfect tender rule does not apply.

The Right to Cure. The UCC does not specifically define the term *cure,* but it refers to the right of the seller or lessor to repair, adjust, or replace defective or nonconforming goods [UCC 2–508, 2A–513]. The seller or lessor can attempt to cure a defect when the following are true:

If the seller ships golf balls that perfectly conform to the sales contract, what must the buyer do?

1. A delivery is rejected because the goods were nonconforming.

2. The time for performance has not yet expired.

3. The seller or lessor provides timely notice to the buyer or lessee of the intention to cure.

4. The cure can be made within the contract time for performance.

Even if the contract time for performance has expired, the seller or lessor can still cure if he or she had *reasonable grounds to believe that the nonconforming tender would be acceptable to the buyer or lessee* [UCC 2–508(2), 2A–513(2)]. **EXAMPLE 18.4** In the past, Reddy Electronics has frequently allowed Topps Company to substitute certain goods when the goods that Reddy ordered were not available. Under a new contract for similar goods, Reddy rejects a shipment of substitute goods. In this situation, Topps had reasonable grounds to believe Reddy would accept a substitute. Therefore, Topps can cure within a reasonable time even if conforming delivery will occur after the contract time for performance has ended. ■

A seller or lessor may tender nonconforming goods with a price allowance (discount). This may also serve as "reasonable grounds" for the seller or lessor to believe that the buyer or lessee will accept the nonconforming tender.

The right to cure substantially restricts the right of the buyer or lessee to reject goods. To reject, the buyer or lessee must inform the seller or lessor of the particular defect. If the defect is not disclosed, and if it is one that the seller or lessor could have cured, the buyer or lessee cannot later assert the defect as a defense. Generally, buyers and lessees must act in good faith and state specific reasons for refusing to accept goods [UCC 2–605, 2A–514].

Substitution of Carriers. An agreed-on manner of delivery (such as which carrier will be used to transport the goods) may become impracticable or unavailable through no fault of either party. In that situation, if a commercially reasonable substitute is available, this substitute must be used and will constitute sufficient tender to the buyer [UCC 2–614(1)]. The seller or lessor is required to arrange for the substitute carrier and normally is responsible for any additional shipping costs (unless the contract states otherwise).

EXAMPLE 18.5 A sales contract calls for a large generator to be delivered via Roadway Trucking Corporation on or before June 1. The contract terms clearly state the importance of the delivery date. The employees of Roadway Trucking go on strike. The seller must make a reasonable substitute tender, by another trucking company or perhaps by rail, if it is available. The seller normally will be responsible for any additional shipping costs. ■

KNOW THIS
If goods never arrive, the buyer or seller usually has at least some recourse against the carrier. Also, a buyer normally insures the goods from the time they leave the seller's possession.

Installment Contracts. An **installment contract** is a single contract that requires or authorizes delivery in two or more separate lots to be accepted and paid for separately. With an installment contract, a buyer or lessee can reject an installment *only if the nonconformity substantially impairs the value* of the installment and cannot be cured [UCC 2–307, 2–612(2), 2A–510(1)]. If the buyer or lessee fails to notify the seller or lessor of the rejection, however, and subsequently accepts a nonconforming installment, the contract is reinstated [UCC 2–612(3), 2A–510(2)].

Installment Contract
A contract that requires or authorizes delivery in two or more separate lots to be accepted and paid for separately.

Unless the contract provides otherwise, the entire installment contract is breached only when one or more nonconforming installments *substantially* impair the value of the *whole contract*. **EXAMPLE 18.6** A contract calls for the parts of a machine to be delivered in installments. The first part is necessary for the operation of the machine, but when it is delivered, it is irreparably defective. The failure of this first installment will be a breach of the whole contract because the machine will not operate without the first part.

In contrast, suppose that a contract calls for twenty carloads of plywood and that 6 percent of one carload deviates from the thickness specifications in the contract. It is unlikely that a court will find that a defect in 6 percent of one installment substantially impairs the value of the whole contract. ■

The point to remember is that the UCC significantly alters the right of the buyer or lessee to reject the entire contract if the contract requires delivery to be made in several installments. The UCC strictly limits rejection to cases of *substantial* nonconformity.

> "Obstacles are those frightful things you see when you take your eyes off your goal."
>
> **HENRY FORD**
> 1863–1947
> (FOUNDER OF FORD MOTOR COMPANY)

Commercial Impracticability. Occurrences unforeseen by either party when a contract was made may make performance commercially impracticable. When this occurs, the rule of perfect tender no longer applies. The seller or lessor must, however, notify the buyer or lessee as soon as practicable that there will be a delay or nondelivery.

EXAMPLE 18.7 Houston Oil Company, which receives its oil from the Middle East, has a contract to supply Northwest Fuels with one hundred thousand barrels of oil. Because of an oil embargo by the Organization of Petroleum Exporting Countries, Houston is unable to secure oil from the Middle East or any other source to meet the terms of the contract. This situation comes fully under the commercial impracticability exception to the perfect tender doctrine because the embargo was unforeseen by either party at the time the contract was made. ■

The doctrine of commercial impracticability does not extend to problems that could have been foreseen, such as an increase in cost resulting from inflation. The nonoccurrence of the contingency must have been a basic assumption on which the contract was made [UCC 2–615, 2A–405].

If a supplier of imported oil is unable to fulfill a contract for delivery in the U.S. because of an oil embargo, does this situation represent commercial impracticability?

Commercial Impracticability and Partial Performance. Sometimes, an unforeseen event only *partially* affects the capacity of the seller or lessor to perform. Therefore, the seller or lessor can *partially* fulfill the contract but cannot tender total performance. In this situation, the seller or lessor is required to distribute any remaining goods or deliveries fairly and reasonably among the parties to whom it is contractually obligated to deliver the goods [UCC 2–615(b), 2A–405(b)]. The buyer or lessee must receive notice of the allocation and has the right to accept or reject it [UCC 2–615(c), 2A–405(c)].

EXAMPLE 18.8 A Florida orange grower, Best Citrus, Inc., contracts to sell this season's crop to a number of customers, including Martin's grocery chain. Martin's contracts to purchase two thousand crates of oranges. Best Citrus has sprayed some of its orange groves with a chemical called Karmoxin. When studies show that persons who eat products sprayed with Karmoxin may develop cancer, the Department of Agriculture issues an order prohibiting the sale of these products. Best Citrus picks only those oranges not sprayed with Karmoxin, but there are not enough to meet all the contracted-for deliveries. In this situation, Best Citrus is required to allocate its production. It notifies Martin's that it cannot deliver the full quantity specified in the contract and indicates the amount it will be able to deliver. Martin's can either accept or reject the allocation, but Best Citrus has no further contractual liability. ■

Destruction of Identified Goods. Sometimes, an unexpected event, such as a fire, totally destroys goods through no fault of either party and before risk passes to the buyer or lessee. In such a situation, *if the goods were identified at the time the contract was formed,* the parties are excused from performance [UCC 2–613, 2A–221]. If the goods are only partially destroyed, however, the buyer or lessee can inspect them and either treat the contract as void or accept the goods with a reduction of the contract price.

EXAMPLE 18.9 Atlas Sporting Equipment agrees to lease to River Bicycles sixty bicycles of a particular model that has been discontinued. No other bicycles of that model are available. River specifies that it needs the bicycles to rent to tourists. Before Atlas can deliver the bicycles, they are destroyed by a fire. In this situation, Atlas is not liable to River for failing to deliver the bicycles. The goods were destroyed through no fault of either party, before the risk of loss passed to the lessee. The loss was total, so the contract is avoided. Clearly, Atlas has no obligation to tender the bicycles, and River has no obligation to make the lease payments for them. ■

The Right of Assurance. Another exception to the perfect tender doctrine is the UCC's right of assurance. If one party to a contract has "reasonable grounds" to believe that the other party will not perform as contracted, he or she may "demand adequate assurance of due performance" from the other party. The demand must be made in writing or in an electronic record. Until such assurance is received, he or she may "suspend" further performance (such as payments due under the contract) without liability.

What constitutes "reasonable grounds" is determined by commercial standards. If such assurances are not forthcoming within a reasonable time (not to exceed thirty days), the failure to respond may be treated as a *repudiation* of the contract [UCC 2–609, 2A–401].

CASE EXAMPLE 18.10 Two companies that made road-surfacing materials, Koch Materials Company and Shore Slurry Seal, Inc., entered into a contract. Koch obtained a license to use Novachip, a special material made by Shore, and Shore agreed to buy all of its asphalt from Koch for the next seven years. A few years into the contract term, Shore notified Koch that it was planning to sell its assets to Asphalt Paving Systems, Inc. Koch demanded assurances that Asphalt Paving would continue the deal, but Shore refused to provide assurances. Koch was able to treat Shore's failure to give assurances as a repudiation and immediately sue Shore for breach of contract.[3] ■

If a seller of oranges cannot deliver the full quantity as specified in the contract, can the buyer reject this smaller amount?

PREVENTING LEGAL DISPUTES

Whenever you have doubts about the other party's ability or willingness to perform a sales contract, you should demand adequate assurances. Rather than requiring a party to "wait and see" (and possibly incur significant losses as a result), the UCC allows a party with reasonable suspicions to seek adequate assurance of performance from the other party. If the other party fails to give assurance, you can treat it as an anticipatory repudiation (a breach, as will be discussed shortly) and pursue damages.

Perhaps more important, the other party's failure to give assurance allows you to suspend further performance, which can save your business from sustaining substantial losses that could be recovered only through costly and lengthy litigation. Ultimately, it may be better simply to withdraw from a deal when the other party will not provide assurances of performance than to continue performing under a contract that is likely to be breached anyway.

The Duty of Cooperation. Sometimes, the performance of one party depends on the cooperation of the other. The UCC provides an exception to the perfect tender doctrine if one party fails to cooperate. When cooperation is not forthcoming, the other party can suspend her or his own performance without liability and hold the uncooperative party in breach or proceed to perform the contract in any reasonable manner [UCC 2–311(3)].

EXAMPLE 18.11 Aman is required by contract to deliver 1,200 Samsung washing machines to various locations in California on or before October 1. Farrell, the buyer, is to specify the

---

3. *Koch Materials Co. v. Shore Slurry Seal, Inc.,* 205 F.Supp.2d 324 (D.N.J. 2002).

Who is liable for nondelivery of washing machines if the buyer does not provide delivery locations?

locations for delivery. Aman repeatedly requests the delivery locations, but Farrell does not respond. The washing machines are ready for shipment on October 1, but Farrell still refuses to give Aman the delivery locations. If Aman does not ship on October 1, he cannot be held liable. Aman is excused for any resulting delay of performance because of Farrell's failure to cooperate. ■

18–1c Obligations of the Buyer or Lessee

The main obligation of the buyer or lessee under a sales or lease contract is to pay for the goods tendered in accordance with the contract. Once the seller or lessor has adequately tendered delivery, the buyer or lessee is obligated to accept the goods and pay for them according to the terms of the contract.

Payment In the absence of any specific agreement, the buyer or lessee must make payment at the time and place the goods are *received* [UCC 2–310(a), 2A–516(1)]. When a sale is made on credit, the buyer is obligated to pay according to the specified credit terms (for instance, 60, 90, or 120 days), not when the goods are received. The credit period usually begins on the *date of shipment* [UCC 2–310(d)]. Under a lease contract, a lessee must make the lease payment that was specified in the contract [UCC 2A–516(1)].

Payment can be made by any means agreed on by the parties—cash or any other method generally acceptable in the commercial world. If the seller demands cash, the seller must give the buyer reasonable time to obtain it [UCC 2–511].

Right of Inspection Unless the parties otherwise agree, or for C.O.D. (collect on delivery) transactions, the buyer or lessee has an absolute right to inspect the goods before making payment. This right allows the buyer or lessee to verify, before making payment, that the goods tendered or delivered are what were contracted for or ordered. If the goods are *not* what were ordered, the buyer or lessee has no duty to pay. *An opportunity for inspection is therefore a condition precedent to the right of the seller or lessor to enforce payment* [UCC 2–513(1), 2A–515(1)].

Inspection can take place at any reasonable place and time and in any reasonable manner. Generally, what is reasonable is determined by custom of the trade, past practices of the parties, and the like. The buyer bears the costs of inspecting the goods (unless otherwise agreed), but if the goods are rejected because they are not conforming, the buyer can recover the costs of inspection from the seller [UCC 2–513(2)].

Acceptance After having had a reasonable opportunity to inspect the goods, the buyer or lessee can demonstrate acceptance in any of the following ways:

1. The buyer or lessee indicates (by words or conduct) to the seller or lessor that the goods are conforming or that he or she will retain them in spite of their nonconformity [UCC 2–606(1)(a), 2A–515(1)(a)].

2. The buyer or lessee *fails to reject* the goods within a reasonable period of time [UCC 2–602(1), 2–606(1)(b), 2A–515(1)(b)].

3. In sales contracts, the buyer *performs any act inconsistent with the seller's ownership*. For instance, any use or resale of the goods—except for the limited purpose of testing or inspecting the goods—generally constitutes an acceptance [UCC 2–606(1)(c)].

Partial Acceptance If some of the goods delivered do not conform to the contract and the seller or lessor has failed to cure, the buyer or lessee can make a *partial* acceptance [UCC 2–601(c), 2A–509(1)]. The same is true if the nonconformity was not reasonably discoverable before acceptance. (In the latter situation, the buyer or lessee may be able to revoke the acceptance, as will be discussed later in this chapter.)

"Death, they say, acquits us of all obligations."

MICHEL DE MONTAIGNE
1533–1592
(FRENCH WRITER AND PHILOSOPHER)

A buyer or lessee cannot accept less than a single commercial unit, however. The UCC defines a *commercial unit* as a unit of goods that, by commercial usage, is viewed as a "single whole" that cannot be divided without material impairment of the character of the unit, its market value, or its use [UCC 2–105(6), 2A–103(1)(c)]. A commercial unit can be a single article (such as a machine), a set of articles (such as a suite of furniture or an assortment of sizes), a quantity (such as a bale, a gross, or a carload), or any other unit treated in the trade as a single whole for purposes of sale.

18-2 Anticipatory Repudiation

What if, before the time for contract performance, one party clearly communicates to the other the intention not to perform? As discussed earlier in this text, such an action is a breach of the contract by anticipatory repudiation.

18-2a Possible Responses to Repudiation

When anticipatory repudiation occurs, the nonbreaching party has a choice of two responses:

1. Treat the repudiation as a final breach by pursuing a remedy.

2. Wait to see if the repudiating party will decide to honor the contract despite the avowed intention to renege [UCC 2–610, 2A–402].

In either situation, the nonbreaching party may *suspend performance*.

EXAMPLE 18.12 On April 1, Cora Lyn, who owns a small inn, purchases a suite of furniture from Tom Horton, proprietor of Horton's Furniture Warehouse. The contract states that "delivery must be made on or before May 1." On April 10, Horton informs Lyn that he cannot make delivery until May 10 and asks her to consent to the modified delivery date. Lyn has two options. She can either treat Horton's notice of late delivery as a final breach of contract and pursue a remedy or agree to the later delivery date. ■

18-2b A Repudiation May Be Retracted

The UCC permits the breaching party to "retract" his or her repudiation (subject to some limitations). This retraction can be done by any method that clearly indicates the party's intent to perform. Once retraction is made, the rights of the repudiating party under the contract are reinstated. There can be no retraction, however, if since the time of the repudiation the other party has canceled or materially changed position or otherwise indicated that the repudiation is final [UCC 2–611, 2A–403].

EXAMPLE 18.13 Suppose that in *Example 18.12,* Lyn does not respond to Horton's repudiation for two weeks. On April 24, Horton informs Lyn that he will be able to deliver the furniture by May 1 after all. In effect, Horton has retracted his repudiation, reinstating the rights and obligations of the parties under the original contract. Note that if Lyn had told Horton that she was canceling the contract after he repudiated, he would not have been able to retract his repudiation. ■

18-3 Remedies for Breach

When one party fails to carry out the performance promised in a contract, a breach occurs, and the aggrieved party looks for remedies. These remedies range from retaining the goods to requiring the breaching party's performance under the contract. The general purpose of these remedies is to put the aggrieved party "in as good a position as if the other party had fully performed."

Remedies under the UCC are *cumulative,* meaning that an innocent party to a breached sales or lease contract is not limited to one exclusive remedy. Of course, a party still may not recover twice for the same harm.

18-3a Remedies of the Seller or Lessor

When the buyer or lessee is in breach, the remedies available to the seller or lessor depend on the circumstances at the time of the breach. Relevant factors include which party has possession of the goods, whether the goods are in transit, and whether the buyer or lessee has rejected or accepted the goods.

When the Goods Are in the Possession of the Seller or Lessor   If the breach occurs *before the goods have been delivered to the buyer or lessee,* the seller or lessor has the right to pursue a number of remedies, which are listed below and discussed in the following subsections.

1. Cancel (rescind) the contract.
2. Withhold delivery of the goods.
3. Resell or dispose of the goods and sue to recover damages.
4. Sue to recover the purchase price or lease payments due.
5. Sue to recover damages for the buyer's nonacceptance.

The Right to Cancel the Contract.   If the buyer or lessee breaches the contract, the seller or lessor can choose to cancel (rescind) the contract [UCC 2–703(f), 2A–523(1)(a)]. The seller must notify the buyer or lessee of the cancellation, and at that point all remaining obligations of the seller or lessor are discharged. The buyer or lessee is not discharged from all remaining obligations, however. She or he is in breach, and the seller or lessor can pursue remedies available under the UCC for breach.

The Right to Withhold Delivery.   In general, sellers and lessors can withhold or discontinue performance of their obligations under sales or lease contracts when the buyers or lessees are in breach. This is true whether a buyer or lessee has wrongfully rejected or revoked acceptance of contract goods (rejection and revocation of acceptance will be discussed later), failed to make a payment, or repudiated the contract [UCC 2–703(a), 2A–523(1)(c)]. The seller or lessor can also refuse to deliver the goods to a buyer or lessee who is insolvent (unable to pay debts as they become due), unless the buyer or lessee pays in cash [UCC 2–702(1), 2A–525(1)].

The Right to Resell or Dispose of the Goods.   When a buyer or lessee breaches or repudiates the contract while the seller or lessor is still in possession of the goods, the seller or lessor can resell or dispose of the goods. Any resale of the goods must be made in good faith and in a commercially reasonable manner. The seller must give the original buyer reasonable notice of the resale, unless the goods are perishable or will rapidly decline in value [UCC 2–706(2), (3)].

The seller or lessor can retain any profits made as a result of the sale or disposition and can hold the buyer or lessee liable for any loss [UCC 2–703(d), 2–706(1), 2A–523(1)(e), 2A–527(1)]. In sales transactions, the seller can recover any deficiency between the resale price and the contract price, and can also recover *incidental damages,* defined as the costs to the seller resulting from the breach [UCC 2–706(1), 2–710]. In lease transactions, the lessor can lease the goods to another party and recover damages from the original lessee. Damages include any unpaid lease payments up to the time the new lease begins. The lessor can also recover any deficiency between the lease payments due under the original lease and those due under the new lease, along with incidental damages [UCC 2A–527(2)].

When the goods are unfinished at the time of breach, the seller or lessor can do either of the following:

1. Cease manufacturing the goods and resell them for scrap or salvage value.

2. Complete the manufacture, resell or dispose of the goods, and hold the buyer or lessee liable for any difference between the contract price and the sale.

In choosing between these two alternatives, the seller or lessor must exercise reasonable commercial judgment to mitigate the loss and obtain maximum value from the unfinished goods [UCC 2–704(2), 2A–524(2)].

The Right to Sue to Recover the Purchase Price or the Lease Payments Due. Under the UCC, an unpaid seller or lessor can bring an action to recover the purchase price or payments due under the lease contract, plus incidental damages [UCC 2–709(1), 2A–529(1)]. If a seller or lessor is unable to resell or dispose of goods and sues for the contract price or lease payments due, the goods must be held for the buyer or lessee. The seller or lessor can resell or dispose of the goods at any time before collecting the judgment from the buyer or lessee. If the goods are resold, the net proceeds from the sale must be credited to the buyer or lessee because of the duty to mitigate damages.

EXAMPLE 18.14 Southern Realty contracts with Gem Point, Inc., to purchase one thousand pens with Southern Realty's name inscribed on them. Gem Point tenders delivery of the pens, but Southern Realty wrongfully refuses to accept them. In this situation, Gem Point can bring an action for the purchase price because it delivered conforming goods, and Southern Realty refused to accept or pay for the goods. Gem Point obviously cannot resell the pens inscribed with the buyer's business name, so this situation falls under UCC 2–709. Gem Point is required to make the pens available for Southern Realty, but can resell them (in the event that it can find a buyer) at any time prior to collecting the judgment from Southern Realty. ■

The Right to Sue to Recover Damages for the Buyer's Nonacceptance. If a buyer or lessee repudiates a contract or wrongfully refuses to accept the goods, a seller or lessor can bring an action to recover the damages sustained. Ordinarily, the amount of damages equals the difference between the contract price or lease payments and the market price or lease payments at the time and place of tender of the goods, plus incidental damages [UCC 2–708(1), 2A–528(1)].

When the ordinary measure of damages is insufficient to put the seller or lessor in the same position as the buyer's or lessee's performance would have, the UCC provides an alternative. In that situation, the proper measure of damages is the lost profits of the seller or lessor, including a reasonable allowance for overhead and other expenses [UCC 2–708(2), 2A–528(2)].

When the Goods Are in Transit

If the seller or lessor has delivered the goods to a carrier or a bailee, but the buyer or lessee has not yet received them, the goods are said to be *in transit*. In limited situations, the seller or lessor can prevent goods in transit from being delivered to the buyer or lessee.

Effect of Insolvency and Breach. If the seller or lessor learns that the buyer or lessee is insolvent, the seller or lessor can stop the carrier or bailee from delivering the goods regardless of the quantity of goods shipped. If the buyer or lessee is in breach but is not insolvent, however, the seller or lessor can stop delivery of goods in transit only if the quantity shipped is at least a carload, a truckload, a planeload, or a larger shipment [UCC 2–705(1), 2A–526(1)].

EXAMPLE 18.15 Arturo Ortega orders a truckload of lumber from Timber Products, Inc., to be shipped to Ortega six weeks later. Ortega, who owes payment to Timber Products for a past shipment, promises to pay the debt immediately and to pay for the current shipment as soon as it is received. After the lumber has been shipped, a bankruptcy court judge notifies Timber Products that Ortega has filed a petition in bankruptcy and listed Timber Products as one of his creditors. If the goods are still in transit, Timber Products can stop the carrier from delivering the lumber to Ortega. ■

If a buyer wrongfully refuses to accept a shipment of blue pens that she ordered, what is the measure of damages that the seller can recover?

Requirements for Stopping Delivery. To stop delivery, the seller or lessor must *timely notify* the carrier or other bailee that the goods are to be returned or held for the seller or lessor. If the carrier has sufficient time to stop delivery, it must hold and deliver the goods according to the instructions of the seller or lessor. The seller or lessor is liable to the carrier for any additional costs incurred [UCC 2–705(3), 2A–526(3)].

The seller or lessor has the right to stop delivery of the goods under UCC 2–705(2) and 2A–526(2) until the time when the following occurs:

1. The buyer or lessee obtains possession of the goods.
2. The carrier or the bailee acknowledges the rights of the buyer or lessee in the goods (by reshipping or holding the goods for the buyer or lessee, for example).
3. A negotiable document of title covering the goods has been properly transferred to the buyer (in sales transactions only), giving the buyer ownership rights in the goods [UCC 2–702].

Once the seller or lessor reclaims the goods in transit, she or he can pursue the remedies allowed to sellers and lessors when the goods are in their possession.

KNOW THIS
Incidental damages include all reasonable expenses incurred because of a breach of contract.

When the Goods Are in the Possession of the Buyer or Lessee

When the buyer or lessee breaches the contract while the goods are in his or her possession, the seller or lessor can sue. The seller or lessor can sue to recover the purchase price of the goods or the lease payments due, plus incidental damages [UCC 2–709(1), 2A–529(1)].

In some situations, a seller may also have a right to reclaim the goods from the buyer. For instance, in a sales contract, if the buyer has received the goods on credit and the seller discovers that the buyer is insolvent, the seller can demand return of the goods [UCC 2–702(2)]. Ordinarily, the demand must be made within ten days of the buyer's receipt of the goods.[4] The seller's right to reclaim the goods is subject to the rights of a good faith purchaser or other subsequent buyer in the ordinary course of business who purchases the goods from the buyer before the seller reclaims them.

A lessor may also have a right to reclaim goods. If the lessee is in default (fails to make payments that are due, for example), the lessor may reclaim leased goods that are in the lessee's possession [UCC 2A–525(2)].

18–3b Remedies of the Buyer or Lessee

When the seller or lessor breaches the contract, the buyer or lessee has numerous remedies available under the UCC. Like the remedies available to sellers and lessors, the remedies of buyers and lessees depend on the circumstances existing at the time of the breach. Relevant factors include whether the seller has refused to deliver conforming goods or delivered nonconforming goods.

When the Seller or Lessor Refuses to Deliver the Goods

If the seller or lessor refuses to deliver the goods, or the buyer or lessee has rightfully rejected the goods, the remedies available to the buyer or lessee include the right to:

1. Cancel (rescind) the contract.
2. Obtain goods that have been paid for if the seller or lessor is insolvent.
3. Sue to obtain specific performance if the goods are unique or damages are an inadequate remedy.
4. Buy other goods (obtain *cover*), and obtain damages from the seller.

---

4. The seller can demand and reclaim the goods at any time, though, if the buyer misrepresented his or her solvency in writing within three months prior to the delivery of the goods.

5. Sue to obtain identified goods held by a third party (*replevy* goods).

6. Sue to obtain damages.

The Right to Cancel the Contract. When a seller or lessor fails to make proper delivery or repudiates the contract, the buyer or lessee can cancel, or rescind, the contract. On notice of cancellation, the buyer or lessee is relieved of any further obligations under the contract but retains all rights to other remedies against the seller [UCC 2–711(1), 2A–508(1)(a)]. (The right to cancel the contract is also available to a buyer or lessee who has rightfully rejected goods or revoked acceptance, as will be discussed shortly.)

The Right to Obtain the Goods on Insolvency. If a buyer or lessee has made a partial or full payment for goods that are in the possession of a seller or lessor who is or becomes insolvent, the buyer or lessee has a right to obtain the goods. For this right to be exercised, the goods must be identified to the contract, and the buyer or lessee must pay any remaining balance of the price to the seller or lessor [UCC 2–502, 2A–522].

The Right to Obtain Specific Performance. A buyer or lessee can obtain specific performance when the goods are unique and the remedy at law is inadequate [UCC 2–716(1), 2A–521(1)]. Ordinarily, a successful suit for monetary damages is sufficient to place a buyer or lessee in the position he or she would have occupied if the seller or lessor had fully performed. When the contract is for the purchase of a particular work of art or a similarly unique item, however, monetary damages may not be sufficient. Under these circumstances, equity requires that the seller or lessor perform exactly by delivering the goods identified to the contract (a remedy of specific performance).

    CASE EXAMPLE 18.16 Doreen Houseman and Eric Dare together bought a house and a pedigreed dog. When the couple separated, they agreed that Dare would keep the house (and pay Houseman for her interest in it) and Houseman would keep the dog. Houseman allowed Dare to take the dog for visits. After one such visit, Dare failed to return the dog. Houseman filed a lawsuit seeking specific performance of their agreement. The court found that because pets have special, subjective value to their owners, a dog can be considered a unique good. Thus, an award of specific performance was appropriate.[5] ▪

The Right to Obtain Cover. In certain situations, buyers and lessees can protect themselves by obtaining **cover**—that is, by purchasing or leasing other goods to substitute for those due under the contract. This option is available when the seller or lessor repudiates the contract or fails to deliver the goods, or when a buyer or lessee has rightfully rejected goods or revoked acceptance. In purchasing or leasing substitute goods, the buyer or lessee must act in good faith and without unreasonable delay [UCC 2–712, 2A–518].

    After obtaining substitute goods, the buyer or lessee can recover the following from the seller or lessor:

1. The difference between the cost of cover and the contract price (or lease payments).

2. Incidental damages that resulted from the breach.

3. Consequential damages to compensate for indirect losses (such as lost profits) resulting from the breach that were reasonably foreseeable at the time of contract formation.

    Buyers and lessees are not required to cover, and failure to do so will not bar them from using any other remedies available under the UCC. A buyer or lessee who fails to cover, however, may not be able to collect consequential damages that he or she could have avoided by purchasing or leasing substitute goods.

---

5. *Houseman v. Dare*, 405 N.J.Super. 538, 966 A.2d 24 (2009).

KNOW THIS

A seller or lessor breaches a contract by wrongfully failing to deliver the goods, delivering nonconforming goods, making an improper tender of the goods, or repudiating the contract.

Cover A remedy that allows the buyer or lessee, on the seller's or lessor's breach, to obtain substitute goods from another seller or lessor.

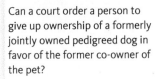

iStockPhoto.com/fotojagodka

Can a court order a person to give up ownership of a formerly jointly owned pedigreed dog in favor of the former co-owner of the pet?

Replevin An action that can be used by a buyer or lessee to recover identified goods from a third party, such as a bailee, who is wrongfully withholding them.

The Right to Replevy Goods. Buyers and lessees also have the right to replevy goods. **Replevin**[6] is an action that a buyer or lessee can use to recover specific goods from a third party, such as a bailee, who is wrongfully withholding them. Under the UCC, the buyer or lessee can replevy goods subject to the contract if the seller or lessor has repudiated or breached the contract. To maintain an action to replevy goods, buyers and lessees usually must show that they are unable to cover for the goods after a reasonable effort [UCC 2–716(3), 2A–521(3)].

The Right to Recover Damages. If a seller or lessor repudiates the contract or fails to deliver the goods, the buyer or lessee can sue for damages. For the buyer (or lessee), the measure of recovery is the difference between the contract price (or lease payments) and the market price (or lease payments) at the time the buyer (or lessee) *learned* of the breach. The market price or market lease payments are determined at the place where the seller or lessor was supposed to deliver the goods. The buyer or lessee can also recover incidental and consequential damages, less the expenses that were saved as a result of the breach [UCC 2–713, 2A–519].

CASE EXAMPLE 18.17 Les Entreprises Jacques Defour & Fils, Inc., contracted to buy a 30,000-gallon industrial tank from Dinsick Equipment Corporation for $70,000. Les Entreprises hired Xaak Transport, Inc., to pick up the tank, but when Xaak arrived at the pickup location, there was no tank. Les Entreprises paid Xaak $7,459 for its services and filed a suit against Dinsick. The court awarded compensatory damages of $70,000 for the tank and incidental damages of $7,459 for the transport. Les Entreprises had agreed to buy a tank and had paid the price. Dinsick had failed to tender or deliver the tank, or to refund the price. The shipping costs were a necessary part of performance, so this was a reasonable expense.[7] ■

If a supplier of industrial storage tanks fails to provide a tank when and where specified in the sales contract, can the buyer recover funds paid to a transport company for its shipment?

When the Seller or Lessor Delivers Nonconforming Goods
When the seller or lessor delivers nonconforming goods, the buyer or lessee has several remedies available under the UCC. The buyer or lessee may reject the goods, revoke acceptance of the goods, and recover damages for accepted goods.

The Right to Reject the Goods. If either the goods or the tender of the goods by the seller or lessor fails to conform to the contract in *any respect,* the buyer or lessee can reject the goods in whole or in part [UCC 2–601, 2A–509]. If the buyer or lessee rejects the goods, she or he may then obtain cover, cancel the contract, or sue for damages for breach of contract, just as if the seller or lessor had refused to deliver the goods (see the earlier discussion of these remedies).

CASE EXAMPLE 18.18 Jorge Jauregui contracted to buy a new Kawai RX5 piano for $24,282 from Bobb's Piano Sales & Service, Inc. When the piano was delivered with "unacceptable damage," Jauregui rejected it and filed a lawsuit for breach of contract. The court ruled that Bobb's had breached the contract by delivering nonconforming goods. Jauregui was entitled to damages equal to the contract price with interest, plus the sales tax, delivery charge, and attorneys' fees.[8] ■

Rejection of Goods: Timeliness and Identification Required. The buyer or lessee must reject the goods within a reasonable amount of time after delivery and must *seasonably* (timely) notify the seller or lessor [UCC 2–602(1), 2A–509(2)]. If the buyer or lessee fails to reject the goods within a reasonable amount of time, acceptance will be presumed.

When rejecting goods, the buyer or lessee must also designate specific defects that would have been apparent to the seller or lessor on reasonable inspection. Failure to do so precludes the buyer or lessee from using such defects to justify rejection or to establish breach when the seller could have cured the defects if they had been disclosed in a timely fashion [UCC 2–605, 2A–514].

---

6. Pronounced ruh-*pleh*-vun. Note that outside the UCC, the term *replevin* refers to a prejudgment process that permits the seizure of specific personal property in which a party claims a right or an interest.
7. *Les Entreprises Jacques Defour & Fils, Inc. v. Dinsick Equipment Corp.,* 2011 WL 307501 (N.D.Ill. 2011).
8. *Jauregui v. Bobb's Piano Sales & Service, Inc.,* 922 So.2d 303 (Fla.App. 2006).

Rejection of Goods: Duties of Merchant Buyers and Lessees. What happens if a *merchant buyer or lessee* rightfully rejects goods and the seller or lessor has no agent or business at the place of rejection? In that situation, the merchant buyer or lessee has a good faith obligation to follow any reasonable instructions received from the seller or lessor with respect to the goods [UCC 2–603, 2A–511]. The buyer or lessee is entitled to be reimbursed for the care and cost entailed in following the instructions. The same requirements hold if the buyer or lessee rightfully revokes his or her acceptance of the goods at some later time [UCC 2–608(3), 2A–517(5)]. (Revocation of acceptance will be discussed shortly.)

If no instructions are forthcoming and the goods are perishable or threaten to decline in value quickly, the buyer can resell the goods in good faith. The buyer can then take the appropriate reimbursement from the proceeds and a selling commission (not to exceed 10 percent of the gross proceeds) [UCC 2–603(1), (2); 2A–511(1), (2)]. If the goods are not perishable, the buyer or lessee may store them for the seller or lessor or reship them to the seller or lessor [UCC 2–604, 2A–512].

Revocation of Acceptance. Acceptance of the goods precludes the buyer or lessee from exercising the right of rejection, but it does not necessarily prevent the buyer or lessee from pursuing other remedies. In certain circumstances, a buyer or lessee is permitted to *revoke* her or his acceptance of the goods.

Acceptance of a lot or a commercial unit can be revoked if the nonconformity *substantially* impairs the value of the lot or unit *and* if one of the following factors is present:

1. Acceptance was predicated on the reasonable assumption that the nonconformity would be cured, and it was not cured within a reasonable time [UCC 2–608(1)(a), 2A–517(1)(a)].

2. The buyer or lessee did not discover the nonconformity before acceptance, either because it was difficult to discover before acceptance or because assurances made by the seller or lessor that the goods were conforming kept the buyer or lessee from inspecting the goods [UCC 2–608(1)(b), 2A–517(1)(b)].

Revocation of acceptance is not effective until notice is given to the seller or lessor. Notice must occur within a reasonable time after the buyer or lessee either discovers or *should have discovered* the grounds for revocation. Additionally, revocation must occur before the goods have undergone any substantial change (such as spoilage) not caused by their own defects [UCC 2–608(2), 2A–517(4)]. Once acceptance is revoked, the buyer or lessee can pursue remedies just as if the goods had been rejected. (See this chapter's *Beyond Our Borders* feature for a glimpse at how international sales law deals with revocation of acceptance.)

BEYOND OUR BORDERS

The CISG's Approach to Revocation of Acceptance

Under the UCC, a buyer or lessee who has accepted goods may be able to revoke acceptance under the circumstances mentioned in the text above. The United Nations Convention on Contracts for the International Sale of Goods (CISG) also allows buyers to rescind their contracts after they have accepted the goods. The CISG, however, takes a somewhat different—and more direct—approach to the problem.

Under the CISG, the buyer can simply declare that the seller has *fundamentally* breached the contract and proceed to sue the seller for the breach. Article 25 of the CISG states that a "breach of contract committed by one of the parties is fundamental if it results in such detriment to the other party as substantially to deprive him [or her] of what he [or she] is entitled to expect under the contract." For example, to revoke acceptance of a shipment under the CISG, a buyer need not prove that the nonconformity of one shipment substantially impaired the value of the whole lot. The buyer can simply file a lawsuit alleging that the seller is in breach.

CRITICAL THINKING

■ What is the essential difference between revoking acceptance and bringing a suit for breach of contract?

The Right to Recover Damages for Accepted Goods. A buyer or lessee who has accepted nonconforming goods may also keep the goods and recover damages caused by the breach. To do so, the buyer or lessee must notify the seller or lessor of the breach within a reasonable time after the defect was or should have been discovered. Failure to give notice of the defect (breach) to the seller or lessor bars the buyer or lessee from pursuing any remedy [UCC 2–607(3), 2A–516(3)]. In addition, the parties to a sales or lease contract can insert a provision requiring the buyer or lessee to give notice of any defects in the goods within a set period.

When the goods delivered are not as promised, the measure of damages equals the difference between the value of the goods as accepted and their value if they had been delivered as warranted [UCC 2–714(2), 2A–519(4)]. The buyer or lessee is also entitled to incidental and consequential damages when appropriate [UCC 2–714(3), 2A–519(3)]. The UCC also permits the buyer or lessee, with proper notice to the seller or lessor, to deduct all or any part of the damages from the price or lease payments still due under the contract [UCC 2–717, 2A–516(1)].

Is two years after a sale of goods a reasonable time period in which to discover a defect in the goods and notify the seller of a breach? That was the question in the following *Spotlight Case*.

SPOTLIGHT ON BASEBALL CARDS: CASE 18.2

Fitl v. Strek

Supreme Court of Nebraska, 269 Neb. 51, 690 N.W.2d 605 (2005).

FACTS In 1995, James Fitl attended a sports-card show in San Francisco, California, where he met Mark Strek, doing business as Star Cards of San Francisco, an exhibitor at the show. Later, on Strek's representation that a certain 1952 Mickey Mantle Topps baseball card was in near-mint condition, Fitl bought the card from Strek for $17,750. Strek delivered the card to Fitl in Omaha, Nebraska, and Fitl placed it in a safe-deposit box.

In May 1997, Fitl sent the card to Professional Sports Authenticators (PSA), a sports-card grading service. PSA told Fitl that the card was ungradable because it had been discolored and doctored. Fitl complained to Strek, who replied that Fitl should have returned the card within "a typical grace period for the unconditional return of a card, . . . 7 days to 1 month" of its receipt. In August, Fitl sent the card to ASA Accugrade, Inc. (ASA), another grading service, for a second opinion of the value. ASA also concluded that the card had been refinished and trimmed. Fitl filed a suit in a Nebraska state court against Strek, seeking damages. The court awarded Fitl $17,750, plus his court costs. Strek appealed to the Nebraska Supreme Court.

ISSUE Was two years after the sale of the baseball card a reasonable time to discover a defect and notify the seller of a breach?

DECISION Yes. The state supreme court affirmed the decision of the lower court.

What is a reasonable time period to discover that a baseball card purchased is not authentic?

JStone/ShutterStock.com

REASON Section 2–607(3)(a) of the UCC states, "Where a tender has been accepted . . . the buyer must within a reasonable time after he discovers or should have discovered any breach notify the seller of breach or be barred from any remedy." Furthermore, "What is a reasonable time for taking any action depends on the nature, purpose and circumstances of such action" [UCC 1–205(a)]. The state supreme court concluded that the buyer (Fitl) had reasonably relied on the seller's (Strek's) representation that the goods were "authentic," which they were not. Fitl had given timely notice when he discovered the defects.

The court reasoned that "the policies behind the notice requirement, to allow the seller to correct a defect, to prepare for negotiation and litigation, and to protect against stale claims at a time beyond which an investigation can be completed, were not unfairly prejudiced by the lack of an earlier notice to Strek. Any problem Strek may have had with the party from whom he obtained the baseball card was a separate matter from his transaction with Fitl, and an investigation into the source of the altered card would not have minimized Fitl's damages."

WHAT IF THE FACTS WERE DIFFERENT? *Suppose that Fitl and Strek had included in their deal a written clause requiring Fitl to give notice of any defect in the card within "7 days to 1 month" of its receipt. Would the result have been different? Why or why not?*

18–3c Limitation of Remedies

The parties to a sales or lease contract can vary their respective rights and obligations by contractual agreement. For example, a seller and buyer can expressly provide for remedies in addition to those provided in the UCC. They can also provide remedies in lieu of those provided in the UCC, or they can change the measure of damages. Any agreed-on remedy is in addition to those provided in the UCC unless the parties expressly agree that the remedy is exclusive of all others [UCC 2–719(1), 2A–503(1), (2)].

Exclusive Remedies If the parties state that a remedy is exclusive, then it is the sole, or exclusive, remedy. **EXAMPLE 18.19** Standard Tool Company agrees to sell a pipe-cutting machine to United Pipe & Tubing Corporation. The contract limits United's remedy exclusively to repair or replacement of any defective parts. Thus, repair or replacement of defective parts is the buyer's exclusive remedy under this contract. ■

When circumstances cause an exclusive remedy to fail in its essential purpose, however, it is no longer exclusive, and the buyer or lessee may pursue other remedies available under the UCC [UCC 2–719(2), 2A–503(2)]. **EXAMPLE 18.20** In *Example 18.19,* suppose that Standard Tool Company is unable to repair a defective part, and no replacement parts are available. In this situation, because the exclusive remedy failed in its essential purpose, the buyer normally will be entitled to seek other remedies provided by the UCC. ■

Limitations on Consequential Damages As discussed previously, *consequential damages* are special damages that compensate for indirect losses (such as lost profits) resulting from a breach of contract that were reasonably foreseeable. Under the UCC, parties to a contract can limit or exclude consequential damages, provided the limitation is not unconscionable.

When the buyer or lessee is a consumer, any limitation of consequential damages for personal injuries resulting from consumer goods is *prima facie* (presumptively, or on its face) unconscionable. The limitation of consequential damages is not necessarily unconscionable when the loss is commercial in nature—such as lost profits and property damage [UCC 2–719(3), 2A–503(3)].

Statute of Limitations An action for breach of contract under the UCC must be commenced *within four years after the cause of action accrues*—that is, a buyer or lessee must file the lawsuit within four years after the breach occurs [UCC 2–725(1)]. In addition, a buyer or lessee who has accepted nonconforming goods usually must notify the breaching party of the breach within a reasonable time, or the aggrieved party is barred from pursuing any remedy [UCC 2–607(3)(a), 2A–516(3)].

The parties can agree in their contract to reduce this period to not less than one year, but cannot extend it beyond four years [UCC 2–725(1), 2A–506(1)]. A cause of action accrues for breach of warranty (discussed next) when the seller or lessor tenders delivery. This is the rule even if the aggrieved party is unaware that the cause of action has accrued [UCC 2–725(2), 2A–506(2)].

If this pipe-cutting machine has defective parts, can the buyer insist on replacement of the entire machine?

iStockPhoto.com/snezhok

18–4 Warranties

The UCC has numerous rules governing product warranties as they occur in sales and lease contracts. Article 2 and Article 2A designate several types of warranties that can arise in a sales or lease contract, including warranties of title, express warranties, and implied warranties.

18–4a Warranties of Title

Under the UCC, three types of title warranties—*good title, no liens,* and *no infringements*—can automatically arise in sales and lease contracts.

Good Title

In most sales, sellers warrant that they have good and valid title to the goods sold and that transfer of the title is rightful [UCC 2–312(1)(a)]. If the buyer subsequently learns that the seller did not have good title to goods that were purchased, the buyer can sue the seller for breach of this warranty.

EXAMPLE 18.21 Alexis steals a diamond ring from Calvin and sells it to Emma, who does not know that the ring is stolen. If Calvin discovers that Emma has the ring, then he has the right to reclaim it from Emma. When Alexis sold Emma the ring, Alexis automatically warranted to Emma that the title conveyed was valid and that its transfer was rightful. Because a thief has no title to stolen goods, Alexis breached the warranty of title imposed by the UCC and became liable to Emma for appropriate damages. ■

There is no warranty of good title in lease contracts because title to the goods does not pass to the lessee.

No Liens

> **Lien** An encumbrance on a property to satisfy a debt or protect a claim for payment of a debt.

A second warranty of title shields buyers and lessees who are unaware of any encumbrances, or **liens** (claims, charges, or liabilities), against goods at the time the contract is made [UCC 2–312(1)(b), 2A–211(1)]. This warranty, for instance, protects buyers who unknowingly purchase goods that are subject to a creditor's *security interest* (an interest in the goods that secures payment or performance). If a creditor legally repossesses the goods from a buyer *who had no actual knowledge of the security interest,* the buyer can recover from the seller for breach of warranty.

No Infringements

A third type of title warranty is a warranty against infringement of any patent, trademark, or copyright. When the seller or lessor is a merchant, he or she automatically warrants that the buyer or lessee takes the goods *free of infringements.* In other words, a merchant promises that the goods delivered are free from any copyright, trademark, or patent claims of a third person [UCC 2–312(3), 2A–211(2)].

18–4b Express Warranties

> **Express Warranty** A seller's or lessor's promise as to the quality, condition, description, or performance of the goods being sold or leased.

A seller or lessor can create an **express warranty** by making representations concerning the quality, condition, description, or performance potential of the goods. Under UCC 2–313 and 2A–210, express warranties arise when a seller or lessor indicates any of the following:

1. That the goods conform to any *affirmation* (declaration that something is true) or *promise* of fact that the seller or lessor makes to the buyer or lessee about the goods. Such affirmations or promises are usually made during the bargaining process. Statements such as "these drill bits will penetrate stainless steel—and without dulling" are express warranties.

2. That the goods conform to any *description* of them. For example, a label that reads "Crate contains one 150-horsepower diesel engine" or a contract that calls for the delivery of a "wool coat" creates an express warranty.

3. That the goods conform to any *sample* or *model* of the goods shown to the buyer or lessee.

Express warranties can be found in a seller's or lessor's advertisement, e-mail, brochure, or promotional materials, in addition to being made orally or set forth in a provision of a contract.

Basis of the Bargain

To create an express warranty, a seller or lessor does not have to use words such as *warrant* or *guarantee* [UCC 2–313(2), 2A–210(2)]. It is only necessary that a reasonable buyer or lessee would regard the representation of fact as part of the basis of the bargain [UCC 2–313(1), 2A–210(1)]. The UCC does not define *basis of the bargain,* however, and it is a question of fact in each case whether a representation was made at such a time and in such a way that it induced the buyer or lessee to enter into the contract.

Statements of Opinion and Value

Only statements of fact create express warranties. If the seller or lessor makes a statement about the supposed value or worth of the goods, or offers an opinion or recommendation about the goods, the seller or lessor is not creating an express warranty [UCC 2–313(2), 2A–210(2)].

EXAMPLE 18.22 A salesperson claims that "this is the best used car to come along in years. It has four new tires and a 250-horsepower engine just rebuilt this year." The seller has made several affirmations of fact that can create a warranty: the automobile has an engine, the engine has 250 horsepower and was rebuilt this year, and there are four new tires on the automobile. The seller's expressed opinion that the vehicle is "the best used car to come along in years," however, is puffery and creates no warranty. ■

As discussed in an earlier chapter, *puffery*—also known as "seller's talk"—is an expression of opinion by a seller or lessor that is not made as a representation of fact. It is not always easy to determine whether a statement constitutes an express warranty or puffery. The reasonableness of the buyer's or lessee's reliance appears to be the controlling criterion in many cases. For instance, a salesperson's statements that a ladder "will never break" and will "last a lifetime" are so clearly improbable that no reasonable buyer should rely on them.

18–4c Implied Warranties

An express warranty is based on the seller's express promise. In contrast, an **implied warranty** is one that *the law derives* by implication or inference because of the circumstances of a sale. In an action based on breach of implied warranty, it is necessary to show that an implied warranty existed and that the breach of the warranty proximately caused[9] the damage sustained. We look here at some of the implied warranties that arise under the UCC.

Implied Warranty of Merchantability Every sale or lease of goods made *by a merchant who deals in goods of the kind sold or leased* automatically gives rise to an **implied warranty of merchantability** [UCC 2–314, 2A–212]. **EXAMPLE 18.23** Colette, a merchant who is in the business of selling ski equipment, makes an implied warranty of merchantability every time she sells a pair of skis. A neighbor selling his skis at a garage sale does not (because he is not in the business of selling goods of this type). ■

Merchantable Goods. Goods that are *merchantable* are "reasonably fit for the ordinary purposes for which such goods are used." They must be of at least average, fair, or medium-grade quality—quality adequate to pass without objection in the trade or market for goods of the same description. The goods must also be adequately packaged and labeled, and they must conform to the promises or affirmations of fact made on the container or label, if any.

The warranty of merchantability may be breached even though the merchant did not know or could not have discovered that a product was defective (not merchantable). Of course, merchants are not absolute insurers against all accidents occurring in connection with their goods. For instance, a bar of soap is not unmerchantable merely because stepping on it could cause a user to slip and fall.

CASE EXAMPLE 18.24 Darrell Shoop bought a Dodge Dakota truck that had been manufactured by DaimlerChrysler Corporation. Almost immediately, he had problems with the truck. During the first eighteen months, the truck's engine, suspension, steering, transmission, and other components required repairs twelve times, including at least five times for the same defect, which remained uncorrected. Shoop eventually traded in the truck and filed a lawsuit against DaimlerChrysler for breach of the implied warranty of merchantability. The court held that Shoop could maintain an action against DaimlerChrysler and use the fact that the truck had required a significant number of repairs as evidence that it was unmerchantable.[10] ■

Implied Warranty A warranty that arises by law because of the circumstances of a sale and not from the seller's express promise.

Implied Warranty of Merchantability A warranty that goods being sold or leased are reasonably fit for the general purpose for which they are sold or leased, are properly packaged and labeled, and are of proper quality.

LEARNING OBJECTIVE 5
What implied warranties arise under the UCC?

---

9. Proximate, or legal, cause exists when the connection between an act and an injury is strong enough to justify imposing liability.
10. *Shoop v. DaimlerChrysler Corp.,* 371 Ill.App.3d 1058, 864 N.E.2d 785 (2007).

Merchantable Food. The UCC recognizes the serving of food or drink to be consumed on or off the premises as a sale of goods subject to the implied warranty of merchantability [UCC 2–314(1)]. "Merchantable" food means food that is fit to eat.

Courts generally determine whether food is fit to eat on the basis of consumer expectations. The courts assume that consumers should reasonably expect on occasion to find bones in fish fillets, cherry pits in cherry pie, or a nutshell in a package of shelled nuts, for example— because such substances are natural incidents of the food. In contrast, consumers would not reasonably expect to find moth larvae in a can of peas or a piece of glass in a soft drink.

In the following *Classic Case,* the court had to determine whether a diner should reasonably expect to find a fish bone in fish chowder.

★★★ CLASSIC CASE 18.3 ★★★

Webster v. Blue Ship Tea Room, Inc.

Supreme Judicial Court of Massachusetts, 347 Mass. 421, 198 N.E.2d 309 (1964).

HISTORICAL AND CULTURAL SETTING *Chowder, a soup or stew made with fresh fish, originated in fishing villages. Recipes for chowder traditionally did not call for the removal of the fish bones. In fact, many recipes specified that the fish head, tail, and backbone were to be broken in pieces and boiled to create the broth of the soup. By the middle of the twentieth century, there was a considerable body of case law concerning implied warranties and foreign and natural substances in food. It was perhaps inevitable that sooner or later, a consumer injured by a fish bone in chowder would challenge the merchantability of chowder containing fish bones.*

Who is liable for fish bones in seafood chowder?

iStockPhoto.com/hipokrat

FACTS Blue Ship Tea Room, Inc., was located in Boston in an old building overlooking the ocean. Priscilla Webster, who had been born and raised in New England, went to the restaurant and ordered fish chowder. The chowder was milky in color. After three or four spoonfuls, she felt something lodged in her throat. As a result, she underwent two esophagoscopies (a procedure in which a telescope-like instrument is used to look into the throat). In the second esophagoscopy, a fish bone was found and removed. Webster filed a lawsuit against the restaurant in a Massachusetts state court for breach of the implied warranty of merchantability. The jury rendered a verdict for Webster, and the restaurant appealed to the state's highest court.

ISSUE Does serving fish chowder that contains a bone constitute a breach of an implied warranty of merchantability by the restaurant?

DECISION No. The Supreme Judicial Court of Massachusetts held that Webster could not recover against Blue Ship Tea Room, because no breach of warranty had occurred.

REASON The court, citing UCC Section 2–314, stated that "a warranty that goods shall be merchantable is implied in a contract for their sale if the seller is a merchant with respect to goods of that kind. Under this section the serving for value of food or drink to be consumed either on the premises or elsewhere is a sale.... Goods to be merchantable must at least be . . . fit for the ordinary purposes for which such goods are used." The question here was whether a fish bone made the chowder unfit for eating. In the judge's opinion, "the joys of life in New England include the ready availability of fresh fish chowder. We should be prepared to cope with the hazards of fish bones, the occasional presence of which in chowders is, it seems to us, to be anticipated, and which, in the light of a hallowed tradition, do not impair their fitness or merchantability."

CRITICAL THINKING—Legal Consideration *If Webster had made the chowder herself from a recipe that she had found on the Internet today, could she have successfully brought an action against its author for a breach of the implied warranty of merchantability? Explain.*

IMPACT OF THIS CASE ON TODAY'S LAW *This classic case, phrased in memorable language, was an early application of the UCC's implied warranty of merchantability to food products. The case established the rule that consumers should expect to occasionally find elements of food products that are natural to the product (such as fish bones in fish chowder). Courts today still apply this rule.*

Implied Warranty of Fitness for a Particular Purpose   The **implied warranty of fitness for a particular purpose** arises in the sale or lease of goods when a seller or lessor (merchant or nonmerchant) knows *both* of the following:

1. The particular purpose for which a buyer or lessee will use the goods.

2. That the buyer or lessee is relying on the skill and judgment of the seller or lessor to select suitable goods [UCC 2–315, 2A–213].

A "particular purpose" of the buyer or lessee differs from the "ordinary purpose for which goods are used" (merchantability). Goods can be merchantable but unfit for a particular purpose. `EXAMPLE 18.25` Cheryl needs a gallon of paint to match the color of her living room walls—a light shade of green. She takes a sample to the local hardware store and requests a gallon of paint of that color. Instead, she is given a gallon of bright blue paint. Here, the salesperson has not breached any warranty of implied merchantability—the bright blue paint is of high quality and suitable for interior walls. The salesperson has breached an implied warranty of fitness for a particular purpose, though, because the paint is not the right color for Cheryl's purpose (to match her living room walls). ■

For this implied warranty to arise, the seller or lessor need not have actual knowledge of the buyer's or lessee's particular purpose. It is sufficient if the seller or lessor "has reason to know" the purpose. The buyer or lessee must have relied on the skill or judgment of the seller or lessor in selecting or furnishing suitable goods, however.

Warranties Implied from Prior Dealings or Trade Custom   Implied warranties can also arise (or be excluded or modified) as a result of course of dealing or usage of trade [UCC 2–314(3), 2A–212(3)]. In the absence of evidence to the contrary, when both parties to a sales or lease contract have knowledge of a well-recognized trade custom, the courts will infer that both parties intended for that trade custom to apply to their contract. `EXAMPLE 18.26` Industry-wide custom is to lubricate new cars before they are delivered to buyers. If a dealer fails to lubricate a car, the dealer can be held liable to a buyer for damages resulting from the breach of an implied warranty. (This, of course, would also be negligence on the part of the dealer.) ■

18–4d Overlapping Warranties

Sometimes, two or more warranties are made in a single transaction. Thus, an implied warranty of merchantability, an implied warranty of fitness for a particular purpose, or both can exist in addition to an express warranty. `EXAMPLE 18.27` A sales contract for a new car states that "this car engine is warranted to be free from defects for 36,000 miles or thirty-six months, whichever occurs first." This statement creates an express warranty against all defects, as well as an implied warranty that the car will be fit for normal use. ■

The rule under the UCC is that express and implied warranties are construed as *cumulative* if they are consistent with one another [UCC 2–317, 2A–215]. If the warranties are inconsistent, courts apply the following rules to establish which warranty has priority:

1. *Express* warranties displace inconsistent *implied* warranties, except for implied warranties of fitness for a particular purpose.

2. Samples take precedence over inconsistent general descriptions.

3. Exact or technical specifications displace inconsistent samples or general descriptions.

18–4e Warranty Disclaimers

The UCC generally permits warranties to be disclaimed or limited by specific and unambiguous language, provided that the buyer or lessee is protected from surprise. Because each type

Implied Warranty of Fitness for a Particular Purpose
A warranty that goods sold or leased are fit for the particular purpose for which the buyer or lessee will use the goods.

KNOW THIS
Express and implied warranties do not necessarily displace each other. More than one warranty can cover the same goods in the same transaction.

Does the normal new car sales contract create express warranties or implied warranties or both?

of warranty is created in a different way, the manner in which a seller or lessor can disclaim warranties varies with the type of warranty.

Express Warranties

A seller or lessor can disclaim all oral express warranties by including a statement in the written contract. The disclaimer must be in language that is clear and conspicuous, and is called to the buyer's or lessee's attention [UCC 2–316(1), 2A–214(1)]. This allows the seller or lessor to avoid false allegations that oral warranties were made, and it ensures that only representations made by properly authorized individuals are included in the bargain.

Note, however, that a buyer or lessee must be made aware of any warranty disclaimers or modifications *at the time the contract is formed.* In other words, the seller or lessor cannot modify any warranties or disclaimers made during the bargaining process without the consent of the buyer or lessee.

Implied Warranties

Generally, unless circumstances indicate otherwise, the implied warranties of merchantability and fitness are disclaimed by the expressions "as is," "with all faults," or other similar phrases. Both parties must be able to clearly understand from the language used that there are no implied warranties [UCC 2–316(3)(a), 2A–214(3)(a)].

CASE EXAMPLE 18.28 Mandy Morningstar advertised a "lovely, eleven-year-old mare" with extensive jumping ability for sale. After examining the horse twice, Sue Hallett contracted to buy it. She signed a contract that described the horse as an eleven-year-old mare that was being sold "as is." Shortly after the purchase, a veterinarian determined that the horse was actually sixteen years old and in no condition for jumping. Hallett stopped payment and tried to return the horse. Morningstar sued for breach of contract.

The court held that the statement in the contract describing the horse as eleven years old constituted an express warranty, which Morningstar had breached. The "as is" clause effectively disclaimed any implied warranties of merchantability and fitness for a particular purpose, such as jumping. Nevertheless, the court ruled that the clause did not disclaim the express warranty concerning the horse's age.[11]

Note that some states have laws that forbid "as is" sales. Other states do not allow disclaimers of warranties of merchantability for consumer goods.

Disclaimer of the Implied Warranty of Merchantability. To specifically disclaim an implied warranty of merchantability, a seller or lessor must mention the word *merchantability* [UCC 2–316(2), 2A–214(2)]. The disclaimer need not be written, but if it is, the writing must be conspicuous [UCC 2–316(2), 2A–214(4)].

Under the UCC, a term or clause is conspicuous when it is written or displayed in such a way that a reasonable person would notice it. Words are conspicuous when they are in capital letters or are in a larger font size or a different color than the surrounding text.

Disclaimer of the Implied Warranty of Fitness. To specifically disclaim an implied warranty of fitness for a particular purpose, the disclaimer must be in a writing and must be conspicuous. The word *fitness* does not have to be mentioned. It is sufficient if, for example, the disclaimer states, "THERE ARE NO WARRANTIES THAT EXTEND BEYOND THE DESCRIPTION ON THE FACE HEREOF."

Buyer's or Lessee's Examination or Refusal to Inspect. If a buyer or lessee examines the goods (or a sample or model) as fully as desired, *there is no implied warranty with respect to defects that a reasonable examination would reveal or defects that are found on examination* [UCC 2–316(3)(b), 2A–214(2)(b)]. Also, if a buyer or lessee refuses to examine the goods on the seller's or lessor's request that he or she do so, there is no implied warranty with respect to reasonably evident defects.

KNOW THIS

Courts generally view warranty disclaimers unfavorably, especially when consumers are involved.

---

11. *Morningstar v. Hallett*, 858 A.2d 125 (Pa.Super.Ct. 2004).

EXAMPLE 18.29 Janna buys a table at Gershwin's Home Store. No express warranties are made. Gershwin asks Janna to inspect the table before buying it, but she refuses. Had Janna inspected the table, she would have noticed that one of its legs was obviously cracked, which made it unstable. Janna takes the table home and sets a lamp on it. The table later collapses, and the lamp starts a fire that causes significant damage. Janna normally will not be able to hold Gershwin's liable for breach of the warranty of merchantability, because she refused to examine the table as Gershwin requested. Janna therefore assumed the risk that the table was defective. ■

18–4f Lemon Laws

Purchasers of defective automobiles—called "lemons"—may pursue remedies in addition to those provided by the UCC under state *lemon laws*. Basically, state lemon laws provide remedies to consumers who buy automobiles that repeatedly fail to meet standards of quality and performance because they are "lemons."

Although lemon laws vary by state, typically they apply to automobiles under warranty that are defective in a way that significantly affects their value or use. Lemon laws do not necessarily cover used-car purchases (unless the car is covered by a manufacturer's extended warranty) or vehicles that are leased.

Generally, the seller or manufacturer of the automobile is given a number of opportunities to remedy the defect (usually four). If the seller fails to cure the problem despite a reasonable number of attempts (as specified by state law), the buyer is entitled to a new car, replacement of defective parts, or return of all consideration paid.

Typically, buyers must submit their complaint to the arbitration program specified in the manufacturer's warranty before taking the case to court. Buyers who prevail in a lemon-law dispute may also be entitled to reimbursement of their attorneys' fees.

iStockPhoto.com/piallnovak

If a buyer refuses to inspect a new table, and it has an obviously cracked leg, can the buyer later argue that the seller breached the warranty of merchantability?

Reviewing . . . Performance and Breach of Sales and Lease Contracts

GFI, Inc., a Hong Kong company, makes audio decoder chips, one of the essential components used in the manufacture of MP3 players. Egan Electronics contracts with GFI to buy 10,000 chips on an installment contract, with 2,500 chips to be shipped every three months, F.O.B. Hong Kong via Air Express. At the time for the first delivery, GFI delivers only 2,400 chips but explains to Egan that even though the shipment is 4 percent short, the chips are of a higher quality than those specified in the contract and are worth 5 percent more than the contract price. Egan accepts the shipment and pays GFI the contract price. At the time for the second shipment, GFI makes a shipment identical to the first. Egan again accepts and pays for the chips. At the time for the third shipment, GFI ships 2,400 of the same chips, but this time GFI sends them via Hong Kong Air instead of Air Express. While in transit, the chips are destroyed. When it is time for the fourth shipment, GFI again sends 2,400 chips, but this time Egan rejects the chips without explanation. Using the information presented in the chapter, answer the following questions.

1. Did GFI have a legitimate reason to expect that Egan would accept the fourth shipment? Why or why not?

2. Does the substitution of carriers for the third shipment constitute a breach of the contract by GFI? Explain.

3. Suppose that the silicon used for the chips becomes unavailable for a period of time and that GFI cannot manufacture enough chips to fulfill the contract but does ship as many as it can to Egan. Under what doctrine might a court release GFI from further performance of the contract?

4. Under the UCC, does Egan have a right to reject the fourth shipment? Why or why not?

DEBATE THIS

■ If a contract specifies a particular carrier, then the shipper must use that carrier or be in breach of the contract—no exceptions should ever be allowed.

Key Terms

conforming goods 434
cover 445
express warranty 450
implied warranty 451

implied warranty of fitness for a
  particular purpose 453
implied warranty of
  merchantability 451

installment contract 437
lien 450
replevin 446
tender of delivery 434

Chapter Summary: Performance and Breach of Sales and Lease Contracts

PERFORMANCE OBLIGATIONS

Obligations of the Seller or Lessor	1. The seller or lessor must tender *conforming* goods to the buyer or lessee. Tender must take place at a *reasonable hour* and in a *reasonable manner*. Under the perfect tender doctrine, the seller or lessor must tender goods that conform exactly to the terms of the contract [UCC 2–503(1), 2A–508(1)]. 2. If the seller or lessor tenders nonconforming goods prior to the performance date and the buyer or lessee rejects them, the seller or lessor may *cure* (repair or replace the goods) within the contract time for performance [UCC 2–508(1), 2A–513(1)]. If the seller or lessor had reasonable grounds to believe that the buyer or lessee would accept the tendered goods, on the buyer's or lessee's rejection the seller or lessor has a reasonable time to substitute conforming goods without liability [UCC 2–508(2), 2A–513(2)]. 3. If the agreed-on means of delivery becomes impracticable or unavailable, the seller must substitute an alternative means (such as a different carrier) if one is available [UCC 2–614(1)]. 4. If a seller or lessor tenders nonconforming goods in any one installment under an installment contract, the buyer or lessee may reject the installment only if its value is substantially impaired and cannot be cured. The entire installment contract is breached only when one or more nonconforming installments *substantially* impair the value of the *whole* contract [UCC 2–612, 2A–510]. 5. When performance becomes commercially impracticable owing to circumstances that were not foreseeable when the contract was formed, the perfect tender rule no longer holds [UCC 2–615, 2A–405].
Obligations of the Buyer or Lessee	1. On tender of delivery by the seller or lessor, the buyer or lessee must pay for the goods at the time and place the goods are *received*, unless the sale is made on credit. Payment may be made by any method generally acceptable in the commercial world unless the seller demands cash [UCC 2–310, 2–511]. In lease contracts, the lessee must make lease payments in accordance with the contract [UCC 2A–516(1)]. 2. Unless otherwise agreed, the buyer or lessee has an absolute right to inspect the goods before acceptance [UCC 2–513(1), 2A–515(1)]. 3. The buyer or lessee can manifest acceptance of delivered goods expressly in words or by conduct, or by failing to reject the goods after a reasonable period of time following inspection or after having had a reasonable opportunity to inspect them [UCC 2–606(1), 2A–515(1)]. A buyer will be deemed to have accepted goods if he or she performs any act inconsistent with the seller's ownership [UCC 2–606(1)(c)]. 4. The buyer or lessee can make a partial acceptance if some of the goods do not conform to the contract and the seller or lessor failed to cure [UCC 2–601(c), 2A–509(1)].
Anticipatory Repudiation	If, before the time for performance, one party clearly indicates to the other an intention not to perform, under UCC 2–610 and 2A–402, the aggrieved party may do the following: 1. Await performance by the repudiating party for a commercially reasonable time. 2. Resort to any remedy for breach. 3. In either situation, suspend performance.

REMEDIES FOR BREACH

Remedies of the Seller or Lessor	1. *When the goods are in the possession of the seller or lessor*—The seller or lessor may do the following:
	  a. Cancel the contract [UCC 2–703(f), 2A–523(1)(a)].
	  b. Withhold delivery [UCC 2–703(a), 2A–523(1)(c)].
	  c. Resell or dispose of the goods [UCC 2–703(d), 2–706(1), 2A–523(1)(e), 2A–527(1)].
	  d. Sue to recover the purchase price or lease payments due [UCC 2–709(1), 2A–529(1)].
	  e. Sue to recover damages [UCC 2–708, 2A–528].
	
	2. *When the goods are in transit*—The seller or lessor may stop the carrier or bailee from delivering the goods under certain conditions [UCC 2–705, 2A–526].
	
	3. *When the goods are in the possession of the buyer or lessee*—The seller or lessor may do the following:
	  a. Sue to recover the purchase price or lease payments due [UCC 2–709(1), 2A–529(1)].
	  b. Reclaim the goods. A seller may reclaim goods received by an insolvent buyer if the demand is made within ten days of receipt (reclaiming goods excludes all other remedies) [UCC 2–702(2)]. A lessor may repossess goods if the lessee is in default [UCC 2A–525(2)].

Remedies of the Buyer or Lessee	1. *When the seller or lessor refuses to deliver the goods*—The buyer or lessee may do the following:
	  a. Cancel the contract [UCC 2–711(1), 2A–508(1)(a)].
	  b. Recover the goods if the seller or lessor becomes insolvent and the goods are identified to the contract [UCC 2–502, 2A–522].
	  c. Obtain specific performance (when the goods are unique and the remedy at law is inadequate) [UCC 2–716(1), 2A–521(1)].
	  d. Obtain cover [UCC 2–712, 2A–518].
	  e. Replevy the goods (if cover is unavailable) [UCC 2–716(3), 2A–521(3)].
	  f. Sue to recover damages [UCC 2–713, 2A–519].
	2. *When the seller or lessor delivers or tenders delivery of nonconforming goods*—The buyer or lessee may do the following:
	  a. Reject the goods [UCC 2–601, 2A–509].
	  b. Revoke acceptance if the nonconformity *substantially* impairs the value of the unit or lot and if one of the following factors is present:
	    (1) Acceptance was predicated on the reasonable assumption that the nonconformity would be cured, and it was not cured within a reasonable time [UCC 2–608(1)(a), 2A–517(1)(a)].
	    (2) The buyer or lessee did not discover the nonconformity before acceptance, either because it was difficult to discover before acceptance or because the seller's or lessor's assurance that the goods were conforming kept the buyer or lessee from inspecting the goods [UCC 2–608(1)(b), 2A–517(1)(b)].
	  c. Accept the goods and recover damages [UCC 2–607, 2–714, 2–717, 2A–519].

Limitation of Remedies	1. Remedies may be limited in sales or lease contracts by agreement of the parties. If the contract states that a remedy is exclusive, then that is the sole remedy unless the remedy fails in its essential purpose. Sellers and lessors can also limit the rights of buyers and lessees to consequential damages unless the limitation is unconscionable [UCC 2–719, 2A–503]. 2. The UCC has a four-year statute of limitations for actions involving breach of contract. By agreement, the parties to a sales or lease contract can reduce this period to not less than one year, but they cannot extend it beyond four years [UCC 2–725(1), 2A–506(1)].

WARRANTIES

Warranties of Title	Under the UCC, three types of title warranties can automatically arise in sales and lease contracts. 1. In most sales, sellers warrant that they have good and valid title to the goods sold and that transfer of the title is rightful [UCC 2–312(1)(a)]. 2. The seller or lessor warrants that the goods are free of any encumbrances, or liens, of which the buyer or lessee is unaware [UCC 2–312(1)(b), 2A–211(1)]. 3. When the seller or lessor is a merchant, he or she warrants that the buyer or lessee takes the goods free of infringements [UCC 2–312(3), 2A–211(2)].
Express Warranties	Under the UCC, an express warranty arises under the UCC when a seller or lessor provides, as part of the basis of the bargain, any of the following [UCC 2–313, 2A–210]: 1. An affirmation or promise of fact. 2. A description of the goods. 3. A sample shown as conforming to the contract goods.
Implied Warranty of Merchantability	When a seller or lessor is a merchant who deals in goods of the kind sold or leased, the seller or lessor warrants that the goods sold or leased are properly packaged and labeled, are of proper quality, and are reasonably fit for the ordinary purposes for which such goods are used [UCC 2–314, 2A–212].
Implied Warranty of Fitness for a Particular Purpose	Arises when the buyer's or lessee's purpose or use is expressly or impliedly known by the seller or lessor, and the buyer or lessee purchases or leases the goods in reliance on the seller's or lessor's selection [UCC 2–315, 2A–213].
Warranties Implied from Prior Dealings or Trade Custom	Implied warranties can arise as a result of course of dealing or usage of trade [UCC 2–314(3), 2A–212(3)].
Overlapping Warranties	The UCC construes warranties as cumulative if they are consistent with each other. If warranties are inconsistent, then express warranties take precedence over implied warranties, except for the implied warranty of fitness for a particular purpose. Also, samples take precedence over general descriptions, and exact or technical specifications displace inconsistent samples or general descriptions.
Warranty Disclaimers	1. Express warranties can be disclaimed if the disclaimer is written in clear language, is conspicuous, and is called to the buyer's or lessee's attention at the time the contract is formed. 2. A disclaimer of the implied warranty of merchantability must specifically mention the word *merchantability*. The disclaimer need not be in writing, but if it is written, it must be conspicuous. 3. A disclaimer of the implied warranty of fitness *must* be in writing and must be conspicuous, though it need not mention the word *fitness*.

Issue Spotters

1. Country Fruit Stand orders eighty cases of peaches from Down Home Farms. Without stating a reason, Down Home untimely delivers thirty cases instead of eighty. Does Country have the right to reject the shipment? Explain. (See *Performance Obligations*.)

2. Brite Images, Inc. (BI), agrees to sell Catalog Corporation (CC) five thousand posters of celebrities, to be delivered on May 1. On April 1, BI repudiates the contract. CC informs BI that it expects delivery. Can CC sue BI without waiting until May 1? Why or why not? (See *Anticipatory Repudiation*.)

   —**Check your answers to the *Issue Spotters* against the answers provided in Appendix D at the end of this text.**

Learning Objectives Check

1. What are the respective obligations of the parties under a contract for the sale or lease of goods?

2. What is the perfect tender rule? What are some important exceptions to this rule that apply to sales and lease contracts?

3. What options are available to the nonbreaching party when the other party to a sales or lease contract repudiates the contract prior to the time for performance?

4. What remedies are available to a seller or lessor when the buyer or lessee breaches the contract?

5. What implied warranties arise under the UCC?

   —**Answers to the even-numbered *Learning Objectives Check* questions can be found in Appendix E at the end of this text.**

Business Scenarios and Case Problems

18–1. Remedies. Genix, Inc., has contracted to sell Larson five hundred washing machines of a certain model at list price. Genix is to ship the goods on or before December 1. Genix produces one thousand washing machines of this model but has not yet prepared Larson's shipment. On November 1, Larson repudiates the contract. Discuss the remedies available to Genix in this situation. (See *Remedies for Breach*.)

18–2. Anticipatory Repudiation. Moore contracted in writing to sell her 2010 Hyundai Santa Fe to Hammer for $16,500. Moore agreed to deliver the car on Wednesday, and Hammer promised to pay the $16,500 on the following Friday. On Tuesday, Hammer informed Moore that he would not be buying the car after all. By Friday, Hammer had changed his mind again and tendered $16,500 to Moore. Although Moore had not sold the car to another party, she refused the tender and refused to deliver. Hammer claimed that Moore had breached their contract. Moore contended that Hammer's repudiation had released her from her duty to perform under the contract. Who is correct, and why? (See *Anticipatory Repudiation*.)

18–3. Right to Recover Damages. Woodridge USA Properties, L.P., bought eighty-seven commercial truck trailers from Southeast Trailer Mart, Inc. (STM). Gerald McCarty, an independent sales agent who arranged the deal, showed Woodridge the documents of title. The documents did not indicate that Woodridge was the buyer. Woodridge then asked McCarty to sell the trailers, and within three months, they were sold. McCarty did not give the proceeds to Woodridge, however. Woodridge—without mentioning the title documents—asked STM to refund the contract price. STM refused. Does Woodridge have a right to recover damages from STM? Explain. [*Woodridge USA Properties, L.P. v. Southeast Trailer Mart, Inc.*, 2011 WL 303204 (11th Cir. 2011)] (See *Remedies for Breach*.)

18–4. Spotlight on Apple—Implied Warranties. Alan Vitt purchased an iBook G4 laptop computer from Apple, Inc. Shortly after the one-year warranty expired, the laptop stopped working due to a weakness in the product manufacture. Vitt sued Apple, arguing that the laptop should have lasted "at least a couple of years," which Vitt believed was a reasonable consumer expectation for a laptop. Vitt claimed that Apple's descriptions of the laptop as "durable," "rugged," "reliable," and "high performance" were affirmative statements concerning the quality and performance of the laptop, which Apple did not meet. How should the court rule? Why? [*Vitt v. Apple Computer, Inc.*, 2012 WL 627702 (9th Cir. 2011)] (See *Warranties*.)

18–5. Business Case Problem with Sample Answer—Nonconforming Goods. Padma Paper Mills, Ltd., converts waste paper into usable paper. In 2007, Padma entered into a contract with Universal Exports, Inc., under which Universal Exports certified that it would ship white envelope cuttings to Padma in exchange for a payment of $131,000. When the shipment arrived, however, Padma discovered that Universal Exports had sent multicolored paper plates and other brightly colored paper products. Padma accepted the goods but notified Universal Exports that they did not conform to the contract. Can Padma recover even though it accepted the goods knowing that they were nonconforming? If so, how? [*Padma Paper Mills, Ltd. v. Universal Exports, Inc.*, 34 Misc.3d 1236(A) (N.Y.Sup. 2012)] (See *Remedies for Breach.*)

—For a sample answer to Problem 18–5, go to Appendix F at the end of this text.

18–6. Implied Warranties. Bariven, S.A., agreed to buy 26,000 metric tons of powdered milk for $123.5 million from Absolute Trading Corp. to be delivered in shipments from China to Venezuela. After the first three shipments, China halted dairy exports due to the presence of melamine in some products. Absolute assured Bariven that its milk was safe, and when China resumed dairy exports, Absolute delivered sixteen more shipments. Tests of samples of the milk revealed that it contained dangerous levels of melamine. Did Absolute breach any implied warranties? Discuss. [*Absolute Trading Corp. v. Bariven S.A.*, 2013 WL 49735 (11th Cir. 2013)] (See *Warranties.*)

18–7. The Right of Rejection. Erb Poultry, Inc., is a distributor of fresh poultry products in Lima, Ohio. CEME, LLC, does business as Bank Shots, a restaurant in Trotwood, Ohio. CEME ordered chicken wings and "dippers" from Erb, which were delivered and for which CEME issued a check in payment. A few days later, CEME stopped payment on the check. When contacted by Erb, CEME alleged that the products were beyond their freshness date, mangled, spoiled, and the wrong sizes. CEME did not provide any evidence to support the claims or arrange to return the products. Is CEME entitled to a full refund of the amount paid for the chicken? Explain. [*Erb Poultry, Inc. v. CEME, LLC*, 20 N.E.3d 1228 (Ohio App. 2 Dist. 2014)] (See *Remedies for Breach.*)

18–8. Remedies for Breach. Reefpoint Brewhouse in Racine, Wisconsin, contracted with Forman Awnings and Construction, LLC, for the fabrication and installation of an awning system over an outdoor seating area. After the system was complete, Reefpoint expressed concerns about the workmanship but did not give Forman a chance to make repairs. The brewhouse used the awning for two months and then had it removed so that siding on the building could be replaced. The parties disagreed about whether cracked and broken welds observed after the removal of the system were due to shoddy workmanship. Reefpoint paid only $400 on the contract price of $8,161. Can Reefpoint rescind the contract and obtain a return of its $400? Is Forman entitled to recover the difference between Reefpoint's payment and the contract price? Discuss. [*Forman Awnings and Construction LLC v. LO Ventures, LLC*, 2015 WL 248034 (2015)] (See *Remedies for Breach.*)

18–9. A Question of Ethics—Lemon Laws. Randal Schweiger bought a 2008 Kia Spectra EX from Kia Motors America, Inc., for his stepdaughter, April Kirichkow. The cost was $17,231, plus sales tax and other charges, and Schweiger financed the entire amount. April soon began having trouble starting the car. The Kia dealership replaced various parts of the motor several times, but was unable to fix the problem. Schweiger sought a refund under the state's lemon law. When Schweiger and Kia could not agree on the amount, Schweiger filed a suit in a Wisconsin state court against Kia. The court ruled in Schweiger's favor, and Kia appealed. [*Schweiger v. Kia Motors America, Inc.*, 347 Wis.2d 550, 830 N.W.2d 723 (Wis.App. 2013)] (See *Warranties.*)

1. Kia offered a refund of $3,306.24. Should this offer bar Schweiger's claim for a refund? Why or why not?

2. Schweiger claimed that Kia's offer did not include the $1,301 cost of a service contract that he purchased with the car. Kia argued that the amount still owed on the purchase, $13,060.16—which Schweiger agreed was the correct amount—"would by definition refund the cost of the service contract." The court found "no logical basis" for this argument. Is it ethical for a party to argue a position for which there is no logical basis? Discuss.

Critical Thinking and Writing Assignments

18–10. Business Law Writing. Suppose that you are a collector of antique cars and you need to purchase spare parts for a 1938 engine. These parts are not made anymore and are scarce. You discover that Beem has the spare parts that you need. You contract with Beem to buy the parts and agree to pay 50 percent of the purchase price in advance. You send the payment on May 1, and Beem receives it on May 2. On May 3, Beem, having found another buyer willing to pay substantially more for the parts, informs you that he will not deliver as contracted. That same day, you learn that Beem is insolvent. Write three paragraphs fully discussing any possible remedies that would enable you to take possession of the parts. (See *Remedies for Breach.*)

18–11. Business Law Critical Thinking Group Assignment. Kodiak agrees to sell one thousand espresso machines to Lin to be delivered on May 1. Due to a strike during the last week of April, there is a temporary shortage of delivery vehicles. Kodiak can deliver the espresso makers two hundred at a time over a period of ten days, with the first delivery on May 1. (See *Performance Obligations.*)

1. The first group will determine if Kodiak has the right to deliver the goods in five lots. What happens if Lin objects to delivery in lots?

2. A second group will analyze whether the doctrine of commercial impracticability applies to this scenario and, if it does, what the result will be.

19

iStockPhoto.com/bluestocking

CHAPTER OUTLINE

- Types of Negotiable Instruments
- Requirements for Negotiability
- Transfer of Instruments
- Holder in Due Course (HDC)
- Signature and Warranty Liability
- Defenses, Limitations, and Discharge

LEARNING OBJECTIVES

The five Learning Objectives *below are designed to help improve your understanding of the chapter. After reading this chapter, you should be able to answer the following questions:*

1. What requirements must an instrument meet to be negotiable?

2. How does the negotiation of order instruments differ from the negotiation of bearer instruments?

3. What are the requirements for attaining the status of a holder in due course (HDC)?

4. What is the difference between signature liability and warranty liability?

5. Name four defenses that can be used against an ordinary holder but are not effective against an HDC.

Negotiable Instrument A signed writing (record) that contains an unconditional promise or order to pay an exact sum on demand or at a specified future time to a specific person or order, or to bearer.

Negotiable Instruments

Most commercial transactions would be inconceivable without negotiable instruments. A **negotiable instrument** is a signed writing that contains an unconditional promise or order to pay an exact amount, either on demand or at a specified future time. Because negotiable instruments originally were (and often still are) paper documents, they are sometimes referred to as *commercial paper.*

As indicated in the chapter-opening quotation, paper was not fully accepted as a substitute for gold or silver in commerce for "many generations." Today, people are experiencing a similar transition as electronic records substitute more and more for paper documents.

A negotiable instrument can function as a substitute for cash or as an extension of credit. For a negotiable instrument to operate *practically* as either a substitute for cash or a credit device, or both, it is essential that the instrument be *easily transferable without danger of being uncollectible.* Each rule described in this chapter can be examined in light of this essential function of negotiable instruments.

> "It took many generations for people to feel comfortable accepting paper in lieu of gold or silver."
>
> **ALAN GREENSPAN**
> 1926–PRESENT
> (CHAIR OF THE BOARD OF GOVERNORS OF THE FEDERAL RESERVE SYSTEM, 1987–2006)

19-1 Types of Negotiable Instruments

The UCC specifies four types of negotiable instruments: *drafts, checks, promissory notes,* and *certificates of deposit* (CDs). These instruments, which are summarized briefly in Exhibit 19–1, are frequently divided into the two classifications that we will discuss in the following subsections: *orders to pay* (drafts and checks) and *promises to pay* (promissory notes and CDs).

Negotiable instruments may also be classified as either demand instruments or time instruments. A *demand instrument* is payable on demand. In other words, it is payable immediately after it is issued and for a reasonable period of time thereafter. A *time instrument* is payable at a future date.

Note that Section 3–104(b) of the Uniform Commercial Code (UCC) defines *instrument* as a "negotiable instrument."[1] For that reason, whenever the term *instrument* is used in this book, it refers to a negotiable instrument.

19-1a Drafts and Checks (Orders to Pay)

A **draft** is an unconditional written order to pay rather than a promise to pay. Drafts involve three parties. The party creating the draft (the **drawer**) orders another party (the **drawee**) to pay funds, usually to a third party (the **payee**). The most common type of draft is a check, but drafts other than checks may be used in commercial transactions.

Time Drafts versus Sight Drafts   A *time draft* is payable at a definite future time. A *sight draft* (or demand draft) is payable on sight—that is, when it is presented to the drawee (usually a bank or financial institution) for payment. A draft can be both a time and a sight draft. Such a draft is payable at a stated time after sight (a draft that states it is payable ninety days after sight, for instance).

Exhibit 19–2 shows a typical time draft. For the drawee to be obligated to honor (pay) the order, the drawee must be obligated to the drawer either by agreement or through a debtor-creditor relationship. EXAMPLE 19.1 On January 16, OurTown Real Estate orders $1,000 worth of office supplies from Eastman Supply Company, with payment due in ninety days. Also on January 16, OurTown sends Eastman a draft drawn on its account with the First National Bank of Whiteacre as payment. In this scenario, the drawer is OurTown, the drawee is OurTown's bank (First National Bank of Whiteacre), and the payee is Eastman Supply Company. ▪

Acceptances   A drawee's written promise to pay a draft when it comes due is called an **acceptance.** Usually, the drawee accepts the instrument by writing the word *accepted* on its face, with a signature and a date. A drawee who has accepted an instrument becomes an **acceptor.**

A *trade acceptance* is a type of draft commonly used in the sale of goods. In this draft, the seller is both the drawer and the payee. The buyer to whom credit is extended is the

Draft Any instrument drawn on a drawee that orders the drawee to pay a certain amount of funds, usually to a third party (the payee), on demand or at a definite future time.

Drawer The party that initiates a draft (such as a check), thereby ordering the drawee to pay.

Drawee The party that is ordered to pay a draft or check. With a check, a bank or a financial institution is always the drawee.

Payee A person to whom an instrument is made payable.

Acceptance In negotiable instruments law, a drawee's signed agreement to pay a draft when it is presented.

Acceptor A drawee that accepts, or promises to pay, an instrument when it is presented later for payment.

---

1. Note that all of the references to Article 3 of the UCC in this chapter are to the 1990 version of Article 3, which has been adopted by nearly every state.

Exhibit 19–1 **Basic Types of Negotiable Instruments**

INSTRUMENTS	CHARACTERISTICS	PARTIES
ORDERS TO PAY:		
Draft	An order by one person to another person or to bearer [UCC 3–104(e)].	Drawer—The person who signs or makes the order to pay [UCC 3–103(a)(3)].
Check	A draft drawn on a bank and payable on demand [UCC 3–104(f)]. (With certain types of checks, such as cashier's checks, the bank is both the drawer and the drawee.)	Drawee—The person to whom the order to pay is made [UCC 3–103(a)(2)]. Payee—The person to whom payment is ordered.
PROMISES TO PAY:		
Promissory note	A promise by one party to pay funds to another party or to bearer [UCC 3–104(e)].	Maker—The person who promises to pay [UCC 3–103(a)(5)].
Certificate of deposit	A note issued by a bank acknowledging a deposit of funds and made payable to the holder of the note [UCC 3–104(j)].	Payee—The person to whom the promise is made.

Exhibit 19–2 A Typical Time Draft

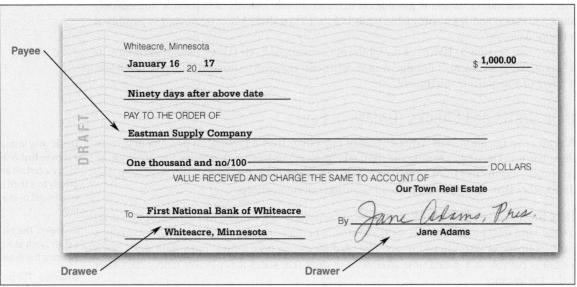

Payee → Eastman Supply Company

Drawee → First National Bank of Whiteacre, Whiteacre, Minnesota

Drawer → Jane Adams

Whiteacre, Minnesota
January 16 20 17 $ 1,000.00

Ninety days after above date

PAY TO THE ORDER OF

Eastman Supply Company

One thousand and no/100————————————————— DOLLARS
VALUE RECEIVED AND CHARGE THE SAME TO ACCOUNT OF
                                        Our Town Real Estate

To   First National Bank of Whiteacre   By *Jane Adams, Pres.*
        Whiteacre, Minnesota   Jane Adams

DRAFT

> "The two most beautiful words in the English language are 'check enclosed.'"
>
> **DOROTHY PARKER**
> 1893–1967
> (AMERICAN AUTHOR AND POET)

Check A draft drawn by a drawer ordering the drawee bank or financial institution to pay a certain amount of funds to the payee on demand.

Promissory Note A written promise made by one person (the maker) to pay a fixed amount of funds to another person (the payee or a subsequent holder) on demand or on a specified date.

Maker One who promises to pay a fixed amount of funds to the holder of a promissory note or a certificate of deposit (CD).

drawee. **EXAMPLE 19.2** Jackson Street Bistro buys its restaurant supplies from Osaka Industries. When Jackson requests supplies, Osaka creates a draft ordering Jackson to pay Osaka for the supplies within ninety days. Jackson accepts the draft by signing its face, which obligates it to make the payment. This is a trade acceptance, and Osaka can sell it to a third party at any time before the payment is due. ■

A *banker's acceptance* is a similar instrument that orders the buyer's bank to pay. Banker's acceptances are often used in international trade.

Checks As mentioned, the most commonly used type of draft is a **check.** The writer of the check is the drawer, the bank on which the check is drawn is the drawee, and the person to whom the check is payable is the payee. Checks are demand instruments because they are payable on demand. Checks will be discussed more fully in the next chapter, but it should be noted here that with certain types of checks, such as *cashier's checks,* the bank is both the drawer and the drawee.

19-1b Promissory Notes (Promises to Pay)

A **promissory note** is a written promise made by one person (the **maker** of the promise to pay) to another (usually a payee). A promissory note, which is often referred to simply as a *note,* can be made payable at a definite time or on demand. It can name a specific payee or merely be payable to bearer (bearer instruments will be discussed later in this chapter). **EXAMPLE 19.3** On April 30, Laurence and Margaret Roberts sign a writing unconditionally promising to pay "to the order of" the First National Bank of Whiteacre $3,000 (with 5 percent interest) on or before June 29. This writing is a promissory note. ■ A typical promissory note is shown in Exhibit 19–3.

Promissory notes are used in a variety of credit transactions. Often, a promissory note will carry the name of the transaction involved. A note secured by personal property, such as an automobile, is referred to as a *collateral note* because property pledged as security for the satisfaction of a debt is called *collateral.*[2] A note payable in installments, such as installment payments for a large-screen television over a twelve-month period, is called an *installment note.*

---
2. To minimize the risk of loss when making a loan, a creditor often requires the debtor to provide some *collateral,* or security, beyond a promise that the debt will be repaid. When this security takes the form of personal property (such as a motor vehicle), the creditor has an interest in the property known as a *security interest.*

Exhibit 19–3 **A Typical Promissory Note**

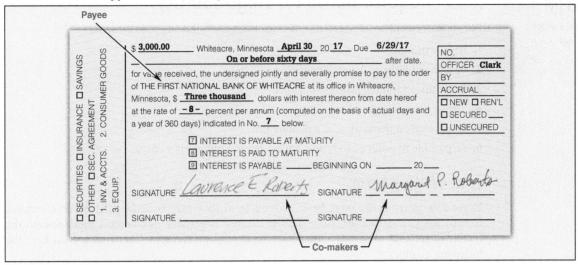

19-1c Certificates of Deposit (Promises to Pay)

A **certificate of deposit (CD)** is a type of note issued when a party deposits funds with a bank that the bank promises to repay, with interest, on a certain date [UCC 3–104(j)]. The bank is the maker of the note, and the depositor is the payee. **EXAMPLE 19.4** On February 15, Sara Levin deposits $5,000 with the First National Bank of Whiteacre. The bank issues a CD, in which it promises to repay the $5,000, plus 1.85 percent annual interest, on August 15. ■

Because CDs are time deposits, the purchaser-payee typically is not allowed to withdraw the funds before the date of maturity (except in limited circumstances, such as disability or death). If a payee wants to access the funds prior to the maturity date, he or she can sell (negotiate) the CD to a third party. Certificates of deposit in small denominations (for amounts up to $100,000) are often sold by savings and loan associations, savings banks, commercial banks, and credit unions. Exhibit 19–4 shows an example of a small CD.

Certificate of Deposit (CD)
A note issued by a bank in which the bank acknowledges the receipt of funds from a party and promises to repay that amount, with interest, to the party on a certain date.

Exhibit 19–4 **A Sample Certificate of Deposit**

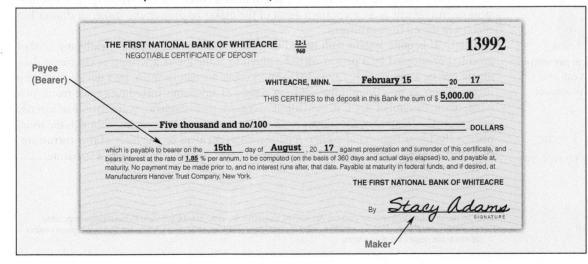

LEARNING OBJECTIVE 1
What requirements must an instrument meet to be negotiable?

19–2 Requirements for Negotiability

For an instrument to be negotiable, it must meet the following requirements:

1. Be in writing.
2. Be signed by the maker or the drawer.
3. Be an unconditional promise or order to pay.
4. State a fixed amount of money.
5. Be payable on demand or at a definite time.
6. Be payable to order or to bearer, unless the instrument is a check.

19–2a Written Form

Negotiable instruments must be in written form (but may be evidenced by an electronic record) [UCC 3–103(a)(6), (9)].[3] This is because negotiable instruments must possess the quality of certainty that only formal, written expression can give. The writing must have the following qualities:

1. The writing must be on material that lends itself to *permanence.* Instruments carved in blocks of ice or recorded on other impermanent surfaces would not qualify as negotiable instruments. **EXAMPLE 19.5** Suzanne writes in the sand, "I promise to pay $500 to the order of Jack." This cannot be a negotiable instrument, because it lacks permanence. ■

2. The writing must also have *portability.* Although the UCC does not explicitly state this requirement, if an instrument is not movable, it obviously cannot meet the requirement that it be freely transferable. **EXAMPLE 19.6** Charles writes on the side of a cow, "I promise to pay $500 to the order of Jason." Technically, this would meet the requirements of a negotiable instrument—except for portability. A cow cannot easily be transferred in the ordinary course of business. Thus, the "instrument" is nonnegotiable. ■

The UCC nevertheless gives considerable leeway as to what can be a negotiable instrument. Courts have found checks and notes written on napkins, menus, tablecloths, shirts, and a variety of other materials to be negotiable.

19–2b Signatures

For an instrument to be negotiable, it must be signed by (1) the maker, if it is a note or a certificate of deposit, or (2) the drawer, if it is a draft or a check [UCC 3–103(a)(3)]. If a person signs an instrument as an authorized agent of the maker or drawer, the maker or drawer has effectively signed the instrument.

The UCC is quite lenient with regard to what constitutes a signature. Nearly any symbol executed or adopted by a person with the intent to authenticate a written or electronic document can be a signature [UCC 1–201(37)]. A signature can be made by a device, such as a rubber stamp, or by a thumbprint, and can consist of any name, including a trade name, or a word, mark, or symbol [UCC 3–401(b)]. If necessary, parol evidence is admissible to identify the signer. The location of the signature on the document is unimportant, although the usual place is the lower right-hand corner. A *handwritten* statement on the body of the instrument, such as "I, Jerome Garcia, promise to pay Elena Greer," is sufficient to act as a signature.

Would a promise to pay written on the side of this calf be negotiable? Why or why not?

"I'm a writer. I write checks. They're not very good."

WENDY LIEBMAN
1961–PRESENT
(AMERICAN COMEDIAN)

---

3. Under the Uniform Electronic Transactions Act (UETA), an electronic record may be sufficient to constitute a negotiable instrument (see UETA Section 16). A small number of states have also adopted amendments to Article 3 that explicitly authorize electronic negotiable instruments.

Although there are almost no limitations on the manner in which a signature can be made, one should be careful about receiving an instrument that has been signed in an unusual way. Oddities on a negotiable instrument can open the door to disputes and lead to litigation. Furthermore, an unusual signature clearly decreases the *marketability* of an instrument because it creates uncertainty.

PREVENTING LEGAL DISPUTES

19-2c Unconditional Promise or Order to Pay

For an instrument to be negotiable, it must contain an express order or promise to pay. The terms of the promise or order must be included in the writing on the face of the instrument. Furthermore, these terms must be unconditional.

KNOW THIS
Negotiable instruments are classified as promises to pay or orders to pay.

Promise The UCC requires that a *promise* be an affirmative (express) undertaking [UCC 3–103(a)(9)]. A mere acknowledgment of a debt, such as an I.O.U., might logically *imply* a promise, but it is *not* sufficient under the UCC. If such words as "to be paid on demand" or "due on demand" are added to an I.O.U., however, the need for an express promise to pay is satisfied.[4]

EXAMPLE 19.7 Kyra executes a promissory note that says "I promise to pay Alvarez $1,000 on demand for the purchase of these goods." These words satisfy the promise-to-pay requirement. ■

Order An *order* is associated with three-party instruments, such as checks, drafts, and trade acceptances. An order directs a third party to pay the instrument as drawn. In the typical check, for instance, the word "pay" (to the order of a payee) is a command to the drawee bank to pay the check when presented—thus, it is an order. "Pay" signifies an order even if it is accompanied by courteous words, as in "Please pay" or "Kindly pay." (In contrast, "I wish you would pay" is not an order.) An order may be addressed to one party or to more than one party, either jointly ("to A *and* B") or alternatively ("to A *or* B") [UCC 3–103(a)(6)].

Unconditionality of Promise or Order Only *unconditional* promises or orders can be negotiable [UCC 3–106(a)]. A promise or order is conditional (and therefore *not* negotiable) if it states *any* of the following:

1. An express condition to payment.
2. That the promise or order is subject to or governed by another writing or record.
3. That the rights or obligations with respect to the promise or order are stated in another writing or record.

A mere reference to another writing, however, does not make the promise or order conditional [UCC 3–106(a)]. For instance, the words "As per contract" or "This debt arises from the sale of goods X and Y" do not render an instrument nonnegotiable. Similarly, a statement in the instrument that payment can be made only out of a particular fund or source will not render the instrument nonnegotiable [UCC 3–106(b)(ii)].

EXAMPLE 19.8 The terms of Biggs's note state that payment will be made out of the proceeds of next year's cotton crop. This does not make the note nonnegotiable. The payee of such a note, however, may find the note commercially unacceptable and refuse to take it. ■

If a note indicates that payment will be made out of the proceeds of the following year's cotton crop, is that note still negotiable?

---

4. A certificate of deposit (CD) is an exception in this respect. A CD does not have to contain an express promise, because the bank's acknowledgment of the deposit and the other terms of the instrument clearly indicate a promise by the bank to repay the funds [UCC 3–104(j)].

In the following case, two notes signed to finance the purchase of a pair of alpacas contained references to the underlying contracts. The court had to determine whether the notes qualified as negotiable instruments.

Alpacas of America, LLC v. Groome

Court of Appeals of Washington, Division 2, 317 P.3d 1103 (2014).

FACTS Sam and Odalis Groome entered into two contracts with Alpacas of America, LLC (AOA) to buy a pair of alpacas—"Phashion Model" and "Black Thunder's Midnight." To finance the purchases, the buyers signed two notes, one for $18,750 and the other for $20,250. Each note included a reference to a contract, outlined a payment schedule, and contained a security agreement that gave AOA an interest in the alpacas. Within a few months, the Groomes stopped making payments.

More than four years later, AOA filed a suit in a Washington state court against the Groomes to collect the unpaid amounts. The court ruled that the notes were not negotiable instruments but were part of the sales contracts. It thus applied the four-year statute of limitations on contract actions in UCC Article 2 to dismiss the suit. AOA appealed, arguing that the notes were negotiable and thus fell within the six-year limit on actions to collect under UCC Article 3.

ISSUE Were the notes negotiable despite containing references to the underlying contracts?

DECISION Yes. A state intermediate appellate court reversed the ruling of the lower court. The notes contained unconditional promises to pay. Because the notes were negotiable, they were subject to Article 3's six-year limit on actions to collect, and AOA could go forward with its claim.

Is a note for funds to purchase alpacas negotiable?

iStockPhoto.com/terrasprite

REASON The Groomes argued that the notes were not negotiable for three reasons. First, each note stated that its indebtedness arose "pursuant to" one of the contracts. UCC 3–106(a), however, provides that "a reference to another writing does not of itself make the promise or order conditional." The words "pursuant to" were only part of a reference to another writing—they did not condition the promise to pay contained in the notes. Second, each note contained a security agreement that referred to its underlying contract as the source to be consulted to determine the property (collateral) covered by the agreement. But UCC 3–106(b) states that a promise is not made conditional by a "reference to another writing for a statement of rights with respect to collateral." Finally, the note to finance the purchase of Black Thunder's Midnight referred to the underlying contract as the source to be consulted to determine the procedure for giving notice to collect. Again, though, this language did not condition the promise to pay.

WHAT IF THE FACTS WERE DIFFERENT? *If AOA's suit had fallen within the four-year statute of limitations of UCC Article 2, could the seller have filed its claim on either the contracts or the notes? Explain.*

19-2d A Fixed Amount of Money

Negotiable instruments must state with certainty a fixed amount of money to be paid at any time the instrument is payable [UCC 3–104(a)]. This requirement ensures that the value of the instrument can be determined with clarity and certainty.

The term *fixed amount* means an amount that is ascertainable from the face of the instrument. A demand note payable with 8 percent interest meets the requirement of a fixed amount because its amount can be determined at the time it is payable or at any time thereafter [UCC 3–104(a)]. The rate of interest may also be determined from information that is not contained in the instrument itself but described by it, such as a formula or a source [UCC 3–112(b)]. For instance, an instrument that is payable at the *legal rate of interest* (a rate of interest fixed by statute) is negotiable. Mortgage notes tied to a variable rate of interest (a rate that fluctuates as a result of market conditions) are also negotiable.

UCC 3–104(a) provides that a fixed amount is to be *payable in money.* The UCC defines money as "a medium of exchange authorized or adopted by a domestic or foreign government

KNOW THIS

Interest payable on an instrument normally cannot exceed the maximum limit on interest under a state's usury statute.

as a part of its currency" [UCC 1–201(24)]. Gold is not a medium of exchange adopted by the U.S. government, so a note payable in gold is nonnegotiable. An instrument payable in the United States with a face amount stated in a foreign currency is negotiable, however, and can be paid in the foreign currency or in the equivalent amount of U.S. dollars [UCC 3–107].

19-2e Payable on Demand or at a Definite Time

A negotiable instrument must "be payable on demand or at a definite time" [UCC 3–104(a)(2)]. To determine the instrument's value, it is necessary to know when the maker, drawee, or acceptor is required to pay. It is also necessary to know when the obligations of secondary parties, such as *indorsers*,[5] will arise. Furthermore, it is necessary to know when an instrument is due in order to calculate when the statute of limitations may apply [UCC 3–118(a)]. Finally, with an interest-bearing instrument, it is necessary to know the exact interval during which interest will accrue to determine the instrument's present value.

Payable on Demand Instruments that are payable on demand include those that contain the words "Payable at sight" or "Payable upon presentment." **Presentment** is a demand made by or on behalf of a person entitled to enforce an instrument to either pay or accept the instrument [UCC 3–501]. Thus, presentment occurs when a person offers the instrument to the appropriate party for payment or acceptance. Presentment can by made by any commercially reasonable means, including oral, written, or electronic communication.

The very nature of the instrument may indicate that it is payable on demand. For instance, a check, by definition, is payable on demand [UCC 3–104(f)]. If no time for payment is specified and the person responsible for payment must pay on the instrument's presentment, the instrument is payable on demand [UCC 3–108(a)].

CASE EXAMPLE 19.9 National City Bank gave Reger Development, LLC, a line of credit to finance potential development opportunities. Reger signed a promissory note requiring it to "pay this loan in full immediately upon Lender's demand." About a year later, the bank asked Reger to pay down the loan and stated that it would be reducing the amount of cash available through the line of credit. Reger sued, alleging that the bank had breached the terms of the note. The court ruled in the bank's favor. The promissory note was a demand instrument because it explicitly set forth the lender's right to demand payment at any time. Thus, National City had the right to collect payment from Reger at any time on demand.[6]

Payable at a Definite Time If an instrument is not payable on demand, to be negotiable it must be payable at a definite time. An instrument is payable at a definite time if it states *any* of the following:

1. That it is payable on a specified date.
2. That it is payable within a definite period of time (such as thirty days) after being presented for payment.
3. That it is payable on a date or time readily ascertainable at the time the promise or order is issued [UCC 3–108(b)].

The maker or drawee in a time draft is under no obligation to pay until the specified time.

When an instrument is payable by the maker or drawer *on or before* a stated date, it is clearly payable at a definite time. The maker or drawer has the *option* of paying before the stated maturity date, but the payee can still rely on payment being made by the maturity date. **EXAMPLE 19.10** Ari gives Ernesto an instrument dated May 1, 2016, that indicates on

Presentment The act of presenting an instrument to the party liable on the instrument in order to collect payment. Presentment also occurs when a person presents an instrument to a drawee for a required acceptance.

---

5. We should note that the UCC uses the spelling *indorse* (*indorsement*, and the like), rather than the more common spelling *endorse* (*endorsement*, and the like). We follow the UCC's spelling here and in other chapters in this text.
6. *Reger Development, LLC v. National City Bank*, 592 F.3d 759 (2010).

its face that it is payable *on or before* May 1, 2017. This instrument satisfies the definite-time requirement. ■

In contrast, an instrument that is undated and made payable "one month after date" is clearly nonnegotiable. There is no way to determine the maturity date from the face of the instrument. If the date is uncertain, the instrument is not payable at a definite time. **EXAMPLE 19.11** An instrument that states, "One year after the death of my grandfather, Jerome Adams, I promise to pay $5,000 to the order of Lucy Harmon. [Signed] Jacqueline Wells," is nonnegotiable. The date on which the instrument becomes payable is uncertain. ■

Acceleration Clause A clause that allows a payee or other holder of a time instrument to demand payment of the entire amount due, with interest, if a certain event occurs, such as a default in the payment of an installment when due.

Acceleration Clause

An **acceleration clause** allows a payee or other holder of a time instrument to demand payment of the entire amount due, with interest, if a certain event occurs. (A **holder** is any person in possession of an instrument drawn, issued, or indorsed to him or her, to his or her order, to bearer, or in blank [UCC 1–201(20)].)

EXAMPLE 19.12 Marta lends $1,000 to Ruth, who makes a negotiable note promising to pay $100 per month (plus interest) for ten months. The note contains an acceleration provision that permits Marta or any holder to immediately demand all the payments plus the interest owed to date if Ruth fails to pay an installment. Ruth fails to make the third payment. Marta accelerates the unpaid balance, and the note becomes due and payable in full. Ruth owes Marta the remaining principal plus any unpaid interest to that date. ■

Holder Any person in possession of an instrument drawn, issued, or indorsed to him or her, to his or her order, to bearer, or in blank.

Instruments that include acceleration clauses are negotiable because the exact value of the instrument can be ascertained. In addition, the instrument will be payable on a specified date if the event allowing acceleration does not occur [UCC 3–108(b)(ii)]. Thus, the specified date is the outside limit used to determine the value and negotiability of the instrument.

Extension Clause A clause in a time instrument that allows the instrument's date of maturity to be extended into the future.

Extension Clause

The reverse of an acceleration clause is an **extension clause,** which allows the date of maturity to be extended into the future [UCC 3–108(b)(iii), (iv)]. If the right to extend the time of payment is given to the maker or drawer, the interval of the extension must be specified to keep the instrument negotiable. If, however, the holder can extend the time of payment, the extended maturity date need not be specified for the instrument to be negotiable.

EXAMPLE 19.13 Alek's note reads, "The holder of this note at the date of maturity, January 1, 2017, can extend the time of payment until the following June 1 or later, if the holder so wishes." This note is negotiable. The length of the extension does not have to be specified, because only the holder has the option to extend. After January 1, 2017, the note is, in effect, a demand instrument. ■

Can a note made in exchange for funds contain an acceleration clause and still be negotiable?

19–2f Payable to Order or to Bearer

Because one of the functions of a negotiable instrument is to serve as a substitute for cash, freedom to transfer is essential. To ensure a proper transfer, the instrument must be "payable to order or to bearer" at the time it is issued or first comes into the possession of the holder [UCC 3–104(a)(1)]. An instrument is not negotiable unless it meets this requirement.

Order Instruments An **order instrument** is an instrument that is payable (1) "to the order of an identified person" or (2) "to an identified person or order" [UCC 3–109(b)]. An identified person is the person "to whom the instrument is initially payable" as determined by the intent of the maker or drawer [UCC 3–110(a)]. The identified person, in turn, may transfer the instrument to whomever he or she wishes. In this way, the instrument retains its transferability.

Order Instrument A negotiable instrument that is payable "to the order of an identified person" or "to an identified person or order."

Note that in an order instrument, the person specified must be identified with *certainty,* because the transfer of the instrument requires the *indorsement,* or signature, of the payee (indorsements will be discussed later in this chapter). An order instrument made "Payable to the order of my nicest cousin," for instance, is not negotiable, because it does not clearly specify the payee.

Bearer Instruments A **bearer instrument** is an instrument that does not designate a specific payee [UCC 3–109(a)]. The term **bearer** refers to a person in possession of an instrument that is payable to bearer or indorsed in blank (with a signature only, as will be discussed shortly) [UCC 1–201(5), 3–109(a), 3–109(c)]. This means that the maker or drawer agrees to pay anyone who presents the instrument for payment.

Any instrument containing terms such as the following is a bearer instrument:

1. "Payable to the order of bearer."

2. "Payable to Simon Reed or bearer."

3. "Payable to bearer."

4. "Pay cash."

5. "Pay to the order of cash."

CASE EXAMPLE 19.14 Amine Nehme applied for credit at the Venetian Resort Hotel Casino in Las Vegas, Nevada, and was granted $500,000 in credit. He signed a marker—that is, a promise to pay a debt—for $500,000. Nehme quickly lost that amount gambling. The Venetian presented the marker for payment to Nehme's bank, Bank of America, which returned it for insufficient funds. The casino's owner, Las Vegas Sands, LLC, filed a suit against Nehme for failure to pay a negotiable instrument.

The court held that the marker fit the UCC's definitions of negotiable instrument and check. It was a means for payment of $500,000 from Bank of America to the order of the Venetian. It did not state a time for payment and thus was payable on demand. It was also unconditional—that is, it stated no promise by Nehme other than the promise to pay a fixed amount of money.[7] ■

19–2g Factors That Do Not Affect Negotiability

Certain ambiguities or omissions will not affect the negotiability of an instrument. The UCC provides the following rules for clearing up ambiguous terms:

1. Unless the date of an instrument is necessary to determine a definite time for payment, the fact that an instrument is *undated* does not affect its negotiability. A typical example is an undated check, which is still negotiable. If a check is not dated, its date is the date of its issue, meaning the date the maker first delivers the check to another person to give that person rights in the check [UCC 3–113(b)].

2. Antedating or postdating an instrument (using a date before or after the actual current date) does not affect the instrument's negotiability [UCC 3–113(a)]. **EXAMPLE 19.15** Crenshaw draws a check on his account at First Bank, payable to Sirah Imports. He postdates the check by fifteen days. Sirah Imports can immediately negotiate the check, and, unless Crenshaw tells First Bank otherwise, the bank can charge the amount of the check to Crenshaw's account [UCC 4–401(c)]. ■

3. Handwritten terms outweigh typewritten and printed terms (preprinted terms on forms, for example), and typewritten terms outweigh printed terms [UCC 3–114]. **EXAMPLE 19.16** Most checks are preprinted "Pay to the order of" followed by a blank line, indicating an order instrument. In handwriting, Chad inserts in the blank, "Anita Delgado or bearer." The handwritten terms will outweigh the printed form, and the check will be a bearer instrument. ■

Bearer Instrument Any instrument that is not payable to a specific person, including instruments payable to the bearer or to "cash."

Bearer A person in possession of an instrument payable to bearer or indorsed in blank.

nito/ShutterStock.com

Can a gambling marker be a negotiable instrument?

KNOW THIS

An instrument that purports to be payable both to order and to bearer contains a contradiction in terms. Such an instrument is a bearer instrument.

---

7. *Las Vegas Sands, LLC v. Nehme*, 632 F.3d 526 (9th Cir. 2011).

4. Words outweigh figures unless the words are ambiguous [UCC 3–114]. This rule is important when the numerical amount and the written amount on a check differ.

5. When an instrument does not specify a particular interest rate but simply states "with interest," the interest rate is the *judgment rate of interest* (a rate of interest fixed by statute that is applied to court judgments) [UCC 3–112(b)].

6. A check is negotiable even if a notation on it states that it is "nonnegotiable" or "not governed by Article 3." Any other instrument, in contrast, can be made nonnegotiable if the maker or drawer conspicuously notes on it that it is "nonnegotiable" or "not governed by Article 3" [UCC 3–104(d)].

In the following case, the court was asked to compare the words and figures in a note to determine its amount.

CASE 19.2

Charles R. Tips Family Trust v. PB Commercial LLC

Court of Appeals of Texas, Houston, First District, __ S.W.3d __, 2015 WL 730481 (2015).

FACTS The Charles R. Tips Family Trust signed a promissory note in favor of Patriot Bank to obtain a loan to buy a house in Harris County, Texas. The note identified the principal amount of the loan as "ONE MILLION SEVEN THOUSAND AND NO/100 ($1,700,000.00) DOLLARS." The trust made payments totaling only $595,586. PB Commercial, LLC (PBC) acquired the note, sold the residence for $874,125, and pursued litigation in a Texas state court against the borrower, alleging default. The defendant argued that the written words in an instrument control and that the note had been satisfied in full by the amount of the payments and the price on the sale of the house—"in fact, PBC has collected a surplus of $189,111." The court entered a judgment in PBC's favor. The trust appealed, arguing one issue—that the amount of the loan must be determined from the printed words in the note.

ISSUE Was the amount of the note "ONE MILLION SEVEN THOUSAND AND NO/100 * * * DOLLARS?"

DECISION Yes. A state intermediate appellate court reversed the judgment of the lower court. "The words 'one million seven thousand' control over the numerals '$1,700,000' to set the amount."

What happens when the numbers in a promissory note differ from the written amount?

REASON To recover on the note, PBC had to prove the balance that was due. Under UCC 3–114, "if an instrument contains contradictory terms, . . . words prevail over numbers." The principle underlying this rule is that words are more likely to represent the parties' actual intent than numbers. In this case, the meaning of the note's phrase "one million seven thousand and no/100 dollars" is unambiguous—it refers to the sum $1,007,000. This phrase obviously conflicted with the note's numerals, differing by $693,000. The court held that the large size of the discrepancy "does not matter" under Texas Business & Commercial Code Section 3.114 (Texas's version of UCC 3–114) or Texas case law. PBC argued that if the phrase had been "one seven hundred thousand," omitting the word "million," the amount of the note would have been ambiguous, and the court would have had to consider the numerals and other evidence to determine it. "But this hypothetical scenario has no bearing on this case because there is no ambiguity . . . here."

WHAT IF THE FACTS WERE DIFFERENT? *Suppose that the note had described the amount of the loan as "ONE MILLION SEVEN HUNDRED THOUSAND AND NO/100 ($1,007,000.00) DOLLARS." What would have been the result?*

19-3 **Transfer of Instruments**

Once issued, a negotiable instrument can be transferred by *assignment* or by *negotiation*. The party receiving the instrument obtains the rights of a holder only if the transfer is by negotiation.

19-3a Transfer by Assignment

Recall that an assignment is a transfer of rights under a contract. Under general contract principles, a transfer by assignment gives the assignee only those rights that the assignor possessed. Any defenses that can be raised against an assignor can normally be raised against the assignee. This same principle applies when a negotiable instrument, such as a promissory note, is transferred by assignment. The transferee is an *assignee* rather than a *holder*.

19-3b Transfer by Negotiation

Negotiation is the transfer of an instrument in such a way that the transferee (the person to whom the instrument is transferred) becomes a holder [UCC 3–201(a)]. Under UCC principles, a transfer by negotiation creates a holder who, at the very least, receives the rights of the previous possessor [UCC 3–203(b)].

Unlike an assignment, a transfer by negotiation can make it possible for a holder to receive more rights in the instrument than the prior possessor had [UCC 3–202(b), 3–305, 3–306]. A holder who receives greater rights is known as a *holder in due course,* a concept we will discuss later in this chapter.

There are two methods of negotiating an instrument so that the receiver becomes a holder. The method used depends on whether the instrument is an *order instrument* or a *bearer instrument*.

Negotiating Order Instruments An order instrument contains the name of a payee capable of indorsing it, as in "Pay to the order of Lloyd Sorenson." If the instrument is an order instrument, it is negotiated by delivery with any necessary indorsements.

EXAMPLE 19.17 National Express Corporation issues a payroll check "to the order of Lloyd Sorenson." Sorenson takes the check to the bank, signs his name on the back (an indorsement), gives it to the teller (a delivery), and receives cash. Sorenson has *negotiated* the check to the bank [UCC 3–201(b)]. ■

Negotiating order instruments requires both delivery and indorsement (indorsements will be discussed shortly). If Sorenson had taken the check to the bank and delivered it to the teller without signing it, the transfer would not qualify as a negotiation. In that situation, the transfer would be treated as an assignment, and the bank would become an assignee rather than a holder.

Negotiating Bearer Instruments If an instrument is payable to bearer, it is negotiated by delivery—that is, by transfer into another person's possession. Indorsement is not necessary [UCC 3–201(b)]. The use of bearer instruments thus involves more risk through loss or theft than the use of order instruments.

EXAMPLE 19.18 Richard Kray writes a check "payable to cash" and hands it to Jessie Arnold (a delivery). Kray has issued the check (a bearer instrument) to Arnold. Arnold places the check in her wallet, which is subsequently stolen. The thief has possession of the check. At this point, the thief has no rights to the check. If the thief "delivers" the check to an innocent third person, however, negotiation will be complete. All rights to the check will be passed absolutely to that third person, and Arnold will lose all rights to recover the proceeds of the check from that person [UCC 3–306]. Of course, Arnold can attempt to recover the amount from the thief if the thief can be found. ■

19-3c Indorsements

An indorsement is required whenever an order instrument is negotiated. An **indorsement** is a signature with or without additional words or statements. It is most often written on the back of the instrument itself. If there is no room on the instrument, the indorsement

---

> "Money has little value to its possessor unless it also has value to others."
>
> **LELAND STANFORD**
> 1824–1893
> (U.S. SENATOR AND FOUNDER OF STANFORD UNIVERSITY)

Negotiation The transfer of an instrument in such form that the transferee (the person to whom the instrument is transferred) becomes a holder.

LEARNING OBJECTIVE 2
How does the negotiation of order instruments differ from the negotiation of bearer instruments?

Is a check made out "payable to cash" a bearer instrument?

Indorsement A signature placed on an instrument for the purpose of transferring ownership rights in the instrument.

can be on a separate piece of paper that is firmly affixed to the instrument, such as with staples [UCC 3–204(a)]. (See this chapter's *Beyond Our Borders* feature for a discussion of the approach to indorsements in France.)

A person who transfers an instrument by signing (indorsing) it and delivering it to another person is an *indorser.* The person to whom the check is indorsed and delivered is the *indorsee.* **EXAMPLE 19.19** Luisa Perez receives a graduation check for $100. She can transfer the check to her mother (or to anyone) by signing it on the back. Luisa is an indorser. If Luisa indorses the check by writing "Pay to Avery Perez," Avery Perez is the indorsee. ■

We examine here the four categories of indorsements: blank, special, qualified, and restrictive. Note that a single indorsement may have characteristics of more than one category.

Blank Indorsements A **blank indorsement** does not specify a particular indorsee and can consist of a mere signature [UCC 3–205(b)]. **EXAMPLE 19.20** A check payable "to the order of Alan Luberda" is indorsed in blank if Luberda simply writes his signature on the back of the check, as shown in Exhibit 19–5. ■

An order instrument indorsed in blank becomes a bearer instrument and can be negotiated by delivery alone, as already discussed. In other words, a blank indorsement converts an order instrument to a bearer instrument, which anybody can cash.

Does an instrument that requires an indorsement for negotiation need to contain a handwritten signature? That was the question in the following case.

Blank Indorsement
An indorsement on an instrument that specifies no indorsee. An order instrument that is indorsed in blank becomes a bearer instrument.

Exhibit 19–5 A Blank Indorsement

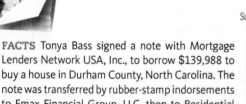

Alan Luberda

CASE 19.3

In re Bass
Supreme Court of North Carolina, 738 S.E.2d 173 (2013).

FACTS Tonya Bass signed a note with Mortgage Lenders Network USA, Inc., to borrow $139,988 to buy a house in Durham County, North Carolina. The note was transferred by rubber-stamp indorsements to Emax Financial Group, LLC, then to Residential Funding Corporation, and finally to U.S. Bank, N.A.

When Bass stopped paying on the note, U.S. Bank filed an action in a North Carolina state court to foreclose. The court issued an order permitting the foreclosure to proceed, and Bass appealed. She argued that the stamp transferring the note from Mortgage Lenders to Emax was invalid because it was not accompanied by a signature. A state intermediate appellate court decided in Bass's favor based on the lack of a "proper indorsement." U.S. Bank appealed.

ISSUE Can an indorsement that does not include a handwritten signature effectively transfer a negotiable instrument?

DECISION Yes. The North Carolina Supreme Court reversed the decision of the lower court, holding that U.S. Bank was the holder of the note.

Can a signature stamp constitute a valid indorsement on a negotiable instrument?

NotarYES/ShutterStock.com

REASON The UCC defines "signature" as "any symbol executed or adopted with present intention to adopt or accept a writing." Under this definition, a handwritten signature is not necessary. A "symbol" can be written, but it may also be printed or stamped. "The question always is whether the symbol was executed or adopted by the party with present intention to adopt or accept the writing." In this case, the stamped indorsement indicates that intent on its face—"Pay to the order of: Emax Financial Group, LLC without recourse By: Mortgage Lenders Network USA, Inc." The stamp's language shows that the indorsement "was executed or adopted by the party with present intention to adopt or accept the writing." Thus, the stamp effectively transferred the note.

CRITICAL THINKING—Economic Consideration *How does presuming that an indorsement is legitimate unless there is evidence to the contrary protect the transferability of a negotiable instrument?*

BEYOND OUR BORDERS

Severe Restrictions on Check Indorsements in France

If you were reading a business law text-book in France, you would find very little on check indorsements. The reason is that checks rarely, if ever, can be indorsed. That means that almost all checks must be deposited in a bank account, rather than transferred to another individual or entity. The French government says that these restrictions on indorsements reduce the risk of loss and theft.

CRITICAL THINKING

■ What would be the cost to individuals and businesses that use checks if a similar rule were passed in this country?

Special Indorsements A **special indorsement** contains the signature of the indorser and identifies the person to whom the instrument is made payable—that is, it names the indorsee [UCC 3–205(a)]. Words such as "Pay to the order of Clay" or "Pay to Clay," followed by the signature of the indorser, create a special indorsement. An instrument indorsed in this way is an order instrument.

To avoid the risk of loss from theft, a holder may convert a blank indorsement to a special indorsement by writing, above the signature of the indorser, words identifying the indorsee [UCC 3–205(c)]. This changes the bearer instrument back to an order instrument.

EXAMPLE 19.21 A check is made payable to Peter Rabe. He indorses the check in blank by signing his name on the back and delivers the check to Anthony Bartomo. Anthony is unable to cash the check immediately and wants to avoid any risk should he lose the check. He therefore prints "Pay to Anthony Bartomo" above Peter's blank indorsement (see Exhibit 19–6). By doing this, Anthony has converted Peter's blank indorsement into a special indorsement. Further negotiation now requires Anthony's indorsement plus delivery. ■

Special Indorsement
An indorsement on an instrument that identifies the specific person to whom the indorser intends to make the instrument payable.

Exhibit 19–6 A Special Indorsement

Pay to Anthony Bartomo

Peter Rabe

Qualified Indorsements Generally, an indorser, *merely by indorsing,* impliedly promises to pay the holder or any subsequent indorser the amount of the instrument in the event that the drawer or maker defaults on the payment [UCC 3–415(a)]. Usually, then, indorsements are *unqualified indorsements,* which means that the indorser is guaranteeing payment of the instrument in addition to transferring title to it.

An indorser who does not wish to be liable on an instrument can use a **qualified indorsement** to disclaim this liability [UCC 3–415(b)]. The notation "without recourse" is commonly used to create a qualified indorsement, such as the one shown in Exhibit 19–7. If an instrument with such an indorsement is later dishonored, the holder cannot recover from the qualified indorser unless the indorser has breached one of the transfer warranties discussed later.

Qualified indorsements are often used by persons (agents) acting in a representative capacity. **EXAMPLE 19.22** Insurance agents sometimes receive checks payable to them that are really intended as payment to the insurance company. The agent is merely indorsing the payment through to the insurance company and should not be required to make good on a check if it is later dishonored. The "without recourse" indorsement relieves the agent from any liability on a check. ■

Qualified Indorsement
An indorsement on a negotiable instrument in which the indorser disclaims any contract liability on the instrument. The notation "without recourse" is commonly used to create a qualified indorsement.

Exhibit 19–7 A Qualified Indorsement

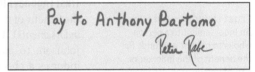

Pay to Elvie Ling, without recourse.

Bridgett Cage

A qualified indorsement can be accompanied by either a special indorsement or a blank indorsement. In either situation, the instrument can be further negotiated.

- A *special qualified indorsement* includes the name of the indorsee as well as the words *without recourse*. The special indorsement makes the instrument an order instrument requiring an indorsement plus delivery for negotiation.
- A *blank qualified indorsement* ("without recourse, [signed] Jennie Cole") makes the instrument a bearer instrument, and only delivery is required for negotiation.

Restrictive Indorsement
An indorsement on a negotiable instrument that requires the indorsee to comply with certain instructions regarding the funds involved.

Restrictive Indorsements A **restrictive indorsement** requires the indorsee to comply with certain instructions regarding the funds involved, but it does not generally prohibit further negotiation of the instrument [UCC 3–206(a)]. Although most indorsements are nonrestrictive, many forms of restrictive indorsements do exist, including those discussed here.

Conditional Indorsements. When payment depends on the occurrence of some event specified in the indorsement, the indorsement is conditional. EXAMPLE 19.23 Ken Barton indorses a check, "Pay to Lars Johansen if he completes the renovation of my kitchen by June 1, 2017 [Signed] Ken Barton." Barton has created a conditional indorsement. ■

Indorsements for Deposit or Collection. A common type of restrictive indorsement is one that makes the indorsee (almost always a bank) a collecting agent of the indorser [UCC 3–206(c)]. EXAMPLE 19.24 Stephanie Mallak has received a check and wants to deposit it into her checking account at the bank. She can indorse the check "For deposit [or collection] only. [Signed] Stephanie Mallak" (see Exhibit 19–8). She may also wish to write her bank account number on the check. A "For deposit" or "For collection" indorsement prohibits further negotiation except by the bank. Following this indorsement, only the bank can acquire the rights of a holder. ■

Trust Indorsement
An indorsement to a person who is to hold or use funds for the benefit of the indorser or a third person. It is also known as an *agency indorsement*.

Trust (Agency) Indorsements. Indorsements to persons who are to hold or use the funds for the benefit of the indorser or a third party are called **trust indorsements** (also known as *agency indorsements*) [UCC 3–206(d), (e)]. EXAMPLE 19.25 Robert Emerson asks his accountant, Ada Johnson, to pay some bills for his invalid wife, Sarah, while he is out of the country. He indorses a check as follows: "Pay to Ada Johnson as Agent for Sarah Emerson." This agency indorsement obligates Johnson to use the funds only for the benefit of Sarah Emerson. ■ Exhibit 19–9 shows sample trust (agency) indorsements.

Exhibit 19–8 "For Deposit" and "For Collection" Indorsements

For deposit only
Stephanie Mallak

or

For Collection only
Stephanie Mallak

Exhibit 19–9 Trust (Agency) Indorsements

Pay to Ada Johnson in trust for Sarah Emerson
Robert Emerson

or

Pay to Ada Johnson as Agent for Sarah Emerson
Robert Emerson

Misspelled Names A payee or indorsee whose name is misspelled can indorse with the misspelled name, the correct name, or both [UCC 3–204(d)]. The usual practice is to indorse with the name as it appears on the instrument, followed by the correct name.

Alternative or Joint Payees An instrument payable to two or more persons *in the alternative* (for example, "Pay to the order of Ramirez or Johnson") requires the indorsement of only one of the payees. In contrast, if an instrument is made payable to two or more persons *jointly* (for example, "Pay to the order of Shari and Bob Covington"), all of the payees' indorsements are necessary for negotiation.

If an instrument payable to two or more persons does not clearly indicate whether it is payable in the alternative or jointly ("Pay to the order of John and/or Sara Fitzgerald" or "Pay to the order of J&D Landscaping, Bryson Maintenance"), then the instrument is payable to the persons alternatively [UCC 3–110(d)]. The same principles apply to special indorsements that identify more than one person to whom the indorser intends to make the instrument payable [UCC 3–205(a)].

19-4 Holder in Due Course (HDC)

Often, whether a holder is entitled to obtain payment will depend on whether the holder is a *holder in due course*. An ordinary holder obtains only those rights that the transferor had in the instrument and normally is subject to any defenses that could be asserted against the transferor. In contrast, a **holder in due course (HDC)** takes an instrument *free* of most of the defenses and claims that could be asserted against the transferor. To become an HDC, a holder must meet certain acquisition requirements.

EXAMPLE 19.26 Marcia Cambry signs a $10,000 note payable to Alex Jerrod in payment for some ancient Roman coins. Jerrod negotiates the note to Alicia Larson, who promises to pay Jerrod for it in sixty days. During the next month, Larson learns that Jerrod has breached his contract with Cambry by delivering coins that were not from the Roman era, as promised, and that for this reason Cambry will not honor the $10,000 note.

Whether Larson can hold Cambry liable on the note depends on whether Larson has met the requirements for HDC status. If Larson has met these requirements, she has HDC status and is entitled to payment on the note. If she has not met the requirements, she has the status of an ordinary holder. In that event, Cambry's defense of breach of contract against payment to Jerrod will also be effective against Larson. ■

19-4a Requirements for HDC Status

The basic requirements for attaining HDC status are set forth in UCC 3–302. A holder of a negotiable instrument is an HDC if she or he takes the instrument (1) for value, (2) in good faith, and (3) without notice that it is defective. Next, we examine each of these requirements.

Taking for Value An HDC must have given *value* for the instrument [UCC 3–302(a)(2)(i)]. A person who receives an instrument as a gift or inherits it has not met the requirement of value. In these situations, the person becomes an ordinary holder and does not possess the rights of an HDC.

Under UCC 3–303(a), a holder takes an instrument for value if the holder has done any of the following:

1. Performed the promise for which the instrument was issued or transferred.

2. Acquired a security interest or other lien in the instrument, excluding a lien obtained by a judicial proceeding.

Holder in Due Course (HDC)
A holder who acquires a negotiable instrument for value, in good faith, and without notice that the instrument is defective.

iStockPhoto.com/paul837

A note is signed for funds to purchase ancient Roman coins. If these coins turn out to be fake, how does that event affect the negotiability of the note?

LEARNING OBJECTIVE 3

What are the requirements for attaining the status of a holder in due course (HDC)?

3. Taken the instrument in payment of, or as security for, a preexisting claim. **EXAMPLE 19.27** Zon owes Dwyer $2,000 on a past-due account. If Zon negotiates a $2,000 note signed by Gordon to Dwyer and Dwyer accepts it to discharge the overdue account balance, Dwyer has given value for the instrument. ▪

4. Given a negotiable instrument as payment for the instrument. **EXAMPLE 19.28** Justin issues a six-month, $5,000 negotiable promissory note to Paige. Paige needs cash and does not want to wait for the maturity date to collect. She negotiates the note to her friend Kristen, who pays her $2,000 in cash and writes her a check—a negotiable instrument—for the balance of $3,000. Kristen has given full value for the note. ▪

5. Given an irrevocable commitment (such as a letter of credit) as payment for the instrument.

If a person promises to perform or give value in the future, that person is not an HDC. A holder takes an instrument for value *only to the extent that the promise has been performed* [UCC 3–303(a)(1)]. Therefore, in *Example 19.26,* Larson is not an HDC, because she did not take the instrument (Cambry's note) for value—she has not yet paid Jerrod for the note. Thus, Cambry's defense of breach of contract is valid against Larson as well as Jerrod. Exhibit 19–10 illustrates these concepts.

Taking in Good Faith
To qualify as an HDC, a holder must take the instrument in *good faith* [UCC 3–302(a)(2)(ii)]. This means that the holder must have acted honestly and observed reasonable commercial standards of fair dealing in the process of acquiring the instrument [UCC 3–103(a)(4)].

The good faith requirement applies only to the *holder.* It is immaterial whether the transferor acted in good faith. Thus, even a person who takes a negotiable instrument from a thief may become an HDC if the person acquired the instrument in good faith and honestly had no reason to be suspicious of the transaction.

CASE EXAMPLE 19.29 Cassandra Demery worked as a bookkeeper at Freestyle until the owner, Clinton Georg, discovered that she had embezzled more than $200,000. Georg fired Demery and demanded repayment. Demery went to work for her parents' firm, Metro Fixtures, where she had some authority to write checks. Without specific authorization, she wrote a check for $189,000 to Freestyle on Metro's account and deposited it in Freestyle's account. She told Georg that the check was a loan to her from her family.

Exhibit 19–10 Taking for Value

By exchanging defective goods for Cambry's note, Jerrod breached his contract with Cambry. Cambry could assert this defense if Jerrod presented the note to her for payment. Cambry can assert the same defense against Larson if Larson submits the note to Cambry for payment. Because Larson took the note in return for her promise to pay in sixty days, she did not take the note for value and is not a holder in due course. In contrast, if Larson had taken the note for value, Cambry could not assert the defense and would be liable to pay the note.

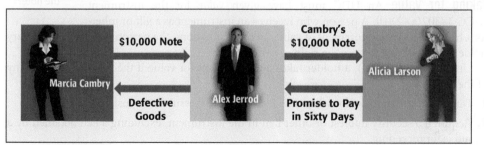

When Metro discovered Demery's theft, it filed a suit against Georg and Freestyle. Freestyle argued that it had taken the check in good faith and was an HDC. The Colorado Supreme Court agreed. Demery was the wrongdoer. She had the authority to issue checks for Metro, and Georg had no reason to know that Demery had lied about this check. Therefore, Freestyle was an HDC, and Metro would bear the loss.[8] ■

Taking without Notice
The final requirement for HDC status involves *notice* [UCC 3–302]. A person will not qualify for HDC protection if he or she is *on notice* (knows or has reason to know) that the instrument being acquired is defective in any one of the following ways [UCC 3–302(a)]:

Can a recipient of a check become an HDC when the person providing the check has check-writing authority?

1. It is overdue.

2. It has been dishonored.

3. It is part of a series of which at least one instrument has an uncured (uncorrected) default.

4. It contains an unauthorized signature or has been altered.

5. There is a defense against the instrument or a claim to it.

6. The instrument is so irregular or incomplete as to call its authenticity into question.

What Constitutes Notice?
Under UCC 1–201(25), a person is considered to have notice in the following circumstances:

1. The person has actual knowledge of the defect.

2. The person has received a notice or notification concerning the defect (such as a letter from a bank identifying the serial numbers of stolen bearer instruments).

3. The person has reason to know that a defect exists, given all the facts and circumstances known at the time in question.

The holder must also have received notice "at a time and in a manner that gives a reasonable opportunity to act on it" [UCC 3–302(f)]. A purchaser's knowledge of certain facts, such as insolvency proceedings against the maker or drawer of the instrument, does not constitute notice that the instrument is defective [UCC 3–302(b)].

Overdue Instruments.
What constitutes notice that an instrument is overdue depends on whether it is a demand instrument or a time instrument.

A purchaser has notice that a *demand instrument* is overdue if she or he either takes the instrument knowing that demand has been made or takes the instrument an unreasonable length of time after its issue. For a check, a "reasonable time" is within ninety days after the date of the check. For all other demand instruments, what will be considered a reasonable time depends on the circumstances [UCC 3–304(a)].

Normally, a *time instrument* is overdue the day after its due date. Anyone who takes a time instrument after the due date is on notice that it is overdue [UCC 3–304(b)(2)]. Thus, if a promissory note due on May 15 is purchased on May 16, the purchaser is an ordinary holder, not an HDC. If an instrument states that it is "Payable in thirty days," counting begins the day after the instrument is dated. Thus, a note dated December 1 that is payable in thirty days is due by midnight on December 31. If the payment date falls on a Sunday or holiday, the instrument is payable on the next business day.

Dishonored Instruments.
An instrument is **dishonored** when the party to whom the instrument is presented refuses to pay it. If a holder knows or has reason to know that an instrument has

Dishonor To refuse to pay or to accept a negotiable instrument that has been presented in a timely and proper manner.

---

8. *Georg v. Metro Fixtures Contractors, Inc.,* 178 P.3d 1209 (Colo.Sup.Ct. 2008).

been dishonored, the holder is on notice and cannot claim HDC status [UCC 3–302(a)(2)]. Thus, a person who takes a check clearly stamped "insufficient funds" is put on notice.

Conversely, if a person purchasing an instrument does not know and has no reason to know that it has been dishonored, the person is *not* put on notice and therefore can become an HDC. **EXAMPLE 19.30** Leah Gonzalez holds a demand note dated September 1 issued by Apex, Inc., a local business firm. On September 17, she demands payment, and Apex refuses (that is, dishonors the instrument). On September 22, Gonzalez negotiates the note to Brenner, a purchaser who lives in another state. Brenner does not know, and has no reason to know, that the note has been dishonored. Because Brenner is *not* put on notice, Brenner can become an HDC. ■

Notice of Claims or Defenses. A holder cannot become an HDC if she or he has notice of any claim to the instrument or any defense against it [UCC 3–302(a)(2)]. Instruments with irregularities and incomplete instruments fall under this rule.

Any *irregularity* on the face of an instrument (such as an obvious forgery or alteration) that calls into question its validity or ownership will bar HDC status. A good forgery of a signature or the careful alteration of an instrument, however, can go undetected by reasonable examination. In that situation, the purchaser can qualify as an HDC.

In addition, a purchaser cannot become an HDC of an instrument so *incomplete* on its face that an element of negotiability is lacking (for instance, the amount is not filled in) [UCC 3–302(a)(1)]. Minor omissions (such as the omission of the date) are permissible, because these do not call into question the validity of the instrument [UCC 3–113(b)].

19–4b Holder through an HDC

A person who does not qualify as an HDC but who derives his or her title through an HDC can acquire the rights and privileges of an HDC. This rule, which is sometimes called the **shelter principle,** is set out in UCC 3–203(b). Under this rule, anyone—no matter how far removed from an HDC—who can ultimately trace his or her title back to an HDC may acquire the rights of an HDC. By extending the benefits of HDC status, the shelter principle promotes the marketability and free transferability of negotiable instruments.

There are some limitations on the shelter principle, though. Certain persons who formerly held instruments cannot improve their positions by later reacquiring the instruments from HDCs [UCC 3–203(b)]. If a holder participated in fraud or illegality affecting the instrument, or had notice of a claim or defense against an instrument, that holder is not allowed to gain the benefits of HDC status by repurchasing the instrument from a later HDC.

19–5 Signature and Warranty Liability

Liability on negotiable instruments can arise either from a person's signature or from the warranties that are implied when the person presents the instrument for negotiation. We discuss signature liability and warranty liability in the subsections that follow.

19–5a Signature Liability

The general rule is that every party, except a qualified indorser,[9] who signs a negotiable instrument is either primarily or secondarily liable for payment of that instrument when it comes due. Signature liability is contractual liability—no person will be held contractually liable for an instrument that he or she has not signed.

---

9. A qualified indorser—one who indorses "without recourse"—undertakes no contractual obligation to pay. A qualified indorser merely assumes warranty liability.

Shelter Principle The principle that the holder of a negotiable instrument who cannot qualify as a holder in due course (HDC), but who derives his or her title through an HDC, acquires the rights of an HDC.

"Most men are admirers of justice—when justice happens to be on their side."

RICHARD WHATELY
1787–1863
(ENGLISH THEOLOGIAN AND LOGICIAN)

Primary Liability A person who is primarily liable on a negotiable instrument is absolutely required to pay the instrument—unless, of course, he or she has a valid defense to payment [UCC 3–305]. Only *makers* and *acceptors* of instruments are primarily liable.

The maker of a promissory note unconditionally promises to pay the note. It is the maker's promise to pay that makes the note a negotiable instrument. If the instrument was incomplete when the maker signed it, the maker is obligated to pay it according to its stated terms or according to terms that were agreed on and later filled in to complete the instrument [UCC 3–115, 3–407(a), 3–412].

EXAMPLE 19.31 Tristan executes a preprinted promissory note to Sharon, without filling in the blank for a due date. If Sharon does not complete the form by adding the date, the note will be payable on demand. If Sharon subsequently fills in a due date that Tristan authorized, the note is payable on the stated due date. In either situation, Tristan (the maker) is obligated to pay the note. ■

As mentioned earlier, an acceptor is a drawee, such as a bank, that promises to pay an instrument when it is presented for payment. Once a drawee accepts a draft, the drawee is obligated to pay the draft when it is presented for payment [UCC 3–409(a)]. Failure to pay an accepted draft when presented leads to primary signature liability.

Secondary Liability *Drawers* and *indorsers* are secondarily liable. On a negotiable instrument, secondary liability is *contingent liability* (similar to that of a guarantor in a contract). In other words, a drawer or an indorser will be liable only if the party that is responsible for paying the instrument dishonors it by refusing to pay.

Parties are secondarily liable on a negotiable instrument *only if* the following events occur:[10]

1. The instrument is properly and timely presented.

2. The instrument is dishonored.

3. Timely notice of dishonor is given to the secondarily liable party.

Proper and Timely Presentment. The holder must present the instrument to the appropriate party in a proper and timely fashion and must give reasonable identification if requested [UCC 3–414(f), 3–415(e), 3–501]. The party to whom the instrument must be presented depends on the type of instrument involved. A note or CD is presented to the maker for payment. A draft is presented to the drawee for acceptance, payment, or both. A check is presented to the drawee for payment [UCC 3–501(a), 3–502(b)].

Presentment can be made by any commercially reasonable means, including oral, written, or electronic communication [UCC 3–501(b)]. Ordinarily, it is effective when received. (If presentment takes place after an established cutoff hour, though, it may be treated as occurring the next business day.)

Timeliness is important for proper presentment [UCC 3–414(f), 3–415(e), 3–501(b)(4)]. Failure to present an instrument on time is the most common reason for improper presentment. If the instrument is payable on demand, the holder should present it for payment or acceptance within a reasonable time. The holder of a domestic check must present that check for payment or collection within thirty days of its *date* to hold the drawer secondarily liable and within thirty days after its indorsement to hold the indorser secondarily liable. The time for proper presentment for various types of instruments is shown in Exhibit 19–11.

Dishonor. As mentioned, an instrument is dishonored when the required acceptance or payment is refused. It is also dishonored when acceptance or payment cannot be obtained within the prescribed time or when the required presentment is excused (as it would be, for instance,

---

10. These requirements are necessary for a secondarily liable party to have signature liability on a negotiable instrument, but they are not necessary for a secondarily liable party to have warranty liability.

Exhibit 19–11 Time for Proper Presentment

TYPE OF INSTRUMENT	FOR ACCEPTANCE	FOR PAYMENT
Time	On or before due date.	On due date.
Demand	Within a reasonable time (after date of issue or after secondary party becomes liable on the instrument).	Within a reasonable time.
Check	Not applicable.	Within thirty days of its date, to hold drawer secondarily liable. Within thirty days of indorsement, to hold indorser secondarily liable.

if the maker had died) and the instrument is not properly accepted or paid [UCC 3–502(e), 3–504].

In certain situations, a delay in payment or a refusal to pay an instrument will not dishonor the instrument.

1. When presentment is made after an established cutoff hour (not earlier than 2:00 P.M.), a bank can postpone payment until the following business day without dishonoring the instrument [UCC 3–501(b)(4)].

2. When the holder refuses to exhibit the instrument, to give reasonable identification, or to sign a receipt for the payment on the instrument, a bank's refusal to pay does not dishonor the instrument [UCC 3–501(b)(2)].

3. When an instrument is returned because it lacks a proper indorsement, the instrument is not dishonored [UCC 3–501(b)(3)(i)].

Proper Notice of Dishonor. Once an instrument has been dishonored, proper notice must be given to secondary parties (drawers and indorsers) for them to be held liable. **EXAMPLE 19.32** Oscar writes a check on his account at People's Bank payable to Bess. Bess indorses the check in blank and cashes it at Midwest Grocery, which transfers it to People's Bank for payment. If People's Bank refuses to pay it, Midwest must timely notify Bess to hold her liable. ■

Notice can be given in any reasonable manner, including an oral, written, or electronic communication, as well as notice written or stamped on the instrument itself. A bank must give any necessary notice before its midnight deadline (midnight of the next banking day after receipt). Notice by any party other than a bank must be given within thirty days following the day of dishonor or the day on which the person who is secondarily liable receives notice of dishonor [UCC 3–503].

Unauthorized Signatures Unauthorized signatures arise in two situations:

1. When a person forges another person's name on a negotiable instrument.

2. When an agent who lacks the authority signs an instrument on behalf of a principal.

The General Rule. The general rule is that an unauthorized signature is wholly inoperative and will not bind the person whose name is signed or forged. **EXAMPLE 19.33** Parker finds Dolby's checkbook lying in the street, writes out a check to himself, and forges Dolby's signature. Banks normally have a duty to determine whether a person's signature on a check is forged. If a bank fails to determine that Dolby's signature is not genuine and cashes the check for Parker, the bank will generally be liable to Dolby for the amount. ■

Who is responsible for validating the signature on a check?

iStockPhoto.com/bluestocking

The general rule also may apply to agents' signatures. If an agent lacks the authority to sign the principal's name or has exceeded the authority given by the principal, the signature does not bind the principal but will bind the "unauthorized signer" [UCC 3–403(a)].

Exceptions to the General Rule. There are two exceptions to the general rule that an unauthorized signature will not bind the person whose name is signed:

1. *Ratification.* When the person whose name is signed ratifies (affirms) the signature, he or she will be bound [UCC 3–403(a)]. For instance, a mother may ratify her daughter's forgery of the mother's signature so that the daughter will not be prosecuted. A person can ratify an unauthorized signature either expressly (by affirming the signature) or impliedly (by other conduct, such as keeping any benefits received in the transaction or failing to repudiate the signature).

2. *Negligence.* When the negligence of the person whose name was forged substantially contributed to the forgery, a court may not allow the person to deny the effectiveness of an unauthorized signature [UCC 3–115, 3–406, 4–401(d)(2)].

Someone finds a checkbook on the sidewalk, writes out a check to himself, and forges the signature of the account holder. Is the bank liable to the true account holder if it cashes the forged check?

Special Rules for Unauthorized Indorsements Generally, when an instrument has a forged or unauthorized indorsement, the burden of loss falls on the first party to take the instrument. The reason for this general rule is that the first party to take an instrument is in the best position to prevent the loss.

EXAMPLE 19.34 Jen Nilson steals a check drawn on Universal Bank that is payable to the order of Inga Leed. Nilson indorses the check "Inga Leed" and presents the check to Universal Bank for payment. The bank, without asking Nilson for identification, pays the check, and Nilson disappears. Leed will not be liable on the check, because her indorsement was forged. The bank will bear the loss, which it might have avoided if it had asked Nilson for identification. ■

This general rule has two important exceptions that cause the loss to fall on the maker or drawer. These exceptions arise when an indorsement is made by an imposter or by a fictitious payee.

Imposter Rule. An **imposter** is one who, through deception, induces a maker or drawer to issue an instrument in the name of an impersonated payee. If the maker or drawer believes the imposter to be the named payee at the time of issue, the indorsement by the imposter is not treated as unauthorized when the instrument is transferred to an innocent party. This is because the maker or drawer *intended* the imposter to receive the instrument.

In these situations, the unauthorized indorsement of a payee's name can be as effective as if the real payee had signed. The *imposter rule* provides that an imposter's indorsement will be effective—that is, not a forgery—insofar as the drawer or maker is concerned [UCC 3–404(a)].

EXAMPLE 19.35 Carol impersonates Donna and induces Edward to write a check payable to the order of Donna. Carol, continuing to impersonate Donna, negotiates the check to First National Bank as payment on her loan there. As the drawer of the check, Edward is liable for its amount to First National. ■

Imposter One who induces a maker or drawer to issue a negotiable instrument in the name of an impersonated payee. Indorsements by imposters are treated as authorized indorsements under UCC Article 3.

Fictitious Payee Rule. When a person causes an instrument to be issued to a payee who will have *no interest* in the instrument, the payee is referred to as a **fictitious payee.** A fictitious payee can be a person or firm that does not exist, or it may be an identifiable party that will not acquire any interest in the instrument. Under the UCC's *fictitious payee rule,* the payee's indorsement is not treated as a forgery, and an innocent holder can hold the maker or drawer liable on the instrument [UCC 3–404(b), 3–405]. Basically, the loss falls on the maker or

Fictitious Payee A payee on a negotiable instrument whom the maker or drawer did not intend to have an interest in the instrument. Indorsements by fictitious payees are treated as authorized indorsements under UCC Article 3.

drawer of the instrument rather than on the third party that accepts it or on the bank that cashes it.

Fictitious payees most often arise in two situations:

1. When a dishonest employee deceives the employer into signing an instrument payable to a party with no right to receive payment on the instrument.

2. When a dishonest employee or agent has the authority to issue an instrument on behalf of the employer and issues a check to a party who has no interest in the instrument.

CASE EXAMPLE 19.36 Braden Furniture Company gave its bookkeeper, Bonnie Manning, general authority to create checks. Over the course of seven years, Manning created more than two hundred unauthorized checks, totaling $470,000, which she deposited in her own account at Union State Bank. Braden Furniture was not a customer of the bank. Most of the checks did not identify a payee (the payee line was left blank). Braden Furniture (the drawer) sued Union State Bank for the loss, claiming that the bank had been negligent in accepting and paying the blank checks. The court, however, held that the fictitious payee rule applied. Therefore, under Alabama's version of the UCC, the loss fell on Braden Furniture, not on Union State Bank.[11] ▪

19–5b Warranty Liability

Signature liability arises from a transferor's signature. Transferors also make certain implied warranties regarding the instruments that they are negotiating. Warranty liability arises even when a transferor does not sign the instrument [UCC 3–416, 3–417].

Warranty liability is particularly important when a holder cannot hold a party liable on her or his signature, such as when a person delivers a bearer instrument. Unlike secondary signature liability, warranty liability is not subject to the conditions of proper presentment, dishonor, or notice of dishonor.

Warranties fall into two categories: those that arise on the *transfer* of a negotiable instrument and those that arise on *presentment*. Both transfer and presentment warranties attempt to shift liability back to a wrongdoer or to the person who dealt face to face with the wrongdoer and thus was in the best position to prevent the wrongdoing.

Transfer Warranties

A person who transfers an instrument *for consideration* makes the following five **transfer warranties** to all subsequent transferees and holders who take the instrument in good faith [UCC 3–416]:[12]

1. The transferor is entitled to enforce the instrument.

2. All signatures are authentic and authorized.

3. The instrument has not been altered.

4. The instrument is not subject to a defense or claim of any party that can be asserted against the transferor.

5. The transferor has no knowledge of any bankruptcy proceedings of the maker, the acceptor, or the drawer of the instrument.

Presentment Warranties

A person who presents an instrument for payment or acceptance makes the following **presentment warranties** to anyone who in good faith pays or accepts the instrument [UCC 3–417(a), 3–417(d)]:

---

11. *Braden Furniture Co. v. Union State Bank*, 109 So.3d 625 (Ala. 2012).

12. An amendment to UCC 3–416(a) adds a sixth warranty "with respect to a remotely created consumer item," such as an electronic check, drawn on a consumer account, that is not created by the payor bank and does not contain the drawer's handwritten signature. Under this amendment, which a few states have adopted, a bank that accepts and pays the instrument warrants to the next bank in the collection chain that the consumer authorized the item in that amount.

"Life is unfair."

MILTON FRIEDMAN
1912–2006
(AMERICAN ECONOMIST)

LEARNING OBJECTIVE 4

What is the difference between signature liability and warranty liability?

Transfer Warranty A person who transfers an instrument for consideration impliedly makes five warranties—relating to good title, authentic signatures, no alterations, defenses, or insolvencies—to all subsequent transferees.

Presentment Warranty A person who presents an instrument for payment or acceptance impliedly makes three warranties relating to good title, no alterations, and no unauthorized signatures.

1. The person obtaining payment or acceptance is entitled to enforce the instrument or is authorized to obtain payment or acceptance on behalf of a person who is entitled to enforce the instrument. (This is, in effect, a warranty that there are no missing or unauthorized indorsements.)

2. The instrument has not been altered.

3. The person obtaining payment or acceptance has no knowledge that the signature of the issuer of the instrument is unauthorized.[13]

The second and third presentment warranties do not apply to makers, acceptors, and drawers when the presenter is an HDC. It is assumed that a drawer or a maker will recognize his or her own signature and that a maker or an acceptor will recognize whether an instrument has been materially altered.

19-6 Defenses, Limitations, and Discharge

Defenses can bar collection from persons who would otherwise be primarily or secondarily liable on a negotiable instrument. There are two general categories of defenses—*universal defenses* and *personal defenses*.

19-6a Universal Defenses

Universal defenses (also called *real defenses*) are valid against *all* holders, including HDCs and holders who take through an HDC. Universal defenses include those described here.

1. *Forgery of a signature on the instrument.* A forged signature will not bind the person whose name is used. Thus, when an instrument is forged, the person whose name is forged normally has no liability to pay any holder the value of the instrument. If the person whose name is forged ratifies the signature, however, he or she may be liable, as discussed earlier.

2. *Fraud in the execution.* If a person is deceived into signing a negotiable instrument, believing that she or he is signing something other than a negotiable instrument (such as a receipt), *fraud in the execution* is committed against the signer [UCC 3–305(a)(1)]. This defense cannot be raised, however, if reasonable inquiry would have revealed the nature and terms of the instrument.
   EXAMPLE 19.37 Connor, a salesperson, asks Javier, a customer, to sign a paper. Connor says that it is a receipt for goods that Javier is picking up from the store. In fact, it is a promissory note, but Javier is unfamiliar with English and does not realize this. Here, even if the note is negotiated to an HDC, Javier has a valid defense against payment. ■

3. *Material alteration.* An alteration is *material* if it changes the obligations of the parties in the instrument *in any way.* Material alterations include completing an incomplete instrument, adding words or numbers, or making any unauthorized changes that affect the obligation of a party [UCC 3–407(a)]. It is not a material alteration, however, to correct the maker's address or to change the figures on a check so that they agree with the written amount.
   Material alteration is a *complete defense* against an ordinary holder, but only a *partial defense* against an HDC. Thus, an ordinary holder can recover nothing on an instrument that has been materially altered. An HDC can enforce the instrument against the maker or drawer according to its original terms but not for the altered amount.

Universal Defense A defense that can be used to avoid payment to all holders of a negotiable instrument, including a holder in due course (HDC) or a holder with the rights of an HDC. Also called a *real defense.*

---

13. Amendments to Article 3 of the UCC provide additional protection for "remotely created" consumer items in the context of presentment also [see Amended UCC 3–417(a)(4)].

4. *Discharge in bankruptcy.* Discharge in bankruptcy is an absolute defense on any instrument, regardless of the status of the holder, because the purpose of bankruptcy is to settle all of the insolvent party's debts [UCC 3–305(a)(1)].

5. *Minority.* Minority, or infancy, is a universal defense only to the extent that state law recognizes it as a defense to a simple contract [UCC 3–305(a)(1)(i)].

6. *Illegality, mental incapacity, or extreme duress.* When the law declares an instrument to be void because it was issued in connection with illegal conduct, illegality is a universal defense. Similarly, if a person who signed the instrument has been declared by a court to be mentally incompetent, or was a under an immediate threat of force or violence, the defense is universal [UCC 3–305(a)(1)(ii)].

19-6b Personal Defenses

Personal defenses (sometimes called *limited defenses*) are effective against an ordinary holder but not against an HDC or a holder through an HDC. Personal defenses include the following:

1. *Breach of contract or breach of warranty.* When there is a breach of the underlying contract for which the negotiable instrument was issued, the maker of a note can refuse to pay it, or the drawer of a check can stop payment.

2. *Lack or failure of consideration.* The absence of consideration may be a successful personal defense in some instances [UCC 3–303(b), 3–305(a)(2)]. **EXAMPLE 19.38** Tara gives Clem, as a gift, a note that states, "I promise to pay you $100,000." Clem accepts the note. Because there is no consideration for Tara's promise, a court will not enforce the promise. ∎

3. *Fraud in the inducement (ordinary fraud).* A person who issues a negotiable instrument based on false statements by the other party will be able to avoid payment on that instrument, unless the holder is an HDC.

4. *Illegality, mental incapacity, or ordinary duress.* If the law declares that an instrument is voidable because of illegality, mental incapacity, or ordinary duress, the defense is personal [UCC 3–305(a)(1)(ii)].

19-6c Federal Limitations on the Rights of HDCs

The federal government limits the rights of HDCs in certain circumstances because of the harsh effects that the HDC rules can sometimes have on consumers. Under the HDC doctrine, a consumer who purchased a defective product (such as a defective automobile) would continue to be liable to HDCs even if the consumer returned the defective product to the retailer.

To protect consumers who purchase defective products, the Federal Trade Commission (FTC) adopted Rule 433, which effectively abolished the HDC doctrine in consumer transactions. How does this rule curb the rights of HDCs? See this chapter's *Landmark in the Law* feature to learn more.

19-6d Discharge from Liability

Discharge from liability on an instrument can come from payment, cancellation, or material alteration. The liability of all parties is discharged when the party primarily liable on the instrument pays to the holder the full amount due [UCC 3–602, 3–603]. Payment by any other party (such as an indorser) discharges only the liability of that party and subsequent parties.

Intentional cancellation by the holder of an instrument discharges the liability of all parties [UCC 3–604]. Intentionally writing "Paid" across the face of an instrument cancels it, as does intentionally tearing it up. If a holder intentionally crosses out a party's signature, that party's

LEARNING OBJECTIVE 5

Name four defenses that can be used against an ordinary holder but are not effective against an HDC.

Personal Defense A defense that can be used to avoid payment to an ordinary holder of a negotiable instrument but not a holder in due course (HDC) or a holder with the rights of an HDC.

If this woman makes a gift by writing out a note that says, "I promise to pay you $1,000," is the note enforceable?

iStockPhoto.com/Giambra

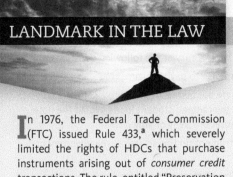

LANDMARK IN THE LAW — Federal Trade Commission Rule 433

In 1976, the Federal Trade Commission (FTC) issued Rule 433,[a] which severely limited the rights of HDCs that purchase instruments arising out of *consumer credit* transactions. The rule, entitled "Preservation of Consumers' Claims and Defenses," applies to any seller or lessor of goods or services who takes or receives a consumer credit contract. The rule also applies to a seller or lessor who accepts as full or partial payment for a sale or lease the proceeds of any purchase-money loan[b] made in connection with any consumer credit contract.

Under the rule, these parties must include the following provision in the consumer credit contract:

NOTICE

ANY HOLDER OF THIS CONSUMER CREDIT CONTRACT IS SUBJECT TO ALL CLAIMS AND DEFENSES WHICH THE DEBTOR COULD ASSERT AGAINST THE SELLER OF GOODS OR SERVICES OBTAINED PURSUANT HERETO OR WITH THE PROCEEDS HEREOF. RECOVERY HEREUNDER BY THE DEBTOR SHALL NOT EXCEED AMOUNTS PAID BY THE DEBTOR HEREUNDER.

Thus, a consumer who is a party to a consumer credit transaction can bring any defense she or he has against the seller of a product against a subsequent holder as well. In essence, the FTC rule places an HDC of the negotiable instrument in the position of a contract assignee. The rule makes the buyer's duty to pay conditional on the seller's full performance of the contract. Finally, the rule clearly reduces the degree of transferability of negotiable instruments resulting from consumer credit contracts.

What if the seller does not include the notice in a promissory note and then sells the note to a third party, such as a bank? In this situation, the seller has violated the rule, but the bank has not. Because the FTC rule does not prohibit third parties from purchasing notes or credit contracts that do *not* contain the required provision, the third party does not become subject to the buyer's defenses against the seller. Thus, a few consumers remain unprotected by the FTC rule.

APPLICATION TO TODAY'S WORLD *The FTC rule has been invoked in many cases involving automobiles that turned out to be "lemons," even when the consumer credit contract did not contain the FTC notice. In these and similar actions, when the notice was not included in the contract, the courts have generally inferred its presence as a contract term.*

---

a. 16 C.F.R. Section 433.2. The rule was enacted pursuant to the FTC's authority under the Federal Trade Commission Act, 15 U.S.C. Sections 41–58.
b. In a *purchase-money loan*, a seller or lessor advances funds to a buyer or lessee, through a credit contract, for the purchase or lease of goods.

---

liability and the liability of subsequent indorsers who have already indorsed the instrument are discharged.

Materially altering an instrument may discharge the liability of any party affected by the alteration, as previously discussed [UCC 3–407(b)]. An HDC may be able to enforce a materially altered instrument against its maker or drawer according to the instrument's original terms, however.

Discharge of liability can also occur when a holder impairs another party's right of recourse (right to seek reimbursement) on the instrument [UCC 3–605]. This occurs when, for instance, the holder releases, or agrees not to sue, a party against whom the indorser has a right of recourse.

Reviewing . . . Negotiable Instruments

Robert Durbin, a student, borrowed funds from a bank for his education and signed a promissory note for their repayment. The bank loaned the funds under a federal program designed to assist students at postsecondary institutions. Under this program, repayment ordinarily begins nine to twelve months after the student borrower fails to carry at least one-half of the normal full-time course load at his or her school. The federal government guarantees that the note will be fully paid. If the student defaults on the payments, the lender presents the current balance—principal, interest, and costs—to the government. When the government pays the balance, it becomes the lender, and the borrower owes the government directly. After Durbin defaulted on his note, the government paid the lender the balance due and took

Continues

possession of the note. Durbin then refused to pay the government, claiming that the government was not the holder of the note. The government filed a suit in a federal district court against Durbin to collect the amount due. Using the information presented in the chapter, answer the following questions.

1. Was the note that Durbin signed an order to pay or a promise to pay? Explain.

2. Suppose that the note did not state a specific interest rate but instead referred to a statute that established the maximum interest rate for government-guaranteed student loans. Would the note fail to meet the requirements for negotiability in that situation? Why or why not?

3. How does a party who is not named in a negotiable instrument (in this situation, the government) obtain a right to enforce the instrument?

4. Now suppose that the school Durbin attended closed down before he could finish his education. In court, Durbin argues that this resulted in a failure of consideration: he did not get something of value in exchange for his promise to pay. Assuming that the government is a holder of the promissory note, will this argument likely be successful against it? Why or why not?

DEBATE THIS

■ We should eliminate the status of holder in due course for those who possess negotiable instruments.

Key Terms

Chapter Summary: Negotiable Instruments

Types of Instruments	The UCC specifies four types of negotiable instruments: drafts, checks, promissory notes, and certificates of deposit (CDs). These instruments fall into two basic classifications: **1.** *Demand instruments versus time instruments*—A demand instrument is payable on demand (when the holder presents it to the maker or drawer). A time instrument is payable at a future date. **2.** *Orders to pay versus promises to pay*—Checks and drafts are *orders* to pay. Promissory notes and CDs are *promises* to pay.

Requirements for Negotiability	To be negotiable, an instrument must meet the following requirements.
	1. *Be in writing*—A writing can be on anything that is readily transferable and has a degree of permanence [UCC 3–103(a)(6), (9)].
	2. *Be signed by the maker or drawer*—The signature can be anyplace on the face of the instrument, can be in any form (including a rubber stamp), and can be made in a representative capacity [UCC 3–103(a)(3), 3–401(b)].
	3. *Be an unconditional promise or order to pay*—
	  a. A promise must be more than a mere acknowledgment of a debt [UCC 3–103(a)(6), (9)].
	  b. Such words as "pay on demand" meet this criterion.
	  c. Payment cannot be expressly conditioned on the occurrence of an event and cannot be made subject to or governed by another contract [UCC 3–106].
	4. *State a fixed amount of money*—
	  a. An amount is considered a fixed sum if it is ascertainable from the face of the instrument or (for an interest rate) readily determinable by a formula described in the instrument [UCC –104(a), 3–112(b)].
	  b. Any medium of exchange recognized as the currency of a government is money [UCC 3—201(24)].
	5. *Be payable on demand or at a definite time*—
	  a. Any instrument that is payable on sight, presentation, or issue, or that does not state any time for payment, is a demand instrument [UCC 3—104(a)(2)].
	  b. An instrument is still payable at a definite time, even if it is payable on or before a stated date or within a fixed period after sight or if the drawer or maker has an option to extend the time for a definite period [UCC 3–108(a), (b), (c)].
	  c. Acceleration clauses do not affect the negotiability of the instrument.
	6. *Be payable to order or bearer*—
	  a. An order instrument must identify the payee with certainty.
	  b. An instrument that indicates it is not payable to an identified person is payable to bearer [UCC 3–109(a)(3)].

Factors That Do Not Affect Negotiability	Certain ambiguities (such as differences between the words and figures) or omissions (such as when an instrument is undated, antedated, or postdated) normally will not affect an instrument's negotiability.

Transfer of Instruments	**1.** *Transfer by assignment*—A transfer by assignment to an assignee gives the assignee only those rights that the assignor possessed. Any defenses against payment that can be raised against an assignor normally can be raised against the assignee.
	2. *Transfer by negotiation*—An order instrument is negotiated by indorsement and delivery. A bearer instrument is negotiated by delivery only.
	3. *Indorsements*—
	  a. Blank indorsements do not specify a particular indorsee and can consist of a mere signature (see Exhibit 19–5).
	  b. Special indorsements contain the signature of the indorser and identify the indorsee (see Exhibit 19–6).
	  c. Qualified indorsements contain language, such as "without recourse," that indicates the indorser is not guaranteeing payment of the instrument (see Exhibit 19–7).
	  d. Restrictive indorsements, such as "For deposit only," require the indorsee to comply with certain instructions regarding the funds involved, but do not prohibit further negotiation of the instrument (see Exhibit 19–8).

Holder in Due Course (HDC)	**1.** *Holder*—A person in possession of an instrument drawn, issued, or indorsed to him or her, to his or her order, to bearer, or in blank. A holder obtains only those rights that the transferor had in the instrument.
	2. *Holder in due course (HDC)*—A holder who, by meeting certain acquisition requirements, takes an instrument free of most defenses and claims to which the transferor was subject.
	3. *Requirements for HDC status*—To be an HDC, a holder must take the instrument:
	  a. For value—A holder can take an instrument for value in five ways: by performing the promise, acquiring a security interest or lien in the instrument, taking the instrument as payment for a preexisting obligation, giving the instrument as payment, or giving an irrevocable commitment as payment [UCC 3–303].
	  b. In good faith—Good faith is defined as "honesty in fact and the observance of reasonable commercial standards of fair dealing" [UCC 3–103(a)(4)].
	  c. Without notice—To be an HDC, a holder must not be on notice that the instrument is defective because it is overdue, has been dishonored, is part of a series of which at least one instrument has a uncured defect, contains an unauthorized signature or has been altered, or is so irregular or incomplete as to call its authenticity into question.
	4. *Shelter principle*—A holder who cannot qualify as an HDC has the *rights* of an HDC if the holder derives her or his title through an HDC, unless the holder engaged in fraud or illegality affecting the instrument [UCC 3–203(b)].

Continues

Signature and Warranty Liability	Liability on negotiable instruments can arise either from a person's signature or from the warranties that are implied when a person presents the instrument for negotiation. 1. *Signature liability*—Every party (except a qualified indorser) who signs a negotiable instrument is either primarily or secondarily liable for payment of the instrument when it comes due. 　a. Primary liability—Makers and acceptors are primarily liable [UCC 3–115, 3–407, 3–409, 3–412]. 　b. Secondary liability—Drawers and indorsers are secondarily liable [UCC 3–412, 3–414, 3–415, 3–501, 3–502, 3–503]. Parties are secondarily liable on an instrument only if (1) presentment is proper and timely, (2) the instrument is dishonored, and (3) they received timely notice of dishonor. 2. *Transfer warranties*—Any person who transfers an instrument for consideration makes five warranties to subsequent transferees and holders [UCC 3–416]. 　a. The transferor is entitled to enforce the instrument. 　b. All signatures are authentic and authorized. 　c. The instrument has not been altered. 　d. The instrument is not subject to a defense or claim of any party that can be asserted against the transferor. 　e. The transferor has no knowledge of any bankruptcy proceedings against the maker, the acceptor, or the drawer of the instrument. 3. *Presentment warranties*—Any person who presents an instrument for payment or acceptance makes three warranties to any person who in good faith pays or accepts the instrument [UCC 3–417(a), 3–417(d)]. 　a. The person is entitled to enforce the instrument or is authorized to act on behalf of a person who is so entitled. 　b. The instrument has not been altered. 　c. The person has no knowledge that the drawer's signature is unauthorized.
Defenses, Limitations, and Discharge	1. *Universal (real) defenses*—The following defenses are valid against all holders, including HDCs and holders with the rights of HDCs [UCC 3–305, 3–403, 3–407]: 　a. Forgery. 　b. Fraud in the execution. 　c. Material alteration. 　d. Discharge in bankruptcy. 　e. Minority—if the contract is voidable under state law. 　f. Illegality, mental incapacity, or extreme duress—if the contract is void under state law. 2. *Personal (limited) defenses*—The following defenses are valid against ordinary holders but not against HDCs or holders with the rights of HDCs [UCC 3–303, 3–305]: 　a. Breach of contract or breach of warranty. 　b. Lack or failure of consideration (value). 　c. Fraud in the inducement. 　d. Illegality, mental incapacity, or ordinary duress—if the contract is voidable. 3. *Federal limitations on the rights of HDCs*—Rule 433 of the Federal Trade Commission, issued in 1976, limits the rights of HDCs who purchase instruments arising out of consumer credit transactions. The rule allows a consumer who is a party to such a transaction to bring any defense he or she has against the seller against a subsequent holder as well, even if the subsequent holder is an HDC. 4. *Discharge from liability*—All parties to a negotiable instrument will be discharged when the party primarily liable on it pays to the holder the full amount due. Discharge can also occur in other circumstances (if the instrument has been canceled or materially altered, for example) [UCC 3–602 through 3–605].

Issue Spotters

1. Sabrina owes $600 to Yale, who asks Sabrina to sign an instrument for the debt. If written on the instrument by Sabrina, which of the following would prevent its negotiability: "I.O.U. $600," "I promise to pay $600," or an instruction to the bank stating, "I wish you would pay $600 to Yale"? Why? (See *Requirements for Negotiability*.)

2. Rye signs corporate checks for Suchin Corporation. Rye writes a check payable to U-All Company, even though Suchin does not owe U-All anything. Rye signs the check, forges U-All's indorsement, and cashes the check at Viceroy Bank, the drawee. Does Suchin have any recourse against the bank for the payment? Why or why not? (See *Signature and Warranty Liability*.)

—**Check your answers to the *Issue Spotters* against the answers provided in Appendix D at the end of this text.**

Learning Objectives Check

1. What requirements must an instrument meet to be negotiable?
2. How does the negotiation of order instruments differ from the negotiation of bearer instruments?
3. What are the requirements for attaining the status of a holder in due course (HDC)?
4. What is the difference between signature liability and warranty liability?
5. Name four defenses that can be used against an ordinary holder but are not effective against an HDC.

—**Answers to the even-numbered** *Learning Objectives Check* **questions can be found in Appendix E in at the end of this text.**

Business Scenarios and Case Problems

19–1. Negotiable Instruments. Muriel Evans writes the following note on the back of an envelope: "I, Muriel Evans, promise to pay Karen Marvin or bearer $100 on demand." Is this a negotiable instrument? Discuss fully. (See *Requirements for Negotiability.*)

19–2. Material Alteration. Williams purchased a used car from Stein for $1,000. Williams paid for the car with a check (written in pencil) payable to Stein for $1,000. Stein, through careful erasures and alterations, changed the amount on the check to read $10,000 and negotiated the check to Boz. Boz took the check for value, in good faith, and without notice of the alteration and thus met the Uniform Commercial Code's requirements for the status of a holder in due course. Can Williams successfully raise the universal (real) defense of material alteration to avoid payment on the check? Explain. (See *Defenses, Limitations, and Discharge.*)

19–3. Payable on Demand or at a Definite Time. Abby Novel signed a handwritten note that read, "Glen Gallwitz 1-8-2002 loaned me $5,000 at 6 percent interest a total of $10,000.00." The note did not state a time for repayment. Novel used the funds to manufacture and market a patented jewelry display design. More than seven years after Novel signed the note, Gallwitz filed a suit to recover the stated amount. Novel claimed that she did not have to pay because the note was not negotiable—it was incomplete. Is she correct? Explain. [*Gallwitz v. Novel,* 2011 Ohio 297 (5 Dist. 2011)] (See *Requirements for Negotiability.*)

19–4. Defenses. Thomas Klutz obtained a franchise from Kahala Franchise Corp. to operate a Samurai Sam's restaurant. Under their agreement, Klutz could transfer the franchise only if he obtained Kahala's approval and paid a transfer fee. Without telling Kahala, Klutz sold the restaurant to William Thorbecke. Thorbecke signed a note for the price. When Kahala learned of the deal, the franchisor told Thorbecke to stop using the Samurai Sam's name. Thorbecke stopped paying on the note, and Klutz filed a claim for the unpaid amount. In defense, Thorbecke asserted breach of contract and fraud. Are these defenses effective against Klutz? Explain. [*Kahala Franchise Corp. v. Hit Enterprises, LLC,* 159 Wash.App. 1013 (Div. 2 2011)] (See *Defenses, Limitations, and Discharge.*)

19–5. Business Case Problem with Sample Answer— Negotiation. Sandra Ford signed a note and a mortgage on her home in Westwood, New Jersey, to borrow $403,750 from Argent Mortgage Co. Argent transferred the note and mortgage to Wells Fargo Bank, N.A., without indorsement. The following spring, Ford stopped making payments on the note. Wells Fargo filed a suit in a New Jersey state court against Ford to foreclose on the mortgage. Ford asserted that Argent had committed fraud in connection with the note by providing misleading information and charging excessive fees. Ford contended that Wells Fargo was subject to these defenses because the bank was not a holder in due course of the note. Was the transfer of the note from Argent to Wells Fargo a negotiation or an assignment? What difference does it make? If Argent indorsed the note to Wells Fargo later, would the bank's status change? Discuss. [*Wells Fargo Bank, N.A. v. Ford,* 418 N.J.Super. 592, 15 A.3d 327 (App.Div. 2011)] (See *Transfer of Instruments.*)

—**For a sample answer to Problem 19–5, go to Appendix F at the end of this text.**

19–6. Indorsements. Angela Brock borrowed $544,000 and signed a note payable to Amerifund Mortgage Services, LLC, to buy a house in Silver Spring, Maryland. The note was indorsed in blank and transferred several times "without recourse" before Brock fell behind on the payments. On behalf of Deutsche Bank National Trust Co., BAC Home Loans Servicing LP initiated foreclosure. Brock filed an action in a Maryland state court to block it, arguing that BAC could not foreclose because Deutsche Bank, not BAC, owned the note. Can BAC enforce the note? Explain. [*Deutsche Bank National Trust Co. v. Brock,* 63 A.3d 40 (Md. 2013)] (See *Transfer of Instruments.*)

19–7. Bearer Instruments. Eligio Gaitan borrowed the funds to buy real property in Downers Grove, Illinois, and signed a note payable to Encore Credit Corp. Encore indorsed the note in blank. Later, when Gaitan defaulted on the payments, an action to foreclose on the property was filed in an Illinois state court by U.S. Bank, N.A. The note was in the bank's possession, but there was no evidence that the note had been transferred or negotiated to the bank. Can U.S. Bank enforce payment of the note? Why or why not? [*U.S. Bank National Association v. Gaitan*, 2013 IL App (2d) 120105-U, 2013 WL 160378 (2013)] (See *Requirements for Negotiability.*)

19–8. Transfer by Negotiation. Thao Thi Duong signed a note in the amount of $200,000 in favor of Country Home Loans, Inc., to obtain a loan to buy a house in Marrero, Louisiana. The note was indorsed "PAY TO THE ORDER OF [blank space] WITHOUT RECOURSE COUNTRY HOME LOANS, INC." Almost five years later, Duong defaulted on the payments. The Federal National Mortgage Association (Fannie Mae) had come into possession of the note. Fannie Mae wanted to foreclose on the house and sell it to recover the balance due. Duong argued that the words "to the order of [blank space]" in the indorsement made the note an incomplete order instrument and that Fannie Mae thus could not enforce it. What is Fannie Mae's best response to this argument? [*Federal National Mortgage Association v. Thao Thi Duong*, __ So.3d __, 2015 WL 629284 (La.App. 5 Cir. 2015)] (See *Transfer of Instruments.*)

19–9. A Question of Ethics—Promissory Notes. Clarence Morgan, Jr., owned Easy Way Automotive, a car dealership in D'Lo, Mississippi. Easy Way sold a truck to Loyd Barnard, who signed a note for the amount of the price payable to Trustmark National Bank in six months. Before the note came due, Barnard returned the truck to Easy Way, which sold it to another buyer. Using some of the proceeds from the second sale, Easy Way sent a check to Trustmark to pay Barnard's note. Meanwhile, Barnard obtained another truck from Easy Way, financed through another six-month note payable to Trustmark. After eight of these deals, some of which involved more than one truck, an Easy Way check to Trustmark was dishonored. In a suit in a Mississippi state court, Trustmark sought to recover the amounts of two of the notes from Barnard. Trustmark had not secured titles to two of the trucks covered by the notes, however, and this complicated Barnard's efforts to reclaim the vehicles from the later buyers. [*Trustmark National Bank v. Barnard*, 930 So.2d 1281 (Miss.App. 2006)] (See *Types of Negotiable Instruments.*)

1. On what basis might Barnard be liable on the Trustmark notes? Would he be primarily or secondarily liable? Could this liability be discharged on the theory that Barnard's right of recourse had been impaired when Trustmark did not secure titles to the trucks covered by the notes? Explain.

2. Easy Way's account had been subject to other recent overdrafts, and a week after the check to Trustmark was returned for insufficient funds, Morgan committed suicide. At the same time, Barnard was unable to obtain a mortgage because the unpaid notes affected his credit rating. How do the circumstances of this case underscore the importance of practicing business ethics?

Critical Thinking and Writing Assignments

19–10. Case Analysis Question. Go to Appendix G at the end of this text and examine the excerpt of Case No. 3, *Mills v. Chauvin*. Review and then brief the case, making sure that your brief answers the following questions. (See *Defenses, Limitations, and Discharge.*)

1. **Issue:** What document was at the center of the dispute in this case?

2. **Rule of Law:** What are the elements of consideration? What are the requirements for attaining the status of a holder in due course (HDC)?

3. **Application:** Did the document at the center of the dispute in this case satisfy the elements of consideration? Did the party in possession of the document take it as an HDC? Explain.

4. **Conclusion:** Who did the court determine was liable? Why?

19–11. Business Law Critical Thinking Group Assignment. Peter Gowin was an employee of a granite countertop business owned by Joann Stathis. In November 2016, Gowin signed a promissory note agreeing to pay $12,500 in order to become a co-owner of the business. The note was dated January 15, 2016 (ten months before it was signed), and required him to make installment payments starting in February 2016. Stathis told Gowin not to worry about the note and never requested any payments. Gowin continued to work at the business until 2018, when he quit, claiming that he owned half of the business. Stathis argued that Gowin was not a co-owner because he had never paid the $12,500 into the business. (See *Requirements for Negotiability.*)

1. The first group will argue in favor of Stathis that Gowin did not own any interest in the business.

2. The second group will evaluate the strength of Gowin's argument. Gowin claimed that because compliance with the stated dates was impossible, the note effectively did not state a date for its payment. It therefore was a demand note under UCC 3–108(a). Because no demand for payment had been made, Gowin's obligation to pay had not arisen, and the termination of his ownership interest was improper.

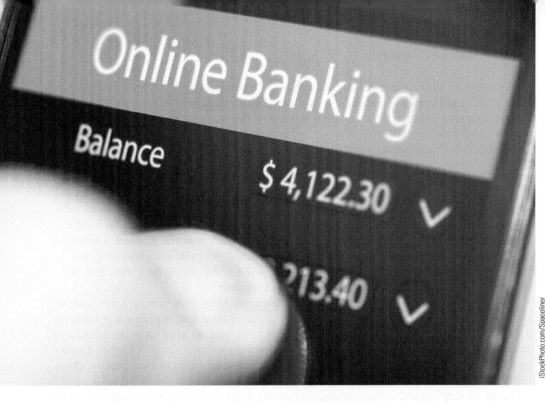

iStockPhoto.com/Spaceliner

20

Banking in the Digital Age

"Money is just what we use to keep tally."

HENRY FORD
1863–1947
(AMERICAN AUTOMOBILE MANUFACTURER)

In the chapter-opening quotation, Henry Ford said that "we use money to keep tally." If we do, then checks help us, because checks serve as a substitute for cash. Checks are the most common type of negotiable instruments regulated by the Uniform Commercial Code (UCC). Many people today use debit cards rather than checks for their retail transactions, and payments are increasingly being made via smartphones, iPads, and other mobile devices. Nonetheless, commercial checks remain an integral part of the U.S. economic system.

Articles 3 and 4 of the UCC govern issues relating to checks. Article 4 of the UCC governs bank deposits and collections as well as bank-customer relationships. Article 4 also regulates the relationships of banks with one another as they process checks for payment, and it establishes a framework for deposit and checking agreements between a bank and its customers. A check therefore may fall within the scope of Article 3 as a negotiable instrument and yet be subject to the provisions of Article 4 while in the course of collection. If a conflict between Article 3 and Article 4 arises, Article 4 controls [UCC 4–102(a)].

20-1 Checks

A *check* is a special type of draft that is drawn on a bank, ordering the bank to pay a fixed amount of funds on demand [UCC 3–104(f)]. Article 4 defines a *bank* as "a person engaged in the business of banking, including a savings bank, savings and loan association, credit union or trust company" [UCC 4–105(1)]. If any other institution (such as a brokerage firm) handles a check for payment or for collection, the check is *not* covered by Article 4.

LEARNING OBJECTIVES

The five Learning Objectives *below are designed to help improve your understanding of the chapter. After reading this chapter, you should be able to answer the following questions:*

1. What type of check does a bank agree in advance to accept when the check is presented for payment?

2. When may a bank properly dishonor a customer's check without being liable to the customer?

3. What duties does the Uniform Commercial Code impose on a bank's customers with regard to forged and altered checks? What are the consequences if a customer is negligent in performing those duties?

4. What is electronic check presentment, and how does it differ from the traditional check-clearing process?

5. What are the four most common types of electronic fund transfers?

A person who writes a check is called the *drawer*. The drawer is a depositor in the bank on which the check is drawn. The person to whom the check is payable is the *payee*. The bank or financial institution on which the check is drawn is the *drawee*. Thus, when Anita Cruzak writes a check from her checking account to pay her college tuition, she is the drawer, her bank is the drawee, and her college is the payee. We now look at some special types of checks.

20-1a Cashier's Checks

Cashier's Check A check drawn by a bank on itself.

Checks usually are three-party instruments, but on certain types of checks, the bank can serve as both the drawer and the drawee. For instance, when a bank draws a check on itself, the check is called a **cashier's check** and is a negotiable instrument at the moment it is issued (see Exhibit 20–1) [UCC 3–104(g)]. Normally, a cashier's check indicates a specific payee. In effect, with a cashier's check, the bank assumes responsibility for paying the check, thus making the check more readily acceptable as a substitute for cash.

EXAMPLE 20.1 Kramer needs to pay a moving company $8,000 for moving his household goods to his new home in another state. The moving company requests payment in the form of a cashier's check. Kramer goes to a bank (he need not have an account at the bank) and purchases a cashier's check, payable to the moving company, in the amount of $8,000. Kramer has to pay the bank the $8,000 for the check, plus a small service fee. He then gives the check to the moving company. ■

Except in very limited circumstances, the issuing bank must honor its cashier's checks when they are presented for payment. If a bank wrongfully dishonors a cashier's check, a holder can recover from the bank all expenses incurred, interest, and consequential damages [UCC 3–411].[1] This same rule applies if a bank wrongfully dishonors a certified check (to be discussed shortly).

---

1. See, for example, *MidAmerica Bank v. Charter One Bank*, 232 Ill.2d 560, 905 N.E.2d 839 (2009).

Exhibit 20–1 A Cashier's Check

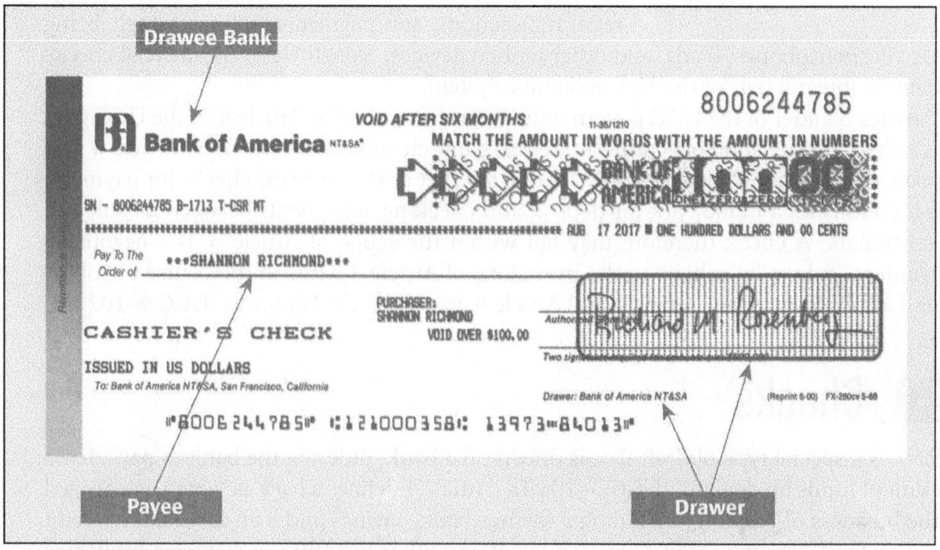

* The abbreviation *NT&SA* stands for National Trust and Savings Association. The Bank of America NT&SA is a subsidiary of Bank of America Corporation, which is engaged in financial services, insurance, investment management, and other businesses.

20-1b Traveler's Checks

A **traveler's check** is an instrument that is payable on demand, drawn on or payable at or through a financial institution (such as a bank), and designated as a traveler's check. The issuing institution is directly obligated to accept and pay its traveler's check according to the check's terms.

Traveler's checks are designed to be a safe substitute for cash for people who are on vacation or traveling. They are issued for fixed amounts, such as $20, $50, or $100. The purchaser is required to sign the check at the time it is bought and again at the time it is used [UCC 3–104(i)]. Most major banks today do not issue their own traveler's checks but, instead, purchase and issue American Express traveler's checks for their customers (see Exhibit 20–2).

Traveler's Check A check that is payable on demand, drawn on or payable through a financial institution, and designated as a traveler's check.

20-1c Certified Checks

A **certified check** is a check that has been accepted in writing by the bank on which it is drawn [UCC 3–409(d)]. When a drawee bank certifies a check, it immediately charges the drawer's account with the amount of the check and transfers those funds to its own certified check account. In effect, the bank is agreeing in advance to accept that check when it is presented for payment and to make payment from those funds reserved in its certified check account. Essentially, certification prevents the bank from denying liability. It is a promise that sufficient funds are on deposit *and have been set aside* to cover the check.

To certify a check, the bank writes or stamps the word *certified* on the face of the check and typically writes the amount that it will pay.[2] Once a check is certified, the drawer and any prior indorsers are completely discharged from liability on the check [UCC 3–414(c), 3–415(d)]. Only the certifying bank is required to pay the instrument.

Either the drawer or the holder (payee) of a check can request certification. The drawee bank is not required to certify the check, however, and the bank's refusal to certify a check is not a dishonor of the check [UCC 3–409(d)].

LEARNING OBJECTIVE 1

What type of check does a bank agree in advance to accept when the check is presented for payment?

Certified Check A check that has been accepted in writing by the bank on which it is drawn. By certifying (accepting) the check, the bank promises to pay the check at the time it is presented.

---

2. If the certification does not state an amount, and the amount is later increased and the instrument negotiated to a holder in due course (HDC), the obligation of the certifying bank is the amount of the instrument when it was taken by the HDC [UCC 3–413(b)].

Exhibit 20–2 A Traveler's Check

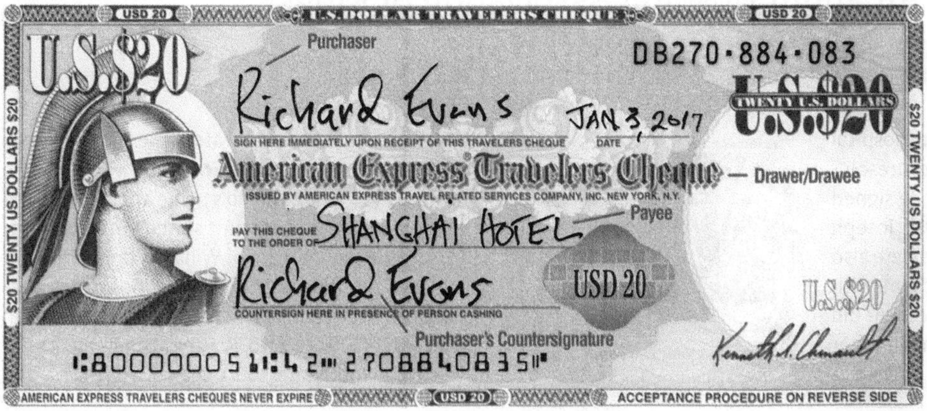

20–2 The Bank-Customer Relationship

The bank-customer relationship begins when the customer opens a checking account and deposits funds that the bank will use to pay for checks written by the customer. Essentially, three types of relationships come into being, as discussed next.

20–2a Creditor-Debtor Relationship

A creditor-debtor relationship is created between a customer and a bank when, for example, the customer makes cash deposits into a checking account. When a customer makes a deposit, the customer becomes a creditor, and the bank a debtor, for the amount deposited.

20–2b Agency Relationship

An agency relationship arises between the customer and the bank when the customer writes a check on his or her account. In effect, the customer is ordering the bank to pay the amount specified on the check to the holder when the holder presents the check to the bank for payment. In this situation, the bank becomes the customer's agent and is obligated to honor the customer's request.

Similarly, if the customer deposits a check into his or her account, the bank, as the customer's agent, is obligated to collect payment on the check from the bank on which the check was drawn. To transfer checking account funds among different banks, each bank acts as the agent of collection for its customer [UCC 4–201(a)].

20–2c Contractual Relationship

When a bank-customer relationship is established, certain contractual rights and duties arise. The contractual rights and duties of the bank and its customer depend on the nature of the transaction. These rights and duties are discussed in detail in the following pages. Another aspect of the bank-customer relationship—deposit insurance—is examined in the *Linking Business Law to Accounting and Finance* feature at the end of this chapter.

The following case arose when a company realized that the balance in its corporate bank account was depleted. In fact, service charges had resulted in a negative balance. Under the parties' account agreement, was the bank liable for the loss of the funds?

CASE 20.1

Royal Arcanum Hospital Association of Kings County, Inc. v. Herrnkind

New York Supreme Court, Appellate Division, Second Department, 113 A.D.3d 672, 978 N.Y.S.2d 355 (2014).

FACTS The board of the Royal Arcanum Hospital Association of Kings County, Inc., passed a resolution to require that all corporate checks be signed by two of three officers—Frank Vassallo, Joseph Rugilio, and William Herrnkind. The three were also named as signatories on the firm's account with Capital One Bank, but the terms of the account did not include the two-signature requirement. After Vassallo and Rugilio died, Herrnkind opened a

Can a customer account require two signatures for any check?

new account in the corporate name that expressly permitted checks to be drawn on it with only one signature. Only Herrnkind's name appeared on the signature card. The account statements were sent to Royal Arcanum "care of William Herrnkind."

Over the next four years, a series of transactions reduced the balance of the account from nearly $200,000 to zero. Royal Arcanum filed a suit in a New York state court against Herrnkind and

Capital One to recover the funds. The court dismissed the complaint against the bank. Royal Arcanum appealed.

ISSUE Was Capital One liable for the payment of unauthorized withdrawals from its customer's corporate accounts?

DECISION No. A state intermediate appellate court affirmed the decision of the lower court to dismiss Royal Arcanum's complaint against Capital One.

REASON The contractual relationship between a bank and its customer includes the understanding that the bank will pay out the customer's funds only as instructed. In this case, although Royal Arcanum's board required two signatures on its corporate checks, the terms of the accounts with Capital Bank did not require two signatures. Because the terms permitted checks to be drawn with only one signature, the bank did not breach its customer's requirement. Also, "insofar as the Bank's transactions with the plaintiff were concerned, the plaintiff conferred, at the least, apparent authority on Herrnkind to act on its behalf."

Under these circumstances, the bank used "due care and diligence," as there was nothing to "arouse the suspicion of its employees." Thus, the bank was not liable for the payment of unauthorized withdrawals from Royal Arcanum's accounts.

CRITICAL THINKING—Legal Consideration *What circumstances indicated that Herrnkind had Royal Arcanum's authority to act on its behalf?*

20-3 The Bank's Duty to Honor Checks

When a banking institution provides checking services, it agrees to honor the checks written by its customers, with the usual stipulation that the account must have sufficient funds available to pay each check [UCC 4–401(a)]. When a drawee bank *wrongfully* fails to honor a check, it is liable to its customer for damages resulting from its refusal to pay [UCC 4–402(b)]. The customer does not have to prove that the bank breached its contractual commitment or was negligent.

The customer's agreement with the bank includes a general obligation to keep sufficient funds on deposit to cover all checks written. The customer is liable to the payee or to the holder of a check in a civil suit if a check is dishonored for insufficient funds. If intent to defraud can be proved, the customer can also be subject to criminal prosecution for writing a bad check.

When the bank properly dishonors a check for insufficient funds, it has no liability to the customer. The bank may rightfully refuse payment on a customer's check in other circumstances as well. We look here at the rights and duties of both the bank and its customers in specific situations.

Can a bank that issues a refund check to a customer then refuse to cash it for that customer? Rarely does a bank draft a check to a customer, but occasionally it does happen—for instance, when the bank is refunding a deposit or closing a customer's account. If the customer presents the check to the same bank that issued it (and the bank is both drawer and drawee), we would expect that the customer would have no trouble cashing it. Not so for Ama Afiriyie.

When Afiriyie first opened checking and savings accounts with Bank of America (BOA), the bank required her to pay a security deposit of $300 to get a "secured" credit card. A year later, BOA upgraded Afiriyie's credit-card account to unsecured status and issued her a refund check for $300. Afiriyie took the check to a BOA branch inside a grocery store, but the branch manager, Diane Lowe, was suspicious and refused to cash it. Lowe also called the police and reported that Afiriyie was trying to pass a fraudulent or counterfeit check.

Afiriyie was arrested, fingerprinted, and held for several hours until police discovered that the check was legitimate and released her. She filed suit against BOA, alleging wrongful dishonor (among other claims). When a jury found in Afiriyie's favor, BOA appealed. The bank argued that there was no wrongful dishonor, because under UCC 3–503(b)(4), it had until the

ETHICAL ISSUE

When you open a checking account, do you establish a contractual relationship?

day after Afiriyie presented the check to process the payment. The court, however, was not persuaded. "BOA cannot, on the one hand, cause plaintiff to be arrested for attempting to pass a fraudulent check, and, on the other hand, claim that they never dishonored that check." BOA's refusal to cash the check constituted wrongful dishonor.[3]

20–3a Overdrafts

When the bank receives an item properly payable from its customer's checking account but the account contains insufficient funds to cover the amount of the check, the bank has two options. It can dishonor the item, or it can pay the item and charge the customer's account, thus creating an **overdraft.** The bank can subtract the amount of the overdraft (plus a service charge) from the customer's next deposit or other customer funds, because a check carries with it an enforceable implied promise to reimburse the bank.

A bank can expressly agree with a customer to accept overdrafts through what is sometimes called an "overdraft protection agreement." If such an agreement is formed, any failure of the bank to honor a check because it would create an overdraft breaches this agreement and is treated as a wrongful dishonor [UCC 4–402(a)].

Overdraft A check that is paid by a bank when the checking account on which the check is written contains insufficient funds to cover the check.

20–3b Postdated Checks

A bank may charge a postdated check against a customer's account, unless the customer notifies the bank, in a timely manner, not to pay the check until the stated date. The notice of postdating must be given in time to allow the bank to act on the notice before it pays the check. If the bank fails to act on the customer's notice and charges the customer's account before the date on the postdated check, the bank may be liable for any damages incurred by the customer [UCC 4–401(c)].[4]

20–3c Stale Checks

Commercial banking practice regards a check that is presented for payment more than six months from its date as a **stale check.** A bank is not obligated to pay an uncertified check presented more than six months from its date [UCC 4–404].

When it receives a stale check for payment, the bank has the option of paying or not paying the check. The bank may consult the customer before paying the check. If a bank pays a stale check in good faith without consulting the customer, the bank has the right to charge the customer's account for the amount of the check.

Stale Check A check, other than a certified check, that is presented for payment more than six months after its date.

20–3d Stop-Payment Orders

A **stop-payment order** is an order by a customer to his or her bank not to pay or certify a certain check. Only a customer (or a person authorized to draw on the account) can order the bank not to pay the check when it is presented for payment [UCC 4–403(a)].[5] A customer has no right to stop payment on a check that has been certified or accepted by a bank, however. In addition, the customer-drawer must have a *valid legal ground* for issuing such an order, or the holder can sue the customer-drawer for payment.

Stop-Payment Order An order by a bank customer to his or her bank not to pay or certify a certain check.

---

3. *Afiriyie v. Bank of America, N.A.,* 2013 WL 451895 (Sup.Ct. N.J. 2013). The intermediate appellate court also affirmed the trial court's finding that the damages awarded by the jury were too high and that a new trial should be held to determine proper damages.

4. Postdating does not affect the negotiability of a check. A check is usually paid without respect to its date.

5. Any person claiming a legitimate interest in the account of a deceased customer may issue a stop-payment order [UCC 4–405].

Reasonable Time and Manner The customer must issue the stop-payment order within a reasonable time and in a reasonable manner to permit the bank to act on it [UCC 4–403(a)]. Most banks allow stop-payment orders to be submitted electronically via the bank's Web site. A written or electronic stop-payment order is effective for six months, at which time it may be renewed [UCC 4–403(b)]. Although a stop-payment order can be given orally over the phone, it is binding on the bank for only fourteen calendar days unless confirmed in writing (or record).[6]

Bank's Liability for Wrongful Payment If the bank pays the check in spite of a stop-payment order, the bank will be obligated to recredit the customer's account. In addition, if the bank's payment over a stop-payment order causes subsequent checks written on the drawer's account to "bounce," the bank will be liable for the resultant costs the drawer incurs. The bank is liable only for the amount of actual damages suffered by the drawer, however [UCC 4–403(c)].

20–3e Death or Incompetence of a Customer

Neither the death nor the incompetence of a customer revokes a bank's authority to pay an item until the bank is informed of the situation and has had a reasonable amount of time to act on the notice. Without this provision, banks would constantly be required to verify the continued life and competence of their drawers.

Thus, if a bank is unaware that a customer who wrote a check has been declared incompetent or has died, the bank can pay the item without incurring liability [UCC 4–405]. Even when a bank knows of the death of its customer, for ten days after the *date of death,* it can pay or certify checks drawn on or before the date of death. An exception to this rule is made if a person claiming an interest in the account, such as an heir, orders the bank to stop payment.

20–3f Checks with Forged Drawers' Signatures

When a bank pays a check on which the drawer's signature is forged, generally the bank is liable. A bank may be able to recover at least some of the loss from the customer, however, if the customer's negligence contributed to the making of the forgery. A bank may also obtain partial recovery from the forger of the check (if he or she can be found) or from the holder who presented the check for payment (if the holder knew that the signature was forged).

The General Rule A forged signature on a check has no legal effect as the signature of a customer-drawer [UCC 3–403(a)]. For this reason, banks require a signature card from each customer who opens a checking account. Signature cards allow the bank to verify whether the signatures on its customers' checks are genuine. (Banks today normally verify signatures only on checks that exceed a certain threshold, such as $2,500 or some higher amount, because it would be too costly to verify every signature.)

The general rule is that the bank must recredit the customer's account when it pays a check with a forged signature. A bank may contractually shift to the customer the risk of forged checks created electronically or by the use other nonmanual signatures. For instance, the contract might stipulate that the customer is solely responsible for maintaining security over the customer's signature stamp for checks.

Customer Negligence When the customer's negligence substantially contributed to the forgery, the bank normally will not be obligated to recredit the customer's account for the amount of the check [UCC 3–406]. The customer's liability may be reduced, however, by the amount

"Canceled checks will be to future historians and cultural anthropologists what the Dead Sea Scrolls and hieroglyphics are to us."

BRENT STAPLES
1951–PRESENT
(AMERICAN JOURNALIST)

---

6. Some states do not recognize oral stop-payment orders.

of loss caused by negligence on the part of the bank (or other person) paying the instrument or taking it for value if the negligence substantially contributed to the loss [UCC 3–406(b)].

CASE EXAMPLE 20.2 Kenneth Wulf worked for Auto-Owners Insurance Company for ten years. During that time, Wulf opened a checking account at Bank One in the name of "Auto-Owners, Kenneth B. Wulf." Over a period of eight years, he deposited $546,000 worth of checks that he had stolen from Auto-Owners and indorsed with a stamp that read "Auto-Owners Insurance Deposit Only." When the scam was finally discovered, Auto-Owners sued Bank One for negligence.

The insurance company claimed that the bank should not have allowed Wulf to open an account in Auto-Owners' name without proof that he was authorized to do so. The court ruled in favor of the bank, though, finding that Bank One's conduct was not a substantial factor in bringing about the loss. The negligence of Auto-Owners—its lack of oversight of its employee—contributed substantially to its own losses. Therefore, the bank did not have to recredit the customer's account.[7] ▦

Timely Examination Required. Banks typically send or provide online monthly statements that detail the activity in their customers' checking accounts. The statements provide customers with information (check number, amount, and date of payment) that will allow them to reasonably identify the checks that the bank has paid [UCC 4–406(a), (b)]. In the past, banks routinely included the canceled checks themselves (or copies of them) with the statement, but that practice is unusual today. If the bank does retain the canceled checks, it must keep the checks—or legible copies—for seven years [UCC 4–406(b)].

The customer has a duty to promptly examine bank statements (and canceled checks or copies) with reasonable care and to report any alterations or forged signatures [UCC 4–406(c)]. This includes forged signatures of indorsers, if discovered (to be discussed shortly). If the customer fails to fulfill this duty and the bank suffers a loss as a result, the customer will be liable for the loss [UCC 4–406(d)].

Consequences of Failing to Detect Forgeries. Sometimes, the same wrongdoer has forged a customer's signature on a series of checks. To recover for all the forged items, the customer must discover and report the *first* forged check to the bank within thirty calendar days of the receipt of the bank statement [UCC 4–406(d)(2)]. Failure to notify the bank within this period of time discharges the bank's liability for *all* of the forged checks that it pays prior to notification.

CASE EXAMPLE 20.3 Joseph Montanez, an employee at Espresso Roma Corporation, used stolen software and blank checks to generate company checks on his home computer. The series of forged checks spanned a period of over two years and totaled more than $330,000. When the bank statements containing the forged checks arrived in the mail, Montanez removed the checks so that the forgeries would go undetected.

Eventually, Espresso Roma discovered the forgeries and asked the bank to recredit its account. The bank refused, and litigation ensued. The court held that the bank was not liable for the forged checks because Espresso Roma had failed to report the first forgeries within the UCC's time period of thirty days.[8] ▦

When the Bank Is Also Negligent If a customer who has been negligent can prove that the bank was also negligent, then the bank will also be liable. In this situation, the loss will be allocated between the bank and the customer on the basis of comparative negligence [UCC 4–406(e)]. In other words, even though a customer may have been negligent, the bank may have to recredit the customer's account for a portion of the loss if the bank also failed to exercise

What is the time limit within which a bank customer must report the first in a series of forged checks?

iStockPhoto.com/Ldf

KNOW THIS
If a bank is forced to recredit a customer's account, the bank may recover from the forger or from the party that cashed the check (usually a different customer or a collecting bank).

---

7. *Auto-Owners Insurance Co. v. Bank One*, 879 N.E.2d 1086 (Ind.Sup.Ct. 2008).
8. *Espresso Roma Corp. v. Bank of America, N.A.*, 100 Cal.App.4th 525, 124 Cal.Rptr.2d 549 (2002).

ordinary care. (*Ordinary care* means the observance of reasonable banking standards prevailing in the relevant geographical area [UCC 3–103].)

One-Year Time Limit Regardless of the degree of care exercised by the customer or the bank, the UCC places an absolute time limit on the liability of a bank for paying a check with a forged customer signature. A customer who fails to report a forged signature within one year from the date of the bank statement loses the legal right to have the bank recredit his or her account [UCC 4–406(f)]. The parties can also agree in their contract to a lower time limit.

Other Parties from Whom the Bank May Recover As noted earlier, a forged signature on a check has no legal effect as the signature of a drawer. Instead, the person who forged the signature is liable [UCC 3–403(a)]. Therefore, when a bank pays a check on which the drawer's signature is forged, the bank has a right to recover from the party who forged the signature (if he or she can be found).

Forgery of checks by employees and embezzlement of company funds are disturbingly common in today's business world. To avoid significant losses due to forgery or embezzlement, as well as litigation, use care in maintaining business bank accounts. Limit access to your business's bank accounts. Never leave company checkbooks or signature stamps in unsecured areas. Use passwords to limit access to computerized check-writing software. Examine bank statements in a timely fashion, and be on the lookout for suspicious transactions. Remember that if a forgery is not reported within thirty days of the first statement in which the forged item appears, you, as the account holder, normally lose the right to hold the bank liable.

20–3g Checks Bearing Forged Indorsements

A bank that pays a customer's check bearing a forged indorsement must recredit the customer's account or be liable to the customer-drawer for breach of contract. **EXAMPLE 20.4** Simon issues a $500 check "to the order of Antonio." Juan steals the check, forges Antonio's indorsement, and cashes the check. When the check reaches Simon's bank, the bank pays it and debits Simon's account. The bank must recredit the $500 to Simon's account because it failed to carry out Simon's order to pay "to the order of Antonio" [UCC 4–401(a)]. ■

Eventually, *the loss usually falls on the first party to take the instrument bearing the forged indorsement* because a forged indorsement does not transfer title. Thus, whoever takes an instrument with a forged indorsement cannot become a holder. In *Example 20.4*, Simon's bank can recover—for breach of warranty—from the bank that cashed the check when Juan presented it [UCC 4–207(a)(2)].

The customer, in any event, has a duty to report forged indorsements promptly. Failure to report forged indorsements within a three-year period after the forged items have been made available to the customer relieves the bank of liability [UCC 4–111].

In the following case, a bank's contract with its customer altered its statutory duties concerning forged indorsements. The court had to decide whether to follow the UCC or enforce the contract as written.

LEARNING OBJECTIVE 3
What duties does the Uniform Commercial Code impose on a bank's customers with regard to forged and altered checks? What are the consequences if a customer is negligent in performing those duties?

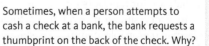

iStockPhoto.com/ziss

Sometimes, when a person attempts to cash a check at a bank, the bank requests a thumbprint on the back of the check. Why?

CASE 20.2

Michigan Basic Property Insurance Association v. Washington

Court of Appeals of Michigan, 2012 WL 205753 (2012).

FACTS The Michigan Basic Property Insurance Association (MBP) issued a check for $69,559.06 from its account with Fifth Third Bank to Joyce Washington, Countrywide Home Loans, and T&C Federal Credit Union as co-payees. Washington indorsed the check herself by signing all three payees' names and did not distribute the proceeds to the co-payees. When the check reached Fifth Third Bank, it notified MBP of the payment through a daily account statement. MBP did not object, so Fifth Third Bank withdrew the funds from MBP's account. Fifth Third Bank also sent information about the check in a monthly account statement. MBP still failed to object, even though the account agreement required it to provide prompt notice of any forgeries. MBP was forced to issue a second check to Countrywide, so it sued Fifth Third Bank and sought to have its account recredited. The trial court found that Fifth Third Bank was liable to MBP, and another party appealed on Fifth Third Bank's behalf.

ISSUE Was Fifth Third Bank liable to MBP for paying a check with forged indorsements?

Checks can be made out to more than one payee.

DECISION No. The Michigan appellate court reversed the trial court's judgment.

REASON The court noted that, under the Uniform Commercial Code (UCC), the check was not properly payable because it had two forged indorsements. When a bank pays a check bearing a forged indorsement, the UCC ordinarily requires the bank to recredit the customer's account. Nevertheless, the court pointed out that the UCC allows parties to change their duties by contract. In this case, the account agreement obligated MBP to carefully review its checking account statements and to notify Fifth Third Bank of any problems within thirty days. In the absence of such notice, the contract provided that MBP, not Fifth Third Bank, was liable for any forged indorsements. Because MBP did not provide prompt notice of the forgeries, Fifth Third Bank was not required to recredit MBP's account.

CRITICAL THINKING—Legal Consideration *As a practical matter, does it make sense for the customer to bear primary responsibility for discovering instances of fraud? Which party is in a better position to detect any irregularities? Explain.*

20–3h Altered Checks

The customer's instruction to the bank is to pay the exact amount on the face of the check to the holder. The bank has a duty to examine each check before making final payment. If the bank fails to detect an alteration, normally it is liable to its customer for the loss because it did not pay as the customer ordered.

The bank's loss is the difference between the original amount of the check and the amount actually paid [UCC 4–401(d)(1)]. **EXAMPLE 20.5** A check written for $11 is altered to $111. The customer's account will be charged $11 (the amount the customer ordered the bank to pay). The bank normally will be responsible for the $100 difference. ■

Customer Negligence As in a situation involving a forged drawer's signature, a customer's negligence can shift the loss when payment is made on an altered check (unless the bank was also negligent). For instance, this may occur when a person carelessly writes a check leaving large gaps where additional numbers and words can be inserted (see Exhibit 20–3).

Similarly, a person who signs a check and leaves the dollar amount for someone else to fill in is barred from protesting when the bank unknowingly and in good faith pays whatever amount is shown [UCC 4–401(d)(2)]. Finally, if the bank can trace its loss on successive altered checks to the customer's failure to discover the initial alteration, the bank can reduce its liability for reimbursing the customer's account [UCC 4–406].

In every situation involving a forged drawer's signature or an alteration, a bank must observe reasonable commercial standards of care in paying on a customer's checks [UCC 4–406(e)]. The customer's negligence can be used as a defense only if the bank has exercised ordinary care.

Exhibit 20–3 A Poorly Filled-Out Check

Other Parties from Whom the Bank May Recover The bank is entitled to recover the amount of loss from the transferor who presented the check for payment. A transferor, by presenting a check for payment, warrants that the check has not been altered.

There are two exceptions to this rule. First, if the bank is also the drawer (as it is on a cashier's check), it cannot recover from the presenting party if the party is a holder in due course (HDC) acting in good faith [UCC 3–417(a)(2), 4–208(a)(2)]. The reason is that an instrument's drawer is in a better position than an HDC to know whether the instrument has been altered.

Second, an HDC who presents a certified check for payment in good faith will not be held liable under warranty principles if the check was altered before the HDC acquired it [UCC 3–417(a)(2), 4–207(a)(2)]. **EXAMPLE 20.6** Jordan draws a check for $500 payable to David. David alters the amount to $5,000. The drawee bank, First National, certifies the check for $5,000. David negotiates the check to Ethan, an HDC. The drawee bank pays Ethan $5,000. On discovering the mistake, the bank cannot recover from Ethan the $4,500 paid by mistake, even though the bank was not in a superior position to detect the alteration. This is in accord with the purpose of certification, which is to obtain the definite obligation of a bank to honor a definite instrument. ■

20-4 The Bank's Duty to Accept Deposits

A bank has a duty to its customer to accept the customer's deposits of cash and checks. When checks are deposited, the bank must make the funds represented by those checks available within certain time frames. A bank also has a duty to collect payment on any checks payable or indorsed to its customers and deposited by them into their accounts. Cash deposits made in U.S. currency are received into customers' accounts without being subject to further collection procedures.

20-4a Availability Schedule for Deposited Checks

The Expedited Funds Availability Act[9] and Regulation CC[10] (the regulation implementing the act) establish when funds from deposited checks must be made available to the customer. The rules are as follows:

---

9. 12 U.S.C. Sections 4001–4010.
10. 12 C.F.R. Sections 229.1–229.42.

1. Any local check (drawn on a bank in the same area) deposited must be available for withdrawal by check or as cash within one business day from the date of deposit.
2. For nonlocal checks, the funds must be available for withdrawal within not more than five business days.
3. Under the Check Clearing in the 21st Century Act[11] (Check 21, which is the subject of this chapter's *Landmark in the Law* feature), a bank must credit a customer's account as soon as the bank receives the funds.
4. For cash deposits, wire transfers, and government checks, funds must be available on the next business day.
5. The first $100 of any deposit must be available for cash withdrawal on the opening of the *next business day* after deposit.

A different availability schedule applies to deposits made at *nonproprietary* automated teller machines (ATMs). These are ATMs that are not owned or operated by the bank receiving the deposits. Basically, a five-day hold is permitted on all deposits, including cash deposits, made at nonproprietary ATMs. Other exceptions also exist. For instance, a banking institution has eight days to make funds available in new accounts (those open less than thirty days).

A bank that places a longer hold on a deposited check than that specified by the rules must notify the customer. A credit union's failure to provide this notice to its customer was at the center of the following case.

If you deposit a check at your bank that is written on another bank, can you withdraw those funds in cash immediately? Why or why not?

---

11. 12 U.S.C. Sections 5001–5018.

CASE 20.3

Shahin v. Delaware Federal Credit Union

United States Court of Appeals, Third Circuit, 2015 WL 509563 (2015).

FACTS Nina Shahin deposited a check in the amount of $2,500 into her checking account at the Delaware Federal Credit Union (DelOne). DelOne placed a two-business-day "local hold" on the check pending verification. Concerned that the drawer's signature did not match the handwriting on the rest of the check, the bank placed it on a fifteen-day "nonverified" hold. Meanwhile, a payment from Shahin's checking account to Bank of America was denied for insufficient funds (NSF), and DelOne transferred funds from her savings account to cover other payments. DelOne then imposed two $30 penalties for NSF, as well as transfer fees totaling $6. Shahin filed a suit in a federal district court against DelOne, alleging that the credit union had failed to give her proper notice of the extended hold. The court issued a summary judgment in Shahin's favor, awarding her the amount of the NSF and transfer fees plus $1,000, the maximum amount of liability for a notice violation under Regulation CC. Shahin appealed, claiming that the amount of damages was insufficient.

ISSUE Did the court award Shahin the proper amount of damages?

DECISION Yes. The U.S Court of Appeals for the Third Circuit affirmed the judgment of the lower court and the amount of the award.

Is the bank liable when it incorrectly returns a check for insufficient funds? If so, what is the proper amount of damages?

REASON Regulation CC sets the requirement for a depositary institution to notify its customer of an extended hold on a deposited check. An institution that fails to comply with this provision is liable to the customer for "any actual damage sustained by that person as a result of the failure" and a penalty of "such additional amount as the court may allow," to a maximum of $1,000. In her motion for summary judgment, Shahin contended that DelOne had imposed $60 in NSF charges and $6 in transfer fees. The lower court found that DelOne was liable to Shahin for these charges and fees—actual damages totaling $66. The court also determined that DelOne was subject to liability to Shahin for a penalty under Regulation CC. The amount of $1,000 was the maximum amount that could be imposed under that provision. On appeal, Shahin claimed that the amount of damages was insufficient. The appellate court pointed out, however, she did not provide evidence to support any other claim for damages.

CRITICAL THINKING—Economic Consideration *Is $1,000 an appropriate penalty for the failure of a depository institution to comply with Regulation CC's notice provision? Why or why not?*

LANDMARK IN THE LAW   Check Clearing in the 21st Century Act (Check 21)

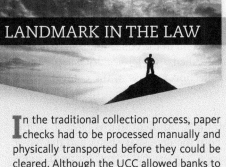

In the traditional collection process, paper checks had to be processed manually and physically transported before they could be cleared. Although the UCC allowed banks to use *electronic presentment*—that is, to transmit check information electronically instead of sending actual paper checks—this method was not widely adopted because it required agreements among individual banks.

PURPOSE OF CHECK 21 To streamline the costly and time-consuming collection process and improve the overall efficiency of the nation's payment system, Congress passed the Check Clearing in the 21st Century Act (Check 21), which went into effect in 2004. Check 21 changed the collection process by creating a new negotiable instrument called a *substitute check*. Although the act did not require banks to change their check-collection practices, the creation of substitute checks has facilitated the use of electronic check processing.

SUBSTITUTE CHECKS A substitute check is a paper reproduction of the front and back of an original check that contains all of the information required for automated processing. A bank creates substitute checks from digital images of original checks. It can then process the check information electronically or deliver substitute checks to banks that wish to continue receiving paper checks. The original check can be destroyed after a substitute check is created, helping to prevent the check from being paid twice and reducing expenses. Nevertheless, at least for a while, not all checks will be converted to substitute checks.

FASTER ACCESS TO FUNDS The Expedited Funds Availability Act requires the Federal Reserve Board to revise the availability schedule for funds from deposited checks to correspond to reductions in check-processing time.[a] Therefore, as the speed of check processing continues to increase under Check 21, the Federal Reserve Board will reduce the maximum time that a bank can hold funds from deposited checks before making them available to the depositors. That means, of course, that account holders will have faster access to their deposited funds. But it also means that they will have less *float time*—the time between when a check is written and when the amount is deducted from the account.

APPLICATION TO TODAY'S WORLD *As more financial institutions transfer digital images of checks, the check-processing system becomes more efficient. Customers are increasingly unable to rely on banking float when they are low on funds, so they should make sure that funds are available to cover checks when they are written. Customers cannot opt out of Check 21. Nor can they refuse to accept a substitute check as proof of payment.*

---

a. 12 U.S.C. Sections 4001–4010.

20–4b The Traditional Collection Process

Usually, deposited checks involve parties that do business at different banks, but sometimes checks are written between customers of the same bank. Either situation brings into play the bank collection process as it operates within the statutory framework of Article 4 of the UCC. Note that the check-collection process described in the following subsections will be modified as the banking industry continues to implement Check 21.

Designations of Banks The first bank to receive a check for payment is the **depositary bank.**[12] For instance, when a person deposits a tax-refund check into a personal checking account at the local bank, that bank is the depositary bank. The bank on which a check is drawn (the drawee bank) is the **payor bank.** Any bank except the payor bank that handles a check during some phase of the collection process is a **collecting bank.** Any bank except the payor bank or the depositary bank to which an item is transferred in the course of this collection process is an **intermediary bank.**

During the collection process, any bank can take on one or more of the various roles of depositary, payor, collecting, and intermediary bank. **EXAMPLE 20.7** A buyer in New York writes

Depositary Bank The first bank to receive a check for payment.

Payor Bank The bank on which a check is drawn (the drawee bank).

Collecting Bank Any bank handling an item for collection, except the payor bank.

Intermediary Bank Any bank to which an item is transferred in the course of collection, except the depositary or payor bank.

---

12. All definitions in this section are found in UCC 4–105. The terms *depositary* and *depository* have different meanings in the banking context. A depository bank refers to a *physical place* (a bank or other institution) in which deposits or funds are held or stored.

a check on her New York bank and sends it to a seller in San Francisco. The seller deposits the check in her San Francisco bank account. The seller's bank is both a *depositary bank* and a *collecting bank*. The buyer's bank in New York is the *payor bank*. As the check travels from San Francisco to New York, any collecting bank handling the item in the collection process (other than the depositary bank and the payor bank) is also called an *intermediary bank*. Exhibit 20–4 illustrates how various banks function in the collection process in the context of this example. ■

Check Collection between Customers of the Same Bank

An item that is payable by the same bank that receives it (which in this situation is both the depositary bank and the payor bank) is called an "on-us item." Usually, the bank issues a "provisional credit" for on-us items within the same day. If the bank does not dishonor the check by the opening of the second banking day following its receipt, the check is considered paid [UCC 4–215(e)(2)].

EXAMPLE 20.8 Pam Otterley and Jenna Merkowitz have checking accounts at First State Bank. On Monday, Merkowitz deposits into her checking account a $300 check from Otterley. That same day, the bank issues Merkowitz a provisional (temporary) credit for $300. When the bank opens on Wednesday, Otterley's check is considered honored, and Merkowitz's provisional credit becomes a final payment. ■

Check Collection between Customers of Different Banks

Once a depositary bank receives a check payable to another bank, it must arrange to present the check, either directly or through intermediary banks, to the appropriate payor bank. Each bank in the collection chain

Exhibit 20–4 The Check-Collection Process

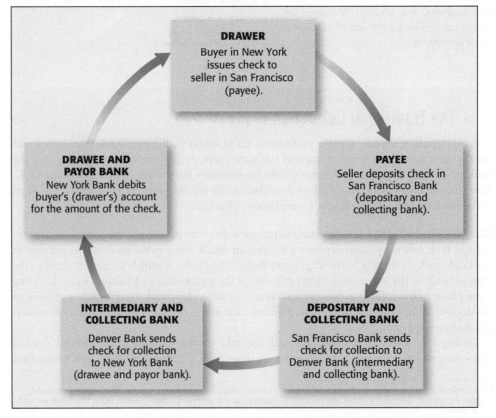

must pass the check on before midnight of the next banking day following its receipt [UCC 4–202(b)].[13] A "banking day" is any part of a day that the bank is open to carry on substantially all of its banking functions. Thus, if only a bank's drive-through facilities are open, a check deposited on Saturday will not trigger the bank's midnight deadline until the following Monday.

The UCC permits what is called *deferred posting*. According to UCC 4–108, "a bank may fix an afternoon hour of 2:00 P.M. or later as a cutoff hour for the handling of money and items and the making of entries on its books." Any checks received after that hour "may be treated as being received at the opening of the next banking day." Thus, if a bank's cutoff hour is 3:00 P.M., a check received by a payor bank at 4:00 P.M. on Monday will be deferred for posting until Tuesday. In this situation, the payor bank's deadline will be midnight Wednesday.

When the check reaches the payor bank, that bank is liable for the face amount of the check, unless the payor bank dishonors the check or returns it by midnight on the next banking day following receipt [UCC 4–302].[14]

How the Federal Reserve System Clears Checks

The **Federal Reserve System** is a network of twelve government banks located around the United States and headed by the Federal Reserve Board of Governors. Most banks in the United States have Federal Reserve accounts. The Federal Reserve System acts as a **clearinghouse**—a system or place where banks exchange checks and drafts drawn on each other and settle daily balances.

EXAMPLE 20.9 Pamela Moy of Philadelphia writes a check to Jeanne Sutton in San Francisco. When Sutton receives the check in the mail, she deposits it in her bank. Her bank then deposits the check in the Federal Reserve Bank of San Francisco, which transfers it to the Federal Reserve Bank of Philadelphia. That Federal Reserve bank then sends the check to Moy's bank, which deducts the amount of the check from Moy's account. ∎

Electronic Check Presentment

In the past, as mentioned, most checks were processed manually. Today, most checks are processed electronically, as discussed in the *Landmark in the Law* feature on Check 21. Whereas manual check processing can take days, *electronic check presentment* can be done on the day of deposit. Check information is encoded, transmitted electronically, and processed by other banks' computers. After encoding a check, a bank may retain it and present only its image or description for payment under an electronic presentment agreement [UCC 4–110].[15]

A bank that encodes information for electronic presentment warrants to any subsequent bank or payor that the encoded information is correct [UCC 4–209]. Similarly, a bank that retains a check and presents its image or description for payment warrants that the image or description is accurate.

Regulation CC, which deals with the availability of deposited funds, provides that a returned check must be encoded with the routing number of the depositary bank, the amount of the check, and other information. The regulation further states that a check must still be returned within the deadlines required by the UCC.

Federal Reserve System
A network of twelve district banks and related branches located around the country and headed by the Federal Reserve Board of Governors. Most banks in the United States have Federal Reserve accounts.

Clearinghouse A system or place where banks exchange checks and drafts drawn on each other and settle daily balances.

LEARNING OBJECTIVE 4
What is electronic check presentment, and how does it differ from the traditional check-clearing process?

Do bank customers directly deposit checks in the closest Federal Reserve bank?

---

13. A bank may take a "reasonably longer time" in certain circumstances, such as when the bank's computer system is down due to a power failure, but the bank must show that its action is still timely [UCC 4–202(b)].

14. Most checks are cleared by a computerized process, and communication and computer facilities may fail because of electrical outages, equipment malfunction, or other conditions. A bank may be "excused" from liability for failing to meet its midnight deadline if such conditions arise and the bank has exercised "such diligence as the circumstances require" [UCC 4–109(d)].

15. This section of the UCC assumes that no bank will participate in an electronic presentment program without an express agreement (which is no longer true since Check 21 went into effect). See Comment 2 to UCC 4–110.

20–5 Electronic Fund Transfers

Electronic Fund Transfer (EFT) A transfer of funds through the use of an electronic terminal, a telephone, a computer, or magnetic tape.

An **electronic fund transfer (EFT)** is a transfer of funds through the use of an electronic terminal, smartphone, tablet, computer, or telephone. The law governing EFTs depends on the type of transfer involved. Consumer fund transfers are governed by the Electronic Fund Transfer Act (EFTA).[16] Commercial fund transfers are governed by Article 4A of the UCC.

Transferring funds electronically offers numerous benefits, but it also poses difficulties on occasion. For instance, it is difficult to issue stop-payment orders with electronic banking. Also, fewer records are available to prove or disprove that a transaction took place. The possibilities for tampering with a person's private banking information have also increased.

KNOW THIS

The EFTA does not provide for the reversal of an electronic transfer of funds once it has occurred.

20–5a Types of EFT Systems

Most banks today offer EFT services. The following are the most common types of EFT systems used by bank customers:

LEARNING OBJECTIVE 5

What are the four most common types of electronic fund transfers?

1. *Automated teller machines (ATMs)*—The machines are connected online to the bank's computers. A customer inserts a plastic card (called an ATM or debit card) issued by the bank and keys in a *personal identification number* (PIN) to access her or his accounts and conduct banking transactions.

2. *Point-of-sale systems*—Online terminals allow consumers to transfer funds to merchants to pay for purchases using a debit card.

3. *Direct deposits and withdrawals*—Customers can authorize the bank to allow another party—such as the government or an employer—to make direct deposits into their accounts. Similarly, customers can request the bank to make automatic payments to a third party at regular, recurrent intervals from the customer's funds (insurance premiums or loan payments, for instance).

4. *Online payment systems*—Many financial institutions permit their customers to access the institution's computer system via the Internet and direct a transfer of funds between accounts or pay a particular bill. Payments can be made on a one-time or a recurring basis.

20–5b Consumer Fund Transfers

Regulation E A set of rules issued by the Federal Reserve System's Board of Governors to protect users of electronic fund transfer systems.

The Electronic Fund Transfer Act (EFTA) provides a basic framework for the rights, liabilities, and responsibilities of users of EFT systems. Additionally, the act gave the Federal Reserve Board authority to issue rules and regulations to help implement the act's provisions. The Federal Reserve Board's implemental regulation is called **Regulation E.**

The EFTA governs financial institutions that offer electronic fund transfers involving consumer accounts. The types of accounts covered include checking accounts, savings accounts, and any other asset accounts established for personal, family, or household purposes.

Disclosure Requirements The EFTA is essentially a disclosure law benefiting consumers. The act requires financial institutions to inform consumers of their rights and responsibilities, including those listed here, with respect to EFT systems.

1. The bank must provide a monthly statement for every month in which there is an electronic transfer of funds. The statement must show the amount and date of the transfer, the names of the retailers or other third parties involved, the location or identification of the terminal, and the fees.

---

16. 15 U.S.C. Sections 1693–1693r. The EFTA amended Title IX of the Consumer Credit Protection Act.

2. If a customer's debit card is lost or stolen and used without his or her permission, the customer will be required to pay no more than $50 if he or she notifies the bank of the loss or theft within two days of learning about it. Otherwise, the liability increases to $500. The customer may be liable for more than $500 if he or she fails to report the unauthorized use within sixty days after it appears on the customer's statement. (If a customer voluntarily gives her or his debit card to another, who then uses it improperly, the protections just mentioned do not apply.)

3. The customer must discover any error on the monthly statement within sixty days and notify the bank. The bank then has ten days to investigate and must report its conclusions to the customer in writing. If the bank takes longer than ten days, it must return the disputed amount to the customer's account until it finds the error. If there is no error, the customer has to return the disputed funds to the bank.

4. The bank must provide receipts for transactions made through computer terminals, but it is not obligated to do so for telephone transfers.

Violations and Damages Unauthorized access to an EFT system constitutes a federal felony, and those convicted may be fined up to $10,000 and sentenced to as long as ten years in prison. Banks must strictly comply with the terms of the EFTA and are liable for any failure to adhere to its provisions.

For a bank's violation of the EFTA, a consumer may recover both actual damages (including attorneys' fees and costs) and punitive damages of not less than $100 and not more than $1,000. Even when a customer has sustained no actual damage, the bank may be liable for legal costs and punitive damages if it fails to follow the proper procedures outlined by the EFTA in regard to error resolution.

20–5c Commercial Fund Transfers

Another way in which funds are transferred electronically is the transfer of funds "by wire" between commercial parties. In fact, the dollar volume of payments by wire transfer is more than $1 trillion a day—an amount that far exceeds the dollar volume of payments made by other means. The two major wire payment systems are the Federal Reserve's wire transfer network (Fedwire) and the New York Clearing House Interbank Payments Systems (CHIPS).

Commercial wire transfers are governed by Article 4A of the UCC, which has been adopted by most states (and is included in Appendix C at the end of this text). Article 4A uses the term *funds transfer* rather than *wire transfer* to describe the overall payment transaction. **EXAMPLE 20.10** Jellux, Inc., owes $5 million to Perot Corporation. Instead of sending Perot a check or some other instrument that would enable Perot to obtain payment, Jellux instructs its bank, East Bank, to credit $5 million to Perot's account in West Bank. East Bank debits Jellux's East Bank account and wires $5 million to Perot's West Bank account. In more complex transactions, additional banks would be involved. ■

20–6 Online Banking and E-Money

Online banking is common in today's world. In a few minutes, anyone with the proper software can access his or her account, transfer funds, write "checks," and pay bills. Also commonplace today is the use of **digital cash,** or **e-money,** which consists of funds stored on microchips in laptops, smartphones, tablets, and other devices. E-money replaces *physical* cash—coins and paper currency—with *virtual* cash in the form of electronic impulses.

KNOW THIS
If any part of an electronic fund transfer is covered by the EFTA, the entire transfer is excluded from UCC Article 4A.

How do businesses transfer large sums of funds among themselves?

Digital Cash Prepaid funds stored on microchips in laptops, smartphones, tablets, and other devices.

E-Money Prepaid funds stored on microchips in laptops, smartphones, tablets, and other devices.

20–6a Online Banking

Most customers use three kinds of online banking services: consolidating bills and making payments, transferring funds among accounts, and applying for loans and credit cards.

Withdrawing and depositing funds are two banking functions not yet widely available online. Nevertheless, there are software applications (apps) that enable customers to make deposits into their accounts using electronic devices. **EXAMPLE 20.11** Bobbi, a Chase Bank customer, downloads its free mobile app. The app allows Bobbi to take a photo of both sides of her endorsed check with her smartphone's camera, follow the on-screen instructions, and submit the check for deposit into her account. ■

Mobile payment apps are also becoming popular, as discussed in this chapter's *Adapting the Law to the Online Environment* feature.

20–6b Stored-Value Cards and Smart Cards

Stored-Value Card A card bearing a magnetic strip that holds magnetically encoded data providing access to stored funds.

The simplest kind of e-money system uses **stored-value cards.** These are plastic cards embossed with magnetic strips containing magnetically encoded data. Frequently, a stored-value card can be used only to purchase specific goods and services offered by the card issuer. An example is a gift card that is only redeemable at a particular retail store or restaurant.

ADAPTING THE LAW TO THE **ONLINE** ENVIRONMENT
Pay with Your Smartphone

A payment revolution is going on right now. Starting in 2009, customers at certain Starbucks locations in New York, San Francisco, and Seattle could use an iPhone app to pay for their lattes. By 2015, some 7,500 Starbucks locations were accepting payments from all types of smartphone-based operating systems. That same year, smartphone point-of-sale payments in the United States reached $4.2 billion. Some experts estimate that the total for 2016 will be $30 billion.

Apple Enters the Mobile Payments Arena
Apple, Inc., provides its own mobile payment and "digital wallet" service, called Apple Pay. Owners of Apple's iPhone 6, iPhone 6 Plus, iPad Air 2, and iPad Mini 3, along with its Apple Watch, have access to the service. Apple Pay enables these devices to communicate wirelessly with special point-of-sale systems using near field communication (NFC) technology. A person using an iPhone holds it close to the point-of-sale terminal and authenticates the transaction by holding a fingerprint to the phone's Touch ID sensor. Customers' payment information is kept private from the retailer. The system generates a "dynamic security code" for each transaction.

Google and Samsung Provide Competition
Google created the Google Wallet wireless payment system even before Apple Pay was launched. Then, in 2015, Google and the mobile payments company Softcard contracted with AT&T, T-Mobile USA, and Verizon Wireless to preinstall Google Wallet in smartphones sold by those three companies.

Google's Android system is used on most Samsung smartphones. Samsung, a fierce competitor of Apple, announced in 2015 its purchase of LoopPay, a mobile payments startup. Also in 2015, Samsung created a direct competitor to Apple Pay called Samsung Pay. It was designed to work with existing magnetic-stripe credit-card machines as well as the newer NFC technology.

Linking Digital Wallets to Other Apps on a Smartphone
The ultimate goal in this modern payment system world is a link from a digital wallet to another app within a single smartphone. For example, Google allows its Google Wallet to link to its Google Offers, which is a discount-deal app. Mobile payment systems will eventually be tied to rewards programs and special offers at individual stores.

CRITICAL THINKING

■ Does having a digital wallet in an iPhone, Android-based smartphone, or other smartphone entail more security risks than carrying a physical wallet? Explain.

Smart cards are plastic cards containing tiny microchips that can hold more information than a magnetic strip can. A smart card carries and processes security programming. This capability gives smart cards a technical advantage over stored-value cards. The microprocessors on smart cards can also authenticate the validity of transactions. Retailers can program electronic cash registers to confirm the authenticity of a smart card by examining a unique digital signature stored on its microchip. Common uses for smart cards are as credit cards and ATM cards.

Smart Card A card containing a microprocessor and typically used for financial transactions, personal identification, and other purposes.

Reviewing . . . Banking in the Digital Age

RPM Pizza, Inc., issued a check for $96,000 to Systems Marketing for an advertising campaign. A few days later, RPM decided not to go through with the deal and placed a written stop-payment order on the check. RPM and Systems had no further contact for many months. Three weeks after the stop-payment order expired, however, Toby Rierson, an employee at Systems, cashed the check. Bank One Cambridge, RPM's bank, paid the check with funds from RPM's account. Because the check was more than six months old, it was stale. Thus, according to standard banking procedures as well as Bank One's own policies, the signature on the check should have been specially verified, but it was not. RPM filed a suit in a federal district court against Bank One to recover the amount of the check. Using the information presented in the chapter, answer the following questions.

1. How long is a written stop-payment order effective? What else could RPM have done to prevent this check from being cashed?

2. What would have happened if RPM had not had a legitimate reason for stopping payment on the check?

3. What are a bank's obligations with respect to stale checks?

4. Would a court be likely to hold the bank liable for the amount of the check because it failed to verify the signature on the check? Why or why not?

DEBATE THIS

- To reduce fraud, checks that utilize mechanical or electronic signature systems should not be honored.

LINKING BUSINESS LAW TO ACCOUNTING AND FINANCE
Banking Risks

In this chapter, you learned about the bank-customer relationship as well as a bank's duty to honor checks and accept deposits. In the macroeconomics courses that your business school offers, the focus on the banking sector is quite different. Among other things, the courses examine banking panics and bank runs and their effects on the economy.

A *bank run* occurs when depositors simultaneously rush to convert their bank deposits into currency because they believe that the assets of their bank are not sufficient to cover its liabilities—the customers' deposits. The largest number of bank runs in modern history occurred during the Great Depression in the 1930s, when nine thousand banks failed.

Federal Deposit Insurance
To prevent bank runs, the federal government set up a system of deposit insurance to assure depositors that their deposits would be safe. The Federal Deposit Insurance

Continues

Corporation (FDIC) and the Federal Savings and Loan Insurance Corporation (FSLIC) were created in the 1930s to insure deposits. In 1971, the National Credit Union Shares Insurance Fund (NCUSIF) was added to insure credit union deposits.

Although the names and form of some of these organizations have changed over the years, the principle remains the same: to insure all accounts in these financial institutions against losses up to a specified limit. In 1933, each account was insured up to $2,500. During the recession that started in December 2007, the federal government wanted to make sure that no banking panics would occur. Therefore, in 2008 the insurance limit was raised to $250,000.

Federal insurance for bank deposits may seem like a good idea. Nevertheless, some problems are associated with it.

Moral Hazard: An Unintended Consequence of Deposit Insurance

In your finance courses, you learn that the riskier a loan is, the higher the interest rate that a lending institution can charge the borrower. Bank managers must weigh the trade-off between risk and return when deciding which loan applicants should receive funds. Loans to poor credit risks offer high profits, assuming that the borrowers actually pay off their debts. Good credit risks are more likely to pay their debts, but can obtain loans at lower rates.

Since the federal deposit insurance limit was increased to $250,000 per account, managers have had a greater incentive to make risky loans. By doing so, in the short run the banks make higher profits, and the managers receive higher salaries and bonuses. If some of these risky loans are not repaid, what is the likely outcome? A bank's losses are limited because the federal government—you, the taxpayer—will cover any shortfall between the bank's assets and its liabilities. Consequently, federal deposit insurance means that banks get to enjoy all of the profits of risk taking without bearing all of the consequences of that risk taking.

In short, an unintended consequence of federal deposit insurance is to encourage *moral hazard*. It creates an incentive for bank managers to take more risks in their lending policies than they would otherwise.

CRITICAL THINKING

- Imagine the United States without federal deposit insurance. What are some of the mechanisms that would arise to "punish" bank managers who acted irresponsibly?

Key Terms

cashier's check 492

certified check 493

clearinghouse 505

collecting bank 503

depositary bank 503

digital cash 507

electronic fund transfer (EFT) 506

e-money 507

Federal Reserve System 505

intermediary bank 503

overdraft 496

payor bank 503

Regulation E 506

smart card 509

stale check 496

stop-payment order 496

stored-value card 508

traveler's check 493

Chapter Summary: Banking in the Digital Age

Checks	1. *Cashier's check*—A check drawn by a bank on itself (the bank is both the drawer and the drawee) and purchased by a customer. In effect, the bank assumes responsibility for paying the check, thus making the check nearly the equivalent of cash.
	2. *Traveler's check*—An instrument on which a financial institution is both the drawer and the drawee. The purchaser is required to sign the check at the time it is bought and again at the time it is used for the check to become a negotiable instrument.
	3. *Certified check*—A check for which the drawee bank certifies in writing that it has set aside funds from the drawer's account to ensure payment of the check on presentation. On certification, the drawer and all prior indorsers are completely discharged from liability on the check.
The Bank-Customer Relationship	1. *Creditor-debtor relationship*—A customer and a bank have a creditor-debtor relationship (the bank is the debtor because it holds the customer's funds on deposit).
	2. *Agency relationship*—Because a bank must act in accordance with the customer's orders in regard to the customer's deposited money, an agency relationship also arises—the bank is the agent for the customer, who is the principal.
	3. *Contractual relationship*—The bank's relationship with its customer is also contractual. Both the bank and the customer assume certain contractual duties when a customer opens a bank account.

The Bank's Duty to Honor Checks	Generally, a bank has a duty to honor its customers' checks, provided that the customers have sufficient funds on deposit to cover the checks [UCC 4–401(a)]. The bank is liable to its customers for actual damages proved to be due to wrongful dishonor [UCC 4–402]. **1.** *Overdraft*—The bank has a right to charge a customer's account for any item properly payable, even if the charge results in an overdraft [UCC 4–401]. **2.** *Postdated check*—The bank may charge a postdated check against a customer's account, unless the customer notifies the bank, in a timely manner, not to pay the check until the stated date [UCC 4–401]. **3.** *Stale check*—The bank is not obligated to pay an uncertified check presented more than six months after its date, but the bank may do so in good faith without liability [UCC 4–404]. **4.** *Stop-payment order*—The customer (or a person authorized to draw on the account) must make a stop-payment order in time for the bank to have a reasonable opportunity to act. Oral orders are binding for only fourteen days unless they are confirmed in writing. Written or electronic orders are effective for six months unless renewed in writing [UCC 4–403]. The bank is liable for wrongful payment over a timely stop-payment order to the extent that the customer suffers a loss. **5.** *Death or incompetence of a customer*—So long as the bank does not know of the death or incompetence of a customer, the bank can pay an item without liability. Even with knowledge of a customer's death, a bank can honor or certify checks (in the absence of a stop-payment order) for ten days after the date of the customer's death [UCC 4–405]. **6.** *Forged signature or alteration*—The customer has a duty to examine account statements with reasonable care on receipt and to notify the bank promptly of any forged signatures or alterations. On a series of forged signatures or alterations by the same wrongdoer, examination and report must be made within thirty calendar days of receipt of the first statement containing a forged or altered item [UCC 4–406]. The customer's failure to comply with these rules releases the bank from liability unless the bank failed to exercise reasonable care, in which case liability may be apportioned according to a comparative negligence standard. Regardless of care or lack of care, the customer is barred from holding the bank liable after one year for forged customer signatures or alterations and after three years for forged indorsements.

The Bank's Duty to Accept Deposits	A bank has a duty to accept deposits made by its customers into their accounts. Funds from deposited checks must be made available to customers according to a schedule mandated by the Expedited Funds Availability Act and Regulation CC. A bank also has a duty to collect payment on any checks deposited by its customers. When checks deposited by customers are drawn on other banks, the check-collection process comes into play.
	1. *Definitions of banks*—UCC 4–105 provides the following definitions of banks involved in the collection process:
	  a. Depositary bank—The first bank to accept a check for payment.
	  b. Payor bank—The bank on which a check is drawn.
	  c. Collecting bank—Any bank except the payor bank that handles a check during the collection process.
	  d. Intermediary bank—Any bank except the payor bank or the depositary bank to which an item is transferred in the course of the collection process.
	2. *Check collection between customers of the same bank*—A check payable by the depositary bank that receives it is an "on-us item." If the bank does not dishonor the check by the opening of the second banking day following its receipt, the check is considered paid [UCC 4–215(e)(2)].
	3. *Check collection between customers of different banks*—Each bank in the collection process must pass the check on to the next appropriate bank before midnight of the next banking day following its receipt [UCC 4–108, 4–202(b), 4–302].
	4. *How the Federal Reserve System clears checks*—The Federal Reserve System facilitates the check-clearing process by serving as a clearinghouse for checks.
	5. *Electronic check presentment*—Check information may be encoded, transmitted electronically, and processed by other banks' computers. After encoding a check, a bank may retain it and present only its image or description for payment under an electronic presentment agreement [UCC 4–110].

Electronic Fund Transfers	**1.** *Types of EFT systems*—
	  a. Automated teller machines (ATMs).
	  b. Point-of-sale systems.
	  c. Direct deposits and withdrawals.
	  d. Online payment systems.
	2. *Consumer fund transfers*—Consumer fund transfers are governed by the Electronic Fund Transfer Act (EFTA). The EFTA is basically a disclosure law that sets forth the rights and duties of the bank and the customer with respect to EFT systems. Banks must comply strictly with EFTA requirements.
	3. *Commercial transfers*—Article 4A of the UCC, which has been adopted by almost all of the states, governs fund transfers not subject to the EFTA or other federal or state statutes.

Online Banking and E-Money	**1.** *Online banking*—Most customers use three kinds of online banking services:
	  a. Bill consolidation and payment.
	  b. Transferring funds among accounts.
	  c. Applying for loans and credit cards.
	2. *E-money*—Types of e-money include stored-value cards and smart cards.

Issue Spotters

1. Lyn writes a check for $900 to Mac, who indorses the check in blank and transfers it to Jan. She presents the check to Omega Bank, the drawee bank, for payment. Omega does not honor the check. Is Lyn liable to Jan? Could Lyn be subject to criminal prosecution? Why or why not? (See *The Bank's Duty to Honor Checks*.)

2. Roni writes a check for $700 to Sela. Sela indorses the check in blank and transfers it to Titus, who alters the check to read $7,000 and presents it to Union Bank, the drawee, for payment. The bank cashes it. Roni discovers the alteration and sues the bank. How much, if anything, can Roni recover? From whom can the bank recover this amount? (See *The Bank's Duty to Honor Checks*.)

—**Check your answers to the *Issue Spotters* against the answers provided in Appendix D at the end of this text.**

Learning Objectives Check

1. What type of check does a bank agree in advance to accept when the check is presented for payment?

2. When may a bank properly dishonor a customer's check without being liable to the customer?

3. What duties does the Uniform Commercial Code impose on a bank's customers with regard to forged and altered checks? What are the consequences if a customer is negligent in performing those duties?

4. What is electronic check presentment, and how does it differ from the traditional check-clearing process?

5. What are the four most common types of electronic fund transfers?

—**Answers to the even-numbered *Learning Objectives Check* questions can be found in Appendix E at the end of this text.**

Business Scenarios and Case Problems

20–1. Forged Checks. Roy Supply, Inc., and R. M. R. Drywall, Inc., had checking accounts at Wells Fargo Bank. Both accounts required all checks to carry two signatures—that of Edward Roy and that of Twila June Moore, both of whom were executive officers of both companies. Between January 2006 and March 2008, the bank honored hundreds of checks on which Roy's signature was forged by Moore. On January 31, 2009, Roy and the two corporations notified the bank of the forgeries and then filed a suit in a California state court against the bank, alleging negligence. Who is liable for the amounts of the forged checks? Why? (See *The Bank's Duty to Honor Checks*.)

20–2. Customer Negligence. Gary goes grocery shopping and carelessly leaves his checkbook in his shopping cart. His checkbook, with two blank checks remaining, is stolen by Dolores. On May 5, Dolores forges Gary's name on a check for $100 and cashes the check at Gary's bank, Citizens Bank of Middletown. Gary has not reported the loss of his blank checks to his bank. On June 1, Gary receives his monthly bank statement from Citizens Bank that includes the forged check, but he does not notice the item, nor does he examine his bank statement. On June 20, Dolores forges Gary's last check. This check is for $1,000 and is cashed at Eastern City Bank, a bank with which Dolores has previously done business. Eastern City Bank puts the check through the collection process, and Citizens Bank honors it. On July 1, on receipt of his bank statement and canceled checks covering June transactions, Gary discovers both forgeries and immediately notifies Citizens Bank. Dolores cannot be found.

Gary claims that Citizens Bank must recredit his account for both checks, as his signature was forged. Discuss fully Gary's claim. (See *The Bank's Duty to Honor Checks*.)

20–3. Forged Drawers' Signatures. Debbie Brooks and Martha Tingstrom lived together. Tingstrom handled their finances. For five years, Brooks did not look at any statements concerning her accounts. When she finally reviewed the statements, she discovered that Tingstrom had taken $85,500 from Brooks's checking account with Transamerica Financial Advisors. Tingstrom had forged Brooks's name on six checks paid between one and two years earlier. Another year passed before Brooks filed a suit against Transamerica. Who is most likely to suffer the loss for the checks paid with Brooks's forged signature? Why? [*Brooks v. Transamerica Financial Advisors*, 57 So.3d 1153 (La.App. 2 Cir. 2011)] (See *The Bank's Duty to Honor Checks*.)

20–4. Business Case Problem with Sample Answer— Honoring Checks. Adley Abdulwahab (Wahab) opened an account on behalf of W Financial Group, LLC, with Wells Fargo Bank. Wahab was one of three authorized signers on the account. Five months later, Wahab withdrew $1,701,250 from W Financial's account to buy a cashier's check payable to Lubna Lateef. Wahab visited a different Wells Fargo branch and deposited the check into the account of CA Houston Investment Center, LLC. Wahab was the only authorized signer on this account. Lateef never received or indorsed the check. W Financial filed a suit to recover the amount. Applying

1. A **secured party** is any creditor who has a *security interest* in the *debtor's collateral*. This creditor can be a seller, a lender, a cosigner, or even a buyer of accounts or chattel paper [UCC 9–102(a)(72)].

2. A **debtor** is a person who *owes payment* or other performance of a secured obligation [UCC 9–102(a)(28)].

3. A **security interest** is the *interest* in the collateral (such as personal property or fixtures) that *secures payment or performance of an obligation* [UCC 1–201(37)].

4. A **security agreement** is an *agreement* that *creates* or provides for a *security interest* [UCC 9–102(a)(73)]. In other words, it is the contract in which a debtor agrees to give a creditor the right to take his or her property in the event of default.

5. **Collateral** is the *subject* of the *security interest* [UCC 9–102(a)(12)].

6. A **financing statement**—referred to as the UCC-1 form—is the *instrument normally filed to give public notice to third parties* of the *secured party's security interest* [UCC 9–102(a)(39)].

Together, these basic definitions form the concept under which a debtor-creditor relationship becomes a secured transaction relationship (see Exhibit 21–1).

21-2 Creating and Perfecting a Security Interest

A creditor has two main concerns if the debtor **defaults** (fails to pay the debt as promised): (1) Can the debt be satisfied through the possession and (usually) sale of the collateral? (2) Will the creditor have priority over any other creditors or buyers who may have rights in the same collateral? These two concerns are met through the creation and perfection of a security interest. We begin this section by examining how a security interest is created.

21-2a Requirements to Create a Security Interest

To become a secured party, the creditor must obtain a security interest in the collateral of the debtor. Three requirements must be met for a creditor to have an enforceable security interest:

1. Unless the creditor has possession of the collateral, there must be a written or authenticated security agreement that clearly describes the collateral subject to the security interest and is signed or authenticated by the debtor.

2. The secured party must give something of value to the debtor.

3. The debtor must have "rights" in the collateral.

Secured Party A creditor who has a security interest in the debtor's collateral, including a seller, lender, cosigner, or buyer of accounts or chattel paper.

Debtor Under Article 9 of the UCC, any party who owes payment or performance of a secured obligation.

Security Interest Any interest in personal property or fixtures that secures payment or performance of an obligation.

Security Agreement An agreement that creates or provides for a security interest between the debtor and a secured party.

Collateral Under Article 9 of the UCC, the property subject to a security interest.

Financing Statement A document filed by a secured creditor with the appropriate official to give notice to the public of the creditor's security interest in collateral belonging to the debtor named in the statement.

Default Failure to pay a debt when it is due.

LEARNING OBJECTIVE 1
What is required to create a security interest?

Exhibit 21–1 Secured Transactions—Concept and Terminology

In a security agreement, a debtor and a creditor agree that the creditor will have a security interest in collateral in which the debtor has rights. In essence, the collateral secures the loan and ensures the creditor of payment should the debtor default.

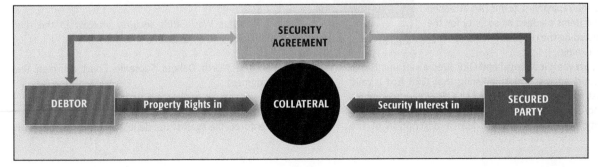

Attachment In a secured transaction, the process by which a secured creditor's interest "attaches" to the collateral and the creditor's security interest becomes enforceable. In the context of judicial liens, a court-ordered seizure of property before a judgment is secured for a past-due debt.

Once these requirements have been met, the creditor's rights are said to attach to the collateral. **Attachment** gives the creditor an enforceable security interest in the collateral [UCC 9–203].[1]

EXAMPLE 21.1 To furnish his new office suite, Bryce applies for a credit card at an office supply store. The application contains a clause stating that the store will retain a security interest in the goods that he buys with the card until he has paid for them in full. This application is a *written security agreement,* which is the first requirement for an enforceable security interest. The goods that Bryce buys with the card are the *something of value* from the secured party (the second requirement). His ownership interest in those goods is the *right* that he has in them (the third requirement). Thus, the requirements for an enforceable security interest are met. When Bryce buys something with the card, the store's rights attach to the purchased goods. ■

If you use a store-provided credit card at that store, does the store automatically have a security interest in what you purchase?

Written or Authenticated Security Agreement

When the collateral is not in the possession of the secured party, the security agreement must be either written or authenticated. It must also describe the collateral.

Here, *authenticate* means to sign, execute, or adopt any symbol on an electronic record that verifies that the person signing has the intent to adopt or accept the record [UCC 9–102(a)(7)(69)]. Authentication provides for electronic filing (the filing process will be discussed later). See this chapter's *Adapting the Law to the Online Environment* feature for a discussion of a type of secured transaction that is performed online.

A security agreement must contain a description of the collateral that reasonably identifies it. Generally, such phrases as "all the debtor's personal property" or "all the debtor's assets" would *not* constitute a sufficient description [UCC 9–108(c)].

If the debtor signs, or otherwise authenticates, a security agreement, does he or she also have to sign an attached list of the collateral to create a valid security interest? That was the question before the court in the following case.

---

1. The term *attachment* has a different meaning in judicial liens, discussed later in this chapter. In that context, it refers to a court-ordered seizure and taking into custody of property before the securing of a court judgment for a past-due debt.

CASE 21.1

Royal Jewelers, Inc. v. Light
Supreme Court of North Dakota, 2015 ND 44, 859 N.W.2d 921 (2015).

FACTS Steven Light bought a $55,050 wedding ring for his wife, Sherri Light, on credit from Royal Jewelers, Inc., a store in Fargo, North Dakota. The receipt granted Royal a security interest in the ring. Later, Royal assigned its interest to GRB Financial Corp. Steven and GRB signed a modification agreement changing the repayment terms. An attached exhibit listed the items pledged as security for the modification, including the ring. Steven did not separately sign the exhibit.

A year later, Steven died. Royal and GRB filed a suit in a North Dakota state court against Sherri, alleging that GRB had a valid security interest in the ring. Sherri cited UCC 9–203, under which there is an enforceable interest only if "the debtor has authenticated a security agreement that provides a description of the

Who retains a security interest in a wedding ring when the buyer dies?

collateral." Sherri argued that the modification agreement did not "properly authenticate" the description of the collateral, including the ring, because Steven had not signed the attached exhibit. The court issued a judgment in GRB's favor. Sherri appealed.

ISSUE Was GRB's security interest in the ring valid and enforceable?

DECISION Yes. The North Dakota Supreme Court affirmed the lower court's judgment.

REASON The court acknowledged that under UCC 9–203, "a security interest is enforceable against the debtor and third parties with respect to the collateral only if . . . the debtor has authenticated a security agreement that provides a description of the collateral." The court explained, however, that under UCC 9–108(2), collateral may be described in a list attached to the security agreement. In fact, several documents may be considered together to comprise a security agreement. Furthermore, "no authority [requires] a debtor to separately sign an exhibit attached to and referenced in a signed security agreement." Here, Steven had granted a valid security interest in the ring. With Steven's knowledge and consent, Royal had assigned the security interest to GRB. Thus, the lower court "did not err in finding GRB Financial had a valid and enforceable security interest in the ring."

CRITICAL THINKING—Ethical Consideration *Under the circumstances, is it ethical for GRB to enforce its security interest in the ring to recover the unpaid amount of the price? Discuss.*

Secured Party Must Give Value The secured party must give something of value to the debtor. Some examples of value include a binding commitment to extend credit or consideration to support a simple contract [UCC 1–204]. Normally, the value given by a secured party is in the form of a direct loan or a commitment to sell goods on credit.

Debtor Must Have Rights in the Collateral The debtor must have rights in the collateral. That means that the debtor must have a current or a future ownership interest in or right to obtain possession of the collateral. For instance, a retail seller-debtor can give a secured party a security interest not only in existing inventory owned by the retailer but also in *future* inventory to be acquired by the retailer. (A common misconception is that the debtor must have title to the collateral to have rights in it, but this is not a requirement.)

ADAPTING THE LAW TO THE **ONLINE** ENVIRONMENT
Secured Transactions Online

When you buy something online, you typically must use your credit card, make an electronic fund transfer, or send a check before the goods that you bought are sent to you. If you are buying an expensive item, such as a car, you are not likely to send funds without being assured that you will receive the item in the condition promised. Enter the concept of escrow.

Escrow Accounts

Escrow accounts are commonly used in real estate transactions, but they are also useful for smaller transactions, particularly those done on the Internet. An escrow account involves three parties—the buyer, the seller, and a trusted third party that collects, holds, and disperses funds according to instructions from the buyer and seller. Escrow services are provided by licensed and regulated escrow companies. For example, if you buy a car on the Internet, you and the seller will agree on an escrow company to which you send the funds. When you receive the car and are satisfied with it, the escrow company will release the funds to the seller. This is a type of secured transaction.

Escrow.com

One of the best-known online escrow firms is Escrow.com, which had provided escrow services for more than $2 billion in secured transactions by 2016. All of its escrow services are offered via its Web site and provided independently by Internet Escrow Services, one of its operating subsidiaries. Escrow.com is particularly useful for transactions that involve an international buyer or seller. It has become the recommended transaction settlement service for AutoTrader, Resale Weekly, Cars.com, eBay Motors, and Flippa.com.

CRITICAL THINKING

- How could online escrow services reduce Internet fraud?

21-2b **Perfecting a Security Interest**

Perfection The legal process by which secured parties protect themselves against the claims of third parties who may wish to have their debts satisfied out of the same collateral. It is usually accomplished by filing a financing statement with the appropriate government official.

Perfection is the legal process by which secured parties protect themselves against the claims of third parties who may wish to have their debts satisfied out of the same collateral. Whether a secured party's security interest is perfected or unperfected can have serious consequences for the secured party.

What if a debtor has borrowed from two different creditors, for instance, using the same property as collateral for both loans? If the debtor defaults on both loans, which of the two creditors has first rights to the collateral? In this situation, the creditor with a perfected security interest will prevail.

Perfection usually is accomplished by filing a financing statement. In some circumstances, however, a security interest becomes perfected even though no financing statement is filed.

When a bank finances the purchase of a tractor, how does it perfect its security interest in that tractor?

Perfection by Filing The most common means of perfection is by filing a *financing statement* with the office of the appropriate government official. A financing statement gives public notice to third parties of the secured party's security interest. The security agreement itself can also be filed to perfect the security interest. The financing statement must provide the names of the debtor and the secured party, and must identify the collateral covered by the financing statement. A uniform financing statement form is now used in all states [see UCC 9–521].

Communication of the financing statement to the appropriate filing office, together with the correct filing fee, or the acceptance of the financing statement by the filing officer constitutes a filing [UCC 9–516(a)]. The filing can be accomplished electronically [UCC 9–102(a)(18)]. In fact, most states use electronic filing systems. A financing statement may be filed even before a security agreement is made or a security interest attaches [UCC 9–502(d)].

The Debtor's Name. The UCC requires that a financing statement be filed under the name of the debtor [UCC 9–502(a)(1)]. Filings are indexed by the name of the debtor so that they can be located by subsequent searchers. Slight variations in names normally will not be considered misleading if a search of the filing office's records, using a standard computer search engine routinely used by that office, would disclose the filings [UCC 9–506(c)].[2]

UCC 9–503 sets out some detailed rules for determining when the debtor's name as it appears on a financing statement is sufficient.

1. *Corporations.* For corporations, which are organizations that have registered with the state, the debtor's name on the financing statement must be "the name of the debtor indicated on the public record of the debtor's jurisdiction of organization" [UCC 9–503(a)(1)].

2. *Trusts.* If the debtor is a trust or a trustee for property held in trust, the financing statement must disclose this information and provide the trust's name as specified in its official documents [UCC 9–503(a)(3)].

3. *Individuals and organizations.* For all others, the financing statement must disclose "the individual or organizational name of the debtor" [UCC 9–503(a)(4)(A)]. The word *organization* includes unincorporated associations, such as clubs, churches, joint ventures, and general partnerships. If an organizational debtor does not have a group name, the names of the individuals in the group must be listed.

4. *Trade names.* When the debtor's trade name is not the legal name of the business, providing only the trade name in a financing statement is *not* sufficient for perfection [UCC 9–503(c)]. The financing statement must also include the owner-debtor's actual name.

---

2. If the name listed in the financing statement is so inaccurate that a search using the standard search engine will not disclose the debtor's name, then the financing statement is deemed seriously misleading under UCC 9–506. See also UCC 9–507, which governs the effectiveness of financing statements found to be seriously misleading.

If the debtor's name changes, the financing statement remains effective for collateral the debtor acquired before or within four months after the name change. Unless an amendment to the financing statement is filed within this four-month period, collateral acquired by the debtor after the four-month period is unperfected [UCC 9–507(b) and (c)]. A one-page uniform financing statement amendment form is available for filing name changes and for other purposes.

PREVENTING LEGAL DISPUTES

Debtors frequently identify themselves by and change their trade names. This can make it difficult to find out whether an individual debtor's collateral is subject to a prior perfected security interest. For instance, suppose that a business named Bob's Automotive has two owners, Bob and Bill. When Bob decides to leave, Bill changes the trade name to Specialized Auto Repair. Searching the records using Bill's name and the new trade name might not reveal a prior perfected security interest from when the business was jointly owned and operating under a different name. Keep this in mind when making loans or extending credit.

When searching the records, find out if the business has used any other names in the past, and include those former names in your search. Remember that the key to determining if a security interest has been perfected is whether the financing statement adequately notifies other potential creditors that a security interest exists. If a search of the records using the debtor's correct name would disclose the interest, the filing is generally sufficient. To prevent legal problems, make sure that no other creditor has a prior interest in the property being used as collateral, and file the financing statement under the correct name.

Description of the Collateral. Both the security agreement and the financing statement must describe the collateral in which the secured party has a security interest. The security agreement must describe the collateral because no security interest in goods can exist unless the parties agree on which goods are subject to the security interest.

The financing statement must describe the collateral to provide public notice of the fact that certain goods of the debtor are subject to a security interest. Other parties who might later wish to lend funds to the debtor or buy the collateral can thus learn of the security interest by checking with the office in which a financing statement would be filed. For land-related security interests, a legal description of the realty is also required [UCC 9–502(b)].

Sometimes, the descriptions in the two documents vary. The description in the security agreement must be more precise than the description in the financing statement. The UCC permits broad, general descriptions in the financing statement, such as "all assets" or "all personal property," as long as they are accurate [UCC 9–504]. **EXAMPLE 21.2** A security agreement for a commercial loan to a manufacturer may list all of the manufacturer's equipment subject to the loan by serial number. The financing statement for the equipment may simply refer to "all equipment owned or hereafter acquired." ■

Where to File. In most states, a financing statement must be filed centrally in the appropriate state office, such as the office of the secretary of state, in the state where the debtor is located. An exception occurs when the collateral consists of timber to be cut, fixtures, or items to be extracted—such as oil, coal, gas, and minerals [UCC 9–301(3) and (4), 9–502(b)]. In those circumstances, the financing statement is filed in the county where the collateral is located.

Note that the state in which a financing statement should be filed depends on the *debtor's location,* not the location of the collateral [UCC 9–301]. The debtor's location is determined as follows [UCC 9–307]:

1. For *individual debtors,* it is the state of the debtor's principal residence.
2. For an *organization that is registered with the state,* such as a corporation or limited liability company, it is the state in which the organization is registered. Thus, if a debtor is incorporated in Maryland and has its

"O.K., folks, let's move along. I'm sure you've all seen someone qualify for a loan before."

chief executive office in New York, a secured party would file the financing statement in Maryland.

3. For *all other entities,* it is the state in which the business is located or, if the debtor has more than one office, the place from which the debtor manages its business operations and affairs.

Consequences of an Improper Filing. Improper filing renders the security interest unperfected and reduces the secured party's claim in bankruptcy to that of an unsecured creditor. For instance, if the debtor's name on the financing statement is seriously misleading or if the collateral is not sufficiently described in the financing statement, the filing may not be effective.

EXAMPLE 21.3 Arthur Mendez Juarez, a strawberry farmer, leases farmland from Morona Fruits, Inc., and borrows funds from Morona for payroll and production expenses. The sublease and other documents set out Juarez's full name, but Juarez generally goes by the name "Mendez" and signs the sublease "Arthur Mendez." To perfect its interests, Morona files financing statements that identify the debtor as "Arthur Mendez."

Then Juarez contracts to sell strawberries to Frozun Foods, Inc., which also advances him funds secured by a financing statement that identifies the debtor as "Arthur Juarez." By the following year, Juarez is unable to pay his debts and owes Morona more than $200,000 and Frozun nearly $50,000. Both Morona and Frozun file a suit against Juarez claiming to have priority under a perfected security interest. In this situation, a properly filed financing statement would identify the debtor's true name (Arthur Juarez). Because a debtor name search for "Arthur Juarez" would not disclose a financing statement in the name of "Arthur Mendez," Morona's financing statement is seriously misleading. Therefore, Frozun's security interest would have priority because its financing statement was recorded properly. ■

Perfection without Filing

In two types of situations, security interests can be perfected without filing a financing statement. The first situation occurs when the collateral is transferred into the possession of the secured party. The second occurs when the security interest can be perfected on attachment (without a filing and without having to possess the goods) [UCC 9–309].

The phrase *perfected on attachment* means that these security interests are automatically perfected at the time of their creation. Two of the more common security interests that are perfected on attachment are a *purchase-money security interest* in consumer goods (discussed shortly) and an assignment of a beneficial interest in a decedent's estate [UCC 9–309(1), (13)].

Perfection by Possession

Pledge A security device in which personal property is transferred into the possession of the creditor as security for the payment of a debt and retained by the creditor until the debt is paid.

In the past, one of the most common means of obtaining financing was to **pledge** certain collateral as security for the debt and transfer the collateral into the creditor's possession. When the debt was paid, the collateral was returned to the debtor. Article 9 of the UCC retained the common law pledge and the principle that the security agreement need not be in writing to be enforceable if the collateral is transferred to the secured party [UCC 9–310, 9–312(b), 9–313].

Certain items, such as stocks, bonds, negotiable instruments, and jewelry, are commonly transferred into the creditor's possession when they are used as collateral for loans. **EXAMPLE 21.4** Sheila needs cash to pay for a medical procedure. She gets a loan for $4,000 from Trent. As security for the loan, she gives him a promissory note on which she is the payee. Even though the agreement to hold the note as collateral was oral, Trent has a perfected security interest and does not need to file a financing statement. No other creditor of Sheila's can attempt to recover the promissory note from Trent in payment for other debts. ■

For most collateral, however, possession by the secured party is impractical because it denies the debtor the right to use or derive income from the property to pay off the debt. **EXAMPLE 21.5** Jed, a farmer, takes out a loan to finance the purchase of a large corn harvester and uses the equipment as collateral. Clearly, the purpose of the purchase would be defeated if Jed transferred the collateral into the creditor's possession, because he would not be able to use the equipment to harvest his corn. ■

Perfection by Attachment—The Purchase-Money Security Interest in Consumer Goods. Under the UCC, fourteen types of security interests are perfected automatically at the time they are created [UCC 9–309]. The most common is the **purchase-money security interest (PMSI)** in *consumer goods* (items bought primarily for personal, family, or household purposes). A PMSI in consumer goods is created when a person buys goods on credit. The entity that extends the credit and obtains the PMSI can be either the seller (a store, for example) or a financial institution that lends the buyer the funds with which to purchase the goods [UCC 9–102(a)(2)].

Automatic Perfection. A PMSI in consumer goods is perfected automatically at the time of a credit sale—that is, at the time the PMSI is created. The seller in this situation does not need to do anything more to perfect her or his interest. **EXAMPLE 21.6** Jami purchases an LG washer and dryer from West Coast Appliance for $2,500. Unable to pay the entire amount in cash, Jami signs a purchase agreement to pay $1,000 down and $100 per month until the balance, plus interest, is fully paid. West Coast Appliance is to retain a security interest in the appliances until full payment has been made. Because the security interest was created as part of a purchase agreement with a consumer, it is a PMSI, and West Coast Appliance's security interest is automatically perfected. ■

Exceptions to the Rule of Automatic Perfection. There are two exceptions to the rule of automatic perfection for PMSIs:

1. Certain types of security interests that are subject to other federal or state laws may require additional steps to be perfected [UCC 9–311]. Many jurisdictions, for instance, have certificate-of-title statutes that establish perfection requirements for security interests in certain goods, including automobiles, trailers, boats, mobile homes, and farm tractors.
   EXAMPLE 21.7 Martin Sedek purchases a boat at a Florida dealership. Florida has a certificate-of-title statute. Sedek obtains financing for his purchase through General Credit Corporation. General Credit Corporation will need to file a certificate of title with the appropriate state official to perfect the PMSI. ■

2. PMSIs in nonconsumer goods, such as a business's inventory or livestock, are not automatically perfected [UCC 9–324]. These types of PMSIs will be discussed later in this chapter in the context of priorities.

Perfection and the Classification of Collateral Where or how to perfect a security interest sometimes depends on the classification or definition of the collateral. Collateral is generally divided into two classifications: *tangible collateral* (collateral that can be seen, felt, and touched) and *intangible collateral* (collateral that consists of or generates rights). Exhibit 21–2 summarizes the various classifications of collateral and the methods of perfecting a security interest in collateral falling within each of those classifications.[3]

Effective Time Duration of Perfection A financing statement is effective for five years from the date of filing [UCC 9–515]. If a **continuation statement** is filed within six months *prior to* the expiration date, the effectiveness of the original statement is continued for another five years, starting with the expiration date of the first five-year period [UCC 9–515(d), (e)]. The effectiveness of the statement can be continued in the same manner indefinitely. Any attempt to file a continuation statement outside the six-month window will render the continuation ineffective, however, and the perfection will lapse at the end of the five-year period.

> **Purchase-Money Security Interest (PMSI)** A security interest that arises when a seller or lender extends credit for part or all of the purchase price of goods purchased by a buyer.

> **LEARNING OBJECTIVE 2**
> How is a purchase-money security interest in consumer goods created?

If this couple buys a 4K Ultra High Definition television on credit, is a PMSI automatically created?

> **Continuation Statement** A statement that, if filed within six months prior to the expiration date of the original financing statement, continues the perfection of the security interest for another five years.

iStockPhoto.com/_shock

---

3. There are additional classifications, such as agricultural liens, commercial tort claims, and investment property. For definitions of these types of collateral, see UCC 9–102(a)(5), (a)(13), and (a)(49).

Exhibit 21–2 Selected Types of Collateral and Their Methods of Perfection

TANGIBLE COLLATERAL		METHOD OF PERFECTION
All things that are movable at the time the security interest attaches or that are attached to land, including timber to be cut and growing crops.		
1. Consumer Goods [UCC 9–301, 9–303, 9–309(1), 9–310(a), 9–313(a)]	Goods used or bought primarily for personal, family, or household purposes—for example, household furniture [UCC 9–102(a)(23)].	For purchase-money security interest, attachment (that is, the creation of a security interest) is sufficient. For boats, motor vehicles, and trailers, filing or compliance with a certificate-of-title statute is required. For other consumer goods, general rules of filing or possession apply.
2. Equipment [UCC 9–301, 9–310(a), 9–313(a)]	Goods bought for or used primarily in business (and not part of inventory or farm products)—for example, a delivery truck [UCC 9–102(a)(33)].	Filing or (rarely) possession by secured party.
3. Farm Products [UCC 9–301, 9–310(a), 9–313(a)]	Crops (including aquatic goods), livestock, or supplies produced in a farming operation—for example, ginned cotton, milk, eggs, and maple syrup [UCC 9–102(a)(34)].	Filing or (rarely) possession by secured party.
4. Inventory [UCC 9–301, 9–310(a), 9–313(a)]	Goods held by a person for sale or under a contract of service or lease; raw materials held for production and work in progress [UCC 9–102(a)(48)].	Filing or (rarely) possession by secured party.
INTANGIBLE COLLATERAL		METHOD OF PERFECTION
Nonphysical property that exists only in connection with something else.		
1. Chattel Paper [UCC 9–301, 9–310(a), 9–312(a), 9–313(a), 9–314(a)]	A writing or electronic record that evidences both a monetary obligation and a security interest in goods and software used in goods—for example, a security agreement [UCC 9–102(a)(11), (a)(31), and (a)(78)].	Filing or possession or control by secured party.
2. Instruments [UCC 9–301, 9–309(4), 9–310(a), 9–312(a) and (e), 9–313(a)]	A negotiable instrument, such as a check, note, certificate of deposit, draft, or other writing that evidences a right to the payment of money and is not a security agreement or lease but rather a type that can ordinarily be transferred (after indorsement, if necessary) by delivery [UCC 9–102(a)(47)].	Normally filing or possession. For the sale of promissory notes, perfection can be by attachment (automatically on the creation of the security interest).
3. Accounts [UCC 9–301, 9–309(2) and (5), 9–310(a)]	Any right to receive payment for property (real or personal), including intellectual licensed property, services, insurance policies, and certain other receivables [UCC 9–102(a)(2) and (a)(46)].	Filing required except for certain assignments that can be perfected by attachment (automatically on the creation of the security interest).
4. Deposit Accounts [UCC 9–104, 9–304, 9–312(b), 9–314(a)]	Any demand, time, savings, passbook, or similar account maintained with a bank [UCC 9–102(a)(29)].	Perfection by control, such as when the secured party is the bank in which the account is maintained or when the parties have agreed that the secured party can direct the disposition of funds in a particular account.

If a financing statement lapses, the security interest that had been perfected by the filing becomes unperfected. A purchaser for value can acquire the collateral as if the security interest had never been perfected [UCC 9–515(c)].

21–3 Scope of a Security Interest

A security interest can cover property in which the debtor has either present or future ownership or possessory rights. Therefore, security agreements can cover not only collateral in the present possession or control of the debtor but also proceeds from the sale of collateral, after-acquired property, and future advances, as discussed next.

21–3a Proceeds

Proceeds are whatever cash or property is received when collateral is sold or disposed of in some other way [UCC 9–102(a)(64)]. A security interest in the collateral gives the secured party a security interest in the proceeds acquired from the sale of that collateral.

EXAMPLE 21.8 People's Bank has a perfected security interest in the inventory of a retail seller of heavy farm machinery. The retailer sells a tractor out of this inventory to Jacob Dunn, a farmer. Dunn agrees, in a security agreement, to make monthly payments to the retailer for a period of twenty-four months. If the retailer goes into default on the loan from the bank, the bank is entitled to the remaining payments Dunn owes to the retailer as proceeds. ■

A security interest in proceeds perfects automatically on the perfection of the secured party's security interest in the original collateral, and it remains perfected for twenty days after the debtor receives the proceeds. The parties can agree to extend the twenty-day automatic perfection period in their original security agreement [UCC 9–315(c), (d)]. This is typically done when the collateral is the type that is likely to be sold, such as a retailer's inventory of tablets or smartphones. The UCC also permits a security interest in identifiable cash proceeds to remain perfected after twenty days [UCC 9–315(d)(2)].

Proceeds Under Article 9 of the UCC, whatever is received when collateral is sold or disposed of in some other way.

21–3b After-Acquired Property

After-acquired property is property that the debtor acquired after the execution of the security agreement. The security agreement may provide for a security interest in after-acquired property, such as a debtor's inventory [UCC 9–204(1)]. Generally, the debtor will purchase new inventory to replace the inventory sold. The secured party wants this newly acquired inventory to be subject to the original security interest. Thus, the after-acquired property clause continues the secured party's claim to any inventory acquired thereafter. (This is not to say that the original security interest will always take priority over the rights of all other creditors with regard to this after-acquired inventory, as will be discussed later.)

EXAMPLE 21.9 Amato buys factory equipment from Bronson on credit, giving as security an interest in all of her equipment—both what she is buying and what she already owns. The security interest with Bronson contains an after-acquired property clause. Six months later, Amato pays cash to another seller of factory equipment for more equipment. Six months after that, Amato goes out of business before she has paid off her debt to Bronson. Bronson has a security interest in all of Amato's equipment, even the equipment bought from the other seller. ■

After-Acquired Property Property that is acquired by the debtor after the execution of a security agreement.

21–3c Future Advances

Often, a debtor will arrange with a bank to have a *continuing line of credit* under which the debtor can borrow funds intermittently. Advances against lines of credit can be subject to a properly perfected security interest in certain collateral. The security agreement may provide that any future advances made against that line of credit are also subject to the security interest in that collateral [UCC 9–204(c)]. Future advances do not have to be of the same type or otherwise related to the original advance to benefit from this type of **cross-collateralization**.[4] Cross-collateralization occurs when an asset that is not the subject of a loan is used to secure that loan.

EXAMPLE 21.10 Stroh is the owner of a small manufacturing plant with equipment valued at $1 million. He has an immediate need for $50,000 of working capital, so he obtains a loan from Midwestern Bank and signs a security agreement, putting up all of his equipment as security. The bank properly perfects its security interest. The security agreement provides that

Cross-Collateralization The use of an asset that is not the subject of a loan to collateralize that loan.

---

4. See official Comment 5 to UCC 9–204.

Can equipment be used as collateral for further advances?

Floating Lien A security interest in proceeds, after-acquired property, or collateral subject to future advances by the secured party (or all three). The security interest is retained even when the collateral changes in character, classification, or location.

Stroh can borrow up to $500,000 in the future, using the same equipment as collateral for any future advances. In this situation, Midwestern Bank does not have to execute a new security agreement and perfect a security interest in the collateral each time an advance is made, up to a cumulative total of $500,000. For priority purposes, each advance is perfected as of the date of the *original* perfection. ■

21–3d The Floating-Lien Concept

A security agreement that provides for a security interest in proceeds, in after-acquired property, or in collateral subject to future advances by the secured party (or in all three) is often characterized as a **floating lien.** This type of security interest continues in the collateral or proceeds even if the collateral is sold, exchanged, or disposed of in some other way.

A Floating Lien in Inventory Floating liens commonly arise in the financing of inventories. A creditor is not interested in *specific* pieces of inventory, which are constantly changing, so the lien "floats" from one item to another as the inventory changes.

EXAMPLE 21.11 Cascade Sports, Inc., an Oregon corporation, operates as a cross-country ski dealer and has a line of credit with Portland First Bank to finance its inventory of cross-country skis. Cascade and Portland First enter into a security agreement that provides for coverage of proceeds, after-acquired inventory, present inventory, and future advances. Portland First perfects its security interest in the inventory by filing centrally with the office of the secretary of state in Oregon.

One day, Cascade sells a new pair of the latest cross-country skis and receives a used pair in trade. That same day, Cascade purchases two new pairs of cross-country skis from a local manufacturer for cash. Later that day, to meet its payroll, Cascade borrows $8,000 from Portland First Bank under the security agreement.

Portland First gets a perfected security interest in the used pair of skis under the proceeds clause and a perfected security interest in the two new pairs of skis under the after-acquired property clause. This collateral, as well as other inventory, secures the new funds advanced to Cascade under the future-advances clause. All of this is accomplished under the original perfected security interest. The various items in the inventory have changed, but Portland First still has a perfected security interest in Cascade's inventory. Hence, it has a floating lien in the inventory. ■

A Floating Lien in a Shifting Stock of Goods The concept of the floating lien can also apply to a shifting stock of goods. The lien can start with raw materials, follow them as they become finished goods and inventories, and continue as the goods are sold and are turned into accounts receivable, chattel paper, or cash.

21–4 Priorities, Rights, and Duties

When more than one party claims an interest in the same collateral, which has priority? The UCC sets out detailed rules to answer this question. Although in many situations the party who has a perfected security interest will have priority, there are exceptions. The UCC also provides certain rights and duties to debtors and secured parties.

21–4a General Rules of Priority

The basic rule is that when more than one security interest has been perfected in the same collateral, the first security interest to be perfected (or filed) has priority over any security

KNOW THIS
Secured creditors—perfected or not—have priority over unsecured creditors.

interests that are perfected later. If only one of the conflicting security interests has been perfected, then that security interest has priority. If none of the security interests have been perfected, then the first security interest that attaches has priority.

The UCC's rules of priority can be summarized as follows:

1. *Perfected security interest versus unsecured creditors and unperfected security interests.* When two or more parties have claims to the same collateral, a perfected secured party's interest has priority over the interests of most other parties [UCC 9–322(a)(2)]. This includes priority to the proceeds from a sale of collateral resulting from a bankruptcy (giving the perfected secured party rights superior to that of a bankruptcy trustee).

2. *Conflicting perfected security interests.* When two or more secured parties have perfected security interests in the same collateral, the first to perfect (by filing or taking possession of the collateral) generally has priority [UCC 9–322(a)(1)].

3. *Conflicting unperfected security interests.* When two conflicting security interests are unperfected, the first to attach (be created) has priority [UCC 9–322(a)(3)]. This is sometimes called the "first-in-time" rule.

CASE EXAMPLE 21.12 Ag Venture Financial Services, Inc., made multiple loans to a family-owned dairy farm, Montagne Heifers, Inc. (MHI). Michael Montagne owned the business, and his wife and son were shareholders and employees. In 2005, MHI executed a promissory note and security agreement in favor of Ag Venture, which listed all of MHI's accounts, equipment, farm products, inventory, livestock, and proceeds as collateral. In 2006, Montagne and his wife separated, and he signed a separation agreement that gave her some funds and certain parcels of land.

In 2007, Montagne gave his son a promissory note for $100,000 in exchange for his shares in MHI. The note listed all of MHI's equipment, inventory, livestock, and proceeds as collateral. Also in 2007, Montagne sold a herd of dairy cows for $500,000 and gave his former wife a check for $240,000. In 2008, Montagne filed a petition for bankruptcy, and a dispute arose over which party (Ag Venture, Montagne's son, or Montagne's former wife) was entitled to the proceeds from the 2007 sale of the cows. The court held that because Ag Venture's security interest in the proceeds was the first in time to *attach* (it was created in 2005), Ag Venture had first priority to the proceeds.[5]

21–4b Exceptions to the General Priority Rules

Under some circumstances, on the debtor's default, the perfection of a security interest will not protect a secured party against certain other third parties having claims to the collateral. For instance, the UCC provides that in some instances a PMSI, properly perfected,[6] will prevail over another security interest in after-acquired collateral, even though the other was perfected first. We discuss some significant exceptions to the general rules of priority next.

Buyers in the Ordinary Course of Business Under the UCC, a person who buys "in the ordinary course of business" takes the goods free from any security interest created by the seller even if the security interest is perfected and the buyer knows of its existence [UCC 9–320(a)]. A *buyer in the ordinary course of business* is a person who in good faith, and without knowledge that the sale violates the rights of another in the goods, buys goods in the ordinary course from a person in the business of selling goods of that kind [UCC 1–201(9)].[7] The rationale for this rule is obvious. If buyers could not obtain the goods free and clear of any

---

5. *In re Montagne*, 417 Bankr. 214 (D.Vt. 2009).
6. Recall that, with some exceptions (such as motor vehicles), a PMSI in *consumer goods* is automatically perfected—no filing is necessary. A PMSI that is *not* in consumer goods must still be perfected, however.
7. Note that even though a buyer may know about the existence of a perfected security interest, he or she must not know that buying the goods violates the rights of any third party.

security interest the merchant had created—for example, in inventory—the free flow of goods in the marketplace would be hindered.

EXAMPLE 21.13 Dubbs Auto grants a security interest in its inventory to Heartland Bank for a $300,000 line of credit. Heartland perfects its security interest by filing financing statements with the appropriate state offices. Dubbs uses $9,000 of its credit to buy two used trucks and delivers the certificates of title, which designate Dubbs as the owner, to Heartland. Later, Dubbs sells one of the trucks to Shea Murdoch and another to Michael Laxton. National City Bank finances both purchases. New certificates of title designate the buyers as the owners and Heartland as the "first lienholder," but Heartland receives none of the funds from the sales. If Heartland sues National City, claiming that its security interest in the vehicles takes priority, it will lose. Because Murdoch and Laxton are buyers in the ordinary course of business, Heartland's security interest in the motor vehicles was extinguished when the vehicles were sold to them. ■

Buyers of the Collateral The UCC recognizes that there are certain types of buyers whose interests in purchased goods could conflict with those of a perfected secured party on the debtor's default. These include not only buyers in the ordinary course of business (as just discussed), but also buyers of farm products, chattel paper, instruments, documents, or securities. The UCC sets down special rules of priority for these types of buyers.

21-4c Rights and Duties of Debtors and Creditors

The security agreement itself determines most of the rights and duties of the debtor and the secured party. The UCC, however, imposes some rights and duties that are applicable unless the security agreement states otherwise.

Information Requests At the time of filing, a secured party can furnish a copy of the financing statement and request that the filing officer note the file number, date, and hour of the original filing on the copy [UCC 9–523(a)]. The filing officer must send this copy to the person designated by the secured party.

The filing officer must also give information to a person who is contemplating obtaining a security interest from a prospective debtor [UCC 9–523(c), (d)]. If requested, the filing officer must issue a certificate (for a fee) that provides information on possible perfected financing statements with respect to the named debtor.

Release, Assignment, and Amendment A secured party can release all or part of any collateral described in the financing statement, thereby terminating its security interest in that collateral. The release is recorded by filing a uniform amendment form [UCC 9–512, 9–521(b)]. A secured party can also assign all or part of the security interest to a third party (the assignee). The assignee becomes the secured party of record if the assignment is filed by use of a uniform amendment form [UCC 9–514, 9–521(a)].

If the debtor and the secured party agree, they can amend the filing—to add or substitute new collateral, for example—by filing a uniform amendment form that indicates the file number of the initial financing statement [UCC 9–512(a)]. The amendment does not extend the time period of perfection, but if new collateral is added, the perfection date (for priority purposes) for the new collateral begins on the date the amendment is filed [UCC 9–512(b), (c)].

Confirmation or Accounting Request by Debtor The debtor may believe that the amount of the unpaid debt or the list of collateral subject to the security interest is inaccurate. The debtor has the right to request a confirmation of the unpaid debt or list of collateral [UCC 9–210]. The debtor is entitled to one request without charge every six months.

The secured party must comply with the debtor's confirmation request by authenticating and sending to the debtor an accounting within fourteen days after the request is received.

Otherwise, the secured party will be held liable for any loss suffered by the debtor, plus $500 [UCC 9–210, 9–625(f)].

Termination Statement When the debtor has fully paid the debt, if the secured party perfected the security interest by filing, the debtor is entitled to have a termination statement filed. Such a statement demonstrates to the public that the filed perfected security interest has been terminated [UCC 9–513].

Whenever consumer goods are involved, the secured party *must* file a termination statement (or, alternatively, a release) within one month of the final payment or within twenty days of receiving the debtor's demand, whichever is earlier [UCC 9–513(b)]. When the collateral is not consumer goods, the secured party is not required to file or to send a termination statement unless the debtor demands one [UCC 9–513(c)].

21–5 Default

Article 9 defines the rights, duties, and remedies of the secured party and of the debtor on the debtor's default. If the secured party fails to comply with his or her duties, the debtor is afforded particular rights and remedies under the UCC.

21–5a What Constitutes Default

What constitutes default is not always clear. In fact, Article 9 does not define the term. Consequently, parties are encouraged in practice—and by the UCC—to include in their security agreements the standards under which their rights and duties will be measured [UCC 9–601, 9–603]. In so doing, parties can stipulate the conditions that will constitute a default. Often, these critical terms are shaped by creditors in an attempt to provide themselves with the maximum protection possible. The terms may not, however, run counter to the UCC's provisions regarding good faith and unconscionability.

Any breach of the terms of the security agreement can constitute default. Nevertheless, default occurs most commonly when the debtor fails to meet the scheduled payments or becomes bankrupt.

21–5b Basic Remedies

UCC 9–601(a) and (b) set out rights and remedies for secured parties, and these rights and remedies are *cumulative* [UCC 9–601(c)]. Therefore, if a creditor is unsuccessful in enforcing rights by one method, he or she can pursue another method. Generally, a secured party's remedies can be divided into the two basic categories discussed next.

Repossession of the Collateral—The Self-Help Remedy On the debtor's default, a secured party can take peaceful possession of the collateral without the use of judicial process [UCC 9–609(b)]. This provision is often referred to as the "self-help" provision of Article 9.

The UCC does not define *peaceful possession,* however. The general rule is that the collateral has been taken peacefully if the secured party can take possession without committing (1) trespass onto land, (2) assault and/or battery, or (3) breaking and entering.

On taking possession, the secured party may either retain the collateral for satisfaction of the debt [UCC 9–620] or resell the goods and apply the proceeds toward the debt [UCC 9–610].

Judicial Remedies Alternatively, a secured party can relinquish the security interest and use any judicial remedy available, such as obtaining a judgment on the underlying debt, followed by execution and levy. (**Execution** is the implementation of a court's decree or judgment. **Levy**

Execution The implementation of a court's decree or judgment.

Levy The legal process of obtaining funds through the seizure and sale of nonexempt property, usually done after a writ of execution has been issued.

haveseen/ShutterStock.com

This man is not stealing this car. What might he be doing instead?

is the legal process of obtaining funds through the seizure and sale of nonexempt property, usually done after a writ of execution has been issued.) Execution and levy are rarely undertaken unless the collateral is no longer in existence or has substantially declined in value and the debtor has other assets available that may be legally seized to satisfy the debt [UCC 9–601(a)].[8]

21-5c Disposition of Collateral

Once default has occurred and the secured party has obtained possession of the collateral, the secured party can:

1. Retain the collateral in full or partial satisfaction of the debt (subject to limitations, discussed next).

2. Sell, lease, license, or otherwise dispose of the collateral in any commercially reasonable manner and apply the proceeds toward satisfaction of the debt [UCC 9–602(7), 9–603, 9–610(a), 9–613, 9–620]. Any sale is always subject to procedures established by state law.

Is the sale of collateral at auction a reasonable means of disposing of that collateral?

Retention of Collateral by the Secured Party Parties are sometimes better off if they do not sell the collateral. Therefore, the UCC generally allows secured parties to retain the collateral (except in certain cases involving consumer goods, discussed shortly). The right to retain the collateral is subject to the following conditions:

1. *Notice to debtor.* The secured party must notify the debtor of its proposal to retain the collateral. Notice is required unless the debtor has signed a statement renouncing or modifying her or his rights *after default* [UCC 9–620(a), 9–621].

2. *Notice to other secured parties.* If the collateral is consumer goods, the secured party does not need to give any other notice. In all other situations, the secured party must also send notice to any other secured party (or lienholder) from whom the secured party has received notice of a claim of interest in the collateral in question.

3. *Waiting period for objections.* If, within twenty days after the notice is sent, the secured party receives an objection from the debtor or another party who was notified, the secured party must sell or otherwise dispose of the collateral. If no objection is received, the secured party may retain the collateral in full or partial satisfaction of the debtor's obligation [UCC 9–620(a), 9–621].

Consumer Goods When the collateral is consumer goods and the debtor has paid 60 percent or more of the purchase price on a PMSI or of the loan amount on a non-PMSI, the secured party must sell or otherwise dispose of the repossessed collateral within ninety days [UCC 9–620(e), (f)]. Failure to comply opens the secured party to an action for conversion or other liability under UCC 9–625(b) and (c). A secured party will not be liable, however, if the consumer-debtor signed a written statement *after default* renouncing or modifying the right to demand the sale of the goods [UCC 9–624].

KNOW THIS

Conversion is a tort that involves depriving an owner of personal property without the owner's permission.

Disposition Procedures A secured party who does not choose to retain the collateral or who is required to sell it must follow the disposition procedures prescribed in the UCC. The secured party may sell, lease, license, or otherwise dispose of any or all of the collateral in its present condition or following any commercially reasonable preparation or processing [UCC 9–610(a)].

---

8. Some assets are exempt from creditors' claims.

Notice Requirement. The secured party must notify the debtor and other specified parties in writing ahead of time about the sale or disposition of the collateral. Notification is not required if the collateral is perishable, will decline rapidly in value, or is a type customarily sold on a recognized market [UCC 9–611(b), (c)]. The debtor may waive the right to receive this notice, but only after default [UCC 9–624(a)].

Commercially Reasonable Manner. Every aspect of the disposition's method, manner, time, and place must be *commercially reasonable* [UCC 9–610(b)]. If the secured party does not dispose of the collateral in a commercially reasonable manner, the price paid for the collateral at the sale may be negatively affected. In that situation, a court can reduce the amount of any deficiency that the debtor owes to the secured party [UCC 9–626(a)(3)].

Although the purpose of requiring a commercially reasonable disposition is to obtain a satisfactory price, the courts look at other factors besides price in determining reasonableness. In the following case, the court considered whether a creditor's sale of the debtors' shares of stock was commercially unreasonable.

> "If you think nobody cares if you're alive, try missing a couple of car payments."
>
> **EARL WILSON**
> 1907–1987
> (AMERICAN JOURNALIST)

CASE 21.2

Smith v. Firstbank Corp.
Court of Appeals of Michigan, 2013 WL 951377 (2013).

COMPANY PROFILE *Since its founding in Jackson, Michigan, in 1900, Sparton Corporation has designed, developed, and manufactured electronic and electromechanical devices. From prototype through shipment, Sparton has worked with diverse companies in the aerospace, medical, defense, security, navigation, exploration, and industrial markets. Today, Sparton is headquartered in Schaumberg, Illinois. It has more than 1,300 employees and maintains production facilities in the United States and in Vietnam.*

When can the debtor who pledged stock as collateral successfully claim that its sale was unreasonable?

FACTS Bradley Smith, on his own behalf and on the behalf of the John J. Smith Revocable Living Trust, borrowed funds from Firstbank Corporation secured with pledges of Sparton Corporation stock and other collateral. When the loans were not paid, Firstbank sold the stock in two private transactions, returned the other collateral, and remitted the excess funds collected to Smith and the trust.

Alleging that the sales were commercially unreasonable because a higher price might have been obtained in a different sale, Smith and the trust filed a suit in a Michigan state court against Firstbank. The court granted the defendant's motion for summary judgment, and the plaintiffs appealed.

ISSUE Were Firstbank's sales of the debtors' Sparton stock commercially reasonable?

DECISION Yes. A state intermediate appellate court affirmed the lower court's summary judgment in the bank's favor.

REASON Firstbank had valid reasons for choosing to sell the debtors' stock in private sales and worked to obtain a reasonable price for the shares. Concern about how public sales might have affected the share price supported the bank's decision to seek a private buyer. In previous sales of Sparton stock in the public market, shares had been sold in a series of transactions at declining prices. Firstbank's decision to use private sales avoided this risk.

The manner in which the sales were conducted was also reasonable. Firstbank sought more than one offer for the stock. Because Sparton shares are thinly traded, however, the bank received only one offer, which was at a discount. Firstbank accepted the offer and later was able to sell additional shares in a second transaction for a somewhat higher price. Because of the bank's efforts, Smith and the trust were able to keep "over five million dollars of collateral, as well as a net surplus on the sale of the stock."

CRITICAL THINKING—Economic Consideration *Why does collateral have to be disposed of in a commercially reasonable way? What factors could courts look at to determine reasonableness?*

Distribution of Proceeds from the Disposition
Proceeds from the disposition of collateral after default on the underlying debt are distributed in the following order:

1. Reasonable expenses incurred by the secured party in repossessing, storing, and reselling the collateral are paid first.

2. The balance of the debt owed to the secured party is then paid.

3. Other lienholders who have made written or authenticated demands.

4. Unless the collateral consists of accounts, payment intangibles, promissory notes, or chattel paper, any surplus goes to the debtor [UCC 9–608(a); 9–615(a), (e)].

Noncash Proceeds

Sometimes the secured party receives noncash proceeds from the disposition of collateral after default. Whenever that occurs, the secured party must make a value determination and apply this value in a commercially reasonable manner [UCC 9–608(a)(3), 9–615(c)].

Deficiency Judgment

Often, after proper disposition of the collateral, the secured party has not collected all that the debtor still owes. Unless otherwise agreed, the debtor normally is liable for any deficiency, and the creditor can obtain a **deficiency judgment** from a court to collect this amount. Practically speaking, though, debtors who have defaulted on a loan rarely have the cash to pay any deficiency.

Note that if the underlying transaction was a sale of accounts, chattel paper, or promissory notes, the debtor is *not* liable for any deficiency. The debtor normally is entitled to any surplus from the disposition of these types of collateral, however [UCC 9–615(e)].

Deficiency Judgment A judgment against a debtor for the amount of a debt remaining unpaid after the collateral has been repossessed and sold.

ETHICAL ISSUE

How long should a secured party have to seek a deficiency judgment? Because of depreciation, the amount received from the sale of collateral is frequently less than the amount the debtor owes the secured party. As noted, the secured party can file a suit against the debtor in an attempt to collect the balance due. Article 9 does not contain a statute of limitations provision, so it is not clear how long a secured party has after default to file a deficiency suit against a debtor. If the secured party waits until the debtor becomes solvent again, though, the court may not allow the suit. When creditors have sued debtors for deficiencies owed on repossessed cars, for instance, many courts have applied the four-year limitation period in Article 2 because the transaction was a sale of goods, even though a security interest was involved.[9] Is this fair?

Redemption Rights

The debtor or any other secured party can exercise the right of *redemption* of the collateral. Redemption may occur at any time before the secured party disposes of the collateral, enters into a contract for its disposition, or discharges the debtor's obligation by retaining the collateral. The debtor or other secured party exercises the redemption right by tendering performance of all obligations secured by the collateral and by paying the expenses reasonably incurred by the secured party in retaking and maintaining the collateral [UCC 9–623].

21-6 Other Laws Assisting Creditors

Both the common law and statutory laws other than Article 9 of the Uniform Commercial Code create rights and remedies for creditors. Here we discuss some of these rights and remedies.

21-6a Liens

A *lien* is an encumbrance on (claim against) property to satisfy a debt or protect a claim for the payment of a debt. Creditors' liens may arise under the common law or under statutory law. Statutory liens include *mechanic's liens,* whereas *artisan's liens* were recognized by common

---

9. See, for example, *Credit Acceptance Corp. v. Coates,* 2008 WL 3889424 (2008), and *Price Automotive II, LLC v. Mass Management, LLC,* 2015 WL 300418 (W.D.Va. 2015).

law. *Judicial liens* arise when a creditor attempts to collect on a debt before or after a judgment is entered by a court.

Liens can be useful because a lien creditor generally has priority over an unperfected secured party. In other words, if a creditor obtains a lien *before* another party perfects a security interest in the same property, the lienholder has priority. If the lien is obtained *after* another's security interest in the property is perfected, the perfected security interest has priority. Mechanic's and artisan's liens are exceptions to this rule. They normally take priority *even over perfected security interests,* unless a statute provides otherwise.

Mechanic's Lien

Sometimes, a person who has contracted for labor, services, or materials to be furnished for making improvements on real property does not immediately pay for the improvements. When that happens, the creditor can place a **mechanic's lien** on the property. A mechanic's lien creates a special type of debtor-creditor relationship in which the real estate itself becomes security for the debt.

EXAMPLE 21.14 Jeff paints a house for Becky, a homeowner, for an agreed-on price to cover labor and materials. If Becky refuses to pay for the work or pays only a portion of the charges, a mechanic's lien against the property can be created. Jeff is then the lienholder, and the real property is encumbered (burdened) with a mechanic's lien for the amount owed. If Becky does not pay the lien, the property can be sold to satisfy the debt. ∎

State law governs the procedures that must be followed to create a mechanic's lien. Generally, the lienholder must file a written notice of lien within a specific time period (usually 60 to 120 days) from the last date that labor or materials were provided. Notice of the foreclosure and sale must be given to the debtor in advance. (*Foreclosure* is the process by which the creditor deprives the debtor of the property.)

Artisan's Lien

When a debtor fails to pay for labor and materials furnished for the repair or improvement of personal property, a creditor can recover payment through an **artisan's lien.** In contrast to a mechanic's lien, an artisan's lien is *possessory*. The lienholder ordinarily must have retained possession of the property and have expressly or impliedly agreed to provide the services on a cash, not a credit, basis. The lien remains in existence as long as the lienholder maintains possession of the property, and the lien is terminated once possession is voluntarily surrendered, unless the surrender is only temporary.

EXAMPLE 21.15 MacKenzie takes a sapphire necklace that she inherited to a jewelry store to have it made into a ring and set of earrings. The store's owner agrees to reset the sapphires into custom jewelry for $4,000. MacKenzie comes to pick up the jewelry but refuses to pay the $4,000 she owes. The jeweler can assert an artisan's lien on the jewelry in his possession until MacKenzie pays. If the jeweler gives the jewelry to MacKenzie (without requiring full payment), the lien disappears. ∎

Modern statutes permit the holder of an artisan's lien to foreclose and sell the property subject to the lien to satisfy payment of the debt. As with a mechanic's lien, the holder of an artisan's lien must give notice to the owner of the property prior to foreclosure and sale. The sale proceeds are used to pay the debt and the costs of the legal proceedings, and the surplus, if any, is paid to the former owner.

Judicial Liens

When a debt is past due, a creditor can bring a legal action against the debtor to collect the debt. If the creditor is successful, the court awards the creditor a judgment against the debtor (usually for the amount of the debt plus any interest and legal costs incurred). Frequently, however, the creditor is unable to collect the awarded amount.

To ensure that a judgment will be collectible, the creditor can request that certain nonexempt property of the debtor be seized to satisfy the debt. (Under state or federal statutes, certain property is exempt from attachment by creditors.) A court's order to seize the debtor's

Mechanic's Lien
A nonpossessory, filed lien on an owner's real estate for labor, services, or materials furnished for making improvements on the realty.

iStockPhoto.com/YinYang

When can a painter place a mechanic's lien on the house?

Artisan's Lien A possessory lien held by a party who has made improvements and added value to the personal property of another party as security for payment for services performed.

property is known as a *writ of attachment* if it is issued before a judgment. If the order is issued after a judgment, it is referred to as a *writ of execution.*

Writ of Attachment.   In the context of judicial liens, *attachment* is a court-ordered seizure of property before a judgment is secured for a past-due debt. Attachment rights are created by state statutes. Because attachment is a *prejudgment* remedy, it occurs either at the time a lawsuit is filed or immediately afterward. The due process clause of the Fourteenth Amendment to the U.S. Constitution requires that the debtor be given notice and an opportunity to be heard before property can be seized.

To use attachment, a creditor must comply with the specific state's statutory restrictions and requirements. The creditor must have an enforceable right to payment of the debt under law and must follow certain procedures. Otherwise, the creditor may be liable for damages for wrongful attachment. The typical procedures for attachment are as follows:

1. The creditor files with the court an *affidavit* (a written statement, made under oath) stating that the debtor has failed to pay and indicating the statutory grounds under which attachment is sought.

2. The creditor must post a bond to cover at least the court costs, the value of the property attached, and the value of the loss of use of that property suffered by the debtor.

3. When the court is satisfied that all the requirements have been met, it issues a **writ of attachment,** which directs the sheriff or other officer to seize the debtor's nonexempt property. If the creditor prevails at trial, the seized property can be sold to satisfy the judgment.

Writ of Execution.   If the creditor wins a judgment against a debtor and the debtor will not or cannot pay the amount due, the creditor can request a **writ of execution.** A writ of execution is an order that directs the sheriff to seize (levy) and sell any of the debtor's nonexempt real or personal property. The writ applies only to property that is within the court's geographic jurisdiction (usually the county in which the courthouse is located).

The proceeds of the sale are used to pay off the judgment, accrued interest, and the costs of the sale. Any excess is paid to the debtor. The debtor can pay the judgment and redeem the nonexempt property any time before the sale takes place. (Because of exemption laws and bankruptcy laws, however, many judgments are uncollectible.)

21–6b Garnishment

Garnishment occurs when a creditor is permitted to collect a debt by seizing property of the debtor (such as wages or funds in a bank account) that is being held by a third party. As a result of a garnishment proceeding, the debtor's employer may be ordered by the court to turn over a portion of the debtor's wages to pay the debt.

   CASE EXAMPLE 21.16   Helen Griffin failed to pay a debt she owed to Indiana Surgical Specialists. When Indiana Surgical filed a lawsuit to collect, the court issued a judgment in favor of Indiana Surgical and a garnishment order to withhold the appropriate amount from Griffin's earnings until her debt was paid. At the time, Griffin was working as an independent contractor driving for a courier service. She claimed that her wages could not be garnished because she was not an employee. The court held that payments for the services of an independent contractor fell within the definition of earnings and could be garnished.[10] ▨

Procedures   Garnishment can be a prejudgment remedy, requiring a hearing before a court, but it is most often a postjudgment remedy. State law governs garnishment, so the procedure varies. In some states, the creditor needs to obtain only one order of garnishment, which will

Writ of Attachment A court order to seize a debtor's nonexempt property prior to a court's final determination of a creditor's rights to the property.

Writ of Execution A court order directing the sheriff to seize (levy) and sell a debtor's nonexempt real or personal property to satisfy a court's judgment in the creditor's favor.

Garnishment A legal process whereby a creditor collects a debt by seizing property of the debtor that is in the hands of a third party.

---

10. *Indiana Surgical Specialists v. Griffin*, 867 N.E.2d 260 (Ind.App. 2007).

then apply continuously to the debtor's wages until the entire debt is paid. In other states, the judgment creditor must go back to court for a separate order of garnishment for each pay period.

Limitations Both federal and state laws limit the amount that can be taken through garnishment proceedings.[11] Federal law provides a framework to protect debtors from suffering unduly when paying judgment debts by setting limits on how much can be garnished per pay period.[12] State laws also provide dollar exemptions, and these amounts are often larger than those provided by federal law. In addition, under federal law, an employer cannot dismiss an employee because his or her wages are being garnished.

21-6c Creditors' Composition Agreements

Creditors may contract with the debtor for discharge of the debtor's liquidated debts (debts that are definite, or fixed, in amount) on payment of a sum less than that owed. These agreements are called **creditors' composition agreements,** or simply *composition agreements,* and usually are held to be enforceable.

21-6d Suretyship and Guaranty

When a third person promises to pay a debt owed by another in the event that the debtor does not pay, either a *suretyship* or a *guaranty* relationship is created. Exhibit 21–3 illustrates these relationships. The third person's income and assets become the security for the debt owed.

Suretyship and guaranty provide creditors with the right to seek payment from the third party if the primary debtor defaults on her or his obligations. At common law, there were significant differences in the liability of a surety and a guarantor, as discussed in the following subsections. Today, however, the distinctions outlined here have been abolished in some states.

Surety A contract of strict **suretyship** is a promise made by a third person to be responsible for the debtor's obligation. It is an express contract between the **surety** (the third party) and the creditor. The surety in the strictest sense is primarily liable for the debt of the principal. The creditor need not exhaust all legal remedies against the principal debtor before holding

> **Creditors' Composition Agreement** A contract between a debtor and his or her creditors in which the creditors agree to discharge the debts on the debtor's payment of a sum less than the amount actually owed.

> **LEARNING OBJECTIVE 5**
> What is a suretyship, and how does it differ from a guaranty?

> **Suretyship** A promise made by a third party to be responsible for a debtor's obligation.

> **Surety** A third party who promises to be responsible for a debtor's obligation under a suretyship arrangement.

---

11. Some states (for example, Texas) do not permit garnishment of wages by private parties except under a child-support order.
12. For example, the federal Consumer Credit Protection Act of 1968, 15 U.S.C. Sections 1601–1693r, provides that a debtor can retain either 75 percent of disposable earnings per week or a sum equivalent to thirty hours of work paid at federal minimum-wage rates, whichever is greater.

Exhibit 21–3 Suretyship and Guaranty Parties

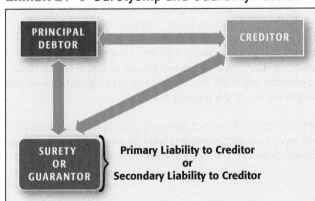

the surety responsible for payment. The creditor can demand payment from the surety from the moment the debt is due.

EXAMPLE 21.17 Roberto Delmar wants to borrow from the bank to buy a used car. Because Roberto is still in college, the bank will not lend him the funds unless his father, José Delmar, who has dealt with the bank before, will cosign the note (add his signature to the note, thereby becoming a surety and thus jointly liable for payment of the debt). When José cosigns the note, he becomes primarily liable to the bank. On the note's due date, the bank can seek payment from either Roberto or José, or both jointly. ■

Guaranty

Guarantor A third party who promises to be responsible for a debtor's obligation under a guaranty arrangement.

With a suretyship arrangement, the surety is *primarily* liable for the debtor's obligation. With a guaranty arrangement, the **guarantor**—the third person making the guaranty—is *secondarily* liable. The guarantor can be required to pay the obligation *only after the principal debtor defaults,* and default usually takes place only after the creditor has made an attempt to collect from the debtor.

EXAMPLE 21.18 BX Enterprises, a small corporation, needs to borrow funds to meet its payroll. The bank is skeptical about the creditworthiness of BX and requires Dawson, who is a wealthy businessperson and the owner of 70 percent of BX Enterprises, to sign an agreement making himself personally liable for payment if BX does not pay off the loan. As a guarantor of the loan, Dawson cannot be held liable until BX Enterprises is in default. ■

The following case concerned a lender's attempt to recover on a loan guaranty.

CASE 21.3

HSBC Realty Credit Corp. (USA) v. O'Neill

United States Court of Appeals, First Circuit, 745 F.3d 564 (2014).

FACTS To finance a development project in Delaware, Brandywine Partners, LLC, borrowed $15.9 million from HSBC Realty Credit Corp. (USA). As part of the deal, Brian O'Neill, principal for Brandywine, signed a guaranty that designated him the "primary obligor" for $8.1 million of the loan. Brandywine defaulted, and HSBC filed a suit in a federal district court against O'Neill to recover on the guaranty. O'Neill filed a counterclaim, alleging fraud.

O'Neill based his fraud claim on two provisions in the loan agreement. The first provision expressed the loan-to-value ratio. O'Neill alleged that this clause valued the property at $26.5 million and that HSBC knew this was not the property's real value. The second provision stated that if Brandywine defaulted, HSBC could recover its loan by selling the property. O'Neill argued that this clause represented that HSBC would try to recover on the property before the guaranty.

The court granted HSBC's motion to dismiss O'Neill's counterclaim and issued a judgment in HSBC's favor. O'Neill appealed, still arguing that HSBC had fraudulently induced him to sign the guaranty.

ISSUE Is a guarantor bound to the clear, unambiguous terms of the guaranty?

When a person signs a personal guaranty to finance his business, can he later get out of paying the debt when his business defaults?

Hatchapong Palurtchaivong/ShutterStock.com

DECISION Yes. The U.S. Court of Appeals for the First Circuit affirmed the lower court's judgment in favor of HSBC. O'Neill's guaranty was enforced according to its express terms.

REASON The court applied the principle that "reliance on supposed misrepresentations that contradict the terms of the parties' agreement is unreasonable as a matter of law and so cannot support a [fraud] claim." O'Neill's claim was "irreconcilably at odds with the guaranty's express terms." The guaranty stated that O'Neill was familiar with the value of the property and that he was not relying on it as an inducement to sign the guaranty. The guaranty also stated that HSBC made no representations to induce O'Neill to sign and provided that HSBC could enforce its rights against him without trying to recover on the property first.

CRITICAL THINKING—E-Commerce Consideration Do the principles applied to a written guaranty in this case also govern electronically recorded agreements and contracts entered into online? Why or why not?

Writing or Record Required Under the Statute of Frauds, a guaranty contract between the guarantor and the creditor normally must be in writing or electronically recorded to be enforceable. A writing or record is required unless the main purpose of the guaranty is to benefit the guarantor. Under common law, a suretyship agreement did not need to be in writing to be enforceable, and oral surety agreements were sufficient. Today, however, some states require a writing or record to enforce a suretyship.

Actions That Release the Surety and Guarantor Basically, the same actions will release a surety or a guarantor from an obligation. In general, the following rules apply to both sureties and guarantors, but for simplicity, we refer just to sureties:

Why might a bank refuse to lend funds to a college student to buy a used car? What can the student do?

1. *Material modification.* Making any material modification to the terms of the original contract without the surety's consent will discharge the surety's obligation. The extent to which the surety is discharged depends on whether he or she was compensated and the amount of the loss suffered as a result of the modification. For instance, a father who receives no consideration in return for acting as a surety on his daughter's loan will be completely discharged if the loan contract is modified without his consent.

2. *Surrender of property.* If a creditor surrenders the collateral to the debtor or impairs the collateral without the surety's consent, these acts can reduce the obligation of the surety. If the creditor's actions reduce the value of the property used as collateral, the surety is released to the extent of any loss suffered.

3. *Payment or tender of payment.* Naturally, any payment of the principal obligation by the debtor or by another person on the debtor's behalf will discharge the surety from the obligation. Even if the creditor refused to accept payment of the principal debt when it was tendered, the obligation of the surety can be discharged (if the creditor knew about the suretyship).

Defenses of the Surety and the Guarantor Generally, the surety (or guarantor) can also assert any of the defenses available to the principal debtor to avoid liability on the obligation to the creditor. A few exceptions do exist, however. The surety cannot assert the principal debtor's incapacity or bankruptcy as a defense. Nor can the surety assert the statute of limitations as a defense.

Obviously, a surety (or guarantor) may also have her or his own defenses. For example, the surety can assert her or his own incapacity or bankruptcy as a defense. Furthermore, if the creditor fraudulently induced the surety to guarantee the debt of the debtor, the surety can assert fraud as a defense. In most states, the creditor has a legal duty to inform the surety, before the formation of the suretyship contract, of material facts known by the creditor that would substantially increase the surety's risk. Failure to so inform may constitute fraud and renders the suretyship obligation voidable.

Rights of the Surety and the Guarantor Usually, when the surety (or guarantor) pays the debt owed to the creditor, the surety (or guarantor) is entitled to certain rights.

The Right of Subrogation. The surety has the legal **right of subrogation,** which means that any right the creditor had against the debtor now becomes the right of the surety. Included are creditor rights in bankruptcy, rights to collateral possessed by the creditor, and rights to judgments secured by the creditor. In short, the surety stands in the shoes of the creditor and may pursue any remedies that were available to the creditor against the debtor.

Right of Subrogation The right of a party to stand in the place of another, giving the substituted party the same legal rights that the original party had.

CASE EXAMPLE 21.19 Guerrero Brothers, Inc. (GBI), contracted with the Public School System (PSS) to build a high school. Century Insurance Company (CIC) agreed to act as a surety of GBI's performance and to finish the project if GBI defaulted. Four years after construction began, PSS canceled GBI's contract, and CIC fulfilled GBI's obligations by finishing construction of the school. Numerous disputes arose, and litigation ensued. Ultimately, PSS agreed to pay GBI $500,000 in contract funds. CIC then filed an action against GBI and PSS to recover $867,000 that it claimed PSS owed it for finishing the school. The court found that CIC, as a performing surety, was entitled to the remaining contract funds through the right of subrogation. It had performed GBI's obligations and therefore stepped into GBI's shoes and had the right to obtain payment from PSS.[13] ■

Right of Reimbursement
The right of a party to be repaid for costs, expenses, or losses incurred on behalf of another.

The Right of Reimbursement. The surety has a **right of reimbursement** from the debtor. Basically, the surety is entitled to receive from the debtor all outlays made on behalf of the suretyship arrangement. Such outlays can include expenses incurred as well as the actual amount of the debt paid to the creditor.

Co-surety A joint surety; a party who assumes liability jointly with another surety for the payment of a debtor's obligation under a suretyship arrangement.

Right of Contribution The right of a co-surety who pays more than his or her proportionate share on a debtor's default to recover the excess paid from other co-sureties.

The Right of Contribution. Two or more sureties are called **co-sureties.** When one co-surety pays more than her or his proportionate share on a debtor's default, she or he is entitled to recover from the other co-sureties the amount paid above her or his obligation. This is the **right of contribution.** Generally, a co-surety's liability either is determined by agreement between the co-sureties or, in the absence of an agreement, is specified in the suretyship contract itself.

EXAMPLE 21.20 Two co-sureties—Yasser and Itzhak—are obligated under a suretyship contract to guarantee the debt of Jules. Itzhak's maximum liability is $15,000, and Yasser's is $10,000. Jules owes $10,000 and is in default. Itzhak pays the creditor the entire $10,000. In the absence of an agreement to the contrary, Itzhak can recover $4,000 from Yasser. The amount of the debt that Yasser agreed to cover is divided by the total amount that Itzhak and Yasser together agreed to cover. The result is multiplied by the amount of the default, yielding the amount that Yasser owes: ($10,000 ÷ $25,000) × $10,000 = $4,000. ■

---

13. *Century Insurance Co. v. Guerrero Brothers, Inc.,* 2010 WL 997112 (N.Mariana Islands 2010).

Reviewing . . . Security Interests and Creditors' Rights

Paul Barton owned a small property-management company, doing business as Brighton Homes. In October, Barton went on a spending spree. First, he bought a Bose surround-sound system for his home from KDM Electronics. The next day, he purchased a Wilderness Systems kayak from Outdoor Outfitters, and the day after that he bought a new Toyota 4-Runner financed through Bridgeport Auto. Two weeks later, Barton purchased six new iMac computers for his office, also from KDM Electronics. Barton bought all of these items under installment sales contracts. Six months later, Barton's property-management business was failing. He could not make the payments due on any of these purchases and thus defaulted on the loans. Using the information presented in the chapter, answer the following questions.

1. For which of Barton's purchases (the surround-sound system, the kayak, the 4-Runner, and the six iMacs) would the creditor need to file a financing statement to perfect its security interest?

2. Suppose that Barton's contract for the office computers mentioned only the name *Brighton Homes.* What would be the consequences if KDM Electronics filed a financing statement that listed only Brighton Homes as the debtor's name?

3. Which of these purchases would qualify as a PMSI in consumer goods?

4. Suppose that after KDM Electronics repossesses the surround-sound system, it decides to keep the system rather than sell it. Can KDM do this under Article 9? Why or why not?

DEBATE THIS

■ A financing statement that does not have the debtor's exact name should still be effective because creditors should always be protected when debtors default.

Key Terms

after-acquired property 523	execution 527	right of contribution 536
artisan's lien 531	financing statement 515	right of reimbursement 536
attachment 516	floating lien 524	right of subrogation 535
collateral 515	garnishment 532	secured party 515
co-surety 536	guarantor 534	secured transaction 514
continuation statement 521	levy 527	security agreement 515
creditors' composition agreement 533	mechanic's lien 531	security interest 515
cross-collateralization 523	perfection 518	surety 533
debtor 515	pledge 520	suretyship 533
default 515	proceeds 523	writ of attachment 532
deficiency judgment 530	purchase-money security interest (PMSI) 521	writ of execution 532

Chapter Summary: Security Interests and Creditors' Rights

Creating a Security Interest	1. Unless the creditor has possession of the collateral, there must be a written or authenticated security agreement that describes the collateral subject to the security interest and is signed or authenticated by the debtor. 2. The secured party must give value to the debtor. 3. The debtor must have rights in the collateral.

Perfecting a Security Interest	1. *Perfection by filing*—The most common method of perfection is by filing a financing statement containing the names of the secured party and the debtor and identifying the collateral covered by the financing statement. The financing statement must be filed under the name of the debtor. Trade names normally are not sufficient.
	 2. *Perfection without filing—*
	   a. By possession—The debtor can transfer possession of the collateral to the secured party. A *pledge* is an example of this type of transfer.
	   b. By attachment—Fourteen types of security interests are perfected automatically when they are created. The most common is the purchase-money security interest (PMSI) in consumer goods.
	 3. *Classification of collateral*—The classification of collateral determines how and where a security interest is perfected (see Exhibit 21–2).

Scope of a Security Interest	A security agreement can cover the following types of property: 1. *Collateral in the present possession or control of the debtor.* 2. *Proceeds from a sale, exchange, or disposition of secured collateral.* 3. *After-acquired property*—A security agreement may provide that property acquired after execution of the agreement will also be secured by the agreement. This provision is often included in security agreements covering a debtor's inventory. 4. *Future advances*—A security agreement may provide that any future advances made against a line of credit will be subject to the initial security interest in the same collateral.

Priorities	1. *General rules—*
	   a. Perfected security interest versus unsecured creditors and unperfected security interests—A perfected secured party's interest has priority over the interests of most other parties.
	   b. Conflicting perfected security interests—When two or more secured parties have perfected security interests in the same collateral, the first to perfect generally has priority [UCC 9–322(a)(1)].
	   c. Conflicting unperfected security interests—When two conflicting security interests are unperfected, the first to attach (be created) has priority [UCC 9–322(a)(3)].
	 2. *Exceptions—*
	   a. In some instances, a PMSI, properly perfected, will prevail over another security interest in after-acquired collateral, even though the other was perfected first.
	   b. A buyer of goods in the ordinary course of the seller's business prevails over a secured party's security interest, even if the security interest is perfected and even if the buyer knows of its existence [UCC 9–320(a)].
	 3. Exceptions also exist for buyers of farm products, chattel paper, instruments, documents, or securities.

Continues

Rights and Duties	1. *Information request*—On request by the filing party, the filing officer must send a statement listing the file number, the date, and the hour of the filing of the financing statement to the person making the request.
	2. *Release, assignment, and amendment*—A secured party may (a) release part or all of the collateral described in a filed financing statement, thus ending the creditor's security interest, or (b) assign part or all of the security interest to another party. If the debtor and the secured party agree, they can also amend the filed statement.
	3. *Confirmation or accounting request by debtor*—If the debtor requests a confirmation of the unpaid debt or a list of the collateral, the secured party must send the debtor an authenticated accounting within fourteen days.
	4. *Termination statement*—When a debt is paid, the secured party generally must file a *termination statement*. If the financing statement covers consumer goods, the termination statement must be filed by the secured party within one month after the debt is paid or within twenty days of receiving the debtor's demand, whichever is earlier.
Default	On the debtor's default, the secured party may do either of the following:
	1. Take peaceful possession of the collateral covered by the security agreement and then pursue one of two alternatives:
	a. Retain the collateral (unless the collateral is consumer goods and the debtor has paid 60 percent or more of the purchase price on a PMSI or of the loan amount on a non-PMSI), subject to certain conditions.
	b. Dispose of the collateral in a commercially reasonable manner in accordance with the requirements prescribed in the UCC.
	2. Relinquish the security interest and use any judicial remedy available, such as proceeding to judgment on the underlying debt, followed by execution and levy on the nonexempt assets of the debtor.
Other Laws Assisting Creditors	1. *Mechanic's lien*—A nonpossessory, filed lien on an owner's real estate for labor, services, or materials furnished for making improvements on the realty.
	2. *Artisan's lien*—A possessory lien on an owner's personal property for labor performed or value added.
	3. *Judicial liens*—
	a. Writ of attachment—A court order to seize a debtor's nonexempt property prior to a court's final determination of a creditor's rights to the property. Attachment is available only if the creditor complies with the applicable state statutes.
	b. Writ of execution—A court order directing the sheriff to seize (levy) and sell a debtor's nonexempt real or personal property to satisfy a court's judgment in the creditor's favor.
	4. *Garnishment*—A collection remedy that allows a creditor to collect a debt by seizing property of the debtor that is being held by a third party.
	5. *Creditors' composition agreements*—Contracts between a debtor and his or her creditors in which the creditors agree to discharge the debts on the debtor's payment of a sum less than the amount actually owed.
	6. *Suretyships and guaranty*—Arrangements by which, under contract, a third person agrees to be primarily or secondarily liable for the debt owed by the principal debtor. A creditor can turn to this third person for satisfaction of the debt.

Issue Spotters

1. Liberty Bank loans Michelle $5,000 to buy a car, which is used as collateral to secure the loan. After repaying less than 50 percent of the loan, Michelle defaults. Liberty could repossess and keep the car, but the bank does not want it. What are the alternatives? (See *Priorities, Rights, and Duties*.)

2. Jorge contracts with Midwest Roofing to fix his roof. Jorge pays half of the contract price in advance. Midwest completes the job, but Jorge refuses to pay the rest of the price. What can Midwest do? (See *Other Laws Assisting Creditors*.)

—**Check your answers to the *Issue Spotters* against the answers provided in Appendix D at the end of this text.**

Learning Objectives Check

1. What is required to create a security interest?

2. How is a purchase-money security interest in consumer goods created?

3. If two parties have perfected security interests in the debtor's collateral, which party has priority on default?

4. How does a mechanic's lien assist creditors?

5. What is a suretyship, and how does it differ from a guaranty?

—**Answers to the even-numbered *Learning Objectives Check* questions can be found in Appendix E at the end of this text.**

Business Scenarios and Case Problems

21–1. Priority Disputes. Redford is a seller of electric generators. He purchases a large quantity of generators from a manufacturer, Mallon Corp., by making a down payment and signing an agreement to pay the balance over a period of time. The agreement gives Mallon Corp. a security interest in the generators and the proceeds. Mallon Corp. properly files a financing statement on its security interest. Redford receives the generators and immediately sells one of them to Garfield on an installment contract with payment to be made in twelve equal installments. At the time of the sale, Garfield knows of Mallon's security interest. Two months later, Redford goes into default on his payments to Mallon. Discuss Mallon's rights against purchaser Garfield in this situation. (See *Priorities, Rights, and Duties*.)

21–2. Perfection. Marsh has a prize horse named Arabian Knight. In need of working capital, Marsh borrows $5,000 from Mendez, who takes possession of Arabian Knight as security for the loan. No written agreement is signed. Discuss whether, in the absence of a written agreement, Mendez has a security interest in Arabian Knight. If Mendez does have a security interest, is it a perfected security interest? Explain. (See *Creating and Perfecting a Security Interest*.)

21–3. Disposition of Collateral. PRA Aviation, LLC, borrowed $3 million from Center Capital Corp. to buy a Gates Learjet 55B. Center perfected a security interest in the plane. Later, PRA defaulted on the loan, and Center obtained possession of the jet. Based on a review of the market for similar aircraft, as well as the jet's design and condition, its value was estimated at $1.45 million. The jet was marketed in trade publications, on the Internet, and by direct advertising to select customers for $1.595 million. There were three offers. Center sold the jet to the highest bidder for $1.3 million. Was the sale commercially reasonable? Explain. [*Center Capital Corp. v. PRA Aviation, LLC,* 2011 WL 867516 (E.D.Pa. 2011)] (See *Default*.)

21–4. Business Case Problem with Sample Answer— Perfecting a Security Interest. Thomas Tille owned M.A.T.T. Equipment Co. To operate the business, Tille borrowed funds from Union Bank. For each loan, Union filed a financing statement that included Tille's signature and address, the bank's address, and a description of the collateral. The first loan covered all of Tille's equipment, including "any after-acquired property." The second loan covered a truck crane "whether owned now or acquired later." The third loan covered a "Bobcat mini-excavator." Did these financing statements perfect Union's security interests? Explain. [*Union Bank Co. v. Heban,* 2012 WL 32102 (Ohio App. 2012) (See *Creating and Perfecting a Security Interest*.)

—**For a sample answer to Problem 21–4, go to Appendix F at the end of this text.**

21–5. Guaranty. Timothy Martinez, owner of Koenig & Vits, Inc. (K&V), guaranteed K&V's debt to Community Bank & Trust. The guaranty stated that the bank was not required to seek payment of the debt from any other source before enforcing the guaranty. K&V defaulted. Through a Wisconsin state court, the bank sought payment of $536,739.40, plus interest at the contract rate of 7.5 percent, from Martinez. Martinez argued that the bank could not enforce his guaranty while other funds were available to satisfy K&V's debt. For example, the debt might be paid out of the proceeds of a sale of corporate assets. Is this an effective defense to a guaranty? Why or why not? [*Community Bank & Trust v. Koenig & Vits, Inc.,* 346 Wis.2d 279 (Wis.App. 2013)] (See *Other Laws Assisting Creditors*.)

21–6. Disposition of Collateral. With a loan of 1.4 million euros from Barclays Bank, PLC, Thomas Poynter bought a yacht. The loan agreement gave Barclays multiple options on default. One option required the lender to give ten days' advance notice of a sale. A different option permitted the lender to avoid this requirement. When Poynter did not repay the loan, Barclays repossessed the yacht, notified Poynter that it would be sold— but did not specify a date, time, or place—and sold the yacht two months later. The sale price was less than Poynter owed, and Barclays filed a suit in a federal district court for the deficiency. Is Barclays entitled to collect even though it did not give Poynter ten days' advance notice of the sale? Explain. [*Barclays Bank PLC v. Poynter,* 710 F.3d 16 (1st Cir. 2013)] (See *Default*.)

21–7. Liens. Daniel and Katherine Balk asked Jirak Construction, LLC, to remodel their farmhouse in Lawler, Iowa. Jirak provided the Balks with an initial estimate of $45,975 for the cost. Over the course of the work, the Balks made significant changes to the plan. Jirak agreed to the changes and regularly advised the Balks about the increasing costs. In mid-project, Jirak provided an itemized breakdown at their request. The Balks paid Jirak $67,000, but refused to pay more. Jirak claimed that they still owed $55,000 in labor and materials. Jirak filed a suit in an Iowa state court against the Balks to collect. Which of the liens discussed in this chapter would be most effective to Jirak in its attempt to collect? How does that type of lien work? Is the court likely to enforce it in this case? Explain. [*Jirak Construction, LLC v. Balk,* __ N.W.2d __, 2015 WL 799786 (Iowa App. 2015)] (See *Other Laws Assisting Creditors*.)

21–8. A Question of Ethics—Guaranty Contracts. 73-75 Main Avenue, LLC, agreed to lease commercial property to PP Door Enterprise, Inc., if its principal officers executed personal guaranties and provided credit information. Nan Zhang signed the lease as manager of PP Door. The principals of PP Door signed the lease and guaranty agreements. When PP Door failed to make monthly payments, the lessor sued

PP Door and its owner, Ping Ying Li. Li testified that she was the sole owner of PP Door but denied that Zhang was its manager. She also denied signing the guaranty agreement. She claimed that she had signed the credit authorization form because Zhang had told her he was too young to have good credit. Li claimed to have no knowledge of the lease agreement. She did admit, however, that she had paid the rent because Zhang had been in a car accident and had asked her to help pay his bills, including the rent. [*73-75 Main Avenue, LLC v. PP Door Enterprise, Inc.*, 120 Conn.App. 150, 991 A.2d 650 (2010)] (See *Other Laws Assisting Creditors*.)

1. Li argued that she was not liable on the lease agreement because Zhang was not authorized to bind her to the lease. Do the facts support Li? Why or why not?

2. Li claimed that the guaranty for rent was not enforceable against her. Why might the court agree?

Critical Thinking and Writing Assignments

21–9. Business Law Writing. Write a few sentences describing the circumstances in which a creditor would resort to each of the following remedies when trying to collect on debt. (See *Other Laws Assisting Creditors*.)

1. Mechanic's lien
2. Artisan's lien
3. Writ of attachment

21–10. Business Law Critical Thinking Group Assignment. Nick Sabol, doing business in the recording industry as Sound Farm Productions, applied to Morton Community Bank for a $58,000 loan to expand his business. Besides the loan application, Sabol signed a promissory note that referred to the bank's rights in "any collateral." Sabol also signed a letter authorizing Morton Community Bank to execute, file, and record all financing statements, amendments, and other documents required by Article 9 to establish a security interest. Sabol did not sign any other documents, including the financing statement, which contained a description of the collateral. Two years later, without having repaid the loan, Sabol filed for bankruptcy. The bank claimed a security interest in Sabol's sound equipment. (See *Creating and Perfecting a Security Interest*.)

1. The first group will list all the requirements of an enforceable security interest and explain why each of these elements is necessary.

2. The second group will determine if Morton Community Bank had a valid security interest.

3. The third group will discuss whether a bank should be able to execute financing statements on a debtor's behalf without the debtor being present or signing them. Are there are any drawbacks to this practice?

Lane V. Erickson/ShutterStock.com

22

Bankruptcy

"Capitalism without bankruptcy is like Christianity without hell."

FRANK BORMAN
1928–PRESENT
(U.S. ASTRONAUT AND BUSINESSMAN)

Many people in today's economy are struggling to pay their monthly bills. In the old days, debtors were punished and sometimes sent to jail for failing to pay their debts. Today, the law provides debtors with numerous rights, including the right to have their debts discharged in bankruptcy.

This chapter discusses bankruptcy—a last resort in resolving debtor-creditor problems. As implied by the chapter-opening quotation, bankruptcy may be a necessary evil in our capitalistic society. Hence, every businessperson should have some understanding of the bankruptcy process.

Often, people end up in bankruptcy because they can no longer afford to make the payments on their homes. We therefore begin this chapter with a discussion of mortgages (the loans that borrowers obtain to purchase homes) and the foreclosure process that occurs when people are no longer able to make their mortgage payments. We also look at laws that assist debtors by providing exemptions that protect certain property from the reach of creditors.

22–1 Mortgages

As noted in the preceding chapter, creditors use various means to ensure that they receive payment from debtors. Creditors financing the purchase of real property are no exception.

LEARNING OBJECTIVES

The five Learning Objectives *below are designed to help improve your understanding of the chapter. After reading this chapter, you should be able to answer the following questions:*

1. What are three ways for a debtor to avoid mortgage foreclosure?

2. In a Chapter 7 bankruptcy, what happens if a court finds that there was "substantial abuse"? How is the means test used?

3. What constitutes a preference in bankruptcy law? When is a trustee able to avoid preferential transfers?

4. In a Chapter 11 reorganization, what is the role of the debtor in possession?

5. How does a Chapter 13 bankruptcy differ from bankruptcy under Chapter 7 and Chapter 11?

Down Payment An initial cash payment made when an expensive item, such as a house, is purchased. The payment represents a percentage of the purchase price, and the remainder is financed.

Mortgage A written instrument that gives a creditor an interest in, or lien on, a debtor's real property as security for a debt.

When individuals purchase real property, they typically make a **down payment** in cash and borrow the remaining funds from a financial institution. A **mortgage** is a written instrument that gives this creditor an interest in, or lien on, the debtor's real property as security for the debt. The creditor is the *mortgagee,* and the debtor is the *mortgagor.*

22–1a Fixed-Rate versus Adjustable-Rate Mortgages

Lenders offer various types of mortgages to meet the needs of different borrowers. A basic distinction is whether the interest rate is fixed or variable.

A *fixed-rate mortgage* has a fixed, or unchanging, rate of interest, so the payments remain the same for the duration of the loan. Lenders determine the interest rate for a standard fixed-rate mortgage loan based on a variety of factors, including the borrower's credit history, credit score, income, and debts.

The rate of interest paid by the borrower changes periodically with an *adjustable-rate mortgage (ARM)*. Typically, the initial interest rate for an ARM is set at a relatively low fixed rate for a specified period, such as a year or three years. After that time, the interest rate adjusts annually or by some other period, such as biannually or monthly. The adjustment is calculated by adding a certain number of percentage points (called the margin) to an index rate (one of various government interest rates).

ARMs contractually shift the risk that the interest rate will change from the lender to the borrower. Borrowers will have lower initial payments if they are willing to assume the risk that interest rates might rise, resulting in higher payments for the borrowers in the future.

22–1b Mortgage Provisions

Because a mortgage involves a transfer of real property, it must be in writing to comply with the Statute of Frauds. Mortgages normally are lengthy and formal documents containing many provisions, including the following:

Prepayment Penalty Clause A mortgage provision requiring the borrower to pay a penalty if the mortgage is repaid in full within a certain period.

1. *The terms of the underlying loan.* These include the loan amount, the interest rate, the period of repayment, and other important financial terms, such as the margin and index rate for an ARM.

2. *A prepayment penalty clause.* A **prepayment penalty clause** requires the borrower to pay a penalty if the mortgage is repaid in full within a certain period. A prepayment penalty helps to protect the lender should the borrower refinance within a short time after obtaining a mortgage.

3. *Provisions relating to the maintenance of the property.* Because the mortgage conveys an interest in the property to the lender, the lender often requires the borrower to maintain the property to protect the lender's collateral.

4. *A statement obligating the borrower to maintain homeowners' insurance on the property.* **Homeowner's insurance** protects the lender's interest in the event of a loss due to certain hazards, such as fire or storm damage.

Homeowner's Insurance A form of property insurance that protects the holder against damage or loss to the holder's home.

5. *A list of the nonloan financial obligations to be borne by the borrower.* For instance, the borrower typically is required to pay all property taxes, assessments, and other claims against the property.

6. *Creditor protections.* When creditors extend mortgages, they are advancing a significant amount of funds for a number of years. Consequently, creditors usually require debtors to obtain *mortgage insurance* if they do not make a down payment of at least 20 percent of the purchase price. Creditors also record the mortgage with the appropriate office in the county where the property is located, so that the creditors' interest in the house is officially on record.

22-1c Mortgage Foreclosure

If a homeowner defaults, or fails to make mortgage payments, the lender has the right to foreclose on the mortgaged property. **Foreclosure** is the legal process by which the lender repossesses and auctions off the property that has secured the loan.

Foreclosure is expensive and time consuming. It generally benefits neither the borrowers, who lose their homes, nor the lenders, which face the prospect of losses on their loans. Therefore, both lenders and borrowers are motivated to avoid foreclosure proceedings if possible.

Ways to Avoid Foreclosure Possible methods of avoiding foreclosure include forbearance, workout agreements, and short sales (see Exhibit 22–1). A **forbearance** is a postponement of part or all of the payments on a loan for a limited time. This option works well when the debtor has short-term financial problems that can likely be solved—for instance, when the debtor has lost a job but is likely to be able to find a new job soon.

A **workout agreement** is a contract that describes the respective rights and responsibilities of the borrower and the lender as they try to resolve the default. Usually, the lender agrees to delay seeking foreclosure in exchange for the borrower's providing additional financial information that might be used to modify the mortgage.

When a borrower is in default, a lender may sometimes agree to a **short sale,** which is a sale of the property for less than the balance due on the mortgage loan. Typically, the borrower

Foreclosure The legal process by which a lender repossesses and disposes of property that has secured a loan.

LEARNING OBJECTIVE 1

What are three ways for a debtor to avoid mortgage foreclosure?

Forbearance A postponement of part or all of the payments on a loan for a limited time.

Workout Agreement A contract that describes the respective rights and responsibilities of a borrower and a lender as they try to resolve the borrower's default.

Short Sale A sale of mortgaged property for less than the balance due on the mortgage loan.

Exhibit 22–1 Methods of Avoiding Foreclosure

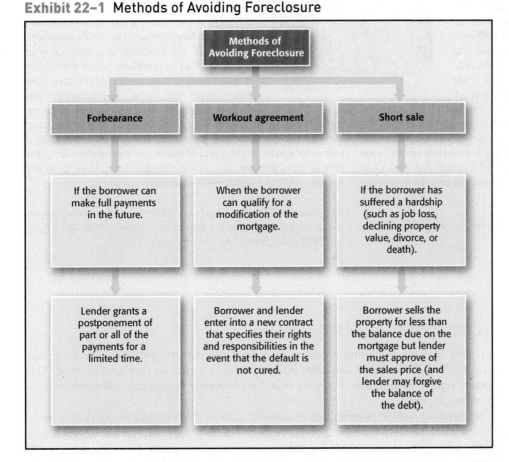

has to show some hardship, such as the loss of job, a decline in the value of the home, a divorce, or a death in the household. The lender often has approval rights in a short sale, so the sale process may take much longer than an ordinary real estate transaction.

Foreclosure Procedure If all efforts to find another solution fail, the lender will proceed to foreclosure. The lender must strictly comply with the state statute governing foreclosures. Many problems arose in the last ten years because lenders, facing a record number of foreclosures during the last recession, had difficulty complying with the required statutory formalities.

To bring a foreclosure action, a bank must have standing to sue. In the following *Spotlight Case,* the court had to decide whether a bank could foreclose a mortgage even though the bank could not prove when it became the owner of the borrower's promissory note.

SPOTLIGHT ON FORECLOSURES: CASE 22.1

McLean v. JPMorgan Chase Bank, N.A.

District Court of Appeal of Florida, 79 So.3d 170 (2012).

FACTS On May 11, 2009, JPMorgan Chase Bank (Chase) filed a foreclosure action against Robert McLean. The complaint alleged that Chase was entitled to enforce the mortgage and promissory note on which McLean had defaulted. Nevertheless, the attached mortgage identified a different mortgagee and lender, and Chase claimed that the note had been "lost, stolen, or destroyed." When McLean filed a motion to dismiss, Chase produced a mortgage assignment dated May 14, 2009, which was three days after it had filed the lawsuit. Eventually, Chase also filed the original note. Although the indorsement to Chase was undated, Chase then filed a motion for summary judgment. The trial court granted Chase's motion even though the accompanying affidavit failed to show that Chase had owned the mortgage or note when it filed the complaint. McLean appealed.

ISSUE Did Chase prove that it had standing to bring a foreclosure action against McLean?

How can Chase Bank foreclose on delinquent mortgages?

iStockPhoto.com/RiverNorthPhotography

DECISION No. The Florida appellate court reversed the trial court's grant of summary judgment to Chase.

REASON A party seeking foreclosure must have standing to foreclose when it files its complaint. In this case, the mortgage was assigned after Chase had filed its complaint. Chase argued that it had standing because the promissory note was indorsed in its name. The indorsement was undated, however, and Chase's affidavit did not show that Chase owned the note when it filed its lawsuit. The court therefore reversed summary judgment and instructed the trial court to find for Chase only if it proved that it had owned the note at the time of the complaint. Otherwise, the case would have to be dismissed, and Chase would need to file a new complaint.

CRITICAL THINKING—Legal Consideration *If Chase cannot prove that it owned the note at the time of its complaint, what will happen next? Will Chase prevail? Why or why not?*

Equitable Right of Redemption The right of a mortgagor who has breached the mortgage agreement to redeem or purchase the mortgaged property prior to foreclosure proceedings.

Statutory Right of Redemption A right provided by statute in some states under which mortgagors can redeem or purchase their property after a judicial foreclosure for a limited time period, such as one year.

22–1d Redemption Rights

Every state allows a defaulting borrower to redeem the property *before the foreclosure sale* by paying the full amount of the debt, plus any interest and costs that have accrued. This **equitable right of redemption** allows the defaulting borrower to gain title and regain possession of the property.

The **statutory right of redemption,** in contrast, entitles the borrower to repurchase property even *after a judicial foreclosure.* In other words, in states that provide for statutory redemption, the homeowner has a right to buy the property back from a third party who bought it at a foreclosure sale. Generally, the borrower may exercise this right for up to one year from the time the house is sold at a foreclosure sale.[1] Some states allow the borrower to retain possession of the property after the foreclosure sale and up until the statutory redemption period ends. If the borrower does not exercise the right of redemption, the new buyer receives title to and possession of the property.

22-2 Laws Assisting Debtors

The preceding chapter emphasized that the law provides many protections for creditors. But the law protects debtors as well. Certain property of the debtor, for instance, is exempt from creditors' actions. Of course, bankruptcy laws are designed specifically to assist debtors, as will be discussed shortly.

In most states, various types of real and personal property are exempt from execution or attachment. State exemption statutes usually include both real and personal property.

22-2a Exempted Real Property

Probably the most familiar real property exemption is the **homestead exemption.** Each state permits the debtor to retain the family home, either in its entirety or up to a specified dollar amount, free from the claims of unsecured creditors or trustees in bankruptcy. The purpose of the homestead exemption is to ensure that the debtor will retain some form of shelter. (As discussed later, federal bankruptcy law limits the amount that debtors can claim under a state's homestead exemption.)

In a few states, statutes allow the homestead exemption only if the judgment debtor has a family. If a judgment debtor does not have a family, a creditor may be entitled to collect the full amount realized from the sale of the debtor's home. In addition, the homestead exemption interacts with other areas of law and can sometimes operate to cancel out a portion of a lien on a debtor's real property.

CASE EXAMPLE 22.1 Antonio Stanley purchased a modular home from Yates Mobile Services Corporation. When Stanley failed to pay the purchase price of the home, Yates obtained a judicial lien against Stanley's property in the amount of $165,138.05. Stanley then filed for bankruptcy and asserted the homestead exemption. The court found that Stanley was entitled to avoid the lien to the extent that it impaired his exemption. Using a bankruptcy law formula, the court determined that the total impairment was $143,639.05 and that Stanley could avoid paying this amount to Yates. Thus, Yates was left with a judicial lien on Stanley's home in the amount of $21,499.[2] ▪

Homestead Exemption A law permitting a debtor to retain the family home, either in its entirety or up to a specified dollar amount, free from the claims of unsecured creditors or trustees in bankruptcy.

How does the homestead exemption help debtors who go into bankruptcy?

22-2b Exempted Personal Property

Personal property that is most often exempt under state law includes the following:

1. Household furniture up to a specified dollar amount.
2. Clothing and certain personal possessions, such as family pictures or a religious text.
3. A vehicle (or vehicles) for transportation (at least up to a specified dollar amount).
4. Certain classified animals, usually livestock but including pets.
5. Equipment that the debtor uses in a business or trade, such as tools or professional instruments, up to a specified dollar amount.

---

1. Some states do not allow a borrower to waive the statutory right of redemption. This means that a buyer at auction must wait one year to obtain title to, and possession of, a foreclosed property.
2. *In re Stanley*, 2010 WL 2103441 (M.D.N.C. 2010).

22-3   The Bankruptcy Code

Bankruptcy relief is provided under federal law. Nevertheless, state laws on secured transactions, liens, judgments, and exemptions also play a role in federal bankruptcy proceedings.

Article I, Section 8, of the U.S. Constitution gave Congress the power to establish "uniform laws on the subject of bankruptcies throughout the United States." Federal bankruptcy legislation was first enacted in 1898 and since then has undergone several modifications, most recently in the 2005 Bankruptcy Reform Act.[3] Federal bankruptcy laws are called the Bankruptcy Code or, more simply, the Code.

22-3a   Goals of Bankruptcy Law

Bankruptcy law in the United States has two main goals:

1. To protect a debtor by giving him or her a fresh start without creditors' claims.

2. To ensure equitable treatment of creditors who are competing for a debtor's assets.

Thus, the law attempts to balance the rights of the debtor and the creditors.

Although the twin goals of bankruptcy remained the same, the balance between them shifted somewhat after the 2005 reform legislation. Because of its significance for creditors and debtors alike, we present the 2005 Bankruptcy Reform Act as this chapter's *Landmark in the Law* feature.

22-3b   Bankruptcy Courts

KNOW THIS

Congress regulates the jurisdiction of the federal courts within the limits set by the U.S. Constitution. Congress can expand or reduce the number of federal courts at any time.

Bankruptcy proceedings are held in federal bankruptcy courts, which are under the authority of U.S. district courts. Rulings by bankruptcy courts can be appealed to the district courts. The bankruptcy court holds proceedings dealing with the procedures required to administer the debtor's estate in bankruptcy (the debtor's assets, as will be discussed shortly).

22-3c   Types of Bankruptcy Relief

The Bankruptcy Code is contained in Title 11 of the *United States Code* (U.S.C.) and has eight "chapters." Chapters 1, 3, and 5 of the Code include general definitions and provisions governing case administration and procedures, creditors, the debtor, and the estate. These three chapters of the Code normally apply to all types of bankruptcies.

Four chapters of the Code set forth the most important types of relief that debtors can seek.

1. Chapter 7 provides for *liquidation* proceedings—that is, the selling of all nonexempt assets and the distribution of the proceeds to the debtor's creditors.

2. Chapter 11 governs reorganizations.

3. Chapter 12 (for family farmers and family fishermen) and Chapter 13 (for individuals) provide for adjustment of the debts of parties with regular income.[4]

Note that a debtor (except for a municipality) need not be insolvent[5] to file for bankruptcy relief under the Bankruptcy Code. Anyone obligated to a creditor can declare bankruptcy.

---

3. The full title of the act is the Bankruptcy Abuse Prevention and Consumer Protection Act of 2005, Pub. L. No. 109-8, 119 Stat. 23 (April 20, 2005).

4. There are no Chapters 2, 4, 6, 8, or 10 in Title 11. Such "gaps" are not uncommon in the *United States Code*. They occur because, when a statute is enacted, chapter numbers (or other subdivisional unit numbers) are sometimes reserved for future use. (A gap may also appear if a law has been repealed.)

5. The inability to pay debts as they come due is known as *equitable* insolvency. A *balance-sheet* insolvency, which exists when a debtor's liabilities exceed assets, is not the test. Thus, it is possible for debtors to petition voluntarily for bankruptcy even though their assets far exceed their liabilities. This situation may occur when a debtor's cash-flow problems become severe.

LANDMARK IN THE LAW

The Bankruptcy Abuse Prevention and Consumer Protection Act

When Congress enacted the first Bankruptcy Reform Act in 1978, many claimed that the law made it too easy for debtors to file for bankruptcy protection. The 2005 Bankruptcy Abuse Prevention and Consumer Protection Act (BAPCPA) was passed, in part, in response to businesses' concerns about the rise in personal bankruptcy filings. From 1978 to 2005, personal bankruptcy filings increased dramatically. Various business groups—including credit-card companies, retailers, and banks—claimed that the bankruptcy process was being abused and that reform was necessary.

MORE REPAYMENT PLANS, FEWER LIQUIDATION BANKRUPTCIES One of the major goals of the BAPCPA is to require consumers to pay as many of their debts as they possibly can instead of having those debts fully discharged in bankruptcy. Before the reforms, the vast majority of bankruptcies

were filed under Chapter 7 of the Bankruptcy Code, which permits debtors, with some exceptions, to have *all* of their debts discharged in bankruptcy. Only about 20 percent of personal bankruptcies were filed under Chapter 13 of the Bankruptcy Code. As you will read later in this chapter, this part of the Bankruptcy Code requires the debtor to establish a repayment plan and pay off as many of his or her debts as possible over a maximum period of five years. Under the BAPCPA, more debtors have to file for bankruptcy under Chapter 13.

OTHER SIGNIFICANT PROVISIONS OF THE ACT BAPCPA also made a number of other changes. One important provision involves the homestead exemption. Before the passage of the act, some states allowed debtors petitioning for bankruptcy to exempt all of the *equity* (the market value minus the outstanding mortgage owed) in their homes during bankruptcy proceedings. The

2005 act leaves these exemptions in place but puts some limits on their use. Another BAPCPA provision gives child-support obligations priority over other debts and allows enforcement agencies to continue efforts to collect child-support payments.

APPLICATION TO TODAY'S WORLD
Under the 2005 bankruptcy reforms, fewer debtors are allowed to have their debts discharged in Chapter 7 liquidation proceedings. At the same time, the act makes it more difficult for debtors to obtain a "fresh start" financially—one of the major goals of bankruptcy law in the United States. Today, more debtors are forced to file under Chapter 13. Additionally, the bankruptcy process has become more time consuming and costly because it requires more extensive documentation and certification. These changes in the law have left many Americans unable to obtain relief from their debts.

22-3d Special Treatment of Consumer-Debtors

A **consumer-debtor** is a debtor whose debts result primarily from the purchase of goods for personal, family, or household use. The Bankruptcy Code requires that the clerk of the court give all consumer-debtors written notice of the general purpose, benefits, and costs of each chapter of bankruptcy under which they may proceed. In addition, the clerk must provide consumer-debtors with information on the types of services available from credit counseling agencies.

Consumer-Debtor One whose debts result primarily from the purchases of goods for personal, family, or household use.

22-4 Chapter 7—Liquidation

Liquidation under Chapter 7 is the most familiar type of bankruptcy proceeding and is often referred to as an *ordinary,* or *straight, bankruptcy*. Put simply, a debtor in a liquidation bankruptcy turns all assets over to a **bankruptcy trustee,** a person appointed by the court to manage the debtor's funds. The trustee sells the nonexempt assets and distributes the proceeds to creditors. With certain exceptions, the remaining debts are then **discharged** (extinguished), and the debtor is relieved of the obligation to pay the debts.

Any "person"—defined as including individuals, partnerships, and corporations[6]—may be a debtor under Chapter 7. Railroads, insurance companies, banks, savings and loan associations,

Liquidation The sale of the nonexempt assets of a debtor and the distribution of the funds received to creditors.

Bankruptcy Trustee A person appointed by the court to manage the debtor's funds.

Discharge The termination of a bankruptcy debtor's obligation to pay debts.

---

6. The definition of *corporation* includes unincorporated companies and associations. It also covers labor unions.

investment companies licensed by the U.S. Small Business Administration, and credit unions *cannot* be Chapter 7 debtors. Other chapters of the Code or other federal or state statutes apply to them. A husband and wife may file jointly for bankruptcy under a single petition.

A straight bankruptcy may be commenced by the filing of either a voluntary or an involuntary **petition in bankruptcy**—the document that is filed with a bankruptcy court to initiate bankruptcy proceedings. If a debtor files the petition, then it is a *voluntary bankruptcy.* If one or more creditors file a petition to force the debtor into bankruptcy, then it is an *involuntary bankruptcy.* We discuss both voluntary and involuntary bankruptcy proceedings under Chapter 7 in the following subsections.

Petition in Bankruptcy
The document that is filed with a bankruptcy court to initiate bankruptcy proceedings.

22–4a Voluntary Bankruptcy

To bring a voluntary petition in bankruptcy, the debtor files official forms designated for that purpose in the bankruptcy court. Before debtors can file a petition, they must receive credit counseling from an approved nonprofit agency. Debtors filing a Chapter 7 petition must thus include a certificate proving that they have received individual or group counseling from an approved agency within the last 180 days (roughly six months).

A consumer-debtor who is filing a voluntary petition must confirm the accuracy of the petition's contents. The debtor must also state in the petition, at the time of filing, that he or she understands the relief available under other chapters of the Code and has chosen to proceed under Chapter 7.

Attorneys representing consumer-debtors must file an affidavit stating that they have informed the debtors of the relief available under each chapter of the Code. In addition, the attorneys must reasonably attempt to verify the accuracy of the consumer-debtors' petitions and schedules (described next). Failure to do so is considered perjury.

Chapter 7 Schedules
The voluntary petition contains the following schedules:

1. A list of both secured and unsecured creditors, their addresses, and the amount of debt owed to each.
2. A statement of the financial affairs of the debtor.
3. A list of all property owned by the debtor, including property claimed by the debtor to be exempt.
4. A list of current income and expenses.
5. A certificate of credit counseling (as mentioned previously).
6. Proof of payments received from employers within sixty days prior to the filing of the petition.
7. A statement of the amount of monthly income, itemized to show how the amount is calculated.
8. A copy of the debtor's federal income tax return for the most recent year ending immediately before the filing of the petition.

The official forms must be completed accurately, sworn to under oath, and signed by the debtor. To conceal assets or knowingly supply false information on these schedules is a crime under the bankruptcy laws.

With the exception of tax returns, failure to file the required schedules within forty-five days after the filing of the petition (unless an extension is granted) will result in an automatic dismissal of the petition. The debtor has up to seven days before the date of the first creditors' meeting to provide a copy of the most recent tax returns to the trustee.

Tax Returns during Bankruptcy
A debtor may be required to file a tax return at the end of each tax year while the case is pending and to provide a copy to the court. A request for a copy

of the debtor's tax return may be made by the court, the trustee, or any *party in interest* (a party, such as a creditor, who has a valid interest in the outcome of the proceedings). Debtors may also be required to file tax returns during Chapter 11 and 13 bankruptcies.

Substantial Abuse and the Means Test
In the past, a bankruptcy court could dismiss a Chapter 7 petition if the use of Chapter 7 would constitute a "substantial abuse" of bankruptcy law. Today, the law provides a *means test* to determine a debtor's eligibility for Chapter 7.

The purpose of the test is to keep upper-income people from abusing the bankruptcy process by filing for Chapter 7, as was thought to have happened in the past. The test forces more people to file for Chapter 13 bankruptcy rather than have their debts discharged under Chapter 7.

LEARNING OBJECTIVE 2

In a Chapter 7 bankruptcy, what happens if a court finds that there was "substantial abuse"? How is the means test used?

The Basic Formula. A debtor wishing to file for bankruptcy must complete the means test to determine whether she or he qualifies for Chapter 7. The debtor's average monthly income in recent months is compared with the median income in the geographic area in which the person lives. (The U.S. Trustee Program provides these data at its Web site, **justice.gov/ust**.) If the debtor's income is below the median income, the debtor usually is allowed to file for Chapter 7 bankruptcy, as there is no presumption of bankruptcy abuse.

Applying the Means Test to Future Disposable Income. If the debtor's income is above the median income, then further calculations must be made. The goal is to determine whether the person will have sufficient disposable income in the future to repay at least some of his or her unsecured debts. As a basis for the calculations, it is presumed that the debtor's recent monthly income will continue for the next sixty months. *Disposable income* is then calculated by subtracting living expenses and interest payments on secured debt, such as mortgage payments, from monthly income.

Living expenses are the amounts allowed under formulas used by the Internal Revenue Service (IRS). The IRS allowances include modest allocations for food, clothing, housing, utilities, transportation (including car payments), health care, and other necessities. (The U.S. Trustee Program's Web site also provides these amounts.) The allowances do not include expenditures for items such as cell phones and cable television service.

Can the Debtor Afford to Pay Unsecured Debts? Once future disposable income has been estimated, that amount is used to determine whether the debtor will have income that could be applied to unsecured debts. The court may also consider the debtor's bad faith or other circumstances indicating abuse.

CASE EXAMPLE 22.2 Christopher Dean Ng and his wife filed for Chapter 7 bankruptcy, hoping primarily to discharge their mortgage debt of $464,830. At the time the petition was filed, Ng was forty-three years old and worked as an electronic technician, earning a monthly salary of $7,439.47, as well as a military pension of $1,439.88 a month. His wife was not employed. From Ng's monthly salary, he made a voluntary contribution of $520 to an employer 401(k) plan and a $343 payment on a pension loan. In calculating his income, Ng excluded these amounts. He also excluded a $300 payment on prepetition income tax liability.

The U.S. trustee filed a motion to dismiss Ng's petition due to substantial abuse, claiming that the retirement contributions should be disallowed. The court agreed and dismissed the Chapter 7 petition. The Ngs appealed, and the appellate court affirmed. Ng's retirement contributions were not reasonably necessary based on his age, his financial circumstances, and his testimony that he was not planning to retire for at least twenty years. The Ngs could afford to repay some of their debts before they made monthly contributions toward retirement.[7]

---

7. *In re Ng*, 422 Bankr. 118 (9th Cir. 2012).

Additional Grounds for Dismissal

As noted, a debtor's voluntary petition for Chapter 7 relief may be dismissed for substantial abuse or for failing to provide the necessary documents (such as schedules and tax returns) within the specified time. In addition, a motion to dismiss a Chapter 7 filing may be granted in two other situations.

1. If the debtor has been convicted of a violent crime or a drug-trafficking offense, the victim can file a motion to dismiss the voluntary petition.[8]
2. If the debtor fails to pay postpetition domestic-support obligations (which include child and spousal support), the court may dismiss the petition.

Order for Relief

If the voluntary petition for bankruptcy is found to be proper, the filing of the petition will itself constitute an **order for relief.** (An order for relief is the court's grant of assistance to a debtor.) Once a consumer-debtor's voluntary petition has been filed, the clerk of the court (or other appointee) must give the trustee and creditors notice of the order for relief by mail not more than twenty days after the entry of the order.

22–4b Involuntary Bankruptcy

An involuntary bankruptcy occurs when the debtor's creditors force the debtor into bankruptcy proceedings. An involuntary petition should not be used as an everyday debt-collection device. The Code provides penalties for the filing of frivolous (unjustified) petitions against debtors. If the court dismisses an involuntary petition, the petitioning creditors may be required to pay the costs and attorneys' fees incurred by the debtor in defending against the petition. If the petition was filed in bad faith, damages can be awarded for injury to the debtor's reputation. Punitive damages may also be awarded.

Requirements

An involuntary case cannot be filed against a charitable institution or a farmer (an individual or business that receives more than 50 percent of gross income from farming operations). For an involuntary action to be filed against other debtors, the following requirements must be met:

1. If the debtor has twelve or more creditors, three or more of those creditors having unsecured claims totaling at least $15,325 must join in the petition.
2. If a debtor has fewer than twelve creditors, one or more creditors having a claim of $15,325 or more may file.[9]

When the Debtor Challenges the Petition

If the debtor challenges the involuntary petition, a hearing will be held. The debtor's challenge will fail if the bankruptcy court finds either of the following:

1. The debtor generally is not paying debts as they become due.
2. A general receiver, assignee, or custodian took possession of, or was appointed to take charge of, substantially all of the debtor's property within 120 days before the filing of the involuntary petition.

If the court allows the bankruptcy to proceed, the debtor will be required to supply the same information in the bankruptcy schedules as in a voluntary bankruptcy.

Order for Relief A court's grant of assistance to a complainant. In bankruptcy proceedings, the order relieves the debtor of the immediate obligation to pay the debts listed in the bankruptcy petition.

"I hope that after I die, people will say of me: 'That guy sure owed me a lot of money.'"

JACK HANDEY
1949–PRESENT
(AMERICAN HUMORIST)

---

8. Note that the court may not dismiss a case on this ground if the debtor's bankruptcy is necessary to satisfy a claim for a domestic-support obligation.

9. 11 U.S.C. Section 303. The amounts stated in this chapter are in accordance with those computed on April 1, 2013.

22–4c Automatic Stay

The moment a petition, either voluntary or involuntary, is filed, an **automatic stay,** or suspension, of almost all actions by creditors against the debtor or the debtor's property normally goes into effect. Until the bankruptcy proceeding is closed or dismissed, the automatic stay prohibits a creditor from taking any act to collect, assess, or recover a claim against the debtor that arose before the filing of the petition.

If a creditor *knowingly* violates the automatic stay (a willful violation), any injured party, including the debtor, is entitled to recover actual damages, costs, and attorneys' fees and may be entitled to punitive damages as well. **CASE EXAMPLE 22.3** Stefanie Kuehn filed for bankruptcy. When she requested a transcript from the university at which she had obtained her master's degree, the university refused because she owed more than $6,000 in tuition. Kuehn complained to the court. The court ruled that the university had violated the automatic stay when it refused to provide a transcript because it was attempting to collect an unpaid tuition debt.[10]

Exceptions to the Automatic Stay The Code provides the following exceptions to the automatic stay:

1. Collection efforts can continue for domestic-support obligations, which include any debt owed to or recoverable by a spouse, a former spouse, a child of the debtor, that child's parent or guardian, or a governmental unit.

2. Proceedings against the debtor related to divorce, child custody or visitation, domestic violence, and support enforcement are not stayed.

3. Investigations by a securities regulatory agency can continue.

4. Certain statutory liens for property taxes are not stayed.

Requests for Relief from the Automatic Stay A secured creditor or other party in interest can petition the bankruptcy court for relief from the automatic stay. If a creditor or other party requests relief from the stay, the stay will automatically terminate sixty days after the request, unless the court grants an extension or the parties agree otherwise.

Secured Property The automatic stay on secured property terminates forty-five days after the creditors' meeting unless the debtor redeems or reaffirms certain debts. (Creditors' meetings and reaffirmation will be discussed later in this chapter.) This means that the debtor cannot keep secured property (such as a financed automobile), even if she or he continues to make payments on it, without reinstating the rights of the secured party to collect on the debt.

Bad Faith If the debtor had two or more bankruptcy petitions dismissed during the prior year, the Code presumes bad faith. In such a situation, the automatic stay does *not* go into effect until the court determines that the petition was filed in good faith.

22–4d Estate in Bankruptcy

On the commencement of a liquidation proceeding under Chapter 7, an **estate in bankruptcy** is created. The estate consists of all the debtor's interests in property currently held, wherever located. The estate in bankruptcy includes all of the following:

1. *Community property* (property jointly owned by a husband and wife in certain states).

2. Property transferred in a transaction voidable by the trustee.

3. Proceeds and profits from the property of the estate.

Automatic Stay In bankruptcy proceedings, the suspension of almost all litigation and other action by creditors against the debtor or the debtor's property. The stay is effective the moment the debtor files a petition in bankruptcy.

Can a university withhold the transcript of a former student who is in bankruptcy?

Estate in Bankruptcy All of the property owned by a person, including real estate and personal property.

---

10. *In re Kuehn*, 563 F.3d 289 (7th Cir. 2009).

Certain after-acquired property—such as gifts, inheritances, property settlements (from divorce), and life insurance death proceeds—to which the debtor becomes entitled *within 180 days after filing* may also become part of the estate. Generally, though, the filing of a bankruptcy petition fixes a dividing line. Property acquired prior to the filing of the petition becomes property of the estate, and property acquired after the filing of the petition, except as just noted, remains the debtor's.

22–4e The Bankruptcy Trustee

Promptly after the order for relief has been entered, a trustee is appointed. The basic duty of the trustee is to collect the debtor's available estate and reduce it to cash for distribution, preserving the interests of both the debtor and the unsecured creditors. This requires that the trustee be accountable for administering the debtor's estate.

To enable the trustee to accomplish this duty, the Code gives the trustee certain powers, stated in both general and specific terms. These powers must be exercised within two years after the order for relief has been entered.

Review for Substantial Abuse

The trustee is required to review promptly all materials filed by the debtor to determine if there is substantial abuse. Within ten days after the first meeting of the creditors, the trustee must file a statement as to whether the case is presumed to be an abuse under the means test. The trustee must provide all creditors with a copy of this statement.

When there is a presumption of abuse, the trustee must either file a motion to dismiss the petition (or convert it to a Chapter 13 case) or file a statement explaining why a motion would not be appropriate. If the debtor owes a domestic-support obligation (such as child support), the trustee must provide written notice of the bankruptcy to the claim holder (a former spouse, for instance).

Trustee's Powers

The trustee has the power to require persons holding the debtor's property at the time the petition is filed to deliver the property to the trustee.[11] To enable the trustee to implement this power, the Code provides that the trustee has rights *equivalent* to those of certain other parties, such as a creditor who has a judicial lien. This power of a trustee, which is equivalent to that of a lien creditor, is known as the *strong-arm power.*

In addition, the trustee has specific *powers of avoidance.* They enable the trustee to set aside (avoid) a sale or other transfer of the debtor's property and take the property back for the debtor's estate. These powers apply to voidable rights available to the debtor, preferences, and fraudulent transfers by the debtor (as discussed in more detail next).

The debtor shares most of the trustee's avoidance powers. Thus, if the trustee does not take action to enforce one of these rights, the debtor in a liquidation bankruptcy can enforce it.

Voidable Rights

A trustee steps into the shoes of the debtor. Thus, any reason that a debtor can use to obtain the return of his or her property can be used by the trustee as well. The grounds for recovery include fraud, duress, incapacity, and mutual mistake.

EXAMPLE 22.4 Ben sells his boat to Inga. Inga gives Ben a check, knowing that she has insufficient funds in her bank account to cover the check. Inga has committed fraud. Ben has the right to avoid that transfer and recover the boat from Inga. If Ben files for Chapter 7 bankruptcy, the trustee can exercise the same right to recover the boat from Inga, and the boat becomes part of the debtor's estate. ■

Preferences

A debtor is not permitted to make a property transfer or a payment that favors—or gives a **preference** to—one creditor over others. The trustee is allowed to recover payments made both voluntarily and involuntarily to one creditor in preference over another.

Preference In bankruptcy proceedings, a property transfer or payment made by the debtor that favors one creditor over others.

---

11. Usually, the trustee takes constructive, rather than actual, possession of the debtor's property. For instance, to obtain possession of a business's inventory, a trustee might change the locks on the doors and hire a security guard.

To have made a recoverable preferential payment, an *insolvent* debtor generally must have transferred property for a *preexisting* debt during the *ninety days* before the filing of the petition in bankruptcy. The transfer must have given the creditor more than the creditor would have received as a result of the bankruptcy proceedings. The Code presumes that the debtor is insolvent during the ninety-day period before filing a petition.

If a **preferred creditor** (one who has received a preferential transfer from the debtor) has sold the property to an innocent third party, the trustee cannot recover the property from the innocent party. The trustee can generally force the preferred creditor to pay the value of the property, however.

Preferences to Insiders. Sometimes, a creditor receiving a preference is an *insider*. An insider is any individual, partner, partnership, or officer or director of a corporation (or a relative of one of these) who has a close relationship with the debtor. In this situation, the avoidance power of the trustee is extended to transfers made within *one year* before filing. (If the transfer was fraudulent, as will be discussed shortly, the trustee can avoid transfers made within *two years* before filing.) However, the trustee must prove that the debtor was insolvent at the time the earlier transfer occurred.

Transfers That Do Not Constitute Preferences. Not all transfers are preferences. To be a preference, the transfer must be made in exchange for something other than current consideration. Most courts do not consider a debtor's payment for services rendered within fifteen days prior to the payment to be a preference. If a creditor receives payment in the ordinary course of business, such as payment of last month's cell phone bill, the trustee in bankruptcy cannot recover the payment. In contrast, a transfer for a preexisting debt, such as a year-old landscaping bill, would be a recoverable preference.

In addition, the Code permits a consumer-debtor to transfer any property to a creditor up to a total value of $6,225 without the transfer constituting a preference. Payments of domestic-support debts do not constitute a preference. Neither do payments required under a plan created by an approved credit-counseling agency.

Fraudulent Transfers   A trustee can avoid (set aside or cancel) fraudulent transfers or obligations if (1) they were made within two years of the filing of the petition or (2) they were made with actual intent to hinder, delay, or defraud a creditor. **EXAMPLE 22.5** April is planning to petition for bankruptcy, so she sells her gold jewelry, worth $10,000, to a friend for $500. The friend agrees that in the future he will "sell" the jewelry back to April for the same amount. This is a fraudulent transfer that the trustee can undo. ◼

22–4f Exemptions

An individual debtor is entitled to exempt certain property from the bankruptcy under federal or state exemption schemes.

Federal Exemptions   The Bankruptcy Code exempts the following property:[12]

1. Up to $22,975 in equity in the debtor's residence and burial plot (the homestead exemption).
2. Interest in a motor vehicle up to $3,675.

12. The dollar amounts stated in the Bankruptcy Code are adjusted automatically every three years on April 1 based on changes in the Consumer Price Index. The adjusted amounts are rounded to the nearest $25. The amounts stated in this chapter are in accordance with those computed on April 1, 2013.

LEARNING OBJECTIVE 3
What constitutes a preference in bankruptcy law? When is a trustee able to avoid preferential transfers?

Under what circumstances might a trustee recover the debtor's boat that was sold prior to the bankruptcy?

Preferred Creditor   In the context of bankruptcy, a creditor who has received a preferential transfer from a debtor.

KNOW THIS
Usually, when property is recovered as a preference, the trustee sells it and distributes the proceeds to the debtor's creditors.

3. Interest, up to $550 for a particular item, in household goods and furnishings, wearing apparel, appliances, books, animals, crops, and musical instruments (the aggregate total of all items is limited to $12,250).

4. Interest in jewelry up to $1,550.

5. Interest in any other property up to $1,225, plus any unused part of the $22,975 homestead exemption up to $11,500.

6. Interest in any tools of the debtor's trade up to $2,300.

7. A life insurance contract owned by the debtor (other than a credit life insurance contract).

8. Certain interests in accrued dividends and interest under life insurance contracts owned by the debtor, not to exceed $12,250.

9. Professionally prescribed health aids.

10. The right to receive Social Security and certain welfare benefits, alimony and support, certain retirement funds and pensions, and education savings accounts held for specific periods of time.

11. The right to receive certain personal-injury and other awards up to $22,975.

State Exemptions Individual states have the power to pass legislation precluding debtors from using the federal exemptions within the state. A majority of the states have done this. In those states, debtors may use only state, not federal, exemptions. In the rest of the states, an individual debtor (or a husband and wife filing jointly) may choose either the exemptions provided under state law or the federal exemptions.

Limitations on the Homestead Exemption The Bankruptcy Code limits the amount that can be claimed in bankruptcy under the homestead exemption of any state. In general, if the debtor acquired the home within three and one-half years preceding the date of filing, the maximum equity exempted is $155,675, even if state law would permit a higher amount.

In addition, the state homestead exemption is available only if the debtor has lived in the state for two years before filing the petition. A debtor who has violated securities law, been convicted of a felony, or engaged in certain other intentional misconduct may not be permitted to claim the homestead exemption at all.

22-4g Creditors' Meeting and Claims

Within a reasonable time after the order of relief has been granted (not more than forty days), the trustee must call a meeting of the creditors listed in the schedules filed by the debtor. The bankruptcy judge does not attend this meeting, but the debtor must attend and submit to an examination under oath. At the meeting, the trustee ensures that the debtor is aware of the potential consequences of bankruptcy and the possibility of filing under a different chapter of the Code.

To be entitled to receive a portion of the debtor's estate, each creditor normally files a *proof of claim* with the bankruptcy court clerk within ninety days of the creditors' meeting. The proof of claim lists the creditor's name and address, as well as the amount that the creditor asserts is owed to the creditor by the debtor.

When the debtor has no assets—called a "no-asset case"—creditors are notified of the debtor's petition for bankruptcy but are instructed not to file a claim. In no-asset cases, the unsecured creditors will receive no payment, and most, if not all, of these debts will be discharged.

22-4h Distribution of Property

The Code provides specific rules for the distribution of the debtor's property to secured and unsecured creditors. If any amount remains after the priority classes of creditors have been satisfied, it is turned over to the debtor. Exhibit 22–2 illustrates the collection and distribution of property in most voluntary bankruptcies.

Distribution to Secured Creditors Secured creditors have priority. The Code requires that consumer-debtors file a statement of intention with respect to the secured collateral. They can choose to pay off the debt and redeem the collateral, claim that it is exempt, reaffirm the debt and continue making payments, or surrender the property to the secured party.

If the collateral is surrendered to the secured party, the secured creditor can either (1) accept the collateral in full satisfaction of the debt or (2) sell the collateral and use the proceeds to pay off the debt. Thus, the secured party has priority over unsecured parties as to the proceeds from the disposition of the collateral. Should the collateral be insufficient to cover the secured debt owed, the secured creditor becomes an unsecured creditor for the difference.

Distribution to Unsecured Creditors Bankruptcy law establishes an order of priority for classes of debts owed to *unsecured* creditors, and they are paid in the order of their priority. Each class must be fully paid before the next class is entitled to any of the remaining proceeds. If there is any balance remaining after all the creditors are paid, it is returned to the debtor.

In almost all Chapter 7 bankruptcies, the funds will be insufficient to pay all creditors. If there are insufficient proceeds to pay the full amount to all the creditors in a class, the proceeds are distributed *proportionately* to the creditors in that class, and classes lower in priority receive nothing. Claims for domestic-support obligations, such as child support and alimony, have the highest priority among unsecured claims, so these debts must be paid first.

Exhibit 22–2 Collection and Distribution of Property in Most Voluntary Bankruptcies

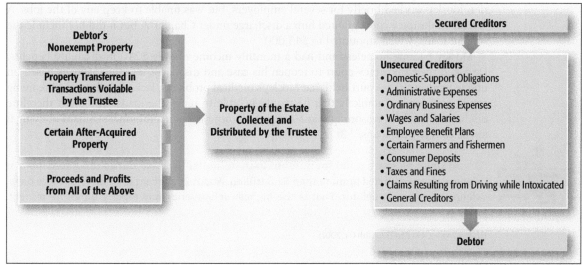

22-4i Discharge

From the debtor's point of view, the primary purpose of liquidation is to obtain a fresh start through the discharge of debts. A discharge voids, or sets aside, any judgment on a discharged debt and prevents any action to collect it. Certain debts, however, are not dischargeable in bankruptcy. Also, certain debtors may not qualify to have all debts discharged in bankruptcy. These situations are discussed next.

Exceptions to Discharge   The most important claims that are not dischargeable under Chapter 7 include the following:

1. Claims for back taxes accruing within two years prior to bankruptcy.
2. Claims for amounts borrowed by the debtor to pay federal taxes or any nondischargeable taxes.
3. Claims against property or funds obtained by the debtor under false pretenses or by false misrepresentations.
4. Claims by creditors who were not notified of the bankruptcy. These claims did not appear on the schedules the debtor was required to file.
5. Claims based on fraud or misuse of funds by the debtor or claims involving the debtor's embezzlement or larceny.
6. Domestic-support obligations and property settlements.
7. Claims for amounts due on a retirement loan account.
8. Claims based on willful or malicious conduct by the debtor toward another or toward the property of another.
9. Certain government fines and penalties.
10. Student loans, unless payment of the loans causes an undue hardship for the debtor and the debtor's dependents.
11. Consumer debts of more than $650 for luxury goods or services owed to a single creditor incurred within ninety days of the order for relief.

> **CASE EXAMPLE 22.6**   Keldric Mosley incurred student loans while attending Alcorn State University and then joined the U.S. Army Reserve Officers' Training Corps. He was injured during training and resigned from the Corps because of medical problems related to his injuries. Mosley worked briefly for several employers, but was unable to keep any of the jobs. A federal bankruptcy court granted him a discharge under Chapter 7, but it did not include the student loans, which amounted to $45,000.
>
> Mosley became homeless and had a monthly income of only $210 in disability benefits. He asked the bankruptcy court to reopen his case and discharge his student loans based on undue hardship. The court held that Mosley's medical problems, lack of skills, and "dire living conditions" made it unlikely that he would be able to repay the loans. The court therefore discharged the debt, reasoning that Mosley could not maintain a minimal standard of living if forced to repay the loans.[13] ▪

ETHICAL ISSUE

Should there be more relief for student loan defaults?   By 2016, outstanding student loan balances were estimated at more than $1.3 trillion. About 20 percent are ninety or more days' delinquent or are in default. That is the highest delinquency rate among all forms of debt,

---

13. *In re Mosley*, 494 F.3d 1320 (11th Cir. 2007).

including credit cards, automobile loans, and mortgages. The average student loan debt is estimated to be more than $30,000.

Any student borrower who has not made regular payments for nine months is in default. If you are in default on a student loan, the U.S. Department of Education can (1) keep your tax refund if you have one, (2) garnish your paycheck without obtaining a court judgment, and (3) take your federal benefits, such as Social Security retirement payments or disability payments. In addition, in some states any professional license that you have can be revoked. The Department of Education can also bring a lawsuit against you. If it wins, it can collect the judgment from your bank accounts or place a lien on any real property that you own.

Recently, Congress attempted to ease the burden on those who have taken out student loans by reducing the interest rates they can be charged. In addition, President Obama signed an executive order putting into place an income-based repayment plan. This plan caps payments at no more than 10 percent of disposable income. Any balance not paid off after twenty years will be forgiven.

Should the federal government go further? Yes, according to the Obama administration. In 2015, Obama signed a presidential memorandum called the "Student Aid Bill of Rights." The Department of Education must now implement actions to ensure that the debt collection process for defaulted student loans "is fair, transparent, [and] charges reasonable fees to defaulted borrowers." Additionally, many politicians are asking Congress to allow federal student loans to be discharged in most bankruptcy proceedings.

Critics point out that such student loan debt forgiveness could have a cost. They claim that colleges and universities might "hint" to potential students that they need not worry about taking on higher student loans because some portion will be forgiven by the federal government.

Can a reservist who is injured during training succeed in discharging his student loans if he can no longer work?

Objections to Discharge

In addition to the exceptions to discharge previously discussed, a bankruptcy court may deny the discharge based on the debtor's *conduct*. Grounds for denial of discharge of the debtor include the following:

1. The debtor's concealment or destruction of property with the intent to hinder, delay, or defraud a creditor.

2. The debtor's fraudulent concealment or destruction of financial records.

3. The granting of a discharge to the debtor within eight years prior to the filing of the petition.

4. The debtor's failure to complete the required consumer education course (unless such a course was not available).

5. The debtor's involvement in proceedings in which the debtor could be found guilty of a felony. (Basically, a court may not discharge any debt until the completion of the felony proceedings against the debtor.)

When a discharge is denied under any of these circumstances, the debtor's assets are still distributed to the creditors. After the bankruptcy proceeding, however, the debtor remains liable for the unpaid portions of all claims.

A discharge may be revoked (taken back) within one year if it is discovered that the debtor acted fraudulently or dishonestly during the bankruptcy proceeding. If that occurs, a creditor whose claim was not satisfied in the distribution of the debtor's property can proceed with his or her claim against the debtor.

Whether a bankruptcy court properly denied a discharge based on the debtors' conduct was the issue in the following case.

CASE 22.2

In re Cummings

United States Court of Appeals, Ninth Circuit, 595 Fed.Appx. 707 (2015).

FACTS Clarence and Pamela Cummings filed a petition for a Chapter 7 bankruptcy in a federal bankruptcy court. After the debtors filed two amended versions of the required schedules, the trustee asked for additional time to investigate. The court granted the request. The debtors then filed a third amended schedule. In it, they disclosed for the first time the existence of First Beacon Management Company, a corporation that they planned to use as part of their postbankruptcy "fresh start." The trustee then claimed that the Cummingses' failure to disclose their interest in First Beacon as debtor property was a "false oath relating to a material fact made knowingly and fraudulently" in violation of the Bankruptcy Code. The court agreed and denied the debtors a discharge. The Bankruptcy Appellate Panel (BAP) affirmed the court's decision. The Cummingses appealed.

ISSUE Did Clarence and Pamela Cummings commit fraud by not disclosing their interest in First Beacon until they filed their third amended schedule?

DECISION Yes. The U.S. Court of Appeals for the Ninth Circuit affirmed the ruling of the Bankruptcy Appellate Panel. "The sequence of debtors' filings substantiates the presence of fraud."

What constitutes a false oath in Chapter 7 proceedings?

REASON The bankruptcy court rejected the Cummingses' testimony as "not credible" and "beyond not credible," and the BAP found "ample evidence" to support these findings. On appeal, the debtors claimed that the bankruptcy court had failed to consider "voluminous independent and undisputed documentary evidence" that "completely obliterated any suggestion of fraudulent intent." The appellate court found, however, that this evidence did not support the debtors' claim. Instead, it clearly showed their ultimate purpose—"to insulate First Beacon Management Co., . . . the new corporate anchor of their post-petition fresh start, from the stigma of bankruptcy." That they eventually disclosed their interest in First Beacon did not eliminate their fraud. They chose twice to amend their schedules without revealing the corporation and finally admitted to its existence only after the bankruptcy court gave the trustee additional time to investigate.

CRITICAL THINKING—Economic Consideration *Why would a debtor risk the denial of a discharge to conceal assets? Discuss.*

22–4j Reaffirmation of Debt

Reaffirmation Agreement
An agreement between a debtor and a creditor in which the debtor voluntarily agrees to pay a debt dischargeable in bankruptcy.

An agreement to pay a debt dischargeable in bankruptcy is called a **reaffirmation agreement.** A debtor may wish to pay a debt—for instance, a debt owed to a family member, physician, bank, or some other creditor—even though the debt could be discharged in bankruptcy. Also, as noted previously, a debtor cannot retain secured property while continuing to pay without entering into a reaffirmation agreement.

Procedures To be enforceable, reaffirmation agreements must be made before the debtor is granted a discharge. The agreement must be signed and filed with the court (along with disclosure documents, as described next). Court approval is required unless the debtor is represented by an attorney during the negotiation of the reaffirmation agreement and submits the proper documents and certifications. Even when the debtor is represented by an attorney, court approval may be required if it appears that the reaffirmation will result in undue hardship to the debtor.

When court approval is required, a separate hearing will take place. The court will approve the reaffirmation only if it finds that the agreement will not result in undue hardship to the debtor and that the reaffirmation is consistent with the debtor's best interests.

Required Disclosures To discourage creditors from engaging in abusive reaffirmation practices, the law provides specific language for disclosures that must be given to debtors entering reaffirmation agreements. Among other things, these disclosures explain that the debtor is not required to reaffirm any debt, but that liens on secured property, such as mortgages and cars, will remain in effect even if the debt is not reaffirmed.

The reaffirmation agreement must disclose the amount of the debt reaffirmed, the rate of interest, the date payments begin, and the right to rescind. The disclosures also caution the debtor: "Only agree to reaffirm a debt if it is in your best interest. Be sure you can afford the payments you agree to make."

The original disclosure documents must be signed by the debtor, certified by the debtor's attorney, and filed with the court at the same time as the reaffirmation agreement. A reaffirmation agreement that is not accompanied by the original signed disclosures will not be effective.

22–5 Chapter 11—Reorganization

The type of bankruptcy proceeding used most commonly by corporate debtors is the Chapter 11 *reorganization*. In a reorganization, the creditors and the debtor formulate a plan under which the debtor pays a portion of its debts and the rest of the debts are discharged. The debtor is allowed to continue in business. This type of bankruptcy is generally a corporate reorganization. Nonetheless, any debtor (except a stockbroker or commodities broker) who is eligible for Chapter 7 relief is normally eligible for relief under Chapter 11. (Railroads are also eligible.)

Congress has established a "fast-track" Chapter 11 procedure for small-business debtors whose liabilities do not exceed $2.49 million and who do not own or manage real estate. The fast track enables a debtor to avoid the appointment of a creditors' committee and also shortens the filing periods and relaxes certain other requirements. Because the process is shorter and simpler, it is less costly. (See the *Linking Business Law to Corporate Management* feature at the end of this chapter for suggestions on how small businesses can prepare for Chapter 11.)

The same principles that govern the filing of a liquidation (Chapter 7) petition apply to reorganization (Chapter 11) proceedings. The case may be brought either voluntarily or involuntarily. The automatic-stay provision and its exceptions apply in reorganizations as well, as do the provisions regarding substantial abuse and additional grounds for dismissal (or conversion) of bankruptcy petitions.

KNOW THIS
Chapter 11 proceedings are typically prolonged and costly. Whether a firm survives depends on its size and its ability to attract new investors despite its Chapter 11 status.

22–5a Workouts

In some instances, to avoid bankruptcy proceedings, creditors may prefer private, negotiated adjustments of creditor-debtor relations, known as *workouts*. Often, these out-of-court workouts are much more flexible and thus conducive to a speedy settlement. Speed is critical because delay is one of the most costly elements in any bankruptcy proceeding. Another advantage of workouts is that they avoid the various administrative costs of bankruptcy proceedings.

22–5b Reasons for Dismissal

Once a petition for Chapter 11 has been filed, a bankruptcy court, after notice and a hearing, can dismiss or suspend all proceedings in a case at any time if dismissal or suspension would better serve the interests of the creditors. The Bankruptcy Code also allows a court, after notice and a hearing, to dismiss a reorganization case "for cause" when there is no reasonable likelihood of rehabilitation. Similarly, a court can dismiss a Chapter 11 petition when there is an inability to effect a plan or an unreasonable delay by the debtor that may harm the interests of creditors. A debtor whose petition is dismissed for these reasons can file a subsequent Chapter 11 petition in the future.[14]

---

14. See 11 U.S.C. Section 1112(b).

LEARNING OBJECTIVE 4

In a Chapter 11 reorganization, what is the role of the debtor in possession?

Debtor in Possession (DIP)
In Chapter 11 bankruptcy proceedings, a debtor who is allowed to continue in possession of the estate in property (the business) and to continue business operations.

22–5c Debtor in Possession

On entry of the order for relief, the debtor in Chapter 11 generally continues to operate the business as a **debtor in possession (DIP).** The court, however, may appoint a trustee (often referred to as a *receiver*) to operate the debtor's business if gross mismanagement of the business is shown or if appointing a trustee is in the best interests of the estate.

The DIP's role is similar to that of a trustee in a liquidation. The DIP is entitled to avoid preferential payments made to creditors and fraudulent transfers of assets. The DIP can also exercise a trustee's strong-arm powers. The DIP has the power to decide whether to cancel or assume prepetition executory contracts (contracts not yet performed) or unexpired leases.

Cancellation of executory contracts or unexpired leases can be of substantial benefit to a Chapter 11 debtor. **EXAMPLE 22.7** Five years ago, APT Corporation leased an office building for a twenty-year term. Now, APT can no longer pay the rent due under the lease and has filed for Chapter 11 reorganization. In this situation, the debtor in possession can cancel the lease so that APT will not be required to continue paying the substantial rent due for fifteen more years. ■

Can a debtor in possession under a Chapter 11 reorganization cancel a long-term lease on an office building?

22–5d Creditors' Committees

As soon as practicable after the entry of the order for relief, a committee of unsecured creditors is appointed.[15] The committee may consult with the trustee or the debtor concerning the administration of the case or the formulation of the plan. Additional creditors' committees may be appointed to represent special interest creditors, and a court may order the trustee to change a committee's membership as needed to ensure adequate representation of the creditors. Generally, no orders affecting the estate will be entered without the consent of the committee or a hearing in which the judge is informed of the position of the committee.

As mentioned earlier, businesses with debts of less than $2.49 million that do not own or manage real estate can avoid creditors' committees. In these fast-track proceedings, orders can be entered without a committee's consent.

22–5e The Reorganization Plan

A reorganization plan is established to conserve and administer the debtor's assets in the hope of an eventual return to successful operation and solvency. The plan must be fair and equitable and must do the following:

1. Designate classes of claims and interests.

2. Specify the treatment to be afforded the classes. (The plan must provide the same treatment for all claims in a particular class.)

3. Provide an adequate means for execution. (Individual debtors must utilize postpetition assets as necessary to execute the plan.)

4. Provide for payment of tax claims over a five-year period.

The plan need not provide for full repayment to unsecured creditors. Instead, creditors receive a percentage of each dollar owed to them by the debtor.

Filing the Plan Only the debtor may file a plan within the first 120 days after the date of the order for relief. This period may be extended, but not beyond eighteen months from the date of the order for relief. If the debtor does not meet the 120-day deadline or obtain an extension,

---

15. If the debtor has filed a plan accepted by the creditors, the trustee may decide not to call a meeting of the creditors.

or if the debtor fails to obtain the required creditor consent (discussed next) within 180 days, any party may propose a plan. If a small-business debtor chooses to avoid a creditors' committee, the time for the debtor's filing is 180 days.

Acceptance and Confirmation of the Plan   Once the plan has been developed, it is submitted to each class of creditors for acceptance. For the plan to be adopted, each class must accept it. A class has accepted the plan when a majority of the creditors, representing two-thirds of the amount of the total claim, vote to approve it.

Even when all classes of creditors accept the plan, the court may refuse to confirm it if it is not "in the best interests of the creditors." In addition, confirmation is conditioned on the debtor's certifying that all postpetition domestic-support obligations have been paid in full. For small-business debtors, if the plan meets the listed requirements, the court must confirm the plan within forty-five days (unless this period is extended).

The plan can also be modified upon the request of the debtor, DIP, trustee, U.S. trustee, or holder of an unsecured claim. If an unsecured creditor objects to the plan, specific rules apply to the value of property to be distributed under the plan. Tax claims must be paid over a five-year period.

Even if only one class of creditors has accepted the plan, the court may still confirm the plan under the Code's so-called **cram-down provision.** In other words, the court may confirm the plan over the objections of a class of creditors. Before the court can exercise this right of cram-down confirmation, it must be demonstrated that the plan is fair and equitable.

Discharge   The plan is binding on confirmation. Nevertheless, the law provides that confirmation of a plan does not discharge an individual debtor. *For individual debtors, the plan must be completed before discharge will be granted,* unless the court orders otherwise. For all other debtors, the court may order discharge at any time after the plan is confirmed.

The debtor is given a reorganization discharge from all claims not protected under the plan. This discharge does not apply to any claims that would be denied discharge under liquidation.

> **Cram-Down Provision**
> A provision of the Bankruptcy Code that allows a court to confirm a debtor's Chapter 11 reorganization plan even though only one class of creditors has accepted it.

22-6 Bankruptcy Relief under Chapter 12 and Chapter 13

In addition to bankruptcy relief through liquidation (Chapter 7) and reorganization (Chapter 11), the Code also provides for family-farmer and family-fisherman debt adjustments (Chapter 12) and individuals' repayment plans (Chapter 13).

22-6a Family Farmers and Fishermen—Chapter 12

To help relieve economic pressure on small farmers, Congress created Chapter 12 of the Bankruptcy Code. In 2005, Congress extended this protection to family fishermen, modified its provisions somewhat, and made it a permanent chapter in the Bankruptcy Code (previously, it had to be periodically renewed by Congress).

For purposes of Chapter 12, a *family farmer* is one whose gross income is at least 50 percent farm dependent and whose debts are at least 50 percent farm related. The total debt must not exceed $4,031,575. A partnership or a close corporation that is at least 50 percent owned by the farm family can also qualify as a family farmer.[16]

A *family fisherman* is one whose gross income is at least 50 percent dependent on commercial fishing operations and whose debts are at least 80 percent related to commercial fishing.

---

16. Note that for a corporation or partnership to qualify under Chapter 12, at least 80 percent of the value of the firm's assets must consist of assets related to the farming operation.

The total debt for a family fisherman must not exceed $1,868,200. As with family farmers, a partnership or close corporation can also qualify.

Filing the Petition The procedure for filing a family-farmer or family-fisherman bankruptcy plan is similar to the procedure for filing a repayment plan under Chapter 13, which will be discussed in detail shortly. The debtor must file a plan not later than ninety days after the order for relief has been entered. The filing of the petition acts as an automatic stay against creditors' and co-obligors' actions against the estate.

A farmer or fisherman who has already filed a reorganization or repayment plan may convert the plan to a Chapter 12 plan. The debtor may also convert a Chapter 12 plan to a liquidation plan.

Content and Confirmation of the Plan The content of a plan under Chapter 12 is basically the same as that of a Chapter 13 repayment plan (described next). Generally, the plan must be confirmed or denied within forty-five days of filing.

The plan must provide for payment of secured debts at the value of the collateral. If the secured debt exceeds the value of the collateral, the remaining debt is unsecured.

For unsecured debtors, the plan must be confirmed if either (1) the value of the property to be distributed under the plan equals the amount of the claim or (2) the plan provides that all of the debtor's disposable income to be received in a three-year period (or longer, by court approval) will be applied to making payments. Completion of payments under the plan discharges all debts provided for by the plan.

22–6b Individuals' Repayment Plan—Chapter 13

Chapter 13 of the bankruptcy code provides for the "adjustment of debts of an individual with regular income." Individuals (not partnerships or corporations) with regular income who owe fixed unsecured debts of less than $383,175 or fixed secured debts of less than $1,149,525 may take advantage of bankruptcy repayment plans.

Among those eligible are salaried employees and sole proprietors, as well as individuals who live on welfare, Social Security, fixed pensions, or investment income. Many small-business debtors have a choice of filing under either Chapter 11 or Chapter 13. Repayment plans offer some advantages because they are typically less expensive and less complicated than reorganization or liquidation proceedings.

Filing the Petition A Chapter 13 repayment plan case can be initiated only by the debtor's filing of a voluntary petition or by court conversion of a Chapter 7 petition (because of a finding of substantial abuse, for instance). Certain liquidation and reorganization cases may be converted to Chapter 13 with the consent of the debtor.[17]

A trustee, who will make payments under the plan, must be appointed. On the filing of a repayment plan petition, an automatic stay takes effect. Although the stay applies to all or part of the debtor's consumer debt, it does not apply to any business debt incurred by the debtor or to any domestic-support obligations.

Good Faith Requirement The Bankruptcy Code imposes the requirement of good faith on a debtor in both the filing of the petition and the filing of the plan. The Code does not define good faith, but if the circumstances as a whole indicate bad faith, a court can dismiss a debtor's Chapter 13 petition.

---

17. A Chapter 13 repayment plan may be converted to a Chapter 7 liquidation either at the request of the debtor or, under certain circumstances, "for cause" by a creditor. A Chapter 13 case may be converted to a Chapter 11 case after a hearing.

LEARNING OBJECTIVE 5

How does a Chapter 13 bankruptcy differ from bankruptcy under Chapter 7 and Chapter 11?

CASE EXAMPLE 22.8 Roger and Pauline Buis formed an air show business, Otto Airshows, which included a helicopter decorated as "Otto the Clown." After a competitor won a defamation lawsuit against the Buises and Otto Airshows, the Buises stopped doing business as Otto Airshows.

The Buises formed a new firm, Prop and Rotor Aviation, Inc., to which they leased the Otto equipment. Within a month, they filed a bankruptcy petition under Chapter 13. The plan and the schedules did not mention the lawsuit, the equipment lease, and several other items. The court dismissed the Buises' petition due to bad faith. The debtors had not included all of their assets and liabilities on their initial petition, and they had timed its filing to avoid payment on the defamation judgment.[18] ▪

In determining whether a Chapter 13 plan was proposed in good faith, should a court consider whether the debtor included his Social Security income in the amount of disposable income available for payment to unsecured creditors? That was the issue in the following case.

Does the owner of an air show have the right to exclude a pending lawsuit when filing bankruptcy papers?

---

18. *In re Buis*, 337 Bankr. 243 (N.D.Fla. 2006).

CASE 22.3

In re Welsh

United States Court of Appeals, Ninth Circuit, 711 F.3d 1120 (2013).

FACTS David and Sharon Welsh filed a Chapter 13 petition. The bankruptcy trustee objected to their proposed plan on the ground that it was not proposed in good faith. Specifically, the Welshes were making "minuscule" payments on unsecured claims while living in a $400,000 home and paying for various luxury items. In addition, they were failing to commit 100 percent of their disposable income to the plan. As a result, the plan would pay off only about $14,700 of their $180,500 unsecured debt.

Must this couple's Social Security income be included in a Chapter 13 petition?

One issue was the fact that David's Social Security income was excluded from the plan. The reformed Bankruptcy Code excludes Social Security income from the current monthly disposable income calculation, however. For that reason and others, the court ruled in the Welshes' favor. The Bankruptcy Appellate Panel for the Ninth Circuit affirmed the ruling. The trustee appealed to the U.S. Court of Appeals for the Ninth Circuit.

ISSUE Did the Welshes propose their plan in good faith despite their failure to include David's Social Security income in their disposable income?

DECISION Yes. The U.S. Court of Appeals for the Ninth Circuit affirmed the Bankruptcy Appellate Panel's judgment in the Welshes' favor. The federal appellate court concluded that the Bankruptcy

Abuse Prevention and Consumer Protection Act (BAPCPA) "forecloses a court's consideration of a debtor's Social Security income . . . as part of the inquiry into good faith."

REASON Before the BAPCPA, bankruptcy judges had the authority to determine a debtor's ability to pay based on the individual circumstances of each debtor. Congress replaced this discretion with a detailed test that requires debtors with a certain amount of "current monthly income" to calculate their disposable income by subtracting specific expenses. Social Security benefits are expressly excluded from current monthly income.

Thus, for a Social Security recipient such as David Welsh, the result of the disposable income calculation may indicate that there is little disposable income to pay debts. But a court cannot recalculate the amount by substituting its judgment for what Congress stipulated. And a court "cannot conclude . . . that a plan prepared completely in accordance with the very detailed calculations that Congress set forth is not proposed in good faith."

CRITICAL THINKING—Legal Consideration *In evaluating a debtor's petition, what factors should be part of a good faith analysis? Should consideration of disposable income play a role? Why or why not?*

The Repayment Plan A plan of rehabilitation by repayment must provide for the following:

1. The turning over to the trustee of future earnings or income of the debtor as necessary for execution of the plan.

2. Full payment through deferred cash payments of all claims entitled to priority, such as taxes.[19]

3. Identical treatment of all claims within a particular class. (The Code permits the debtor to list co-debtors, such as guarantors or sureties, as a separate class.)

The repayment plan may provide either for payment of all obligations in full or for payment of a lesser amount. The debtor must begin making payments under the proposed plan within thirty days after the plan has been filed and must continue to make "timely" payments from her or his disposable income. If the debtor fails to make timely payments or does not commence payments within the thirty-day period, the court can convert the case to a liquidation bankruptcy or dismiss the petition.

In putting together a repayment plan, a debtor must apply the means test to identify the amount of disposable income that will be available to repay creditors. The debtor is allowed to deduct certain expenses from monthly income to arrive at this amount. For instance, a debtor can claim a car-ownership deduction if the debtor is making payments on a car. When the debtor owns the car free and clear, however, the debtor cannot claim the car-ownership deduction, according to the United States Supreme Court.[20]

The Length of the Plan. The length of the payment plan can be three or five years, depending on the debtor's family income. If the debtor's family income is less than the median family income in the relevant geographic area under the means test, the term of the proposed plan must be three years.[21] The term may not exceed five years.

Confirmation of the Plan. After the plan is filed, the court holds a confirmation hearing, at which interested parties (such as creditors) may object to the plan. The hearing must be held at least twenty days, but no more than forty-five days, after the meeting of the creditors. The debtor must have filed all prepetition tax returns and paid all postpetition domestic-support obligations before a court will confirm the plan.

The court will confirm a plan with respect to each claim of a secured creditor under any of the following circumstances:

1. If the secured creditors have accepted the plan.

2. If the plan provides that secured creditors retain their liens until there is payment in full or until the debtor receives a discharge.

3. If the debtor surrenders the property securing the claims to the creditors.

In addition, for a motor vehicle purchased within 910 days before the petition is filed, the plan must provide that a creditor with a purchase-money security interest (PMSI) retains its lien until the entire debt is paid. For PMSIs on other personal property, the payment plan must cover debts incurred within a one-year period preceding the filing.

Discharge After the debtor has completed all payments, the court grants a discharge of all debts provided for by the repayment plan. Generally, all debts are dischargeable except the following:

1. Allowed claims not provided for by the plan.

2. Certain long-term debts provided for by the plan.

---

19. As with a Chapter 11 reorganization plan, full repayment of all claims is not always required.
20. *Ransom v. FIA Card Services, N.A.*, 562 U.S. 61, 131 S.Ct. 716, 178 L.Ed.2d 603 (2011).
21. See 11 U.S.C. Section 1322(d) for details on when a court will find that the Chapter 13 plan should extend to a five-year period.

3. Certain tax claims and payments on retirement accounts.

4. Claims for domestic-support obligations.

5. Debts related to injury or property damage caused while driving under the influence of alcohol or drugs.

An order granting discharge is final as to the debts listed in the repayment plan. **CASE EXAMPLE 22.9** Francisco Espinosa filed a petition for an individual repayment plan under Chapter 13 of the Bankruptcy Code. His plan proposed to pay only the principal on his student loan and to discharge the interest. United Student Aid Funds, Inc. (the creditor), had notice of the plan and did not object. Without finding that payment of the interest would cause undue hardship (as required under the Code), the court confirmed the plan.

Years later, United filed a motion asking the bankruptcy court to rule that its order confirming the plan was void because it was in violation of the rules governing bankruptcy. The court denied United's petition and ordered the creditor to cease its collection efforts. United appealed, and the case ultimately reached the United States Supreme Court. The Court affirmed the decision of the lower court that the bankruptcy court's order was not void. Thus, the student loan debt was discharged.[22] ∎

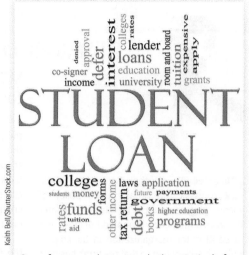

Can a former student pay only the principal of a student loan under Chapter 13?

Keith Bell/ShutterStock.com

_____

22. _United Student Aid Funds, Inc. v. Espinosa,_ 559 U.S. 260, 130 S.Ct. 1367, 176 L.Ed.2d 158 (2010).

Reviewing . . . Bankruptcy

Three months ago, Janet Hart's husband of twenty years died of cancer. Although he had medical insurance, he left Janet with outstanding medical bills of more than $50,000. Janet has worked at the local library for the past ten years, earning $1,500 per month. Since her husband's death, Janet also has received $1,500 in Social Security benefits and $1,100 in life insurance proceeds every month, giving her a monthly income of $4,100. After she pays the mortgage payment of $1,500 and the amounts due on other debts each month, Janet barely has enough left over to buy groceries for her family (she has two teenage daughters at home). She decides to file for Chapter 7 bankruptcy, hoping for a fresh start. Using the information provided in the chapter, answer the following questions.

1. Under the Bankruptcy Code after the reform act, what must Janet do before filing a petition for relief under Chapter 7?

2. How much time does Janet have after filing the bankruptcy petition to submit the required schedules? What happens if Janet does not meet the deadline?

3. Assume that Janet files a petition under Chapter 7. Further assume that the median family income in the state in which Janet lives is $49,300. What steps would a court take to determine whether Janet's petition is presumed to be substantial abuse under the means test?

4. Suppose the court determines that no presumption of substantial abuse applies in Janet's case. Nevertheless, the court finds that Janet does have the ability to pay at least a portion of the medical bills out of her disposable income. What would the court likely order in that situation?

DEBATE THIS

■ Rather than being allowed to file Chapter 7 bankruptcy petitions, individuals and couples should always be forced to make an effort to pay off their debts through Chapter 13.

LINKING BUSINESS LAW TO CORPORATE MANAGEMENT

What Can You Do to Prepare for a Chapter 11 Reorganization?

Chapter 11 of the Bankruptcy Code expresses the broad public policy of encouraging commerce. To this end, Chapter 11 allows a financially troubled business firm to petition for reorganization in bankruptcy while it is still solvent so that the firm's business can continue. Small businesses, however, do not fare very well under Chapter 11. Although some corporations that enter into Chapter 11 emerge as functioning entities, only a small number of companies survive the process.

Plan Ahead

If you ever are a small-business owner contemplating Chapter 11 reorganization, you can improve your chances of being among the survivors by planning ahead. To ensure the greatest possibility of success, you should take action before, not after, entering bankruptcy proceedings. Discuss your financial troubles openly and cooperatively with creditors to see if you can agree on a workout or some other arrangement.

If you appear to have no choice but to file for Chapter 11 protection, try to persuade a lender to loan you funds to see you through the bankruptcy. If your business is a small corporation, you might try to negotiate a favorable deal with a major investor. For example, a small business could offer to transfer ownership of stock to the investor in return for a loan to pay the costs of the bankruptcy proceedings and an option to repurchase the stock when the firm becomes profitable again.

Consult with Creditors

Most important, you should form a Chapter 11 plan before entering bankruptcy proceedings. Consult with creditors in advance to see what kind of plan would be acceptable to them, and prepare your plan accordingly. Having an acceptable plan prepared before you file will expedite the proceedings and thus save substantially on costs.

CRITICAL THINKING

- Filing for bankruptcy under Chapter 11 may involve a time-consuming process. How might this affect the likelihood that a firm will be able to negotiate a workout agreement with its creditors?

Key Terms

automatic stay 551	equitable right of redemption 544	petition in bankruptcy 548
bankruptcy trustee 547	forbearance 543	preference 552
consumer-debtor 547	foreclosure 543	preferred creditor 553
cram-down provision 561	homeowner's insurance 542	prepayment penalty clause 542
debtor in possession (DIP) 560	homestead exemption 545	reaffirmation agreement 558
discharge 547	liquidation 547	short sale 543
down payment 542	mortgage 542	statutory right of redemption 544
estate in bankruptcy 551	order for relief 550	workout agreement 543

Chapter Summary: Bankruptcy

PROTECTION FOR DEBTORS

Mortgages	When individuals purchase real estate, they typically make a down payment and take out a mortgage loan for the balance of the purchase price. Loan types include fixed-rate and adjustable-rate mortgages. Several protections, such as mortgage insurance, exist for lenders, but if the borrower defaults, the entire mortgage debt is due and payable, and the lender can foreclose on the mortgaged property.
Laws Assisting Debtors	Certain property of a debtor is exempt from creditors' actions under state laws. Each state permits a debtor to retain the family home, either in its entirety or up to a specified dollar amount, free from the claims of unsecured creditors or trustees in bankruptcy (homestead exemption).

BANKRUPTCY—A COMPARISON OF CHAPTERS 7, 11, 12, AND 13

Issue	Chapter 7	Chapter 11	Chapters 12 and 13
Who Can Petition	Debtor (voluntary) or creditors (involuntary).	Debtor (voluntary) or creditors (involuntary).	Debtor (voluntary) only.
Who Can Be a Debtor	Any "person" (including partnerships and corporations) except railroads, insurance companies, banks, savings and loan institutions, investment companies licensed by the U.S. Small Business Administration, and credit unions. Farmers and charitable institutions cannot be involuntarily petitioned.	Any debtor eligible for Chapter 7 relief; railroads are also eligible.	*Chapter 12*—Any family farmer (one whose gross income is at least 50 percent farm dependent and whose debts are at least 50 percent farm related) or family fisherman (one whose gross income is at least 50 percent dependent on and whose debts are at least 80 percent related to commercial fishing) or any partnership or close corporation at least 50 percent owned by a family farmer or fisherman, when total debt does not exceed a specified amount. *Chapter 13*—Any individual (not partnerships or corporations) with regular income who owes fixed (liquidated) unsecured debts of less than $383,175 or fixed secured debts of less than $1,149,525.
Procedure Leading to Discharge	Nonexempt property is sold with proceeds to be distributed (in order) to priority groups. Dischargeable debts are terminated.	Plan is submitted. If it is approved and followed, debts are discharged.	Plan is submitted and must be approved if the value of the property to be distributed equals the amount of the claims or if the debtor turns over disposable income for a three-year or five-year period. If the plan is followed, debts are discharged.
Advantages	On liquidation and distribution, most debts are discharged, and the debtor has an opportunity for a fresh start.	Debtor continues in business. Creditors can either accept the plan, or it can be "crammed down" on them. The plan allows for the reorganization and liquidation of debts over the plan period.	Debtor continues in business or possession of assets. If the plan is approved, most debts are discharged after the specified period.

Issue Spotters

1. After graduating from college, Tina works briefly as a salesperson and then files for bankruptcy. As part of her petition, Tina reveals that her only debts are student loans, taxes accruing within the last year, and a claim against her based on her misuse of funds during her employment. Are these debts dischargeable in bankruptcy? Explain. (See *Chapter 7—Liquidation*.)

2. Ogden is a vice president of Plumbing Service, Inc. (PSI). On May 1, Ogden loans PSI $10,000. On June 1, the firm repays the loan. On July 1, PSI files for bankruptcy. Quentin is appointed trustee. Can Quentin recover the $10,000 paid to Ogden on June 1? Why or why not? (See *Chapter 7—Liquidation*.)

   —**Check your answers to the *Issue Spotters* against the answers provided in Appendix D at the end of this text.**

Learning Objectives Check

1. What are three ways for a debtor to avoid mortgage foreclosure?
2. In a Chapter 7 bankruptcy, what happens if a court finds that there was "substantial abuse"? How is the means test used?
3. What constitutes a preference in bankruptcy law? When is a trustee able to avoid preferential transfers?
4. In a Chapter 11 reorganization, what is the role of the debtor in possession?
5. How does a Chapter 13 bankruptcy differ from bankruptcy under Chapter 7 and Chapter 11?

Answers to the even-numbered *Learning Objectives Check* questions can be found in Appendix E at the end of this text.

Business Scenarios and Case Problems

22–1. Voluntary versus Involuntary Bankruptcy. Burke has been a rancher all her life, raising cattle and crops. Her ranch is valued at $500,000, almost all of which is exempt under state law. Burke has eight creditors and a total indebtedness of $70,000. Two of her largest creditors are Oman ($30,000 owed) and Sneed ($25,000 owed). The other six creditors have claims of less than $5,000 each. A drought has ruined all of Burke's crops and forced her to sell many of her cattle at a loss. She cannot pay off her creditors. (See *Chapter 7—Liquidation.*)

1. Under the Bankruptcy Code, can Burke, with a $500,000 ranch, voluntarily petition herself into bankruptcy? Explain.

2. Could either Oman or Sneed force Burke into involuntary bankruptcy? Explain.

22–2. Distribution of Property. Montoro petitioned himself into voluntary bankruptcy. There were three major claims against his estate. One was made by Carlton, a friend who held Montoro's negotiable promissory note for $2,500. Another was made by Elmer, Montoro's employee, who claimed that Montoro owed him three months' back wages of $4,500. The last major claim was made by the United Bank of the Rockies on an unsecured loan of $5,000. In addition, Dietrich, an accountant retained by the trustee, was owed $500, and property taxes of $1,000 were owed to Rock County. Montoro's nonexempt property was liquidated, with proceeds of $5,000. Discuss fully what amount each party will receive, and why. (See *Chapter 7—Liquidation.*)

22–3. Protection for Debtors. Bill and Betty Ma owned half of a two-unit residential building. Betty lived in the unit, but Bill did not. To collect a judgment against the Mas, Mei-Fang Zhang obtained a writ of execution directing the sheriff to seize and sell the building. State law allowed a $100,000 homestead exemption if the debtor lived in the home and $175,000 if the debtor was also disabled and "unable to engage in gainful employment." Bill argued that he could not work because of "gout and dizziness." How much of an exemption were the Mas allowed? Why? [*Zhang v. Tse,* 2011 WL 500196 (N.D.Cal. 2011)] (See *Laws Assisting Debtors.*)

22–4. Business Case Problem with Sample Answer— Automatic Stay. Michelle Gholston leased a Chevy Impala from EZ Auto Van Rentals. In November 2011, Gholston filed for bankruptcy. Around November 21, the bankruptcy court notified EZ Auto of Gholston's bankruptcy and the imposition of an automatic stay. Nevertheless, because Gholston had fallen behind on her payments, EZ Auto repossessed the vehicle on November 28. Gholston's attorney then reminded EZ Auto about the automatic stay, but the company failed to return the car. As a result of the car's repossession, Gholston suffered damages that included emotional distress, lost wages, attorneys' fees, and car rental expenses. Can Gholston recover from EZ Auto? Why or why not? [*In re Gholston,* 2012 WL 639288 (M.D.Fla. 2012)] (See *Chapter 7— Liquidation.*)

—For a sample answer to Problem 22–4, go to Appendix F at the end of this text.

22–5. Discharge in Bankruptcy. Like many students, Barbara Hann financed her education partially through loans. These loans included three federally insured Stafford Loans of $7,500 each ($22,500 in total). Hann believed that she had repaid the loans, but later, when she filed a Chapter 13 petition, Educational Credit Management Corp. (ECMC) filed an unsecured proof of claim based on the loans. Hann objected. At a hearing at which ECMC failed to appear, Hann submitted correspondence from the lender that indicated the loans had been paid. The court entered an order sustaining Hann's objection. Despite the order, can ECMC resume its effort to collect on Hann's loans? Explain. [*In re Hann,* 711 F.3d 235 (1st Cir. 2013)] (See *Bankruptcy Relief under Chapter 12 and Chapter 13.*)

22–6. Discharge. Michael and Dianne Shankle divorced. An Arkansas state court ordered Michael to pay Dianne alimony and child support, as well as half of the $184,000 in their investment accounts. Instead, Michael withdrew more than half of the investment funds and spent them. Over the next several years, the court repeatedly held Michael in contempt for failing to pay Dianne. Six years later, Michael filed for Chapter 7 bankruptcy, including in the petition's schedule the debt to Dianne of unpaid alimony, child support, and investment funds. Is Michael entitled to a discharge of this debt, or does it qualify as an exception? Explain. [*In re Shankle*, 554 Fed.Appx. 264 (5th Cir. 2014)] (See *Chapter 7—Liquidation.*)

22–7. Discharge under Chapter 13. James Thomas and Jennifer Clark married and had two children. They bought a home in Ironton, Ohio, with a loan secured by a mortgage. Later, they took out a second mortgage. On their divorce, the court gave Clark custody of the children and required Clark to pay the first mortgage. The divorce decree also required Thomas and Clark to make equal payments on the second mortgage and provided that Clark would receive all proceeds on the sale of the home. Thomas failed to make any payments, and Clark sold the home. At that point, she learned that Auto Now had a lien on the home because Thomas had not made payments on his car. Clark used all the sale proceeds to pay off the lien and the mortgages. When Thomas filed a petition for a Chapter 13 bankruptcy in a federal bankruptcy court, Clark filed a proof of claim for the mortgage and lien debts. Clark claimed that Thomas should not be able to discharge these debts because they were part of his domestic-support obligations. Are these debts dischargeable? Explain. [*In re Thomas*, 591 Fed.Appx. 443 (6th Cir. 2015)] (See *Bankruptcy Relief under Chapter 12 and Chapter 13.*)

22–8. A Question of Ethics—Discharge in Bankruptcy. Monica Sexton filed a petition for Chapter 13 reorganization. One of her creditors was Friedman's Jewelers. Her petition misclassified Friedman's claim as $800 of unsecured debt. Within days, Friedman's filed proof of a secured claim for $300 and an unsecured claim for $462. Eventually, Friedman's was sent payments of about $300 by check. None of the checks were cashed. By then, Friedman's had filed its own petition under Chapter 11, Bankruptcy Receivables Management (BRM) had bought Friedman's unpaid accounts, and the checks had not been forwarded. Sexton received a discharge on the completion of her plan. BRM was not notified. BRM wrote to Sexton's attorney to ask about the status of her case, but received no response. BRM demanded that Sexton surrender the collateral on its claim. Sexton asked the court to impose sanctions on BRM for violating the discharge order. [*In re Sexton*, 2011 WL 284180 (E.D.N.C. 2011)] (See *Chapter 7—Liquidation.*)

1. Was Sexton's debt to Friedman's dischargeable? Discuss.
2. Should BRM be sanctioned for willfully violating the discharge order? Why or why not?

Critical Thinking and Writing Assignments

22–9. Business Law Critical Thinking Group Assignment. Cathy Coleman took out loans to complete her college education. After graduation, Coleman was irregularly employed as a teacher. Eventually, she filed a petition in a federal bankruptcy court under Chapter 13. The court confirmed a five-year plan under which Coleman was required to commit all of her disposable income to paying the student loans. Less than a year later, when Coleman was laid off, she still owed more than $100,000 to Educational Credit Management Corp. Coleman asked the court to discharge the debt on the ground that it would be an undue hardship for her to pay it. (See *Bankruptcy Relief under Chapter 12 and Chapter 13.*)

1. The first group will explain when a debtor normally is entitled to a discharge under Chapter 13.
2. The second group will discuss whether student loans are dischargeable and when "undue hardship" is a legitimate ground for an exception.
3. The third group will outline the goals of bankruptcy law and make an argument, based on these facts and principles, in support of Coleman's request.

Unit Three—Business Case Study with Dissenting Opinion

First Bank v. Fischer & Frichtel, Inc.

When a borrower defaults on a mortgage, the lender may recover the remaining debt by foreclosing on the mortgaged property. In a judicial foreclosure—the method used in most states—the property is sold at auction under court supervision. If the proceeds are enough to cover the borrower's debt, the lender gets the proceeds, and the debt is satisfied. But if the proceeds are insufficient to cover the debt, the lender may obtain a deficiency judgment for the difference between the sale price and the amount owed.

In this *Business Case Study with Dissenting Opinion,* we review *First Bank v. Fischer & Frichtel, Inc.*[1] In this case, the lender was the only bidder at a judicial sale and bought the mortgaged property for far less than its fair market value. The Missouri Supreme Court had to determine the amount of the deficiency.

iStockPhoto.com/Cvisphoto

How is the deficiency in a foreclosure sale calculated?

CASE BACKGROUND

Fischer & Frichtel, Inc., is an experienced real estate developer based in Missouri. In June 2000, Fischer & Frichtel borrowed $2.58 million from First Bank in order to buy twenty-one lots of property for a residential development. Over the next five years, Fischer & Frichtel paid First Bank as it sold the lots, which served as collateral for the loan. When the housing market collapsed, however, Fischer & Frichtel was unable to pay First Bank for nine unsold lots.

Through a series of negotiations, First Bank extended the loan's maturity date from July 1, 2003, to September 1, 2008. When the loan matured, Fischer & Frichtel defaulted, still owing $1.13 million. First Bank foreclosed on the unsold lots and was the only bidder at the judicial sale. First Bank's winning bid of $466,000 was based on its estimate of the lots' value, the depressed state of the real estate market, and the fact that it would have to sell the lots in bulk rather than individually.

First Bank filed a suit seeking to recover the unpaid principal and interest on the loan. At trial, Fischer & Frichtel presented expert testimony showing that the lots' fair market value was $918,000. The trial judge instructed the jury that, if it found for First Bank, it "must award . . . the balance due . . . on the date of maturity, less the fair market value of the property at the time of the foreclosure sale, plus interest." Following the judge's instructions, the jury awarded First Bank $215,875. First Bank then moved for a new trial, arguing that it was entitled to the full difference between the sale price and the amount owed. The trial court granted First Bank's motion, and Fischer & Frichtel appealed to the Missouri Supreme Court.

MAJORITY OPINION

Laura Denvir *STITH,* Judge.

* * * *

Missouri and many * * * other states * * * require a debtor to pay as a deficiency the full difference between the debt and the foreclosure sale price. They do not permit a debtor to attack the sufficiency of the foreclosure sale price *as part of the deficiency proceeding* even if the debtor believes that the foreclosure sale price was inadequate.

This does not mean Missouri does not give a debtor a mechanism for attacking an inadequate foreclosure sale price. Rather, a debtor who believes that the foreclosure sale price was inadequate can bring an action to void the *foreclosure sale* itself. If the sale stands, then it has been thought fair to require the debtor to pay any deficiency remaining based on the foreclosure sale price.

* * * *

*Missouri permits the debtor to void a properly noticed and carried out foreclosure sale only by showing that "the inadequacy [of the sale price is] so gross that it shocks the conscience * * * and is in itself evidence of fraud."* * * * Missouri's standard for proving that a foreclosure sale "shocks the conscience" is among the strictest in the country; more than one Missouri case has refused to set aside a sale that was only 20 to 30 percent of the fair market value * * * . [Emphasis added.]

Fischer & Frichtel argues that this standard * * * almost inevitably leads to windfalls for lenders. Fischer & Frichtel suggests that the foreclosure process is unfair in part because cash must be offered for the property by the bidder. This is a problem for the ordinary bidder, particularly a homeowner or small business owner, because the

---

1. 364 S.W.3d 216 (Mo. 2012).

statutory minimum time period between notice of foreclosure and the actual sale is often less than a month, an insufficient amount of time to allow potential bidders to secure financing.

Fischer & Frichtel notes that the lender does not have this financing problem, as it does not have to pay with cash, but instead simply may deduct the purchase price from the amount of principal the borrower owes. Because realistically the lender often will be the sole bidder, it can buy the foreclosed property for far less than market value, sell the property at a profit and then collect a deficiency from the borrower based on the below-market value it paid for the property.

* * * *

* * * While the foreclosure sale price was barely more than 50 percent of the fair market value later determined by the jury, the lender gave cogent reasons for its lower bid due to the depressed real estate market and the bulk nature of the sale, as of trial the lender had not been able to sell the property, and Fischer & Frichtel has not argued it could not have purchased the property at the foreclosure sale * * * .

This is not a case, therefore, in which to consider a modification of the standard for setting aside a foreclosure sale solely due to inadequacy of price or whether a change should be made in the manner of determining a deficiency where the foreclosure price is less than the fair market value.

* * * *

For the reasons stated, the judgment of the trial court awarding a new trial is affirmed.

DISSENTING OPINION
Richard B. *TEITELMAN*, Chief Justice.

I respectfully dissent. The purpose of a damage award is to make the injured party whole without creating a windfall. Accordingly, in nearly every context in which a party sustains damage to or the loss of a property or business interest, Missouri law measures damages by reference to fair market value. Yet in the foreclosure context, Missouri law ignores the fair market value of the foreclosed property and, instead, measures the lender's damages with reference to the foreclosure sale price. Rather than making the injured party whole, this anomaly in the law of damages, in many cases, will require the defaulting party to subsidize a substantial windfall to the lender. Aside from the fact that this anomaly long has been a part of Missouri law, there is no other compelling reason for continued adherence to a measure of damages that too often enriches one party at the expense of another. Consequently, I would hold that damages in a deficiency action should be measured by reference to the fair market value of the foreclosed property.

* * * *

I would reverse the judgment sustaining First Bank's motion for a new trial and order the trial court to enter judgment consistent with the jury's finding that the fair market value of the foreclosed property was $918,000 and that Fischer & Fritchel therefore owed First Bank a deficiency of $215,875.

QUESTIONS FOR ANALYSIS

1. *Law.* What was the majority's decision? What were the reasons for its decision?

2. *Law.* Why did the dissent disagree with the majority? If the court had adopted the dissent's position, how would this have affected the result?

3. *Ethics.* Suppose that First Bank, the only bidder at the judicial sale, had submitted a winning bid of $1,000. Would First Bank's conduct have been ethical? Why or why not?

4. *Economic Dimensions.* Are there any reasons why the dissent's position might be more favorable for economic recovery from a recession? Explain your answer.

5. *Implications for the Businessperson.* What does the majority's ruling mean for a mortgagee that bids on a foreclosed property at a judicial sale? Explain your answer.

Unit Three—Business Scenario

Sonja owns a bakery in San Francisco.

1. **Performance of Sales Contracts.** Sonja orders two new model X23 McIntyre ovens from Western Heating Appliances for $16,000. Sonja and Western Heating agree orally, on the telephone, that Western will deliver the ovens within two weeks and that Sonja will pay for the ovens when they are delivered. Two days later, Sonja receives a fax from Western confirming her order. Before delivery, Sonja learns that she can obtain the same ovens from another company at a much lower price. Sonja wants to cancel her order, but Western refuses. Is the contract enforceable against Sonja? Why or why not?

2. **Banking.** To pay a supplier, Sonja issues a check to Milled Grains Co. that is drawn on United First Bank. A Milled Grains employee, with authorization, indorses the check and transfers it to Milled Grains' financial institution, Second Federal Bank. Second Federal puts the check into the regular bank collection process. If United First refuses to honor the check, who will ultimately suffer the loss? Could Sonja be subject to criminal prosecution if United First refuses to honor the check?

Continues

Amin Akhavan/ShutterStock.com

3. Security Interests. Sonja wants to borrow $40,000 from Credit National Bank to buy coffee-brewing equipment. If Credit National accepts Sonja's equipment as collateral for the loan, how does it let other potential creditors know of its interest? If Sonja fails to repay the loan, what are Credit National's alternatives with respect to collecting the amount due?

4. Creditors' Rights. Sonya borrows $20,000 from Ace Loan Co. to remodel the bakery and gives it to Jones Construction, a contractor, to do the work. The amount covers only half of the cost, but when Jones finishes the work, Sonja fails to pay the rest. Sonja also does not repay Ace for the loan. What can Jones do to collect what it is owed? What can Ace do?

Unit Three—Group Project

Sara contracted to buy a new Steinway grand piano for $52,400 from InTune Pianos. InTune delivered a piano that had been in storage for a year and had been moved at least six times. Sara considered the piano to be unacceptably damaged.

1. The first group will determine whether Sara can reject the piano.

2. The second group will assume that Sara sued InTune and will decide what would be the proper measure of recovery (what types of damages should be sought and what costs should be covered).

3. A third group will determine what types of warranties were implied in the sale of the piano and consider whether Sara could sue InTune based on breach of warranty.

30

CHAPTER OUTLINE

- Securities Act of 1933
- Securities Exchange Act of 1934
- State Securities Laws
- Corporate Governance

LEARNING OBJECTIVES

The five Learning Objectives *below are designed to help improve your understanding of the chapter. After reading this chapter, you should be able to answer the following questions:*

1. What is meant by the term *securities?*

2. What are the two major statutes regulating the securities industry?

3. What is insider trading? Why is it prohibited?

4. What are some of the features of state securities laws?

5. What certification requirements does the Sarbanes-Oxley Act impose on corporate executives?

Investor Protection, Insider Trading, and Corporate Governance

"You are remembered for the rules you break."

GENERAL DOUGLAS MACARTHUR
1880–1964
(U.S. ARMY GENERAL)

After the stock market crash of 1929, Congress enacted legislation to regulate securities markets. *Securities* generally are defined as any instruments representing corporate ownership (stock) or debts (bonds). The goal of regulation was to provide investors with more information to help them make buying and selling decisions about securities and to prohibit deceptive, unfair, and manipulative practices.

Today, the sale and transfer of securities are heavily regulated by federal and state statutes and by government agencies. Moreover, the Securities and Exchange Commission (SEC) has implemented new regulations since Congress passed the Dodd-Frank Wall Street Reform and Consumer Protection Act in 2010.[1] We discuss the role of the SEC in the regulation of securities laws in this chapter's *Landmark in the Law* feature.

Despite all efforts to regulate the securities markets, people continue to break the rules and are often remembered for it, as observed in the chapter-opening quotation. Consider Keith Seilhan, a former employee of BP. Seilhan was the person in charge of coordinating the company's clean-up efforts after the *Deepwater Horizon* oil spill in the Gulf of Mexico. When Seilhan realized how much oil was flowing into the Gulf—and before that information was released to

---

1. Pub. L. No. 111-203, July 21, 2010, 124 Stat. 1376; 12 U.S.C. Sections 5301 *et seq.*

LANDMARK IN THE LAW   The Securities and Exchange Commission

In 1931, in the wake of the stock market crash of 1929, the U.S. Senate passed a resolution calling for an extensive investigation of securities trading. The investigation led, ultimately, to the enactment of the Securities Act of 1933, which is also known as the *truth-in-securities* bill. In the following year, Congress passed the Securities Exchange Act. This 1934 act created the Securities and Exchange Commission (SEC).

MAJOR RESPONSIBILITIES OF THE SEC
The SEC was created as an independent regulatory agency with the function of administering the 1933 and 1934 acts. Its major responsibilities in this respect are as follows:

1. To interpret federal securities laws and investigate securities law violations.

2. To issue new rules and amend existing rules.

3. To oversee the inspection of securities firms, brokers, investment advisers, and ratings agencies.

4. To oversee private regulatory organizations in the securities, accounting, and auditing fields.

5. To coordinate U.S. securities regulation with federal, state, and foreign authorities.

THE SEC'S EXPANDING REGULATORY POWERS Since its creation, the SEC's regulatory functions have gradually been increased by legislation granting it authority in different areas. For instance, the Securities Enforcement Remedies and Penny Stock Reform Act of 1990[a] allowed SEC administrative law judges to hear cases involving more types of alleged securities law violations. In addition, the act gave courts the authority to prevent persons who have engaged in securities fraud from serving as officers and directors of publicly held corporations. The Securities Acts Amendments of 1993[b] authorized the SEC to seek sanctions against those who violate foreign securities laws.

The National Securities Markets Improvement Act of 1996[c] expanded the power of the SEC to exempt persons, securities, and transactions from the requirements of the securities laws. (This act is also known as the

Capital Markets Efficiency Act.) The act also limited the authority of the states to regulate certain securities transactions and investment advisory firms.[d] The Sarbanes-Oxley Act of 2002,[e] which you will read about later in this chapter, further expanded the authority of the SEC by directing it to issue new rules relating to corporate disclosure requirements.

APPLICATION TO TODAY'S WORLD *The SEC is working to make the regulatory process more efficient and more relevant to today's securities trading practices. To this end, the SEC has embraced modern technology and the Internet more completely than many other federal agencies have. For example, the agency now requires companies to file certain information electronically so that it can be posted on the SEC's EDGAR (Electronic Data Gathering, Analysis, and Retrieval) database.*

---

a. 15 U.S.C. Section 77g.
b. 15 U.S.C. Section 78a.
c. 15 U.S.C. Sections 77z-3, 78mm.

---

d. 15 U.S.C. Section 80b-3a.
e. 15 U.S.C. Sections 7201 *et seq.*

---

the public—he sold $1 million of his family's BP securities. By doing so, he avoided significant losses, because when the news came out about the magnitude of the oil spill, BP stock prices dropped by around 48 percent. The SEC charged Seilhan with insider trading in 2014, and he agreed to settle the case and return the ill-gotten gains, plus interest and penalties.

30-1 Securities Act of 1933

LEARNING OBJECTIVE 1

What is meant by the term *securities?*

The Securities Act of 1933[2] governs initial sales of stock by businesses. The act was designed to prohibit various forms of fraud and to stabilize the securities industry by requiring that all essential information concerning the issuance of securities be made available to the investing public. Basically, the purpose of this act is to require disclosure. The act provides that all securities transactions must be registered with the SEC unless they qualify for an exemption.

---

2. 15 U.S.C. Sections 77–77aa.

30–1a What Is a Security?

Section 2(1) of the Securities Act contains a broad definition of securities, which generally include the following:[3]

1. Instruments and interests commonly known as securities, such as preferred and common stocks, treasury stocks, bonds, debentures, and stock warrants.

2. Any interests, such as stock options, puts, calls, or other types of privilege on a security or on the right to purchase a security or a group of securities on a national security exchange.

3. Notes, instruments, or other evidence of indebtedness, including certificates of interest in a profit-sharing agreement and certificates of deposit.

4. Any fractional undivided interest in oil, gas, or other mineral rights.

5. Investment contracts, which include interests in limited partnerships and other investment schemes.

During the stock market crash of 1929, hordes of investors crowded Wall Street to find out the latest news. How did the "crash" affect stock trading in the years thereafter?

The Howey Test In interpreting the act, the United States Supreme Court has held that an **investment contract** is any transaction in which a person (1) invests (2) in a common enterprise (3) reasonably expecting profits (4) derived *primarily* or *substantially* from others' managerial or entrepreneurial efforts. Known as the *Howey* test, this definition continues to guide the determination of what types of contracts can be considered securities.[4]

CASE EXAMPLE 30.1 James Nistler and his wife bought undeveloped land in Jackson County, Oregon, and created an LLC to develop it. The property, called Tennessee Acres, was divided into six lots. Nistler obtained investors for the development by telling them that they would earn 12 to 15 percent interest on their investment and be repaid in full within a specified time. The property was never developed, the investors were never paid, and a substantial part of the funds provided by investors were used to pay Nistler and his wife.

Nistler was convicted of securities fraud. He appealed, claiming that the investments at issue did not involve "securities," but a state appellate court affirmed his conviction. The court found that there had been a pooling of funds from a group of investors, whose interests had been secured by the same land. The value of that land had been highly dependent on Nistler's use of the investors' funds to develop the land. In other words, the investors had engaged in a common enterprise from which they reasonably expected to profit, and that profit would be derived from the development efforts of Nistler.[5] ▪

Many Types of Securities For our purposes, it is probably convenient to think of securities in their most common forms—stocks and bonds issued by corporations. Bear in mind, though, that securities can take many forms, including interests in whiskey, cosmetics, worms, beavers, boats, vacuum cleaners, muskrats, and cemetery lots. Almost any stake in the ownership or debt of a company can be considered a security. Investment contracts in condominiums, franchises, limited partnerships in real estate, and oil or gas or other mineral rights have qualified as securities as well.

> **Investment Contract**
> In securities law, a transaction in which a person invests in a common enterprise reasonably expecting profits that are derived primarily from the efforts of others.

Securities are not limited to stocks and bonds but can encompass a wide variety of legal claims. The analysis hinges on the nature of the transaction rather than on the particular instrument or rights involved. Because Congress enacted securities laws to regulate

PREVENTING LEGAL DISPUTES

---

3. 15 U.S.C. Section 77b(1). Amendments in 1982 added stock options.
4. *SEC v. W. J. Howey Co.,* 328 U.S. 293, 66 S.Ct. 1100, 90 L.Ed. 1244 (1946).
5. *State v. Nistler,* 286 Or.App. 470, 342 P.3d 1035 (2015).

investments, in whatever form and by whatever name they are called, almost any type of security that might be sold as an investment can be subject to securities laws. When in doubt about whether an investment transaction involves securities, seek the advice of a specialized attorney.

30-1b Registration Statement

Section 5 of the Securities Act of 1933 broadly provides that a security must be *registered* before being offered to the public unless it qualifies for an exemption. The issuing corporation must file a *registration statement* with the SEC and must provide all investors with a *prospectus*.

A **prospectus** is a written disclosure document that describes the security being sold, the financial operations of the issuing corporation, and the investment or risk attaching to the security. The prospectus also serves as a selling tool for the issuing corporation. The SEC now allows an issuer to deliver its prospectus to investors electronically via the Internet.[6]

In principle, the registration statement and the prospectus supply sufficient information to enable unsophisticated investors to evaluate the financial risk involved.

Contents of the Registration Statement
The registration statement must be written in plain English and fully describe the following:

1. The securities being offered for sale, including their relationship to the issuer's other securities.

2. The corporation's properties and business (including a financial statement certified by an independent public accounting firm).

3. The management of the corporation, including managerial compensation, stock options, pensions, and other benefits. Any interests of directors or officers in any material transactions with the corporation must be disclosed.

4. How the corporation intends to use the proceeds of the sale.

5. Any pending lawsuits or special risk factors.

All companies, both domestic and foreign, must file their registration statements electronically so that they can be posted on the SEC's EDGAR (Electronic Data Gathering, Analysis, and Retrieval) database. The EDGAR database includes material on initial public offerings, proxy statements, corporations' annual reports, registration statements, and other documents that have been filed with the SEC. Investors can access the database via the Internet (**www .sec.gov/edgar.shtml**) to obtain information that can be used to make investment decisions.

The Registration Process
The registration statement does not become effective until after it has been reviewed and approved by the SEC (unless it is filed by a *well-known seasoned issuer,* as will be discussed shortly). The process includes several stages, and the 1933 act restricts the types of activities that an issuer can engage in at each stage.

Prefiling Period. During the *prefiling period* (before the registration statement is filed), the issuer normally cannot sell or offer to sell the securities. Once the registration statement has been filed, a waiting period begins while the SEC reviews the registration statement for completeness.[7]

Prospectus A written document required by securities laws when a security is being sold. The prospectus describes the security, the financial operations of the issuing corporation, and the risk attaching to the security.

KNOW THIS
The purpose of the Securities Act of 1933 is disclosure. The SEC does not consider whether a security is worth the investment price.

What act requires securities to be registered?

---

6. Basically, an electronic prospectus must meet the same requirements as a printed prospectus. The SEC has special rules that address situations in which the graphics, images, or audio files in a printed prospectus cannot be reproduced in an electronic form. 17 C.F.R. Section 232.304.

7. The waiting period must last at least twenty days but always extends much longer because the SEC invariably requires numerous changes and additions to the registration statement.

Waiting Period. During the *waiting period,* or *quiet period,* the securities can be offered for sale but cannot legally be sold. Only certain types of offers are allowed during this period.

All issuers can now distribute a *preliminary prospectus,* which contains most of the information that will be included in the final prospectus but often does not include a price. Most issuers can also distribute a *free-writing prospectus.*[8] A **free-writing prospectus** is any type of written, electronic, or graphic offer that describes the issuer or its securities and includes a legend indicating that the investor may obtain the prospectus at the SEC's Web site.

Posteffective Period. Once the SEC has reviewed and approved the registration statement and the waiting period is over, the registration is effective, and the *posteffective period* begins. The issuer can now offer and sell the securities without restrictions. If the company issued a preliminary or free-writing prospectus to investors, it must provide those investors with a final prospectus either before or at the time they purchase the securities. The issuer can force investors to download the final prospectus from a Web site if it notifies them of the appropriate Internet address.

Well-Known Seasoned Issuers
In 2005, the SEC revised the registration process and loosened some of the restrictions on large, experienced issuers.[9] The rules created new categories of issuers depending on their size and presence in the market and provided a simplified registration process for these issuers. The large, well-known firms that issue most securities have the greatest flexibility.

A firm that has issued at least $1 billion in securities in the previous three years or has at least $700 million of value of outstanding stock in the hands of the public is considered a *well-known seasoned issuer* (WKSI). WKSIs can file registration statements the day they announce a new offering and are not required to wait for SEC review and approval. They can also use a free-writing prospectus at any time, even during the prefiling period.

30–1c Exempt Securities and Transactions

Certain types of securities are exempt from the registration requirements of the Securities Act. These securities—which generally can also be resold without being registered—are summarized in Exhibit 30–1 under the "Exempt Securities" heading.[10]

The exhibit also lists and describes certain transactions that are exempt from registration requirements under various SEC regulations. The transaction exemptions are the most important because they are very broad and can enable an issuer to avoid the high cost and complicated procedures associated with registration. Because the coverage of the exemptions overlaps somewhat, an offering may qualify for more than one. Therefore, many sales of securities occur without registration. Even when a transaction is exempt from the registration requirements, the offering is still subject to the antifraud provisions of the 1933 act (as well as those of the 1934 act, to be discussed later in this chapter).

Regulation A Offerings
Securities issued by an issuer that has offered less than $50 million in securities during any twelve-month period are exempt from registration.[11] (The cap was $5 million until 2015, when the SEC approved rule changes to make it easier for small and midsized businesses to raise capital. These changes were made in connection with the Jumpstart Our Business Startups, or JOBS, Act.[12] Expanding the issuers that qualify for exemption under Regulation A will eventually decrease the significance of the other exemptions listed in Exhibit 30–1.)

Free-Writing Prospectus
A written, electronic, or graphic communication associated with the offer to sell a security and used during the waiting period to supplement other information about the security.

KNOW THIS
The issuer of an exempt security does not have to disclose the same information as other issuers.

---

8. See SEC Rules 164 and 433.
9. Securities Offering Reform, codified at 17 C.F.R. Sections 200, 228, 229, 230, 239, 240, 243, 249, and 274.
10. 15 U.S.C. Section 77c.
11. 15 U.S.C. Section 77c(b).
12. Pub. L. No. 112-106 (April 5, 2012).

Exhibit 30–1 Exemptions for Securities Offerings under the 1933 Securities Act

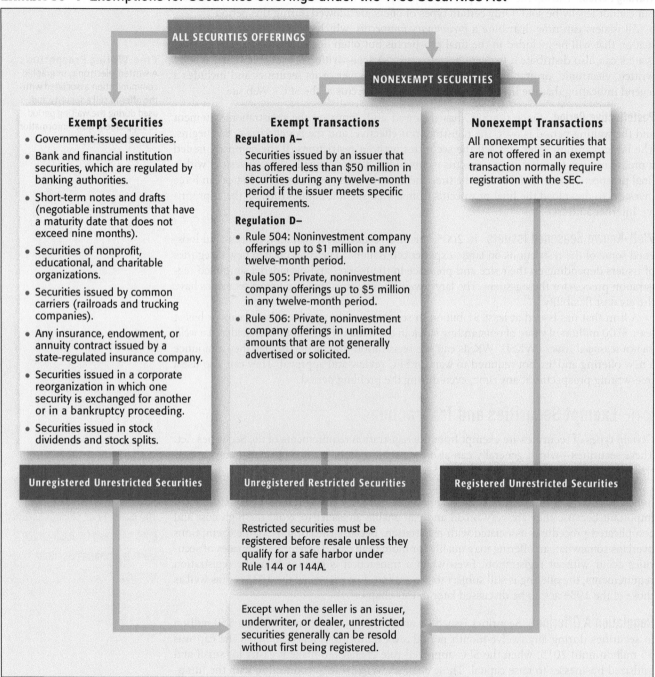

Under Regulation A,[13] the issuer must file with the SEC a notice of the issue and an offering circular, which must also be provided to investors before the sale. Additional review requirements apply to issuers raising between $20 and $50 million. Overall, Regulation A provides a process much simpler and less expensive than full registration.

13. 17 C.F.R. Sections 230.251–230.263.

Companies are allowed to "test the waters" for potential interest before preparing the offering circular. To *test the waters* means to determine potential interest without actually selling any securities or requiring any commitment on the part of those who express interest.

Some companies have sold their securities via the Internet under Regulation A. **EXAMPLE 30.2** The Spring Street Brewing Company became the first company to sell securities via an online initial public offering (IPO). Spring Street raised about $1.6 million—without having to pay any commissions to brokers or underwriters. ■ Such online IPOs are particularly attractive to small companies and start-up ventures that may find it difficult to raise capital from institutional investors or through underwriters.

Small Offerings—Regulation D

The SEC's Regulation D contains several exemptions from registration requirements (Rules 504, 505, and 506) for offers that either involve a small dollar amount or are made in a limited manner.

Rule 504. Rule 504 is the exemption used by most small businesses. It provides that noninvestment company offerings up to $1 million in any twelve-month period are exempt. Noninvestment companies are firms that are not engaged primarily in the business of investing or trading in securities. (In contrast, an **investment company** is a firm that buys a large portfolio of securities and professionally manages it on behalf of many smaller shareholders/owners. A **mutual fund** is a type of investment company.)

EXAMPLE 30.3 Zeta Enterprises is a limited partnership that develops commercial property. Zeta intends to offer $600,000 of its limited partnership interests for sale between June 1 and May 31. According to the definition of a security (discussed earlier in this chapter), this offering would be subject to the registration and prospectus requirements of the 1933 Securities Act.

Under Rule 504, however, the sales of Zeta's interests are exempt from these requirements because Zeta is a noninvestment company making an offering of less than $1 million in a twelve-month period. Therefore, Zeta can sell its limited partnership interests without filing a registration statement with the SEC or issuing a prospectus to any investor. ■

Rule 505. Another exemption is available under Rule 505 for private, noninvestment company offerings up to $5 million in any twelve-month period. The offer may be made to an unlimited number of *accredited investors* and up to thirty-five unaccredited investors. **Accredited investors** include banks, insurance companies, investment companies, employee benefit plans, the issuer's executive officers and directors, and persons whose income or net worth exceeds a certain threshold.

The SEC must be notified of the sales, and precautions must be taken, because these restricted securities may be resold only by registration or in an exempt transaction. No general solicitation or advertising is allowed. The issuer must provide any unaccredited investors with disclosure documents that generally are the same as those used in registered offerings.

Rule 506—Private Placement Exemption. Rule 506 exempts private, noninvestment company offerings in unlimited amounts that are not generally solicited or advertised. This exemption is often referred to as the *private placement* exemption because it exempts "transactions not involving any public offering."[14] To qualify for the exemption, the issuer must believe that each unaccredited investor has sufficient knowledge or experience in financial matters to be capable of evaluating the investment's merits and risks.[15]

The private placement exemption is perhaps most important to firms that want to raise funds through the sale of securities without registering them. **EXAMPLE 30.4** Citco Corporation needs to raise capital to expand its operations. Citco decides to make a private $10 million offering of its common stock directly to two hundred accredited investors and thirty highly

---

14. 15 U.S.C. Section 77d(2).
15. 17 C.F.R. Section 230.506.

Investment Company
A company that acts on the behalf of many smaller shareholders-owners by buying a large portfolio of securities and professionally managing that portfolio.

Mutual Fund A specific type of investment company that continually buys or sells to investors shares of ownership in a portfolio.

iStockPhoto.com/g-stockstudio

How did the Spring Street Brewing Company avoid paying commissions to brokers and underwriters when it held its initial public offering (IPO)?

Accredited Investor In the context of securities offerings, sophisticated investors, such as banks, insurance companies, investment companies, the issuer's executive officers and directors, and persons whose income or net worth exceeds certain limits.

KNOW THIS

An investor can be "sophisticated" by virtue of his or her education and experience or by virtue of investing through a knowledgeable, experienced representative.

sophisticated, but unaccredited, investors. Citco provides all of these investors with a prospectus and material information about the firm, including its most recent financial statements.

As long as Citco notifies the SEC of the sale, this offering will likely qualify for the private placement exemption. The offering is nonpublic and not generally advertised. There are fewer than thirty-five unaccredited investors, and each of them possesses sufficient knowledge and experience to evaluate the risks involved. The issuer has provided all purchasers with the necessary material information. Thus, Citco will *not* be required to comply with the registration requirements of the Securities Act of 1933. ■

Resales and Safe Harbor Rules Most securities can be resold without registration. The Securities Act provides exemptions for resales by most persons other than issuers or underwriters. Thus, the average investor who sells shares of stock does not have to file a registration statement with the SEC.

Resales of restricted securities, however, trigger the registration requirements unless the party selling them complies with Rule 144 or Rule 144A. These rules are sometimes referred to as "safe harbors."

Rule 144. Rule 144 exempts restricted securities from registration on resale if all of the following conditions are met:

1. There is adequate current public information about the issuer. ("Adequate current public information" refers to the reports that certain companies are required to file under the 1934 Securities Exchange Act.)

2. The person selling the securities has owned them for at least six months, if the issuer is subject to the reporting requirements of the 1934 act.[16] If the issuer is not subject to the 1934 act's reporting requirements, the seller must have owned the securities for at least one year.

3. The securities are sold in certain limited amounts in unsolicited brokers' transactions.

4. The SEC is notified of the resale.[17]

Rule 144A. Securities that at the time of issue are not of the same class as securities listed on a national securities exchange or quoted in a U.S. automated interdealer quotation system may be resold under Rule 144A.[18] They may be sold only to a qualified institutional buyer (an institution, such as an insurance company or a bank, that owns and invests at least $100 million in securities). The seller must take reasonable steps to ensure that the buyer knows that the seller is relying on the exemption under Rule 144A.

30–1d Violations of the 1933 Act

It is a violation of the Securities Act to intentionally defraud investors by misrepresenting or omitting facts in a registration statement or prospectus. Liability may also be imposed on those who are negligent with respect to the preparation of these publications. Selling securities before the effective date of the registration statement or under an exemption for which the securities do not qualify also results in liability.

Can the omission of a fact make a statement of opinion misleading to an ordinary investor? That was the question before the United States Supreme Court in the following case.

---

16. Before 2008, when amendments to Rule 144 became effective, the holding period was one year if the issuer was subject to the reporting requirements of the 1934 act. See the revised SEC Rules and Regulations at 72 Federal Rules 71546-01, 2007 WL 4368599, Release No. 33-8869. This reduced holding period allows nonpublic issuers to raise capital electronically from private and overseas sources more quickly.
17. 17 C.F.R. Section 230.144.
18. 17 C.F.R. Section 230.144A.

CASE 30.1

Omnicare, Inc. v. Laborers District Council Construction Industry Pension Fund

Supreme Court of the United States, __ U.S. __, 135 S.Ct. 1318, 191 L.Ed.2d 253 (2015).

FACTS Omnicare, Inc., a pharmacy services company, filed a registration statement in connection with a public offering. The statement expressed the company's opinion that it was in compliance with federal and state laws. Later, the federal government accused Omnicare of receiving kickbacks from pharmaceutical manufacturers. The Laborers District Council Construction Industry Pension Fund and others (the Funds), who had bought the stock, filed a suit in a federal district court against Omnicare.

The plaintiffs alleged that Omnicare's legal-compliance opinion was "untrue" and that Omnicare had, in violation of the Securities Act, "omitted to state [material] facts necessary" to make that opinion not misleading. Omnicare claimed that "no reasonable person, in any context, can understand a pure statement of opinion to convey anything more than the speaker's own mindset." The court dismissed the suit. The U.S. Court of Appeals for the Sixth Circuit reversed the dismissal in part and affirmed in part. The Funds appealed to the United States Supreme Court.

ISSUE If a registration statement omits material facts about the issuer's inquiry into or knowledge concerning a statement of opinion, and those facts conflict with what a reasonable investor would understand from the statement, is the issuer liable under the Securities Act?

DECISION Yes. The Court vacated the lower courts' decision. But because "neither court . . . considered the Funds' omissions theory with the right standard in mind," the Court remanded the case "for

What requirements does a drug company need to satisfy to file an accurate registration statement?

a determination of whether the Funds have stated a viable omissions claim (or, if not, whether they should have a chance to replead)."

REASON Whether a statement is "misleading" depends on the perspective of a reasonable investor. A reasonable investor may, depending on the circumstances, understand a statement of opinion to convey particular facts about the speaker's basis for holding that view. If the real facts are otherwise, and are not provided, the statement will mislead its audience. An opinion statement is not misleading, however, simply because an issuer knows "some fact cutting the other way" and fails to disclose it. A reasonable investor does not expect that every fact known to an issuer supports the issuer's opinion. Moreover, whether an omission of fact makes a statement of opinion misleading depends on the context.

Registration statements are formal documents—a reasonable investor would expect an opinion in such a statement to be more carefully considered than an opinion casually expressed in daily life. In addition, the investor reads the statement "in light of all its surrounding text, including hedges, disclaimers, and apparently conflicting information," as well as the customs and practices of the issuer's business. The Securities Act "creates liability only for the omission of material facts that cannot be squared with such a fair reading."

CRITICAL THINKING—Legal Consideration *Would a reasonable investor have cause to complain if an issuer, without having consulted a lawyer, states, "We believe our conduct is lawful"? Explain.*

Remedies Criminal violations are prosecuted by the U.S. Department of Justice. Violators may be fined up to $10,000, imprisoned for up to five years, or both.

The SEC is authorized to seek civil sanctions against those who willfully violate the 1933 act. It can request an injunction to prevent further sales of the securities involved or ask the court to grant other relief, such as an order to a violator to refund profits. Parties who purchase securities and suffer harm as a result of false or omitted statements may also bring suits in a federal court to recover their losses and other damages.

Defenses There are three basic defenses to charges of violations under the 1933 act. A defendant can avoid liability by proving any of the following:

1. The statement or omission was not material.

2. The plaintiff knew about the misrepresentation at the time of purchasing the stock.

3. The defendant exercised *due diligence* in preparing the registration and reasonably believed at the time that the statements were true and there were no omissions of material facts.

CASE EXAMPLE 30.5 In preparation for an initial public offering (IPO), Blackstone Group, LP, filed a registration statement with the SEC. At the time, Blackstone's corporate private equity investments included FGIC Corporation (which insured investments in subprime mortgages) and Freescale Semiconductor, Inc. Before the IPO, FGIC's customers began to suffer large losses, and Freescale lost an exclusive contract to make wireless 3G chipsets for Motorola, Inc. (its largest customer). The losses suffered by these two companies would affect Blackstone. Nevertheless, Blackstone's registration statement did not mention the impact on its revenues of the investments in FGIC and Freescale.

Martin Litwin and others who invested in Blackstone's IPO filed a suit in a federal district court against Blackstone and its officers, alleging material omissions from the statement. Blackstone argued as a defense that the omissions were not material, and the lower court dismissed the case. The plaintiffs appealed. A federal appellate court ruled in favor of the plaintiffs that the alleged omissions were reasonably likely to be material, and remanded the case. The plaintiffs were entitled to the opportunity to prove at a trial that Blackstone had omitted material information that it was required to disclose.[19] ■

LEARNING OBJECTIVE 2
What are the two major statutes regulating the securities industry?

Blackstone Group, LP, owned a large interest in Freescale Semiconductor, Inc. Should Blackstone have revealed in its registration statement that Freescale had lost a major 3G chipset order?

SEC Rule 10b-5 A rule of the Securities and Exchange Commission that prohibits the commission of fraud in connection with the purchase or sale of any security.

30-2 Securities Exchange Act of 1934

The 1934 Securities Exchange Act provides for the regulation and registration of securities exchanges, brokers, dealers, and national securities associations, such as the National Association of Securities Dealers (NASD). Unlike the 1933 act, which is a one-time disclosure law, the 1934 act provides for continuous periodic disclosures by publicly held corporations to enable the SEC to regulate subsequent trading.

The Securities Exchange Act applies to companies that have assets in excess of $10 million and five hundred or more shareholders. These corporations are referred to as *Section 12 companies* because they are required to register their securities under Section 12 of the 1934 act. Section 12 companies must file reports with the SEC annually and quarterly, and sometimes even monthly if specified events occur (such as a merger). Other provisions in the 1934 act require all securities brokers and dealers to be registered, to keep detailed records of their activities, and to file annual reports with the SEC.

The act also authorizes the SEC to engage in market surveillance to deter undesirable market practices such as fraud, market manipulation (attempts at illegally influencing stock prices), and misrepresentation. In addition, the act provides for the SEC's regulation of proxy solicitations for voting.

30-2a Section 10(b), SEC Rule 10b-5, and Insider Trading

Section 10(b) is an especially important section of the Securities Exchange Act. This section proscribes the use of any manipulative or deceptive mechanism in violation of SEC rules and regulations. Among the rules that the SEC has promulgated pursuant to Section 10(b) is **SEC Rule 10b-5,** which prohibits the commission of fraud in connection with the purchase or sale of any security.

SEC Rule 10b-5 applies to almost all cases concerning the trading of securities, whether on organized exchanges, in over-the-counter markets, or in private transactions. Generally, the rule covers just about any form of security, and the securities need not be registered under the 1933 act for the 1934 act to apply.

---

19. *Litwin v. Blackstone Group, LP,* 634 F.3d 706 (2d Cir. 2011).

Private parties can sue for securities fraud under the 1934 act and SEC Rule 10b-5. The basic elements of a securities fraud action are as follows:

1. A *material misrepresentation* (or omission) in connection with the purchase and sale of securities.
2. *Scienter* (a wrongful state of mind).
3. *Reliance* by the plaintiff on the material misrepresentation.
4. An *economic loss*.
5. *Causation*, meaning that there is a causal connection between the misrepresentation and the loss.

Insider Trading One of the major goals of Section 10(b) and SEC Rule 10b-5 is to prevent so-called **insider trading,** which occurs when persons buy or sell securities on the basis of information that is not available to the public. Corporate directors, officers, and majority shareholders, for instance, often have advance inside information that can affect the future market value of the corporate stock. Obviously, if they act on this information, their positions give them a trading advantage over the general public and other shareholders.

The 1934 act defines inside information and extends liability to those who take advantage of such information in their personal transactions when they know that the information is unavailable to those with whom they are dealing. Section 10(b) of the 1934 act and SEC Rule 10b-5 apply to anyone who has access to or receives information of a nonpublic nature on which trading is based—not just to corporate "insiders."

Disclosure under SEC Rule 10b-5 Any material omission or misrepresentation of material facts in connection with the purchase or sale of a security may violate not only the Securities Act of 1933 but also the antifraud provisions of Section 10(b) of the 1934 act and SEC Rule 10b-5. The key to liability (which can be civil or criminal) under Section 10(b) and SEC Rule 10b-5 is whether the insider's information is *material.*

The following are some examples of material facts calling for disclosure under SEC Rule 10b-5:

1. Fraudulent trading in the company's stock by a broker-dealer.
2. A dividend change (whether up or down).
3. A contract for the sale of corporate assets.
4. A new discovery, a new process, or a new product.
5. A significant change in the firm's financial condition.
6. Potential litigation against the company.

Note that any one of these facts, by itself, is not *automatically* considered a material fact. Rather, it will be regarded as a material fact if it is significant enough that it would likely affect an investor's decision as to whether to purchase or sell the company's securities.

EXAMPLE 30.6 Sheen, Inc., is the defendant in a class-action product liability suit that its attorney, Paula Frasier, believes that the company will lose. Frasier has advised Sheen's directors, officers, and accountants that the company will likely have to pay a substantial damages award. Sheen plans to make a $5 million offering of newly issued stock before the date when the trial is expected to end. Sheen's potential liability and the financial consequences to the firm are material facts that must be disclosed, because they are significant enough to affect an investor's decision as to whether to purchase the stock. ■

The following is a *Classic Case* interpreting materiality under SEC Rule 10b-5.

KNOW THIS
A required element in any fraud claim is reliance. The innocent party must justifiably have relied on the misrepresentation.

LEARNING OBJECTIVE 3
What is insider trading? Why is it prohibited?

Insider Trading The purchase or sale of securities on the basis of information that has not been made available to the public.

★★★ CLASSIC CASE 30.2 ★★★

Securities and Exchange Commission v. Texas Gulf Sulphur Co.

United States Court of Appeals, Second Circuit, 401 F.2d 833 (1968).

HISTORICAL AND ENVIRONMENTAL SETTING *In 1957, the Texas Gulf Sulphur Company began exploring for minerals in eastern Canada. In March 1959, aerial geophysical surveys were conducted over more than fifteen thousand square miles of the area. The operations revealed numerous variations in the conductivity of the rock, which indicated a remarkable concentration of commercially exploitable minerals. One site of such variations was near Timmins, Ontario. On October 29 and 30, 1963, a ground survey of the site near Timmins indicated a need to drill for further evaluation.*

FACTS On November 12, 1963, the Texas Gulf Sulphur Company (TGS) drilled a hole that appeared to yield a core with an exceedingly high mineral content, although further drilling would be necessary to establish whether there was enough ore to be mined commercially. TGS kept secret the results of the core sample.

After learning of the ore discovery, officers and employees of the company made substantial purchases of TGS's stock or accepted stock options (rights to purchase stock). On April 11, 1964, an unauthorized report of the mineral find appeared in the newspapers. On the following day, April 12, TGS issued a press release that played down the discovery and stated that it was too early to tell whether the ore find would be significant.

Later on, TGS announced a strike of at least 25 million tons of ore. The news led to a substantial increase in the price of TGS stock. The Securities and Exchange Commission (SEC) brought a suit in a federal district court against the officers and employees of TGS for violating the insider-trading prohibition of SEC Rule 10b-5. The officers and employees argued that the prohibition did not apply. They reasoned that the information on which they had traded was not material, as the find had not been commercially proved. The trial court held that most of the defendants had not violated SEC Rule 10b-5, and the SEC appealed.

ISSUE Did the officers and employees of TGS violate SEC Rule 10b-5 by buying the stock, even though they did not know the full extent

After sample drilling revealed potential mineral deposits, company executives made large stock purchases. Did they violate insider trading laws?

and profit potential of the ore discovery at the time of their purchases?

DECISION Yes. The U.S. Court of Appeals for the Second Circuit reversed the lower court's decision and remanded the case for further proceedings, holding that the employees and officers had violated SEC Rule 10b-5's prohibition against insider trading.

REASON For SEC Rule 10b-5 purposes, the test of materiality is whether the information would affect the judgment of reasonable investors. Reasonable investors include speculative as well as conservative investors. "A major factor in determining whether the . . . discovery [of the ore] was a material fact is the importance attached to the drilling results by those who knew about it. . . . The timing by those who knew of it of their stock purchases and their purchases of short-term calls [rights to buy shares at a specified price within a specified time period]—purchases in some cases by individuals who had never before purchased calls or even TGS stock— virtually compels the inference that the insiders were influenced by the drilling results. . . . We hold, therefore, that all transactions in TGS stock or calls by individuals apprised of the drilling results . . . were made in violation of Rule 10b-5."

IMPACT OF THIS CASE ON TODAY'S LAW *This landmark case affirmed the principle that the test of whether information is "material," for SEC Rule 10b-5 purposes, is whether it would affect the judgment of reasonable investors. The corporate insiders' purchases of stock and stock options indicated that they were influenced by the results and that the information about the drilling results was material. The courts continue to cite this case when applying SEC Rule 10b-5 to cases of alleged insider trading.*

Outsiders and SEC Rule 10b-5 The traditional insider-trading case involves true insiders— corporate officers, directors, and majority shareholders who have access to (and trade on) inside information. Increasingly, liability under Section 10(b) of the 1934 act and SEC Rule 10b-5 is being extended to certain "outsiders"—persons who trade on inside information acquired indirectly. Two theories have been developed under which outsiders may be held liable for insider trading: the *tipper/tippee theory* and the *misappropriation theory.*

Tipper/Tippee Theory. Anyone who acquires inside information as a result of a corporate insider's breach of his or her fiduciary duty can be liable under SEC Rule 10b-5. This liability extends to **tippees** (those who receive "tips" from insiders) and even remote tippees (tippees of tippees).

Tippee A person who receives inside information.

The key to liability under this theory is that the inside information must be obtained as a result of someone's breach of a fiduciary duty to the corporation whose shares are involved in the trading. The tippee is liable under this theory only if the following requirements are met:

1. There is a breach of a duty not to disclose inside information.

2. The disclosure is in exchange for personal benefit.

3. The tippee knows (or should know) of this breach and benefits from it.

CASE EXAMPLE 30.7 Eric McPhail was a member of the same country club as an executive at American Superconductor. While they were golfing, the executive shared information with McPhail about the company's expected earnings, contracts, and other major developments, trusting that McPhail would keep the information confidential. Instead, McPhail repeatedly tipped six of his other golfing buddies at the country club, and they all used the nonpublic information to their advantage in trading. In this situation, the executive breached his duty not to disclose the information, which McPhail knew. McPhail (the tippee) is liable under SEC Rule 10b-5, and so are his other golfing buddies (remote tippees). All traded on inside information to their benefit.[20] ■

Misappropriation Theory. Liability for insider trading may also be established under the misappropriation theory. Under this theory, an individual who wrongfully obtains (misappropriates) inside information and trades on it for her or his personal gain should be held liable because, in essence, she or he stole information rightfully belonging to another.

The misappropriation theory has been controversial because it significantly extends the reach of SEC Rule 10b-5 to outsiders who ordinarily would *not* be deemed fiduciaries of the corporations in whose stock they trade. It is not always wrong to disclose material, nonpublic information about a company to another person. Nevertheless, a person who obtains the information and trades securities on it can be liable.[21]

Insider Reporting and Trading—Section 16(b)

Section 16(b) of the 1934 act provides for the recapture by the corporation of all profits realized by an insider on a purchase and sale, or sale and purchase, of the corporation's stock within any six-month period.[22] It is irrelevant whether the insider actually uses inside information—all such **short-swing profits** must be returned to the corporation.

In this context, *insiders* means officers, directors, and large stockholders of Section 12 corporations. (Large stockholders are those owning at least 10 percent of the class of equity securities registered under Section 12 of the 1934 act.) To discourage such insiders from using nonpublic information about their companies for their personal benefit in the stock market, the SEC requires them to file reports concerning their ownership and trading of the corporation's securities.

Section 16(b) applies not only to stock but also to stock warrants, options, and securities convertible into stock. In addition, the courts have fashioned complex rules for determining profits. Note, however, that the SEC exempts a number of transactions under Rule 16b-3.[23]

> "The way to stop financial 'joy-riding' is to arrest the chauffeur, not the automobile."
>
> **WOODROW WILSON**
> 1856–1924
> (TWENTY-EIGHTH PRESIDENT OF THE UNITED STATES, 1913–1921)

A golfer obtains inside information while playing with an executive of a listed company. The golfer then tells his friends about this valuable information. What are the friends called in securities law?

Short-Swing Profits Profits earned by a purchase and sale, or sale and purchase, of the same security within a six-month period.

---

20. Three of the defendants in this case agreed to settle with the SEC and return the trading profits. See SEC press release 2014-134 "SEC Charges Group of Amateur Golfers in Insider Trading Ring."

21. See, for example, *United States v. Gansman*, 657 F.3d 85 (2d Cir. 2011).

22. A person who expects the price of a particular stock to decline can realize profits by "selling short"—selling at a high price and repurchasing later at a lower price to cover the "short sale."

23. 17 C.F.R. Section 240.16b-3.

Exhibit 30–2 Comparison of Coverage, Application, and Liability under SEC Rule 10b-5 and Section 16(b)

AREA OF COMPARISON	SEC RULE 10b-5	SECTION 16(b)
What is the subject matter of the transaction?	Any security (does not have to be registered).	Any security (does not have to be registered).
What transactions are covered?	Purchase or sale.	Short-swing purchase and sale or short-swing sale and purchase.
Who is subject to liability?	Almost anyone with inside information under a duty to disclose—including officers, directors, controlling shareholders, and tippees.	Officers, directors, and shareholders who own 10 percent or more of the relevant class of securities.
Is omission or misrepresentation necessary for liability?	Yes.	No.
Are there any exempt transactions?	No.	Yes, there are a number of exemptions.
Who may bring an action?	A person transacting with an insider, the SEC, or a purchaser or seller damaged by a wrongful act.	A corporation or a shareholder by derivative action.

Exhibit 30–2 compares the effects of SEC Rule 10b-5 and Section 16(b). Because of these and other effects, corporate insiders are wise to seek specialized counsel before trading in the corporation's stock.

The Private Securities Litigation Reform Act
The disclosure requirements of SEC Rule 10b-5 had the unintended effect of deterring the disclosure of forward-looking information. To understand why, consider an example. **EXAMPLE 30.8** BT Company announces that its projected earnings in a future time period will be a certain amount, but the forecast turns out to be wrong. The earnings are in fact much lower, and the price of BT's stock is affected negatively. The shareholders then file suit against BT, claiming that its directors violated SEC Rule 10b-5 by disclosing misleading financial information. ■

To encourage companies to make earnings projections, Congress passed the Private Securities Litigation Reform Act (PSLRA) in 1995.[24] The PSLRA provides a "safe harbor" for publicly held companies that make forward-looking statements, such as financial forecasts. Those who make such statements are protected against liability for securities fraud if they include "meaningful cautionary statements identifying important factors that could cause actual results to differ materially from those in the forward-looking statement."[25]

The PSLRA also affected the level of detail required in securities fraud complaints. Plaintiffs must specify each purportedly misleading statement and say how it led them to a mistaken belief.

Limitations on Class Actions
After the PSLRA was passed, a number of securities class-action suits were filed in state courts to skirt its requirements. In response, Congress passed the Securities Litigation Uniform Standards Act (SLUSA).[26] The act placed stringent limits on the ability of plaintiffs to bring class-action suits in state courts against firms whose securities are traded on national stock exchanges. SLUSA applies to plaintiffs who claim fraud in the purchase or sale of securities and also applies to investors who claim that they were fraudulently induced to hold on to their securities.[27]

---

24. Pub. L. No. 104-67, 109 Stat. 737 (codified in scattered sections of Title 15 of the *United States Code*).
25. 15 U.S.C. Sections 77z-2, 78u-5.
26. Pub. L. No. 105-353. This act amended many sections of Title 15 of the *United States Code*.
27. *Merrill Lynch, Pierce, Fenner & Smith, Inc. v. Dabit,* 547 U.S. 71, 126 S.Ct. 1503, 164 L.Ed.2d 179 (2006).

30–2b Regulation of Proxy Statements

Section 14(a) of the Securities Exchange Act of 1934 regulates the solicitation of proxies (authorization to vote shares) from shareholders of Section 12 companies. The SEC regulates the content of proxy statements. Whoever solicits a proxy must fully and accurately disclose in the proxy statement all of the facts that are pertinent to the matter on which the shareholders are to vote. SEC Rule 14a-9 is similar to the antifraud provisions of SEC Rule 10b-5. Remedies for violations range from injunctions to prevent a vote from being taken to monetary damages.

30–2c Violations of the 1934 Act

As mentioned earlier, violations of Section 10(b) of the Securities Exchange Act and SEC Rule 10b-5, including insider trading, may be subject to criminal or civil liability.

Scienter Requirement For either criminal or civil sanctions to be imposed, *scienter* must exist—that is, the violator must have had an intent to defraud or knowledge of her or his misconduct. *Scienter* can be proved by showing that the defendant made false statements or wrongfully failed to disclose material facts. In some situations, *scienter* can even be proved by showing that the defendant was consciously reckless as to the truth or falsity of his or her statements.

CASE EXAMPLE 30.9 Alvin Gebhart and Jack Archer started a business venture purchasing mobile home parks (MHPs) from owners and converting them to resident ownership. They formed MHP Conversions, LP, to facilitate the conversion process and issue promissory notes that were sold to investors to raise funds for the purchases. Archer ran the MHP program, and Gebhart sold the promissory notes. Gebhart sold nearly $2.4 million in MHP promissory notes to clients, who bought notes based on Gebhart's positive statements about the investment.

During the time Gebhart was selling the notes, however, he never actually looked into the finances of the MHP program. He relied entirely on information that Archer gave him, some of which was not true. When Gebhart was later sued for securities fraud, a federal appellate court concluded that there was sufficient evidence of *scienter*. Gebhart knew that he had no knowledge of the financial affairs of MHP, and he had been consciously reckless as to the truth or falsity of his statements about investing in MHP.[28] ■

Scienter Not Required for Section 16(b) Violations Violations of Section 16(b) include the sale by insiders of stock acquired less than six months before the sale (or less than six months after the sale if selling short). These violations are subject to civil sanctions. Liability under Section 16(b) is strict liability. Neither *scienter* nor negligence is required.

Criminal Penalties For violations of Section 10(b) and Rule 10b-5, an individual may be fined up to $5 million, imprisoned for up to twenty years, or both. A partnership or a corporation may be fined up to $25 million. Section 807 of the Sarbanes-Oxley Act provides that for a *willful* violation of the 1934 act, the violator may be imprisoned for up to twenty-five years in addition to being fined.

For a defendant to be convicted in a criminal prosecution under the securities laws, there can be no reasonable doubt that

Does a man selling promissory notes based on mobile home park conversions have a duty to investigate his statements about the financial soundness of those conversions?

iStockPhoto.com/Marje

---

28. *Gebhart v. SEC*, 595 F.3d 1034 (9th Cir. 2010).

the defendant knew he or she was acting wrongfully. A jury is not allowed merely to speculate that the defendant may have acted willfully.

CASE EXAMPLE 30.10 Martha Stewart, founder of a well-known media and homemaking empire, was charged with intentionally deceiving investors based on public statements she made. In 2001, Stewart's stockbroker allegedly had informed Stewart that the head of ImClone Systems, Inc., was selling his shares in that company. Stewart then sold her ImClone shares. The next day, ImClone announced that the U.S. Food and Drug Administration had not approved Erbitux, an experimental cancer drug that the company was developing.

After the government began investigating Stewart's ImClone trades, she publicly stated that she had previously instructed her stockbroker to sell her ImClone stock if the price fell to $60 per share. The government prosecutor claimed that this statement was false and that Stewart made it with the intent to deceive investors in her own corporation, Martha Stewart Living Omnimedia, Inc., by offering an explanation for the stock sale. The court, however, acquitted Stewart on this charge because "to find the essential element of criminal intent beyond a reasonable doubt, a rational juror would have to speculate."[29] ■

In the following case, the defendant argued that he should not have been convicted for securities fraud because the government had failed to prove its case.

---

29. *United States v. Stewart*, 305 F.Supp.2d 368 (S.D.N.Y. 2004). Stewart was convicted on other charges relating to her ImClone trading that did not require proof of intent.

CASE 30.3

United States v. Newton

United States Court of Appeals, Eleventh Circuit, 559 Fed.Appx. 902 (2014).

FACTS Douglas Newton was the president and sole director of Real American Brands, Inc. (RLAB), which owned the Billy Martin's USA brand and operated a Billy Martin's retail boutique at the Trump Plaza in New York City. (Billy Martin, the one-time manager of the New York Yankees, co-founded Billy Martin's, a Western wear store.)

Newton agreed to pay kickbacks to Chris Russo, whom he believed to be the manager of a pension fund, to induce the fund to buy shares of RLAB stock. Newton later arranged for his friend Yan Skwara to pay similar kickbacks for the fund's purchase of stock in U.S. Farms, Inc. Skwara was the chief executive officer and president of U.S. Farms. In reality, the pension fund was fictitious, and Newton and Skwara had been dealing with agents of the Federal Bureau of Investigation (FBI). Consequently, Newton and Skwara were charged with securities fraud. Skwara pleaded guilty, and a federal district court jury convicted Newton. Sentenced to thirty months in prison, Newton appealed.

ISSUE Did the government prove beyond a reasonable doubt that Newton knew that the shares of RLAB and U.S. Farms stock were being sold at artificially inflated prices because of the kickbacks?

DECISION Yes. The U.S. Court of Appeals for the Eleventh Circuit affirmed Newton's conviction and sentence for securities fraud.

What does the government have to prove to show that a corporate director intended to defraud a pension fund by paying kickbacks?

iStockPhoto.com/wdstock

REASON The evidence established that in each transaction, the amount of the kickback was added to the price of the stock, which artificially increased the stock price. Because of the kickbacks, the pension fund paid the same price for restricted shares as it would have paid for freely traded shares, although the price of the restricted shares should have been less. The evidence also proved that Newton had engaged in a scheme to defraud the pension fund. The FBI agents had initiated the deal, but Newton had joined the scheme voluntarily and had urged Skwara to participate.

In addition, Newton had tried to conceal the scheme with a false consulting agreement, as shown by e-mail that referred to advice he never actually received. His words and conduct, which were revealed on video at the trial, also showed his intent to defraud the pension fund investors. Thus, the evidence supported the conviction beyond a reasonable doubt. "Accordingly, there was no miscarriage of justice."

CRITICAL THINKING—Ethical Consideration *What is the difference between a sales commission or a transaction fee and a kickback? Why is a kickback unethical? Discuss.*

Civil Sanctions The SEC can also bring suit in a federal district court against anyone violating or aiding in a violation of the 1934 act or SEC rules by purchasing or selling a security while in the possession of material nonpublic information.[30] The violation must occur on or through the facilities of a national securities exchange or through a broker or dealer. A court may assess a penalty for as much as triple the profits gained or the loss avoided by the guilty party.[31] In addition, the 1988 Insider Trading and Securities Fraud Enforcement Act increased the number of persons who may be subject to civil liability for insider trading and gave the SEC authority to pay monetary rewards to informants.[32]

Private parties may also sue violators of Section 10(b) and Rule 10b-5. A private party may obtain rescission (cancellation) of a contract to buy securities or damages to the extent of the violator's illegal profits. Those found liable have a right to seek contribution from those who share responsibility for the violations, including accountants, attorneys, and corporations. For violations of Section 16(b), a corporation can bring an action to recover the short-swing profits.

Martha Stewart is shown here leaving a federal courthouse. On appeal, why did the court affirm her acquittal on the charge that she had engaged in a criminal action?

30–2d Online Securities Fraud

A problem facing the SEC today is how to enforce the antifraud provisions of the securities laws in the online environment. Internet-related forms of securities fraud include many types of investment scams. Spam, online newsletters and bulletin boards, chat rooms, blogs, social media, and tweets can all be used to spread false information and perpetrate fraud. For a relatively small cost, fraudsters can even build sophisticated Web pages to facilitate their investment scams.

Consider investment newsletters as an example. Hundreds of online investment newsletters provide free information on stocks. Legitimate online newsletters can help investors gather valuable information, but some e-newsletters are used for fraud. The law allows companies to pay the people who write these newsletters to tout their securities, but the newsletters are required to disclose who paid for the advertising. Many newsletters do not follow that law, however. Thus, an investor reading an online newsletter may believe that the information is unbiased, when in fact the fraudsters will directly profit by convincing investors to buy or sell particular stocks.

30–3 State Securities Laws

Today, every state has its own corporate securities laws, or "blue sky laws," that regulate the offer and sale of securities within its borders. (The phrase *blue sky laws* dates to a 1917 decision by the United States Supreme Court in which the Court declared that the purpose of such laws was to prevent "speculative schemes which have no more basis than so many feet of 'blue sky.'")[33] Article 8 of the Uniform Commercial Code, which has been adopted by all of the states, also imposes various requirements relating to the purchase and sale of securities.

30–3a Requirements under State Securities Laws

State securities laws apply mainly to intrastate transactions. Typically, state laws have disclosure requirements and antifraud provisions, many of which are patterned after Section 10(b)

LEARNING OBJECTIVE 4
What are some of the features of state securities laws?

---

30. The Insider Trading Sanctions Act of 1984, 15 U.S.C. Section 78u(d).
31. Profit or loss is defined as "the difference between the purchase or sale price of the security and the value of that security as measured by the trading price of the security at a reasonable period of time after public dissemination of the nonpublic information." 15 U.S.C. Section 78u(d)(3)(C).
32. 15 U.S.C. Section 78u-1.
33. *Hall v. Geiger-Jones Co.*, 242 U.S. 539, 37 S.Ct. 217, 61 L.Ed. 480 (1917).

of the Securities Exchange Act and SEC Rule 10b-5. State laws also provide for the registration of securities offered or issued for sale within the state and impose disclosure requirements.

CASE EXAMPLE 30.11 Randall Fincke was the founder, director, and officer of Access Cardiosystems, Inc., a small startup company that sold portable automated external heart defibrillators. Fincke prepared a business plan that stated Access's "patent counsel" had advised the firm "its product does not infringe any patents." This statement was false—patent counsel never offered Access any opinion on the question of infringement.

Fincke gave this plan to potential investors, including Joseph Zimmel who bought $1.5 million in Access shares. When the company later filed for Chapter 11 bankruptcy protection, Zimmel filed a complaint with the federal bankruptcy court, alleging that Fincke had violated the Massachusetts blue sky law. The court awarded Zimmel $1.5 million in damages, and the award was affirmed on appeal. Fincke had solicited investors "by means of" a false statement of material fact, in violation of the fraud provisions in the state's securities laws.[34] ▪

Methods of registration, required disclosures, and exemptions from registration vary among states. Unless an exemption from registration is applicable, issuers must register or qualify their stock with the appropriate state official, often called a *corporations commissioner.* Additionally, most state securities laws regulate securities brokers and dealers.

30–3b Concurrent Regulation

Since the adoption of the 1933 and 1934 federal securities acts, the state and federal governments have regulated securities concurrently. Issuers must comply with both federal and state securities laws, and exemptions from federal law are not exemptions from state laws.

The dual federal and state system has not always worked well, particularly during the early 1990s, when the securities markets underwent considerable expansion. Today, most duplicate regulations have been eliminated, and the SEC has exclusive power to regulate most national securities activities. The National Conference of Commissioners on Uniform State Laws also substantially revised the Uniform Securities Act in 2002 to coordinate state and federal securities regulation and enforcement efforts. Seventeen states have adopted the most recent version of the Uniform Securities Act.[35]

30–4 Corporate Governance

Corporate governance can be narrowly defined as the relationship between a corporation and its shareholders. Some argue for a broader definition—that corporate governance specifies the rights and responsibilities among different participants in the corporation, such as the board of directors, managers, shareholders, and other stakeholders, and spells out the rules and procedures for making decisions on corporate affairs. Regardless of the way it is defined, effective corporate governance requires more than just compliance with laws and regulations. (For a discussion of corporate governance in other nations, see this chapter's *Beyond Our Borders* feature.)

Effective corporate governance is essential in large corporations because corporate ownership (by shareholders) is separated from corporate control (by officers and managers). Under these circumstances, officers and managers may attempt to advance their own interests at the expense of the shareholders. The well-publicized corporate scandals in the first decade of the 2000s clearly illustrate the reasons for concern about managerial opportunism.

Corporate Governance A set of policies specifying the rights and responsibilities of the various participants in a corporation and spelling out the rules and procedures for making corporate decisions.

---

34. *In re Access Cardiosystems, Inc.,* 776 F.3d 30 (1st Cir. 2015).

35. At the time this book went to press, the Uniform Securities Act had been adopted in Georgia, Hawaii, Idaho, Indiana, Iowa, Kansas, Maine, Michigan, Minnesota, Mississippi, Missouri, New Mexico, Oklahoma, South Carolina, South Dakota, Vermont, and Wisconsin, as well as the U.S. Virgin Islands.

BEYOND OUR BORDERS — Corporate Governance in Other Nations

Corporate governance has become an issue of concern not only for U.S. corporations, but also for corporate entities around the world. With the globalization of business, a corporation's bad acts (or lack of control systems) can have far-reaching consequences.

Different models of corporate governance exist in different nations, often depending on the degree of capitalism in the particular nation. In the United States, corporate governance tends to give priority to shareholders' interests. This approach encourages significant innovation, as well as cost and quality competition.

In contrast, the coordinated model of governance that prevails in continental Europe and Japan gives priority to the interests of so-called stakeholders—employees, managers, suppliers, customers, and the community. The coordinated model still encourages innovation and cost and quality competition, but not to the same extent as the U.S. model.

CRITICAL THINKING

■ Why does the presence of a capitalist system affect a nation's perspective on corporate governance?

30–4a Aligning the Interests of Officers and Shareholders

Some corporations have sought to align the financial interests of their officers with those of the company's shareholders by providing the officers with **stock options,** which enable them to purchase shares of the corporation's stock at a set price. When the market price rises above that level, the officers can sell their shares for a profit. Because a stock's market price generally increases as the corporation prospers, the options give the officers a financial stake in the corporation's well-being and supposedly encourage them to work hard for the benefit of the shareholders.

Stock Option A right to buy a given number of shares of stock at a set price, usually within a specified time period.

Problems with Stock Options Options have turned out to be an imperfect device for encouraging effective governance, however. Executives in some companies have been tempted to "cook" the company's books in order to keep share prices higher so that they could sell their stock for a profit. Executives in other corporations have experienced no losses when share prices dropped because their options were "repriced" so that they did not suffer from the share price decline. Thus, although stock options theoretically can motivate officers to protect shareholder interests, stock option plans have sometimes become a way for officers to take advantage of shareholders.

Outside Directors With stock options generally failing to work as planned, there has been an outcry for more outside directors (those with no formal employment affiliation with the company). The theory is that independent directors will more closely monitor the actions of corporate officers. Hence, today we see more boards with outside directors. Note, though, that outside directors may not be truly independent of corporate officers. They may be friends or business associates of the leading officers.

Should shareholders have more control over corporate officers' compensation? Over the last several years, executive compensation has become a hotly debated issue. Many critics argue that the chief executive officers (CEOs) of public companies are paid too much, especially in comparison with the wages earned by the average worker.

The Dodd-Frank Wall Street Reform and Consumer Protection Act includes a "say-on-pay" provision that gives shareholders the right to vote on compensation for senior executives at every public U.S. company. These votes are nonbinding, however—the board of directors does not have to abide by them. Furthermore, more than 90 percent of shareholder votes on

ETHICAL
ISSUE

executive pay have been in favor of the proposed compensation plans. Despite the "say on pay" provision, the average compensation for a CEO in 2014 was more than $10.5 million, up 13 percent from the previous year. A typical U.S. employee would have to work about a month to earn what a CEO earns in an hour.

30-4b Promoting Accountability

Effective corporate governance standards are designed to address problems and to motivate officers to make decisions that promote the financial interests of the company's shareholders. Generally, corporate governance entails corporate decision-making structures that monitor employees (particularly officers) to ensure that they are acting for the benefit of the shareholders. Firms that are more accountable to shareholders typically report higher profits, higher sales growth, higher firm value, and other economic advantages. Thus, corporate governance involves, at a minimum:

1. The audited reporting of the corporation's financial progress, so managers can be evaluated.
2. Legal protections for shareholders, so violators of the law who attempt to take advantage of shareholders can be punished for misbehavior and victims may recover damages for any associated losses.

> "Honesty is the single most important factor having a direct bearing on the final success of an individual, corporation, or product."
>
> **ED MCMAHON**
> 1923–2009
> (AMERICAN ENTERTAINER)

Governance and Corporation Law State corporation statutes set up the legal framework for corporate governance. Under the corporate law of Delaware, where most major companies incorporate, all corporations must have certain structures of corporate governance in place. The most important structure, of course, is the board of directors because the board makes the major decisions about the future of the corporation.

The Board of Directors Under corporate law, a corporation must have a board of directors elected by the shareholders. Directors are responsible for ensuring that the corporation's officers are operating wisely and in the exclusive interest of shareholders. The directors receive reports from the officers and give them managerial direction. In reality, though, corporate directors devote a relatively small amount of time to monitoring officers.

Ideally, shareholders would monitor the directors' supervision of the officers. In practice, however, it can be difficult for shareholders to monitor directors and hold them responsible for corporate failings. Although the directors can be sued for failing to do their jobs effectively, directors are rarely held personally liable.

The Audit Committee. A crucial committee of the board of directors is the *audit committee,* which oversees the corporation's accounting and financial reporting processes, including both internal and outside auditors. Unless the committee members have sufficient expertise and are willing to spend the time to carefully examine the corporation's bookkeeping methods, however, the audit committee may be ineffective.

The audit committee also oversees the corporation's "internal controls," which are the measures taken to ensure that reported results are accurate. As an example, these controls—carried out largely by the company's internal auditing staff—help to determine whether a corporation's debts are collectible. If the debts are not collectible, it is up to the audit committee to make sure that the corporation's financial officers do not simply pretend that payment will eventually be made.

The Compensation Committee. Another important committee of the board of directors is the *compensation committee.* This committee monitors and determines the compensation of the company's officers. As part of this process, it is responsible for assessing the officers' performance and for designing a compensation system that will better align the officers' interests with those of the shareholders.

30-4c The Sarbanes-Oxley Act

In 2002, following a series of corporate scandals, Congress passed the Sarbanes-Oxley Act,[36] which addresses certain issues relating to corporate governance. Generally, the act attempts to increase corporate accountability by imposing strict disclosure requirements and harsh penalties for violations of securities laws. The act requires chief corporate executives to take responsibility for the accuracy of financial statements and reports that are filed with the SEC.

Additionally, the act requires that certain financial and stock-transaction reports be filed with the SEC earlier than was required under the previous rules. The act also created a new entity, called the Public Company Accounting Oversight Board, to regulate and oversee public accounting firms. Other provisions of the act established private civil actions and expanded the SEC's remedies in administrative and civil actions.

Because of the importance of this act for corporate leaders and for those dealing with securities transactions, we highlight some of its key provisions relating to corporate accountability in Exhibit 30–3.

---

36. 15 U.S.C. Sections 7201 *et seq.*

Exhibit 30–3 Some Key Provisions of the Sarbanes-Oxley Act Relating to Corporate Accountability

Certification Requirements—Under Section 906 of the Sarbanes-Oxley Act, the chief executive officers (CEOs) and chief financial officers (CFOs) of most major companies listed on public stock exchanges must certify financial statements that are filed with the SEC. CEOs and CFOs must certify that filed financial reports "fully comply" with SEC requirements and that all of the information reported "fairly represents in all material respects, the financial conditions and results of operations of the issuer."

Under Section 302 of the act, CEOs and CFOs of reporting companies are required to certify that a signing officer reviewed each quarterly and annual filing with the SEC and that none contained untrue statements of material fact. Also, the signing officer or officers must certify that they have established an internal control system to identify all material information and that any deficiencies in the system were disclosed to the auditors.

Effectiveness of Internal Controls on Financial Reporting—Under Section 404(a), all public companies are required to assess the effectiveness of their internal control over financial reporting. Section 404(b) requires independent auditors to report on management's assessment of internal controls, but companies with a public float (price times total shares publicly owned) of less than $75 million are exempted from this requirement.

Loans to Directors and Officers—Section 402 prohibits any reporting company, as well as any private company that is filing an initial public offering, from making personal loans to directors and executive officers (with a few limited exceptions, such as for certain consumer and housing loans).

Protection for Whistleblowers—Section 806 protects whistleblowers—employees who report ("blow the whistle" on) securities violations by their employers—from being fired or in any way discriminated against by their employers.

Blackout Periods—Section 306 prohibits certain types of securities transactions during "blackout periods"—periods during which the issuer's ability to purchase, sell, or otherwise transfer funds in individual account plans (such as pension funds) is suspended.

Enhanced Penalties for—
- *Violations of Section 906 Certification Requirements*—A CEO or CFO who certifies a financial report or statement filed with the SEC knowing that the report or statement does not fulfill all of the requirements of Section 906 will be subject to criminal penalties of up to $1 million in fines, ten years in prison, or both. *Willful* violators of the certification requirements may be subject to $5 million in fines, twenty years in prison, or both.
- *Violations of the 1934 Securities Exchange Act*—Penalties for securities fraud under the 1934 act were increased (as discussed earlier in this chapter). Individual violators may be fined up to $5 million, imprisoned for up to twenty years, or both. *Willful* violators may be imprisoned for up to twenty-five years in addition to being fined.
- *Destruction or Alteration of Documents*—Anyone who alters, destroys, or conceals documents or otherwise obstructs any official proceeding will be subject to fines, imprisonment for up to twenty years, or both.
- *Other Forms of White-Collar Crime*—The act stiffened the penalties for certain criminal violations, such as federal mail and wire fraud, and ordered the U.S. Sentencing Commission to revise the sentencing guidelines for white-collar crimes.

Statute of Limitations for Securities Fraud—Section 804 provides that a private right of action for securities fraud may be brought no later than two years after the discovery of the violation or five years after the violation, whichever is earlier.

More Internal Controls and Accountability

The Sarbanes-Oxley Act introduced direct *federal* corporate governance requirements for public companies (companies whose shares are traded in the public securities markets). The law addressed many of the corporate governance procedures discussed here and created new requirements in an attempt to make the system work more effectively. The requirements deal with independent monitoring of company officers by both the board of directors and auditors.

Sections 302 and 404 of Sarbanes-Oxley require high-level managers (the most senior officers) to establish and maintain an effective system of internal controls. The system must include "disclosure controls and procedures" to ensure that company financial reports are accurate and timely and to document financial results prior to reporting.

Senior management must reassess the system's effectiveness annually. Some companies had to take expensive steps to bring their internal controls up to the new federal standard. After the act was passed, hundreds of companies reported that they had identified and corrected shortcomings in their internal control systems.

Exemptions for Smaller Companies

The Sarbanes-Oxley Act initially required all public companies to have an independent auditor file a report with the SEC on management's assessment of internal controls. In 2010, however, Congress enacted an exemption for smaller companies in an effort to reduce compliance costs. Public companies with a market capitalization, or public float (price times total shares publicly owned), of less than $75 million no longer need to have an auditor report on management's assessment of internal controls.

Certification and Monitoring Requirements

Section 906 requires that chief executive officers (CEOs) and chief financial officers (CFOs) certify that the information in the corporate financial statements "fairly represents in all material respects, the financial conditions and results of operations of the issuer." This requirement makes officers directly accountable for the accuracy of their financial reporting and avoids any "ignorance defense" if shortcomings are later discovered.

Sarbanes-Oxley also includes requirements to improve directors' monitoring of officers' activities. All members of the corporate audit committee for public companies must be outside directors. The audit committee must have a written charter that sets out its duties and provides for performance appraisal. At least one "financial expert" must serve on the audit committee, which must hold executive meetings without company officers present. In addition to reviewing the internal controls, the committee also monitors the actions of the outside auditor.

LEARNING OBJECTIVE 5

What certification requirements does the Sarbanes-Oxley Act impose on corporate executives?

Reviewing . . . Investor Protection, Insider Trading, and Corporate Governance

Dale Emerson served as the chief financial officer for Reliant Electric Company, a distributor of electricity serving portions of Montana and North Dakota. Reliant was in the final stages of planning a takeover of Dakota Gasworks, Inc., a natural gas distributor that operated solely within North Dakota. On a weekend fishing trip with his uncle, Ernest Wallace, Emerson mentioned that he had been putting in a lot of extra hours at the office planning a takeover of Dakota Gasworks. When he returned from the fishing trip, Wallace purchased $20,000 worth of Reliant stock. Three weeks later, Reliant made a tender offer to Dakota Gasworks stockholders and purchased 57 percent of Dakota Gasworks stock. Over the next two weeks, the price of Reliant stock rose 72 percent before leveling out. Wallace sold his Reliant stock for a gross profit of $14,400. Using the information presented in the chapter, answer the following questions.

1. Would registration with the SEC be required for Dakota Gasworks securities? Why or why not?

2. Did Emerson violate Section 10(b) of the Securities Exchange Act of 1934 and SEC Rule 10b-5? Why or why not?

3. What theory or theories might a court use to hold Wallace liable for insider trading?

4. Under the Sarbanes-Oxley Act, who would be required to certify the accuracy of financial statements filed with the SEC?

DEBATE THIS

■ Insider trading should be legalized.

Key Terms

accredited investor 753
corporate governance 764
free-writing prospectus 751
insider trading 757

investment company 753
investment contract 749
mutual fund 753
prospectus 750

SEC Rule 10b-5 756
short-swing profits 759
stock option 765
tippee 758

Chapter Summary: Investor Protection, Insider Trading, and Corporate Governance

Securities Act of 1933	Prohibits fraud and stabilizes the securities industry by requiring disclosure of all essential information relating to the issuance of securities to the investing public. 1. *Registration requirements*—Securities, unless exempt, must be registered with the SEC before being offered to the public. The *registration statement* must include detailed financial information about the issuing corporation; the intended use of the proceeds of the securities being issued; and certain disclosures, such as interests of directors or officers and pending lawsuits. 2. *Prospectus*—The issuer must provide investors with a *prospectus* that describes the security being sold, the issuing corporation, and the risk attaching to the security. 3. *Exemptions*—The SEC has exempted certain offerings from the requirements of the Securities Act of 1933. Exemptions may be determined on the basis of the size of the issue, whether the offering is private or public, and whether advertising is involved. Exemptions are summarized in Exhibit 30–1.

Securities Exchange Act of 1934	Provides for the regulation and registration of securities exchanges, brokers, dealers, and national securities associations. Maintains a continuous disclosure system for all corporations with securities on the securities exchanges and for companies that have assets in excess of $10 million and five hundred or more shareholders (Section 12 companies).
	1. *SEC Rule 10b-5 [under Section 10(b) of the 1934 act]*—
	  a. Applies to almost all trading of securities—a firm's securities do not have to be registered under the 1933 act for the 1934 act to apply.
	  b. Applies to insider trading by corporate officers, directors, majority shareholders, and any persons receiving inside information (information not available to the public) who base their trading on this information.
	  c. Liability for insider trading may be based on the tipper/tippee or the misappropriation theory.
	  d. May be violated by failing to disclose "material facts" that must be disclosed under this rule.
	  e. Liability for violations can be civil or criminal.
	2. *Insider trading [under Section 16(b) of the 1934 act]*—To prevent corporate insiders from taking advantage of inside information, the 1934 act requires officers, directors, and shareholders owning 10 percent or more of the issued stock of a corporation to turn over to the corporation all short-term profits (called *short-swing profits*) realized from the purchase and sale or sale and purchase of corporate stock within any six-month period.
	3. *Regulation of proxies*—The SEC regulates the content of proxy statements sent to shareholders of Section 12 companies. Section 14(a) is essentially a disclosure law, with provisions similar to the antifraud provisions of SEC Rule 10b-5.

Continues

State Securities Laws	All states have corporate securities laws (*blue sky laws*) that regulate the offer and sale of securities within state borders. These laws are designed to prevent "speculative schemes which have no more basis than so many feet of 'blue sky.'" States regulate securities concurrently with the federal government. The Uniform Securities Act is designed to promote coordination and reduce duplication between state and federal securities regulation.
Corporate Governance	1. *Definition*—Corporate governance involves a set of policies specifying the rights and responsibilities of the various participants in a corporation and spelling out the rules and procedures for making decisions on corporate affairs.
	2. *The need for corporate governance*—Corporate governance is necessary in large corporations because corporate ownership (by the shareholders) is separated from corporate control (by officers and managers). This separation of corporate ownership and control can often result in conflicting interests. Corporate governance standards address such issues.
	3. *Sarbanes-Oxley Act*—This act attempts to increase corporate accountability by imposing strict disclosure requirements and harsh penalties for violations of securities laws.

Issue Spotters

1. When a corporation wishes to issue certain securities, it must provide sufficient information for an unsophisticated investor to evaluate the financial risk involved. Specifically, the law imposes liability for making a false statement or omission that is "material." What sort of information would an investor consider material? (See *Securities Exchange Act of 1934*.)

2. Lee is an officer of Magma Oil, Inc. Lee knows that a Magma geologist has just discovered a new deposit of oil. Can Lee take advantage of this information to buy and sell Magma stock? Why or why not? (See *Securities Exchange Act of 1934*.)

　—**Check your answers to the *Issue Spotters* against the answers provided in Appendix D at the end of this text.**

Learning Objectives Check

1. What is meant by the term *securities?*
2. What are the two major statutes regulating the securities industry?
3. What is insider trading? Why is it prohibited?
4. What are some of the features of state securities laws?
5. What certification requirements does the Sarbanes-Oxley Act impose on corporate executives?

　—**Answers to the even-numbered *Learning Objectives Check* questions can be found in Appendix E at the end of this text.**

Business Scenarios and Case Problems

30–1. Registration Requirements. Langley Brothers, Inc., a corporation incorporated and doing business in Kansas, decides to sell common stock worth $1 million to the public. The stock will be sold only within the state of Kansas. Joseph Langley, the chair of the board, says the offering need not be registered with the Securities and Exchange Commission. His brother, Harry, disagrees. Who is right? Explain. (See *Securities Act of 1933*.)

30–2. Insider Trading. David Gain is the chief executive officer (CEO) of Forest Media Corp., which is interested in acquiring RS Communications, Inc. To initiate negotiations, Gain meets with RS's CEO, Gill Raz, on Friday, July 12. Two days later, Gain phones his brother, Mark, who buys 3,800 shares of RS stock on the following Monday. Mark discusses the deal with their father, Jordan, who buys 20,000 RS shares on Thursday. On July 25, the day before the RS bid is due, Gain phones his parents' home, and Mark buys another 3,200 RS shares. Over the next few days, Gain periodically phones Mark and Jordan, both of whom

continued to buy RS shares. On August 5, RS refuses Forest's bid and announces that it is merging with another company. The price of RS stock rises 30 percent, increasing the value of Mark's and Jordan's shares by nearly $660,000 and $400,000, respectively. Is Gain guilty of insider trading? What is required to impose sanctions for this offense? Could a court hold Gain liable? Why or why not? (See *Securities Exchange Act of 1934*.)

30–3. Business Case Problem with Sample Answer— Violations of the 1934 Act. Matrixx Initiatives, Inc., makes and sells over-the-counter pharmaceutical products. Its core brand is Zicam, which accounts for 70 percent of its sales. Matrixx received reports that some consumers had lost their sense of smell (a condition called *anosmia*) after using Zicam Cold Remedy. Four product liability suits were filed against Matrixx, seeking damages for anosmia. In public statements relating to revenues and product safety, however, Matrixx did not reveal this information.

James Siracusano and other Matrixx investors filed a suit in a federal district court against the company and its executives under Section 10(b) of the Securities Exchange Act of 1934 and SEC Rule 10b-5, claiming that the statements were misleading because they did not disclose the information about the product liability suits. Matrixx argued that to be material, information must consist of a statistically significant number of adverse events that require disclosure. Because Siracusano's claim did not allege that Matrixx knew of a statistically significant number of adverse events, the company contended that the claim should be dismissed. What is the standard for materiality in this context? Should Siracusano's claim be dismissed? Explain. [*Matrixx Initiatives, Inc. v. Siracusano,* __U.S. __, 131 S.Ct. 1309, 179 L.Ed.2d 398 (2011)] (See *Securities Exchange Act of 1934.*)

—For a sample answer to Problem 30–3, go to Appendix F at the end of this text.

30–4. Disclosure under SEC Rule 10b-5. Dodona I, LLC, invested $4 million in two securities offerings from Goldman, Sachs & Co. The investments were in collateralized debt obligations (CDOs). Their value depended on residential mortgage-backed securities (RMBSs), whose value in turn depended on the performance of subprime residential mortgages. Before marketing the CDOs, Goldman had noticed several "red flags" relating to investments in the subprime market, in which it had invested heavily. To limit its risk, Goldman began betting against subprime mortgages, RMBSs, and CDOs, including the CDOs it had sold to Dodona. In an internal e-mail, one Goldman official commented that the company had managed to "make some lemonade from some big old lemons." Nevertheless, Goldman's marketing materials provided only boilerplate statements about the risks of investing in the securities. The CDOs were later downgraded to junk status, and Dodona suffered a major loss while Goldman profited. Assuming that Goldman did not affirmatively misrepresent any facts about the CDOs, can Dodona still recover under SEC Rule 10b-5? If so, how? [*Dodona I, LLC v. Goldman, Sachs & Co.,* 847 F.Supp.2d 624 (S.D.N.Y. 2012)] (See *Securities Exchange Act of 1934.*)

30–5. Violations of the 1933 Act. Three shareholders of iStorage sought to sell their stock through World Trade Financial Corp. The shares were *restricted securities*—that is, securities acquired in an unregistered, private sale. Restricted securities typically bear a "restrictive" legend clearly stating that they cannot be resold in the public marketplace. This legend had been wrongly removed from the iStorage shares, however. Information about the company that was publicly available included the fact that, despite a ten-year life, it had no operating history or earnings. In addition, it had net losses of about $200,000, and its stock was thinly traded. Without investigating the company or the status of its stock, World Trade sold more than 2.3 million shares to the public on behalf of the three customers. Did World Trade violate the Securities Act of 1933? Discuss. [*World*

Trade Financial Corp. v. Securities and Exchange Commission, 739 F.3d 1243 (9th Cir. 2014)] (See *Securities Act of 1933.*)

30–6. Securities Act of 1933. Big Apple Consulting USA, Inc., provided small publicly traded companies with a variety of services, including marketing, business planning, and Web site development and maintenance. CyberKey Corp. sold customizable USB drives. CyberKey falsely informed Big Apple that CyberKey had been awarded a $25 million contract with the Department of Homeland Security (DHS). Big Apple used this information in aggressively promoting CyberKey's stock and was compensated for the effort in the form of CyberKey shares. When the Securities and Exchange Commission (SEC) began to investigate, Big Apple sold its shares for $7.8 million. The SEC filed an action in a federal district court against Big Apple, alleging a violation of the Securities Act of 1933. Can liability be imposed on a seller for a false statement that was made by someone else? Explain. [*U.S. Securities and Exchange Commission v. Big Apple Consulting USA, Inc.,* 783 F.3d 786 (11th Cir. 2015)] (See *Securities Act of 1933.*)

30–7. A Question of Ethics—Violations of the 1934 Act. Melvin Lyttle told John Montana and Paul Knight about a "Trading Program" that purportedly would buy and sell securities in deals that were fully insured, as well as monitored and controlled by the Federal Reserve Board. Without checking the details or even verifying whether the Program existed, Montana and Knight, with Lyttle's help, began to sell interests in the Program to investors.

For a minimum investment of $1 million, the investors were promised extraordinary rates of return—from 10 percent to as much as 100 percent per week—without risk. They were also told that the Program would "utilize banks that can ensure full bank integrity of The Transaction whose undertaking[s] are in complete harmony with international banking rules and protocol and who guarantee maximum security of a Funder's Capital Placement Amount." Nothing was required but the investors' funds and their silence—the Program was to be kept secret. Over a four-month period, Montana raised nearly $23 million from twenty-two investors. The promised gains did not accrue, however. Instead, Montana, Lyttle, and Knight depleted the investors' funds in high-risk trades or spent the funds on themselves. [*SEC v. Montana,* 464 F.Supp.2d 772 (S.D.Ind. 2006)] (See *Securities Exchange Act of 1934.*)

1. The Securities and Exchange Commission (SEC) filed a suit against Montana alleging violations of Section 10(b) and SEC Rule 10b-5. What is required to establish a violation of these laws? Explain how and why the facts in this case meet, or fail to meet, these requirements.

2. Ultimately, about half of the investors recouped the amount they had invested. Should the others be considered at least partly responsible for their own losses? Discuss.

Critical Thinking and Writing Assignments

30–8. Case Analysis Question. Go to Appendix G at the end of this text and examine the excerpt of Case No. 5, *City of Livonia Employees' Retirement System and Local 295/Local 851 v. Boeing Co.* Review and then brief the case, making sure that your brief answers the following questions. (See *Securities Exchange Act of 1934.*)

1. **Issue:** Which pleading was at the center of the dispute in this case? What aspect of this pleading was at issue? Why?

2. **Rule of Law:** What must this pleading state in a suit alleging violations of Section 10(b) and Rule 10b-5?

3. **Applying the Rule of Law:** How did the source of the plaintiffs' allegations and the motive for the defendants' actions influence the result in this case?

4. **Conclusion:** Did the court conclude that the pleading here met the requirement for a suit alleging violations of Section 10(b) and Rule 10b-5?

30–9. Business Law Critical Thinking Group Assignment. Karel Svoboda, a credit officer for Rogue Bank, evaluated and approved his employer's extensions of credit to clients. These responsibilities gave Svoboda access to nonpublic information about the clients' earnings, performance, acquisitions, and business plans from confidential memos, e-mail, and other sources. Svoboda devised a scheme with Alena Robles, an independent accountant, to use this information to trade securities. Pursuant to their scheme, Robles traded in the securities of more than twenty different companies and profited by more than $2 million. Svoboda also executed trades for his own profit of more than $800,000, despite their agreement that Robles would do all of the trading. Aware that their scheme violated Rogue Bank's policy, they attempted to conduct their trades in such a way as to avoid suspicion. When the bank questioned Svoboda about his actions, he lied, refused to cooperate, and was fired. (See *Securities Exchange Act of 1934.*)

1. The first group will determine whether Svoboda or Robles committed any crimes.

2. The second group will decide whether Svoboda or Robles is subject to civil liability. If so, who could file a suit and on what ground? What are the possible sanctions?

3. A third group will identify any defenses that Svoboda or Robles could raise and determine whether the defenses would be likely to succeed.

Unit Five—Business Case Study with Dissenting Opinion

Notz v. Everett Smith Group, Ltd.

This *Business Case Study with Dissenting Opinion* examines *Notz v. Everett Smith Group, Ltd.*[1] in which a minority shareholder claimed that he had been excluded from some of the benefits of participating in the corporation. The shareholder asserted that the majority shareholder and the board of directors, which was controlled by the majority shareholder, had breached their fiduciary duties to the minority shareholder and to the firm. The court had to answer this question: Could the minority shareholder bring a suit directly to recover personally from the directors, or was he limited to bringing a shareholder's derivative suit on behalf of the corporation?

iStockPhoto.com/imtmphoto

What does a minority shareholder have to do to show that the majority shareholder and the board of directors breached their fiduciary duties to that shareholder?

CASE BACKGROUND

Albert Trostel & Sons (ATS) began as a tannery in Milwaukee, Wisconsin, in the 1800s. Over the decades, ATS acquired subsidiaries and expanded into the production of rubber and plastics. Everett Smith came to work for ATS in 1938, later became its president, and eventually gained control of the company. Smith formed Everett Smith Group, Ltd., which owned 88.9 percent of ATS by 2003. Edward Notz owned 5.5 percent, and others owned the rest. All of the members of ATS's board of directors were either officers or directors of the Smith Group.

In 2004, ATS had an opportunity to acquire Dickten & Masch, a competing thermoplastics maker. The ATS board chose not to act. Instead, the Smith Group, which had no direct holdings in the plastics field, acquired Dickten & Masch. Within months, the Smith Group's new affiliate bought the assets of ATS's plastics subsidiary, Trostel Specialty Elastomers Group, Inc. (Trostel SEG), from ATS.

Notz filed a suit in a Wisconsin state court against the Smith Group, alleging breach of fiduciary duty for stripping ATS of its most important assets and diverting the corporate opportunity to buy Dickten & Masch. The court dismissed the claim, and a state intermediate appellate court affirmed. Notz appealed to the Wisconsin Supreme Court.

MAJORITY OPINION

N. Patrick *CROOKS*, J. [Judge]
* * * *

Notz's claims of breach of fiduciary duty are primarily based on the series of transactions in which the Smith Group acquired two plastics companies. The allegations are that the Smith Group, as

ATS's majority shareholder, rejected the opportunity ATS had to buy Dickten & Masch; the Smith Group subsequently bought Dickten & Masch itself; and the Smith Group, in its capacity as majority shareholder, orchestrated the sale of ATS's valuable plastics group, Trostel SEG, to its own new acquisition.

The question is whether those allegations support direct claims for breach of fiduciary duty to a minority shareholder. * * * The Smith Group argues that * * * these are derivative claims; Notz argues that * * * these are direct claims.

* * * *Though each shareholder has an individual right to be treated fairly by the board of directors, when the injury from such actions is primarily to the corporation, there can be no direct claim by minority shareholders.* [Emphasis added.]

* * * It is true the fiduciary duty of a director is owed to the individual stockholders as well as to the corporation. Directors in this state may not use their position of trust to further their private interests. Thus, where some individual right of a stockholder is being impaired by the improper acts of a director, the stockholder can bring a direct suit on his own behalf because it is his individual right that is being violated. However, a right of action that belongs to the corporation cannot be pursued as a direct claim by an individual stockholder. * * * *Even where the injury to the corporation results in harm to a shareholder, it won't transform an action from a derivative to a direct one* * * * . That such primary and direct injury to a corporation may have a subsequent impact on the value of the stockholders' shares is clear, but that is not enough to create a right to bring a direct, rather than derivative, action. Where the injury to the corporation is the primary injury, and any injury to stockholders secondary, it is the derivative action alone that can be brought and maintained. That

---

1. 316 Wis.2d 640, 764 N.W.2d 904 (2009).

Continues

is the general rule, and, if it were to be abandoned, there would be no reason left for the concept of derivative actions for the redress of wrongs to a corporation. [Emphasis added.]

* * * *

Notz alleges self-dealing on the part of the majority shareholder, but * * * a shareholder-director's self-dealing [does not] transform an action that primarily injures the corporation into one that primarily injures a shareholder.

We agree with the Smith Group that breach of fiduciary duty claims, based on the lost opportunity to purchase one company and the sale of a subsidiary with great growth potential, are [derivative claims]. Our analysis * * * centers on a determination of whether the primary injury is to the corporation or to the shareholder. * * * An injury primarily * * * to an individual shareholder [is] one which affects a shareholder's rights in a manner distinct from the effect upon other shareholders. We agree with the court of appeals that the allegations here are essentially that the Smith Group stripped ATS of its most important assets and engaged in various acts of self-dealing, and that those are allegations of injury primarily to ATS. * * * All of the shareholders of ATS were affected equally by the loss of the opportunity to acquire Dickten & Masch and by the sale of Trostel SEG, the plastics division.

* * * *

* * * We agree with the court of appeals that the claims of harm alleged—the loss of a corporate opportunity and the sale of a subsidiary with high growth potential—caused harm primarily to the corporation, and thus we affirm the dismissal of Notz's direct claim of breach of fiduciary duty as to those allegations.

DISSENTING OPINION

Ann Walsh BRADLEY, J. [Judge] (* * * DISSENTING * * *).

* * * *

* * * I disagree with the majority * * * that Notz's claim for breach of fiduciary duty arising out of corporate usurpation is a derivative rather than a direct claim and that it thus must be dismissed.

Instead, * * * I conclude that Notz states a direct claim for breach of fiduciary duty arising out of the defendants' usurpation of a corporate opportunity.

* * * *

* * * Officers and directors owe a fiduciary duty to shareholders to act in good faith and to treat each shareholder fairly. The directors and officers of a corporation owe a fiduciary duty to not use their positions for their own personal advantage * * * to the detriment of the interests of the stockholders of the corporation.

That same fiduciary duty is also owed by majority shareholders to minority shareholders.

Officers, directors, and controlling shareholders breach their fiduciary duties when they treat minority shareholders differently, and inequitably, or when they use their position of trust to further their private interests. If through that control a sale of the corporate property is made and the property acquired by the majority, the minority may not be excluded from a fair participation in the fruits of the sale.

* * * *

[The majority's] conclusion is antithetical to the facts. It is true that all shareholders suffered a common injury in that the value of their investment in ATS depreciated. Nonetheless, Notz suffered an additional injury that was unique to the minority shareholders. The Smith Group who planned and executed these transactions received a net gain, but Notz suffered a net loss. * * * Notz's injury was distinct from the injury to the controlling shareholder—unlike the defendants, Notz was denied continued participation in a thriving growth industry.

QUESTIONS FOR ANALYSIS

1. **Law.** *What did the majority rule with respect to the dispute before the court? On what reasoning did the majority base its ruling?*

2. **Law.** *What was the dissent's interpretation of the facts in this case? How would the dissent have applied the law to these facts? Why?*

3. **Ethics.** *From an ethical perspective, should ATS's directors have made different decisions on the choices that came before the board? Discuss.*

4. **Economic Dimensions.** *Could a shareholder in the position of the minority shareholder in this case seek a judicial dissolution? If so, what would be the likely result?*

5. **Implications for the Shareholder.** *Can a shareholder pursue a derivative claim on behalf of a corporation? If so, what steps must the shareholder take? Why might a shareholder be reluctant to take these steps?*

Unit Five—Business Scenario

John leases an office and buys computer equipment. Initially, to pay for the lease and the equipment, he goes into the business of designing applications for smartphones. He also has an idea for a new software product that he hopes will be more profitable than designing apps. Whenever he has time, he works on the software.

1. **Selecting a Business Organization.** After six months, Mary and Paul come to work in the office to help develop John's idea. John continues to pay the rent and other expenses, including salaries for Mary and Paul. John does not expect to make a profit until the software is developed, which could take months. Even then, there may be very little profit unless the product is marketed successfully. If the software is successful, though, John believes that the firm will be able to follow up with other products. In choosing a form of business organization for this firm, what are the important considerations? What are the advantages and disadvantages of each basic option?

2. **Corporate Nature and Classification.** It is decided that the organizational form for this firm should provide limited liability for the owners. The owners will include John, Mary, Paul, and some members of their respective families. Limited liability is one of the features of the corporate form. Ordinarily, however, corporate income is taxed at both the corporate level and the shareholder level. Which corporate form could the firm use to avoid this double taxation? Which other forms of business organization provide limited liability? What factors, other than liability and taxation, influence a firm's choice among these forms?

3. **Duties of Corporate Directors.** The firm is incorporated as Digital Software, Inc. (DSI). The software is developed and marketed successfully, and DSI prospers. John, Mary, and Paul become directors of DSI. At a board meeting, Paul proposes a marketing strategy for DSI's next product, and John and Mary approve it. Implementing the strategy causes DSI's profits to drop. If the shareholders accuse Paul of breaching his fiduciary duty to DSI, what is Paul's most likely defense? If the shareholders accuse John and Mary of the same breach, what is their best defense? In either case, if the shareholders file a suit, how is a court likely to rule?

4. **Securities Regulation.** Mary and Paul withdraw from DSI to set up their own firm. To obtain operating capital, they solicit investors, who agree to become "general partners." Mary and Paul designate themselves "managing partners." The investors are spread over a wide area geographically and learn about Mary and Paul's business only through contact from Mary and Paul. Are Mary and Paul truly soliciting partners, or are they selling securities? What are the criteria for determining whether an investment is a security? What are the advantages and disadvantages of selling securities versus soliciting partners?

Unit Five—Group Project

iStockPhoto.com/Avalon_Studio

Although a limited liability company (LLC) may be the best organizational form for most businesses, a significant number of firms may be better off as a corporation or some other form of organization.

1. The first group will outline several reasons why a firm might be better off as a corporation than as an LLC.

2. The second group will discuss whether it is preferable for a five-member LLC to be member managed or manager managed and will identify some of the factors that should be taken into consideration.

33

iStockPhoto.com/opolja

Liability of Accountants and Other Professionals

LEARNING OBJECTIVES

The four Learning Objectives *below are designed to help improve your understanding of the chapter. After reading this chapter, you should be able to answer the following questions:*

1. Under what common law theories may professionals be liable to clients?

2. What are the rules concerning an auditor's liability to third parties?

3. How might an accountant violate federal securities laws?

4. What crimes might an accountant commit under the Internal Revenue Code?

Professionals, such as accountants, attorneys, physicians, and architects, are increasingly faced with the threat of liability. In part, this is because the public has become more aware that professionals are required to deliver competent services and adhere to certain standards of performance within their professions.

The standard of due care to which the members of the American Institute of Certified Public Accountants are expected to adhere is set out in the chapter-opening quotation. Investors rely heavily on the opinions of certified public accountants when making decisions about whether to invest in a company.

The failure of several major companies and leading public accounting firms in the past twenty years has focused attention on the importance of abiding by professional accounting standards. Numerous corporations—from American International Group (AIG, the world's largest insurance company), to HealthSouth, Goldman Sachs, Lehman Brothers, Tyco International, and India-based Satyam Computer Services—have been accused of engaging in accounting fraud. These companies may have reported fictitious revenues, concealed liabilities or debts, or artificially inflated their assets.

Considering the many potential sources of legal liability that they face, accountants, attorneys, and other professionals should be aware of their legal obligations. In this chapter, we look at the potential liability of professionals under both the common law and

> "A member should observe the profession's technical and ethical standards . . . and discharge professional responsibility to the best of the member's ability."
>
> ARTICLE V, CODE OF PROFESSIONAL CONDUCT, AMERICAN INSTITUTE OF CERTIFIED PUBLIC ACCOUNTANTS

statutory law. We conclude the chapter with a brief examination of the relationships of professionals, particularly accountants and attorneys, with their clients.

33-1 Potential Liability to Clients

Under the common law, professionals may be liable to clients for breach of contract, negligence, or fraud.

LEARNING OBJECTIVE 1
Under what common law theories may professionals be liable to clients?

33-1a Liability for Breach of Contract

Accountants and other professionals face liability under the common law for any breach of contract. A professional owes a duty to his or her client to honor the terms of their contract and to perform the contract within the stated time period. If the professional fails to perform as agreed, then he or she has breached the contract, and the client has the right to pursue recovery of damages.

Possible damages include expenses incurred by the client in securing another professional to provide the contracted-for services and any other reasonable and foreseeable losses that arise from the professional's breach. For instance, if the client had to pay penalties for failing to meet deadlines, the court may order the professional to pay an equivalent amount in damages to the client.

33-1b Liability for Negligence

Accountants and other professionals may also be held liable under the common law for negligence in the performance of their services. Recall that the following elements must be proved to establish negligence:

1. A duty of care existed.

2. That duty of care was breached.

3. The plaintiff suffered an injury.

4. The injury was proximately caused by the defendant's breach of the duty of care.

Negligence cases against professionals often focus on the standard of care exercised by the professional. All professionals are subject to standards of conduct established by codes of professional ethics, by state statutes, and by judicial decisions. They are also governed by the contracts they enter into with their clients.

In performing their contracts, professionals must exercise the established standards of care, knowledge, and judgment generally accepted by members of their professional group. Here, we look at the duty of care owed by two groups of professionals that frequently perform services for business firms: accountants and attorneys.

Accountant's Duty of Care Accountants play a major role in a business's financial system. Accountants establish and maintain financial records and design, control, and audit record-keeping systems. They also prepare statements that reflect an individual's or a business's financial status, give tax advice, and prepare tax returns.

Generally, an accountant must possess the skills that an ordinarily prudent accountant would have and must exercise the degree of care that an ordinarily prudent accountant would exercise. The level of skill expected of accountants and the degree of care that they should exercise in performing their services are reflected in the standards discussed next.

GAAP and GAAS. When performing their services, accountants must comply with **generally accepted accounting principles (GAAP)** and **generally accepted auditing standards (GAAS)**. The Financial Accounting Standards Board (FASB, usually pronounced "faz-bee") determines

Generally Accepted Accounting Principles (GAAP) The conventions, rules, and procedures developed by the Financial Accounting Standards Board to define accepted accounting practices at a particular time.

Generally Accepted Auditing Standards (GAAS) Standards established by the American Institute of Certified Public Accountants to define the professional qualities and judgment that should be exercised by an auditor in performing an audit.

what accounting conventions, rules, and procedures constitute GAAP at a given point in time. GAAS, established by the American Institute of Certified Public Accountants, set forth the professional qualities and judgment that an auditor should exercise in performing an audit. Normally, if an accountant conforms to generally accepted standards and acts in good faith, he or she will not be held liable to the client for incorrect judgment.

A violation of GAAP and GAAS is considered *prima facie* evidence of negligence on the part of the accountant. Compliance with GAAP and GAAS, however, does not *necessarily* relieve an accountant from potential legal liability. An accountant may be held to a higher standard of conduct established by state statute or by judicial decisions.

For a discussion of how global accounting rules are replacing GAAP, see this chapter's *Landmark in the Law* feature.

Defalcation Embezzlement or misappropriation of funds.

International Financial Reporting Standards (IFRS) A set of global accounting standards that are being phased in by companies in the United States.

Discovering Improprieties. An accountant is not required to discover every impropriety, defalcation[1] (embezzlement), or fraud in her or his client's books. If, however, the impropriety, defalcation, or fraud has gone undiscovered because of the accountant's negligence or failure to perform an express or implied duty, the accountant will be liable for any resulting

---

1. This term, pronounced deh-fal-*kay*-shun, is derived from the Latin *de* ("off") and *falx* ("sickle"—a tool from cutting grain or tall grass). As used here, the term refers to the act of an embezzler.

LANDMARK IN THE LAW

The SEC Adopts Global Accounting Rules

At one time, investors and companies considered U.S. accounting rules, known as generally accepted accounting principles (GAAP), to be the gold standard—the best system for reporting earnings and other financial information. Then came the subprime mortgage meltdown and a global economic crisis, which caused many to question the effectiveness and superiority of GAAP.

In 2008, the Securities and Exchange Commission (SEC) unanimously approved a plan to require U.S. companies to use a set of global accounting rules known as **International Financial Reporting Standards (IFRS)**. These rules, which are established by the London-based International Accounting Standards Board, are being phased in and will be required for all financial reports filed with the SEC.

WHY SHIFT TO GLOBAL ACCOUNTING STANDARDS? The SEC decided to replace the GAAP with the IFRS for several reasons. GAAP rules are detailed and fill nearly

25,000 pages. The IFRS are simpler and more straightforward, filling only 2,500 pages, and they focus more on general principles than on specific rules. Consequently, companies should eventually find it less difficult to comply with the international rules, and this should lead to cost savings.

Another benefit is that investors will find it easier to make cross-country comparisons between, say, a technology company in Silicon Valley and one in Germany or Japan. Furthermore, having uniform accounting rules that apply to all nations makes sense in a global economy. The European Union and 113 other nations—including nearly all of the United States' trading partners—already use the IFRS.

THE DOWNSIDE TO ADOPTING GLOBAL RULES Despite these benefits, the shift to the global rules has had some drawbacks. Making the change has proven to be both costly and time consuming. Companies have had to upgrade their communications and software systems, study and implement the new rules, and train their employees, accountants, and tax attorneys in the rules'

use. Some smaller U.S. firms have found it difficult to absorb the costs of converting to the IFRS.

Another concern is that although the IFRS are simpler than GAAP, they may not be better. Because the global rules are broader and less detailed, they give companies more leeway in reporting, so less financial information may be disclosed. There are also indications that using the IFRS can lead to wide variances in profit reporting and may tend to boost earnings above what they would have been under GAAP. Finally, the role of the U.S. Financial Accounting Standards Board and the SEC in shaping and overseeing accounting standards will necessarily be reduced because the London-based International Accounting Standards Board sets the IFRS.

APPLICATION TO TODAY'S WORLD *The shift to IFRS received broad bipartisan political support even during the economic recession. Nevertheless, it will take years for the United States to completely implement global accounting rules. Business students should study and understand the IFRS so that they are prepared to use these rules in their future careers.*

losses suffered by the client. Therefore, an accountant who uncovers suspicious financial transactions and fails to investigate the matter fully or to inform the client of the discovery can be held liable to the client for the resulting loss.

Audits. One of the most important tasks that an accountant may perform for a business is an audit. An *audit* is a systematic inspection, by analyses and tests, of a business's financial records. An accountant qualified to perform audits is often called an **auditor.** After performing an audit, the auditor issues an opinion letter stating whether, in his or her opinion, the financial statements fairly present the business's financial position.

Auditor An accountant qualified to perform audits (systematic inspections) of a business's financial records.

The purpose of an audit is to provide the auditor with evidence to support an opinion on the reliability of the business's financial statements. A normal audit is not intended to uncover fraud or other misconduct. Nevertheless, an accountant may be liable for failing to detect misconduct if a normal audit would have revealed it. Also, if the auditor agreed to examine the records for evidence of fraud or other obvious misconduct and then failed to detect it, he or she may be liable.

Qualified Opinions and Disclaimers. In issuing an opinion letter, an auditor may *qualify* the opinion or include a *disclaimer.* In a disclaimer, the auditor basically states that she or he does not have sufficient information to issue an opinion. A qualified opinion or a disclaimer must be specific and must identify the reason for the qualification or disclaimer.

EXAMPLE 33.1 Richard Zehr performs an audit of Lacey Corporation. In the opinion letter, Zehr qualifies his opinion by stating that there is uncertainty about how a lawsuit against the firm will be resolved. In this situation, Zehr will not be liable if the outcome of the suit is unfavorable for the firm. Zehr could still be liable, however, for failing to discover other problems that an audit in compliance with IFRS or GAAS would have revealed. ■

Unaudited Financial Statements. Sometimes, accountants are called on to prepare unaudited financial statements. (A financial statement is considered unaudited if incomplete auditing procedures have been used in its preparation or if insufficient procedures have been used to justify an opinion.) Lesser standards of care are typically required in this situation.

Nevertheless, accountants may be liable for omissions from unaudited statements. Accountants may be subject to liability for failing, in accordance with standard accounting procedures, to designate a balance sheet as "unaudited." An accountant will also be held liable for failure to disclose to a client any facts or circumstances that give reason to believe that misstatements have been made or that a fraud has been committed.

> "Never call an accountant a credit to his profession; a good accountant is a debit to his profession."
>
> **ATTRIBUTED TO CHARLES J. C. LYELL**
> 1943–1996
> (AMERICAN COMMENTATOR)

Defenses to Negligence. If an accountant is found guilty of negligence, the client can collect damages for losses that arose from the accountant's negligence. An accountant facing a claim of negligence, however, has several possible defenses, including the following:

1. The accountant was not negligent.

2. If the accountant was negligent, this negligence was not the proximate cause of the client's losses.

3. The client was also negligent (depending on whether state law allows contributory negligence as a defense).

CASE EXAMPLE 33.2 Coopers & Lybrand, LLP, provided accounting services for Oregon Steel Mills, Inc. (OSM). Coopers advised OSM to report a certain transaction as a $12.3 million gain on its financial statements. Later, when OSM planned to make a public offering of its stock, the Securities and Exchange Commission (SEC) reviewed its financial statements and concluded that the transaction had been treated improperly. OSM then had to correct the statements.

Because of the delay caused by the correction, the public offering did not occur on May 2, when OSM's stock was selling for $16 per share. Instead, it took place on June 13, when, due

Assume that the accounting firm for this steel manufacturer makes an error in a registration statement. If the initial public offering is delayed and the stock price falls in the meantime, is the accounting firm liable for the lower price?

to unrelated factors, the price was $13.50. OSM filed a lawsuit against Coopers, claiming that negligent accounting had resulted in the stock's being sold at a lower price. The court held, however, that although the accounting firm's negligence had delayed the stock offering, the negligence was not the proximate cause of the decline in the stock price. Thus, Coopers could not be held liable for damages based on the price decline.[2] ■

Attorney's Duty of Care

The conduct of attorneys is governed by rules established by each state and by the American Bar Association's Code of Professional Responsibility and Model Rules of Professional Conduct. All attorneys owe a duty to provide competent and diligent representation.

Attorneys are required to be familiar with well-settled principles of law applicable to a case and to find relevant law that can be discovered through a reasonable amount of research. They must also investigate and discover facts that could materially affect clients' legal rights.

Normally, an attorney's performance is expected to be that of a reasonably competent general practitioner of ordinary skill, experience, and capacity. An attorney who holds himself or herself out as having expertise in a particular area of law (such as intellectual property) is held to a higher standard of care in that area of the law than attorneys without such expertise.

ETHICAL ISSUE

What are an attorney's responsibilities with respect to protecting data stored in the cloud? To achieve both cost savings and better security, more and more attorneys are storing their data, including confidential client information, on the cloud. Sometimes, professionals assume that once their data have migrated to the cloud, they no longer have to be concerned with keeping the information secure. But cloud computing is simply the virtualization of the computing process. In other words, the professional is still ultimately responsible for the information.

Attorneys' obligations for their clients' information are spelled out in the American Bar Association's Model Rules of Professional Conduct, which serve as the basis for the ethics rules for attorneys adopted by most states. Comment 17 to Model Rule 1.6 states, "The lawyer must take reasonable precautions to prevent the [client's] information from coming into the hands of unintended recipients." Thus, lawyers have an ethical duty to safeguard confidential client information, whether it is stored as documents in a filing cabinet or as electromagnetic impulses on a server that might be located anywhere. (Note that Rule 1.6 does not require an attorney to *guarantee* that a breach of confidentiality will never occur.)

Certainly, it is harder to maintain control over information stored on the cloud. Although the attorney "owns" the data, he or she probably does not even know the location of the computer where the information is stored. Furthermore, a provider of cloud computing services may move data from one server to another. Nevertheless, attorneys should be aware of jurisdictional issues and make sure that their cloud computing service provider is complying with data protection regulations and privacy notification requirements wherever the provider's servers are located.

Misconduct.

Typically, a state's rules of professional conduct for attorneys provide that committing a criminal act that reflects adversely on the person's "honesty or trustworthiness, or fitness as a lawyer in other respects" is professional misconduct. The rules often further provide that a lawyer should not engage in conduct involving "dishonesty, fraud, deceit, or misrepresentation." Under these rules, state authorities can discipline attorneys for many types of misconduct.

CASE EXAMPLE 33.3 Michael Inglimo, who was licensed to practice law in Wisconsin, occasionally used marijuana with a person who later became his client in a criminal case. After the trial, the client claimed that Inglimo had been high on drugs during the trial and had not

---

2. *Oregon Steel Mills, Inc. v. Coopers & Lybrand, LLP,* 336 Or. 329, 83 P.3d 322 (2004).

adequately represented him. Two years later, Inglimo was convicted for misdemeanor possession of marijuana. State authorities also discovered that Inglimo had commingled client funds and written several checks for personal expenses out of his client trust account.

The state initiated disciplinary proceedings to have Inglimo's license to practice suspended. Inglimo argued that he should not be suspended, because his misconduct was related to his past use of controlled substances and he no longer used drugs. The court, however, concluded that the suspension was necessary to protect the public in light of Inglimo's "disturbing pattern of disregard" for his professional obligations.[3] ■

Malpractice Professional negligence, or failure to exercise reasonable care and professional judgment, that results in injury, loss, or damage to those relying on the professional.

Liability for Malpractice. When an attorney fails to exercise reasonable care and professional judgment, she or he breaches the duty of care and can be held liable for **malpractice** (professional negligence). In malpractice cases—as in all cases involving allegations of negligence—the plaintiff must prove that the attorney's breach of the duty of care actually caused the plaintiff to suffer some injury.

EXAMPLE 33.4 Attorney Lynette Boehmer allows the statute of limitations to lapse on the claim of Karen Anderson, a client. Boehmer can be held liable for malpractice because Anderson can no longer pursue her claim and has lost a potential award of damages. ■

An attorney has a responsibility to advocate on the behalf of his or her client. In the following case, an attorney was accused of failing to fulfill this responsibility.

When does an attorney's recreational use of illegal drugs rise to the level of disregarding professional obligations?

---

3. *In re Disciplinary Proceedings against Inglimo*, 2007 WI 126, 305 Wis.2d 71, 740 N.W.2d 125 (2007).

CASE 33.1

In re B.L.H.
Court of Appeals of North Carolina, 767 S.E.2d 905 (2015).

FACTS The parents of B.L.H. (Barbara) lived in Virginia until their divorce, when primary custody of Barbara was granted to the mother. The mother and Barbara moved to North Carolina. Two years later, the father was convicted of drug-related offenses and incarcerated in a federal prison in Texas. Meanwhile, the mother remarried. Her new spouse sought to adopt Barbara. The mother filed a petition in a North Carolina state court to terminate the father's parental rights.

The summons served on the father notified him that the court had appointed an attorney to represent him in the proceeding. The father responded that he opposed the termination. The response was addressed to the court in care of the attorney. The attorney did not contact the father or present any evidence on his behalf at the hearing. The court terminated the father's parental rights. He appealed the termination, arguing that he had received ineffective assistance of counsel.

ISSUE Did the failure of the father's attorney to make an effort to communicate with the father before the hearing constitute ineffective representation?

DECISION Yes. A state intermediate appellate court vacated the lower court's judgment and ordered a new hearing on the termination of the father's parental rights.

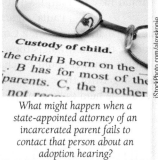

What might happen when a state-appointed attorney of an incarcerated parent fails to contact that person about an adoption hearing?

REASON The appellate court concluded that the failure of the attorney to make an effort to communicate with the father before the hearing deprived the father of a fair procedure. A parent has a "commanding" interest in a decision to terminate his or her parental rights. For this reason, a North Carolina statute provides an indigent parent with a right to counsel in a termination of parental rights proceeding. This includes a right to effective assistance of counsel.

A parent who claims to have received ineffective assistance must show that an attorney's deficient performance deprived the parent of a fair hearing. Here, the father did not have any contact with his attorney—no letter, e-mail, phone call, or conversation. The attorney's only arguable attempt to communicate was to contact the federal prison in which the father was incarcerated to learn about its e-mail system. "A lawyer cannot properly represent a client with whom he has no contact." And, in fact, at the termination hearing, the attorney presented no evidence and declined to make any argument on the father's behalf.

WHAT IF THE FACTS WERE DIFFERENT? *Suppose that the father had failed to cooperate with his attorney or had declined to respond to inquiries from him. Would the result have been different? Explain.*

33-1c Liability for Fraud

Recall that fraud, or fraudulent misrepresentation, involves the following elements:

1. A misrepresentation of a material fact.

2. An intent to deceive.

3. Justifiable reliance by the innocent party on the misrepresentation.

In addition, to obtain damages, the innocent party must have been injured. Both actual and constructive fraud are potential sources of legal liability for an accountant or other professional.

Actual Fraud   A professional may be held liable for *actual fraud* when he or she (1) intentionally misstates a material fact to mislead a client and (2) the client is injured as a result of justifiably relying on the misstated fact. A material fact is one that a reasonable person would consider important in deciding whether to act.

Among other penalties, an accountant guilty of fraudulent conduct may suffer penalties imposed by a state board of accountancy. **CASE EXAMPLE 33.5** Michael Walsh, a certified public accountant (CPA), impersonated his brother-in-law, Stephen Teiper, on the phone to obtain financial information from Teiper's insurance company. Teiper wrote a letter reporting Walsh's conduct to the Nebraska Board of Public Accountancy. After a hearing, the board reprimanded Walsh, placed him on probation for three months, and ordered him to attend four hours of ethics training. He also had to pay the costs of the hearing. The Nebraska Supreme Court affirmed the board's decision on appeal.[4] ■

Constructive Fraud   A professional may sometimes be held liable for **constructive fraud** whether or not he or she acted with fraudulent intent. Liability arises because the professional has a duty to the client and violates that duty by making a material misrepresentation. The client must be injured as a result of justifiably relying on the professional's misstatements to obtain damages.

Constructive fraud may be found when an accountant is grossly negligent in performing his or her duties. **EXAMPLE 33.6** Paula, an accountant, is conducting an audit of ComCo, Inc. Paula accepts the explanations of Ron, a ComCo officer, regarding certain financial irregularities, despite evidence that contradicts those explanations and indicates that the irregularities may be illegal. Paula's conduct could be characterized as an intentional failure to perform a duty in reckless disregard of the consequences of such failure. This would constitute gross negligence and could be held to be constructive fraud. ■

Constructive Fraud Conduct that is treated as fraud under the law even when there is no proof of intent to defraud, usually because of the existence of a special relationship or fiduciary duty.

33-2 Potential Liability to Third Parties

Traditionally, an accountant or other professional owed a duty only to those with whom she or he had a direct contractual relationship—that is, those with whom she or he was in *privity of contract*. A professional's duty was solely to her or his client. Violations of statutes, fraud, and other intentional or reckless acts of wrongdoing were the only exceptions to this general rule.

Today, numerous third parties—including investors, shareholders, creditors, corporate managers and directors, and regulatory agencies—rely on the opinions of auditors when making decisions. In view of this extensive reliance, many courts have all but abandoned the privity requirement in regard to accountants' liability to third parties.

What sanctions are there for a CPA who impersonates someone else over the phone to obtain financial information?

---

4. *Walsh v. State,* 276 Neb. 1034, 759 N.W.2d 100 (2009).

In this section, we focus primarily on the potential liability of auditors to third parties. The majority of courts now hold that auditors can be held liable to third parties for negligence, but the standard for the imposition of this liability varies.

33–2a The *Ultramares* Rule

LEARNING OBJECTIVE 2
What are the rules concerning an auditor's liability to third parties?

The traditional rule regarding an accountant's liability to third parties is based on privity of contract and was enunciated by Chief Judge Benjamin Cardozo in 1931. **CASE EXAMPLE 33.7** Fred Stern & Company hired the public accounting firm of Touche, Niven & Company to review Stern's financial records and prepare a balance sheet for the year ending December 31, 1923.[5] Touche prepared the balance sheet and supplied Stern with thirty-two certified copies. According to the certified balance sheet, Stern had a net worth (assets less liabilities) of $1,070,715.26.

In reality, however, Stern's liabilities exceeded its assets. The company's records had been falsified by insiders at Stern so that assets exceeded liabilities, resulting in a positive net worth. In reliance on the certified balance sheets, Ultramares Corporation loaned substantial amounts to Stern. After Stern was declared bankrupt, Ultramares brought an action against Touche for negligence in an attempt to recover damages.

The New York Court of Appeals (that state's highest court) refused to impose liability on Touche. The court concluded that Touche's accountants owed a duty of care only to those persons for whose "primary benefit" the statements were intended. In this case, the statements were intended only for the primary benefit of Stern. The court held that in the absence of privity or a relationship "so close as to approach that of privity," a party could not recover from an accountant.[6]

The Requirement of Privity The requirement of privity has since been referred to as the *Ultramares* rule, or the New York rule. It continues to be used in some states. **CASE EXAMPLE 33.8** Toro Company supplied equipment and credit to Summit Power Equipment Distributors and required Summit to submit audited reports indicating its financial condition. Accountants at Krouse, Kern & Company prepared the reports, which allegedly contained mistakes and omissions regarding Summit's financial condition.

Toro extended large amounts of credit to Summit in reliance on the audited reports. When Summit was unable to repay the loans, Toro brought a negligence action against the accounting firm and proved that accountants at Krouse knew the reports would be used by Summit to induce Toro to extend credit. Nevertheless, under the *Ultramares* rule, the court refused to hold the accounting firm liable because the firm was not in privity with Toro.[7]

To what extent is an accounting firm liable for incorrect balance-sheet information that is distributed to the public?

"Near Privity" Modification The *Ultramares* rule was modified somewhat in a 1985 New York case, *Credit Alliance Corp. v. Arthur Andersen & Co.*[8] In that case, the court held that if a third party has a sufficiently close relationship or *nexus* (link or connection) with an accountant, then the *Ultramares* privity requirement may be satisfied without the establishment of an accountant-client relationship. The rule enunciated in the *Credit Alliance* case is often referred to as the "near privity" rule. Only a minority of states have adopted this rule.

5. Banks, creditors, stockholders, purchasers, or sellers often rely on a balance sheet as a basis for making decisions relating to a company's business.
6. *Ultramares Corp. v. Touche*, 255 N.Y. 170, 174 N.E. 441 (1931).
7. *Toro Co. v. Krouse, Kern & Co.*, 827 F.2d 155 (7th Cir. 1987).
8. 66 N.Y.2d 812, 489 N.E.2d 249, 498 N.Y.S.2d 362 (1985).

33-2b The *Restatement* Rule

The *Ultramares* rule has been severely criticized. Because much of the work performed by auditors is intended for use by persons who are not parties to the contract, many argue that auditors should owe a duty to these third parties. As support for this position has grown, there has been an erosion of the *Ultramares* rule to expose accountants to liability to third parties in some situations.

The majority of courts have adopted the position taken by the *Restatement (Third) of Torts,* which states that accountants are subject to liability for negligence not only to their clients but also to foreseen or *known* users—or classes of users—of their reports or financial statements. Under the *Restatement (Third) of Torts,* an accountant's liability extends to the following:

1. Persons for whose benefit and guidance the accountant "intends to supply the information or knows that the recipient intends to supply it."

2. Persons that the accountant "intends the information to influence or knows that the recipient so intends."

EXAMPLE 33.9 Steve, an accountant, prepares a financial statement for Tech Software, Inc., a client, knowing that Tech Software will submit the statement when it applies for a loan from First National Bank. If Steve makes negligent misstatements or omissions in the statement, he may be held liable to the bank because he knew that the bank would rely on his work product when deciding whether to make the loan. ■

33-2c The "Reasonably Foreseeable Users" Rule

A small minority of courts hold accountants liable to any users whose reliance on an accountant's statements or reports was *reasonably foreseeable*. This standard has been criticized as extending liability too far and exposing accountants to massive liability.

The majority of courts have concluded that the *Restatement's* approach is more reasonable because it allows accountants to control their exposure to liability. Liability is "fixed by the accountants' particular knowledge at the moment the audit is published," not by the foreseeability of the harm that might occur to a third party after the report is released. Exhibit 33–1 summarizes the three different views of accountants' liability to third parties.

33-2d Liability of Attorneys to Third Parties

Like accountants, attorneys may be held liable under the common law to third parties who rely on legal opinions to their detriment. Generally, an attorney is not liable to a nonclient

Exhibit 33–1 Three Basic Rules of Accountant's Liability to Third Parties

RULE	DESCRIPTION	APPLICATION
Ultramares rule	Liability is imposed only if the accountant is in privity, or near privity, with the third party.	A minority of courts apply this rule.
Restatement rule	Liability is imposed only if the third party's reliance is foreseen, or known, or if the third party is among a class of foreseen, or known, users.	The majority of courts have adopted this rule.
"Reasonably foreseeable users" rule	Liability is imposed if the third party's use was reasonably foreseeable.	A small minority of courts use this rule.

unless there is fraud (or malicious conduct) by the attorney. The liability principles stated in the *Restatement (Third) of Torts,* however, may apply to attorneys as well as to accountants.

Should an attorney's duty of care extend to third party beneficiaries whose rights were harmed by the attorney's malpractice? That question was at issue in the following case.

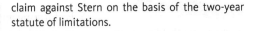

CASE 33.2

Pereza v. Stern

Nebraska Supreme Court, 279 Neb. 187, 777 N.W.2d 545 (2010).

FACTS Domingo Martinez and Reyna Guido had two minor children when Martinez was killed in a hit-and-run accident. Guido became the personal representative of Martinez's estate and retained attorney Sandra Stern to file a wrongful death lawsuit. Stern did so, but because the complaint was not served within six months of filing, the case was dismissed.

Several years later, Guido filed a legal malpractice suit against Stern on behalf of herself, the children, and the estate. Stern moved for summary judgment on the ground that the malpractice claim was barred by the Nebraska two-year statute of limitations for professional negligence. The trial court found that the estate's claim against Stern was barred. The court granted summary judgment in favor of Stern and dismissed the case. Guido appealed, claiming that the trial court had erred in granting Stern's motion for summary judgment.

ISSUE Can the minor children of a decedent sue the attorney who failed to properly file a wrongful death claim on their behalf for malpractice?

DECISION Yes. The Nebraska Supreme Court reversed the part of the trial court's ruling that pertained to Martinez's minor children and remanded the case for further proceedings. The court affirmed the lower court's dismissal of Guido's individual claim and the estate's

If a parent is killed in an auto accident, what duty does an attorney have to the children?

claim against Stern on the basis of the two-year statute of limitations.

REASON The question was whether Stern owed an independent duty to the children, who were Martinez's next of kin, to prosecute the underlying wrongful death claim in a timely manner. The reviewing court pointed out that a lawyer's duty does not extend to third parties in most situations. "Courts have repeatedly emphasized that the starting point for analyzing an attorney's duty to a third party is determining whether the third party was a direct and intended beneficiary of the attorney services."

In this situation, Stern did owe a duty to the children to represent their interests competently. "To hold otherwise would deny a legal recourse to the children for whose benefit Stern was hired in the first place." The court concluded that the children had standing to sue Stern for neglecting that duty. The claim was not barred by the statute of limitations because the statutory period did not run while the children were minors.b

CRITICAL THINKING—Ethical Consideration *If one of the children had not been a minor at the time of the father's death, the court would have dismissed his or her claims against Stern, even though he or she was an intended beneficiary. Is it fair for the law to treat minors differently than other children with regard to a statute of limitations? Why or why not?*

---

a. Esteban Perez was one of the minor children of Domingo Martinez, the man killed in the accident.

b. In most states, the law allows a person's status as a minor to toll (or stop) the statute of limitations period from running.

33–3 The Sarbanes-Oxley Act

The Sarbanes-Oxley Act of 2002 imposes a number of strict requirements on both domestic and foreign public accounting firms. These requirements apply to firms that provide auditing services to companies ("issuers") whose securities are sold to public investors. The act defines an *issuer* as a company that has securities that are registered under Section 12 of the Securities Exchange Act of 1934, that is required to file reports under Section 15(d) of the 1934 act, or that files—or has filed—a registration statement that has not yet become effective under the Securities Act of 1933.

To the extent that Deloitte & Touche engages in auditing public companies, its procedures are overseen by the Public Company Accounting Oversight Board. What law requires this oversight?

Working Papers
The documents used and developed by an accountant during an audit, such as notes, computations, and memoranda.

33–3a The Public Company Accounting Oversight Board

The Sarbanes-Oxley Act increased government oversight of public accounting practices by creating the Public Company Accounting Oversight Board, which reports to the Securities and Exchange Commission. The board oversees the audit of public companies that are subject to securities laws. The goal is to protect public investors and to ensure that public accounting firms comply with the provisions of the act. The act defines *public accounting firms* as firms "engaged in the practice of public accounting or preparing or issuing audit reports." The key provisions relating to the duties of the oversight board and the requirements relating to public accounting firms are summarized in Exhibit 33–2.

33–3b Requirements for Maintaining Working Papers

Performing an audit for a client involves an accumulation of **working papers**—the documents used and developed during the audit. These include notes, computations, memoranda, copies, and other papers that make up the work product of an accountant's services to a client.

Under the common law, which in this instance has been codified in a number of states, working papers remain the accountant's property. It is important for accountants to retain such records in the event that they need to defend against lawsuits for negligence or other actions in which their competence is challenged. The client also has a right to access an accountant's working papers because they reflect the client's financial situation. On a client's request, an accountant must return to the client any of the client's records or journals, and failure to do so may result in liability.

Section 802(a)(1) of the Sarbanes-Oxley Act required accountants to maintain working papers relating to an audit or review for five years from the end of the fiscal period in which the audit or review was concluded. The requirement was subsequently extended to seven

Exhibit 33–2 Key Provisions of the Sarbanes-Oxley Act Relating to Public Accounting Firms

AUDITOR INDEPENDENCE

To help ensure that auditors remain independent of the firms that they audit, Title II of the Sarbanes-Oxley Act does the following:

1. Makes it unlawful for Registered Public Accounting Firms (RPAFs) to perform both audit and nonaudit services for the same company at the same time. Nonaudit services include the following:
   - Bookkeeping or other services related to the accounting records or financial statements of the audit client.
   - Financial information systems design and implementation.
   - Appraisal or valuation services.
   - Fairness opinions.
   - Management functions.
   - Broker or dealer, investment adviser, or investment banking services.
2. Requires preapproval for most auditing services from the issuer's (the corporation's) audit committee.
3. Requires audit partner rotation by prohibiting RPAFs from providing audit services to an issuer if either the lead audit partner or the audit partner responsible for reviewing the audit has provided such services to that corporation in each of the prior five years.
4. Requires RPAFs to make timely reports to the audit committees of the corporations. The report must indicate all critical accounting policies and practices to be used; all alternative treatments of financial information within generally accepted accounting principles that have been discussed with the corporation's management officials, the ramifications of the use of such alternative treatments, and the treatment preferred by the auditor; and other material written communications between the auditor and the corporation's management.
5. Makes it unlawful for an RPAF to provide auditing services to an issuer if the corporation's chief executive officer, chief financial officer, chief accounting officer, or controller was previously employed by the auditor and participated in any capacity in the audit of the corporation during the one-year period preceding the date that the audit began.

DOCUMENT INTEGRITY AND RETENTION

1. The act provides that anyone who destroys, alters, or falsifies records with the intent to obstruct or influence a federal investigation or in relation to bankruptcy proceedings can be criminally prosecuted and sentenced to a fine, imprisonment for up to twenty years, or both.
2. The act requires accountants who audit or review publicly traded companies to retain all working papers related to the audit or review for a period of five years (amended to seven years). Violators can be sentenced to a fine, imprisonment for up to ten years, or both.

years. A knowing violation of this requirement will subject the accountant to a fine, imprisonment for up to ten years, or both.

33-4 Potential Liability of Accountants under Securities Laws

Both civil and criminal liability may be imposed on accountants under the Securities Act of 1933, the Securities Exchange Act of 1934, and the 1995 Private Securities Litigation Reform Act.[9]

33-4a Liability under the Securities Act of 1933

The Securities Act requires issuers to file registration statements with the Securities and Exchange Commission (SEC) prior to an offering of securities.[10] Accountants frequently prepare and certify the financial statements that are included in the issuer's registration statement.

Liability under Section 11 Section 11 of the Securities Act of 1933 imposes civil liability on accountants for misstatements and omissions of material facts in registration statements. Accountants may be liable if a financial statement they prepared for inclusion "contained an untrue statement of a material fact or omitted to state a material fact required to be stated therein or necessary to make the statements therein not misleading."[11]

An accountant's liability for a misstatement or omission of a material fact in a registration statement extends to anyone who acquires a security covered by the registration statement. A purchaser of a security need only demonstrate that she or he has suffered a loss on the security. Proof of reliance on the materially false statement or misleading omission ordinarily is not required. Nor is there a requirement of privity between the accountant and the security purchaser.

The Due Diligence Standard. Section 11 imposes a duty on accountants to use **due diligence** in preparing the financial statements included in registration statements. Thus, after a purchaser has proved a loss on a security, the accountant has the burden of showing that he or she exercised due diligence in preparing the financial statements.

To prove due diligence, an accountant must demonstrate that she or he followed generally accepted standards and did not commit negligence or fraud. Specifically, to avoid liability, the accountant must show that he or she did the following:

1. Conducted a reasonable investigation.

2. Had reasonable grounds to believe and did believe, at the time the registration statement became effective, that the statements therein were true and that there was no omission of a material fact that would be misleading.[12]

In particular, the due diligence standard places a burden on accountants to verify information furnished by a corporation's officers and directors. Merely asking questions is not always sufficient to satisfy the requirement. Accountants have been held liable for failing to detect danger signals in documents that, according to GAAS, require further investigation under the circumstances.[13]

LEARNING OBJECTIVE 3
How might an accountant violate federal securities laws?

"Destroy the old files, but make copies first."

SAMUEL GOLDWYN
1879–1974
(AMERICAN MOTION PICTURE PRODUCER)

Due Diligence A required standard of care that certain professionals, such as accountants, must meet to avoid liability for securities violations.

---

9. Civil and criminal liability may also be imposed on accountants and other professionals under other statutes, including the Racketeer Influenced and Corrupt Organizations Act (RICO), which was discussed in the criminal law chapter.
10. Many securities and transactions are expressly exempted from the 1933 act.
11. 15 U.S.C. Section 77k(a).
12. 15 U.S.C. Section 77k(b)(3).
13. See *In re Cardinal Health, Inc. Securities Litigation*, 426 F.Supp.2d 688 (S.D. Ohio 2006); and *In re WorldCom, Inc. Securities Litigation*, 352 F.Supp.2d 472 (S.D.N.Y. 2005).

PREVENTING LEGAL DISPUTES

When "danger signals" exist, the responsibility to investigate extends beyond accountants. Persons other than accountants, including corporate directors, officers, and managers, can also be liable for failing to perform due diligence. Courts are more likely to impose liability on someone who has ignored warning signs or red flags that suggest accounting errors or misstatements are present. To avoid liability, always investigate the facts underlying financial statements that appear "too good to be true." Compare recent financial statements with earlier ones, read minutes of shareholders' and directors' meetings, and inspect changes in material contracts, bad debts, and newly discovered liabilities. Know what is required to meet due diligence standards in the relevant jurisdiction, and conduct yourself in a manner that is above reproach.

Other Defenses to Liability. Besides proving that he or she has acted with due diligence, an accountant can raise the following defenses to Section 11 liability:

1. There were no misstatements or omissions.

2. The misstatements or omissions were not of material facts.

3. The misstatements or omissions had no causal connection to the plaintiff's loss.

4. The plaintiff-purchaser invested in the securities knowing of the misstatements or omissions.

Liability under Section 12(2)

Section 12(2) of the 1933 Securities Act imposes civil liability for fraud in relation to offerings or sales of securities.[14] Liability arises when an oral statement to an investor or a written prospectus[15] includes an untrue statement or omits a material fact. Some courts have applied Section 12(2) to accountants who aided and abetted (assisted) the seller or the offeror of the securities in violating Section 12(2).

Those who purchase securities and suffer harm as a result of a false or omitted statement, or some other violation, may bring a suit in a federal court to recover their losses and other damages. The U.S. Department of Justice brings criminal actions against those who commit willful violations.

The penalties include fines of up to $10,000, imprisonment for up to five years, or both. The SEC is authorized to seek an injunction against a willful violator to prevent further violations. The SEC can also ask a court to grant other relief, such as an order to a violator to refund profits derived from an illegal transaction.

33-4b Liability under the Securities Exchange Act of 1934

Under Sections 18 and 10(b) of the Securities Exchange Act and SEC Rule 10b-5, an accountant may be found liable for fraud. A plaintiff has a substantially heavier burden of proof under the 1934 act than under the 1933 act because an accountant does not have to prove due diligence to escape liability under the 1934 act.

Liability under Section 18

Section 18 of the 1934 act imposes civil liability on an accountant who makes or causes to be made in any application, report, or document a statement that at the time and in light of the circumstances was false or misleading with respect to any material fact.[16]

Section 18 liability is narrow in that it applies only to applications, reports, documents, and registration statements filed with the SEC. This remedy is further limited in that it applies

---

14. 15 U.S.C. Section 77l.

15. A *prospectus* contains financial disclosures about the corporation for the benefit of potential investors.

16. 15 U.S.C. Section 78r(a).

only to sellers and purchasers. Under Section 18, a seller or purchaser must prove one of the following:

1. That the false or misleading statement affected the price of the security.

2. That the purchaser or seller relied on the false or misleading statement in making the purchase or sale and was not aware of the inaccuracy of the statement.

Good Faith Defense. An accountant will not be liable for violating Section 18 if he or she acted in good faith in preparing the financial statement. To demonstrate good faith, an accountant must show that he or she had no knowledge that the financial statement was false and misleading. In addition, the accountant must have had no intent to deceive, manipulate, defraud, or seek unfair advantage over another party.

Note that "mere" negligence in preparing a financial statement does not lead to liability under the 1934 act. This differs from the 1933 act, under which an accountant is liable for *all* negligent acts.

Other Defenses. In addition to the good faith defense, accountants can escape liability by proving that the buyer or seller of the security in question knew that the financial statement was false and misleading. Also, the statute of limitations may be asserted as a defense to liability under the 1934 act. Sellers and purchasers must bring a cause of action "within one year after the discovery of the facts constituting the cause of action and within three years after such cause of action accrued."[17]

Liability under Section 10(b) and Rule 10b-5
Accountants additionally face potential legal liability under the antifraud provisions contained in the Securities Exchange Act and SEC Rule 10b-5. The scope of these antifraud provisions is very broad and allows private parties to bring civil actions against violators.

Prohibited Conduct. Section 10(b) makes it unlawful for any person, including accountants, to use, in connection with the purchase or sale of any security, any manipulative or deceptive device or contrivance in contravention of SEC rules and regulations.[18] Rule 10b-5 further makes it unlawful for any person, by use of any means or instrumentality of interstate commerce, to do the following:

1. Employ any device, scheme, or artifice (pretense) to defraud.

2. Make any untrue statement of a material fact or omit a material fact necessary to ensure that the statements made were not misleading, in light of the circumstances.

3. Engage in any act, practice, or course of business that operates or would operate as a fraud or deceit on any person, in connection with the purchase or sale of any security.[19]

Extent of Liability. Accountants may be held liable only to sellers or purchasers of securities under Section 10(b) and Rule 10b-5. Privity is not necessary for a recovery.

An accountant may be found liable not only for fraudulent misstatements of material facts in written material filed with the SEC, but also for any fraudulent oral statements or omissions made in connection with the purchase or sale of any security. For a plaintiff to succeed in recovering damages under these antifraud provisions, he or she must prove intent (*scienter*) to commit the fraudulent or deceptive act. Ordinary negligence is not enough.

---

17. 15 U.S.C. Section 17r(c).
18. 15 U.S.C. Section 78j(b)
19. 17 C.F.R. Section 240.10b-5.

Do accountants have a duty to correct misstatements that they discover in *previous* financial statements? What if they know that potential investors are relying on those statements? Those were the questions in the following *Spotlight Case.*

SPOTLIGHT ON AN ACCOUNTANT'S DUTY TO CORRECT MISTAKES: CASE 33.3

Overton v. Todman & Co., CPAs

United States Court of Appeals, Second Circuit, 478 F.3d 479 (2007).

FACTS From 1999 through 2002, Todman & Company, CPAs, audited the financial statements of Direct Brokerage, Inc. (DBI), a broker-dealer in New York registered with the Securities and Exchange Commission (SEC). Each year, Todman issued an unqualified opinion that DBI's financial statements were accurate. DBI filed its statements and Todman's opinions with the SEC.

Despite the certifications of accuracy, Todman made significant errors that concealed DBI's largest liability—its payroll taxes—in the 1999 and 2000 audits. The errors came to light in 2003 when the New York State Division of Taxation subpoenaed DBI's payroll records. It became clear that the company had not filed or paid its payroll taxes for 1999 and 2000. This put DBI in a precarious financial position, owing the state more than $3 million in unpaid taxes, interest, and penalties.

To meet its needs, DBI sought outside investors, including David Overton, who relied on DBI's statements and Todman's opinion for 2002 to invest in DBI. When DBI collapsed under the weight of its liabilities in 2004, Overton and others filed a suit in a federal district court against Todman, asserting, among other things, fraud under Section 10(b) and Rule 10b-5. The court dismissed the complaint. The plaintiffs appealed.

ISSUE Is an accountant liable for securities fraud if the accountant certified a financial statement containing a misstatement and later learned of the misstatement but failed to correct it, even though the accountant knew that investors were relying on the statement?

DECISION Yes. The federal appellate court held that an accountant is liable in these circumstances under Section 10(b) and Rule 10b-5.

Must an accounting firm make public its new knowledge of prior misstatements?

The court vacated the lower court's dismissal and remanded the case for further proceedings.

REASON The court pointed out that any person or entity, including an accountant, "who employs a manipulative device or makes a material misstatement (or omission) on which a purchaser or seller of securities relies may be liable as a primary violator under [Section] 10b-5, assuming all of the requirements for primary liability under Rule 10b-5 are met." One of the requirements is a "duty to speak." Such a duty arises "when one party has information that the other party is entitled to know because of a fiduciary or other similar relation of trust and confidence between them."

When accountants issue a certified opinion, they create the required special relationship with investors. Thus, accountants have a duty to take reasonable steps to correct misstatements that they discover in previous financial statements on which they know the public is relying. Silence in this situation can constitute a false or misleading statement under Section 10(b) and Rule 10b-5. Among other authorities, the court cited Section 10(b), which covers "any person," a United States Supreme Court decision that "labeled a critical element under [Section] 10(b) and Rule 10b-5: reliance by potential investors on the accountant's omission."[a]

WHAT IF THE FACTS WERE DIFFERENT? *If Todman had conducted an audit for DBI but had not issued a certified opinion about DBI's financial statements, would the result have been the same? Explain.*

a. See *Central Bank of Denver v. First Interstate Bank of Denver*, 511 U.S. 164, 114 S.Ct. 1439, 128 L.Ed.2d 119 (1994).

33-4c The Private Securities Litigation Reform Act

The 1995 Private Securities Litigation Reform Act made some changes to the potential liability of accountants and other professionals in securities fraud cases. Among other things, the act imposed a statutory obligation on accountants. An auditor must use adequate procedures in an audit to detect any illegal acts of the company being audited. If something illegal is detected, the auditor must disclose it to the company's board of directors, the audit committee, or the SEC, depending on the circumstances.[20]

---

20. 15 U.S.C. Section 78j-1.

Proportionate Liability The act provides that, in most situations, a party is liable only for the proportion of damages for which he or she is responsible.[21] An accountant who participates in, but is unaware of, illegal conduct may not be liable for the entire loss caused by the illegality.

EXAMPLE 33.10 Nina, an accountant, helps the president and owner of Midstate Trucking company draft financial statements. The statements misrepresent Midstate's financial condition, but Nina is not aware of the fraud. Nina might be held liable, but the amount of her liability could be proportionately less than the entire loss. ■

Aiding and Abetting The act also made it a separate crime to aid and abet a violation of the Securities Exchange Act. Aiding and abetting might include knowingly participating in such an act, assisting in it, or keeping quiet about it. If an accountant knowingly aids and abets a primary violator, the SEC can seek an injunction or monetary damages.

EXAMPLE 33.11 Smith & Jones, an accounting firm, performs an audit for ABC Sales Company that is so inadequate as to constitute gross negligence. ABC uses the materials provided by Smith & Jones as part of a scheme to defraud investors. When the scheme is uncovered, the SEC can bring an action against Smith & Jones for aiding and abetting on the ground that the firm knew or should have known of the material misrepresentations that were in its audit and on which investors were likely to rely. ■

If an accountant is unaware of a company officer's fraud, will she still be held fully liable for any losses caused by the misstatements?

33–5 Potential Criminal Liability

An accountant may be found criminally liable for violations of securities laws and tax laws. In addition, most states make it a crime to (1) knowingly certify false reports, (2) falsify, alter, or destroy books of account, and (3) obtain property or credit through the use of false financial statements.

33–5a Criminal Violations of Securities Laws

Accountants may be subject to criminal penalties for *willful* violations of the 1933 Securities Act and the 1934 Securities Exchange Act. If convicted, they face imprisonment for up to five years and/or a fine of up to $10,000 under the 1933 act, and imprisonment for up to ten years and a fine of $100,000 under the 1934 act. Under the Sarbanes-Oxley Act, if an accountant's false or misleading certified audit statement is used in a securities filing, the accountant may be fined up to $5 million, imprisoned for up to twenty years, or both.

33–5b Criminal Violations of Tax Laws

The Internal Revenue Code makes it a felony to willfully make false statements in a tax return or to willfully aid or assist others in preparing a false tax return. Felony violations are punishable by a fine of $100,000 ($500,000 in the case of a corporation) and imprisonment for up to three years.[22] This provision applies to anyone who prepares tax returns for others for compensation—not just to accountants.[23]

A penalty of $250 per tax return is levied on tax preparers for negligent understatement of the client's tax liability. For willful understatement of tax liability or reckless or intentional disregard of rules or regulations, a penalty of $1,000 is imposed.[24] A tax preparer may also be

LEARNING OBJECTIVE 4
What crimes might an accountant commit under the Internal Revenue Code?

---

21. 15 U.S.C. Section 78u-4(g).
22. 26 U.S.C. Section 7206(2).
23. 26 U.S.C. Section 7701(a)(36).
24. 26 U.S.C. Section 6694.

subject to penalties for failing to furnish the taxpayer with a copy of the return, failing to sign the return, or failing to furnish the appropriate tax identification numbers.

In addition, a tax preparer may be fined $1,000 per document for aiding and abetting another's understatement of tax liability (the penalty is increased to $10,000 in corporate cases).[25] The tax preparer's liability is limited to one penalty per taxpayer per tax year.

33–6 Confidentiality and Privilege

Professionals are restrained by the ethical tenets of their professions to keep all communications with their clients confidential.

33–6a Attorney-Client Relationships

The confidentiality of attorney-client communications is protected by law, which confers a privilege on such communications. This privilege exists because of the client's need to fully disclose the facts of his or her case to the attorney.

To encourage frankness, confidential attorney-client communications relating to representation are normally held in strictest confidence and protected by law. The attorney and her or his employees may not discuss the client's case with anyone—even under court order—without the client's permission. The client holds the privilege, and only the client may waive it—by disclosing privileged information to someone outside the privilege, for instance.

Note, however, that the SEC has implemented rules requiring attorneys who become aware that a client has violated securities laws to report the violation to the SEC. Because reporting a client's misconduct can be a breach of the attorney-client privilege, these rules have created potential conflicts for some attorneys.

33–6b Accountant-Client Relationships

In a few states, accountant-client communications are privileged by state statute. In these states, accountant-client communications may not be revealed even in court or in court-sanctioned proceedings without the client's permission.

The majority of states, however, abide by the common law, which provides that, if a court so orders, an accountant must disclose information about his or her client to the court. Physicians and other professionals may similarly be compelled to disclose in court information given to them in confidence by patients or clients.

Communications between professionals and their clients—other than those between an attorney and her or his client—are not privileged under federal law. In cases involving federal law, state-provided rights to confidentiality of accountant-client communications are not recognized. Thus, in those cases, an accountant must provide all information requested in a court order.

---

25. 26 U.S.C. Section 6701.

Reviewing . . . Liability of Accountants and Other Professionals

Superior Wholesale Corporation planned to purchase Regal Furniture, Inc., and wished to determine Regal's net worth. Superior hired Lynette Shuebke, of the accounting firm Shuebke Delgado, to review an audit that had been prepared by Norman Chase, the accountant for Regal. Shuebke advised Superior that Chase had performed a high-quality audit and that Regal's inventory on the audit dates was stated accurately on the general ledger. As a result of these representations, Superior went forward with its purchase of Regal.

 After the purchase, Superior discovered that the audit by Chase had been materially inaccurate and misleading, primarily because the inventory had been grossly overstated on the balance sheet. Later, a former Regal employee who had begun working for Superior exposed an e-mail exchange between Chase and former Regal chief executive officer Buddy Gantry. The exchange revealed that Chase had cooperated in overstating the inventory and understating Regal's tax liability. Using the information presented in the chapter, answer the following questions.

1. If Shuebke's review was conducted in good faith and conformed to generally accepted accounting principles, could Superior hold Shuebke Delgado liable for negligently failing to detect material omissions in Chase's audit? Why or why not?

2. According to the rule adopted by the majority of courts to determine accountants' liability to third parties, could Chase be liable to Superior? Explain.

3. Generally, what requirements must be met before Superior can recover damages under Section 10(b) of the Securities Exchange Act of 1934 and SEC Rule 10b-5? Can Superior meet these requirements?

4. Suppose that a court determined that Chase had aided Regal in willfully understating its tax liability. What is the maximum penalty that could be imposed on Chase?

DEBATE THIS

■ Only the largest publicly held companies should be subject to the Sarbanes-Oxley Act.

Key Terms

auditor 833	generally accepted accounting principles (GAAP) 831	International Financial Reporting Standards (IFRS) 832
constructive fraud 836		
defalcation 832	generally accepted auditing standards (GAAS) 831	malpractice 835
due diligence 841		working papers 840

Chapter Summary: Liability of Accountants and Other Professionals

COMMON LAW LIABILITY	
Potential Liability to Clients	1. *Breach of contract*—A professional who fails to fulfill contractual obligations can be held liable for breach of contract and resulting damages.
	2. *Negligence*—An accountant, attorney, or other professional, in performing of her or his duties, must use the care, knowledge, and judgment generally used by professionals in the same or similar circumstances. Failure to do so is negligence. An accountant's violation of generally accepted accounting principles and generally accepted auditing standards is *prima facie* evidence of negligence.
	3. *Fraud*—Intentionally misrepresenting a material fact to a client, when the client relies on the misrepresentation, is fraud. Gross negligence in performance of duties is constructive fraud.

Continues

Potential Liability to Third Parties	An accountant may be liable for negligence to any third person the accountant knows or should have known will benefit from the accountant's work. The standard for imposing this liability varies, but generally courts follow one of the following rules (see Exhibit 33–1): 1. *Ultramares rule*—Liability will be imposed only if the accountant is in privity, or near privity, with the third party. 2. *Restatement rule*—Liability will be imposed only if the third party's reliance is foreseen or known, or if the third party is among a class of foreseen or known users. The majority of courts have adopted this rule. 3. *"Reasonably foreseeable users" rule*—Liability will be imposed if the third party's use was reasonably foreseeable.
STATUTORY LIABILITY	
The Sarbanes-Oxley Act	1. *Purpose*—The Sarbanes-Oxley Act imposed requirements on public accounting firms that provide auditing services to companies whose securities are sold to public investors. 2. *Government oversight*—The act created the Public Company Accounting Oversight Board to provide government oversight over public accounting practices. 3. *Working papers*—The act requires accountants to maintain working papers relating to an audit or review for seven years from the end of the fiscal period in which the audit or review was concluded. 4. *Other requirements*—See Exhibit 33–2.
Securities Act of 1933—Section 11	An accountant who makes a false statement or omits a material fact in audited financial statements required for registration of securities under the act may be liable to anyone who acquires securities covered by the registration statement. The accountant's defense is basically the use of due diligence and the reasonable belief that the work was complete and correct. The burden of proof is on the accountant. Willful violations of this act may be subject to criminal penalties.
Securities Act of 1933—Section 12(2)	An accountant may be liable when a prospectus or other communication presented to an investor contained an untrue statement or omitted a material fact.
Securities Exchange Act of 1934— Sections 10(b) and 18	Accountants may be held liable for false and misleading applications, reports, and documents required under the act. The burden is on the plaintiff, and the accountant has numerous defenses, including good faith and lack of knowledge that what was submitted was false.
Potential Criminal Liability	1. Willful violations of the Securities Act of 1933 and the Securities Exchange Act of 1934 may be subject to criminal penalties. 2. Willfully making false statements in or willfully aiding or assisting in the preparation of a false tax return is a felony. Aiding and abetting an individual's understatement of tax liability is a separate crime.

Issue Spotters

1. Dave, an accountant, prepares a financial statement for Excel Company, a client, knowing that Excel will use the statement to obtain a loan from First National Bank. Dave makes negligent omissions in the statement that result in a loss to the bank. Can the bank successfully sue Dave? Why or why not? (See *Potential Liability to Third Parties*.)

2. Nora, an accountant, prepares a financial statement as part of a registration statement that Omega, Inc., files with the Securities and Exchange Commission before making a public offering of securities. The statement contains a misstatement of material fact that is not attributable to Nora's fraud or negligence. Pat relies on the misstatement, buys some of the securities, and suffers a loss. Can Nora be held liable to Pat? Explain. (See *Potential Liability of Accountants under Securities Laws*.)

—**Check your answers to the *Issue Spotters* against the answers provided in Appendix D at the end of this text.**

Learning Objectives Check

1. Under what common law theories may professionals be liable to clients?
2. What are the rules concerning an auditor's liability to third parties?
3. How might an accountant violate federal securities laws?
4. What crimes might an accountant commit under the Internal Revenue Code?

—**Answers to the even-numbered *Learning Objectives Check* questions can be found in Appendix E at the end of this text.**

Business Scenarios and Case Problems

33–1. The *Ultramares* Rule. Larkin, Inc., retains Howard Perkins to manage its books and prepare its financial statements. Perkins, a certified public accountant, lives in Indiana and practices there. After twenty years, Perkins has become a bit bored with generally accepted accounting principles (GAAP) and has adopted more creative accounting methods. Now, though, Perkins has a problem. He is being sued by Molly Tucker, one of Larkin's creditors. Tucker alleges that Perkins either knew or should have known that Larkin's financial statements would be distributed to various individuals. Furthermore, she asserts that these financial statements were negligently prepared and seriously inaccurate. What are the consequences of Perkins's failure to follow GAAP? Under the traditional *Ultramares* rule, can Tucker recover damages from Perkins? Explain. (See *Potential Liability to Third Parties*.)

33–2. The Restatement Rule. The accounting firm of Goldman, Walters, Johnson & Co. prepared financial statements for Lucy's Fashions, Inc. After reviewing the financial statements, Happydays State Bank agreed to loan Lucy's Fashions $35,000 for expansion. When Lucy's Fashions declared bankruptcy under Chapter 11 six months later, Happydays State Bank filed an action against Goldman, Walters, Johnson & Co., alleging negligent preparation of financial statements. Assuming that the court has abandoned the *Ultramares* approach, what is the result? What are the policy reasons for holding accountants liable to third parties with whom they are not in privity? (See *Potential Liability to Third Parties*.)

33–3. Accountant's Liability under Rule 10b-5. In early 2016, Bennett, Inc., offered a substantial number of new common shares to the public. Harvey Helms had a long-standing interest in Bennett because his grandfather had once been president of the company. On receiving Bennett's prospectus, Helms was dismayed by the pessimism it embodied, so he decided to delay purchasing stock in the company. Later, Helms asserted that the prospectus prepared by the accountants had been overly pessimistic and had contained materially misleading statements. Discuss fully how successful Helms would be in bringing a suit under Rule 10b-5 against Bennett's accountants. (See *Potential Liability of Accountants under Securities Laws*.)

33–4. Accountant's Liability for Audit. A West Virginia bank ran its asset value from $100 million to $1 billion over seven years by aggressively marketing subprime loans. The Office of the Comptroller of the Currency, a federal regulator, audited the bank and discovered that the books had been falsified for several years and that the bank was insolvent. The Comptroller closed the bank and brought criminal charges against its managers.

The Comptroller fined Grant Thornton, LLP, the bank's accounting firm, $300,000 for recklessly failing to meet generally accepted auditing standards during the years it audited the bank. The Comptroller claimed that Thornton had violated federal law by "participating in . . . unsafe and unsound banking practice." Thornton appealed, contending that its audit function did not qualify as "participating in . . . unsafe and unsound banking practice." What would be the key to determining if the accounting firm could be held liable for the specified violation of federal law? [*Grant Thornton, LLP v. Office of the Comptroller of the Currency,* 514 F.3d 1328 (D.C.Cir. 2008)] (See *Potential Liability of Accountants under Securities Law*.)

33–5. Professional's Liability. Soon after Teresa DeYoung's husband died, her mother-in-law also died, leaving an inheritance of more than $400,000 for DeYoung's children. DeYoung hired John Ruggerio, an attorney, to ensure that her children would receive it. Ruggerio advised her to invest the funds in his real estate business. She declined. A few months later, $300,000 of the inheritance was sent to Ruggerio. Without telling DeYoung, he deposited the $300,000 in his account and began to use the funds in his real estate business. Nine months later, $109,000 of the inheritance was sent to Ruggerio. He paid this to DeYoung. She asked about the remaining amount. Ruggerio lied to hide his theft. Unable to access these funds, DeYoung's children changed their college plans to attend less expensive institutions. Nearly three years later, DeYoung learned the truth. Can she bring a suit against Ruggerio? If so, on what ground? If not, why not? Did Ruggerio violate any standard of professional ethics? Discuss. [*DeYoung v. Ruggerio,* 2009 VT 9, 971 A.2d 627 (2009)] (See *Potential Liability to Clients*.)

33–6. Professional Malpractice. Jeffery Guerrero hired James McDonald, a certified public accountant, to represent him and his business in an appeal to the Internal Revenue Service. The appeal concerned audits that showed Guerrero owed more taxes. When the appeal failed, McDonald assisted in preparing materials for an appeal to the Tax Court, which was not successful. Guerrero then sued McDonald for professional negligence in the preparation of his evidence for the court. Specifically, Guerrero claimed that he would have won the case if McDonald had adequately prepared witnesses and had presented all the arguments that could have been made on his behalf. Guerrero contended that McDonald was liable for all of the additional taxes he was required to pay. Is Guerrero's claim likely to result in liability on McDonald's part? What factors would the court consider? [*Guerrero v. McDonald,* 302 Ga.App. 164, 690 S.E.2d 486 (2010)] (See *Potential Liability to Clients*.)

33–7. Business Case Problem with Sample Answer—Potential Liability to Third Parties. In 2006, twenty-seven parties became limited partners in two hedge funds that had invested with Bernard Madoff and his investment firm. The partners' investment adviser gave them various investment information, including a memorandum indicating that an independent certified public accountant, KPMG, LLP, had audited the hedge funds' annual reports. Since 2004, KPMG had also prepared annual reports addressed to the funds' "partners." Each report stated that KPMG had investigated the funds' financial statements, had followed generally accepted auditing principles, and had concluded that the statements fairly summarized the funds' financial conditions. Moreover, KPMG used the information from its audits to prepare individual tax statements for each fund partner.

In 2008, Madoff was charged with securities fraud for running a massive Ponzi scheme. In a 2009 report, the Securities and Exchange Commission identified numerous "red flags" that should have been discovered by investment advisers and auditors. Unfortunately, they were not, and the hedge funds' partners lost millions of dollars. Is KPMG potentially liable to the funds' partners under the *Restatement (Third) of Torts?* Why or why not? [*Askenazy v. Tremont Group Holdings, Inc.,* 2012 WL 440675 (Mass.Super. 2012)] (See *Potential Liability to Third Parties.*)

—**For a sample answer to Problem 33–7, go to Appendix F at the end of this text.**

33–8. Attorney's Duty of Care. Luis and Maria Rojas contracted to buy a house in Westchester County, New York, from Andrew and Karen Paine. The house was on property designated as "Lot No. 8" on a subdivision map filed in the county clerk's office. The Paines had acquired the property in two parts by the transfer of two separate deeds. At the closing, they delivered a deed stating that it covered "the same property." In fact, however, the legal description attached to the deed covered only the portion of Lot No. 8 described in one of the two previous deeds. Attorney Paul Herrick represented the Rojases in the deal with the Paines. When the Rojases sought to sell the property two years later, the title search revealed that they owned only part of Lot No. 8, and the buyer refused to go through with the sale. Is Herrick liable for malpractice? Explain. [*Rojas v. Paine,* 125 A.D.3d 745, 4 N.Y.S.3d 223 (2 Dept. 2015)] (See *Potential Liability to Clients.*)

33–9. A Question of Ethics—Securities Laws. Portland Shellfish Co. processes live shellfish in Maine. As one of the firm's two owners, Frank Wetmore held 300 voting and 150 nonvoting shares of the stock. Donna Holden held the other 300 voting shares. Donna's husband, Jeff, managed the company's daily operations, including production, procurement, and sales. The board of directors consisted of Frank and Jeff. In 2001, disagreements arose over the company's management. The Holdens invoked the "Shareholders' Agreement," which provided that "in the event of a deadlock, the directors shall hire an accountant at [MacDonald, Page, Schatz, Fletcher & Co., LLC] to determine the value of the outstanding shares. . . . Each shareholder shall have the right to buy out the other shareholder(s)' interest."

MacDonald Page estimated the stock's "fair market value" to be $1.09 million. Donna offered to buy Frank's shares at a price equal to his proportionate share. Frank countered by offering $1.25 million for Donna's shares. Donna rejected Frank's offer and insisted that he sell his shares to her or she would sue. In the face of this threat, Frank sold his shares to Donna for $750,705. Believing the stock to be worth more than twice MacDonald Page's estimate, Frank filed a suit in a federal district court against the accounting firm. [*Wetmore v. MacDonald, Page, Schatz, Fletcher & Co., LLC,* 476 F.3d 1 (1st Cir. 2007)] (See *Potential Liability of Accountants under Securities Law.*)

1. Frank claimed that in valuing the stock, the accounting firm had disregarded "commonly accepted and reliable methods of valuation in favor of less reliable methods." He alleged negligence, among other things. MacDonald Page filed a motion to dismiss the complaint. What are the elements that establish negligence? Which is the most critical element in this case?

2. MacDonald Page evaluated the company's stock by identifying its "fair market value," defined as "[t]he price at which the property would change hands between a willing buyer and a willing seller, neither being under a compulsion to buy or sell and both having reasonable knowledge of relevant facts." The firm knew that the shareholders would use its estimate to determine the price that one would pay to the other. Under these circumstances, was Frank's injury foreseeable? Explain.

3. What factor might have influenced Frank to sell his shares to Donna even if he believed that MacDonald Page's "fair market value" figure was less than half what it should have been? Does this factor represent an unfair, or unethical, advantage? Why or why not?

Critical Thinking and Writing Assignments

33–10. Business Law Critical Thinking Group Assignment.
Napster, Inc., offered a service that allowed its users to browse digital music files on other users' computers and download selections for free. Music industry principals sued Napster for copyright infringement, and the court ordered Napster to remove files that were identified as infringing from its service. When Napster failed to comply, it was shut down.

A few months later, Bertelsmann, a German corporation, loaned Napster $85 million to fund its anticipated transition to a licensed digital music distribution system. The terms allowed Napster to spend the loan on "general, administrative and overhead expenses." In an e-mail, Napster's chief executive officer referred to a "side deal" under which Napster could use up to $10 million of the loan to pay litigation expenses. Napster failed to launch the new system before declaring bankruptcy. The plaintiffs filed a suit against Bertelsmann, alleging that its loan had prolonged Napster's infringement. The plaintiffs asked the court to order the disclosure of all attorney-client communications related to the loan. (See *Confidentiality and Privilege*.)

1. The first group will identify the principle that Bertelsmann could assert to protect these communications and outline the purpose of this protection.

2. The second group will decide whether this principle should protect a client who consults an attorney for advice that will help the client commit fraud.

3. A third group will determine whether the court should grant the plaintiffs' request.

Unit Six—Business Case Study with Dissenting Opinion

Yates v. United States

In this unit, we outlined provisions of the Sarbanes-Oxley Act of 2002 that apply to corporate governance. Congress's passage of this act was prompted by the exposure of Enron Corporation's massive accounting fraud and revelations that the company's outside auditor, Arthur Andersen LLP, had systematically destroyed potentially incriminating documents.

Later, Congress enacted 18 U.S.C. Section 1519 as part of the act. That section provides that a person may be fined or imprisoned for up to twenty years for knowingly destroying, concealing, or covering up "any record, document, or tangible object" to impede a federal investigation. Congress intended to prohibit, in particular, corporate document-shredding to hide evidence of financial wrongdoing.

In this *Business Case Study with Dissenting Opinion,* we focus on *Yates v. United States.*[1] In this decision, the United States Supreme Court considered how broadly to interpret the term "tangible object" as that term is used in Section 1519.

Is the disposal of undersized fish after a government inspection a violation of the Sarbanes-Oxley Act?

CASE BACKGROUND

An inspection of *Miss Katie,* a commercial fishing vessel, in the Gulf of Mexico by John Jones, a deputized agent of the National Marine Fisheries Service, revealed that the ship's catch contained undersized red grouper in violation of federal regulations. Jones told the ship's captain, John Yates, to keep the undersized fish segregated from the rest of the catch until the ship returned to port. Instead, after the officer left, Yates told the crew to throw the fish overboard.

For this offense, Yates was charged with, and convicted of, violating Section 1519. Yates argued that the statute's reference to "tangible object" includes objects used to store information, such as computer hard drives, not fish. The U.S. Court of Appeals for the Eleventh Circuit affirmed the conviction, concluding that the reference includes any object having physical form. Yates appealed to the United States Supreme Court.

MAJORITY OPINION

Justice *GINSBURG* announced the judgment of the Court and delivered an opinion * * * .
* * * *

The ordinary meaning of an "object" that is "tangible," as stated in dictionary definitions, is "a discrete * * * thing" that "possesses physical form."

Whether a statutory term is unambiguous, however, does not turn solely on dictionary definitions of its component words * * * but as well by the specific context in which that language is used, and the broader context of the statute as a whole. * * * In law as in life,

* * * the same words, placed in different contexts, sometimes mean different things.
* * * *

We note first Section 1519's caption: "Destruction, alteration, or falsification of records in Federal investigations and bankruptcy." That heading conveys no suggestion that the section prohibits spoliation [alteration or destruction] of any and all physical evidence, however remote from records. Neither does the title of the section of the Sarbanes-Oxley Act in which Section 1519 was placed, Section 802: "Criminal penalties for altering documents." Furthermore, Section 1520, the only other provision passed as part of Section 802, is titled "Destruction of corporate audit records" and addresses only that specific subset of records and documents. While these headings are not commanding, they supply cues that Congress did not intend "tangible object" in Section 1519 to sweep within its reach physical objects of every kind, including things no one would describe as records, documents, or devices closely associated with them. *If Congress indeed meant to make Section 1519 an all-encompassing ban on the spoliation of evidence, * * * one would have expected a clearer indication of that intent.* [Emphasis added.]

Section 1519's position within * * * Title 18 further signals that Section 1519 was not intended to serve as a cross-the-board ban on the destruction of physical evidence of every kind. Congress placed Section 1519 (and its companion provision Section 1520) * * * following immediately after * * * Section 1516, Section 1517, and Section 1518, each of them prohibiting obstructive acts in specific contexts. See Section 1516 (audits of recipients of federal funds); Section 1517

---

1. 135 S.Ct. 1074, __ U.S. __, 191 L.Ed.2d 64 (2015).

(federal examinations of financial institutions); [and] Section 1518 (criminal investigations of federal health care offenses).

* * * *

The contemporaneous [concurrent] passage of Section 1512(c)(1), which was contained in a section of the Sarbanes-Oxley Act discrete from the section embracing Section 1519 and Section 1520, is also instructive. Section 1512(c)(1) [prohibits a person from "altering, destroying, mutilating, or concealing a record, document, or other object * * * with the intent to impair the object's integrity or availability for use in an official proceeding."]

* * * If Section 1519's reference to "tangible object" already included all physical objects, * * * then Congress had no reason to enact Section 1512(c)(1).

* * * *

The words immediately surrounding "tangible object" in Section 1519—"falsifies, or makes a false entry in any record [or] document"—also cabin [restrain] the contextual meaning of that term. We rely on the principle [that] a word is known by the company it keeps to avoid ascribing to one word a meaning so broad that it is inconsistent with its accompanying words.

* * * "Tangible object" is the last in a list of terms that begins "any record [or] document." The term is therefore appropriately read to refer, not to any tangible object, but specifically to the subset of tangible objects involving records and documents, *i.e.,* objects used to record or preserve information.

This moderate interpretation of "tangible object" accords with the list of actions Section 1519 proscribes. The section applies to anyone who "alters, destroys, mutilates, conceals, covers up, falsifies, or makes a false entry in any record, document, or tangible object" with the requisite obstructive intent. The last two verbs, "falsif[y]" and "mak[e] a false entry in," typically take as grammatical objects records, documents, or things used to record or preserve information, such as logbooks or hard drives.

* * * *

For the reasons stated, * * * we hold that a "tangible object" within Section 1519's compass is one used to record or preserve information. The judgment of the U.S. Court of Appeals for the Eleventh Circuit is therefore reversed, and the case is remanded for further proceedings.

DISSENTING OPINION

Justice *KAGAN,* * * * dissenting.

A criminal law, 18 U.S.C. Section 1519, prohibits tampering with "any record, document, or tangible object" in an attempt to obstruct a federal investigation. This case raises the question whether the term "tangible object" means the same thing in Section 1519 as it means in everyday language—any object capable of being touched.

The answer should be easy: Yes. The term "tangible object" is broad, but clear. Throughout the U.S. Code and many States' laws, it invariably covers physical objects of all kinds. And in Section 1519, context confirms what bare text says: All the words surrounding "tangible object" show that Congress meant the term to have a wide range. That fits with Congress's evident purpose in enacting Section 1519: to punish those who alter or destroy physical evidence—*any* physical evidence—with the intent of thwarting federal law enforcement.

The plurality instead interprets "tangible object" to cover "only objects one can use to record or preserve information." * * * In my view, conventional tools of statutory construction all lead to a more conventional result: A "tangible object" is an object that's tangible. I would apply the statute that Congress enacted and affirm the judgment below.

* * * *

* * * The ordinary meaning of "tangible object" is "a discrete thing that possesses physical form." A fish is, of course, a discrete thing that possesses physical form. So the ordinary meaning of the term "tangible object" in Section 1519 * * * covers fish (including too-small red grouper).

That interpretation accords with endless uses of the term in statute and rule books as construed by courts. Dozens of federal laws and rules of procedure (and hundreds of state enactments) include the term "tangible object" or its first cousin "tangible thing"—some in association with documents, others not. To my knowledge, no court has ever read any such provision to exclude things that don't record or preserve data; rather, all courts have adhered to the statutory language's ordinary * * * meaning. * * * No surprise, then, that—until today—courts have uniformly applied the term "tangible object" in Section 1519 in the same way.

QUESTIONS FOR ANALYSIS

1. *Law.* How did the Court interpret the term "tangible object" in this case? Why?

2. *Law.* Why did the dissent disagree with the Court's interpretation? If the Court had adopted the dissent's position, how would this have affected the result?

3. *Ethics.* Was the ship captain's decision to throw the undersized fish overboard a breach of ethics? Explain.

4. *Political Dimension.* How could a party who disagrees with certain provisions of the Sarbanes-Oxley Act affect a change to those provisions?

5. *Implications for the Business Owner.* How does the Court's interpretation of the term "tangible object" affect businesses' use of computers, servers, and other media on which information is stored?

Unit Six—Business Scenario

Alpha Software, Inc., and Beta Products Corporation—both small firms—are competitors in the business of software research, development, and production.

1. **Antitrust Law.** Alpha and Beta form a joint venture to research, develop, and produce new software for a particular line of computers. Does this business combination violate the antitrust laws? If so, is it a *per se* violation, or is it subject to the rule of reason? Alpha and Beta decide to merge. After the merger, Beta is the surviving firm. What aspect of this firm's presence in the market will be assessed to decide whether this merger is in violation of any antitrust laws?

2. **Consumer Law.** To market its products profitably, Beta considers a number of advertising and labeling proposals. One proposal is that Beta suggest in its advertising that one of its software products has a certain function even though the product does not actually have that capability. Another suggestion is that Beta sell half of a certain program in packaging that misleads the buyer into believing the entire program is included. To obtain the entire program, customers would need to buy a second product. Can Beta implement these suggestions or otherwise market its products in any way it likes? If not, why not?

3. **Environmental Law.** The production part of Beta's operations generates hazardous waste. Gamma Transport Company transports the waste to Omega Waste Corporation, which owns and operates a hazardous waste disposal site. At the site, some containers leak hazardous waste, and the Environmental Protection Agency (EPA) cleans it up. From whom can the EPA recover the cost of the clean-up?

4. **Liability of Accountants.** Beta hires a certified public accountant, Aaron Schleger, to prepare its financial reports and issue opinion letters based on those reports. One year, Beta falls into serious financial trouble, but this is not reflected in Schleger's reports and opinion letters. Relying on Schleger's portrayal of the company's fiscal health, Beta borrows substantial amounts to develop a new product. The bank, in lending funds to Beta, relies on an opinion letter from Schleger, and Schleger is aware of the bank's reliance. Assuming that Schleger was negligent but did not engage in intentional fraud, what is his potential liability in this situation? Discuss fully.

Unit Six—Group Project

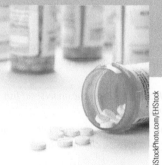

Pharma, Inc., made Cancera, a prescription drug that helped in the treatment of certain forms of cancer. When Cancera's patent was about to expire, Synthetic Chemix Corporation developed a generic version of Cancera and prepared to enter the market. Within weeks of this drug's debut, Pharma offered to pay Synthetic $50 million per year *not* to market the generic version. Synthetic accepted the offer.

1. The first group will determine whether the agreement between Pharma and Synthetic was a violation of antitrust law.

2. The second group will examine the impact of delaying entry of the generic version of Cancera into the market and determine its effect on competition.

3. The third group will decide whether a court, in considering these issues, would apply the *per se* rule or the rule of reason.

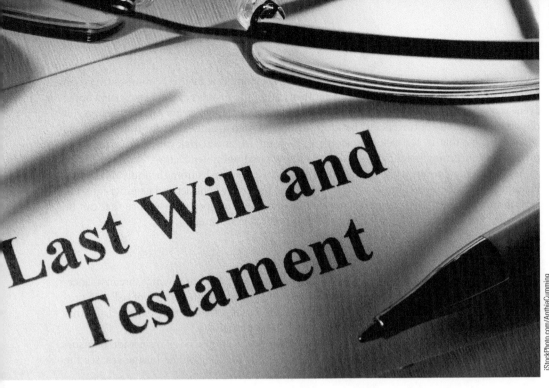

36

Insurance, Wills, and Trusts

LEARNING OBJECTIVES

The five Learning Objectives *below are designed to help improve your understanding of the chapter. After reading this chapter, you should be able to answer the following questions:*

1. What is an insurable interest? When must an insurable interest exist?

2. How do courts interpret ambiguities in an insurance policy?

3. What are the basic requirements for executing a will?

4. What is the difference between a *per stirpes* distribution and a *per capita* distribution of an estate to the grandchildren of the deceased?

5. What are the four essential elements of a trust?

> "Insurance is part charity and part business, but all common sense."
>
> **CALVIN COOLIDGE**
> 1872–1933
> (THIRTIETH PRESIDENT OF THE UNITED STATES, 1923–1929)

Most individuals insure their real and personal property (as well as their lives). As Calvin Coolidge asserted in the chapter-opening quotation, insurance is "all common sense"—by insuring our property, we protect ourselves against damage and loss. In the first part of this chapter, we focus on insurance, which is a foremost concern of all property owners.

In the remainder of the chapter, we examine how property is transferred on the death of its owner. Certainly, the laws governing such transfers are a necessary corollary to the concept of private ownership of property. Our laws require that on death, title to the property of the decedent (the one who has died) must be delivered in full somewhere. This can be done through wills, trusts, or state laws prescribing distribution of property among heirs or next of kin.

In today's world, a person's property may include social media. We discuss social media estate planning later in the chapter.

36-1 Insurance

Many precautions may be taken to protect against the hazards of life. For instance, an individual may wear a seat belt to protect against injuries from automobile accidents and install smoke detectors to guard against injury from fire. Of course, no one can predict whether an accident or a fire will ever occur, but individuals and businesses must establish plans to protect their personal and financial interests should some event threaten to undermine their security.

Insurance A contract by which the insurer promises to reimburse the insured or a beneficiary in the event that the insured is injured, dies, or sustains damage to property as a result of particular, stated contingencies.

Risk Management In the context of insurance, the transfer of certain risks from the insured to the insurance company by contractual agreement.

Risk A prediction concerning potential loss based on known and unknown factors.

Insurance is a contract by which the insurance company (the insurer) promises to pay an amount or to give something of value to another (either the insured or the beneficiary) in the event that the insured is injured, dies, or sustains damage to her or his property as a result of particular, stated contingencies. Basically, insurance is an arrangement for *transferring and allocating risk*—that is, for **risk management.** In many instances, **risk** can be described as a prediction concerning potential loss based on known and unknown factors.

Risk management normally involves the transfer of certain risks from the individual to the insurance company by a contractual agreement. The insurance contract and its provisions will be examined shortly. First, however, we look at the different types of insurance that can be obtained, insurance terminology, and the concept of insurable interest.

36–1a Classifications of Insurance

Insurance is classified according to the nature of the risk involved. For instance, fire insurance, casualty insurance, life insurance, and title insurance apply to different types of risk and protect different interests. This is reasonable because the types of losses that are expected and that are foreseeable or unforeseeable vary with the nature of the activity.

Exhibit 36–1 presents a list of selected insurance classifications. For a discussion of insurance policies designed to cover the special kinds of risks faced by online businesses, see the *Business Application* feature at the end of this chapter.

36–1b Insurance Terminology

Policy In insurance law, the contract between the insurer and the insured.

Premium In insurance law, the price paid by the insured for insurance protection for a specified period of time.

Underwriter In insurance law, the insurer, or the one assuming a risk in return for the payment of a premium.

An insurance contract is called a **policy,** the consideration paid to the insurer is called a **premium,** and the insurance company is sometimes called an **underwriter.** The parties to an insurance policy are the *insurer* (the insurance company) and the *insured* (the person covered by its provisions or the holder of the policy).

Insurance contracts are usually obtained through an *agent,* who ordinarily works for the insurance company, or through a *broker,* who is ordinarily an *independent contractor.* When a broker deals with an applicant for insurance, the broker is, in effect, the applicant's agent and not an agent of the insurance company. In contrast, an insurance agent is an agent of the insurance company, not of the applicant. Thus, the agent owes fiduciary duties to the insurance company, but not to the person who is applying for insurance. As a general rule, the insurance company is bound by the acts of its agents when they act within the scope of the agency relationship.

36–1c Insurable Interest

LEARNING OBJECTIVE 1

What is an insurable interest? When must an insurable interest exist?

A person can insure anything in which she or he has an **insurable interest.** Without an insurable interest, there is no enforceable insurance contract, and a transaction to purchase insurance coverage would have to be treated as a wager.

Life Insurance In regard to life insurance, a person must have a reasonable expectation of benefit from the continued life of another in order to have an insurable interest in that person's life. The insurable interest must exist *at the time the policy is obtained.* The benefit may be pecuniary (monetary) or it may be founded on the relationship between the parties (by blood or affinity).

Insurable Interest An interest that exists when a person benefits from the preservation of the health or life of the insured or the property to be insured.

Key-person insurance is a type of life insurance obtained by an organization on the life of a person (such as a talented executive) who is important to that organization. Because the organization expects to experience some financial gain from the continuation of the key person's life or some financial loss from the key person's death, the organization has an insurable interest.

Exhibit 36–1 Selected Insurance Classifications

TYPE OF INSURANCE	COVERAGE
Accident	Covers expenses, losses, and suffering incurred by the insured because of accidents causing physical injury and any consequent disability; sometimes includes a specified payment to heirs of the insured if death results from an accident.
All-risk	Covers all losses that the insured may incur except those that are specifically excluded. Typical exclusions are war, pollution, earthquakes, and floods.
Automobile	May cover damage to automobiles resulting from specified hazards or occurrences (such as fire, vandalism, theft, or collision); normally provides protection against liability for personal injuries and property damage resulting from the operation of the vehicle.
Casualty	Protects against losses incurred by the insured as a result of being held liable for personal injuries or property damage sustained by others.
Disability	Replaces a portion of the insured's monthly income from employment in the event that illness or injury causes a short- or long-term disability. Some states require employers to provide short-term disability insurance. Benefits typically last a set period of time, such as six months for short-term coverage or five years for long-term coverage.
Fire	Covers losses incurred by the insured as a result of fire.
Floater	Covers movable property, as long as the property is within the territorial boundaries specified in the contract.
Homeowners'	Protects homeowners against some or all risks of loss to their residences and the residences' contents or liability arising from the use of the property.
Key-person	Protects a business in the event of the death or disability of a key employee.
Liability	Protects against liability imposed on the insured as a result of injuries to the person or property of another.
Life	Covers the death of the policyholder. On the death of the insured, the insurer pays the amount specified in the policy to the insured's beneficiary.
Major medical	Protects the insured against major hospital, medical, or surgical expenses.
Malpractice	Protects professionals (physicians, lawyers, and others) against malpractice claims brought against them by their patients or clients; a form of liability insurance.
Term life	Provides life insurance for a specified period of time (term) with no cash surrender value; usually renewable.

Property Insurance In regard to real and personal property, an insurable interest exists when the insured derives a pecuniary (monetary) benefit from the preservation and continued existence of the property. Put another way, a person has an insurable interest in property when she or he would sustain a financial loss from its destruction. For property insurance, the insurable interest must exist at the time the loss occurs but need not exist when the policy is purchased.

The existence of an insurable interest is a primary concern in determining liability under an insurance policy. **CASE EXAMPLE 36.1** ABM Industries, Inc., leased office and storage space in the World Trade Center (WTC) in New York City in 2001. ABM also ran the building's heating, ventilation, and air-conditioning systems, and maintained all of the WTC's common areas. At the time, ABM employed more than eight hundred workers at the WTC. Zurich American Insurance Company insured ABM against losses resulting from "business interruption" caused by direct physical loss or damage "to property owned, controlled, used, leased or intended for use" by ABM.

After the World Trade Center was destroyed on September 11, 2001, should the company providing maintenance have been reimbursed by its insurance company for all of its income losses?

After the terrorist attacks on September 11, 2001, ABM filed a claim with Zurich to recover for the loss of all income derived from ABM's WTC operations. Zurich argued that ABM's recovery should be limited to the income lost as a result of the destruction of ABM's office and storage space and supplies. A court, however, ruled that ABM was entitled to compensation for the loss of all of its WTC operations. The court reasoned that the "policy's scope expressly includes real or personal property that the insured 'used,' 'controlled,' or 'intended for use.'" Because ABM's income depended on "the common areas and leased premises in the WTC complex," it had an insurable interest in that property at the time of the loss.[1]

In the following case, the plaintiff sought to retain his insurable interest in a home he no longer owned.

CASE 36.1

Breeden v. Buchanan

Court of Appeals of Mississippi, __ So. 3d __, 2015 WL 433621 (2015).

FACTS Donald Breeden and Willie Buchanan were married in Marion County, Mississippi. They lived in a home in Sandy Hook. Nationwide Property & Casualty Insurance Company insured the home under a policy bought by Breeden that named him as the insured. The policy provided that the spouse of the named insured was covered as an insured. After eight years of marriage, Breeden and Buchanan divorced. Breeden transferred his interest in the home to Buchanan as part of the couple's property settlement. Less than a year later, a fire completely destroyed the home. A claim was filed with Nationwide. Nationwide paid Buchanan. Breeden filed a suit in a Mississippi state court against Buchanan and Nationwide, asserting claims for breach of contract and bad faith, and seeking to recover the proceeds under the policy. The court dismissed the suit. Breeden appealed.

A year after a couple divorces, fire destroys their house. Who should obtain the insurance proceeds?

ISSUE Did Breeden's one-time right to the proceeds continue after he transferred his interest in the home to his spouse on their divorce?

DECISION No. A state intermediate appellate court affirmed the lower court's dismissal of Breeden's suit. Buchanan, not Breeden, was entitled to the proceeds of the claim filed with Nationwide.

REASON Breeden's claims against Nationwide were based on the insurance policy. The policy provided that the spouse of the named insured who resided at the premises was also covered. At the beginning of the policy period, both Breeden and Buchanan had an insurable interest in the home because they were married and lived together in it. Later, Breeden transferred his interest in the insured property to Buchanan as part of a property settlement agreement on their divorce. This occurred several months before the fire that caused the loss of the property. For this reason, the lower court ruled that Breeden did not have an "insurable interest" in the property at the time of the loss and thus had no right to the proceeds of the policy. Because Breeden had no insurable interest in the property, Nationwide did not breach the insurance contract or act in bad faith by failing to pay Breeden the insurance proceeds. Based on these circumstances, "there was simply nothing further that Nationwide owed under the insurance policy."

CRITICAL THINKING—Economic Consideration *Why is an insurable interest required for the enforcement of an insurance contract?*

36–1d The Insurance Contract

An insurance contract is governed by the general principles of contract law, although the insurance industry is heavily regulated by the states.[2] Customarily, a party offers to purchase

---

1. *Zurich American Insurance Co. v. ABM Industries, Inc.*, 397 F.3d 158 (2d Cir. 2005).

2. The states were given authority to regulate the insurance industry by the McCarran-Ferguson Act of 1945, 15 U.S.C. Sections 1011–1015.

insurance by submitting an application to the insurance company. The company can either accept or reject the offer. For the contract to be binding, consideration (in the form of a premium) must be given, and the parties forming the contract must have the required contractual capacity to do so.

Application

The filled-in application form for insurance is usually attached to the policy and made a part of the insurance contract. The person applying for insurance normally is bound by any false statements that appear in the application (subject to certain exceptions). Because the insurance company evaluates the risk factors based on the information included in the insurance application, misstatements or misrepresentations can void a policy. This is particularly true if the insurance company can show that it would not have extended insurance if it had known the true facts.

Effective Date

The effective date of an insurance contract—the date on which the insurance coverage begins—is important. In some situations, the insurance applicant is not protected until a formal written policy is issued. In other situations, the applicant is protected between the time the application is received and the time the insurance company either accepts or rejects it. Four facts should be kept in mind:

1. As stated earlier, a broker is an agent of the applicant, not an agent of the insurance company. Therefore, if a person hires a broker to obtain insurance, and the broker fails to procure a policy, the applicant normally is not insured.

2. A person who seeks insurance from an insurance company's agent is usually protected from the moment the application is made, provided—for life insurance—that some form of premium has been paid. Usually, the agent will write a memorandum, or **binder**, indicating that a policy is pending and stating its essential terms.

3. If the parties agree that the policy will be issued and delivered at a later time, the contract is not effective until the policy is issued and delivered. Thus, any loss sustained between the time of application and the delivery of the policy is not covered.

4. Parties may agree that a life insurance policy will be binding at the time the insured pays the first premium, or the policy may be expressly contingent on the applicant's passing a physical examination. If the applicant pays the premium and passes the examination, then the policy coverage is continuously in effect.

If the applicant pays the premium but dies before having the physical examination, the policy may still be effective. Then, in order to collect, the applicant's estate normally must show that the applicant *would have passed* the examination had he or she not died.

Coinsurance Clauses

Often, when taking out fire insurance policies, property owners insure their property for less than full value because most fires do not result in a total loss. To encourage owners to insure their property for an amount as close to full value as possible, fire insurance policies commonly include a coinsurance clause.

Typically, a *coinsurance clause* provides that if the owner insures the property up to a specified percentage—usually 80 percent—of its value, she or he will recover any loss up to the face amount of the policy. If the insurance is for less than the specified percentage, the owner is responsible for a proportionate share of the loss.

Coinsurance applies only in instances of partial loss. The amount of the recovery is calculated by using the following formula:

$$\text{Loss} \times \left(\frac{\text{Amount of Insurance Coverage}}{\text{Coinsurance Percentage} \times \text{Property Value}} \right) = \text{Amount of Recovery}$$

Binder A written, temporary insurance policy.

EXAMPLE 36.2 Madison, who owns property valued at $200,000, takes out a policy in the amount of $100,000. If Madison then suffers a loss of $80,000, her recovery will be $50,000. Madison will be responsible for (coinsure) the balance of the loss, or $30,000, which is the amount of loss ($80,000) minus the amount of recovery ($50,000).

$$\$80,000 \times \left(\frac{\$100,000}{0.8 \times \$200,000} \right) = \$50,000$$

If Madison had taken out a policy in the amount of 80 percent of the value of the property, or $160,000, then according to the same formula, she would have recovered the full amount of the loss (the face amount of the policy). ■

Incontestability Clauses Statutes commonly require that a policy for life or health insurance include an **incontestability clause.** Under this clause, after the policy has been in force for a specified length of time—often two or three years—the insurer cannot contest statements made in the application. Once a policy becomes incontestable, the insurer cannot later avoid a claim on the basis of, for instance, fraud on the part of the insured, unless the clause provides an exception for that circumstance.

Some important provisions and clauses that are frequently included in insurance contracts are described in Exhibit 36–2.

Interpreting the Insurance Contract The courts recognize that most people do not have the special training necessary to understand the intricate terminology used in insurance policies. Therefore, when disputes arise, the courts will interpret the words used in an insurance contract according to their ordinary meanings in light of the nature of the coverage involved.

When there is an ambiguity in the policy, the provision generally is interpreted *against the insurance company*. Also, when it is unclear whether an insurance contract actually exists because the written policy has not been delivered, the uncertainty normally is resolved against the insurance company. The court presumes that the policy is in effect unless the company can show otherwise. Similarly, an insurer must make sure that the insured is adequately notified of any change in coverage under an existing policy.

Incontestability Clause
A clause in a policy for life or health insurance stating that after the policy has been in force for a specified length of time (usually two or three years), the insurer cannot contest statements made in the policyholder's application.

LEARNING OBJECTIVE 2
How do courts interpret ambiguities in an insurance policy?

Exhibit 36–2 Insurance Contract Provisions and Clauses

TYPE OF CLAUSE	DESCRIPTION
Antilapse clause	An antilapse clause provides that the policy will not automatically lapse if no payment is made on the date due. Ordinarily, under such a provision, the insured has a *grace period* of thirty or thirty-one days within which to pay an overdue premium before the policy is canceled.
Appraisal clause	Insurance policies frequently provide that if the parties cannot agree on the amount of a loss covered under the policy or the value of the property lost, an appraisal, or estimate, by an impartial and qualified third party can be demanded.
Arbitration clause	Many insurance policies include clauses that call for arbitration of any disputes that arise between the insurer and the insured concerning the settlement of claims.
Incontestability clause	An incontestability clause provides that after a policy has been in force for a specified length of time—usually two or three years—the insurer cannot contest statements made in the application.
Multiple insurance	Many insurance policies include a clause providing that if the insured has multiple insurance policies that cover the same property and the amount of coverage exceeds the loss, the loss will be shared proportionately by the insurance companies.

Disputes over insurance often focus on the application of an exclusion in the policy, as the following case illustrates.

CASE 36.2

Valero v. Florida Insurance Guaranty Association, Inc.

District Court of Appeal of Florida, Fourth District, 59 So.3d 1166 (2011).

FACTS Alberto and Karelli Mila were insured under a homeowners' liability policy. "Exclusion k" of the policy stated that coverage did not apply to "bodily injury arising out of sexual molestation, corporal punishment or physical or mental abuse." Verushka Valero, on behalf of her child, filed a suit in a Florida state court against the Milas, charging them with negligent supervision of a perpetrator who had sexually molested Valero's child.

What acts can be excluded from a homeowner's liability policy?

iStockPhoto.com/Kirby Hamilton

The Milas filed a claim asking their insurer to defend against the charges. The insurer had become insolvent, so the claim was submitted to the Florida Insurance Guaranty Association, Inc. (FIGA). FIGA is a nonprofit corporation created by the Florida legislature to evaluate and resolve claims when insurance companies become insolvent (a similar insurance guaranty association exists in nearly every state). FIGA refused to pay the Milas' claim and asked the court to rule that it had no obligation under the policy to provide such a defense. The court issued a summary judgment in FIGA's favor. Valero and the Milas appealed, arguing that exclusion k was ambiguous.

ISSUE Was the term of the Milas' insurance policy that excluded coverage for "bodily injury arising out of sexual molestation" ambiguous as to whether it covered acts by someone under their supervision?

DECISION No. A state intermediate appellate court affirmed the lower court's judgment. The exclusion applied to preclude coverage in this case.

REASON The Milas pointed out that a different exclusion, exclusion l, used the phrase "by any person," and exclusion k did not. Thus, the Milas contended, it was not clear whether exclusion k applied only to acts of an insured. The court read the entire list of twelve exclusions together and concluded that the phrase in exclusion l was "superfluous." Even if the phrase "by any person" had been used in exclusion k, coverage might still have been denied, as in this case. Valero and the Milas also cited decisions from other jurisdictions to support their argument. The court found these decisions to be "not helpful" because they considered exclusions in isolation, not in the context of other exclusions.

WHAT IF THE FACTS WERE DIFFERENT? *Suppose that exclusion k, instead of exclusion l, had used the phrase "by any person." Would the result have been different? Explain.*

Cancellation The insured can cancel a policy at any time, and the insurer can cancel under certain circumstances. When an insurance company can cancel its insurance contract, the policy or a state statute usually requires that the insurer give advance written notice of the cancellation to the insured. The same requirement applies when only part of a policy is canceled. Any premium paid in advance may be refundable on the policy's cancellation. The insured may also be entitled to a life insurance policy's cash surrender value.

The insurer may cancel an insurance policy for various reasons, depending on the type of insurance. Following are some examples:

1. Automobile insurance can be canceled for nonpayment of premiums or suspension of the insured's driver's license.

2. Property insurance can be canceled for nonpayment of premiums or for other reasons, including the insured's fraud or misrepresentation, gross negligence, or conviction for a crime that increases the risk assumed by the insurer.

3. Life and health policies can be canceled because of false statements made by the insured in the application, but the cancellation must take place before the effective date of an incontestability clause.

An insurer cannot cancel—or refuse to renew—a policy for discriminatory reasons or other reasons that violate public policy. Also, an insurer cannot cancel a policy because the insured has appeared as a witness in a case brought against the company.

Duties and Obligations of the Parties
Both parties to an insurance contract are responsible for the obligations they assume under the contract. In addition, both the insured and the insurer have an implied duty to act in good faith.

Duties of the Insured. Good faith requires the party who is applying for insurance to reveal everything necessary for the insurer to evaluate the risk. The applicant must disclose all material facts, including all facts that an insurer would consider in determining whether to charge a higher premium or to refuse to issue a policy altogether. Many insurance companies today require that an applicant give the company permission to access other information, such as private medical records and credit ratings, for the purpose of evaluating the risk.

Once the insurance policy is issued, the insured has three basic duties under the contract:

1. To pay the premiums as stated in the contract.

2. To notify the insurer within a reasonable time if an event occurs that gives rise to a claim.

3. To cooperate with the insurer during any investigation or litigation.

Duties of the Insurer. Once the insurer has accepted the risk, and some event occurs that gives rise to a claim, the insurer has a *duty to investigate* to determine the facts. When a policy provides insurance against third party claims, the insurer is obligated to make reasonable efforts to settle such a claim.

If a settlement cannot be reached, then regardless of the claim's merit, the insurer has a *duty to defend* any suit against the insured. Usually, a policy provides that in this situation the insured must cooperate in the defense and attend hearings and trials if necessary. An insurer has a duty to provide or pay an attorney to defend its insured when a complaint alleges facts that could, if proved, impose liability on the insured within the policy's coverage.

CASE EXAMPLE 36.3 Dentist Robert Woo installed implants for one of his employees, Tina Alberts, whose family raised potbellied pigs. As a joke, while Alberts was anesthetized, Woo installed a set of "flippers" (temporary partial bridges) shaped like boar tusks and took photos. A month later, Woo's staff showed the photos to Alberts at a party. Alberts refused to return to work. She filed a suit against Woo for battery.

Woo's insurance company refused to defend him in the suit, and he ended up paying Alberts $250,000 to settle her claim. Woo then sued the insurance company and won. The court held that the insurance company had a duty to defend Woo under the professional liability provision of his policy because Woo's practical joke took place during a routine dental procedure.[3] ▪

Bad Faith Actions. Although insurance law generally follows contract law, most states now recognize a "bad faith" tort action against insurers. Thus, if an insurer in bad faith denies coverage of a claim, the insured may recover in tort in an amount exceeding the policy's coverage limits and may also recover punitive damages. Some courts have held insurers liable for bad faith refusals to settle claims for reasonable amounts within the policy limits.

Defenses against Payment
An insurance company can raise any of the defenses that would be valid in an ordinary action on a contract, as well as some defenses that do not apply in ordinary contract actions.

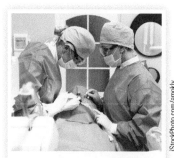

If a dentist plays a practical joke on a patient for which he is sued, does the dentist's insurance company have to defend him? Why or why not?

---

3. *Woo v. Fireman's Fund Insurance Co.,* 161 Wash.2d 43, 164 P.3d 454 (2007).

1. *Fraud or misrepresentation.* If the insurance company can show that the policy was procured by fraud or misrepresentation, it may have a valid defense for not paying on a claim. (The insurance company may also have the right to disaffirm or rescind the insurance contract.)

2. *Lack of an insurable interest.* An absolute defense exists if the insurer can show that the insured lacked an insurable interest—thus rendering the policy void from the beginning.

3. *Illegal actions of the insured.* Improper actions, such as those that are against public policy or that are otherwise illegal, can also give the insurance company a defense against the payment of a claim or allow it to rescind the contract.

An insurance company can be prevented, or estopped, from asserting some defenses that are usually available. For instance, an insurance company normally cannot escape payment on the death of an insured on the ground that the person's age was stated incorrectly on the application. Also, incontestability clauses prevent the insurer from asserting certain defenses.

36-2 Wills

Not only do the owners of property want to protect it during their lifetime through insurance coverage, but they typically also wish to transfer it to their loved ones at the time of their death. A **will** is the final declaration of how a person desires to have her or his property disposed of after death. It is a formal instrument that must follow exactly the requirements of state law to be effective. A will is referred to as a *testamentary disposition* of property, and one who dies after having made a valid will is said to have died **testate.**

A will can serve other purposes besides the distribution of property. It can appoint a guardian for minor children or incapacitated adults. It can also appoint a personal representative to settle the affairs of the deceased. Exhibit 36–3 presents excerpts from the will of Michael Jackson, the "King of Pop," who died from cardiac arrest at the age of fifty. Jackson held a substantial amount of tangible and intangible property, including the publishing rights to most of the Beatles' music catalogue. The will is a "pour-over" will, meaning that it transfers all of Jackson's property (that is not already held in the name of the trust) into the Michael Jackson Family Trust (trusts are discussed later in this chapter). Jackson's will also appoints his mother, Katherine Jackson, as the guardian of his three minor children.

36-2a Terminology of Wills

A person who makes out a will is known as a **testator** (from the Latin *testari,* "to make a will"). The court responsible for administering any legal problems surrounding a will is called a *probate court.*

When a person dies, a personal representative administers the estate and settles all of the decedent's affairs. An **executor** is a personal representative named in the will, whereas an **administrator** is a personal representative appointed by the court for a decedent who dies without a will. The court will also appoint an administrator if the will does not name an executor or if the named person lacks the capacity to serve as an executor.

A person who dies without having created a valid will is said to have died **intestate.** In this situation, state **intestacy laws** (sometimes referred to as *laws of descent*) prescribe the distribution of the property among heirs or next of kin (relatives). If no heirs or kin can be found, title to the property will be transferred to the state.

A gift of real estate by will is generally called a **devise,** and a gift of personal property by will is called a **bequest,** or **legacy.** The recipient of a gift by will is a **devisee** or a **legatee,** depending on whether the gift was a devise or a legacy.

Will An instrument made by a testator directing what is to be done with her or his property after death.

Testate Having left a will at death.

Testator One who makes and executes a will.

Executor A person appointed by a testator in a will to administer her or his estate.

Administrator One who is appointed by a court to administer a person's estate if the decedent died without a valid will or if the executor named in the will cannot serve.

Intestate As a noun, one who has died without having created a valid will. As an adjective, the state of having died without a will.

Intestacy Laws State statutes that specify how property will be distributed when a person dies intestate (without a valid will).

Devise A gift of real property by will, or the act of giving real property by will.

Bequest A gift of personal property by will (from the verb *to bequeath*).

Legacy A gift of personal property under a will.

Devisee One designated in a will to receive a gift of real property.

Legatee One designated in a will to receive a gift of personal property.

Exhibit 36–3 Excerpts from Michael Jackson's Will

LAST WILL OF MICHAEL JOSEPH JACKSON

I, MICHAEL JOSEPH JACKSON, a resident of the State of California, declare this to be my last Will, and do hereby revoke all former wills and codicils made by me.

I.   I declare that I am not married. My marriage to DEBORAH JEAN ROWE JACKSON has been dissolved. I have three children now living, PRINCE MICHAEL JACKSON, JR., PARIS MICHAEL KATHERINE JACKSON and PRINCE MICHAEL JOSEPH JACKSON, II. I have no other children, living or deceased.

II.   It is my intention by this Will to dispose of all property which I am entitled to dispose of by will. I specifically refrain from exercising all powers of appointment that I may possess at the time of my death.

III.   I give my entire estate to the Trustee or Trustees then acting under that certain Amended and Restated Declaration of Trust executed on March 22, 2002 by me as Trustee and Trustor which is called the MICHAEL JACKSON FAMILY TRUST, giving effect to any amendments thereto made prior to my death. All such assets shall be held, managed and distributed as a part of said Trust according to its terms and not as a separate testamentary trust.

        If for any reason this gift is not operative or is invalid, or if the aforesaid Trust fails or has been revoked, I give my residuary estate to the Trustee or Trustees named to act in the MICHAEL JACKSON FAMILY TRUST, as Amended and Restated on March 22, 2002, and I direct said Trustee or Trustees to divide, administer, hold and distribute the trust estate pursuant to the provisions of said Trust * * * .

        * * * *

IV.   I direct that all federal estate taxes and state inheritance or succession taxes payable upon or resulting from or by reason of my death (herein "Death Taxes") attributable to property which is part of the trust estate of the MICHAEL JACKSON FAMILY TRUST, including property which passes to said trust from my probate estate shall be paid by the Trustee of said trust in accordance with its terms. Death Taxes attributable to property passing outside this Will, other than property constituting the trust estate of the trust mentioned in the preceding sentence, shall be charged against the taker of said property.

V.   I appoint JOHN BRANCA, JOHN McCLAIN and BARRY SIEGEL as co-Executors of this Will. In the event of any of their deaths, resignations, inability, failure or refusal to serve or continue to serve as a co-Executor, the other shall serve and no replacement need be named. The co-Executors serving at any time after my death may name one or more replacements to serve in the event that none of the three named individuals is willing or able to serve at any time.

        The term "my executors" as used in this Will shall include any duly acting personal representative or representatives of my estate. No individual acting as such need past a bond.

        I hereby give to my Executors, full power and authority at any time or times to sell, lease, mortgage, pledge, exchange or otherwise dispose of the property, whether real or personal comprising my estate, upon such terms as my Executors shall deem best, to continue any business enterprises, to purchase assets from my estate, to continue in force and pay any insurance policy * * * .

VI.   Except as otherwise provided in this Will or in the Trust referred to in Article III hereof, I have intentionally omitted to provide for my heirs. I have intentionally omitted to provide for my former wife, DEBORAH JEAN ROWE JACKSON.

        * * * *

VIII.   If any of my children are minors at the time of my death, I nominate my mother, KATHERINE JACKSON as guardian of the persons and estates of such minor children. If KATHERINE JACKSON fails to survive me, or is unable or unwilling to act as guardian, I nominate DIANA ROSS as guardian of the persons and estates of such minor children.

36–2b Types of Gifts

Gifts by will can be specific, general, or residuary. If a decedent's assets are not sufficient to cover all the gifts identified in the will, an abatement is necessary.

Specific and General Devises
A *specific* devise or bequest (legacy) describes particular property (such as "Eastwood Estate" or "my gold pocket watch") that can be distinguished from all the rest of the testator's property.

A *general* devise or bequest (legacy) does not single out any particular item of property to be transferred by will. For instance, "I devise all my lands" is a general devise. A general bequest may specify the property's value in monetary terms (such as "two diamonds worth $10,000") or simply state a dollar amount (such as "$30,000 to my nephew, Carleton").

Residuary Clause
Sometimes, a will provides that any assets remaining after the estate's debts have been paid and specific gifts have been made are to be distributed in a specific way through a *residuary clause*. Residuary clauses are often used when the exact amount to be distributed cannot be determined until all of the other gifts and payouts have been made. If the testator has not indicated what party or parties should receive the residuary of the estate, the residuary passes according to state laws of intestacy.

"If you want to see a man's true character, watch him divide an estate."

BENJAMIN FRANKLIN
1706–1790
(AMERICAN DIPLOMAT, AUTHOR, AND SCIENTIST)

Abatement If the assets of an estate are insufficient to pay in full all general bequests provided for in the will, an *abatement* takes place. In an abatement, the legatees receive reduced benefits. **EXAMPLE 36.4** Julie's will leaves $15,000 each to her children, Tamara and Stan. On Julie's death, only $10,000 is available to honor these bequests. By abatement, each child will receive $5,000. ■ If bequests are more complicated, abatement may be more complex. The testator's intent, as expressed in the will, controls.

36-2c Requirements for a Valid Will

A will must comply with statutory formalities designed to ensure that the testator understood his or her actions at the time the will was made. These formalities are intended to help prevent fraud. Unless they are followed, the will is declared void, and the decedent's property is distributed according to the laws of intestacy of that state, as discussed later in this chapter.

Although the required formalities vary among jurisdictions, most states have certain basic requirements for executing a will. The National Conference of Commissioners on Uniform State Laws has issued the Uniform Probate Code (UPC) to govern various aspects of wills, inheritance, and estates. Almost half of the states have enacted some part of the UPC and incorporated it into their own probate codes.

For a valid will, most states require proof of (1) the testator's capacity, (2) testamentary intent, (3) a written document, (4) the testator's signature, and (5) the signatures of persons who witnessed the testator's signing of the will.

LEARNING OBJECTIVE 3
What are the basic requirements for executing a will?

Testamentary Capacity and Intent To have testamentary capacity, a testator must be of legal age and sound mind *at the time the will is made.* The minimum legal age for executing a will in most states and under the UPC is eighteen years [UPC 2–501]. Thus, the will of a twenty-one-year-old decedent written when the person was sixteen is invalid if, under state law, the legal age for executing a will is eighteen.

The concept of "being of sound mind" refers to the testator's ability to formulate and to comprehend a personal plan for the disposition of property. Persons who have been declared incompetent in a legal proceeding do not meet the sound mind requirement.

Related to the requirement of capacity is the concept of intent. A valid will is one that represents the maker's intention to transfer and distribute her or his property. Generally, a testator must:

If this couple leaves a sum of money to each child, but there are not enough assets to pay the amount specified in the will, what happens?

1. Know the nature of the act (of making a will).

2. Comprehend and remember the people to whom the testator would naturally leave his or her estate (such as family members and friends).

3. Know the nature and extent of her or his property.

4. Understand the distribution of assets called for by the will.

Undue Influence. When it can be shown that the decedent's plan of distribution was the result of fraud or of undue influence, the will is declared invalid. A court may sometimes infer undue influence when the named beneficiary was in a position to influence the making of the will. If the testator ignored blood relatives and named as a beneficiary a nonrelative who was in constant close contact with the testator, for instance, a court might infer undue influence.

CASE EXAMPLE 36.5 Belton Johnson, whose family owned the famous King Ranch in Texas, was married three times. He had three children from his first marriage and eight grandchildren. While married to his second wife, he executed a will that provided for her during her lifetime and left the remainder of his estate in a trust for his children and grandchildren. When his second wife died, he changed the will to give $1 million to each grandchild and the remainder

KNOW THIS
In most states, the age of majority for contractual purposes is eighteen years.

to five charities. His children were provided for in a separate trust. While married to his third wife, Laura, he executed a will that left $1 million to each grandchild and the rest to Laura. Later, another will left his entire estate in trust to Laura for her life and then to a foundation that she controlled. After Johnson's death, a dispute arose over the validity of the latest will.

The court concluded that Johnson's last will was invalid due to Laura's undue influence. Johnson was an admitted alcoholic with permanent cognitive defects and memory problems that would have caused him to be more susceptible to undue influence. Evidence suggested that Laura had exerted substantial control over many aspects of Johnson's life. Other evidence established that Johnson wanted to provide for his descendants, as well as for the charities named in the earlier will.[4]

How would the fact that the rich owner of this ranch was an alcoholic make him more susceptible to undue influence?

Disinheritance. Although a testator must be able to remember the persons who would naturally be heirs to the estate, there is no requirement that testators give their estates to the natural heirs. A testator may decide to disinherit, or leave nothing to, an individual for various reasons. Most states have laws that attempt to prevent accidental disinheritance, however. There are also laws that protect minor children from loss of the family residence. Therefore, the testator's intent to disinherit needs to be clear.

The following case involved a will in the form of a testamentary letter that left the decedent's entire estate to a friend and explicitly disinherited his family. The friend died before the decedent, so the court had to decide whether to follow the state's intestacy laws or enforce the disinheritance clause.

---

4. *In re Estate of Johnson*, 340 S.W.3d 769 (Tex.App.—San Antonio 2011).

CASE 36.3

In re Estate of Melton
Supreme Court of Nevada, 272 P.3d 668 (2012).

FACTS In 1975, William Melton executed a will that, among other things, stated that his daughter, Vicki Palm, was to receive nothing. In 1979, he added a handwritten note to the will, saying that his friend, Alberta Kelleher, was to receive a small portion of his estate. In 1995, Melton sent a signed, handwritten letter to Kelleher. In the letter, Melton said he was returning from his mother's funeral and, because she had died in an automobile accident, he wanted to put "something in writing" leaving Kelleher his "entire estate." Melton also said, "I do not want my brother Larry J. Melton or Vicki Palm or any of my other relatives to have one penny of my estate." When Melton died in 2008, Kelleher had already passed away, and Palm was his only natural heir. The state of Nevada argued that it should receive everything because Palm had been disinherited. Nevertheless, the trial court applied the state's intestacy laws and distributed the entire estate to Palm. The state appealed.

Can a person disinherit his or her daughter?

ISSUE Could Melton bypass Nevada's intestacy laws through a will that disinherited his family but failed to dispose of his property?

DECISION Yes. The Nevada Supreme Court reversed the judgment of the lower court. It held that the disinheritance clause was enforceable and that Melton's estate should go to the state of Nevada.

REASON Under the common law, the courts have developed two rules to determine whether a disinheritance clause should apply to any property that is not distributed by the will. Under the English rule, a disinheritance clause is enforceable only if "at least one . . . heir remain[s] eligible to receive the intestate property." Under the American rule, the testator must "affirmatively dispos[e] of the entire estate through a will." Many courts follow the American rule because disinheritance clauses create complications when they are applied to intestate property. For example, some courts say that such clauses "create an undesirable 'mixing' of the probate and intestacy systems by requiring courts to alter the distribution scheme provided in the intestacy statute." The state of Nevada, however, has rejected the common law rule by defining a will to include a "testamentary instrument that merely . . . excludes or limits the right of an individual or class to succeed to property of the decedent passing by intestate succession." As a result, Melton could disinherit his family without giving his property to someone else. Therefore, the state was entitled to Melton's property.

CRITICAL THINKING—Legal Consideration *Based on the information presented here, did Melton have testamentary intent when he wrote his letter? Why or why not?*

Writing Requirements Generally, a will must be in writing. The writing itself can be informal as long as it substantially complies with the statutory requirements. In some states, a will can be handwritten in crayon or ink. It can be written on a sheet or scrap of paper, on a paper bag, or on a piece of cloth. A will that is completely in the handwriting of the testator is called a **holographic will** (sometimes referred to as an *olographic will*).

A **nuncupative will** is an oral will made before witnesses. Oral wills are not permitted in most states. Where authorized by statute, such wills are generally valid only if made during the last illness of the testator and are therefore sometimes referred to as *deathbed wills*. Normally, only personal property can be transferred by a nuncupative will. Statutes may also permit members of the military to make nuncupative wills when on active duty.

Signature Requirements A fundamental requirement is that the testator's signature must appear on the will, generally at the end. Each jurisdiction dictates by statute and court decision what constitutes a signature. Initials, an X or other mark, and words such as "Mom" have all been upheld as valid when it was shown that the testators *intended* them to be signatures.

Witness Requirements A will usually must be attested (sworn to) by two, and sometimes three, witnesses. The number of witnesses, their qualifications, and the manner in which the witnessing must be done are generally set out in a statute. A witness can be required to be disinterested—that is, not a beneficiary under the will. The UPC, however, allows even interested witnesses to attest to a will [UPC 2–505]. There are no age requirements for witnesses, but they must be mentally competent.

The purpose of the witnesses is to verify that the testator actually executed (signed) the will and had the requisite intent and capacity at the time. A witness does not have to read the contents of the will. Usually, the testator and all witnesses sign in the sight or the presence of one another. The UPC does not require all parties to sign in the presence of one another, however, and deems it sufficient if the testator acknowledges her or his signature to the witnesses [UPC 2–502]. The UPC also provides an alternative to traditional witnesses—the signature may be acknowledged by the testator before a notary public.

36–2d Revocation of Wills

The testator can revoke a will at any time during his or her life, either by a physical act or by a subsequent writing. Wills can also be revoked by operation of law. Revocation can be partial or complete, and must follow certain strict formalities.

Revocation by a Physical Act A testator can revoke a will by *intentionally* burning, tearing, canceling, obliterating, or otherwise destroying it.[5] A testator can also revoke a will by intentionally having someone else destroy it in the testator's presence and at the testator's direction.

In some states, a testator can partially revoke a will by the physical act of crossing out some provisions in the will. Then, those portions that are crossed out are dropped, and the remaining parts of the will are valid. In no circumstances, however, can a provision be crossed out and an additional or substitute provision written in its place. Such altered portions require reexecution (re-signing) and reattestation (rewitnessing).

To revoke a will by physical act, it is necessary to follow the mandates of a state statute exactly. When a state statute prescribes the specific methods for revoking a will by physical act, only those methods can be used to revoke the will.

Revocation by a Subsequent Writing A will may be wholly or partially revoked by a **codicil,** a written instrument separate from the will that amends or revokes provisions in the will. A codicil eliminates the necessity of redrafting an entire will merely to add to it or amend it. It can also be used to revoke an entire will. The codicil must be executed with the same

Holographic Will A will written entirely in the testator's handwriting.

Nuncupative Will An oral will (often called a *deathbed will*) made before witnesses. Usually, such wills are limited to transfers of personal property.

Codicil A written supplement or modification to a will. A codicil must be executed with the same formalities as a will.

---

5. The destruction cannot be inadvertent. The testator must have the intent to revoke the will.

Is tearing up a will a legally recognized method of revoking that will?

formalities required for a will, and it must refer expressly to the will. In effect, it updates a will, because the will is "incorporated by reference" into the codicil.

A new will (second will) can be executed that may or may not revoke the first or a prior will, depending on the language used. To revoke a prior will, the second will must use language specifically revoking other wills, such as "This will hereby revokes all prior wills." If the express *declaration of revocation* is missing, then both wills are read together. If there are any discrepancies between the wills, the second will controls.

Revocation by Operation of Law
Revocation by *operation of law* occurs when marriage, divorce or annulment, or the birth of a child takes place after a will has been executed.

Marriage and Divorce. In most states, when a testator marries after executing a will that does not include the new spouse, the spouse can still receive a share of the testator's estate. On the testator's death, the surviving spouse can receive the amount he or she would have taken had the testator died intestate (intestacy laws will be discussed shortly). The rest of the estate is passed under the will [UPC 2–301, 2–508].

If, however, the new spouse is otherwise provided for in the will (or by transfer of property outside the will), he or she will not be given an intestate amount. Also, if the parties had a valid *prenuptial agreement* (a contract made prior to marriage), its provisions dictate what the surviving spouse receives.

Divorce or annulment does not necessarily revoke the entire will. Rather, a divorce or an annulment occurring after a will has been executed revokes those dispositions of property made under the will to the former spouse [UPC 2–508].

Children. If a child is born after a will has been executed, that child may be entitled to a portion of the estate. Most state laws allow a child of the deceased to receive some portion of a parent's estate even if no provision is made in the parent's will. This is true *unless it is clear from the will's terms that the testator intended to disinherit the child* (see Case 36.3 for an example of disinheritance). Under the UPC, the rule is the same.

36–2e Probate Procedures and Estate Planning

Probate The process of proving and validating a will and settling all matters pertaining to an estate.

To **probate** a will means to establish its validity and to carry the administration of the estate through a court process. Probate laws vary from state to state. Typically, the procedure depends on the size and complexity of the decedent's estate.

People commonly engage in estate planning in an attempt to avoid formal probate procedures and to maximize the value of their estate by reducing taxes and other expenses. Individuals should also consider formulating a social media estate plan, as discussed in this chapter's *Adapting the Law to the Online Environment* feature.

Informal Probate
For smaller estates, most state statutes provide for the distribution of assets without formal probate proceedings. Faster and less expensive methods are then used. Property can be transferred by *affidavit* (a written statement taken before a person who has authority to affirm it). Problems or questions can be handled during an administrative hearing. Some state statutes allow car titles, savings and checking accounts, and certain other property to be transferred simply by filling out forms.

A majority of states also provide for *family settlement agreements,* which are private agreements among the beneficiaries. Once a will is admitted to probate, the family members can agree among themselves on how to distribute the decedent's assets. Although a family settlement agreement speeds the settlement process, a court order is still needed to protect the estate from future creditors and to clear title to the assets involved.

Formal Probate
For larger estates, formal probate proceedings normally are undertaken, and the probate court supervises every aspect of the process. Additionally, in some situations—such

ADAPTING THE LAW TO THE **ONLINE** ENVIRONMENT
Social Media Estate Planning

People are generally quite careful about choosing the personal representatives who will deal with their real estate, bank accounts, and investments after they are gone. Today, the same care should be taken in choosing an online executor to deal with a deceased's online identity, particularly in social media.

What an Online Executor Should Do

An online executor is responsible for dealing with a decedent's e-mail addresses, social media profiles, and blogs. E-mail accounts should be closed, but some people do not want their social media profiles to be erased

after they die. They want the profiles to be maintained, at least for some specified time after death, so that family and friends can visit them. Some people ask that their online executors place a memorial profile in their social media accounts.

Why Social Media Estate Planning Is Important

Online estate planning is essential because the deceased can still be a victim of identity theft. Unscrupulous fraudsters often use dead people's online identities to defraud private companies, individuals, and federal and state governments. If all of a person's

e-mail addresses and social media accounts are closed, it is harder for online fraudsters to use them for identity theft.

In addition, closing an e-mail account not only protects family members from being harassed with continuing spam after the person's death but also prevents spammers from hijacking the account. Spammers can use a dead person's e-mail account as the sender of billions of unwanted bulk e-mails.

CRITICAL THINKING

- Why might an online executor need a copy of the deceased's death certificate?

---

as when a guardian for minor children must be appointed—more formal probate procedures cannot be avoided.

Formal probate proceedings may take several months or several years to complete, depending on the size and complexity of the estate and whether the will is contested. As a result, a sizable portion of the decedent's assets (as much as 10 percent) may go toward payment of court costs and fees charged by attorneys and personal representatives.

Property Transfers outside the Probate Process
Often, people can avoid the cost of probate by employing various **will substitutes.** Examples include *living trusts* (discussed later in this chapter), life insurance policies, and individual retirement accounts (IRAs) with named beneficiaries.

One way to transfer property outside the probate process is to make gifts to children or others while one is still living. Another way is to own property in a joint tenancy. As previously discussed, in a joint tenancy, when one joint tenant dies, the other joint tenant or tenants automatically inherit the deceased tenant's share of the property. This is true even if the deceased tenant has provided otherwise in her or his will. Not all alternatives to formal probate administration are suitable to every estate, however.

Will Substitutes Various instruments, such as living trusts and life insurance plans, that may be used to avoid the formal probate process.

For most people, estate planning involves not only ensuring that, after they die, their property goes to the intended recipients, but also avoiding probate and maximizing their estates. To this end, many choose to set up living trusts, establish joint tenancies, or use other will substitutes.

If you use will substitutes, though, you should be aware that a court will not apply the same principles in reviewing a transfer outside the probate process as it would apply to a testamentary transfer. Therefore, any such arrangements should be carefully drafted by an attorney and must comply with all legal requirements. To avoid disputes between beneficiaries after your death, make sure that your words and actions in such property transfers are clear and represent the final expression of your intent.

PREVENTING LEGAL DISPUTES

36–2f Intestacy Laws

As mentioned, each state regulates by statute how property will be distributed when a person dies intestate (without a valid will). Intestacy laws attempt to carry out the likely intent and wishes of the decedent. These laws assume that deceased persons would have intended that their natural heirs (spouses, children, grandchildren, or other family members) inherit their property. Therefore, intestacy statutes set out rules and priorities under which these heirs inherit the property. If no heirs exist, the state will assume ownership of the property. The rules of descent vary widely from state to state.

Surviving Spouse and Children   Usually, state statutes provide that the estate must be used to satisfy first the debts of the decedent. Then, the remaining assets pass to the surviving spouse and to the children. A surviving spouse usually receives only a share of the estate—one-half if there is also a surviving child and one-third if there are two or more children. Only if no children or grandchildren survive the decedent will a surviving spouse be entitled to the entire estate.

EXAMPLE 36.6 Allen dies intestate and is survived by his wife, Beth, and his children, Duane and Tara. Allen's property passes according to intestacy laws. After his outstanding debts are paid, Beth will receive the family home (either in fee simple or as a life estate) and ordinarily a one-third interest in all other property. The remaining real and personal property will pass to Duane and Tara in equal portions. ■

Under most state intestacy laws and under the UPC, in-laws do not share in an estate. Thus, if a child dies before his or her parents, the child's spouse will not receive an inheritance on the parents' death. For instance, if Duane died before his father (Allen) in *Example 36.6*, Duane's spouse would not inherit Duane's share of Allen's estate.

When There Is No Surviving Spouse or Child   When there is no surviving spouse or child, the order of inheritance is grandchildren, then brothers and sisters, and, in some states, parents of the decedent. These relatives are usually called *lineal descendants*.

If there are no lineal descendants, then *collateral heirs*—nieces, nephews, aunts, and uncles of the decedent—make up the next group to share. If there are no survivors in any of these groups, most statutes provide for the property to be distributed among the next of kin of the collateral heirs.

Stepchildren, Adopted Children, and Illegitimate Children   Under intestacy laws, stepchildren are not considered kin. Legally adopted children, however, are recognized as lawful heirs of their adoptive parents (as are children who are in the process of being adopted at the time of the parents' death).

Statutes vary from state to state in regard to the inheritance rights of illegitimate children (children born out of wedlock). In some states, an illegitimate child has the right to inherit only from the mother and her relatives, unless the father's paternity has been established by a legal proceeding. In the majority of states, however, a child born of any union that has the characteristics of a formal marriage relationship (such as unmarried parents who cohabit) is considered to be legitimate. Under the revised UPC, a child is the child of his or her natural (biological) parents, regardless of their marital status, as long as the natural parent has openly treated the child as her or his child [UPC 2–114]. Although illegitimate children may have inheritance rights in most states, their rights are not necessarily identical to those of legitimate children.

Grandchildren   Usually, a decedent's will provides for how the estate will be distributed to descendants of deceased children—that is, to the decedent's grandchildren. If a will does not include such a provision—or if a person dies intestate—the question arises as to what share the grandchildren of the decedent will receive. Each state uses one of two methods of distributing the assets of intestate decedents—*per stirpes* or *per capita*.

Per Stirpes* Distribution.** Under the ***per stirpes[6] method, within a class or group of distributees (such as grandchildren), the children of a descendant take the share that their deceased parent *would have been* entitled to inherit. Thus, a grandchild with no siblings inherits all of his or her parent's share, while grandchildren with siblings divide their parent's share.

EXAMPLE 36.7 Michael, a widower, has two children, Scott and Jonathan. Scott has two children (Becky and Holly), and Jonathan has one child (Paul). Scott and Jonathan die before their father, and then Michael dies. If Michael's estate is distributed *per stirpes,* Becky and Holly each receive one-fourth of the estate (dividing Scott's one-half share). Paul receives one-half of the estate (taking Jonathan's one-half share). ■ Exhibit 36–4 illustrates the *per stirpes* method of distribution.

Per Capita* Distribution.** An estate may also be distributed on a ***per capita[7] basis, which means that each person in a class or group takes an equal share of the estate. In *Example 36.7,* if Michael's estate is distributed *per capita,* Becky, Holly, and Paul each receive a one-third share. Exhibit 36–5 illustrates the *per capita* method of distribution.

Per Stirpes A method of distributing an intestate's estate so that each heir in a certain class (such as grandchildren) takes the share to which her or his deceased ancestor (such as a mother or father) would have been entitled.

Per Capita A method of distributing an intestate's estate so that each heir in a certain class (such as grandchildren) receives an equal share.

36-3 Trusts

A **trust** is any arrangement through which property is transferred from one person to a trustee to be administered for the transferor's or another party's benefit. It can also be defined as a right of property held by one party for the benefit of another. A trust can be created for any purpose that is not illegal or against public policy, and it can be express or implied.

The essential elements of a trust are as follows:

1. A designated beneficiary.

2. A designated trustee.

3. A fund sufficiently identified to enable title to pass to the trustee.

4. Actual delivery by the *grantor* (or *settlor,* the person creating the trust) to the trustee with the intention of passing title.

Trust An arrangement in which title to property is held by one person (a trustee) for the benefit of another (a beneficiary).

LEARNING OBJECTIVE 5
What are the four essential elements of a trust?

---

6. *Per stirpes* is a Latin term meaning "by the roots" or "by stock." When used in estate law, it means proportionally divided among beneficiaries according to their deceased ancestor's share.

7. *Per capita* is a Latin term meaning "per person" or "for each head." When used in estate law, it means equally divided among beneficiaries.

Exhibit 36–4 *Per Stirpes* Distribution

Under this method of distribution, an heir takes the share that his or her deceased parent would have been entitled to inherit had the parent lived. This may mean that a class of distributees—the grandchildren in this example—will not inherit in equal portions. Note that Becky and Holly receive only one-fourth of Michael's estate while Paul inherits one-half.

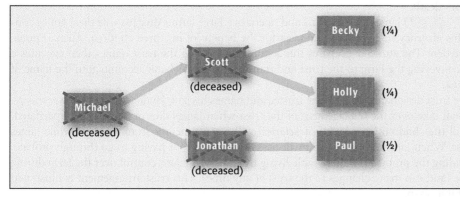

In what two ways will the proceeds from the sale of this property be divided to heirs after the owner's death?

Exhibit 36–5 *Per Capita* **Distribution**

Under this method of distribution, all heirs in a certain class—in this example, the grandchildren—inherit equally. Note that Becky and Holly in this situation each inherit one-third, as does Paul.

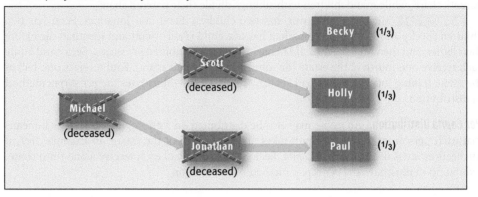

36-3a Express Trusts

An express trust is created or declared in explicit terms, usually in writing. There are many types of express trusts, each with its own special characteristics.

Living Trusts   A **living (*inter vivos*) trust**—*inter vivos* is Latin for "between or among the living"—is a trust created by a grantor during her or his lifetime. Living trusts have become a popular estate-planning option because at the grantor's death, assets held in a living trust can pass to the heirs without going through probate.

Note, however, that living trusts do not shelter assets from estate taxes. Furthermore, the grantor may have to pay income taxes on trust earnings, depending on whether the trust is revocable or irrevocable.

Revocable Living Trusts. Living trusts can be revocable or irrevocable. In a *revocable* living trust, which is the most common type, the grantor retains control over the trust property. The grantor deeds the property to the trust but retains the power to amend, alter, or revoke the trust during her or his lifetime.

The grantor may also serve as a trustee or co-trustee and can arrange to receive income earned by the trust assets during her or his lifetime. Because the grantor is in control of the funds, she or he is required to pay income taxes on the trust earnings. Unless the trust is revoked, the principal of the trust is transferred to the trust beneficiary or beneficiaries on the grantor's death.

EXAMPLE 36.8 James Cortez owns and operates a large farm. After his wife dies, James contacts his attorney to create a living trust for the benefit of his three children, Alicia, Emma, and Jayden. The attorney prepares the documents creating the trust. James then executes a deed conveying the farm to the trust and transfers the farm's bank accounts into the name of the trust.

The trust designates James as the trustee and names his son, Jayden, as the *successor trustee,* who will take over the management of the trust when James dies or becomes incapacitated. Each of the children (as *income beneficiaries*) will receive income from the trust while James is alive. When James dies, the farm will pass to them without having to go through probate. By holding the property in a revocable living trust, James retains control over the farm during his life (and can make changes to the trust at any time). This trust arrangement is illustrated in Exhibit 36–6. ■

Living (*Inter Vivos*) Trust
A trust created by the grantor (settlor) and effective during his or her lifetime.

Exhibit 36–6 A Revocable Living Trust Arrangement

Grantor	Trust Property	Trustee	Income Beneficiary	Remainder Beneficiaries
James Cortez	**Farm and Accounts**	**James Cortez** as Trustee of the James Cortez Living Trust	**James Cortez** during his lifetime	On the grantor's death, the trust property will be distributed to Alicia, Emma, and Jayden.

Irrevocable Living Trusts. In an *irrevocable* living trust, the grantor permanently gives up control over the property to the trustee. The grantor executes a trust deed, and legal title to the trust property passes to the named trustee. The trustee has a duty to administer the property as directed by the grantor for the benefit and in the interest of the beneficiaries.

The trustee must preserve the trust property and make it productive. If required by the terms of the trust agreement, the trustee must pay income to the beneficiaries in accordance with the terms of the trust. Because the grantor has, in effect, given over the property for the benefit of the beneficiaries, he or she is no longer responsible for paying income taxes on the trust earnings.

iStockPhoto.com/DNY59

When a living trust is created, who is normally named as the trustee?

Testamentary Trusts

A **testamentary trust** is created by will and comes into existence on the grantor's death. Although a testamentary trust has a trustee who maintains legal title to the trust property, the trustee's actions are subject to judicial approval. This trustee can be named in the will or be appointed by the court (if not named in the will). The legal responsibilities of the trustee are the same as in a living trust.

If a court finds that the will setting up a testamentary trust is invalid, then the trust will also be invalid. The property that was supposed to be in the trust will then pass according to intestacy laws, not according to the terms of the trust.

Testamentary Trust A trust that is created by will and therefore does not take effect until the death of the testator.

Charitable Trusts

A **charitable trust** is an express trust designed for the benefit of a segment of the public or the public in general. It differs from other types of trusts in that the identities of the beneficiaries are uncertain and it can be established to last indefinitely. Usually, to be deemed a charitable trust, a trust must be created for charitable, educational, religious, or scientific purposes.

Charitable Trust A trust in which the property held by the trustee must be used for a charitable purpose, such as the advancement of health, education, or religion.

Spendthrift Trusts

A **spendthrift trust** is created to provide for the maintenance of a beneficiary by preventing him or her from being careless with the bestowed funds. Unlike the beneficiaries of other trusts, the beneficiary in a spendthrift trust is not permitted to transfer or assign his or her right to the trust's principal or future payments from the trust. Essentially, the beneficiary can withdraw only a certain portion of the total amount to which he or she is entitled at any one time. The majority of states allow spendthrift trust provisions that prohibit creditors from attaching such trusts.

Spendthrift Trust A trust created to protect the beneficiary from spending all the funds to which she or he is entitled. Only a certain portion of the total amount is given to the beneficiary at any one time, and most states prohibit creditors from attaching assets of the trust.

Totten Trusts

A **Totten trust**[8] is created when a grantor deposits funds in her or his own name with instructions that on the grantor's death, whatever is in that account should go to a specific beneficiary. This type of trust is revocable at will until the depositor dies or completes the gift during her or his lifetime (by delivering the funds to the intended beneficiary,

Totten Trust A trust created when a person deposits funds in his or her own name for a specific beneficiary, who will receive the funds on the depositor's death. The trust is revocable at will until the depositor dies or completes the gift.

---

8. This type of trust derives its unusual name from the case *In re Totten*, 179 N.Y. 112, 71 N.E. 748 (1904).

for instance). The beneficiary has no access to the funds until the depositor's death, when the beneficiary obtains property rights to the balance on hand.

36-3b Implied Trusts

Sometimes, a trust will be imposed (implied) by law, even in the absence of an express trust. Implied trusts include resulting trusts and constructive trusts.

Constructive Trust
An equitable trust that is imposed in the interests of fairness and justice when someone wrongfully holds legal title to property.

Constructive Trusts
A **constructive trust** is an equitable trust imposed by a court in the interests of fairness and justice. In a constructive trust, the owner of the property is declared to be a trustee for the parties who are, in fairness, actually entitled to the benefits that flow from the property.

Courts often impose constructive trusts when someone who is in a confidential or fiduciary relationship with another person, such as a guardian to a ward, has breached a duty to that person. A court may also impose a constructive trust when someone wrongfully holds legal title to property—because the property was obtained through fraud or in breach of a legal duty, for instance.

CASE EXAMPLE 36.9 Stella Jankowski added her niece Genevieve Viarengo as a joint owner on bank accounts and other financial assets valued at $500,000. Jankowski also executed a will that divided her estate equally among her ten nieces, nephews, and cousins, and named Viarengo and Richard Golebiewski as coexecutors. She did not tell the attorney who drafted the will about the jointly held accounts.

When Jankowski died, Viarengo emptied her safe, removed her financial records, and claimed that the funds in the accounts were hers. Jankowski's other relatives filed a suit and asked the court to impose a constructive trust. The court found that Viarengo had committed fraud in obtaining the assets that she had held jointly with Jankowski and would be unjustly enriched if she were allowed to retain them. Therefore, the court imposed a constructive trust.[9]

Resulting Trust An implied trust that arises when one party holds the legal title to another's property only for that other's benefit.

Resulting Trusts
A **resulting trust** arises from the conduct of the parties. When circumstances raise an inference that one party holds legal title to the property for the benefit of another, a court may infer a resulting trust.

EXAMPLE 36.10 Gabriela Fuentes wants to put one acre of land she owns on the market for sale. Because she is going out of the country for two years and will not be able to deed the property to a buyer during that period, Fuentes conveys (transfers) the property to her good friend Oswald. Oswald can then attempt to sell the property while Fuentes is gone.

The transaction in which Fuentes conveyed the property to Oswald was intended to be neither a sale nor a gift. Consequently, Oswald will hold the property in a resulting trust for the benefit of Fuentes. When Fuentes returns, Oswald will be required either to deed the property back to her or, if the property has been sold, to turn over the proceeds (held in trust) to her. ■

36-3c The Trustee

The *trustee* is the person holding the trust property. Anyone legally capable of holding title to, and dealing in, property can be a trustee. If a trust fails to name a trustee, or if a named trustee cannot or will not serve, the trust does not fail—an appropriate court can appoint a trustee.

Trustee's Duties
A trustee must act with honesty, good faith, and prudence in administering the trust and must exercise a high degree of loyalty toward the trust beneficiary. The general standard of care is the degree of care a prudent person would exercise in his or her personal affairs.[10] The duty of loyalty requires that the trustee act in the exclusive interest of the beneficiary.

---

9. *Garrigus v. Viarengo*, 112 Conn.App. 655, 963 A.2d 1065 (2009).
10. Revised Uniform Principal and Income Act, Section 2(a)(3); *Restatement (Third) of Trusts (Prudent Investor Rule)*, Section 227. This rule is in force in the majority of states by statute and in a small number of states under the common law.

A trustee's specific duties include the following:

1. Maintain clear and accurate accounts of the trust's administration.

2. Furnish complete and correct information to the beneficiary.

3. Keep trust assets separate from her or his own assets.

4. Pay to an income beneficiary the net income of the trust assets at reasonable intervals.

5. Limit the risk of loss from investments by reasonable diversification and dispose of assets that do not represent prudent investments. (Prudent investment choices might include federal, state, or municipal bonds and some corporate bonds and stocks.)

Trustee's Powers

When a grantor creates a trust, he or she may set forth the trustee's powers and performance. State law governs in the absence of specific terms in the trust, and the states often restrict the trustee's investment of trust funds.

Typically, statutes confine trustees to investments in conservative debt securities such as government, utility, and railroad bonds. Frequently, though, a grantor gives a trustee discretionary investment power. In that circumstance, any statute may be considered only advisory, with the trustee's decisions subject in most states to the prudent person rule.

Of course, a trustee is responsible for carrying out the purposes of the trust. If the trustee fails to comply with the terms of the trust or the controlling statute, he or she is personally liable for any loss.

Allocations between Principal and Income

Often, a grantor will provide one beneficiary with a life estate and another beneficiary with the remainder interest in a trust. A farmer, for instance, may create a testamentary trust providing that the farm's income be paid to the surviving spouse and that on the surviving spouse's death, the farm be given to their children. In this situation, the surviving spouse has a *life estate* in the farm's income, and the children have a *remainder interest* in the farm (the principal).

When a trust is set up in this manner, questions may arise as to how the receipts and expenses for the farm's management and the trust's administration should be allocated between income and principal. When a trust instrument does not provide instructions, a trustee must refer to applicable state law.

The general rule is that ordinary receipts and expenses are chargeable to the income beneficiary, whereas extraordinary receipts and expenses are allocated to the principal beneficiaries.[11] The receipt of rent from trust realty would be ordinary, as would the expense of paying the property's taxes. The cost of long-term improvements and proceeds from the property's sale, however, would be extraordinary.

36-3d Trust Termination

The terms of a trust should expressly state the event on which the grantor wishes it to terminate—for instance, the beneficiary's or the trustee's death. If the trust instrument does not provide for termination on the beneficiary's death, the beneficiary's death will not end the trust. Similarly, without an express provision, a trust will not terminate on the trustee's death.

Typically, a trust instrument specifies a termination date. For instance, a trust created to educate the grantor's child may provide that the trust ends when the beneficiary reaches the age of twenty-five. If the trust's purpose is fulfilled before that date, a court may order the trust's termination. If no date is specified, a trust will terminate when its purpose has been fulfilled. Of course, if a trust's purpose becomes impossible or illegal, the trust will terminate.

> "Put not your trust in money, but put your money in trust."
>
> **OLIVER WENDELL HOLMES, JR.**
> 1841–1935
> (ASSOCIATE JUSTICE OF THE UNITED STATES SUPREME COURT, 1902–1932)

---

11. Revised Uniform Principal and Income Act, Sections 3, 6, 8, and 13; *Restatement (Second) of Trusts*, Section 233.

Reviewing . . . Insurance, Wills, and Trusts

In June 2015, Bernard Ramish set up a $48,000 trust fund through West Plains Credit Union to provide tuition for his nephew, Nathan Covacek, to attend Tri-State Polytechnic Institute. The trust was established under Ramish's control and went into effect that August. In December, Ramish suffered a brain aneurysm that caused frequent, severe headaches but no other symptoms. In August 2016, Ramish developed heat stroke and collapsed on the golf course at La Prima Country Club.

After recuperating at the clubhouse, Ramish quickly wrote his will on the back of a wine list. It stated, "My last will and testament: Upon my death, I give all of my personal property to my friend Bernard Eshom and my home to Lizzie Johansen." He signed the will at the bottom in the presence of five men in the La Prima clubhouse, and all five men signed as witnesses.

A week later, Ramish suffered a second aneurysm and died in his sleep. He was survived by his mother (Dorris Ramish), his nephew (Nathan Covacek), his son-in-law (Bruce Lupin), and his granddaughter (Tori Lupin). Using the information presented in the chapter, answer the following questions.

1. Does Ramish's testament on the back of the wine list meet the requirements for a valid will?

2. Suppose that after Ramish's first aneurysm in 2016, Covacek contacted an insurance company to obtain a life insurance policy on Ramish's life. Would Covacek have had an insurable interest in his uncle's life? Why or why not?

3. What would the order of inheritance have been if Ramish had died intestate?

4. What will most likely happen to the trust fund established for Covacek on Ramish's death?

DEBATE THIS

- Any changes to existing, fully witnessed wills should also have to be witnessed.

BUSINESS APPLICATION

How Can You Manage Risk in Cyberspace?*

Companies doing business online face many risks that are not covered by traditional types of insurance (listed in Exhibit 36–1). Not surprisingly, a growing number of companies are now offering policies designed to cover Web-related risks.

Insurance Coverage for Web-Related Risks

Insurance to cover Web-related incidents is frequently referred to as *network intrusion insurance*. Such insurance protects companies from losses stemming from hacking and computer viruses, programming errors, and network and Web site disruptions. It also protects against losses from theft of electronic data and assets, including intellectual property, and losses arising from claims of Web-related defamation, copyright infringement, false advertising, and violations of users' privacy rights.

InsureTrust.com, an insurer affiliated with three leading insurance companies—

American International Group, Lloyd's of London, and Reliance National—is a leading provider of network intrusion insurance. Other insurers, such as Hartford Insurance and the Chubb Group of Insurance Companies, have also added insurance for Web-related perils to their offerings. Clearly, the market for network intrusion insurance is evolving rapidly, and new policies will continue to appear.

Customized Policies

Unlike traditional insurance policies, which are generally drafted by insurance companies and presented to insurance applicants on a take-it-or-leave-it basis, network

---

* This *Business Application* is not meant to substitute for the services of an attorney who is licensed to practice law in your state.

intrusion insurance policies are usually customized to provide protection against specific risks faced by a particular type of business. For example, an Internet service provider will face different risks than an online merchant, and a banking institution will face different risks than a law firm. The specific business-related risks are taken into consideration when determining the policy premium.

Qualifying Criteria

Many companies that offer network intrusion insurance require applicants to meet high security standards. In other words, to qualify for a policy, a business must have Web-related security measures in place. Several companies assess an applicant's security system before underwriting a policy. The insurer might, for example, refuse to provide coverage unless the business scores higher than 60 percent in such an assessment. If the business does not score that high, it can contract with the company to improve its Web-related security.

CHECKLIST for the Businessperson:

1. Determine the types of risks that your Web business is exposed to, and try to obtain an insurance policy that protects you against those specific risks.
2. As when procuring any type of insurance, read the policy carefully, including any exclusions contained in the fine print, before committing to it.
3. Do not be "penny wise and pound foolish" when it comes to insurance protection. Though insurance coverage may seem expensive, it may be much less costly than the loss of intellectual property or the cost of defending against a lawsuit. Opting for a higher deductible can reduce the amount you pay in premiums.
4. Find out what the company's underwriting standards are, and determine whether your Web security measures meet its standards.

Key Terms

administrator 907
bequest 907
binder 903
charitable trust 917
codicil 911
constructive trust 918
devise 907
devisee 907
executor 907
holographic will 911
incontestability clause 904
insurable interest 900

insurance 900
intestacy laws 907
intestate 907
legacy 907
legatee 907
living (*inter vivos*) trust 916
nuncupative will 911
per capita 915
per stirpes 915
policy 900
premium 900
probate 912

resulting trust 918
risk 900
risk management 900
spendthrift trust 917
testamentary trust 917
testate 907
testator 907
Totten trust 917
trust 915
underwriter 900
will 907
will substitutes 913

Chapter Summary: Insurance, Wills, and Trusts

INSURANCE	
Classifications	See Exhibit 36–1 for a list of types of insurance.
Terminology	1. *Policy*—The insurance contract. 2. *Premium*—The consideration paid to the insurer for a policy. 3. *Underwriter*—The insurance company. 4. *Parties*—Include the insurer (the insurance company), the insured (the person covered by insurance), an agent (a representative of the insurance company) or a broker (ordinarily an independent contractor), and a beneficiary (a person to receive proceeds under the policy).
Insurable Interest	An insurable interest exists whenever an individual or entity benefits from the preservation of the health or life of the insured or the property to be insured. For life insurance, an insurable interest must exist at the time the policy is issued. For property insurance, an insurable interest must exist at the time of the loss.

Continues

The Insurance Contract	1. *Laws governing*—The general principles of contract law are applied. The insurance industry is also heavily regulated by the states.
	2. *Application*—An insurance applicant is bound by any false statements that appear in the application (subject to certain exceptions), which is part of the insurance contract. Misstatements or misrepresentations may be grounds for voiding the policy.
	3. *Effective date*—Coverage on an insurance policy can begin when a *binder* (a written memorandum indicating that a formal policy is pending and stating its essential terms) is written; when the policy is issued; at the time of contract formation; or, depending on the terms of the contract, when certain conditions are met.
	4. *Provisions and clauses*—See Exhibit 36–2 for specific provisions. Words will be given their ordinary meanings, and any ambiguity in the policy will be interpreted against the insurance company. When the written policy has not been delivered and it is unclear whether an insurance contract actually exists, the uncertainty will be resolved against the insurance company. The court will presume that the policy is in effect unless the company can show otherwise.
	5. *Defenses against payment to the insured*—Defenses include misrepresentation or fraud by the applicant.

WILLS

Terminology	1. *Intestate*—One who dies without a valid will.
	2. *Testator*—A person who makes out a will.
	3. *Personal representative*—A person appointed in a will or by a court to settle the affairs of a decedent. A personal representative named in the will is an *executor*. A personal representative appointed by the court for an intestate decedent is an *administrator*.
	4. *Devise*—A gift of real estate by will; may be general or specific. The recipient of a devise is a *devisee*.
	5. *Bequest, or legacy*—A gift of personal property by will; may be general or specific. The recipient of a bequest (legacy) is a *legatee*.
Requirements for a Valid Will	1. The testator must have testamentary capacity (be of legal age and sound mind at the time the will is made).
	2. The testator must have the necessary intent to transfer and distribute his or her property.
	3. A will must be in writing (except for nuncupative wills). A holographic will is completely in the handwriting of the testator.
	4. A will must be signed by the testator. What constitutes a signature varies from jurisdiction to jurisdiction.
	5. A nonholographic will (an attested will) must be witnessed in the manner prescribed by state statute.
Revocation of Wills	1. *By physical act of the maker*—Tearing up, canceling, obliterating, or deliberately destroying part or all of a will.
	2. *By subsequent writing*—
	a. Codicil—A formal, separate document to amend or revoke an existing will.
	b. Second will or new will—A new, properly executed will expressly revoking the existing will.
	3. *By operation of law*—
	a. Marriage—Generally revokes part of a will written before the marriage.
	b. Divorce or annulment—Revokes dispositions of property made under a will to a former spouse.
	c. Subsequently born child—Most states allow the child to receive a portion of the estate.
Probate Procedures and Estate Planning	To probate a will means to establish its validity and to carry the administration of the estate through a state court process. Probate procedures may be informal or formal, depending on the size of the estate and other factors, such as whether a guardian for minor children must be appointed.
Intestacy Laws	1. Intestacy laws vary widely from state to state. Usually, the law provides that the surviving spouse and children inherit the property of the decedent (after the decedent's debts are paid). The spouse usually inherits the entire estate if there are no children, one-half of the estate if there is one child, and one-third of the estate if there are two or more children.
	2. If there is no surviving spouse or child, then, in order, lineal descendants (grandchildren, brothers and sisters, and—in some states—parents of the decedent) inherit. If there are no lineal descendants, then collateral heirs (nieces, nephews, aunts, and uncles of the decedent) inherit.

TRUSTS

Definition	A trust is any arrangement through which property is transferred from one person to a trustee to be administered for another party's benefit. The essential elements of a trust are (1) a designated beneficiary, (2) a designated trustee, (3) a fund sufficiently identified to enable title to pass to the trustee, and (4) actual delivery to the trustee with the intention of passing title.
Express Trusts	Express trusts are created by explicit terms, usually in writing, and include the following:
	1. *Living (inter vivos) trust*—A trust created by a grantor during her or his lifetime.
	2. *Testamentary trust*—A trust that is created by will and comes into existence on the death of the grantor.
	3. *Charitable trust*—A trust designed for the benefit of a public group or the public in general.
	4. *Spendthrift trust*—A trust created to provide for a beneficiary by allowing the beneficiary to withdraw only a certain amount at any one time.
	5. *Totten trust*—A trust created when one person deposits funds in his or her own name as a trustee for another.
Implied Trusts	Implied trusts, which are imposed by law in the interests of fairness and justice, include the following:
	1. *Constructive trust*—Arises by operation of law when a person wrongfully takes title to property. A court may require the owner to hold the property in trust for those who, in equity, are entitled to enjoy the benefits from the trust.
	2. *Resulting trust*—Arises from the conduct of the parties when an apparent intention to create a trust is present.

Issue Spotters

1. Sheila makes out a will, leaving her property in equal thirds to Toby and Uma, her children, and Velda, her niece. Two years later, Sheila is adjudged mentally incompetent, and that same year, she dies. Can Toby and Uma have Sheila's will revoked on the ground that she did not have the capacity to make a will? Why or why not? (See *Wills*.)

2. When Ralph dies, he has not made a will and is survived by many relatives—a spouse, children, adopted children, sisters, brothers, uncles, aunts, cousins, nephews, and nieces. What determines who inherits what? (See *Wills*.)

—**Check your answers to the *Issue Spotters* against the answers provided in Appendix D at the end of this text.**

Learning Objectives Check

1. What is an insurable interest? When must an insurable interest exist?

2. How do courts interpret ambiguities in an insurance policy?

3. What are the basic requirements for executing a will?

4. What is the difference between a *per stirpes* distribution and a *per capita* distribution of an estate to the grandchildren of the deceased?

5. What are the four essential elements of a trust?

—**Answers to the even-numbered *Learning Objectives Check* questions can be found in Appendix E at the end of this text.**

Business Scenarios and Case Problems

36–1. Timing of Insurance Coverage. On October 10, Joleen Vora applied for a $50,000 life insurance policy with Magnum Life Insurance Co. She named her husband, Jay, as the beneficiary. Joleen paid the insurance company the first year's premium on making the application. Two days later, before she had a chance to take the physical examination required by the insurance company and before the policy was issued, Joleen was killed in an automobile accident. Jay submitted a claim to the insurance company for $50,000. Can Jay collect? Explain. (See *Insurance*.)

36–2. Wills and Intestacy Laws. Benjamin is a widower who has two married children, Edward and Patricia. Patricia has two children, Perry and Paul. Edward has no children. Benjamin makes a will leaving all his property equally to Edward and Patricia. The will provides that should a child predecease him, the grandchildren are to take *per stirpes*. The will is witnessed by Patricia and by Benjamin's lawyer and is signed by Benjamin in their presence. Benjamin dies, and Patricia has predeceased him. Edward claims the will is invalid. (See *Wills*.)

1. Discuss whether the will is valid.

2. Discuss the distribution of Benjamin's estate if the will is invalid.

3. Discuss the distribution of Benjamin's estate if the will is valid.

36–3. Intestacy Laws. A Florida statute provides that the right of election of a surviving spouse can be waived by written agreement: "A waiver of 'all rights,' or equivalent language, in the property or estate of a present or prospective spouse . . . is a waiver of all rights to elective share." The day before Mary Ann Taylor married Louis Taylor in Florida, they entered into a prenuptial agreement. The agreement stated that all property belonging to each spouse would "forever remain his or her personal estate," "said property shall remain forever free of claim by the other," and the parties would retain "full rights and authority" over their property as they would have as "if not married." After Louis's death, his only child, Joshua Taylor, filed a petition in a Florida state court for a determination of the beneficiaries of Louis's estate. How much of the estate can Mary Ann elect to receive? Explain. [*Taylor v. Taylor,* 1 So.3d 348 (Fla.App. 1 Dist. 2009)] (See *Wills*.)

36–4. Revocation of a Will. Marion Peterson executed a will that contained a bequest to Vasta Lucas in the form of a trust. On Lucas's death, the trustee was to distribute the assets to four beneficiaries, including Peterson's brother and sister, Arvin and Carolyn. Later, without witnesses, Peterson crossed out the beneficiaries' names, but she left the bequest to Lucas intact. After Peterson's death, Arvin and Carolyn contended that the will had been completely revoked. Were they correct? Explain. [*Peterson v. Harrell,* 286 Ga. 546, 690 S.E.2d 151 (2010)] (See *Wills*.)

36–5. Business Case Problem with Sample Answer—Undue **Influence.** Susie Walker executed a will that left her entire estate to her grandson. When her grandson died, Susie executed a new will that named her great-grandson as her sole beneficiary and specifically disinherited her son,

Tommy. At the time, Tommy's ex-wife was living with Susie. After Susie died, Tommy filed a suit, claiming that her will was the product of undue influence on the part of his ex-wife. Several witnesses testified that Susie had been mentally competent when she executed her will. Does undue influence appear likely based on these facts? Why or why not? [*In re Estate of Walker*, 80 A.D.3d 865, 914 N.Y.S.2d 379 (3 Dept. 2011)] (See *Wills*.)

—For a sample answer to Problem 36–5, go to Appendix F at the end of this text.

36–6. Insurance Provisions and Clauses. Darling's Rent-a-Car carried property insurance on its cars under a policy issued by Philadelphia Indemnity Insurance Co. The policy listed Darling's as the "insured." Darling's rented a car to Joshuah Farrington. In the rental contract, Farrington agreed to be responsible for any damage to the car and declined the optional insurance. Later, Farrington collided with a moose. Philadelphia paid Darling's for the damage to the car and sought to collect this amount from Farrington. Farrington argued that he was an "insured" under Darling's policy. How should "insured" be interpreted in this case? Why? [*Philadelphia Indemnity Insurance Co. v. Farrington*, 37 A.3d 305 (Me. 2012)] (See *Insurance*.)

36–7. Requirements of a Will. Sherman Hemsley was a well-known actor from the 1970s. Most notably, he played George Jefferson on the television shows *All in the Family* and *The Jeffersons*. He was born to Arsena Chisolm and William Thornton. Thornton was married to another woman, and Hemsley never had a relationship with his father or that side of the family. Hemsley never married and had no children. He lived with Flora Bernal, his business manager. Diagnosed with cancer, Hemsley executed a will naming Bernal the sole beneficiary of his estate. At the signing, Hemsley indicated that he knew he was executing his will and that he had deliberately chosen Bernal, but he did not discuss his relatives or the nature of his property with his attorney or the witnesses. After his death, the Thorntons challenged the will. Was Hemsley of sound mind? Discuss. [*In re Estate of Hemsley*, __ S.W.3d __, 2014 WL 5854220 (Tex.App.—El Paso 2014)] (See *Wills*.)

36–8. Wills. Andrew Walker executed a will giving a certain parcel of real estate in fee simple to his three children from a previous marriage, Mark Walker, Michelle Peters, and Andrea Knox, with a "life use" in the property granted to his current spouse, Nora Walker. A year later, Andrew, who suffered from asbestosis, was discharged from a hospital to spend his last days at home. He told Nora that he wished to execute a new will to change the disposition of the property to devise half of it to her. Nora recorded his wish and took her notes to the office of attorney Frederick Meagher to have the document drafted. Meagher did not see Nora's notes, he did not talk to Walker, no one from his office was present at the signing of the document, and, when Walker signed it, he did not declare that it was his will, as required by state law. Is the document a valid will? Explain. [*In re Estate of Walker*, 124 A.D.3d 970, 2 N.Y.S.3d 628 (3 Dept. 2015)] (See *Wills*.)

36–9. A Question of Ethics—Will Requirements. Vickie Lynn Smith, an actress and model also known as Anna Nicole Smith, met J. Howard Marshall II in 1991. During their courtship, J. Howard lavished gifts and large sums of money on Anna Nicole, and they married on June 27, 1994. J. Howard died on August 4, 1995. According to Anna Nicole, J. Howard intended to provide for her financial security through a trust, but under the terms of his will, all of his assets were transferred to a trust for the benefit of E. Pierce Marshall, one of J. Howard's sons. While J. Howard's estate was subject to probate proceedings in a Texas state court, Anna Nicole filed for bankruptcy in a federal bankruptcy court. Pierce filed a claim in the bankruptcy proceeding, alleging that Anna Nicole had defamed him when her lawyers told the media that Pierce had engaged in forgery and fraud to gain control of his father's assets. Anna Nicole filed a counterclaim, alleging that Pierce prevented the transfer of his father's assets to a trust for her by, among other things, imprisoning J. Howard against his wishes, surrounding him with security guards to prevent contact with her, and transferring property against his wishes. [*Marshall v. Marshall*, 547 U.S. 293, 126 S.Ct. 1735, 164 L.Ed.2d 480 (2006)] (See *Wills*.)

1. What is the purpose underlying the requirements for a valid will? Which of these requirements might be at issue in this case? How should it apply here? Why?

2. State courts generally have jurisdiction over the probate of a will and the administration of an estate. Does the Texas state court thus have the sole authority to adjudicate all of the claims in this case? Why or why not?

3. How should Pierce's claim against Anna Nicole and her counterclaim be resolved?

4. Anna Nicole executed her will in 2001. The beneficiary—Daniel, her son, who was not J. Howard's child—died in 2006, shortly after Anna Nicole gave birth to a daughter, Dannielynn. In 2007, before executing a new will, Anna Nicole died. What happens if a will's beneficiary dies before the testator? What happens if a child is born after a will is executed?

Critical Thinking and Writing Assignments

36–10. Business Law Critical Thinking Group Assignment.
PAJ, Inc., a jewelry company, had a commercial general liability (CGL) policy from Hanover Insurance Company. The policy required PAJ to notify Hanover of any claim or suit against PAJ "as soon as practicable." Yurman Designs sued PAJ for copyright infringement because of the design of a particular jewelry line. Because PAJ did not realize that the CGL policy had a clause that covered infringement claims, it did not notify Hanover of the suit until four to six months after litigation began. Hanover contended that the policy did not apply to this incident because the late notification had violated its terms.

PAJ sued Hanover, seeking a declaration that it was obligated to defend and indemnify PAJ. (See *Insurance*.)

1. The first group will decide whether Hanover had an obligation to provide PAJ with legal assistance.

2. The second group will determine the effect that PAJ's late notice to the insurance company had on the insurance company's ability to provide assistance and mount a defense. Should the court require the insurance company to indemnify PAJ in this situation? Why or why not?

Unit Seven—Business Case Study with Dissenting Opinion

Kovarik v. Kovarik

When a couple divorces, the division of the marital estate—all of the property that the parties accumulated during their marriage—often leads to disputes. Questions of ownership frequently arise in divorce proceedings: Who owned what property, and how did she or he acquire it? If property was allegedly acquired by gift, did the transfer satisfy the requirements for a valid gift?

Those questions arose in *Kovarik v. Kovarik*,[1] which we examine in this *Business Case Study with Dissenting Opinion*. During a divorce, a dispute arose over whether the couple's marital estate included several certificates of deposit worth about $60,000 in which one spouse allegedly had an interest. The acquisition, division, and transfer of ownership of personal property, as well as other types of property transfers, were covered in this unit.

alexmillos/ShutterStock.com

Are certificates of deposit (CDs) part of the marital estate?

CASE BACKGROUND

Jennifer Stahl and Bradly Kovarik were married in North Dakota in July 2001. A few months later, Bradly's parents, Dennis and Marlene, liquidated their farm business and invested the proceeds in certificates of deposit (CDs). Four of the CDs were in the names of Bradly and his sister, Wanda Morstad, but were retained by their parents.

Jennifer and Bradly separated in August 2007. Jennifer filed for divorce in a North Dakota state court. In a list of their marital property, she included the four CDs. Bradly denied any interest in those items.

At the trial, Bradly testified that he had learned about the CDs from his sister, who had cashed one without giving him any of the proceeds after Jennifer filed for divorce. At their mother's request, his sister had also negotiated the other three CDs before the divorce trial.

The court did not include the CDs in valuing and distributing the Kovariks' marital estate. Jennifer appealed to the North Dakota Supreme Court, arguing that Bradly's interest in the CDs should have been included.

MAJORITY OPINION

SANDSTROM, Justice.

* * * *

A [trial] court's decisions regarding the division of marital property are findings of fact and may be reversed on appeal only if clearly erroneous. A finding of fact is clearly erroneous if it is induced by an erroneous view of the law, if there is no evidence to support it, or if, after reviewing the entirety of the evidence, this Court is left with a definite and firm conviction a mistake has been made. A [trial] court's

findings of fact are presumed correct, and we view the evidence in the light most favorable to its findings.

Division of marital property upon divorce must be equitable. Although the division does not have to be equal, a substantial disparity must be explained. *All of the real and personal property accumulated by the parties, regardless of source, must be included in the marital estate.* [Emphasis added.]

* * * *

A * * * court may consider property to be part of the marital estate, if supported by evidence, even if a party claims it is owned by a nonparty. The principles applicable to *inter vivos* gifts in general apply as well to purported gifts of certificates of deposit. A valid gift made during the donor's lifetime must satisfy certain requirements—donative intent, delivery, actual or constructive, and acceptance by donee. A donor's intent is a question of fact. The actual or constructive delivery must be of a nature sufficient to divest the owner of all dominion [control] over the property and to invest the donee therewith.

Bradly Kovarik's parents testified that after liquidating their farm and equipment * * *, they placed four certificates of deposit in Bradly Kovarik's and his sister's names—"Wanda Morstad or Bradly Kovarik." They also testified they did not intend to give Bradly Kovarik and Morstad any present interest in the certificates. Moreover, Bradly Kovarik's father testified that the certificates, prior to having been cashed out, had been locked in a safe in their home and neither Bradly Kovarik nor his sister could just come and take the certificates.

Bradly Kovarik testified he had no knowledge of the certificates' existence until his sister told him she cashed one out and used some of the proceeds for home repairs. He also testified he did not receive

---

1. 2009 ND 82, 765 N.W.2d 511 (2009).

any of the remaining proceeds. Wanda Morstad testified she did not expect the certificates of deposit to belong to her. When requested, she assisted her parents in cashing out the certificates, which she did with respect to the remaining three certificates.

The [trial] court found Bradly Kovarik's parents did not intend to gift the certificates to him and his sister. The court further found the certificates were never delivered to either Bradly Kovarik or his sister but were retained in their parents' possession. The record does not reflect donative intent or delivery of the certificates to Bradly Kovarik, either actual or constructive. *In the absence of a donative intent and delivery, the [trial] court's finding that there was no valid gift is not clearly erroneous.* [Emphasis added.]

* * * *

We hold the [trial] court's property distribution and property valuation is not clearly erroneous, and affirm.

DISSENTING OPINION

MARING, Justice, dissenting.

I respectfully dissent from * * * the Majority opinion because the [trial] court * * * erred in concluding Bradly Kovarik's parents never gave him the certificates of deposit.

* * * *

First, the [trial] court found Bradly Kovarik's parents did not intend to give the certificates of deposit to Bradly Kovarik or his sister. This finding is not supported by the record. Bradly Kovarik admits that he and his sister were the co-owners of the certificates of deposit. Bradly Kovarik's sister also testified * * * that she was the co-owner of the certificates of deposit with her brother.

* * * *

Dennis Kovarik's testimony establishes that he knew Bradly Kovarik was a joint owner of the certificates of deposit * * *. Marlene Kovarik's testimony establishes that Bradly Kovarik was the joint owner of the certificates of deposit.

These admissions by Bradly Kovarik and his family that he owned the certificates of deposits are supported by the law. The parties do not dispute that Bradly Kovarik's name was on the certificate of deposit together with his sister's name or that neither of his parents' names were on the certificates of deposit. It is presumed that a certificate of deposit belongs to the person whose name appears on the certificate. * * * Bradly Kovarik's parents gave up their exclusive dominion and control over their assets when they placed the money in certificates of deposit in their children's names.

* * * *

The [trial] court found the certificates of deposit were never delivered to Bradly Kovarik or his sister because the parents kept possession of the certificates of deposit. This finding is not supported by the record.

* * * *

* * * Bradly Kovarik's parents divested themselves of the control of the certificates of deposit by first solely placing their children's names on the certificates of deposit and then delivering the certificates of deposit to Wanda Morstad to be cashed.

* * * *

In conclusion, I dissent because the certificates of deposit were completed gifts to Bradly Kovarik and must be included in the marital estate.

QUESTIONS FOR ANALYSIS

1. *Law.* How does the majority respond to the appellant's argument in this case? What is the majority's reasoning?

2. *Law.* How does the dissent analyze the issue before the court?

3. *Ethics.* According to Marlene Kovarik, the CDs were obtained in her children's names in an effort to avoid the parents' tax obligations, rather than to give the funds to the children. Is this ethical? Explain.

4. *Social Dimensions.* If the Kovariks had invested their funds in real estate in their children's names, instead of CDs, would the result in this case have been the same? Why or why not?

5. *Implications for the Estate Planner.* How might Marlene and Dennis Kovarik have avoided the question that Jennifer raised here? Discuss.

Unit Seven—Business Scenario

iStockPhoto.com/proxyminder

Dave graduates from State University with an engineering degree and goes into business as a self-employed computer programmer.

1. **Ownership of Personal Property.** To advertise his services on the Internet, Dave creates and produces a short digital video. Venture Films, Inc., sees the video and hires Dave to program the special effects for a short sequence in a Venture Films movie. Their contract states that all rights to the sequence

Continues

belong to Venture Films. What belongs to Dave: the digital video, the movie sequence, both, or neither? Explain.

2. **Landlord-Tenant Law.** Dave leases an office in Carl's Riverside Plaza office building for a two-year term. What is Dave's obligation for the rent if he moves out before the end of the term? If Dave dies during the term, who is entitled to possession of the office? What is Dave's obligation for the rent if Carl sells the building to Commercial Investments, Inc., before Dave's lease is up?

3. **Real Property Deeds.** At the end of the lease term, Dave buys the office building from Carl, who gives Dave a warranty deed. Commercial Investments later challenges Dave's ownership of the building and presents its own allegedly valid deed. What will it mean if a court rules that Dave owns the building in fee simple? If Commercial Investments is successful, can Dave recover anything from Carl? Explain.

4. **Insurance.** Dave's programming business expands, and he hires Mary as an employee. Mary becomes invaluable to the business, and Dave obtains a key-person insurance policy on her life. She dies six years later. If the insurance company discovers that Dave understated Mary's age when applying for the policy (which includes an incontestability clause), can the insurer legitimately refuse payment? If Mary had resigned to start her own programming firm one year before she died, could Dave have collected payment under the policy? Why or why not?

5. **Wills and Trusts.** Over time, Dave acquires other commercial property, which eventually becomes the most lucrative part of his business. Dave wants his adult children, Frank and Terry, to get the benefit of this property when he dies. Dave does not think that Frank and Terry can manage the property, however, because they have their own careers and live in other states. How can Dave provide for them to get the benefit of the property under someone else's management? In his will, Dave designates Hal, his attorney, as executor. What does an executor do?

Unit Seven—Group Project

iStockPhoto.com/petekarici

Hobie and Colleen designed and developed a smartphone app called Do It. Do It is a game in which players cooperate rather than compete to complete a task, such as draw a picture, play a tune, or score a point. Documents evidence each party's investment, ownership, and share of profits and losses in the app. In the documents, Hobie and Colleen are referred to as "joint owners" and "tenants."

1. The first group will determine whether the ownership interest of each party is a tenancy in common or a joint tenancy. Is there a presumption that applies? Discuss.

2. The second group will describe the differences between a tenancy in common and a joint tenancy. What happens to Colleen's interest if Hobie dies?

3. The third group will assume that Hobie and Colleen are not married but live together and hold the property as tenants in common. If Hobie has no children and dies without a will, does Colleen inherit his interest in the Do It app? Why or why not? How would most states' intestate succession laws distribute Hobie's property?

How to Brief Cases and Analyze Case Problems

How to Brief Cases

To fully understand the law with respect to business, you need to be able to read and understand court decisions. To make this task easier, you can use a method of case analysis that is called *briefing*. There is a fairly standard procedure that you can follow when you "brief" any court case. You must first read the case opinion carefully. When you feel you understand the case, you can prepare a brief of it.

Although the format of the brief may vary, typically it will present the essentials of the case under headings such as those listed below.

1. **Citation.** Give the full citation for the case, including the name of the case, the date it was decided, and the court that decided it.
2. **Facts.** Briefly indicate (a) the reasons for the lawsuit; (b) the identity and arguments of the plaintiff(s) and defendant(s), respectively; and (c) the lower court's decision—if appropriate.
3. **Issue.** Concisely phrase, in the form of a question, the essential issue before the court. (If more than one issue is involved, you may have two—or even more—questions here.)
4. **Decision.** Indicate here—with a "yes" or "no," if possible—the court's answer to the question (or questions) in the Issue section above.
5. **Reason.** Summarize as briefly as possible the reasons given by the court for its decision (or decisions) and the case or statutory law relied on by the court in arriving at its decision.

For a case-specific example of what should be included under each of the above headings when briefing a case, see the review of the sample court case presented in the appendix to Chapter 1 of this text.

Analyzing Case Problems

In addition to learning how to brief cases, students of business law and the legal environment also find it helpful to know how to analyze case problems. Part of the study of business law and the legal environment usually involves analyzing case problems, such as those included in this text at the end of each chapter.

For each case problem in this book, we provide the relevant background and facts of the lawsuit and the issue before the court.

When you are assigned one of these problems, your job will be to determine how the court should decide the issue, and why. In other words, you will need to engage in legal analysis and reasoning. Here, we offer some suggestions on how to make this task less daunting. We begin by presenting a sample case problem:

> While Janet Lawson, a famous pianist, was shopping in Quality Market, she slipped and fell on a wet floor in one of the aisles. The floor had recently been mopped by one of the store's employees, but there were no signs warning customers that the floor in that area was wet. As a result of the fall, Lawson injured her right arm and was unable to perform piano concerts for the next six months. Had she been able to perform the scheduled concerts, she would have earned approximately $60,000 over that period of time. Lawson sued Quality Market for this amount, plus another $10,000 in medical expenses. She claimed that the store's failure to warn customers of the wet floor constituted negligence and therefore the market was liable for her injuries. Will the court agree with Lawson? Discuss.

Understand the Facts

This may sound obvious, but before you can analyze or apply the relevant law to a specific set of facts, you must clearly understand those facts. In other words, you should read through the case problem carefully—more than once, if necessary—to make sure you understand the identity of the plaintiff(s) and defendant(s) in the case and the progression of events that led to the lawsuit.

In the sample case problem just given, the identity of the parties is fairly obvious. Janet Lawson is the one bringing the suit; therefore, she is the plaintiff. Lawson is bringing the suit against Quality Market, so it is the defendant. Some of the case problems you may work on have multiple plaintiffs or defendants. Often, it is helpful to use abbreviations for the parties. To indicate a reference to a plaintiff, for example, the *pi* symbol—π—is often used, and a defendant is denoted by a *delta*—Δ—a triangle.

The events leading to the lawsuit are also fairly straightforward. Lawson slipped and fell on a wet floor, and she contends that Quality Market should be liable for her injuries because it was negligent in not posting a sign warning customers of the wet floor.

When you are working on case problems, realize that the facts should be accepted as they are given. For instance, in our sample problem, it should be accepted that the floor was wet and that there was no sign. In other words, avoid making conjectures, such as "Maybe the floor wasn't too wet," or "Maybe an employee was getting a sign to put up," or "Maybe someone stole the sign." Questioning the facts as they are presented only adds confusion to your analysis.

Legal Analysis and Reasoning

Once you understand the facts given in the case problem, you can begin to analyze the case. The **IRAC method** is a helpful tool to use in the legal analysis and reasoning process. IRAC is an acronym for Issue, Rule, Application, Conclusion. Applying this method to our sample problem would involve the following steps:

1. First, you need to decide what legal **issue** is involved in the case. In our sample case, the basic issue is whether Quality Market's failure to warn customers of the wet floor constituted negligence. Negligence is a *tort*—a civil wrong. In a tort lawsuit, the plaintiff seeks to be compensated for another's wrongful act. A defendant will be deemed negligent if he or she breached a duty of care owed to the plaintiff and the breach of that duty caused the plaintiff to suffer harm.

2. Once you have identified the issue, the next step is to determine what **rule of law** applies to the issue. To make this determination, you will want to carefully review the text discussion relating to the issue involved in the problem. Our sample case problem involves the tort of negligence. The applicable rule of law is the tort law principle that business owners owe a duty to exercise reasonable care to protect their customers (*business invitees*). Reasonable care, in this context, includes either removing—or warning customers of—*foreseeable* risks about which the owner *knew* or *should have known*. Business owners need not warn customers of "open and obvious" risks, however. If a business owner breaches this duty of care (fails to exercise the appropriate degree of care toward customers), and the breach of duty causes a customer to be injured, the business owner will be liable to the customer for the customer's injuries.

3. The next—and usually the most difficult—step in analyzing case problems is the **application** of the relevant rule of law to the specific facts of the case you are studying. In our sample problem, applying the tort law principle just discussed presents few difficulties. An employee of the store had mopped the floor in the aisle where Lawson slipped and fell, but no sign was present indicating that the floor was wet. That a customer might fall on a wet floor is clearly a foreseeable risk. Therefore, the failure to warn customers about the wet floor was a breach of the duty of care owed by the business owner to the store's customers.

4. Once you have completed Step 3 in the IRAC method, you should be ready to draw your **conclusion.** In our sample problem, Quality Market is liable to Lawson for her injuries because the market's breach of its duty of care caused Lawson's injuries.

The fact patterns in the case problems presented in this text are not always as simple as those presented in our sample problem. Often, a case has more than one plaintiff or defendant. A case may also involve more than one issue and have more than one applicable rule of law. Furthermore, in some case problems the facts may indicate that the general rule of law should not apply. Suppose that a store employee told Lawson about the wet floor and advised her not to walk in that aisle, but Lawson decided to walk there anyway. This fact could alter the outcome of the case because the store could then raise the defense of *assumption of risk*. Nonetheless, a careful review of the chapter should always provide you with the knowledge you need to analyze the problem thoroughly and arrive at accurate conclusions.

The Constitution of the United States

Preamble

We the People of the United States, in Order to form a more perfect Union, establish Justice, insure domestic Tranquility, provide for the common defence, promote the general Welfare, and secure the Blessings of Liberty to ourselves and our Posterity, do ordain and establish this Constitution for the United States of America.

Article I

Section 1. All legislative Powers herein granted shall be vested in a Congress of the United States, which shall consist of a Senate and House of Representatives.

Section 2. The House of Representatives shall be composed of Members chosen every second Year by the People of the several States, and the Electors in each State shall have the Qualifications requisite for Electors of the most numerous Branch of the State Legislature.

No Person shall be a Representative who shall not have attained to the Age of twenty five Years, and been seven Years a Citizen of the United States, and who shall not, when elected, be an Inhabitant of that State in which he shall be chosen.

Representatives and direct Taxes shall be apportioned among the several States which may be included within this Union, according to their respective Numbers, which shall be determined by adding to the whole Number of free Persons, including those bound to Service for a Term of Years, and excluding Indians not taxed, three fifths of all other Persons. The actual Enumeration shall be made within three Years after the first Meeting of the Congress of the United States, and within every subsequent Term of ten Years, in such Manner as they shall by Law direct. The Number of Representatives shall not exceed one for every thirty Thousand, but each State shall have at Least one Representative; and until such enumeration shall be made, the State of New Hampshire shall be entitled to chuse three, Massachusetts eight, Rhode Island and Providence Plantations one, Connecticut five, New York six, New Jersey four, Pennsylvania eight, Delaware one, Maryland six, Virginia ten, North Carolina five, South Carolina five, and Georgia three.

When vacancies happen in the Representation from any State, the Executive Authority thereof shall issue Writs of Election to fill such Vacancies.

The House of Representatives shall chuse their Speaker and other Officers; and shall have the sole Power of Impeachment.

Section 3. The Senate of the United States shall be composed of two Senators from each State, chosen by the Legislature thereof, for six Years; and each Senator shall have one Vote.

Immediately after they shall be assembled in Consequence of the first Election, they shall be divided as equally as may be into three Classes. The Seats of the Senators of the first Class shall be vacated at the Expiration of the second Year, of the second Class at the Expiration of the fourth Year, and of the third Class at the Expiration of the sixth Year, so that one third may be chosen every second Year; and if Vacancies happen by Resignation, or otherwise, during the Recess of the Legislature of any State, the Executive thereof may make temporary Appointments until the next Meeting of the Legislature, which shall then fill such Vacancies.

No Person shall be a Senator who shall not have attained to the Age of thirty Years, and been nine Years a Citizen of the United States, and who shall not, when elected, be an Inhabitant of that State for which he shall be chosen.

The Vice President of the United States shall be President of the Senate, but shall have no Vote, unless they be equally divided.

The Senate shall chuse their other Officers, and also a President pro tempore, in the Absence of the Vice President, or when he shall exercise the Office of President of the United States.

The Senate shall have the sole Power to try all Impeachments. When sitting for that Purpose, they shall be on Oath or Affirmation. When the President of the United States is tried, the Chief Justice shall preside: And no Person shall be convicted without the Concurrence of two thirds of the Members present.

Judgment in Cases of Impeachment shall not extend further than to removal from Office, and disqualification to hold and enjoy any Office of honor, Trust, or Profit under the United States: but the Party convicted shall nevertheless be liable and subject to Indictment, Trial, Judgment, and Punishment, according to Law.

Section 4. The Times, Places and Manner of holding Elections for Senators and Representatives, shall be prescribed in each State by the Legislature thereof; but the Congress may at any time by Law make or alter such Regulations, except as to the Places of chusing Senators.

The Congress shall assemble at least once in every Year, and such Meeting shall be on the first Monday in December, unless they shall by Law appoint a different Day.

Section 5. Each House shall be the Judge of the Elections, Returns, and Qualifications of its own Members, and a Majority of each shall constitute a Quorum to do Business; but a smaller Number may adjourn from day to day, and may be authorized to compel the Attendance of absent Members, in such Manner, and under such Penalties as each House may provide.

Each House may determine the Rules of its Proceedings, punish its Members for disorderly Behavior, and, with the Concurrence of two thirds, expel a Member.

Each House shall keep a Journal of its Proceedings, and from time to time publish the same, excepting such Parts as may in their Judgment require Secrecy; and the Yeas and Nays of the Members of either House on any question shall, at the Desire of one fifth of those Present, be entered on the Journal.

Neither House, during the Session of Congress, shall, without the Consent of the other, adjourn for more than three days, nor to any other Place than that in which the two Houses shall be sitting.

Section 6. The Senators and Representatives shall receive a Compensation for their Services, to be ascertained by Law, and paid out of the Treasury of the United States. They shall in all Cases, except Treason, Felony and Breach of the Peace, be privileged from Arrest during their Attendance at the Session of their respective Houses, and in going to and returning from the same; and for any Speech or Debate in either House, they shall not be questioned in any other Place.

No Senator or Representative shall, during the Time for which he was elected, be appointed to any civil Office under the Authority of the United States, which shall have been created, or the Emoluments whereof shall have been increased during such time; and no Person holding any Office under the United States, shall be a Member of either House during his Continuance in Office.

Section 7. All Bills for raising Revenue shall originate in the House of Representatives; but the Senate may propose or concur with Amendments as on other Bills.

Every Bill which shall have passed the House of Representatives and the Senate, shall, before it become a Law, be presented to the President of the United States; If he approve he shall sign it, but if not he shall return it, with his Objections to the House in which it shall have originated, who shall enter the Objections at large on their Journal, and proceed to reconsider it. If after such Reconsideration two thirds of that House shall agree to pass the Bill, it shall be sent together with the Objections, to the other House, by which it shall likewise be reconsidered, and if approved by two thirds of that House, it shall become a Law. But in all such Cases the Votes of both Houses shall be determined by Yeas and Nays, and the Names of the Persons voting for and against the Bill shall be entered on the Journal of each House respectively. If any Bill shall not be returned by the President within ten Days (Sundays excepted) after it shall have been presented to him, the Same shall be a Law, in like Manner as if he had signed it, unless the Congress by their Adjournment prevent its Return in which Case it shall not be a Law.

Every Order, Resolution, or Vote, to which the Concurrence of the Senate and House of Representatives may be necessary (except on a question of Adjournment) shall be presented to the President of the United States; and before the Same shall take Effect, shall be approved by him, or being disapproved by him, shall be repassed by two thirds of the Senate and House of Representatives, according to the Rules and Limitations prescribed in the Case of a Bill.

Section 8. The Congress shall have Power To lay and collect Taxes, Duties, Imposts and Excises, to pay the Debts and provide for the common Defence and general Welfare of the United States; but all Duties, Imposts and Excises shall be uniform throughout the United States;

To borrow Money on the credit of the United States;

To regulate Commerce with foreign Nations, and among the several States, and with the Indian Tribes;

To establish an uniform Rule of Naturalization, and uniform Laws on the subject of Bankruptcies throughout the United States;

To coin Money, regulate the Value thereof, and of foreign Coin, and fix the Standard of Weights and Measures;

To provide for the Punishment of counterfeiting the Securities and current Coin of the United States;

To establish Post Offices and post Roads;

To promote the Progress of Science and useful Arts, by securing for limited Times to Authors and Inventors the exclusive Right to their respective Writings and Discoveries;

To constitute Tribunals inferior to the supreme Court;

To define and punish Piracies and Felonies committed on the high Seas, and Offenses against the Law of Nations;

To declare War, grant Letters of Marque and Reprisal, and make Rules concerning Captures on Land and Water;

To raise and support Armies, but no Appropriation of Money to that Use shall be for a longer Term than two Years;

To provide and maintain a Navy;

To make Rules for the Government and Regulation of the land and naval Forces;

To provide for calling forth the Militia to execute the Laws of the Union, suppress Insurrections and repel Invasions;

To provide for organizing, arming, and disciplining, the Militia, and for governing such Part of them as may be employed in the Service of the United States, reserving to the States respectively, the Appointment of the Officers, and the Authority of training the Militia according to the discipline prescribed by Congress;

To exercise exclusive Legislation in all Cases whatsoever, over such District (not exceeding ten Miles square) as may, by Cession of particular States, and the Acceptance of Congress, become the Seat of the Government of the United States, and to exercise like Authority over all Places purchased by the Consent of the Legislature of the State in which the Same shall be, for the Erection of Forts, Magazines, Arsenals, dock-Yards, and other needful Buildings;—And

To make all Laws which shall be necessary and proper for carrying into Execution the foregoing Powers, and all other Powers vested by this Constitution in the Government of the United States, or in any Department or Officer thereof.

Section 9. The Migration or Importation of such Persons as any of the States now existing shall think proper to admit, shall not be prohibited by the Congress prior to the Year one thousand eight hundred and eight, but a Tax or duty may be imposed on such Importation, not exceeding ten dollars for each Person.

The privilege of the Writ of Habeas Corpus shall not be suspended, unless when in Cases of Rebellion or Invasion the public Safety may require it.

No Bill of Attainder or ex post facto Law shall be passed.

No Capitation, or other direct, Tax shall be laid, unless in Proportion to the Census or Enumeration herein before directed to be taken.

No Tax or Duty shall be laid on Articles exported from any State.

No Preference shall be given by any Regulation of Commerce or Revenue to the Ports of one State over those of another: nor shall Vessels bound to, or from, one State be obliged to enter, clear, or pay Duties in another.

No Money shall be drawn from the Treasury, but in Consequence of Appropriations made by Law; and a regular Statement and Account of the Receipts and Expenditures of all public Money shall be published from time to time.

No Title of Nobility shall be granted by the United States: And no Person holding any Office of Profit or Trust under them, shall, without the Consent of the Congress, accept of any present, Emolument, Office, or Title, of any kind whatever, from any King, Prince, or foreign State.

Section 10. No State shall enter into any Treaty, Alliance, or Confederation; grant Letters of Marque and Reprisal; coin Money; emit Bills of Credit; make any Thing but gold and silver Coin a Tender in Payment of Debts; pass any Bill of Attainder, ex post facto Law, or Law impairing the Obligation of Contracts, or grant any Title of Nobility.

No State shall, without the Consent of the Congress, lay any Imposts or Duties on Imports or Exports, except what may be absolutely necessary for executing its inspection Laws: and the net Produce of all Duties and Imposts, laid by any State on Imports or Exports, shall be for the Use of the Treasury of the United States; and all such Laws shall be subject to the Revision and Controul of the Congress.

No State shall, without the Consent of Congress, lay any Duty of Tonnage, keep Troops, or Ships of War in time of Peace, enter into any Agreement or Compact with another State, or with a foreign Power, or engage in War, unless actually invaded, or in such imminent Danger as will not admit of delay.

Article II

Section 1. The executive Power shall be vested in a President of the United States of America. He shall hold his Office during the Term of four Years, and, together with the Vice President, chosen for the same Term, be elected, as follows:

Each State shall appoint, in such Manner as the Legislature thereof may direct, a Number of Electors, equal to the whole Number of Senators and Representatives to which the State may be entitled in the Congress; but no Senator or Representative, or Person holding an Office of Trust or Profit under the United States, shall be appointed an Elector.

The Electors shall meet in their respective States, and vote by Ballot for two Persons, of whom one at least shall not be an Inhabitant of the same State with themselves. And they shall make a List of all the Persons voted for, and of the Number of Votes for each; which List they shall sign and certify, and transmit sealed to the Seat of the Government of the United States, directed to the President of the Senate. The President of the Senate shall, in the Presence of the Senate and House of Representatives, open all the Certificates, and the Votes shall then be counted. The Person having the greatest Number of Votes shall be the President, if such Number be a Majority of the whole Number of Electors appointed; and if there be more than one who have such Majority, and have an equal Number of Votes, then the House of Representatives shall immediately chuse by Ballot one of them for President; and if no Person have a Majority, then from the five highest on the List the said House shall in like Manner chuse the President. But in chusing the President, the Votes shall be taken by States, the Representation from each State having one Vote; A quorum for this Purpose shall consist of a Member or Members from two thirds of the States, and a Majority of all the States shall be necessary to a Choice. In every Case, after the Choice of the President, the Person having the greater Number of Votes of the Electors shall be the Vice President. But if there should remain two or more who have equal Votes, the Senate shall chuse from them by Ballot the Vice President.

The Congress may determine the Time of chusing the Electors, and the Day on which they shall give their Votes; which Day shall be the same throughout the United States.

No person except a natural born Citizen, or a Citizen of the United States, at the time of the Adoption of this Constitution, shall be eligible to the Office of President; neither shall any Person be eligible to that Office who shall not have attained to the Age of thirty five Years, and been fourteen Years a Resident within the United States.

In Case of the Removal of the President from Office, or of his Death, Resignation or Inability to discharge the Powers and Duties of the said Office, the same shall devolve on the Vice President, and the Congress may by Law provide for the Case of Removal, Death, Resignation or Inability, both of the President and Vice President, declaring what Officer shall then act as President, and such Officer shall act accordingly, until the Disability be removed, or a President shall be elected.

The President shall, at stated Times, receive for his Services, a Compensation, which shall neither be increased nor diminished during the Period for which he shall have been elected, and he shall not receive within that Period any other Emolument from the United States, or any of them.

Before he enter on the Execution of his Office, he shall take the following Oath or Affirmation: "I do solemnly swear (or affirm) that I will faithfully execute the Office of President of the United States, and will to the best of my Ability, preserve, protect and defend the Constitution of the United States."

Section 2. The President shall be Commander in Chief of the Army and Navy of the United States, and of the Militia of the several States, when called into the actual Service of the United States; he may require the Opinion, in writing, of the principal Officer in each of the executive Departments, upon any Subject relating to the Duties of their respective Offices, and he shall have Power to grant Reprieves and Pardons for Offenses against the United States, except in Cases of Impeachment.

He shall have Power, by and with the Advice and Consent of the Senate to make Treaties, provided two thirds of the Senators present concur; and he shall nominate, and by and with the Advice and Consent of the Senate, shall appoint Ambassadors, other public Ministers and Consuls, Judges of the supreme Court, and all other Officers of the United States, whose Appointments are not herein otherwise provided for, and which shall be established by Law; but the Congress may by Law vest the Appointment of such inferior Officers, as they think proper, in the President alone, in the Courts of Law, or in the Heads of Departments.

The President shall have Power to fill up all Vacancies that may happen during the Recess of the Senate, by granting Commissions which shall expire at the End of their next Session.

Section 3. He shall from time to time give to the Congress Information of the State of the Union, and recommend to their Consideration such Measures as he shall judge necessary and expedient; he may, on extraordinary Occasions, convene both Houses, or either of them, and in Case of Disagreement between them, with Respect to the Time of Adjournment, he may adjourn them to such Time as he shall think proper; he shall receive Ambassadors and other public Ministers; he shall take Care that the Laws be faithfully executed, and shall Commission all the Officers of the United States.

Section 4. The President, Vice President and all civil Officers of the United States, shall be removed from Office on Impeachment for, and Conviction of, Treason, Bribery, or other high Crimes and Misdemeanors.

Article III

Section 1. The judicial Power of the United States, shall be vested in one supreme Court, and in such inferior Courts as the Congress may from time to time ordain and establish. The Judges, both of the supreme and inferior Courts, shall hold their Offices during good Behaviour, and shall, at stated Times, receive for their Services a Compensation, which shall not be diminished during their Continuance in Office.

Section 2. The judicial Power shall extend to all Cases, in Law and Equity, arising under this Constitution, the Laws of the United States, and Treaties made, or which shall be made, under their Authority;—to all Cases affecting Ambassadors, other public Ministers and Consuls;—to all Cases of admiralty and maritime Jurisdiction;—to Controversies to which the United States shall be a Party;—to Controversies between two or more States;—between a State and Citizens of another State;—between Citizens of different States;—between Citizens of the same State claiming Lands under Grants of different States, and between a State, or the Citizens thereof, and foreign States, Citizens or Subjects.

In all Cases affecting Ambassadors, other public Ministers and Consuls, and those in which a State shall be a Party, the supreme Court shall have original Jurisdiction. In all the other Cases before mentioned, the supreme Court shall have appellate Jurisdiction, both as to Law and Fact, with such Exceptions, and under such Regulations as the Congress shall make.

The Trial of all Crimes, except in Cases of Impeachment, shall be by Jury; and such Trial shall be held in the State where the said Crimes shall have been committed; but when not committed within any State, the Trial shall be at such Place or Places as the Congress may by Law have directed.

Section 3. Treason against the United States, shall consist only in levying War against them, or, in adhering to their Enemies, giving them Aid and Comfort. No Person shall be convicted of Treason unless on the Testimony of two Witnesses to the same overt Act, or on Confession in open Court.

The Congress shall have Power to declare the Punishment of Treason, but no Attainder of Treason shall work Corruption of Blood, or Forfeiture except during the Life of the Person attainted.

Article IV

Section 1. Full Faith and Credit shall be given in each State to the public Acts, Records, and judicial Proceedings of every other State. And the Congress may by general Laws prescribe the Manner in which such Acts, Records and Proceedings shall be proved, and the Effect thereof.

Section 2. The Citizens of each State shall be entitled to all Privileges and Immunities of Citizens in the several States.

A Person charged in any State with Treason, Felony, or other Crime, who shall flee from Justice, and be found in another State, shall on Demand of the executive Authority of the State from which he fled, be delivered up, to be removed to the State having Jurisdiction of the Crime.

No Person held to Service or Labour in one State, under the Laws thereof, escaping into another, shall, in Consequence of any Law or Regulation therein, be discharged from such Service or Labour, but shall be delivered up on Claim of the Party to whom such Service or Labour may be due.

Section 3. New States may be admitted by the Congress into this Union; but no new State shall be formed or erected within the Jurisdiction of any other State; nor any State be formed by the Junction of two or more States, or Parts of States, without the Consent of the Legislatures of the States concerned as well as of the Congress.

The Congress shall have Power to dispose of and make all needful Rules and Regulations respecting the Territory or other Property belonging to the United States; and nothing in this Constitution shall be so construed as to Prejudice any Claims of the United States, or of any particular State.

Section 4. The United States shall guarantee to every State in this Union a Republican Form of Government, and shall protect each of them against Invasion; and on Application of the Legislature, or of the Executive (when the Legislature cannot be convened) against domestic Violence.

Article V

The Congress, whenever two thirds of both Houses shall deem it necessary, shall propose Amendments to this Constitution, or, on the Application of the Legislatures of two thirds of the several States, shall call a Convention for proposing Amendments, which, in either Case, shall be valid to all Intents and Purposes, as part of this Constitution, when ratified by the Legislatures of three fourths of the several States, or by Conventions in three fourths thereof, as the one or the other Mode of Ratification may be proposed by the Congress; Provided that no Amendment which may be made prior to the Year One thousand eight hundred and eight shall in any Manner affect the first and fourth Clauses in the Ninth Section of the first Article; and that no State, without its Consent, shall be deprived of its equal Suffrage in the Senate.

Article VI

All Debts contracted and Engagements entered into, before the Adoption of this Constitution shall be as valid against the United States under this Constitution, as under the Confederation.

This Constitution, and the Laws of the United States which shall be made in Pursuance thereof; and all Treaties made, or which shall be made, under the Authority of the United States, shall be the supreme Law of the Land; and the Judges in every State shall be bound thereby, any Thing in the Constitution or Laws of any State to the Contrary notwithstanding.

The Senators and Representatives before mentioned, and the Members of the several State Legislatures, and all executive and judicial Officers, both of the United States and of the several States, shall be bound by Oath or Affirmation, to support this Constitution; but no religious Test shall ever be required as a Qualification to any Office or public Trust under the United States.

Article VII

The Ratification of the Conventions of nine States shall be sufficient for the Establishment of this Constitution between the States so ratifying the Same.

Amendment I [1791]

Congress shall make no law respecting an establishment of religion, or prohibiting the free exercise thereof; or abridging the freedom of speech, or of the press; or the right of the people peaceably to assembly, and to petition the Government for a redress of grievances.

Amendment II [1791]

A well regulated Militia, being necessary to the security of a free State, the right of the people to keep and bear Arms, shall not be infringed.

Amendment III [1791]

No Soldier shall, in time of peace be quartered in any house, without the consent of the Owner, nor in time of war, but in a manner to be prescribed by law.

Amendment IV [1791]

The right of the people to be secure in their persons, houses, papers, and effects, against unreasonable searches and seizures, shall not be violated, and no Warrants shall issue, but upon probable cause, supported by Oath or affirmation, and particularly describing the place to be searched, and the persons or things to be seized.

Amendment V [1791]

No person shall be held to answer for a capital, or otherwise infamous crime, unless on a presentment or indictment of a Grand Jury, except in cases arising in the land or naval forces, or in the Militia, when in actual service in time of War or public danger; nor shall any person be subject for the same offence to be twice put in jeopardy of life or limb; nor shall be compelled in any criminal case to be a witness against himself, nor be deprived of life, liberty, or property, without due process of law; nor shall private property be taken for public use, without just compensation.

Amendment VI [1791]

In all criminal prosecutions, the accused shall enjoy the right to a speedy and public trial, by an impartial jury of the State and district wherein the crime shall have been committed, which district shall have been previously ascertained by law, and to be informed of the nature and cause of the accusation; to be confronted with the witnesses against him; to have compulsory process for obtaining witnesses in his favor, and to have the Assistance of Counsel for his defence.

Amendment VII [1791]

In Suits at common law, where the value in controversy shall exceed twenty dollars, the right of trial by jury shall be preserved, and no fact tried by jury, shall be otherwise re-examined in any Court of the United States, than according to the rules of the common law.

Amendment VIII [1791]

Excessive bail shall not be required, nor excessive fines imposed, nor cruel and unusual punishments inflicted.

Amendment IX [1791]

The enumeration in the Constitution, of certain rights, shall not be construed to deny or disparage others retained by the people.

Amendment X [1791]

The powers not delegated to the United States by the Constitution, nor prohibited by it to the States, are reserved to the States respectively, or to the people.

Amendment XI [1795]

The Judicial power of the United States shall not be construed to extend to any suit in law or equity, commenced or prosecuted against one of the United States by Citizens of another State, or by Citizens or Subjects of any Foreign State.

Amendment XII [1804]

The Electors shall meet in their respective states, and vote by ballot for President and Vice-President, one of whom, at least, shall not be an inhabitant of the same state with themselves; they shall name in their ballots the person voted for as President, and in distinct ballots the person voted for as Vice-President, and they shall make distinct lists of all persons voted for as President, and of all persons voted for as Vice-President, and of the number of votes for each, which lists they shall sign and certify, and transmit sealed to the seat of the government of the United States, directed to the President of the Senate;—The President of the Senate shall, in the presence of the Senate and House of Representatives, open all the certificates and the votes shall then be counted;—The person having the greatest number of votes for President, shall be the President, if such number be a majority of the whole number of Electors appointed; and if no person have such majority, then from the persons having the highest numbers not exceeding three on the list of those voted for as President, the House of Representatives shall choose immediately, by ballot, the President. But in choosing the President, the votes shall be taken by states, the representation from each state having one vote; a quorum for this purpose shall consist of a member or members from two-thirds of the states, and a majority of all states shall be necessary to a choice. And if the House of Representatives shall not choose a President whenever the right of choice shall devolve upon them, before the fourth day of March next following, then the Vice-President shall act as President, as in the case of the death or other constitutional disability of the President.—The person having the greatest number of votes as Vice-President, shall be the Vice-President, if such number be a majority of the whole number of Electors appointed, and if no person have a majority, then from the two highest numbers on the list, the Senate shall choose the Vice-President; a quorum for the purpose shall consist of two-thirds of the whole number of Senators, and a majority of the whole number shall be necessary to a choice. But no person constitutionally ineligible to the office of President shall be eligible to that of Vice-President of the United States.

Amendment XIII [1865]

Section 1. Neither slavery nor involuntary servitude, except as a punishment for crime whereof the party shall have been duly convicted, shall exist within the United States, or any place subject to their jurisdiction.

Section 2. Congress shall have power to enforce this article by appropriate legislation.

Amendment XIV [1868]

Section 1. All persons born or naturalized in the United States, and subject to the jurisdiction thereof, are citizens of the United States and of the State wherein they reside. No State shall make or enforce any law which shall abridge the privileges or immunities of citizens of the United States; nor shall any State deprive any person of life, liberty, or property, without due process of law; nor deny to any person within its jurisdiction the equal protection of the laws.

Section 2. Representatives shall be apportioned among the several States according to their respective numbers, counting the whole number of persons in each State, excluding Indians not taxed. But when the right to vote at any election for the choice of electors for President and Vice President of the United States, Representatives in Congress, the Executive and Judicial officers of a State, or the members of the Legislature thereof, is denied to any of the male inhabitants of such State, being twenty-one years of age, and citizens of the United States, or in any way abridged, except for participation in rebellion, or other crime, the basis of representation therein shall be reduced in the proportion which the number of such male citizens shall bear to the whole number of male citizens twenty-one years of age in such State.

Section 3. No person shall be a Senator or Representative in Congress, or elector of President and Vice President, or hold any office, civil or military, under the United States, or under any State, who having previously taken an oath, as a member of Congress, or as an officer of the United States, or as a member of any State legislature, or as an executive or judicial officer of any State, to support the Constitution of the United States, shall have engaged in insurrection or rebellion against the same, or given aid or comfort to the enemies thereof. But Congress may by a vote of two-thirds of each House, remove such disability.

Section 4. The validity of the public debt of the United States, authorized by law, including debts incurred for payment of pensions and bounties for services in suppressing insurrection or rebellion, shall not be questioned. But neither the United States nor any State shall assume or pay any debt or obligation incurred in aid of insurrection or rebellion against the United States, or any claim for the loss or emancipation of any slave; but all such debts, obligations and claims shall be held illegal and void.

Section 5. The Congress shall have power to enforce, by appropriate legislation, the provisions of this article.

Amendment XV [1870]

Section 1. The right of citizens of the United States to vote shall not be denied or abridged by the United States or by any State on account of race, color, or previous condition of servitude.

Section 2. The Congress shall have power to enforce this article by appropriate legislation.

Amendment XVI [1913]

The Congress shall have power to lay and collect taxes on incomes, from whatever source derived, without apportionment among the several States, and without regard to any census or enumeration.

Amendment XVII [1913]

Section 1. The Senate of the United States shall be composed of two Senators from each State, elected by the people thereof, for six years; and each Senator shall have one vote. The electors in each State shall have the qualifications requisite for electors of the most numerous branch of the State legislatures.

Section 2. When vacancies happen in the representation of any State in the Senate, the executive authority of such State shall issue writs of election to fill such vacancies: *Provided,* That the legislature of any State may empower the executive thereof to make temporary appointments until the people fill the vacancies by election as the legislature may direct.

Section 3. This amendment shall not be so construed as to affect the election or term of any Senator chosen before it becomes valid as part of the Constitution.

Amendment XVIII [1919]

Section 1. After one year from the ratification of this article the manufacture, sale, or transportation of intoxicating liquors within, the importation thereof into, or the exportation thereof from the United States and all territory subject to the jurisdiction thereof for beverage purposes is hereby prohibited.

Section 2. The Congress and the several States shall have concurrent power to enforce this article by appropriate legislation.

Section 3. This article shall be inoperative unless it shall have been ratified as an amendment to the Constitution by the legislatures of the several States, as provided in the Constitution, within seven years from the date of the submission hereof to the States by the Congress.

Amendment XIX [1920]

Section 1. The right of citizens of the United States to vote shall not be denied or abridged by the United States or by any State on account of sex.

Section 2. Congress shall have power to enforce this article by appropriate legislation.

Amendment XX [1933]

Section 1. The terms of the President and Vice President shall end at noon on the 20th day of January, and the terms of Senators and Representatives at noon on the 3d day of January, of the years in which such terms would have ended if this article had not been ratified; and the terms of their successors shall then begin.

Section 2. The Congress shall assemble at least once in every year, and such meeting shall begin at noon on the 3d day of January, unless they shall by law appoint a different day.

Section 3. If, at the time fixed for the beginning of the term of the President, the President elect shall have died, the Vice President elect shall become President. If the President shall not have been chosen before the time fixed for the beginning of his term, or if the President elect shall have failed to qualify, then the Vice President elect shall act as President until a President shall have qualified; and the Congress may by law provide for the case wherein neither a President elect nor a Vice President elect shall have qualified, declaring who shall then act as President, or the manner in which one who is to act shall be selected, and such person shall act accordingly until a President or Vice President shall have qualified.

Section 4. The Congress may by law provide for the case of the death of any of the persons from whom the House of Representatives may choose a President whenever the right of choice shall have devolved upon them, and for the case of the death of any of the persons from whom the Senate may choose a Vice President whenever the right of choice shall have devolved upon them.

Section 5. Sections 1 and 2 shall take effect on the 15th day of October following the ratification of this article.

Section 6. This article shall be inoperative unless it shall have been ratified as an amendment to the Constitution by the legislatures of three-fourths of the several States within seven years from the date of its submission.

Amendment XXI [1933]

Section 1. The eighteenth article of amendment to the Constitution of the United States is hereby repealed.

Section 2. The transportation or importation into any State, Territory, or possession of the United States for delivery or use therein of intoxicating liquors, in violation of the laws thereof, is hereby prohibited.

Section 3. This article shall be inoperative unless it shall have been ratified as an amendment to the Constitution by conventions in the several States, as provided in the Constitution, within seven years from the date of the submission hereof to the States by the Congress.

Amendment XXII [1951]

Section 1. No person shall be elected to the office of the President more than twice, and no person who has held the office of President, or acted as President, for more than two years of a term to which some other person was elected President shall be elected to the office of President more than once. But this Article shall not apply to any person holding the office of President when this Article was proposed by the Congress, and shall not prevent any person who may be holding the office of President, or acting as President, during the term within which this Article becomes operative from holding the office of President or acting as President during the remainder of such term.

Section 2. This article shall be inoperative unless it shall have been ratified as an amendment to the Constitution by the legislatures of three-fourths of the several States within seven years from the date of its submission to the States by the Congress.

Amendment XXIII [1961]

Section 1. The District constituting the seat of Government of the United States shall appoint in such manner as the Congress may direct:

A number of electors of President and Vice President equal to the whole number of Senators and Representatives in Congress to which the District would be entitled if it were a State, but in no event more than the least populous state; they shall be in addition to those appointed by the states, but they shall be considered, for the purposes of the election of President and Vice President, to be electors appointed by a state; and they shall meet in the District and perform such duties as provided by the twelfth article of amendment.

Section 2. The Congress shall have power to enforce this article by appropriate legislation.

Amendment XXIV [1964]

Section 1. The right of citizens of the United States to vote in any primary or other election for President or Vice President, for electors for President or Vice President, or for Senator or Representative in Congress, shall not be denied or abridged by the United States, or any State by reason of failure to pay any poll tax or other tax.

Section 2. The Congress shall have power to enforce this article by appropriate legislation.

Amendment XXV [1967]

Section 1. In case of the removal of the President from office or of his death or resignation, the Vice President shall become President.

Section 2. Whenever there is a vacancy in the office of the Vice President, the President shall nominate a Vice President who shall take office upon confirmation by a majority vote of both Houses of Congress.

Section 3. Whenever the President transmits to the President pro tempore of the Senate and the Speaker of the House of Representatives his written declaration that he is unable to discharge the powers and duties of his office, and until he transmits to them a written declaration to the contrary, such powers and duties shall be discharged by the Vice President as Acting President.

Section 4. Whenever the Vice President and a majority of either the principal officers of the executive departments or of such other body as Congress may by law provide, transmit to the President pro tempore of the Senate and the Speaker of the House of Representatives their written declaration that the President is unable to discharge the powers and duties of his office, the Vice President shall immediately assume the powers and duties of the office as Acting President.

Thereafter, when the President transmits to the President pro tempore of the Senate and the Speaker of the House of Representatives his written declaration that no inability exists, he shall resume the powers and duties of his office unless the Vice President and a majority of either the principal officers of the executive department or of such other body as Congress may by law provide, transmit within four days to the President pro tempore of the Senate and the Speaker of the House of Representatives their written declaration

that the President is unable to discharge the powers and duties of his office. Thereupon Congress shall decide the issue, assembling within forty-eight hours for that purpose if not in session. If the Congress, within twenty-one days after receipt of the latter written declaration, or, if Congress is not in session, within twenty-one days after Congress is required to assemble, determines by two-thirds vote of both Houses that the President is unable to discharge the powers and duties of his office, the Vice President shall continue to discharge the same as Acting President; otherwise, the President shall resume the powers and duties of his office.

Amendment XXVI [1971]

Section 1. The right of citizens of the United States, who are eighteen years of age or older, to vote shall not be denied or abridged by the United States or by any State on account of age.

Section 2. The Congress shall have power to enforce this article by appropriate legislation.

Amendment XXVII [1992]

No law, varying the compensation for the services of the Senators and Representatives, shall take effect, until an election of Representatives shall have intervened.

The Uniform Commercial Code (Excerpts)

(Adopted in fifty-two jurisdictions; all fifty States, although Louisiana has adopted only Articles 1, 3, 4, 7, 8, and 9; the District of Columbia; and the Virgin Islands.)

The Uniform Commercial Code consists of the following articles:

Articles:

1. **General Provisions**
2. **Sales**
2A. **Leases**
3. **Negotiable Instruments**
4. **Bank Deposits and Collections**
4A. **Fund Transfers**
5. **Letters of Credit**
6. **Repealer of Article 6—Bulk Transfers and [Revised] Article 6—Bulk Sales**
7. **Warehouse Receipts, Bills of Lading and Other Documents of Title**
8. **Investment Securities**
9. **Secured Transactions**
10. **Effective Date and Repealer**
11. **Effective Date and Transition Provisions**

Article 1
GENERAL PROVISIONS

Part 1   General Provisions

§ 1–101.   Short Titles.

(a) This [Act] may be cited as Uniform Commercial Code.

(b) This article may be cited as Uniform Commercial Code–Uniform Provisions.

§ 1–102.   Scope of Article.

This article applies to a transaction to the extent that it is governed by another article of [the Uniform Commercial Code].

§ 1–103.   Construction of [Uniform Commercial Code] to Promote Its Purpose and Policies; Applicability of Supplemental Principles of Law.

(a) [The Uniform Commercial Code] must be liberally construed and applied to promote its underlying purposes and policies, which are:

(1) to simplify, clarify, and modernize the law governing commercial transactions;

(2) to permit the continued expansion of commercial practices through custom, usage, and agreement of the parties; and

(3) to make uniform the law among the various jurisdictions.

(b) Unless displaced by the particular provisions of [the Uniform Commercial Code], the principles of law and equity, including the law merchant and the law relative to capacity to contract, principal and agent, estoppel, fraud, misrepresentation, duress, coercion, mistake, bankruptcy, and other validating or invalidating cause, supplement its provisions.

§ 1–104.   Construction Against Implicit Repeal.

This Act being a general act intended as a unified coverage of its subject matter, no part of it shall be deemed to be impliedly repealed by subsequent legislation if such construction can reasonably be avoided.

§ 1–105.   Severability.

If any provision or clause of [the Uniform Commercial Code] or its application to any person or circumstance is held invalid, the invalidity does not affect other provisions or applications of [the Uniform Commercial Code] which can be given effect without the invalid provision or application, and to this end the provisions of [the Uniform Commercial Code] are severable.

§ 1–106.   Use of Singular and Plural; Gender.

In [the Uniform Commercial Code], unless the statutory context otherwise requires:

(1) words in the singular number include the plural, and those in the plural include the singular; and

(2) words of any gender also refer to any other gender.

§ 1–107.   Section Captions.

Section captions are part of [the Uniform Commercial Code].

§ 1–108.   Relation to Electronic Signatures in Global and National Commerce Act.

This article modifies, limits, and supersedes the Federal Electronic Signatures in Global and National Commerce Act, 15 U.S.C. Sections 7001 *et seq.*, except that nothing in this article modifies, limits, or supersedes section 7001(c) of that act or authorizes electronic delivery of any of the notices described in section 7003(b) of that Act.

Part 2   General Definitions and Principles of Interpretation

§ 1–201.   General Definitions.

Subject to additional definitions contained in the subsequent Articles of this Act which are applicable to specific Articles or Parts thereof, and unless the context otherwise requires, in this Act:

(1) "Action", in the sense of a judicial proceeding, includes recoupment, counterclaim, set-off, suit in equity, and any other proceedings in which rights are determined.

(2) "Aggrieved party" means a party entitled to resort to a remedy.

(3) "Agreement", as distinguished from "contract", means the bargain of the parties in fact, as found in their language or by implication from other circumstances, including course of performance, course of dealing, or usage of trade as provided in Section 1–303.

(4) "Bank" means a person engaged in the business of banking and includes a savings bank, savings and loan association, credit union, and trust company.

(5) "Bearer" means a person in control of a negotiable electronic document of title or a person in possession of a negotiable instrument, negotiable tangible document of title, or certificated security that is payable to bearer or indorsed in blank.

(6) "Bill of lading" means a document of title evidencing the receipt of goods for shipment issued by a person engaged in the business of directly or indirectly transporting or forwarding goods. The term does not include a warehouse receipt.

(7) "Branch" includes a separately incorporated foreign branch of a bank.

(8) "Burden of establishing" a fact means the burden of persuading the trier of fact that the existence of the fact is more probable than its nonexistence.

(9) "Buyer in ordinary course of business" means a person that buys goods in good faith, without knowledge that the sale violates the rights of another person in the goods, and in the ordinary course from a person, other than a pawnbroker, in the business of selling goods of that kind. A person buys goods in the ordinary course if the sale to the person comports with the usual or customary practices in the kind of business in which the seller is engaged or with the seller's own usual or customary practices. A person that sells oil, gas, or other minerals at the wellhead or minehead is a person in the business of selling goods of that kind. A buyer in ordinary course of business may buy for cash, by exchange of other property, or on secured or unsecured credit, and may acquire goods or documents of title under a pre-existing contract for sale. Only a buyer that takes possession of the goods or has a right to recover the goods from the seller under Article 2 may be a buyer in ordinary course of business. A person that acquires goods in a transfer in bulk or as security for or in total or partial satisfaction of a money debt is not a buyer in ordinary course of business.

(10) "Conspicuous", with reference to a term, means so written, displayed, or presented that a reasonable person against which it is to operate ought to have noticed it. Whether a term is "conspicuous" or not is a decision for the court. Conspicuous terms include the following:

(A) a heading in capitals equal to or greater in size than the surrounding text, or in contrasting type, font, or color to the surrounding text of the same or lesser size; and

(B) language in the body of a record or display in larger type than the surrounding text, or in contrasting type, font, or color to the surrounding text of the same size, or set off from surrounding text of the same size by symbols or other marks that call attention to the language.

(11) "Consumer" means an individual who enters into a transaction primarily for personal, family, or household purposes.

(12) "Contract", as distinguished from "agreement", means the total legal obligation that results from the parties' agreement as determined by [the Uniform Commercial Code] as supplemented by any other laws.

(13) "Creditor" includes a general creditor, a secured creditor, a lien creditor and any representative of creditors, including an assignee for the benefit of creditors, a trustee in bankruptcy, a receiver in equity and an executor or administrator of an insolvent debtor's or assignor's estate.

(14) "Defendant" includes a person in the position of defendant in a counterclaim, cross-action, or third-party claim.

(15) "Delivery" with respect to an electronic document of title means voluntary transfer of control and with respect to an instrument, a tangible document of title, or chattel paper means voluntary transfer of possession.

(16) "Document of title" means a record (i) that in regular course of business or financing is treated as adequately evidencing that the person in possession or control of the record is entitled to receive, control, hold, and dispose of the record and the goods the record covers and (ii) that purports to be issued by or addressed to a bailee and to cover goods in the bailee's possession which are either identified or are fungible portions of an identified mass. The term includes a bill of lading, transport document, dock warrant, dock receipt, warehouse receipt, and order for delivery of goods. An electronic document of title means a document of title evidenced by a record consisting of information stored in an electronic medium. A tangible document of title means a document of title evidenced by a record consisting of information that is inscribed on a tangible medium.

(17) "Fault" means a default, breach, or wrongful act or omission.

(18) "Fungible goods" means:

(A) goods of which any unit, by nature or usage of trade, is the equivalent of any other like unit; or

(B) goods that by agreement are treated as equivalent.

(19) "Genuine" means free of forgery or counterfeiting.

(20) "Good faith," except as otherwise provided in Article 5, means honesty in fact and the observance of reasonable commercial standards of fair dealing.

(21) "Holder" means:

(A) the person in possession of a negotiable instrument that is payable either to bearer or to an identified person that is the person in possession;

(B) the person in possession of a negotiable tangible document of title if the goods are deliverable either to bearer or to the order of the person in possession; or

(C) the person in control of a negotiable electronic document of title.

(22) "Insolvency proceeding" includes an assignment for the benefit of creditors or other proceeding intended to liquidate or rehabilitate the estate of the person involved.

(23) "Insolvent" means:

(A) having generally ceased to pay debts in the ordinary course of business other than as a result of bona fide dispute;

(B) being unable to pay debts as they become due; or

(C) being insolvent within the meaning of federal bankruptcy law.

(24) "Money" means a medium of exchange currently authorized or adopted by a domestic or foreign government. The term includes a monetary unit of account established by an intergovernmental organization or by agreement between two or more countries.

(25) "Organization" means a person other than an individual.

(26) "Party", as distinguished from "third party", means a person that has engaged in a transaction or made an agreement subject to [the Uniform Commercial Code].

(27) "Person" means an individual, corporation, business trust, estate, trust, partnership, limited liability company, association, joint venture, government, governmental subdivision, agency, or instrumentality, public corporation, or any other legal or commercial entity.

(28) "Present value" means the amount as of a date certain of one or more sums payable in the future, discounted to the date certain by use of either an interest rate specified by the parties if that rate is not manifestly unreasonable at the time the transaction is entered into or, if an interest rate is not so specified, a commercially reasonable rate that takes into account the facts and circumstances at the time the transaction is entered into.

(29) "Purchase" means taking by sale, lease, discount, negotiation, mortgage, pledge, lien, security interest, issue or reissue, gift, or any other voluntary transaction creating an interest in property.

(30) "Purchaser" means a person that takes by purchase.

(31) "Record" means information that is inscribed on a tangible medium or that is stored in an electronic or other medium and is retrievable in perceivable form.

(32) "Remedy" means any remedial right to which an aggrieved party is entitled with or without resort to a tribunal.

(33) "Representative" means a person empowered to act for another, including an agent, an officer of a corporation or association, and a trustee, executor, or administrator of an estate.

(34) "Right" includes remedy.

(35) "Security interest" means an interest in personal property or fixtures which secures payment or performance of an obligation. "Security interest" includes any interest of a consignor and a buyer of accounts, chattel paper, a payment intangible, or a promissory note in a transaction that is subject to Article 9. "Security interest" does not include the special property interest of a buyer of goods on identification of those goods to a contract for sale under Section 2–401, but a buyer may also acquire a "security interest" by complying with Article 9. Except as otherwise provided in Section 2–505, the right of a seller or lessor of goods under Article 2 or 2A to retain or acquire possession of the goods is not a "security interest", but a seller or lessor may also acquire a "security interest" by complying with Article 9. The retention or reservation of title by a seller of goods notwithstanding shipment or delivery to the buyer under Section 2–401 is limited in effect to a reservation of a "security interest." Whether a transaction in the form of a lease creates a "security interest" is determined pursuant to Section 1–203.

(36) "Send" in connection with a writing, record, or notice means:

(A) to deposit in the mail or deliver for transmission by any other usual means of communication with postage or cost of transmission provided for and properly addressed and, in the case of an instrument, to an address specified thereon or otherwise agreed, or if there be none to any address reasonable under the circumstances; or

(B) in any other way to cause to be received any record or notice within the time it would have arrived if properly sent.

(37) "Signed" includes using any symbol executed or adopted with present intention to adopt or accept a writing.

(38) "State" means a State of the United States, the District of Columbia, Puerto Rico, the United States Virgin Islands, or any territory or insular possession subject to the jurisdiction of the United States.

(39) "Surety" includes a guarantor or other secondary obligor.

(40) "Term" means a portion of an agreement that relates to a particular matter.

(41) "Unauthorized signature" means a signature made without actual, implied, or apparent authority. The term includes a forgery.

(42) "Warehouse receipt" means a document of title issued by a person engaged in the business of storing goods for hire.

(43) "Writing" includes printing, typewriting, or any other intentional reduction to tangible form. "Written" has a corresponding meaning.

As amended in 2003.

* * * *

§ 1–205. Reasonable Time; Seasonableness.

(a) Whether a time for taking an action required by [the Uniform Commercial Code] is reasonable depends on the nature, purpose, and circumstances of the action.

(b) An action is taken seasonally if it is taken at or within the time agreed or, if no time is agreed, at or within a reasonable time.

* * * *

Part 3   Territorial Applicability and General Rules

* * * *

§ 1–303.   Course of Performance, Course of Dealing, and Usage of Trade.

(a) A "course of performance" is a sequence of conduct between the parties to a particular transaction that exists if:

(1) the agreement of the parties with respect to the transaction involves repeated occasions for performance by a party; and

(2) the other party, with knowledge of the nature of the performance and opportunity for objection to it, accepts the performance or acquiesces in it without objection.

(b) A "course of dealing" is a sequence of conduct concerning previous transactions between the parties to a particular transaction that is fairly to be regarded as establishing a common basis of understanding for interpreting their expressions and other conduct.

(c) A "usage of trade" is any practice or method of dealing having such regularity of observance in a place, vocation, or trade as to justify an expectation that it will be observed with respect to the transaction in question. The existence and scope of such a usage must be proved as facts. If it is established that such a usage is embodied in a trade code or similar record, the interpretation of the record is a question of law.

(d) A course of performance or course of dealing between the parties or usage of trade in the vocation or trade in which they are engaged or of which they are or should be aware is relevant in ascertaining the meaning of the parties' agreement, may give particular meaning to specific terms of the agreement, and may supplement or qualify the terms of the agreement. A usage of trade applicable in the place in which part of the performance under the agreement is to occur may be so utilized as to that part of the performance.

(e) Except as otherwise provided in subsection (f), the express terms of an agreement and any applicable course of performance, course of dealing, or usage of trade must be construed whenever reasonable as consistent with each other. If such a construction is unreasonable:

(1) express terms prevail over course of performance, course of dealing, and usage of trade;

(2) course of performance prevails over course of dealing and usage of trade; and

(3) course of dealing prevails over usage of trade.

(f) Subject to Section 2–209 and Section 2A–208, a course of performance is relevant to show a waiver or modification of any term inconsistent with the course of performance.

(g) Evidence of a relevant usage of trade offered by one party is not admissible unless that party has given the other party notice that the court finds sufficient to prevent unfair surprise to the other party.

§ 1–304.   Obligation of Good Faith.

Every contract or duty within [the Uniform Commercial Code] imposes an obligation of good faith in its performance and enforcement.

* * * *

§ 1–309.   Option to Accelerate at Will.

A term providing that one party or that party's successor in interest may accelerate payment or performance or require collateral or additional collateral "at will" or when the party "deems itself insecure," or words of similar import, means that the party has power to do so only if that party in good faith believes that the prospect of payment or performance is impaired. The burden of establishing lack of good faith is on the party against which the power has been exercised.

§ 1–310.   Subordinated Obligations.

An obligation may be issued as subordinated to performance of another obligation of the person obligated, or a creditor may subordinate its right to performance of an obligation by agreement with either the person obligated or another creditor of the person obligated. Subordination does not create a security interest as against either the common debtor or a subordinated creditor.

Article 2
SALES

Part 1   Short Title, General Construction and Subject Matter

§ 2–101.   Short Title.

This Article shall be known and may be cited as Uniform Commercial Code—Sales.

§ 2–102.   Scope; Certain Security and Other Transactions Excluded From This Article.

Unless the context otherwise requires, this Article applies to transactions in goods; it does not apply to any transaction which although in the form of an unconditional contract to sell or present sale is intended to operate only as a security transaction nor does this Article impair or repeal any statute regulating sales to consumers, farmers or other specified classes of buyers.

§ 2–103.   Definitions and Index of Definitions.

(1) In this Article unless the context otherwise requires

(a) "Buyer" means a person who buys or contracts to buy goods.

(b) "Good faith" in the case of a merchant means honesty in fact and the observance of reasonable commercial standards of fair dealing in the trade.

(c) "Receipt" of goods means taking physical possession of them.

(d) "Seller" means a person who sells or contracts to sell goods.

(2) Other definitions applying to this Article or to specified Parts thereof, and the sections in which they appear are:

"Acceptance". Section 2–606.

"Banker's credit". Section 2–325.

"Between merchants". Section 2–104.

"Cancellation". Section 2–106(4).

"Commercial unit". Section 2–105.

"Confirmed credit". Section 2–325.

"Conforming to contract". Section 2–106.

"Contract for sale". Section 2–106.

"Cover". Section 2–712.

"Entrusting". Section 2–403.

"Financing agency". Section 2–104.

"Future goods". Section 2–105.

"Goods". Section 2–105.

"Identification". Section 2–501.

"Installment contract". Section 2–612.

"Letter of Credit". Section 2–325.

"Lot". Section 2–105.

"Merchant". Section 2–104.

"Overseas". Section 2–323.

"Person in position of seller". Section 2–707.

"Present sale". Section 2–106.

"Sale". Section 2–106.

"Sale on approval". Section 2–326.

"Sale or return". Section 2–326.

"Termination". Section 2–106.

(3) The following definitions in other Articles apply to this Article:

"Check". Section 3–104.

"Consignee". Section 7–102.

"Consignor". Section 7–102.

"Consumer goods". Section 9–109.

"Dishonor". Section 3–507.

"Draft". Section 3–104.

(4) In addition Article 1 contains general definitions and principles of construction and interpretation applicable throughout this Article. As amended in 1994 and 1999.

§ 2–104.   Definitions: "Merchant"; "Between Merchants"; "Financing Agency".

(1) "Merchant" means a person who deals in goods of the kind or otherwise by his occupation holds himself out as having knowledge or skill peculiar to the practices or goods involved in the transaction or to whom such knowledge or skill may be attributed by his employment of an agent or broker or other intermediary who by his occupation holds himself out as having such knowledge or skill.

(2) "Financing agency" means a bank, finance company or other person who in the ordinary course of business makes advances against goods or documents of title or who by arrangement with either the seller or the buyer intervenes in ordinary course to make or collect payment due or claimed under the contract for sale, as by purchasing or paying the seller's draft or making advances against it or by merely taking it for collection whether or not documents of title accompany the draft. "Financing agency" includes also a bank or other person who similarly intervenes between persons who are in the position of seller and buyer in respect to the goods (Section 2–707).

(3) "Between merchants" means in any transaction with respect to which both parties are chargeable with the knowledge or skill of merchants.

§ 2–105.   Definitions: Transferability; "Goods"; "Future" Goods; "Lot"; "Commercial Unit".

(1) "Goods" means all things (including specially manufactured goods) which are movable at the time of identification to the contract for sale other than the money in which the price is to be paid, investment securities (Article 8) and things in action. "Goods" also includes the unborn young of animals and growing crops and other identified things attached to realty as described in the section on goods to be severed from realty (Section 2–107).

(2) Goods must be both existing and identified before any interest in them can pass. Goods which are not both existing and identified are "future" goods. A purported present sale of future goods or of any interest therein operates as a contract to sell.

(3) There may be a sale of a part interest in existing identified goods.

(4) An undivided share in an identified bulk of fungible goods is sufficiently identified to be sold although the quantity of the bulk is not determined. Any agreed proportion of such a bulk or any quantity thereof agreed upon by number, weight or other measure may to the extent of the seller's interest in the bulk be sold to the buyer who then becomes an owner in common.

(5) "Lot" means a parcel or a single article which is the subject matter of a separate sale or delivery, whether or not it is sufficient to perform the contract.

(6) "Commercial unit" means such a unit of goods as by commercial usage is a single whole for purposes of sale and division of which materially impairs its character or value on the market or in use. A commercial unit may be a single article (as a machine) or a set of articles (as a suite of furniture or an assortment of sizes) or a quantity (as a bale, gross, or carload) or any other unit treated in use or in the relevant market as a single whole.

§ 2–106.   Definitions: "Contract"; "Agreement"; "Contract for Sale"; "Sale"; "Present Sale"; "Conforming" to Contract; "Termination"; "Cancellation".

(1) In this Article unless the context otherwise requires "contract" and "agreement" are limited to those relating to the present or future sale of goods. "Contract for sale" includes both a present sale of goods and a contract to sell goods at a future time. A "sale" consists in the passing of title from the seller to the buyer for a price (Section 2–401). A "present sale" means a sale which is accomplished by the making of the contract.

(2) Goods or conduct including any part of a performance are "conforming" or conform to the contract when they are in accordance with the obligations under the contract.

(3) "Termination" occurs when either party pursuant to a power created by agreement or law puts an end to the contract otherwise than for its breach. On "termination" all obligations which are still executory on both sides are discharged but any right based on prior breach or performance survives.

(4) "Cancellation" occurs when either party puts an end to the contract for breach by the other and its effect is the same as that of "termination" except that the cancelling party also retains any remedy for breach of the whole contract or any unperformed balance.

§ 2–107.   Goods to Be Severed From Realty: Recording.

(1) A contract for the sale of minerals or the like (including oil and gas) or a structure or its materials to be removed from realty is a contract for the sale of goods within this Article if they are to be severed by the seller but until severance a purported present sale thereof which is not effective as a transfer of an interest in land is effective only as a contract to sell.

(2) A contract for the sale apart from the land of growing crops or other things attached to realty and capable of severance without material harm thereto but not described in subsection (1) or of timber to be cut is a contract for the sale of goods within this Article whether the subject matter is to be severed by the buyer or by the seller even though it forms part of the realty at the time of contracting, and the parties can by identification effect a present sale before severance.

(3) The provisions of this section are subject to any third party rights provided by the law relating to realty records, and the contract for sale may be executed and recorded as a document transferring an interest in land and shall then constitute notice to third parties of the buyer's rights under the contract for sale.

As amended in 1972.

Part 2   Form, Formation and Readjustment of Contract

§ 2–201.   Formal Requirements; Statute of Frauds.

(1) Except as otherwise provided in this section a contract for the sale of goods for the price of $500 or more is not enforceable by way of action or defense unless there is some writing sufficient to indicate that a contract for sale has been made between the parties and signed by the party against whom enforcement is sought or by his authorized agent or broker. A writing is not insufficient because it omits or incorrectly states a term agreed upon but the contract is not enforceable under this paragraph beyond the quantity of goods shown in such writing.

(2) Between merchants if within a reasonable time a writing in confirmation of the contract and sufficient against the sender is received and the party receiving it has reason to know its contents, its satisfies the requirements of subsection (1) against such party unless written notice of objection to its contents is given within ten days after it is received.

(3) A contract which does not satisfy the requirements of subsection (1) but which is valid in other respects is enforceable

(a) if the goods are to be specially manufactured for the buyer and are not suitable for sale to others in the ordinary course of the seller's business and the seller, before notice of repudiation is received and under circumstances which reasonably indicate that the goods are for the buyer, has made either a substantial beginning of their manufacture or commitments for their procurement; or

(b) if the party against whom enforcement is sought admits in his pleading, testimony or otherwise in court that a contract for sale was made, but the contract is not enforceable under this provision beyond the quantity of goods admitted; or

(c) with respect to goods for which payment has been made and accepted or which have been received and accepted (Sec. 2–606).

§ 2–202.   Final Written Expression: Parol or Extrinsic Evidence.

Terms with respect to which the confirmatory memoranda of the parties agree or which are otherwise set forth in a writing intended by the parties as a final expression of their agreement with respect to such terms as are included therein may not be contradicted by evidence of any prior agreement or of a contemporaneous oral agreement but may be explained or supplemented

(a) by course of dealing or usage of trade (Section 1–205) or by course of performance (Section 2–208); and

(b) by evidence of consistent additional terms unless the court finds the writing to have been intended also as a complete and exclusive statement of the terms of the agreement.

§ 2–203.   Seals Inoperative.

The affixing of a seal to a writing evidencing a contract for sale or an offer to buy or sell goods does not constitute the writing a sealed instrument and the law with respect to sealed instruments does not apply to such a contract or offer.

§ 2–204.   Formation in General.

(1) A contract for sale of goods may be made in any manner sufficient to show agreement, including conduct by both parties which recognizes the existence of such a contract.

(2) An agreement sufficient to constitute a contract for sale may be found even though the moment of its making is undetermined.

(3) Even though one or more terms are left open a contract for sale does not fail for indefiniteness if the parties have intended to make a contract and there is a reasonably certain basis for giving an appropriate remedy.

§ 2–205.   Firm Offers.

An offer by a merchant to buy or sell goods in a signed writing which by its terms gives assurance that it will be held open is not revocable, for lack of consideration, during the time stated or if no time is stated for a reasonable time, but in no event may such period of irrevocability exceed three months; but any such term of assurance on a form supplied by the offeree must be separately signed by the offeror.

§ 2–206.   Offer and Acceptance in Formation of Contract.

(1) Unless other unambiguously indicated by the language or circumstances

(a) an offer to make a contract shall be construed as inviting acceptance in any manner and by any medium reasonable in the circumstances;

(b) an order or other offer to buy goods for prompt or current shipment shall be construed as inviting acceptance either by a prompt promise to ship or by the prompt or current shipment of conforming or nonconforming goods, but such a shipment of non-conforming goods does not constitute an acceptance if the seller seasonably notifies the buyer that the shipment is offered only as an accommodation to the buyer.

(2) Where the beginning of a requested performance is a reasonable mode of acceptance an offeror who is not notified of acceptance within a reasonable time may treat the offer as having lapsed before acceptance.

§ 2–207.   Additional Terms in Acceptance or Confirmation.

(1) A definite and seasonable expression of acceptance or a written confirmation which is sent within a reasonable time operates as an acceptance even though it states terms additional to or different from those offered or agreed upon, unless acceptance is expressly made conditional on assent to the additional or different terms.

(2) The additional terms are to be construed as proposals for addition to the contract. Between merchants such terms become part of the contract unless:

(a) the offer expressly limits acceptance to the terms of the offer;

(b) they materially alter it; or

(c) notification of objection to them has already been given or is given within a reasonable time after notice of them is received.

(3) Conduct by both parties which recognizes the existence of a contract is sufficient to establish a contract for sale although the writings of the parties do not otherwise establish a contract. In such case the terms of the particular contract consist of those terms on which the writings of the parties agree, together with any supplementary terms incorporated under any other provisions of this Act.

§ 2–208.   Course of Performance or Practical Construction.

(1) Where the contract for sale involves repeated occasions for performance by either party with knowledge of the nature of the performance and opportunity for objection to it by the other, any course of performance accepted or acquiesced in without objection shall be relevant to determine the meaning of the agreement.

(2) The express terms of the agreement and any such course of performance, as well as any course of dealing and usage of trade, shall be construed whenever reasonable as consistent with each other; but when such construction is unreasonable, express terms shall control course of performance and course of performance shall control both course of dealing and usage of trade (Section 1–205).

(3) Subject to the provisions of the next section on modification and waiver, such course of performance shall be relevant to show a waiver or modification of any term inconsistent with such course of performance.

§ 2–209.   Modification, Rescission and Waiver.

(1) An agreement modifying a contract within this Article needs no consideration to be binding.

(2) A signed agreement which excludes modification or rescission except by a signed writing cannot be otherwise modified or rescinded, but except as between merchants such a requirement on a form supplied by the merchant must be separately signed by the other party.

(3) The requirements of the statute of frauds section of this Article (Section 2–201) must be satisfied if the contract as modified is within its provisions.

(4) Although an attempt at modification or rescission does not satisfy the requirements of subsection (2) or (3) it can operate as a waiver.

(5) A party who has made a waiver affecting an executory portion of the contract may retract the waiver by reasonable notification received by the other party that strict performance will be required of any term waived, unless the retraction would be unjust in view of a material change of position in reliance on the waiver.

§ 2–210.   Delegation of Performance; Assignment of Rights.

(1) A party may perform his duty through a delegate unless otherwise agreed or unless the other party has a substantial interest in having his original promisor perform or control the acts required by the contract. No delegation of performance relieves the party delegating of any duty to perform or any liability for breach.

(2) Except as otherwise provided in Section 9–406, unless otherwise agreed, all rights of either seller or buyer can be assigned except where the assignment would materially change the duty of the other party, or increase materially the burden or risk imposed on him by his contract, or impair materially his chance of obtaining return performance. A right to damages for breach of the whole contract or a right arising out of the assignor's due performance of his entire obligation can be assigned despite agreement otherwise.

(3) The creation, attachment, perfection, or enforcement of a security interest in the seller's interest under a contract is not a transfer that materially changes the duty of or increases materially the burden or risk imposed on the buyer or impairs materially the buyer's chance of obtaining return performance within the purview of subsection (2) unless, and then only to the extent that, enforcement actually results in a delegation of material performance of the seller. Even in that event, the creation, attachment, perfection, and enforcement of the security interest remain effective, but (i) the seller is liable to the buyer for damages caused by the delegation to the extent that the damages could not reasonably by prevented by the buyer, and (ii) a court having jurisdiction may grant other appropriate relief, including cancellation of the contract for sale or an injunction against enforcement of the security interest or consummation of the enforcement.

(4) Unless the circumstances indicate the contrary a prohibition of assignment of "the contract" is to be construed as barring only the delegation to the assignee of the assignor's performance.

(5) An assignment of "the contract" or of "all my rights under the contract" or an assignment in similar general terms is an assignment of rights and unless the language or the circumstances (as in an assignment for security) indicate the contrary, it is a delegation of performance of the duties of the assignor and its acceptance by the assignee constitutes a promise by him to perform those duties. This promise is enforceable by either the assignor or the other party to the original contract.

(6) The other party may treat any assignment which delegates performance as creating reasonable grounds for insecurity and may

without prejudice to his rights against the assignor demand assurances from the assignee (Section 2–609).

As amended in 1999.

Part 3   General Obligation and Construction of Contract

§ 2–301.   General Obligations of Parties.

The obligation of the seller is to transfer and deliver and that of the buyer is to accept and pay in accordance with the contract.

§ 2–302.   Unconscionable Contract or Clause.

(1) If the court as a matter of law finds the contract or any clause of the contract to have been unconscionable at the time it was made the court may refuse to enforce the contract, or it may enforce the remainder of the contract without the unconscionable clause, or it may so limit the application of any unconscionable clause as to avoid any unconscionable result.

(2) When it is claimed or appears to the court that the contract or any clause thereof may be unconscionable the parties shall be afforded a reasonable opportunity to present evidence as to its commercial setting, purpose and effect to aid the court in making the determination.

§ 2–303.   Allocations or Division of Risks.

Where this Article allocates a risk or a burden as between the parties "unless otherwise agreed", the agreement may not only shift the allocation but may also divide the risk or burden.

§ 2–304.   Price Payable in Money, Goods, Realty, or Otherwise.

(1) The price can be made payable in money or otherwise. If it is payable in whole or in part in goods each party is a seller of the goods which he is to transfer.

(2) Even though all or part of the price is payable in an interest in realty the transfer of the goods and the seller's obligations with reference to them are subject to this Article, but not the transfer of the interest in realty or the transferor's obligations in connection therewith.

§ 2–305.   Open Price Term.

(1) The parties if they so intend can conclude a contract for sale even though the price is not settled. In such a case the price is a reasonable price at the time for delivery if

(a) nothing is said as to price; or

(b) the price is left to be agreed by the parties and they fail to agree; or

(c) the price is to be fixed in terms of some agreed market or other standard as set or recorded by a third person or agency and it is not so set or recorded.

(2) A price to be fixed by the seller or by the buyer means a price for him to fix in good faith.

(3) When a price left to be fixed otherwise than by agreement of the parties fails to be fixed through fault of one party the other may at his option treat the contract as cancelled or himself fix a reasonable price.

(4) Where, however, the parties intend not to be bound unless the price be fixed or agreed and it is not fixed or agreed there is no contract. In such a case the buyer must return any goods already received or if unable so to do must pay their reasonable value at the time of delivery and the seller must return any portion of the price paid on account.

§ 2–306.   Output, Requirements and Exclusive Dealings.

(1) A term which measures the quantity by the output of the seller or the requirements of the buyer means such actual output or requirements as may occur in good faith, except that no quantity unreasonably disproportionate to any stated estimate or in the absence of a stated estimate to any normal or otherwise comparable prior output or requirements may be tendered or demanded.

(2) A lawful agreement by either the seller or the buyer for exclusive dealing in the kind of goods concerned imposes unless otherwise agreed an obligation by the seller to use best efforts to supply the goods and by the buyer to use best efforts to promote their sale.

§ 2–307.   Delivery in Single Lot or Several Lots.

Unless otherwise agreed all goods called for by a contract for sale must be tendered in a single delivery and payment is due only on such tender but where the circumstances give either party the right to make or demand delivery in lots the price if it can be apportioned may be demanded for each lot.

§ 2–308.   Absence of Specified Place for Delivery.

Unless otherwise agreed

(a) the place for delivery of goods is the seller's place of business or if he has none his residence; but

(b) in a contract for sale of identified goods which to the knowledge of the parties at the time of contracting are in some other place, that place is the place for their delivery; and

(c) documents of title may be delivered through customary banking channels.

§ 2–309.   Absence of Specific Time Provisions; Notice of Termination.

(1) The time for shipment or delivery or any other action under a contract if not provided in this Article or agreed upon shall be a reasonable time.

(2) Where the contract provides for successive performances but is indefinite in duration it is valid for a reasonable time but unless otherwise agreed may be terminated at any time by either party.

(3) Termination of a contract by one party except on the happening of an agreed event requires that reasonable notification be received by the other party and an agreement dispensing with notification is invalid if its operation would be unconscionable.

§ 2–310.   Open Time for Payment or
Running of Credit; Authority to Ship Under Reservation.

Unless otherwise agreed

(a) payment is due at the time and place at which the buyer is to receive the goods even though the place of shipment is the place of delivery; and

(b) if the seller is authorized to send the goods he may ship them under reservation, and may tender the documents of title, but the buyer may inspect the goods after their arrival before payment is due unless such inspection is inconsistent with the terms of the contract (Section 2–513); and

(c) if delivery is authorized and made by way of documents of title otherwise than by subsection (b) then payment is due at the time and place at which the buyer is to receive the documents regardless of where the goods are to be received; and

(d) where the seller is required or authorized to ship the goods on credit the credit period runs from the time of shipment but post-dating the invoice or delaying its dispatch will correspondingly delay the starting of the credit period.

§ 2-311.   Options and Cooperation Respecting Performance.

(1) An agreement for sale which is otherwise sufficiently definite (subsection (3) of Section 2-204) to be a contract is not made invalid by the fact that it leaves particulars of performance to be specified by one of the parties. Any such specification must be made in good faith and within limits set by commercial reasonableness.

(2) Unless otherwise agreed specifications relating to assortment of the goods are at the buyer's option and except as otherwise provided in subsections (1)(c) and (3) of Section 2-319 specifications or arrangements relating to shipment are at the seller's option.

(3) Where such specification would materially affect the other party's performance but is not seasonably made or where one party's cooperation is necessary to the agreed performance of the other but is not seasonably forthcoming, the other party in addition to all other remedies

(a) is excused for any resulting delay in his own performance; and

(b) may also either proceed to perform in any reasonable manner or after the time for a material part of his own performance treat the failure to specify or to cooperate as a breach by failure to deliver or accept the goods.

§ 2-312.   Warranty of Title and Against Infringement; Buyer's Obligation Against Infringement.

(1) Subject to subsection (2) there is in a contract for sale a warranty by the seller that

(a) the title conveyed shall be good, and its transfer rightful; and

(b) the goods shall be delivered free from any security interest or other lien or encumbrance of which the buyer at the time of contracting has no knowledge.

(2) A warranty under subsection (1) will be excluded or modified only by specific language or by circumstances which give the buyer reason to know that the person selling does not claim title in himself or that he is purporting to sell only such right or title as he or a third person may have.

(3) Unless otherwise agreed a seller who is a merchant regularly dealing in goods of the kind warrants that the goods shall be delivered free of the rightful claim of any third person by way of infringement or the like but a buyer who furnishes specifications to the seller must hold the seller harmless against any such claim which arises out of compliance with the specifications.

§ 2-313.   Express Warranties by Affirmation, Promise, Description, Sample.

(1) Express warranties by the seller are created as follows:

(a) Any affirmation of fact or promise made by the seller to the buyer which relates to the goods and becomes part of the basis of the bargain creates an express warranty that the goods shall conform to the affirmation or promise.

(b) Any description of the goods which is made part of the basis of the bargain creates an express warranty that the goods shall conform to the description.

(c) Any sample or model which is made part of the basis of the bargain creates an express warranty that the whole of the goods shall conform to the sample or model.

(2) It is not necessary to the creation of an express warranty that the seller use formal words such as "warrant" or "guarantee" or that he have a specific intention to make a warranty, but an affirmation merely of the value of the goods or a statement purporting to be merely the seller's opinion or commendation of the goods does not create a warranty.

§ 2-314.   Implied Warranty: Merchantability; Usage of Trade.

(1) Unless excluded or modified (Section 2-316), a warranty that the goods shall be merchantable is implied in a contract for their sale if the seller is a merchant with respect to goods of that kind. Under this section the serving for value of food or drink to be consumed either on the premises or elsewhere is a sale.

(2) Goods to be merchantable must be at least such as

(a) pass without objection in the trade under the contract description; and

(b) in the case of fungible goods, are of fair average quality within the description; and

(c) are fit for the ordinary purposes for which such goods are used; and

(d) run, within the variations permitted by the agreement, of even kind, quality and quantity within each unit and among all units involved; and

(e) are adequately contained, packaged, and labeled as the agreement may require; and

(f) conform to the promises or affirmations of fact made on the container or label if any.

(3) Unless excluded or modified (Section 2-316) other implied warranties may arise from course of dealing or usage of trade.

§ 2-315.   Implied Warranty: Fitness for Particular Purpose.

Where the seller at the time of contracting has reason to know any particular purpose for which the goods are required and that the buyer is relying on the seller's skill or judgment to select or furnish suitable goods, there is unless excluded or modified under the next section an implied warranty that the goods shall be fit for such purpose.

§ 2-316.   Exclusion or Modification of Warranties.

(1) Words or conduct relevant to the creation of an express warranty and words or conduct tending to negate or limit warranty shall be construed wherever reasonable as consistent with each other; but subject to the provisions of this Article on parol or extrinsic evidence (Section 2-202) negation or limitation is inoperative to the extent that such construction is unreasonable.

(2) Subject to subsection (3), to exclude or modify the implied warranty of merchantability or any part of it the language must

mention merchantability and in case of a writing must be conspicuous, and to exclude or modify any implied warranty of fitness the exclusion must be by a writing and conspicuous. Language to exclude all implied warranties of fitness is sufficient if it states, for example, that "There are no warranties which extend beyond the description on the face hereof."

(3) Notwithstanding subsection (2)

(a) unless the circumstances indicate otherwise, all implied warranties are excluded by expressions like "as is", "with all faults" or other language which in common understanding calls the buyer's attention to the exclusion of warranties and makes plain that there is no implied warranty; and

(b) when the buyer before entering into the contract has examined the goods or the sample or model as fully as he desired or has refused to examine the goods there is no implied warranty with regard to defects which an examination ought in the circumstances to have revealed to him; and

(c) an implied warranty can also be excluded or modified by course of dealing or course of performance or usage of trade.

(4) Remedies for breach of warranty can be limited in accordance with the provisions of this Article on liquidation or limitation of damages and on contractual modification of remedy (Sections 2–718 and 2–719).

§ 2–317.   Cumulation and Conflict of Warranties Express or Implied.

Warranties whether express or implied shall be construed as consistent with each other and as cumulative, but if such construction is unreasonable the intention of the parties shall determine which warranty is dominant. In ascertaining that intention the following rules apply:

(a) Exact or technical specifications displace an inconsistent sample or model or general language of description.

(b) A sample from an existing bulk displaces inconsistent general language of description.

(c) Express warranties displace inconsistent implied warranties other than an implied warranty of fitness for a particular purpose.

§ 2–318.   Third Party Beneficiaries of Warranties Express or Implied.

Note: If this Act is introduced in the Congress of the United States this section should be omitted. (States to select one alternative.)

Alternative A

A seller's warranty whether express or implied extends to any natural person who is in the family or household of his buyer or who is a guest in his home if it is reasonable to expect that such person may use, consume or be affected by the goods and who is injured in person by breach of the warranty. A seller may not exclude or limit the operation of this section.

Alternative B

A seller's warranty whether express or implied extends to any natural person who may reasonably be expected to use, consume or be affected by the goods and who is injured in person by breach of the warranty. A seller may not exclude or limit the operation of this section.

Alternative C

A seller's warranty whether express or implied extends to any person who may reasonably be expected to use, consume or be affected by the goods and who is injured by breach of the warranty. A seller may not exclude or limit the operation of this section with respect to injury to the person of an individual to whom the warranty extends.

As amended 1966.

§ 2–319.   F.O.B. and F.A.S. Terms.

(1) Unless otherwise agreed the term F.O.B. (which means "free on board") at a named place, even though used only in connection with the stated price, is a delivery term under which

(a) when the term is F.O.B. the place of shipment, the seller must at that place ship the goods in the manner provided in this Article (Section 2–504) and bear the expense and risk of putting them into the possession of the carrier; or

(b) when the term is F.O.B. the place of destination, the seller must at his own expense and risk transport the goods to that place and there tender delivery of them in the manner provided in this Article (Section 2–503);

(c) when under either (a) or (b) the term is also F.O.B. vessel, car or other vehicle, the seller must in addition at his own expense and risk load the goods on board. If the term is F.O.B. vessel the buyer must name the vessel and in an appropriate case the seller must comply with the provisions of this Article on the form of bill of lading (Section 2–323).

(2) Unless otherwise agreed the term F.A.S. vessel (which means "free alongside") at a named port, even though used only in connection with the stated price, is a delivery term under which the seller must

(a) at his own expense and risk deliver the goods alongside the vessel in the manner usual in that port or on a dock designated and provided by the buyer; and

(b) obtain and tender a receipt for the goods in exchange for which the carrier is under a duty to issue a bill of lading.

(3) Unless otherwise agreed in any case falling within subsection (1)(a) or (c) or subsection (2) the buyer must seasonably give any needed instructions for making delivery, including when the term is F.A.S. or F.O.B. the loading berth of the vessel and in an appropriate case its name and sailing date. The seller may treat the failure of needed instructions as a failure of cooperation under this Article (Section 2–311). He may also at his option move the goods in any reasonable manner preparatory to delivery or shipment.

(4) Under the term F.O.B. vessel or F.A.S. unless otherwise agreed the buyer must make payment against tender of the required documents and the seller may not tender nor the buyer demand delivery of the goods in substitution for the documents.

§ 2–320.   C.I.F. and C. & F. Terms.

(1) The term C.I.F. means that the price includes in a lump sum the cost of the goods and the insurance and freight to the named destination. The term C. & F. or C.F. means that the price so includes cost and freight to the named destination.

(2) Unless otherwise agreed and even though used only in connection with the stated price and destination, the term C.I.F. destination or its equivalent requires the seller at his own expense and risk to

(a) put the goods into the possession of a carrier at the port for shipment and obtain a negotiable bill or bills of lading covering the entire transportation to the named destination; and

(b) load the goods and obtain a receipt from the carrier (which may be contained in the bill of lading) showing that the freight has been paid or provided for; and

(c) obtain a policy or certificate of insurance, including any war risk insurance, of a kind and on terms then current at the port of shipment in the usual amount, in the currency of the contract, shown to cover the same goods covered by the bill of lading and providing for payment of loss to the order of the buyer or for the account of whom it may concern; but the seller may add to the price the amount of the premium for any such war risk insurance; and

(d) prepare an invoice of the goods and procure any other documents required to effect shipment or to comply with the contract; and

(e) forward and tender with commercial promptness all the documents in due form and with any indorsement necessary to perfect the buyer's rights.

(3) Unless otherwise agreed the term C. & F. or its equivalent has the same effect and imposes upon the seller the same obligations and risks as a C.I.F. term except the obligation as to insurance.

(4) Under the term C.I.F. or C. & F. unless otherwise agreed the buyer must make payment against tender of the required documents and the seller may not tender nor the buyer demand delivery of the goods in substitution for the documents.

§ 2–321.   C.I.F. or C. & F.: "Net Landed Weights"; "Payment on Arrival"; Warranty of Condition on Arrival.

Under a contract containing a term C.I.F. or C. & F.

(1) Where the price is based on or is to be adjusted according to "net landed weights", "delivered weights", "out turn" quantity or quality or the like, unless otherwise agreed the seller must reasonably estimate the price. The payment due on tender of the documents called for by the contract is the amount so estimated, but after final adjustment of the price a settlement must be made with commercial promptness.

(2) An agreement described in subsection (1) or any warranty of quality or condition of the goods on arrival places upon the seller the risk of ordinary deterioration, shrinkage and the like in transportation but has no effect on the place or time of identification to the contract for sale or delivery or on the passing of the risk of loss.

(3) Unless otherwise agreed where the contract provides for payment on or after arrival of the goods the seller must before payment allow such preliminary inspection as is feasible; but if the goods are lost delivery of the documents and payment are due when the goods should have arrived.

§ 2–322.   Delivery "Ex-Ship".

(1) Unless otherwise agreed a term for delivery of goods "ex-ship" (which means from the carrying vessel) or in equivalent language is not restricted to a particular ship and requires delivery from a ship which has reached a place at the named port of destination where goods of the kind are usually discharged.

(2) Under such a term unless otherwise agreed

(a) the seller must discharge all liens arising out of the carriage and furnish the buyer with a direction which puts the carrier under a duty to deliver the goods; and

(b) the risk of loss does not pass to the buyer until the goods leave the ship's tackle or are otherwise properly unloaded.

§ 2–323.   Form of Bill of Lading Required in Overseas Shipment; "Overseas".

(1) Where the contract contemplates overseas shipment and contains a term C.I.F. or C. & F. or F.O.B. vessel, the seller unless otherwise agreed must obtain a negotiable bill of lading stating that the goods have been loaded on board or, in the case of a term C.I.F. or C. & F., received for shipment.

(2) Where in a case within subsection (1) a bill of lading has been issued in a set of parts, unless otherwise agreed if the documents are not to be sent from abroad the buyer may demand tender of the full set; otherwise only one part of the bill of lading need be tendered. Even if the agreement expressly requires a full set

(a) due tender of a single part is acceptable within the provisions of this Article on cure of improper delivery (subsection (1) of Section 2–508); and

(b) even though the full set is demanded, if the documents are sent from abroad the person tendering an incomplete set may nevertheless require payment upon furnishing an indemnity which the buyer in good faith deems adequate.

(3) A shipment by water or by air or a contract contemplating such shipment is "overseas" insofar as by usage of trade or agreement it is subject to the commercial, financing or shipping practices characteristic of international deep water commerce.

§ 2–324.   "No Arrival, No Sale" Term.

Under a term "no arrival, no sale" or terms of like meaning, unless otherwise agreed,

(a) the seller must properly ship conforming goods and if they arrive by any means he must tender them on arrival but he assumes no obligation that the goods will arrive unless he has caused the non-arrival; and

(b) where without fault of the seller the goods are in part lost or have so deteriorated as no longer to conform to the contract or arrive after the contract time, the buyer may proceed as if there had been casualty to identified goods (Section 2–613).

§ 2–325.   "Letter of Credit" Term; "Confirmed Credit".

(1) Failure of the buyer seasonably to furnish an agreed letter of credit is a breach of the contract for sale.

(2) The delivery to seller of a proper letter of credit suspends the buyer's obligation to pay. If the letter of credit is dishonored, the

seller may on seasonable notification to the buyer require payment directly from him.

(3) Unless otherwise agreed the term "letter of credit" or "banker's credit" in a contract for sale means an irrevocable credit issued by a financing agency of good repute and, where the shipment is overseas, of good international repute. The term "confirmed credit" means that the credit must also carry the direct obligation of such an agency which does business in the seller's financial market.

§ 2–326.   Sale on Approval and Sale or Return; Rights of Creditors.

(1) Unless otherwise agreed, if delivered goods may be returned by the buyer even though they conform to the contract, the transaction is

(a) a "sale on approval" if the goods are delivered primarily for use, and

(b) a "sale or return" if the goods are delivered primarily for resale.

(2) Goods held on approval are not subject to the claims of the buyer's creditors until acceptance; goods held on sale or return are subject to such claims while in the buyer's possession.

(3) Any "or return" term of a contract for sale is to be treated as a separate contract for sale within the statute of frauds section of this Article (Section 2–201) and as contradicting the sale aspect of the contract within the provisions of this Article or on parol or extrinsic evidence (Section 2–202).

As amended in 1999.

§ 2–327.   Special Incidents of Sale on Approval and Sale or Return.

(1) Under a sale on approval unless otherwise agreed

(a) although the goods are identified to the contract the risk of loss and the title do not pass to the buyer until acceptance; and

(b) use of the goods consistent with the purpose of trial is not acceptance but failure seasonably to notify the seller of election to return the goods is acceptance, and if the goods conform to the contract acceptance of any part is acceptance of the whole; and

(c) after due notification of election to return, the return is at the seller's risk and expense but a merchant buyer must follow any reasonable instructions.

(2) Under a sale or return unless otherwise agreed

(a) the option to return extends to the whole or any commercial unit of the goods while in substantially their original condition, but must be exercised seasonably; and

(b) the return is at the buyer's risk and expense.

§ 2–328.   Sale by Auction.

(1) In a sale by auction if goods are put up in lots each lot is the subject of a separate sale.

(2) A sale by auction is complete when the auctioneer so announces by the fall of the hammer or in other customary manner. Where a bid is made while the hammer is falling in acceptance of a prior bid the auctioneer may in his discretion reopen the bidding or declare the goods sold under the bid on which the hammer was falling.

(3) Such a sale is with reserve unless the goods are in explicit terms put up without reserve. In an auction with reserve the auctioneer may withdraw the goods at any time until he announces completion of the sale. In an auction without reserve, after the auctioneer calls for bids on an article or lot, that article or lot cannot be withdrawn unless no bid is made within a reasonable time. In either case a bidder may retract his bid until the auctioneer's announcement of completion of the sale, but a bidder's retraction does not revive any previous bid.

(4) If the auctioneer knowingly receives a bid on the seller's behalf or the seller makes or procures such as bid, and notice has not been given that liberty for such bidding is reserved, the buyer may at his option avoid the sale or take the goods at the price of the last good faith bid prior to the completion of the sale. This subsection shall not apply to any bid at a forced sale.

Part 4   Title, Creditors and Good Faith Purchasers

§ 2–401.   Passing of Title; Reservation
for Security; Limited Application of This Section.

Each provision of this Article with regard to the rights, obligations and remedies of the seller, the buyer, purchasers or other third parties applies irrespective of title to the goods except where the provision refers to such title. Insofar as situations are not covered by the other provisions of this Article and matters concerning title became material the following rules apply:

(1) Title to goods cannot pass under a contract for sale prior to their identification to the contract (Section 2–501), and unless otherwise explicitly agreed the buyer acquires by their identification a special property as limited by this Act. Any retention or reservation by the seller of the title (property) in goods shipped or delivered to the buyer is limited in effect to a reservation of a security interest. Subject to these provisions and to the provisions of the Article on Secured Transactions (Article 9), title to goods passes from the seller to the buyer in any manner and on any conditions explicitly agreed on by the parties.

(2) Unless otherwise explicitly agreed title passes to the buyer at the time and place at which the seller completes his performance with reference to the physical delivery of the goods, despite any reservation of a security interest and even though a document of title is to be delivered at a different time or place; and in particular and despite any reservation of a security interest by the bill of lading

(a) if the contract requires or authorizes the seller to send the goods to the buyer but does not require him to deliver them at destination, title passes to the buyer at the time and place of shipment; but

(b) if the contract requires delivery at destination, title passes on tender there.

(3) Unless otherwise explicitly agreed where delivery is to be made without moving the goods,

(a) if the seller is to deliver a document of title, title passes at the time when and the place where he delivers such documents; or

(b) if the goods are at the time of contracting already identified and no documents are to be delivered, title passes at the time and place of contracting.

(4) A rejection or other refusal by the buyer to receive or retain the goods, whether or not justified, or a justified revocation of acceptance revests title to the goods in the seller. Such revesting occurs by operation of law and is not a "sale".

§ 2–402.   Rights of Seller's Creditors Against Sold Goods.

(1) Except as provided in subsections (2) and (3), rights of unsecured creditors of the seller with respect to goods which have been identified to a contract for sale are subject to the buyer's rights to recover the goods under this Article (Sections 2–502 and 2–716).

(2) A creditor of the seller may treat a sale or an identification of goods to a contract for sale as void if as against him a retention of possession by the seller is fraudulent under any rule of law of the state where the goods are situated, except that retention of possession in good faith and current course of trade by a merchant-seller for a commercially reasonable time after a sale or identification is not fraudulent.

(3) Nothing in this Article shall be deemed to impair the rights of creditors of the seller

(a) under the provisions of the Article on Secured Transactions (Article 9); or

(b) where identification to the contract or delivery is made not in current course of trade but in satisfaction of or as security for a pre-existing claim for money, security or the like and is made under circumstances which under any rule of law of the state where the goods are situated would apart from this Article constitute the transaction a fraudulent transfer or voidable preference.

§ 2–403.   Power to Transfer; Good Faith Purchase of Goods; "Entrusting".

(1) A purchaser of goods acquires all title which his transferor had or had power to transfer except that a purchaser of a limited interest acquires rights only to the extent of the interest purchased. A person with voidable title has power to transfer a good title to a good faith purchaser for value. When goods have been delivered under a transaction of purchase the purchaser has such power even though

(a) the transferor was deceived as to the identity of the purchaser, or

(b) the delivery was in exchange for a check which is later dishonored, or

(c) it was agreed that the transaction was to be a "cash sale", or

(d) the delivery was procured through fraud punishable as larcenous under the criminal law.

(2) Any entrusting of possession of goods to a merchant who deals in goods of that kind gives him power to transfer all rights of the entruster to a buyer in ordinary course of business.

(3) "Entrusting" includes any delivery and any acquiescence in retention of possession regardless of any condition expressed between the parties to the delivery or acquiescence and regardless of whether the procurement of the entrusting or the possessor's disposition of the goods have been such as to be larcenous under the criminal law.

(4) The rights of other purchasers of goods and of lien creditors are governed by the Articles on Secured Transactions (Article 9), Bulk Transfers (Article 6) and Documents of Title (Article 7).

As amended in 1988.

Part 5   Performance

§ 2–501.   Insurable Interest in Goods; Manner of Identification of Goods.

(1) The buyer obtains a special property and an insurable interest in goods by identification of existing goods as goods to which the contract refers even though the goods so identified are nonconforming and he has an option to return or reject them. Such identification can be made at any time and in any manner explicitly agreed to by the parties. In the absence of explicit agreement identification occurs

(a) when the contract is made if it is for the sale of goods already existing and identified;

(b) if the contract is for the sale of future goods other than those described in paragraph (c), when goods are shipped, marked or otherwise designated by the seller as goods to which the contract refers;

(c) when the crops are planted or otherwise become growing crops or the young are conceived if the contract is for the sale of unborn young to be born within twelve months after contracting or for the sale of crops to be harvested within twelve months or the next normal harvest season after contracting whichever is longer.

(2) The seller retains an insurable interest in goods so long as title to or any security interest in the goods remains in him and where the identification is by the seller alone he may until default or insolvency or notification to the buyer that the identification is final substitute other goods for those identified.

(3) Nothing in this section impairs any insurable interest recognized under any other statute or rule of law.

§ 2–502.   Buyer's Right to Goods on Seller's Insolvency.

(1) Subject to subsections (2) and (3) and even though the goods have not been shipped a buyer who has paid a part or all of the price of goods in which he has a special property under the provisions of the immediately preceding section may on making and keeping good a tender of any unpaid portion of their price recover them from the seller if:

(a) in the case of goods bought for personal, family, or household purposes, the seller repudiates or fails to deliver as required by the contract; or

(b) in all cases, the seller becomes insolvent within ten days after receipt of the first installment on their price.

(2) The buyer's right to recover the goods under subsection (1)(a) vests upon acquisition of a special property, even if the seller had not then repudiated or failed to deliver.

(3) If the identification creating his special property has been made by the buyer he acquires the right to recover the goods only if they conform to the contract for sale.

As amended in 1999.

§ 2–503. Manner of Seller's Tender of Delivery.

(1) Tender of delivery requires that the seller put and hold conforming goods at the buyer's disposition and give the buyer any notification reasonably necessary to enable him to take delivery. The manner, time and place for tender are determined by the agreement and this Article, and in particular

(a) tender must be at a reasonable hour, and if it is of goods they must be kept available for the period reasonably necessary to enable the buyer to take possession; but

(b) unless otherwise agreed the buyer must furnish facilities reasonably suited to the receipt of the goods.

(2) Where the case is within the next section respecting shipment tender requires that the seller comply with its provisions.

(3) Where the seller is required to deliver at a particular destination tender requires that he comply with subsection (1) and also in any appropriate case tender documents as described in subsections (4) and (5) of this section.

(4) Where goods are in the possession of a bailee and are to be delivered without being moved

(a) tender requires that the seller either tender a negotiable document of title covering such goods or procure acknowledgment by the bailee of the buyer's right to possession of the goods; but

(b) tender to the buyer of a non-negotiable document of title or of a written direction to the bailee to deliver is sufficient tender unless the buyer seasonably objects, and receipt by the bailee of notification of the buyer's rights fixes those rights as against the bailee and all third persons; but risk of loss of the goods and of any failure by the bailee to honor the non-negotiable document of title or to obey the direction remains on the seller until the buyer has had a reasonable time to present the document or direction, and a refusal by the bailee to honor the document or to obey the direction defeats the tender.

(5) Where the contract requires the seller to deliver documents

(a) he must tender all such documents in correct form, except as provided in this Article with respect to bills of lading in a set (subsection (2) of Section 2–323); and

(b) tender through customary banking channels is sufficient and dishonor of a draft accompanying the documents constitutes non-acceptance or rejection.

§ 2–504. Shipment by Seller.

Where the seller is required or authorized to send the goods to the buyer and the contract does not require him to deliver them at a particular destination, then unless otherwise agreed he must

(a) put the goods in the possession of such a carrier and make such a contract for their transportation as may be reasonable having regard to the nature of the goods and other circumstances of the case; and

(b) obtain and promptly deliver or tender in due form any document necessary to enable the buyer to obtain possession of the goods or otherwise required by the agreement or by usage of trade; and

(c) promptly notify the buyer of the shipment.

Failure to notify the buyer under paragraph (c) or to make a proper contract under paragraph (a) is a ground for rejection only if material delay or loss ensues.

§ 2–505. Seller's Shipment under Reservation.

(1) Where the seller has identified goods to the contract by or before shipment:

(a) his procurement of a negotiable bill of lading to his own order or otherwise reserves in him a security interest in the goods. His procurement of the bill to the order of a financing agency or of the buyer indicates in addition only the seller's expectation of transferring that interest to the person named.

(b) a non-negotiable bill of lading to himself or his nominee reserves possession of the goods as security but except in a case of conditional delivery (subsection (2) of Section 2–507) a non-negotiable bill of lading naming the buyer as consignee reserves no security interest even though the seller retains possession of the bill of lading.

(2) When shipment by the seller with reservation of a security interest is in violation of the contract for sale it constitutes an improper contract for transportation within the preceding section but impairs neither the rights given to the buyer by shipment and identification of the goods to the contract nor the seller's powers as a holder of a negotiable document.

§ 2–506. Rights of Financing Agency.

(1) A financing agency by paying or purchasing for value a draft which relates to a shipment of goods acquires to the extent of the payment or purchase and in addition to its own rights under the draft and any document of title securing it any rights of the shipper in the goods including the right to stop delivery and the shipper's right to have the draft honored by the buyer.

(2) The right to reimbursement of a financing agency which has in good faith honored or purchased the draft under commitment to or authority from the buyer is not impaired by subsequent discovery of defects with reference to any relevant document which was apparently regular on its face.

§ 2–507. Effect of Seller's Tender; Delivery on Condition.

(1) Tender of delivery is a condition to the buyer's duty to accept the goods and, unless otherwise agreed, to his duty to pay for them. Tender entitles the seller to acceptance of the goods and to payment according to the contract.

(2) Where payment is due and demanded on the delivery to the buyer of goods or documents of title, his right as against the seller to retain or dispose of them is conditional upon his making the payment due.

§ 2–508. Cure by Seller of Improper Tender or Delivery; Replacement.

(1) Where any tender or delivery by the seller is rejected because non-conforming and the time for performance has not yet expired,

the seller may seasonably notify the buyer of his intention to cure and may then within the contract time make a conforming delivery.

(2) Where the buyer rejects a non-conforming tender which the seller had reasonable grounds to believe would be acceptable with or without money allowance the seller may if he seasonably notifies the buyer have a further reasonable time to substitute a conforming tender.

§ 2–509.   Risk of Loss in the Absence of Breach.

(1) Where the contract requires or authorizes the seller to ship the goods by carrier

(a) if it does not require him to deliver them at a particular destination, the risk of loss passes to the buyer when the goods are duly delivered to the carrier even though the shipment is under reservation (Section 2–505); but

(b) if it does require him to deliver them at a particular destination and the goods are there duly tendered while in the possession of the carrier, the risk of loss passes to the buyer when the goods are there duly so tendered as to enable the buyer to take delivery.

(2) Where the goods are held by a bailee to be delivered without being moved, the risk of loss passes to the buyer

(a) on his receipt of a negotiable document of title covering the goods; or

(b) on acknowledgment by the bailee of the buyer's right to possession of the goods; or

(c) after his receipt of a non-negotiable document of title or other written direction to deliver, as provided in subsection (4)(b) of Section 2–503.

(3) In any case not within subsection (1) or (2), the risk of loss passes to the buyer on his receipt of the goods if the seller is a merchant; otherwise the risk passes to the buyer on tender of delivery.

(4) The provisions of this section are subject to contrary agreement of the parties and to the provisions of this Article on sale on approval (Section 2–327) and on effect of breach on risk of loss (Section 2–510).

§ 2–510.   Effect of Breach on Risk of Loss.

(1) Where a tender or delivery of goods so fails to conform to the contract as to give a right of rejection the risk of their loss remains on the seller until cure or acceptance.

(2) Where the buyer rightfully revokes acceptance he may to the extent of any deficiency in his effective insurance coverage treat the risk of loss as having rested on the seller from the beginning.

(3) Where the buyer as to conforming goods already identified to the contract for sale repudiates or is otherwise in breach before risk of their loss has passed to him, the seller may to the extent of any deficiency in his effective insurance coverage treat the risk of loss as resting on the buyer for a commercially reasonable time.

§ 2–511.   Tender of Payment by Buyer; Payment by Check.

(1) Unless otherwise agreed tender of payment is a condition to the seller's duty to tender and complete any delivery.

(2) Tender of payment is sufficient when made by any means or in any manner current in the ordinary course of business unless the seller demands payment in legal tender and gives any extension of time reasonably necessary to procure it.

(3) Subject to the provisions of this Act on the effect of an instrument on an obligation (Section 3–310), payment by check is conditional and is defeated as between the parties by dishonor of the check on due presentment.

As amended in 1994.

§ 2–512.   Payment by Buyer Before Inspection.

(1) Where the contract requires payment before inspection non-conformity of the goods does not excuse the buyer from so making payment unless

(a) the non-conformity appears without inspection; or

(b) despite tender of the required documents the circumstances would justify injunction against honor under this Act (Section 5–109(b)).

(2) Payment pursuant to subsection (1) does not constitute an acceptance of goods or impair the buyer's right to inspect or any of his remedies.

As amended in 1995.

§ 2–513.   Buyer's Right to Inspection of Goods.

(1) Unless otherwise agreed and subject to subsection (3), where goods are tendered or delivered or identified to the contract for sale, the buyer has a right before payment or acceptance to inspect them at any reasonable place and time and in any reasonable manner. When the seller is required or authorized to send the goods to the buyer, the inspection may be after their arrival.

(2) Expenses of inspection must be borne by the buyer but may be recovered from the seller if the goods do not conform and are rejected.

(3) Unless otherwise agreed and subject to the provisions of this Article on C.I.F. contracts (subsection (3) of Section 2–321), the buyer is not entitled to inspect the goods before payment of the price when the contract provides

(a) for delivery "C.O.D." or on other like terms; or

(b) for payment against documents of title, except where such payment is due only after the goods are to become available for inspection.

(4) A place or method of inspection fixed by the parties is presumed to be exclusive but unless otherwise expressly agreed it does not postpone identification or shift the place for delivery or for passing the risk of loss. If compliance becomes impossible, inspection shall be as provided in this section unless the place or method fixed was clearly intended as an indispensable condition failure of which avoids the contract.

§ 2–514.   When Documents Deliverable on Acceptance; When on Payment.

Unless otherwise agreed documents against which a draft is drawn are to be delivered to the drawee on acceptance of the draft if it is payable more than three days after presentment; otherwise, only on payment.

§ 2–515.   Preserving Evidence of Goods in Dispute.

In furtherance of the adjustment of any claim or dispute

(a) either party on reasonable notification to the other and for the purpose of ascertaining the facts and preserving evidence has the right to inspect, test and sample the goods including such of them as may be in the possession or control of the other; and

(b) the parties may agree to a third party inspection or survey to determine the conformity or condition of the goods and may agree that the findings shall be binding upon them in any subsequent litigation or adjustment.

Part 6   Breach, Repudiation and Excuse

§ 2-601.   Buyer's Rights on Improper Delivery.

Subject to the provisions of this Article on breach in installment contracts (Section 2-612) and unless otherwise agreed under the sections on contractual limitations of remedy (Sections 2-718 and 2-719), if the goods or the tender of delivery fail in any respect to conform to the contract, the buyer may

(a) reject the whole; or

(b) accept the whole; or

(c) accept any commercial unit or units and reject the rest.

§ 2-602.   Manner and Effect of Rightful Rejection.

(1) Rejection of goods must be within a reasonable time after their delivery or tender. It is ineffective unless the buyer seasonably notifies the seller.

(2) Subject to the provisions of the two following sections on rejected goods (Sections 2-603 and 2-604),

(a) after rejection any exercise of ownership by the buyer with respect to any commercial unit is wrongful as against the seller; and

(b) if the buyer has before rejection taken physical possession of goods in which he does not have a security interest under the provisions of this Article (subsection (3) of Section 2-711), he is under a duty after rejection to hold them with reasonable care at the seller's disposition for a time sufficient to permit the seller to remove them; but

(c) the buyer has no further obligations with regard to goods rightfully rejected.

(3) The seller's rights with respect to goods wrongfully rejected are governed by the provisions of this Article on Seller's remedies in general (Section 2-703).

§ 2-603.   Merchant Buyer's Duties as to Rightfully Rejected Goods.

(1) Subject to any security interest in the buyer (subsection (3) of Section 2-711), when the seller has no agent or place of business at the market of rejection a merchant buyer is under a duty after rejection of goods in his possession or control to follow any reasonable instructions received from the seller with respect to the goods and in the absence of such instructions to make reasonable efforts to sell them for the seller's account if they are perishable or threaten to decline in value speedily. Instructions are not reasonable if on demand indemnity for expenses is not forthcoming.

(2) When the buyer sells goods under subsection (1), he is entitled to reimbursement from the seller or out of the proceeds for reasonable expenses of caring for and selling them, and if the expenses include no selling commission then to such commission as is usual

in the trade or if there is none to a reasonable sum not exceeding ten per cent on the gross proceeds.

(3) In complying with this section the buyer is held only to good faith and good faith conduct hereunder is neither acceptance nor conversion nor the basis of an action for damages.

§ 2-604.   Buyer's Options as to Salvage of Rightfully Rejected Goods.

Subject to the provisions of the immediately preceding section on perishables if the seller gives no instructions within a reasonable time after notification of rejection the buyer may store the rejected goods for the seller's account or reship them to him or resell them for the seller's account with reimbursement as provided in the preceding section. Such action is not acceptance or conversion.

§ 2-605.   Waiver of Buyer's Objections by Failure to Particularize.

(1) The buyer's failure to state in connection with rejection a particular defect which is ascertainable by reasonable inspection precludes him from relying on the unstated defect to justify rejection or to establish breach

(a) where the seller could have cured it if stated seasonally; or

(b) between merchants when the seller has after rejection made a request in writing for a full and final written statement of all defects on which the buyer proposes to rely.

(2) Payment against documents made without reservation of rights precludes recovery of the payment for defects apparent on the face of the documents.

§ 2-606.   What Constitutes Acceptance of Goods.

(1) Acceptance of goods occurs when the buyer

(a) after a reasonable opportunity to inspect the goods signifies to the seller that the goods are conforming or that he will take or retain them in spite of their nonconformity; or

(b) fails to make an effective rejection (subsection (1) of Section 2-602), but such acceptance does not occur until the buyer has had a reasonable opportunity to inspect them; or

(c) does any act inconsistent with the seller's ownership; but if such act is wrongful as against the seller it is an acceptance only if ratified by him.

(2) Acceptance of a part of any commercial unit is acceptance of that entire unit.

§ 2-607.   Effect of Acceptance; Notice of Breach; Burden of Establishing Breach After Acceptance; Notice of Claim or Litigation to Person Answerable Over.

(1) The buyer must pay at the contract rate for any goods accepted.

(2) Acceptance of goods by the buyer precludes rejection of the goods accepted and if made with knowledge of a non-conformity cannot be revoked because of it unless the acceptance was on the reasonable assumption that the non-conformity would be seasonably cured but acceptance does not of itself impair any other remedy provided by this Article for non-conformity.

(3) Where a tender has been accepted

(a) the buyer must within a reasonable time after he discovers or should have discovered any breach notify the seller of breach or be barred from any remedy; and

(b) if the claim is one for infringement or the like (subsection (3) of Section 2–312) and the buyer is sued as a result of such a breach he must so notify the seller within a reasonable time after he receives notice of the litigation or be barred from any remedy over for liability established by the litigation.

(4) The burden is on the buyer to establish any breach with respect to the goods accepted.

(5) Where the buyer is sued for breach of a warranty or other obligation for which his seller is answerable over

(a) he may give his seller written notice of the litigation. If the notice states that the seller may come in and defend and that if the seller does not do so he will be bound in any action against him by his buyer by any determination of fact common to the two litigations, then unless the seller after seasonable receipt of the notice does come in and defend he is so bound.

(b) if the claim is one for infringement or the like (subsection (3) of Section 2–312) the original seller may demand in writing that his buyer turn over to him control of the litigation including settlement or else be barred from any remedy over and if he also agrees to bear all expense and to satisfy any adverse judgment, then unless the buyer after seasonable receipt of the demand does turn over control the buyer is so barred.

(6) The provisions of subsections (3), (4) and (5) apply to any obligation of a buyer to hold the seller harmless against infringement or the like (subsection (3) of Section 2–312).

§ 2–608.   Revocation of Acceptance in Whole or in Part.

(1) The buyer may revoke his acceptance of a lot or commercial unit whose non-conformity substantially impairs its value to him if he has accepted it

(a) on the reasonable assumption that its nonconformity would be cured and it has not been seasonably cured; or

(b) without discovery of such non-conformity if his acceptance was reasonably induced either by the difficulty of discovery before acceptance or by the seller's assurances.

(2) Revocation of acceptance must occur within a reasonable time after the buyer discovers or should have discovered the ground for it and before any substantial change in condition of the goods which is not caused by their own defects. It is not effective until the buyer notifies the seller of it.

(3) A buyer who so revokes has the same rights and duties with regard to the goods involved as if he had rejected them.

§ 2–609.   Right to Adequate Assurance of Performance.

(1) A contract for sale imposes an obligation on each party that the other's expectation of receiving due performance will not be impaired. When reasonable grounds for insecurity arise with respect to the performance of either party the other may in writing demand adequate assurance of due performance and until he receives such assurance may if commercially reasonable suspend any performance for which he has not already received the agreed return.

(2) Between merchants the reasonableness of grounds for insecurity and the adequacy of any assurance offered shall be determined according to commercial standards.

(3) Acceptance of any improper delivery or payment does not prejudice the party's right to demand adequate assurance of future performance.

(4) After receipt of a justified demand failure to provide within a reasonable time not exceeding thirty days such assurance of due performance as is adequate under the circumstances of the particular case is a repudiation of the contract.

§ 2–610.   Anticipatory Repudiation.

When either party repudiates the contract with respect to a performance not yet due the loss of which will substantially impair the value of the contract to the other, the aggrieved party may

(a) for a commercially reasonable time await performance by the repudiating party; or

(b) resort to any remedy for breach (Section 2–703 or Section 2–711), even though he has notified the repudiating party that he would await the latter's performance and has urged retraction; and

(c) in either case suspend his own performance or proceed in accordance with the provisions of this Article on the seller's right to identify goods to the contract notwithstanding breach or to salvage unfinished goods (Section 2–704).

§ 2–611.   Retraction of Anticipatory Repudiation.

(1) Until the repudiating party's next performance is due he can retract his repudiation unless the aggrieved party has since the repudiation cancelled or materially changed his position or otherwise indicated that he considers the repudiation final.

(2) Retraction may be by any method which clearly indicates to the aggrieved party that the repudiating party intends to perform, but must include any assurance justifiably demanded under the provisions of this Article (Section 2–609).

(3) Retraction reinstates the repudiating party's rights under the contract with due excuse and allowance to the aggrieved party for any delay occasioned by the repudiation.

§ 2–612.   "Installment Contract"; Breach.

(1) An "installment contract" is one which requires or authorizes the delivery of goods in separate lots to be separately accepted, even though the contract contains a clause "each delivery is a separate contract" or its equivalent.

(2) The buyer may reject any installment which is non-conforming if the non-conformity substantially impairs the value of that installment and cannot be cured or if the non-conformity is a defect in the required documents; but if the non-conformity does not fall within subsection (3) and the seller gives adequate assurance of its cure the buyer must accept that installment.

(3) Whenever non-conformity or default with respect to one or more installments substantially impairs the value of the whole contract there is a breach of the whole. But the aggrieved party reinstates the contract if he accepts a non-conforming installment without seasonably notifying of cancellation or if he brings an action with respect only to past installments or demands performance as to future installments.

§ 2–613.   Casualty to Identified Goods.

Where the contract requires for its performance goods identified when the contract is made, and the goods suffer casualty without fault of either party before the risk of loss passes to the buyer, or in a proper case under a "no arrival, no sale" term (Section 2–324) then

(a) if the loss is total the contract is avoided; and

(b) if the loss is partial or the goods have so deteriorated as no longer to conform to the contract the buyer may nevertheless demand inspection and at his option either treat the contract as voided or accept the goods with due allowance from the contract price for the deterioration or the deficiency in quantity but without further right against the seller.

§ 2–614.   Substituted Performance.

(1) Where without fault of either party the agreed berthing, loading, or unloading facilities fail or an agreed type of carrier becomes unavailable or the agreed manner of delivery otherwise becomes commercially impracticable but a commercially reasonable substitute is available, such substitute performance must be tendered and accepted.

(2) If the agreed means or manner of payment fails because of domestic or foreign governmental regulation, the seller may withhold or stop delivery unless the buyer provides a means or manner of payment which is commercially a substantial equivalent. If delivery has already been taken, payment by the means or in the manner provided by the regulation discharges the buyer's obligation unless the regulation is discriminatory, oppressive or predatory.

§ 2–615.   Excuse by Failure of Presupposed Conditions.

Except so far as a seller may have assumed a greater obligation and subject to the preceding section on substituted performance:

(a) Delay in delivery or non-delivery in whole or in part by a seller who complies with paragraphs (b) and (c) is not a breach of his duty under a contract for sale if performance as agreed has been made impracticable by the occurrence of a contingency the nonoccurrence of which was a basic assumption on which the contract was made or by compliance in good faith with any applicable foreign or domestic governmental regulation or order whether or not it later proves to be invalid.

(b) Where the causes mentioned in paragraph (a) affect only a part of the seller's capacity to perform, he must allocate production and deliveries among his customers but may at his option include regular customers not then under contract as well as his own requirements for further manufacture. He may so allocate in any manner which is fair and reasonable.

(c) The seller must notify the buyer seasonably that there will be delay or non-delivery and, when allocation is required under paragraph (b), of the estimated quota thus made available for the buyer.

§ 2–616.   Procedure on Notice Claiming Excuse.

(1) Where the buyer receives notification of a material or indefinite delay or an allocation justified under the preceding section he may by written notification to the seller as to any delivery concerned, and where the prospective deficiency substantially impairs the value of the whole contract under the provisions of this Article relating to breach of installment contracts (Section 2–612), then also as to the whole,

   (a) terminate and thereby discharge any unexecuted portion of the contract; or

   (b) modify the contract by agreeing to take his available quota in substitution.

(2) If after receipt of such notification from the seller the buyer fails so to modify the contract within a reasonable time not exceeding thirty days the contract lapses with respect to any deliveries affected.

(3) The provisions of this section may not be negated by agreement except in so far as the seller has assumed a greater obligation under the preceding section.

Part 7   Remedies

§ 2–701.   Remedies for Breach of Collateral Contracts Not Impaired.

Remedies for breach of any obligation or promise collateral or ancillary to a contract for sale are not impaired by the provisions of this Article.

§ 2–702.   Seller's Remedies on Discovery of Buyer's Insolvency.

(1) Where the seller discovers the buyer to be insolvent he may refuse delivery except for cash including payment for all goods theretofore delivered under the contract, and stop delivery under this Article (Section 2–705).

(2) Where the seller discovers that the buyer has received goods on credit while insolvent he may reclaim the goods upon demand made within ten days after the receipt, but if misrepresentation of solvency has been made to the particular seller in writing within three months before delivery the ten day limitation does not apply. Except as provided in this subsection the seller may not base a right to reclaim goods on the buyer's fraudulent or innocent misrepresentation of solvency or of intent to pay.

(3) The seller's right to reclaim under subsection (2) is subject to the rights of a buyer in ordinary course or other good faith purchaser under this Article (Section 2–403). Successful reclamation of goods excludes all other remedies with respect to them.

§ 2–703.   Seller's Remedies in General.

Where the buyer wrongfully rejects or revokes acceptance of goods or fails to make a payment due on or before delivery or repudiates with respect to a part or the whole, then with respect to any goods directly affected and, if the breach is of the whole contract (Section 2–612), then also with respect to the whole undelivered balance, the aggrieved seller may

(a) withhold delivery of such goods;

(b) stop delivery by any bailee as hereafter provided (Section 2–705);

(c) proceed under the next section respecting goods still unidentified to the contract;

(d) resell and recover damages as hereafter provided (Section 2–706);

(e) recover damages for non-acceptance (Section 2–708) or in a proper case the price (Section 2–709);

(f) cancel.

§ 2–704.   Seller's Right to Identify Goods to the Contract Notwithstanding Breach or to Salvage Unfinished Goods.

(1) An aggrieved seller under the preceding section may

(a) identify to the contract conforming goods not already identified if at the time he learned of the breach they are in his possession or control;

(b) treat as the subject of resale goods which have demonstrably been intended for the particular contract even though those goods are unfinished.

(2) Where the goods are unfinished an aggrieved seller may in the exercise of reasonable commercial judgment for the purposes of avoiding loss and of effective realization either complete the manufacture and wholly identify the goods to the contract or cease manufacture and resell for scrap or salvage value or proceed in any other reasonable manner.

§ 2–705.   Seller's Stoppage of Delivery in Transit or Otherwise.

(1) The seller may stop delivery of goods in the possession of a carrier or other bailee when he discovers the buyer to be insolvent (Section 2–702) and may stop delivery of carload, truckload, planeload or larger shipments of express or freight when the buyer repudiates or fails to make a payment due before delivery or if for any other reason the seller has a right to withhold or reclaim the goods.

(2) As against such buyer the seller may stop delivery until

(a) receipt of the goods by the buyer; or

(b) acknowledgment to the buyer by any bailee of the goods except a carrier that the bailee holds the goods for the buyer; or

(c) such acknowledgment to the buyer by a carrier by reshipment or as warehouseman; or

(d) negotiation to the buyer of any negotiable document of title covering the goods.

(3) (a) To stop delivery the seller must so notify as to enable the bailee by reasonable diligence to prevent delivery of the goods.

(b) After such notification the bailee must hold and deliver the goods according to the directions of the seller but the seller is liable to the bailee for any ensuing charges or damages.

(c) If a negotiable document of title has been issued for goods the bailee is not obliged to obey a notification to stop until surrender of the document.

(d) A carrier who has issued a non-negotiable bill of lading is not obliged to obey a notification to stop received from a person other than the consignor.

§ 2–706.   Seller's Resale Including Contract for Resale.

(1) Under the conditions stated in Section 2–703 on seller's remedies, the seller may resell the goods concerned or the undelivered balance thereof. Where the resale is made in good faith and in a commercially reasonable manner the seller may recover the difference between the resale price and the contract price together with any incidental damages allowed under the provisions of this Article (Section 2–710), but less expenses saved in consequence of the buyer's breach.

(2) Except as otherwise provided in subsection (3) or unless otherwise agreed resale may be at public or private sale including sale by way of one or more contracts to sell or of identification to an existing contract of the seller. Sale may be as a unit or in parcels and at any time and place and on any terms but every aspect of the sale including the method, manner, time, place and terms must be commercially reasonable. The resale must be reasonably identified as referring to the broken contract, but it is not necessary that the goods be in existence or that any or all of them have been identified to the contract before the breach.

(3) Where the resale is at private sale the seller must give the buyer reasonable notification of his intention to resell.

(4) Where the resale is at public sale

(a) only identified goods can be sold except where there is a recognized market for a public sale of futures in goods of the kind; and

(b) it must be made at a usual place or market for public sale if one is reasonably available and except in the case of goods which are perishable or threaten to decline in value speedily the seller must give the buyer reasonable notice of the time and place of the resale; and

(c) if the goods are not to be within the view of those attending the sale the notification of sale must state the place where the goods are located and provide for their reasonable inspection by prospective bidders; and

(d) the seller may buy.

(5) A purchaser who buys in good faith at a resale takes the goods free of any rights of the original buyer even though the seller fails to comply with one or more of the requirements of this section.

(6) The seller is not accountable to the buyer for any profit made on any resale. A person in the position of a seller (Section 2–707) or a buyer who has rightfully rejected or justifiably revoked acceptance must account for any excess over the amount of his security interest, as hereinafter defined (subsection (3) of Section 2–711).

§ 2–707.   "Person in the Position of a Seller".

(1) A "person in the position of a seller" includes as against a principal an agent who has paid or become responsible for the price of goods on behalf of his principal or anyone who otherwise holds a security interest or other right in goods similar to that of a seller.

(2) A person in the position of a seller may as provided in this Article withhold or stop delivery (Section 2–705) and resell (Section 2–706) and recover incidental damages (Section 2–710).

§ 2–708.   Seller's Damages for Non-Acceptance or Repudiation.

(1) Subject to subsection (2) and to the provisions of this Article with respect to proof of market price (Section 2–723), the measure of damages for non-acceptance or repudiation by the buyer is the difference between the market price at the time and place for tender and the unpaid contract price together with any incidental damages provided in this Article (Section 2–710), but less expenses saved in consequence of the buyer's breach.

(2) If the measure of damages provided in subsection (1) is inadequate to put the seller in as good a position as performance would have

done then the measure of damages is the profit (including reasonable overhead) which the seller would have made from full performance by the buyer, together with any incidental damages provided in this Article (Section 2–710), due allowance for costs reasonably incurred and due credit for payments or proceeds of resale.

§ 2–709. Action for the Price.

(1) When the buyer fails to pay the price as it becomes due the seller may recover, together with any incidental damages under the next section, the price

(a) of goods accepted or of conforming goods lost or damaged within a commercially reasonable time after risk of their loss has passed to the buyer; and

(b) of goods identified to the contract if the seller is unable after reasonable effort to resell them at a reasonable price or the circumstances reasonably indicate that such effort will be unavailing.

(2) Where the seller sues for the price he must hold for the buyer any goods which have been identified to the contract and are still in his control except that if resale becomes possible he may resell them at any time prior to the collection of the judgment. The net proceeds of any such resale must be credited to the buyer and payment of the judgment entitles him to any goods not resold.

(3) After the buyer has wrongfully rejected or revoked acceptance of the goods or has failed to make a payment due or has repudiated (Section 2–610), a seller who is held not entitled to the price under this section shall nevertheless be awarded damages for non-acceptance under the preceding section.

§ 2–710. Seller's Incidental Damages.

Incidental damages to an aggrieved seller include any commercially reasonable charges, expenses or commissions incurred in stopping delivery, in the transportation, care and custody of goods after the buyer's breach, in connection with return or resale of the goods or otherwise resulting from the breach.

§ 2–711. Buyer's Remedies in General; Buyer's Security Interest in Rejected Goods.

(1) Where the seller fails to make delivery or repudiates or the buyer rightfully rejects or justifiably revokes acceptance then with respect to any goods involved, and with respect to the whole if the breach goes to the whole contract (Section 2–612), the buyer may cancel and whether or not he has done so may in addition to recovering so much of the price as has been paid

(a) "cover" and have damages under the next section as to all the goods affected whether or not they have been identified to the contract; or

(b) recover damages for non-delivery as provided in this Article (Section 2–713).

(2) Where the seller fails to deliver or repudiates the buyer may also

(a) if the goods have been identified recover them as provided in this Article (Section 2–502); or

(b) in a proper case obtain specific performance or replevy the goods as provided in this Article (Section 2–716).

(3) On rightful rejection or justifiable revocation of acceptance a buyer has a security interest in goods in his possession or control

for any payments made on their price and any expenses reasonably incurred in their inspection, receipt, transportation, care and custody and may hold such goods and resell them in like manner as an aggrieved seller (Section 2–706).

§ 2–712. "Cover"; Buyer's Procurement of Substitute Goods.

(1) After a breach within the preceding section the buyer may "cover" by making in good faith and without unreasonable delay any reasonable purchase of or contract to purchase goods in substitution for those due from the seller.

(2) The buyer may recover from the seller as damages the difference between the cost of cover and the contract price together with any incidental or consequential damages as hereinafter defined (Section 2–715), but less expenses saved in consequence of the seller's breach.

(3) Failure of the buyer to effect cover within this section does not bar him from any other remedy.

§ 2–713. Buyer's Damages for Non-Delivery or Repudiation.

(1) Subject to the provisions of this Article with respect to proof of market price (Section 2–723), the measure of damages for non-delivery or repudiation by the seller is the difference between the market price at the time when the buyer learned of the breach and the contract price together with any incidental and consequential damages provided in this Article (Section 2–715), but less expenses saved in consequence of the seller's breach.

(2) Market price is to be determined as of the place for tender or, in cases of rejection after arrival or revocation of acceptance, as of the place of arrival.

§ 2–714. Buyer's Damages for Breach in Regard to Accepted Goods.

(1) Where the buyer has accepted goods and given notification (subsection (3) of Section 2–607) he may recover as damages for any non-conformity of tender the loss resulting in the ordinary course of events from the seller's breach as determined in any manner which is reasonable.

(2) The measure of damages for breach of warranty is the difference at the time and place of acceptance between the value of the goods accepted and the value they would have had if they had been as warranted, unless special circumstances show proximate damages of a different amount.

(3) In a proper case any incidental and consequential damages under the next section may also be recovered.

§ 2–715. Buyer's Incidental and Consequential Damages.

(1) Incidental damages resulting from the seller's breach include expenses reasonably incurred in inspection, receipt, transportation and care and custody of goods rightfully rejected, any commercially reasonable charges, expenses or commissions in connection with effecting cover and any other reasonable expense incident to the delay or other breach.

(2) Consequential damages resulting from the seller's breach include

(a) any loss resulting from general or particular requirements and needs of which the seller at the time of contracting had reason to know and which could not reasonably be prevented by cover or otherwise; and

(b) injury to person or property proximately resulting from any breach of warranty.

§ 2–716.   Buyer's Right to Specific Performance or Replevin.

(1) Specific performance may be decreed where the goods are unique or in other proper circumstances.

(2) The decree for specific performance may include such terms and conditions as to payment of the price, damages, or other relief as the court may deem just.

(3) The buyer has a right of replevin for goods identified to the contract if after reasonable effort he is unable to effect cover for such goods or the circumstances reasonably indicate that such effort will be unavailing or if the goods have been shipped under reservation and satisfaction of the security interest in them has been made or tendered. In the case of goods bought for personal, family, or household purposes, the buyer's right of replevin vests upon acquisition of a special property, even if the seller had not then repudiated or failed to deliver.

As amended in 1999.

§ 2–717.   Deduction of Damages From the Price.

The buyer on notifying the seller of his intention to do so may deduct all or any part of the damages resulting from any breach of the contract from any part of the price still due under the same contract.

§ 2–718.   Liquidation or Limitation of Damages; Deposits.

(1) Damages for breach by either party may be liquidated in the agreement but only at an amount which is reasonable in the light of the anticipated or actual harm caused by the breach, the difficulties of proof of loss, and the inconvenience or nonfeasibility of otherwise obtaining an adequate remedy. A term fixing unreasonably large liquidated damages is void as a penalty.

(2) Where the seller justifiably withholds delivery of goods because of the buyer's breach, the buyer is entitled to restitution of any amount by which the sum of his payments exceeds

(a) the amount to which the seller is entitled by virtue of terms liquidating the seller's damages in accordance with subsection (1), or

(b) in the absence of such terms, twenty per cent of the value of the total performance for which the buyer is obligated under the contract or $500, whichever is smaller.

(3) The buyer's right to restitution under subsection (2) is subject to offset to the extent that the seller establishes

(a) a right to recover damages under the provisions of this Article other than subsection (1), and

(b) the amount or value of any benefits received by the buyer directly or indirectly by reason of the contract.

(4) Where a seller has received payment in goods their reasonable value or the proceeds of their resale shall be treated as payments for the purposes of subsection (2); but if the seller has notice of the buyer's breach before reselling goods received in part performance, his resale is subject to the conditions laid down in this Article on resale by an aggrieved seller (Section 2–706).

§ 2–719.   Contractual Modification or Limitation of Remedy.

(1) Subject to the provisions of subsections (2) and (3) of this section and of the preceding section on liquidation and limitation of damages,

(a) the agreement may provide for remedies in addition to or in substitution for those provided in this Article and may limit or alter the measure of damages recoverable under this Article, as by limiting the buyer's remedies to return of the goods and repayment of the price or to repair and replacement of nonconforming goods or parts; and

(b) resort to a remedy as provided is optional unless the remedy is expressly agreed to be exclusive, in which case it is the sole remedy.

(2) Where circumstances cause an exclusive or limited remedy to fail of its essential purpose, remedy may be had as provided in this Act.

(3) Consequential damages may be limited or excluded unless the limitation or exclusion is unconscionable. Limitation of consequential damages for injury to the person in the case of consumer goods is prima facie unconscionable but limitation of damages where the loss is commercial is not.

§ 2–720.   Effect of "Cancellation" or "Rescission" on Claims for Antecedent Breach.

Unless the contrary intention clearly appears, expressions of "cancellation" or "rescission" of the contract or the like shall not be construed as a renunciation or discharge of any claim in damages for an antecedent breach.

§ 2–721.   Remedies for Fraud.

Remedies for material misrepresentation or fraud include all remedies available under this Article for non-fraudulent breach. Neither rescission or a claim for rescission of the contract for sale nor rejection or return of the goods shall bar or be deemed inconsistent with a claim for damages or other remedy.

§ 2–722.   Who Can Sue Third Parties for Injury to Goods.

Where a third party so deals with goods which have been identified to a contract for sale as to cause actionable injury to a party to that contract

(a) a right of action against the third party is in either party to the contract for sale who has title to or a security interest or a special property or an insurable interest in the goods; and if the goods have been destroyed or converted a right of action is also in the party who either bore the risk of loss under the contract for sale or has since the injury assumed that risk as against the other;

(b) if at the time of the injury the party plaintiff did not bear the risk of loss as against the other party to the contract for sale and there is no arrangement between them for disposition of the recovery, his suit or settlement is, subject to his own interest, as a fiduciary for the other party to the contract;

(c) either party may with the consent of the other sue for the benefit of whom it may concern.

§ 2–723.   Proof of Market Price: Time and Place.

(1) If an action based on anticipatory repudiation comes to trial before the time for performance with respect to some or all of the goods, any damages based on market price (Section 2–708 or Section 2–713) shall be determined according to the price of such goods prevailing at the time when the aggrieved party learned of the repudiation.

(2) If evidence of a price prevailing at the times or places described in this Article is not readily available the price prevailing within any reasonable time before or after the time described or at any other

place which in commercial judgment or under usage of trade would serve as a reasonable substitute for the one described may be used, making any proper allowance for the cost of transporting the goods to or from such other place.

(3) Evidence of a relevant price prevailing at a time or place other than the one described in this Article offered by one party is not admissible unless and until he has given the other party such notice as the court finds sufficient to prevent unfair surprise.

§ 2–724.   Admissibility of Market Quotations.

Whenever the prevailing price or value of any goods regularly bought and sold in any established commodity market is in issue, reports in official publications or trade journals or in newspapers or periodicals of general circulation published as the reports of such market shall be admissible in evidence. The circumstances of the preparation of such a report may be shown to affect its weight but not its admissibility.

§ 2–725.   Statute of Limitations in Contracts for Sale.

(1) An action for breach of any contract for sale must be commenced within four years after the cause of action has accrued. By the original agreement the parties may reduce the period of limitation to not less than one year but may not extend it.

(2) A cause of action accrues when the breach occurs, regardless of the aggrieved party's lack of knowledge of the breach. A breach of warranty occurs when tender of delivery is made, except that where a warranty explicitly extends to future performance of the goods and discovery of the breach must await the time of such performance the cause of action accrues when the breach is or should have been discovered.

(3) Where an action commenced within the time limited by subsection (1) is so terminated as to leave available a remedy by another action for the same breach such other action may be commenced after the expiration of the time limited and within six months after the termination of the first action unless the termination resulted from voluntary discontinuance or from dismissal for failure or neglect to prosecute.

(4) This section does not alter the law on tolling of the statute of limitations nor does it apply to causes of action which have accrued before this Act becomes effective.

Article 2A
LEASES

Part 1   General Provisions

§ 2A–101.   Short Title.

This Article shall be known and may be cited as the Uniform Commercial Code—Leases.

§ 2A–102.   Scope.

This Article applies to any transaction, regardless of form, that creates a lease.

§ 2A–103.   Definitions and Index of Definitions.

(1) In this Article unless the context otherwise requires:

(a) "Buyer in ordinary course of business" means a person who in good faith and without knowledge that the sale to him [or her] is in violation of the ownership rights or security interest or leasehold interest of a third party in the goods buys in ordinary course from a person in the business of selling goods of that kind but does not include a pawnbroker. "Buying" may be for cash or by exchange of other property or on secured or unsecured credit and includes receiving goods or documents of title under a pre-existing contract for sale but does not include a transfer in bulk or as security for or in total or partial satisfaction of a money debt.

(b) "Cancellation" occurs when either party puts an end to the lease contract for default by the other party.

(c) "Commercial unit" means such a unit of goods as by commercial usage is a single whole for purposes of lease and division of which materially impairs its character or value on the market or in use. A commercial unit may be a single article, as a machine, or a set of articles, as a suite of furniture or a line of machinery, or a quantity, as a gross or carload, or any other unit treated in use or in the relevant market as a single whole.

(d) "Conforming" goods or performance under a lease contract means goods or performance that are in accordance with the obligations under the lease contract.

(e) "Consumer lease" means a lease that a lessor regularly engaged in the business of leasing or selling makes to a lessee who is an individual and who takes under the lease primarily for a personal, family, or household purpose [, if the total payments to be made under the lease contract, excluding payments for options to renew or buy, do not exceed $_____].

(f) "Fault" means wrongful act, omission, breach, or default.

(g) "Finance lease" means a lease with respect to which:

(i) the lessor does not select, manufacture or supply the goods;

(ii) the lessor acquires the goods or the right to possession and use of the goods in connection with the lease; and

(iii) one of the following occurs:

(A) the lessee receives a copy of the contract by which the lessor acquired the goods or the right to possession and use of the goods before signing the lease contract;

(B) the lessee's approval of the contract by which the lessor acquired the goods or the right to possession and use of the goods is a condition to effectiveness of the lease contract;

(C) the lessee, before signing the lease contract, receives an accurate and complete statement designating the promises and warranties, and any disclaimers of warranties, limitations or modifications of remedies, or liquidated damages, including those of a third party, such as the manufacturer of the goods, provided to the lessor by the person supplying the goods in connection with or as part of the contract by which the lessor acquired the goods or the right to possession and use of the goods; or

(D) if the lease is not a consumer lease, the lessor, before the lessee signs the lease contract, informs the lessee in writing (a) of the identity of the person supplying the goods to the lessor, unless the lessee has selected that person and directed the lessor to acquire the goods or the right to possession and use of the goods from that person, (b) that the lessee is entitled under this Article to any promises and warranties, including those of any third party, provided to the lessor by the person supplying the goods in connection with or as part of the contract by which the lessor acquired the goods or the right to possession and use of the goods, and (c) that the lessee may communicate with the person supplying the goods to the lessor and receive an accurate and complete statement of those promises and warranties, including any disclaimers and limitations of them or of remedies.

(h) "Goods" means all things that are movable at the time of identification to the lease contract, or are fixtures (Section 2A–309), but the term does not include money, documents, instruments, accounts, chattel paper, general intangibles, or minerals or the like, including oil and gas, before extraction. The term also includes the unborn young of animals.

(i) "Installment lease contract" means a lease contract that authorizes or requires the delivery of goods in separate lots to be separately accepted, even though the lease contract contains a clause "each delivery is a separate lease" or its equivalent.

(j) "Lease" means a transfer of the right to possession and use of goods for a term in return for consideration, but a sale, including a sale on approval or a sale or return, or retention or creation of a security interest is not a lease. Unless the context clearly indicates otherwise, the term includes a sublease.

(k) "Lease agreement" means the bargain, with respect to the lease, of the lessor and the lessee in fact as found in their language or by implication from other circumstances including course of dealing or usage of trade or course of performance as provided in this Article. Unless the context clearly indicates otherwise, the term includes a sublease agreement.

(l) "Lease contract" means the total legal obligation that results from the lease agreement as affected by this Article and any other applicable rules of law. Unless the context clearly indicates otherwise, the term includes a sublease contract.

(m) "Leasehold interest" means the interest of the lessor or the lessee under a lease contract.

(n) "Lessee" means a person who acquires the right to possession and use of goods under a lease. Unless the context clearly indicates otherwise, the term includes a sublessee.

(o) "Lessee in ordinary course of business" means a person who in good faith and without knowledge that the lease to him [or her] is in violation of the ownership rights or security interest or leasehold interest of a third party in the goods, leases in ordinary course from a person in the business of selling or leasing goods of that kind but does not include a pawnbroker. "Leasing" may be for cash or by exchange of other property or on secured or unsecured credit and includes receiving goods or documents of title under a pre-existing lease contract but does not include a transfer in bulk or as security for or in total or partial satisfaction of a money debt.

(p) "Lessor" means a person who transfers the right to possession and use of goods under a lease. Unless the context clearly indicates otherwise, the term includes a sublessor.

(q) "Lessor's residual interest" means the lessor's interest in the goods after expiration, termination, or cancellation of the lease contract.

(r) "Lien" means a charge against or interest in goods to secure payment of a debt or performance of an obligation, but the term does not include a security interest.

(s) "Lot" means a parcel or a single article that is the subject matter of a separate lease or delivery, whether or not it is sufficient to perform the lease contract.

(t) "Merchant lessee" means a lessee that is a merchant with respect to goods of the kind subject to the lease.

(u) "Present value" means the amount as of a date certain of one or more sums payable in the future, discounted to the date certain. The discount is determined by the interest rate specified by the parties if the rate was not manifestly unreasonable at the time the transaction was entered into; otherwise, the discount is determined by a commercially reasonable rate that takes into account the facts and circumstances of each case at the time the transaction was entered into.

(v) "Purchase" includes taking by sale, lease, mortgage, security interest, pledge, gift, or any other voluntary transaction creating an interest in goods.

(w) "Sublease" means a lease of goods the right to possession and use of which was acquired by the lessor as a lessee under an existing lease.

(x) "Supplier" means a person from whom a lessor buys or leases goods to be leased under a finance lease.

(y) "Supply contract" means a contract under which a lessor buys or leases goods to be leased.

(z) "Termination" occurs when either party pursuant to a power created by agreement or law puts an end to the lease contract otherwise than for default.

(2) Other definitions applying to this Article and the sections in which they appear are:

"Accessions". Section 2A–310(1).

"Construction mortgage". Section 2A–309(1)(d).

"Encumbrance". Section 2A–309(1)(e).

"Fixtures". Section 2A–309(1)(a).

"Fixture filing". Section 2A-309(1)(b).

"Purchase money lease". Section 2A-309(1)(c).

(3) The following definitions in other Articles apply to this Article:

"Accounts". Section 9-106.

"Between merchants". Section 2-104(3).

"Buyer". Section 2-103(1)(a).

"Chattel paper". Section 9-105(1)(b).

"Consumer goods". Section 9-109(1).

"Document". Section 9-105(1)(f).

"Entrusting". Section 2-403(3).

"General intangibles". Section 9-106.

"Good faith". Section 2-103(1)(b).

"Instrument". Section 9-105(1)(i).

"Merchant". Section 2-104(1).

"Mortgage". Section 9-105(1)(j).

"Pursuant to commitment". Section 9-105(1)(k).

"Receipt". Section 2-103(1)(c).

"Sale". Section 2-106(1).

"Sale on approval". Section 2-326.

"Sale or return". Section 2-326.

"Seller". Section 2-103(1)(d).

(4) In addition Article 1 contains general definitions and principles of construction and interpretation applicable throughout this Article.

As amended in 1990 and 1999.

§ 2A-104.   Leases Subject to Other Law.

(1) A lease, although subject to this Article, is also subject to any applicable:

    (a) certificate of title statute of this State: (list any certificate of title statutes covering automobiles, trailers, mobile homes, boats, farm tractors, and the like);

    (b) certificate of title statute of another jurisdiction (Section 2A-105); or

    (c) consumer protection statute of this State, or final consumer protection decision of a court of this State existing on the effective date of this Article.

(2) In case of conflict between this Article, other than Sections 2A-105, 2A-304(3), and 2A-305(3), and a statute or decision referred to in subsection (1), the statute or decision controls.

(3) Failure to comply with an applicable law has only the effect specified therein.

As amended in 1990.

§ 2A-105.   Territorial Application of
Article to Goods Covered by Certificate of Title.

Subject to the provisions of Sections 2A-304(3) and 2A-305(3), with respect to goods covered by a certificate of title issued under a statute of this State or of another jurisdiction, compliance and the effect of compliance or noncompliance with a certificate of title statute are governed by the law (including the conflict of laws rules) of the jurisdiction issuing the certificate until the earlier of

(a) surrender of the certificate, or (b) four months after the goods are removed from that jurisdiction and thereafter until a new certificate of title is issued by another jurisdiction.

§ 2A-106.   Limitation on Power of Parties to
Consumer Lease to Choose Applicable Law and Judicial Forum.

(1) If the law chosen by the parties to a consumer lease is that of a jurisdiction other than a jurisdiction in which the lessee resides at the time the lease agreement becomes enforceable or within 30 days thereafter or in which the goods are to be used, the choice is not enforceable.

(2) If the judicial forum chosen by the parties to a consumer lease is a forum that would not otherwise have jurisdiction over the lessee, the choice is not enforceable.

§ 2A-107.   Waiver or Renunciation of Claim or Right After Default.

Any claim or right arising out of an alleged default or breach of warranty may be discharged in whole or in part without consideration by a written waiver or renunciation signed and delivered by the aggrieved party.

§ 2A-108.   Unconscionability.

(1) If the court as a matter of law finds a lease contract or any clause of a lease contract to have been unconscionable at the time it was made the court may refuse to enforce the lease contract, or it may enforce the remainder of the lease contract without the unconscionable clause, or it may so limit the application of any unconscionable clause as to avoid any unconscionable result.

(2) With respect to a consumer lease, if the court as a matter of law finds that a lease contract or any clause of a lease contract has been induced by unconscionable conduct or that unconscionable conduct has occurred in the collection of a claim arising from a lease contract, the court may grant appropriate relief.

(3) Before making a finding of unconscionability under subsection (1) or (2), the court, on its own motion or that of a party, shall afford the parties a reasonable opportunity to present evidence as to the setting, purpose, and effect of the lease contract or clause thereof, or of the conduct.

(4) In an action in which the lessee claims unconscionability with respect to a consumer lease:

    (a) If the court finds unconscionability under subsection (1) or (2), the court shall award reasonable attorney's fees to the lessee.

    (b) If the court does not find unconscionability and the lessee claiming unconscionability has brought or maintained an action he [or she] knew to be groundless, the court shall award reasonable attorney's fees to the party against whom the claim is made.

    (c) In determining attorney's fees, the amount of the recovery on behalf of the claimant under subsections (1) and (2) is not controlling.

§ 2A-109.   Option to Accelerate at Will.

(1) A term providing that one party or his [or her] successor in interest may accelerate payment or performance or require collateral or additional collateral "at will" or "when he [or she] deems himself [or

herself] insecure" or in words of similar import must be construed to mean that he [or she] has power to do so only if he [or she] in good faith believes that the prospect of payment or performance is impaired.

(2) With respect to a consumer lease, the burden of establishing good faith under subsection (1) is on the party who exercised the power; otherwise the burden of establishing lack of good faith is on the party against whom the power has been exercised.

Part 2   Formation and Construction of Lease Contract

§ 2A–201.   Statute of Frauds.

(1) A lease contract is not enforceable by way of action or defense unless:

(a) the total payments to be made under the lease contract, excluding payments for options to renew or buy, are less than $1,000; or

(b) there is a writing, signed by the party against whom enforcement is sought or by that party's authorized agent, sufficient to indicate that a lease contract has been made between the parties and to describe the goods leased and the lease term.

(2) Any description of leased goods or of the lease term is sufficient and satisfies subsection (1)(b), whether or not it is specific, if it reasonably identifies what is described.

(3) A writing is not insufficient because it omits or incorrectly states a term agreed upon, but the lease contract is not enforceable under subsection (1)(b) beyond the lease term and the quantity of goods shown in the writing.

(4) A lease contract that does not satisfy the requirements of subsection (1), but which is valid in other respects, is enforceable:

(a) if the goods are to be specially manufactured or obtained for the lessee and are not suitable for lease or sale to others in the ordinary course of the lessor's business, and the lessor, before notice of repudiation is received and under circumstances that reasonably indicate that the goods are for the lessee, has made either a substantial beginning of their manufacture or commitments for their procurement;

(b) if the party against whom enforcement is sought admits in that party's pleading, testimony or otherwise in court that a lease contract was made, but the lease contract is not enforceable under this provision beyond the quantity of goods admitted; or

(c) with respect to goods that have been received and accepted by the lessee.

(5) The lease term under a lease contract referred to in subsection (4) is:

(a) if there is a writing signed by the party against whom enforcement is sought or by that party's authorized agent specifying the lease term, the term so specified;

(b) if the party against whom enforcement is sought admits in that party's pleading, testimony, or otherwise in court a lease term, the term so admitted; or

(c) a reasonable lease term.

§ 2A–202.   Final Written Expression: Parol or Extrinsic Evidence.

Terms with respect to which the confirmatory memoranda of the parties agree or which are otherwise set forth in a writing intended by the parties as a final expression of their agreement with respect to such terms as are included therein may not be contradicted by evidence of any prior agreement or of a contemporaneous oral agreement but may be explained or supplemented:

(a) by course of dealing or usage of trade or by course of performance; and

(b) by evidence of consistent additional terms unless the court finds the writing to have been intended also as a complete and exclusive statement of the terms of the agreement.

§ 2A–203.   Seals Inoperative.

The affixing of a seal to a writing evidencing a lease contract or an offer to enter into a lease contract does not render the writing a sealed instrument and the law with respect to sealed instruments does not apply to the lease contract or offer.

§ 2A–204.   Formation in General.

(1) A lease contract may be made in any manner sufficient to show agreement, including conduct by both parties which recognizes the existence of a lease contract.

(2) An agreement sufficient to constitute a lease contract may be found although the moment of its making is undetermined.

(3) Although one or more terms are left open, a lease contract does not fail for indefiniteness if the parties have intended to make a lease contract and there is a reasonably certain basis for giving an appropriate remedy.

§ 2A–205.   Firm Offers.

An offer by a merchant to lease goods to or from another person in a signed writing that by its terms gives assurance it will be held open is not revocable, for lack of consideration, during the time stated or, if no time is stated, for a reasonable time, but in no event may the period of irrevocability exceed 3 months. Any such term of assurance on a form supplied by the offeree must be separately signed by the offeror.

§ 2A–206.   Offer and Acceptance in Formation of Lease Contract.

(1) Unless otherwise unambiguously indicated by the language or circumstances, an offer to make a lease contract must be construed as inviting acceptance in any manner and by any medium reasonable in the circumstances.

(2) If the beginning of a requested performance is a reasonable mode of acceptance, an offeror who is not notified of acceptance within a reasonable time may treat the offer as having lapsed before acceptance.

§ 2A–207.   Course of Performance or Practical Construction.

(1) If a lease contract involves repeated occasions for performance by either party with knowledge of the nature of the performance and opportunity for objection to it by the other, any course of performance accepted or acquiesced in without objection is relevant to determine the meaning of the lease agreement.

(2) The express terms of a lease agreement and any course of performance, as well as any course of dealing and usage of trade, must be construed whenever reasonable as consistent with each other; but if that construction is unreasonable, express terms control course of performance, course of performance controls both course of dealing and usage of trade, and course of dealing controls usage of trade.

(3) Subject to the provisions of Section 2A–208 on modification and waiver, course of performance is relevant to show a waiver or modification of any term inconsistent with the course of performance.

§ 2A–208.   Modification, Rescission and Waiver.

(1) An agreement modifying a lease contract needs no consideration to be binding.

(2) A signed lease agreement that excludes modification or rescission except by a signed writing may not be otherwise modified or rescinded, but, except as between merchants, such a requirement on a form supplied by a merchant must be separately signed by the other party.

(3) Although an attempt at modification or rescission does not satisfy the requirements of subsection (2), it may operate as a waiver.

(4) A party who has made a waiver affecting an executory portion of a lease contract may retract the waiver by reasonable notification received by the other party that strict performance will be required of any term waived, unless the retraction would be unjust in view of a material change of position in reliance on the waiver.

§ 2A–209.   Lessee under Finance Lease as Beneficiary of Supply Contract.

(1) The benefit of the supplier's promises to the lessor under the supply contract and of all warranties, whether express or implied, including those of any third party provided in connection with or as part of the supply contract, extends to the lessee to the extent of the lessee's leasehold interest under a finance lease related to the supply contract, but is subject to the terms warranty and of the supply contract and all defenses or claims arising therefrom.

(2) The extension of the benefit of supplier's promises and of warranties to the lessee (Section 2A–209(1)) does not: (i) modify the rights and obligations of the parties to the supply contract, whether arising therefrom or otherwise, or (ii) impose any duty or liability under the supply contract on the lessee.

(3) Any modification or rescission of the supply contract by the supplier and the lessor is effective between the supplier and the lessee unless, before the modification or rescission, the supplier has received notice that the lessee has entered into a finance lease related to the supply contract. If the modification or rescission is effective between the supplier and the lessee, the lessor is deemed to have assumed, in addition to the obligations of the lessor to the lessee under the lease contract, promises of the supplier to the lessor and warranties that were so modified or rescinded as they existed and were available to the lessee before modification or rescission.

(4) In addition to the extension of the benefit of the supplier's promises and of warranties to the lessee under subsection (1), the lessee retains all rights that the lessee may have against the supplier which arise from an agreement between the lessee and the supplier or under other law.

As amended in 1990.

§ 2A–210.   Express Warranties.

(1) Express warranties by the lessor are created as follows:

(a) Any affirmation of fact or promise made by the lessor to the lessee which relates to the goods and becomes part of the basis of the bargain creates an express warranty that the goods will conform to the affirmation or promise.

(b) Any description of the goods which is made part of the basis of the bargain creates an express warranty that the goods will conform to the description.

(c) Any sample or model that is made part of the basis of the bargain creates an express warranty that the whole of the goods will conform to the sample or model.

(2) It is not necessary to the creation of an express warranty that the lessor use formal words, such as "warrant" or "guarantee," or that the lessor have a specific intention to make a warranty, but an affirmation merely of the value of the goods or a statement purporting to be merely the lessor's opinion or commendation of the goods does not create a warranty.

§ 2A–211.   Warranties Against Interference and Against Infringement; Lessee's Obligation Against Infringement.

(1) There is in a lease contract a warranty that for the lease term no person holds a claim to or interest in the goods that arose from an act or omission of the lessor, other than a claim by way of infringement or the like, which will interfere with the lessee's enjoyment of its leasehold interest.

(2) Except in a finance lease there is in a lease contract by a lessor who is a merchant regularly dealing in goods of the kind a warranty that the goods are delivered free of the rightful claim of any person by way of infringement or the like.

(3) A lessee who furnishes specifications to a lessor or a supplier shall hold the lessor and the supplier harmless against any claim by way of infringement or the like that arises out of compliance with the specifications.

§ 2A–212.   Implied Warranty of Merchantability.

(1) Except in a finance lease, a warranty that the goods will be merchantable is implied in a lease contract if the lessor is a merchant with respect to goods of that kind.

(2) Goods to be merchantable must be at least such as

(a) pass without objection in the trade under the description in the lease agreement;

(b) in the case of fungible goods, are of fair average quality within the description;

(c) are fit for the ordinary purposes for which goods of that type are used;

(d) run, within the variation permitted by the lease agreement, of even kind, quality, and quantity within each unit and among all units involved;

(e) are adequately contained, packaged, and labeled as the lease agreement may require; and

(f) conform to any promises or affirmations of fact made on the container or label.

(3) Other implied warranties may arise from course of dealing or usage of trade.

§ 2A–213. Implied Warranty of Fitness for Particular Purpose.

Except in a finance of lease, if the lessor at the time the lease contract is made has reason to know of any particular purpose for which the goods are required and that the lessee is relying on the lessor's skill or judgment to select or furnish suitable goods, there is in the lease contract an implied warranty that the goods will be fit for that purpose.

§ 2A–214. Exclusion or Modification of Warranties.

(1) Words or conduct relevant to the creation of an express warranty and words or conduct tending to negate or limit a warranty must be construed wherever reasonable as consistent with each other; but, subject to the provisions of Section 2A–202 on parol or extrinsic evidence, negation or limitation is inoperative to the extent that the construction is unreasonable.

(2) Subject to subsection (3), to exclude or modify the implied warranty of merchantability or any part of it the language must mention "merchantability", be by a writing, and be conspicuous. Subject to subsection (3), to exclude or modify any implied warranty of fitness the exclusion must be by a writing and be conspicuous. Language to exclude all implied warranties of fitness is sufficient if it is in writing, is conspicuous and states, for example, "There is no warranty that the goods will be fit for a particular purpose".

(3) Notwithstanding subsection (2), but subject to subsection (4),

(a) unless the circumstances indicate otherwise, all implied warranties are excluded by expressions like "as is" or "with all faults" or by other language that in common understanding calls the lessee's attention to the exclusion of warranties and makes plain that there is no implied warranty, if in writing and conspicuous;

(b) if the lessee before entering into the lease contract has examined the goods or the sample or model as fully as desired or has refused to examine the goods, there is no implied warranty with regard to defects that an examination ought in the circumstances to have revealed; and

(c) an implied warranty may also be excluded or modified by course of dealing, course of performance, or usage of trade.

(4) To exclude or modify a warranty against interference or against infringement (Section 2A–211) or any part of it, the language must be specific, be by a writing, and be conspicuous, unless the circumstances, including course of performance, course of dealing, or usage of trade, give the lessee reason to know that the goods are being leased subject to a claim or interest of any person.

§ 2A–215. Cumulation and Conflict of Warranties Express or Implied.

Warranties, whether express or implied, must be construed as consistent with each other and as cumulative, but if that construction is unreasonable, the intention of the parties determines which warranty is dominant. In ascertaining that intention the following rules apply:

(a) Exact or technical specifications displace an inconsistent sample or model or general language of description.

(b) A sample from an existing bulk displaces inconsistent general language of description.

(c) Express warranties displace inconsistent implied warranties other than an implied warranty of fitness for a particular purpose.

§ 2A–216. Third-Party Beneficiaries of Express and Implied Warranties.

Alternative A

A warranty to or for the benefit of a lessee under this Article, whether express or implied, extends to any natural person who is in the family or household of the lessee or who is a guest in the lessee's home if it is reasonable to expect that such person may use, consume, or be affected by the goods and who is injured in person by breach of the warranty. This section does not displace principles of law and equity that extend a warranty to or for the benefit of a lessee to other persons. The operation of this section may not be excluded, modified, or limited, but an exclusion, modification, or limitation of the warranty, including any with respect to rights and remedies, effective against the lessee is also effective against any beneficiary designated under this section.

Alternative B

A warranty to or for the benefit of a lessee under this Article, whether express or implied, extends to any natural person who may reasonably be expected to use, consume, or be affected by the goods and who is injured in person by breach of the warranty. This section does not displace principles of law and equity that extend a warranty to or for the benefit of a lessee to other persons. The operation of this section may not be excluded, modified, or limited, but an exclusion, modification, or limitation of the warranty, including any with respect to rights and remedies, effective against the lessee is also effective against the beneficiary designated under this section.

Alternative C

A warranty to or for the benefit of a lessee under this Article, whether express or implied, extends to any person who may reasonably be expected to use, consume, or be affected by the goods and who is injured by breach of the warranty. The operation of this section may not be excluded, modified, or limited with respect to injury to the person of an individual to whom the warranty extends, but an exclusion, modification, or limitation of the warranty, including any with respect to rights and remedies, effective against the lessee is also effective against the beneficiary designated under this section.

§ 2A–217. Identification.

Identification of goods as goods to which a lease contract refers may be made at any time and in any manner explicitly agreed to by the parties. In the absence of explicit agreement, identification occurs:

(a) when the lease contract is made if the lease contract is for a lease of goods that are existing and identified;

(b) when the goods are shipped, marked, or otherwise designated by the lessor as goods to which the lease contract refers, if the lease contract is for a lease of goods that are not existing and identified; or

(c) when the young are conceived, if the lease contract is for a lease of unborn young of animals.

§ 2A–218.   Insurance and Proceeds.

(1) A lessee obtains an insurable interest when existing goods are identified to the lease contract even though the goods identified are nonconforming and the lessee has an option to reject them.

(2) If a lessee has an insurable interest only by reason of the lessor's identification of the goods, the lessor, until default or insolvency or notification to the lessee that identification is final, may substitute other goods for those identified.

(3) Notwithstanding a lessee's insurable interest under subsections (1) and (2), the lessor retains an insurable interest until an option to buy has been exercised by the lessee and risk of loss has passed to the lessee.

(4) Nothing in this section impairs any insurable interest recognized under any other statute or rule of law.

(5) The parties by agreement may determine that one or more parties have an obligation to obtain and pay for insurance covering the goods and by agreement may determine the beneficiary of the proceeds of the insurance.

§ 2A–219.   Risk of Loss.

(1) Except in the case of a finance lease, risk of loss is retained by the lessor and does not pass to the lessee. In the case of a finance lease, risk of loss passes to the lessee.

(2) Subject to the provisions of this Article on the effect of default on risk of loss (Section 2A–220), if risk of loss is to pass to the lessee and the time of passage is not stated, the following rules apply:

(a) If the lease contract requires or authorizes the goods to be shipped by carrier

(i) and it does not require delivery at a particular destination, the risk of loss passes to the lessee when the goods are duly delivered to the carrier; but

(ii) if it does require delivery at a particular destination and the goods are there duly tendered while in the possession of the carrier, the risk of loss passes to the lessee when the goods are there duly so tendered as to enable the lessee to take delivery.

(b) If the goods are held by a bailee to be delivered without being moved, the risk of loss passes to the lessee on acknowledgment by the bailee of the lessee's right to possession of the goods.

(c) In any case not within subsection (a) or (b), the risk of loss passes to the lessee on the lessee's receipt of the goods if the lessor, or, in the case of a finance lease, the supplier, is a merchant; otherwise the risk passes to the lessee on tender of delivery.

§ 2A–220.   Effect of Default on Risk of Loss.

(1) Where risk of loss is to pass to the lessee and the time of passage is not stated:

(a) If a tender or delivery of goods so fails to conform to the lease contract as to give a right of rejection, the risk of their loss remains with the lessor, or, in the case of a finance lease, the supplier, until cure or acceptance.

(b) If the lessee rightfully revokes acceptance, he [or she], to the extent of any deficiency in his [or her] effective insurance coverage, may treat the risk of loss as having remained with the lessor from the beginning.

(2) Whether or not risk of loss is to pass to the lessee, if the lessee as to conforming goods already identified to a lease contract repudiates or is otherwise in default under the lease contract, the lessor, or, in the case of a finance lease, the supplier, to the extent of any deficiency in his [or her] effective insurance coverage may treat the risk of loss as resting on the lessee for a commercially reasonable time.

§ 2A–221.   Casualty to Identified Goods.

If a lease contract requires goods identified when the lease contract is made, and the goods suffer casualty without fault of the lessee, the lessor or the supplier before delivery, or the goods suffer casualty before risk of loss passes to the lessee pursuant to the lease agreement or Section 2A–219, then:

(a) if the loss is total, the lease contract is avoided; and

(b) if the loss is partial or the goods have so deteriorated as to no longer conform to the lease contract, the lessee may nevertheless demand inspection and at his [or her] option either treat the lease contract as avoided or, except in a finance lease that is not a consumer lease, accept the goods with due allowance from the rent payable for the balance of the lease term for the deterioration or the deficiency in quantity but without further right against the lessor.

Part 3   Effect of Lease Contract

§ 2A–301.   Enforceability of Lease Contract.

Except as otherwise provided in this Article, a lease contract is effective and enforceable according to its terms between the parties, against purchasers of the goods and against creditors of the parties.

§ 2A–302.   Title to and Possession of Goods.

Except as otherwise provided in this Article, each provision of this Article applies whether the lessor or a third party has title to the goods, and whether the lessor, the lessee, or a third party has possession of the goods, notwithstanding any statute or rule of law that possession or the absence of possession is fraudulent.

§ 2A–303.   Alienability of Party's Interest Under Lease Contract or of Lessor's Residual Interest in Goods; Delegation of Performance; Transfer of Rights.

(1) As used in this section, "creation of a security interest" includes the sale of a lease contract that is subject to Article 9, Secured Transactions, by reason of Section 9–109(a)(3).

(2) Except as provided in subsections (3) and Section 9–407, a provision in a lease agreement which (i) prohibits the voluntary or involuntary transfer, including a transfer by sale, sublease, creation or enforcement of a security interest, or attachment, levy, or other judicial process, of an interest of a party under the lease contract or of the lessor's residual interest in the goods, or (ii) makes such a transfer an event of default, gives rise to the rights and remedies provided in subsection (4), but a transfer that is prohibited or is an event of default under the lease agreement is otherwise effective.

(3) A provision in a lease agreement which (i) prohibits a transfer of a right to damages for default with respect to the whole lease contract or of a right to payment arising out of the transferor's due performance of the transferor's entire obligation, or (ii) makes such a transfer an event of default, is not enforceable, and such a transfer is not a transfer that materially impairs the propsect of obtaining return performance by, materially changes the duty of, or materially increases the burden or risk imposed on, the other party to the lease contract within the purview of subsection (4).

(4) Subject to subsection (3) and Section 9–407:

(a) if a transfer is made which is made an event of default under a lease agreement, the party to the lease contract not making the transfer, unless that party waives the default or otherwise agrees, has the rights and remedies described in Section 2A–501(2);

(b) if paragraph (a) is not applicable and if a transfer is made that (i) is prohibited under a lease agreement or (ii) materially impairs the prospect of obtaining return performance by, materially changes the duty of, or materially increases the burden or risk imposed on, the other party to the lease contract, unless the party not making the transfer agrees at any time to the transfer in the lease contract or otherwise, then, except as limited by contract, (i) the transferor is liable to the party not making the transfer for damages caused by the transfer to the extent that the damages could not reasonably be prevented by the party not making the transfer and (ii) a court having jurisdiction may grant other appropriate relief, including cancellation of the lease contract or an injunction against the transfer.

(5) A transfer of "the lease" or of "all my rights under the lease", or a transfer in similar general terms, is a transfer of rights and, unless the language or the circumstances, as in a transfer for security, indicate the contrary, the transfer is a delegation of duties by the transferor to the transferee. Acceptance by the transferee constitutes a promise by the transferee to perform those duties. The promise is enforceable by either the transferor or the other party to the lease contract.

(6) Unless otherwise agreed by the lessor and the lessee, a delegation of performance does not relieve the transferor as against the other party of any duty to perform or of any liability for default.

(7) In a consumer lease, to prohibit the transfer of an interest of a party under the lease contract or to make a transfer an event of default, the language must be specific, by a writing, and conspicuous.
As amended in 1990 and 1999.

§ 2A–304.   Subsequent Lease of Goods by Lessor.

(1) Subject to Section 2A–303, a subsequent lessee from a lessor of goods under an existing lease contract obtains, to the extent of the leasehold interest transferred, the leasehold interest in the goods that the lessor had or had power to transfer, and except as provided in subsection (2) and Section 2A–527(4), takes subject to the existing lease contract. A lessor with voidable title has power to transfer a good leasehold interest to a good faith subsequent lessee for value, but only to the extent set forth in the preceding sentence. If goods have been delivered under a transaction of purchase the lessor has that power even though:

(a) the lessor's transferor was deceived as to the identity of the lessor;

(b) the delivery was in exchange for a check which is later dishonored;

(c) it was agreed that the transaction was to be a "cash sale"; or

(d) the delivery was procured through fraud punishable as larcenous under the criminal law.

(2) A subsequent lessee in the ordinary course of business from a lessor who is a merchant dealing in goods of that kind to whom the goods were entrusted by the existing lessee of that lessor before the interest of the subsequent lessee became enforceable against that lessor obtains, to the extent of the leasehold interest transferred, all of that lessor's and the existing lessee's rights to the goods, and takes free of the existing lease contract.

(3) A subsequent lessee from the lessor of goods that are subject to an existing lease contract and are covered by a certificate of title issued under a statute of this State or of another jurisdiction takes no greater rights than those provided both by this section and by the certificate of title statute.
As amended in 1990.

§ 2A–305.   Sale or Sublease of Goods by Lessee.

(1) Subject to the provisions of Section 2A–303, a buyer or sublessee from the lessee of goods under an existing lease contract obtains, to the extent of the interest transferred, the leasehold interest in the goods that the lessee had or had power to transfer, and except as provided in subsection (2) and Section 2A–511(4), takes subject to the existing lease contract. A lessee with a voidable leasehold interest has power to transfer a good leasehold interest to a good faith buyer for value or a good faith sublessee for value, but only to the extent set forth in the preceding sentence. When goods have been delivered under a transaction of lease the lessee has that power even though:

(a) the lessor was deceived as to the identity of the lessee;

(b) the delivery was in exchange for a check which is later dishonored; or

(c) the delivery was procured through fraud punishable as larcenous under the criminal law.

(2) A buyer in the ordinary course of business or a sublessee in the ordinary course of business from a lessee who is a merchant dealing in goods of that kind to whom the goods were entrusted by

the lessor obtains, to the extent of the interest transferred, all of the lessor's and lessee's rights to the goods, and takes free of the existing lease contract.

(3) A buyer or sublessee from the lessee of goods that are subject to an existing lease contract and are covered by a certificate of title issued under a statute of this State or of another jurisdiction takes no greater rights than those provided both by this section and by the certificate of title statute.

§ 2A–306.　Priority of Certain Liens Arising by Operation of Law.

If a person in the ordinary course of his [or her] business furnishes services or materials with respect to goods subject to a lease contract, a lien upon those goods in the possession of that person given by statute or rule of law for those materials or services takes priority over any interest of the lessor or lessee under the lease contract or this Article unless the lien is created by statute and the statute provides otherwise or unless the lien is created by rule of law and the rule of law provides otherwise.

§ 2A–307.　Priority of Liens Arising by Attachment or Levy on, Security Interests in, and Other Claims to Goods.

(1) Except as otherwise provided in Section 2A–306, a creditor of a lessee takes subject to the lease contract.

(2) Except as otherwise provided in subsection (3) and in Sections 2A–306 and 2A–308, a creditor of a lessor takes subject to the lease contract unless the creditor holds a lien that attached to the goods before the lease contract became enforceable.

(3) Except as otherwise provided in Sections 9–317, 9–321, and 9–323, a lessee takes a leasehold interest subject to a security interest held by a creditor of the lessor.

As amended in 1990 and 1999.

§ 2A–308.　Special Rights of Creditors.

(1) A creditor of a lessor in possession of goods subject to a lease contract may treat the lease contract as void if as against the creditor retention of possession by the lessor is fraudulent under any statute or rule of law, but retention of possession in good faith and current course of trade by the lessor for a commercially reasonable time after the lease contract becomes enforceable is not fraudulent.

(2) Nothing in this Article impairs the rights of creditors of a lessor if the lease contract (a) becomes enforceable, not in current course of trade but in satisfaction of or as security for a pre-existing claim for money, security, or the like, and (b) is made under circumstances which under any statute or rule of law apart from this Article would constitute the transaction a fraudulent transfer or voidable preference.

(3) A creditor of a seller may treat a sale or an identification of goods to a contract for sale as void if as against the creditor retention of possession by the seller is fraudulent under any statute or rule of law, but retention of possession of the goods pursuant to a lease contract entered into by the seller as lessee and the buyer as lessor in connection with the sale or identification of the goods is not fraudulent if the buyer bought for value and in good faith.

§ 2A–309.　Lessor's and Lessee's Rights When Goods Become Fixtures.

(1) In this section:

(a) goods are "fixtures" when they become so related to particular real estate that an interest in them arises under real estate law;

(b) a "fixture filing" is the filing, in the office where a mortgage on the real estate would be filed or recorded, of a financing statement covering goods that are or are to become fixtures and conforming to the requirements of Section 9–502(a) and (b);

(c) a lease is a "purchase money lease" unless the lessee has possession or use of the goods or the right to possession or use of the goods before the lease agreement is enforceable;

(d) a mortgage is a "construction mortgage" to the extent it secures an obligation incurred for the construction of an improvement on land including the acquisition cost of the land, if the recorded writing so indicates; and

(e) "encumbrance" includes real estate mortgages and other liens on real estate and all other rights in real estate that are not ownership interests.

(2) Under this Article a lease may be of goods that are fixtures or may continue in goods that become fixtures, but no lease exists under this Article of ordinary building materials incorporated into an improvement on land.

(3) This Article does not prevent creation of a lease of fixtures pursuant to real estate law.

(4) The perfected interest of a lessor of fixtures has priority over a conflicting interest of an encumbrancer or owner of the real estate if:

(a) the lease is a purchase money lease, the conflicting interest of the encumbrancer or owner arises before the goods become fixtures, the interest of the lessor is perfected by a fixture filing before the goods become fixtures or within ten days thereafter, and the lessee has an interest of record in the real estate or is in possession of the real estate; or

(b) the interest of the lessor is perfected by a fixture filing before the interest of the encumbrancer or owner is of record, the lessor's interest has priority over any conflicting interest of a predecessor in title of the encumbrancer or owner, and the lessee has an interest of record in the real estate or is in possession of the real estate.

(5) The interest of a lessor of fixtures, whether or not perfected, has priority over the conflicting interest of an encumbrancer or owner of the real estate if:

(a) the fixtures are readily removable factory or office machines, readily removable equipment that is not primarily used or leased for use in the operation of the real estate, or readily removable replacements of domestic appliances that are goods subject to a consumer lease, and before the goods become fixtures the lease contract is enforceable; or

(b) the conflicting interest is a lien on the real estate obtained by legal or equitable proceedings after the lease contract is enforceable; or

(c) the encumbrancer or owner has consented in writing to the lease or has disclaimed an interest in the goods as fixtures; or

(d) the lessee has a right to remove the goods as against the encumbrancer or owner. If the lessee's right to remove terminates, the priority of the interest of the lessor continues for a reasonable time.

(6) Notwithstanding paragraph (4)(a) but otherwise subject to subsections (4) and (5), the interest of a lessor of fixtures, including the lessor's residual interest, is subordinate to the conflicting interest of an encumbrancer of the real estate under a construction mortgage recorded before the goods become fixtures if the goods become fixtures before the completion of the construction. To the extent given to refinance a construction mortgage, the conflicting interest of an encumbrancer of the real estate under a mortgage has this priority to the same extent as the encumbrancer of the real estate under the construction mortgage.

(7) In cases not within the preceding subsections, priority between the interest of a lessor of fixtures, including the lessor's residual interest, and the conflicting interest of an encumbrancer or owner of the real estate who is not the lessee is determined by the priority rules governing conflicting interests in real estate.

(8) If the interest of a lessor of fixtures, including the lessor's residual interest, has priority over all conflicting interests of all owners and encumbrancers of the real estate, the lessor or the lessee may (i) on default, expiration, termination, or cancellation of the lease agreement but subject to the agreement and this Article, or (ii) if necessary to enforce other rights and remedies of the lessor or lessee under this Article, remove the goods from the real estate, free and clear of all conflicting interests of all owners and encumbrancers of the real estate, but the lessor or lessee must reimburse any encumbrancer or owner of the real estate who is not the lessee and who has not otherwise agreed for the cost of repair of any physical injury, but not for any diminution in value of the real estate caused by the absence of the goods removed or by any necessity of replacing them. A person entitled to reimbursement may refuse permission to remove until the party seeking removal gives adequate security for the performance of this obligation.

(9) Even though the lease agreement does not create a security interest, the interest of a lessor of fixtures, including the lessor's residual interest, is perfected by filing a financing statement as a fixture filing for leased goods that are or are to become fixtures in accordance with the relevant provisions of the Article on Secured Transactions (Article 9).

As amended in 1990 and 1999.

§ 2A–310.   Lessor's and Lessee's Rights When Goods Become Accessions.

(1) Goods are "accessions" when they are installed in or affixed to other goods.

(2) The interest of a lessor or a lessee under a lease contract entered into before the goods became accessions is superior to all interests in the whole except as stated in subsection (4).

(3) The interest of a lessor or a lessee under a lease contract entered into at the time or after the goods became accessions is superior to

all subsequently acquired interests in the whole except as stated in subsection (4) but is subordinate to interests in the whole existing at the time the lease contract was made unless the holders of such interests in the whole have in writing consented to the lease or disclaimed an interest in the goods as part of the whole.

(4) The interest of a lessor or a lessee under a lease contract described in subsection (2) or (3) is subordinate to the interest of

(a) a buyer in the ordinary course of business or a lessee in the ordinary course of business of any interest in the whole acquired after the goods became accessions; or

(b) a creditor with a security interest in the whole perfected before the lease contract was made to the extent that the creditor makes subsequent advances without knowledge of the lease contract.

(5) When under subsections (2) or (3) and (4) a lessor or a lessee of accessions holds an interest that is superior to all interests in the whole, the lessor or the lessee may (a) on default, expiration, termination, or cancellation of the lease contract by the other party but subject to the provisions of the lease contract and this Article, or (b) if necessary to enforce his [or her] other rights and remedies under this Article, remove the goods from the whole, free and clear of all interests in the whole, but he [or she] must reimburse any holder of an interest in the whole who is not the lessee and who has not otherwise agreed for the cost of repair of any physical injury but not for any diminution in value of the whole caused by the absence of the goods removed or by any necessity for replacing them. A person entitled to reimbursement may refuse permission to remove until the party seeking removal gives adequate security for the performance of this obligation.

§ 2A–311.   Priority Subject to Subordination.

Nothing in this Article prevents subordination by agreement by any person entitled to priority.

As added in 1990.

Part 4   Performance of Lease Contract: Repudiated, Substituted and Excused

§ 2A–401.   Insecurity: Adequate Assurance of Performance.

(1) A lease contract imposes an obligation on each party that the other's expectation of receiving due performance will not be impaired.

(2) If reasonable grounds for insecurity arise with respect to the performance of either party, the insecure party may demand in writing adequate assurance of due performance. Until the insecure party receives that assurance, if commercially reasonable the insecure party may suspend any performance for which he [or she] has not already received the agreed return.

(3) A repudiation of the lease contract occurs if assurance of due performance adequate under the circumstances of the particular case is not provided to the insecure party within a reasonable time, not to exceed 30 days after receipt of a demand by the other party.

(4) Between merchants, the reasonableness of grounds for insecurity and the adequacy of any assurance offered must be determined according to commercial standards.

(5) Acceptance of any nonconforming delivery or payment does not prejudice the aggrieved party's right to demand adequate assurance of future performance.

§ 2A-402.   Anticipatory Repudiation.

If either party repudiates a lease contract with respect to a performance not yet due under the lease contract, the loss of which performance will substantially impair the value of the lease contract to the other, the aggrieved party may:

(a) for a commercially reasonable time, await retraction of repudiation and performance by the repudiating party;

(b) make demand pursuant to Section 2A-401 and await assurance of future performance adequate under the circumstances of the particular case; or

(c) resort to any right or remedy upon default under the lease contract or this Article, even though the aggrieved party has notified the repudiating party that the aggrieved party would await the repudiating party's performance and assurance and has urged retraction. In addition, whether or not the aggrieved party is pursuing one of the foregoing remedies, the aggrieved party may suspend performance or, if the aggrieved party is the lessor, proceed in accordance with the provisions of this Article on the lessor's right to identify goods to the lease contract notwithstanding default or to salvage unfinished goods (Section 2A-524).

§ 2A-403.   Retraction of Anticipatory Repudiation.

(1) Until the repudiating party's next performance is due, the repudiating party can retract the repudiation unless, since the repudiation, the aggrieved party has cancelled the lease contract or materially changed the aggrieved party's position or otherwise indicated that the aggrieved party considers the repudiation final.

(2) Retraction may be by any method that clearly indicates to the aggrieved party that the repudiating party intends to perform under the lease contract and includes any assurance demanded under Section 2A-401.

(3) Retraction reinstates a repudiating party's rights under a lease contract with due excuse and allowance to the aggrieved party for any delay occasioned by the repudiation.

§ 2A-404.   Substituted Performance.

(1) If without fault of the lessee, the lessor and the supplier, the agreed berthing, loading, or unloading facilities fail or the agreed type of carrier becomes unavailable or the agreed manner of delivery otherwise becomes commercially impracticable, but a commercially reasonable substitute is available, the substitute performance must be tendered and accepted.

(2) If the agreed means or manner of payment fails because of domestic or foreign governmental regulation:

  (a) the lessor may withhold or stop delivery or cause the supplier to withhold or stop delivery unless the lessee provides a means or manner of payment that is commercially a substantial equivalent; and

  (b) if delivery has already been taken, payment by the means or in the manner provided by the regulation discharges the lessee's obligation unless the regulation is discriminatory, oppressive, or predatory.

§ 2A-405.   Excused Performance.

Subject to Section 2A-404 on substituted performance, the following rules apply:

(a) Delay in delivery or nondelivery in whole or in part by a lessor or a supplier who complies with paragraphs (b) and (c) is not a default under the lease contract if performance as agreed has been made impracticable by the occurrence of a contingency the nonoccurrence of which was a basic assumption on which the lease contract was made or by compliance in good faith with any applicable foreign or domestic governmental regulation or order, whether or not the regulation or order later proves to be invalid.

(b) If the causes mentioned in paragraph (a) affect only part of the lessor's or the supplier's capacity to perform, he [or she] shall allocate production and deliveries among his [or her] customers but at his [or her] option may include regular customers not then under contract for sale or lease as well as his [or her] own requirements for further manufacture. He [or she] may so allocate in any manner that is fair and reasonable.

(c) The lessor seasonably shall notify the lessee and in the case of a finance lease the supplier seasonably shall notify the lessor and the lessee, if known, that there will be delay or nondelivery and, if allocation is required under paragraph (b), of the estimated quota thus made available for the lessee.

§ 2A-406.   Procedure on Excused Performance.

(1) If the lessee receives notification of a material or indefinite delay or an allocation justified under Section 2A-405, the lessee may by written notification to the lessor as to any goods involved, and with respect to all of the goods if under an installment lease contract the value of the whole lease contract is substantially impaired (Section 2A-510):

  (a) terminate the lease contract (Section 2A-505(2)); or

  (b) except in a finance lease that is not a consumer lease, modify the lease contract by accepting the available quota in substitution, with due allowance from the rent payable for the balance of the lease term for the deficiency but without further right against the lessor.

(2) If, after receipt of a notification from the lessor under Section 2A-405, the lessee fails so to modify the lease agreement within a reasonable time not exceeding 30 days, the lease contract lapses with respect to any deliveries affected.

§ 2A-407.   Irrevocable Promises: Finance Leases.

(1) In the case of a finance lease that is not a consumer lease the lessee's promises under the lease contract become irrevocable and independent upon the lessee's acceptance of the goods.

(2) A promise that has become irrevocable and independent under subsection (1):

  (a) is effective and enforceable between the parties, and by or against third parties including assignees of the parties, and

  (b) is not subject to cancellation, termination, modification, repudiation, excuse, or substitution without the consent of the party to whom the promise runs.

(3) This section does not affect the validity under any other law of a covenant in any lease contract making the lessee's promises

irrevocable and independent upon the lessee's acceptance of the goods.

As amended in 1990.

Part 5   Default

A. In General

§ 2A–501.   Default: Procedure.

(1) Whether the lessor or the lessee is in default under a lease contract is determined by the lease agreement and this Article.

(2) If the lessor or the lessee is in default under the lease contract, the party seeking enforcement has rights and remedies as provided in this Article and, except as limited by this Article, as provided in the lease agreement.

(3) If the lessor or the lessee is in default under the lease contract, the party seeking enforcement may reduce the party's claim to judgment, or otherwise enforce the lease contract by self-help or any available judicial procedure or nonjudicial procedure, including administrative proceeding, arbitration, or the like, in accordance with this Article.

(4) Except as otherwise provided in Section 1–106(1) or this Article or the lease agreement, the rights and remedies referred to in subsections (2) and (3) are cumulative.

(5) If the lease agreement covers both real property and goods, the party seeking enforcement may proceed under this Part as to the goods, or under other applicable law as to both the real property and the goods in accordance with that party's rights and remedies in respect of the real property, in which case this Part does not apply.

As amended in 1990.

§ 2A–502.   Notice After Default.

Except as otherwise provided in this Article or the lease agreement, the lessor or lessee in default under the lease contract is not entitled to notice of default or notice of enforcement from the other party to the lease agreement.

§ 2A–503.   Modification or Impairment of Rights and Remedies.

(1) Except as otherwise provided in this Article, the lease agreement may include rights and remedies for default in addition to or in substitution for those provided in this Article and may limit or alter the measure of damages recoverable under this Article.

(2) Resort to a remedy provided under this Article or in the lease agreement is optional unless the remedy is expressly agreed to be exclusive. If circumstances cause an exclusive or limited remedy to fail of its essential purpose, or provision for an exclusive remedy is unconscionable, remedy may be had as provided in this Article.

(3) Consequential damages may be liquidated under Section 2A–504, or may otherwise be limited, altered, or excluded unless the limitation, alteration, or exclusion is unconscionable. Limitation, alteration, or exclusion of consequential damages for injury to the person in the case of consumer goods is prima facie unconscionable but limitation, alteration, or exclusion of damages where the loss is commercial is not prima facie unconscionable.

(4) Rights and remedies on default by the lessor or the lessee with respect to any obligation or promise collateral or ancillary to the lease contract are not impaired by this Article.

As amended in 1990.

§ 2A–504.   Liquidation of Damages.

(1) Damages payable by either party for default, or any other act or omission, including indemnity for loss or diminution of anticipated tax benefits or loss or damage to lessor's residual interest, may be liquidated in the lease agreement but only at an amount or by a formula that is reasonable in light of the then anticipated harm caused by the default or other act or omission.

(2) If the lease agreement provides for liquidation of damages, and such provision does not comply with subsection (1), or such provision is an exclusive or limited remedy that circumstances cause to fail of its essential purpose, remedy may be had as provided in this Article.

(3) If the lessor justifiably withholds or stops delivery of goods because of the lessee's default or insolvency (Section 2A–525 or 2A–526), the lessee is entitled to restitution of any amount by which the sum of his [or her] payments exceeds:

(a) the amount to which the lessor is entitled by virtue of terms liquidating the lessor's damages in accordance with subsection (1); or

(b) in the absence of those terms, 20 percent of the then present value of the total rent the lessee was obligated to pay for the balance of the lease term, or, in the case of a consumer lease, the lesser of such amount or $500.

(4) A lessee's right to restitution under subsection (3) is subject to offset to the extent the lessor establishes:

(a) a right to recover damages under the provisions of this Article other than subsection (1); and

(b) the amount or value of any benefits received by the lessee directly or indirectly by reason of the lease contract.

§ 2A–505.   Cancellation and Termination and Effect of Cancellation, Termination, Rescission, or Fraud on Rights and Remedies.

(1) On cancellation of the lease contract, all obligations that are still executory on both sides are discharged, but any right based on prior default or performance survives, and the cancelling party also retains any remedy for default of the whole lease contract or any unperformed balance.

(2) On termination of the lease contract, all obligations that are still executory on both sides are discharged but any right based on prior default or performance survives.

(3) Unless the contrary intention clearly appears, expressions of "cancellation," "rescission," or the like of the lease contract may not be construed as a renunciation or discharge of any claim in damages for an antecedent default.

(4) Rights and remedies for material misrepresentation or fraud include all rights and remedies available under this Article for default.

(5) Neither rescission nor a claim for rescission of the lease contract nor rejection or return of the goods may bar or be deemed inconsistent with a claim for damages or other right or remedy.

§ 2A–506. Statute of Limitations.

(1) An action for default under a lease contract, including breach of warranty or indemnity, must be commenced within 4 years after the cause of action accrued. By the original lease contract the parties may reduce the period of limitation to not less than one year.

(2) A cause of action for default accrues when the act or omission on which the default or breach of warranty is based is or should have been discovered by the aggrieved party, or when the default occurs, whichever is later. A cause of action for indemnity accrues when the act or omission on which the claim for indemnity is based is or should have been discovered by the indemnified party, whichever is later.

(3) If an action commenced within the time limited by subsection (1) is so terminated as to leave available a remedy by another action for the same default or breach of warranty or indemnity, the other action may be commenced after the expiration of the time limited and within 6 months after the termination of the first action unless the termination resulted from voluntary discontinuance or from dismissal for failure or neglect to prosecute.

(4) This section does not alter the law on tolling of the statute of limitations nor does it apply to causes of action that have accrued before this Article becomes effective.

§ 2A–507. Proof of Market Rent: Time and Place.

(1) Damages based on market rent (Section 2A–519 or 2A–528) are determined according to the rent for the use of the goods concerned for a lease term identical to the remaining lease term of the original lease agreement and prevailing at the times specified in Sections 2A–519 and 2A–528.

(2) If evidence of rent for the use of the goods concerned for a lease term identical to the remaining lease term of the original lease agreement and prevailing at the times or places described in this Article is not readily available, the rent prevailing within any reasonable time before or after the time described or at any other place or for a different lease term which in commercial judgment or under usage of trade would serve as a reasonable substitute for the one described may be used, making any proper allowance for the difference, including the cost of transporting the goods to or from the other place.

(3) Evidence of a relevant rent prevailing at a time or place or for a lease term other than the one described in this Article offered by one party is not admissible unless and until he [or she] has given the other party notice the court finds sufficient to prevent unfair surprise.

(4) If the prevailing rent or value of any goods regularly leased in any established market is in issue, reports in official publications or trade journals or in newspapers or periodicals of general circulation published as the reports of that market are admissible in evidence. The circumstances of the preparation of the report may be shown to affect its weight but not its admissibility.

As amended in 1990.

B. Default by Lessor

§ 2A–508. Lessee's Remedies.

(1) If a lessor fails to deliver the goods in conformity to the lease contract (Section 2A–509) or repudiates the lease contract (Section 2A–402), or a lessee rightfully rejects the goods (Section 2A–509) or

justifiably revokes acceptance of the goods (Section 2A–517), then with respect to any goods involved, and with respect to all of the goods if under an installment lease contract the value of the whole lease contract is substantially impaired (Section 2A–510), the lessor is in default under the lease contract and the lessee may:

(a) cancel the lease contract (Section 2A–505(1));

(b) recover so much of the rent and security as has been paid and is just under the circumstances;

(c) cover and recover damages as to all goods affected whether or not they have been identified to the lease contract (Sections 2A–518 and 2A–520), or recover damages for nondelivery (Sections 2A–519 and 2A–520);

(d) exercise any other rights or pursue any other remedies provided in the lease contract.

(2) If a lessor fails to deliver the goods in conformity to the lease contract or repudiates the lease contract, the lessee may also:

(a) if the goods have been identified, recover them (Section 2A–522); or

(b) in a proper case, obtain specific performance or replevy the goods (Section 2A–521).

(3) If a lessor is otherwise in default under a lease contract, the lessee may exercise the rights and pursue the remedies provided in the lease contract, which may include a right to cancel the lease, and in Section 2A–519(3).

(4) If a lessor has breached a warranty, whether express or implied, the lessee may recover damages (Section 2A–519(4)).

(5) On rightful rejection or justifiable revocation of acceptance, a lessee has a security interest in goods in the lessee's possession or control for any rent and security that has been paid and any expenses reasonably incurred in their inspection, receipt, transportation, and care and custody and may hold those goods and dispose of them in good faith and in a commercially reasonable manner, subject to Section 2A–527(5).

(6) Subject to the provisions of Section 2A–407, a lessee, on notifying the lessor of the lessee's intention to do so, may deduct all or any part of the damages resulting from any default under the lease contract from any part of the rent still due under the same lease contract.

As amended in 1990.

§ 2A–509. Lessee's Rights on Improper Delivery; Rightful Rejection.

(1) Subject to the provisions of Section 2A–510 on default in installment lease contracts, if the goods or the tender or delivery fail in any respect to conform to the lease contract, the lessee may reject or accept the goods or accept any commercial unit or units and reject the rest of the goods.

(2) Rejection of goods is ineffective unless it is within a reasonable time after tender or delivery of the goods and the lessee seasonably notifies the lessor.

§ 2A–510. Installment Lease Contracts: Rejection and Default.

(1) Under an installment lease contract a lessee may reject any delivery that is nonconforming if the nonconformity substantially impairs the value of that delivery and cannot be cured or the nonconformity is a defect in the required documents; but if the

nonconformity does not fall within subsection (2) and the lessor or the supplier gives adequate assurance of its cure, the lessee must accept that delivery.

(2) Whenever nonconformity or default with respect to one or more deliveries substantially impairs the value of the installment lease contract as a whole there is a default with respect to the whole. But, the aggrieved party reinstates the installment lease contract as a whole if the aggrieved party accepts a nonconforming delivery without seasonably notifying of cancellation or brings an action with respect only to past deliveries or demands performance as to future deliveries.

§ 2A–511. Merchant Lessee's Duties as to Rightfully Rejected Goods.

(1) Subject to any security interest of a lessee (Section 2A–508(5)), if a lessor or a supplier has no agent or place of business at the market of rejection, a merchant lessee, after rejection of goods in his [or her] possession or control, shall follow any reasonable instructions received from the lessor or the supplier with respect to the goods. In the absence of those instructions, a merchant lessee shall make reasonable efforts to sell, lease, or otherwise dispose of the goods for the lessor's account if they threaten to decline in value speedily. Instructions are not reasonable if on demand indemnity for expenses is not forthcoming.

(2) If a merchant lessee (subsection (1)) or any other lessee (Section 2A–512) disposes of goods, he [or she] is entitled to reimbursement either from the lessor or the supplier or out of the proceeds for reasonable expenses of caring for and disposing of the goods and, if the expenses include no disposition commission, to such commission as is usual in the trade, or if there is none, to a reasonable sum not exceeding 10 percent of the gross proceeds.

(3) In complying with this section or Section 2A–512, the lessee is held only to good faith. Good faith conduct hereunder is neither acceptance or conversion nor the basis of an action for damages.

(4) A purchaser who purchases in good faith from a lessee pursuant to this section or Section 2A–512 takes the goods free of any rights of the lessor and the supplier even though the lessee fails to comply with one or more of the requirements of this Article.

§ 2A–512. Lessee's Duties as to Rightfully Rejected Goods.

(1) Except as otherwise provided with respect to goods that threaten to decline in value speedily (Section 2A–511) and subject to any security interest of a lessee (Section 2A–508(5)):

(a) the lessee, after rejection of goods in the lessee's possession, shall hold them with reasonable care at the lessor's or the supplier's disposition for a reasonable time after the lessee's seasonable notification of rejection;

(b) if the lessor or the supplier gives no instructions within a reasonable time after notification of rejection, the lessee may store the rejected goods for the lessor's or the supplier's account or ship them to the lessor or the supplier or dispose of them for the lessor's or the supplier's account with reimbursement in the manner provided in Section 2A–511; but

(c) the lessee has no further obligations with regard to goods rightfully rejected.

(2) Action by the lessee pursuant to subsection (1) is not acceptance or conversion.

§ 2A–513. Cure by Lessor of Improper Tender or Delivery; Replacement.

(1) If any tender or delivery by the lessor or the supplier is rejected because nonconforming and the time for performance has not yet expired, the lessor or the supplier may seasonably notify the lessee of the lessor's or the supplier's intention to cure and may then make a conforming delivery within the time provided in the lease contract.

(2) If the lessee rejects a nonconforming tender that the lessor or the supplier had reasonable grounds to believe would be acceptable with or without money allowance, the lessor or the supplier may have a further reasonable time to substitute a conforming tender if he [or she] seasonably notifies the lessee.

§ 2A–514. Waiver of Lessee's Objections.

(1) In rejecting goods, a lessee's failure to state a particular defect that is ascertainable by reasonable inspection precludes the lessee from relying on the defect to justify rejection or to establish default:

(a) if, stated seasonably, the lessor or the supplier could have cured it (Section 2A–513); or

(b) between merchants if the lessor or the supplier after rejection has made a request in writing for a full and final written statement of all defects on which the lessee proposes to rely.

(2) A lessee's failure to reserve rights when paying rent or other consideration against documents precludes recovery of the payment for defects apparent on the face of the documents.

§ 2A–515. Acceptance of Goods.

(1) Acceptance of goods occurs after the lessee has had a reasonable opportunity to inspect the goods and

(a) the lessee signifies or acts with respect to the goods in a manner that signifies to the lessor or the supplier that the goods are conforming or that the lessee will take or retain them in spite of their nonconformity; or

(b) the lessee fails to make an effective rejection of the goods (Section 2A–509(2)).

(2) Acceptance of a part of any commercial unit is acceptance of that entire unit.

§ 2A–516. Effect of Acceptance of Goods; Notice of Default; Burden of Establishing Default after Acceptance; Notice of Claim or Litigation to Person Answerable Over.

(1) A lessee must pay rent for any goods accepted in accordance with the lease contract, with due allowance for goods rightfully rejected or not delivered.

(2) A lessee's acceptance of goods precludes rejection of the goods accepted. In the case of a finance lease, if made with knowledge of a nonconformity, acceptance cannot be revoked because of it. In any other case, if made with knowledge of a nonconformity, acceptance cannot be revoked because of it unless the acceptance was on the reasonable assumption that the nonconformity would be seasonably cured. Acceptance does not of itself impair any other remedy provided by this Article or the lease agreement for nonconformity.

(3) If a tender has been accepted:

(a) within a reasonable time after the lessee discovers or should have discovered any default, the lessee shall notify the lessor and the supplier, if any, or be barred from any remedy against the party notified;

(b) except in the case of a consumer lease, within a reasonable time after the lessee receives notice of litigation for infringement or the like (Section 2A–211) the lessee shall notify the lessor or be barred from any remedy over for liability established by the litigation; and

(c) the burden is on the lessee to establish any default.

(4) If a lessee is sued for breach of a warranty or other obligation for which a lessor or a supplier is answerable over the following apply:

(a) The lessee may give the lessor or the supplier, or both, written notice of the litigation. If the notice states that the person notified may come in and defend and that if the person notified does not do so that person will be bound in any action against that person by the lessee by any determination of fact common to the two litigations, then unless the person notified after seasonable receipt of the notice does come in and defend that person is so bound.

(b) The lessor or the supplier may demand in writing that the lessee turn over control of the litigation including settlement if the claim is one for infringement or the like (Section 2A–211) or else be barred from any remedy over. If the demand states that the lessor or the supplier agrees to bear all expense and to satisfy any adverse judgment, then unless the lessee after seasonable receipt of the demand does turn over control the lessee is so barred.

(5) Subsections (3) and (4) apply to any obligation of a lessee to hold the lessor or the supplier harmless against infringement or the like (Section 2A–211).

As amended in 1990.

§ 2A–517.   Revocation of Acceptance of Goods.

(1) A lessee may revoke acceptance of a lot or commercial unit whose nonconformity substantially impairs its value to the lessee if the lessee has accepted it:

(a) except in the case of a finance lease, on the reasonable assumption that its nonconformity would be cured and it has not been seasonably cured; or

(b) without discovery of the nonconformity if the lessee's acceptance was reasonably induced either by the lessor's assurances or, except in the case of a finance lease, by the difficulty of discovery before acceptance.

(2) Except in the case of a finance lease that is not a consumer lease, a lessee may revoke acceptance of a lot or commercial unit if the lessor defaults under the lease contract and the default substantially impairs the value of that lot or commercial unit to the lessee.

(3) If the lease agreement so provides, the lessee may revoke acceptance of a lot or commercial unit because of other defaults by the lessor.

(4) Revocation of acceptance must occur within a reasonable time after the lessee discovers or should have discovered the ground for it and before any substantial change in condition of the goods

which is not caused by the nonconformity. Revocation is not effective until the lessee notifies the lessor.

(5) A lessee who so revokes has the same rights and duties with regard to the goods involved as if the lessee had rejected them.

As amended in 1990.

§ 2A–518.   Cover; Substitute Goods.

(1) After a default by a lessor under the lease contract of the type described in Section 2A–508(1), or, if agreed, after other default by the lessor, the lessee may cover by making any purchase or lease of or contract to purchase or lease goods in substitution for those due from the lessor.

(2) Except as otherwise provided with respect to damages liquidated in the lease agreement (Section 2A–504) or otherwise determined pursuant to agreement of the parties (Sections 1–102(3) and 2A–503), if a lessee's cover is by lease agreement substantially similar to the original lease agreement and the new lease agreement is made in good faith and in a commercially reasonable manner, the lessee may recover from the lessor as damages (i) the present value, as of the date of the commencement of the term of the new lease agreement, of the rent under the new lease agreement applicable to that period of the new lease term which is comparable to the then remaining term of the original lease agreement minus the present value as of the same date of the total rent for the then remaining lease term of the original lease agreement, and (ii) any incidental or consequential damages, less expenses saved in consequence of the lessor's default.

(3) If a lessee's cover is by lease agreement that for any reason does not qualify for treatment under subsection (2), or is by purchase or otherwise, the lessee may recover from the lessor as if the lessee had elected not to cover and Section 2A–519 governs.

As amended in 1990.

§ 2A–519.   Lessee's Damages for Non-Delivery, Repudiation, Default, and Breach of Warranty in Regard to Accepted Goods.

(1) Except as otherwise provided with respect to damages liquidated in the lease agreement (Section 2A–504) or otherwise determined pursuant to agreement of the parties (Sections 1–102(3) and 2A–503), if a lessee elects not to cover or a lessee elects to cover and the cover is by lease agreement that for any reason does not qualify for treatment under Section 2A–518(2), or is by purchase or otherwise, the measure of damages for non-delivery or repudiation by the lessor or for rejection or revocation of acceptance by the lessee is the present value, as of the date of the default, of the then market rent minus the present value as of the same date of the original rent, computed for the remaining lease term of the original lease agreement, together with incidental and consequential damages, less expenses saved in consequence of the lessor's default.

(2) Market rent is to be determined as of the place for tender or, in cases of rejection after arrival or revocation of acceptance, as of the place of arrival.

(3) Except as otherwise agreed, if the lessee has accepted goods and given notification (Section 2A–516(3)), the measure of damages for non-conforming tender or delivery or other default by a lessor is the loss resulting in the ordinary course of events from the lessor's default as determined in any manner that is reasonable together

with incidental and consequential damages, less expenses saved in consequence of the lessor's default.

(4) Except as otherwise agreed, the measure of damages for breach of warranty is the present value at the time and place of acceptance of the difference between the value of the use of the goods accepted and the value if they had been as warranted for the lease term, unless special circumstances show proximate damages of a different amount, together with incidental and consequential damages, less expenses saved in consequence of the lessor's default or breach of warranty.

As amended in 1990.

§ 2A–520.   Lessee's Incidental and Consequential Damages.

(1) Incidental damages resulting from a lessor's default include expenses reasonably incurred in inspection, receipt, transportation, and care and custody of goods rightfully rejected or goods the acceptance of which is justifiably revoked, any commercially reasonable charges, expenses or commissions in connection with effecting cover, and any other reasonable expense incident to the default.

(2) Consequential damages resulting from a lessor's default include:

   (a) any loss resulting from general or particular requirements and needs of which the lessor at the time of contracting had reason to know and which could not reasonably be prevented by cover or otherwise; and

   (b) injury to person or property proximately resulting from any breach of warranty.

§ 2A–521.   Lessee's Right to Specific Performance or Replevin.

(1) Specific performance may be decreed if the goods are unique or in other proper circumstances.

(2) A decree for specific performance may include any terms and conditions as to payment of the rent, damages, or other relief that the court deems just.

(3) A lessee has a right of replevin, detinue, sequestration, claim and delivery, or the like for goods identified to the lease contract if after reasonable effort the lessee is unable to effect cover for those goods or the circumstances reasonably indicate that the effort will be unavailing.

§ 2A–522.   Lessee's Right to Goods on Lessor's Insolvency.

(1) Subject to subsection (2) and even though the goods have not been shipped, a lessee who has paid a part or all of the rent and security for goods identified to a lease contract (Section 2A–217) on making and keeping good a tender of any unpaid portion of the rent and security due under the lease contract may recover the goods identified from the lessor if the lessor becomes insolvent within 10 days after receipt of the first installment of rent and security.

(2) A lessee acquires the right to recover goods identified to a lease contract only if they conform to the lease contract.

C. Default by Lessee

§ 2A–523.   Lessor's Remedies.

(1) If a lessee wrongfully rejects or revokes acceptance of goods or fails to make a payment when due or repudiates with respect to a part or the whole, then, with respect to any goods involved, and with respect to all of the goods if under an installment lease contract the value of the whole lease contract is substantially impaired (Section 2A–510), the lessee is in default under the lease contract and the lessor may:

   (a) cancel the lease contract (Section 2A–505(1));

   (b) proceed respecting goods not identified to the lease contract (Section 2A–524);

   (c) withhold delivery of the goods and take possession of goods previously delivered (Section 2A–525);

   (d) stop delivery of the goods by any bailee (Section 2A–526);

   (e) dispose of the goods and recover damages (Section 2A–527), or retain the goods and recover damages (Section 2A–528), or in a proper case recover rent (Section 2A–529)

   (f) exercise any other rights or pursue any other remedies provided in the lease contract.

(2) If a lessor does not fully exercise a right or obtain a remedy to which the lessor is entitled under subsection (1), the lessor may recover the loss resulting in the ordinary course of events from the lessee's default as determined in any reasonable manner, together with incidental damages, less expenses saved in consequence of the lessee's default.

(3) If a lessee is otherwise in default under a lease contract, the lessor may exercise the rights and pursue the remedies provided in the lease contract, which may include a right to cancel the lease. In addition, unless otherwise provided in the lease contract:

   (a) if the default substantially impairs the value of the lease contract to the lessor, the lessor may exercise the rights and pursue the remedies provided in subsections (1) or (2); or

   (b) if the default does not substantially impair the value of the lease contract to the lessor, the lessor may recover as provided in subsection (2).

As amended in 1990.

§ 2A–524.   Lessor's Right to Identify Goods to Lease Contract.

(1) After default by the lessee under the lease contract of the type described in Section 2A–523(1) or 2A–523(3)(a) or, if agreed, after other default by the lessee, the lessor may:

   (a) identify to the lease contract conforming goods not already identified if at the time the lessor learned of the default they were in the lessor's or the supplier's possession or control; and

   (b) dispose of goods (Section 2A–527(1)) that demonstrably have been intended for the particular lease contract even though those goods are unfinished.

(2) If the goods are unfinished, in the exercise of reasonable commercial judgment for the purposes of avoiding loss and of effective realization, an aggrieved lessor or the supplier may either complete manufacture and wholly identify the goods to the lease contract or cease manufacture and lease, sell, or otherwise dispose of the goods for scrap or salvage value or proceed in any other reasonable manner.

As amended in 1990.

§ 2A–525.   Lessor's Right to Possession of Goods.

(1) If a lessor discovers the lessee to be insolvent, the lessor may refuse to deliver the goods.

(2) After a default by the lessee under the lease contract of the type described in Section 2A-523(1) or 2A-523(3)(a) or, if agreed, after other default by the lessee, the lessor has the right to take possession of the goods. If the lease contract so provides, the lessor may require the lessee to assemble the goods and make them available to the lessor at a place to be designated by the lessor which is reasonably convenient to both parties. Without removal, the lessor may render unusable any goods employed in trade or business, and may dispose of goods on the lessee's premises (Section 2A-527).

(3) The lessor may proceed under subsection (2) without judicial process if that can be done without breach of the peace or the lessor may proceed by action.

As amended in 1990.

§ 2A-526.   Lessor's Stoppage of Delivery in Transit or Otherwise.

(1) A lessor may stop delivery of goods in the possession of a carrier or other bailee if the lessor discovers the lessee to be insolvent and may stop delivery of carload, truckload, planeload, or larger shipments of express or freight if the lessee repudiates or fails to make a payment due before delivery, whether for rent, security or otherwise under the lease contract, or for any other reason the lessor has a right to withhold or take possession of the goods.

(2) In pursuing its remedies under subsection (1), the lessor may stop delivery until

    (a) receipt of the goods by the lessee;

    (b) acknowledgment to the lessee by any bailee of the goods, except a carrier, that the bailee holds the goods for the lessee; or

    (c) such an acknowledgment to the lessee by a carrier via reshipment or as warehouseman.

(3) (a) To stop delivery, a lessor shall so notify as to enable the bailee by reasonable diligence to prevent delivery of the goods.

    (b) After notification, the bailee shall hold and deliver the goods according to the directions of the lessor, but the lessor is liable to the bailee for any ensuing charges or damages.

    (c) A carrier who has issued a nonnegotiable bill of lading is not obliged to obey a notification to stop received from a person other than the consignor.

§ 2A-527.   Lessor's Rights to Dispose of Goods.

(1) After a default by a lessee under the lease contract of the type described in Section 2A-523(1) or 2A-523(3)(a) or after the lessor refuses to deliver or takes possession of goods (Section 2A-525 or 2A-526), or, if agreed, after other default by a lessee, the lessor may dispose of the goods concerned or the undelivered balance thereof by lease, sale, or otherwise.

(2) Except as otherwise provided with respect to damages liquidated in the lease agreement (Section 2A-504) or otherwise determined pursuant to agreement of the parties (Sections 1-102(3) and 2A-503), if the disposition is by lease agreement substantially similar to the original lease agreement and the new lease agreement is made in good faith and in a commercially reasonable manner, the lessor may recover from the lessee as damages (i) accrued and unpaid rent as of the date of the commencement of the term of the new lease agreement, (ii) the present value, as of the same date, of the total rent for the then remaining lease term of the original lease agreement minus the present value, as of the same date, of the rent under the new lease agreement applicable to that period of the new lease term which is comparable to the then remaining term of the original lease agreement, and (iii) any incidental damages allowed under Section 2A-530, less expenses saved in consequence of the lessee's default.

(3) If the lessor's disposition is by lease agreement that for any reason does not qualify for treatment under subsection (2), or is by sale or otherwise, the lessor may recover from the lessee as if the lessor had elected not to dispose of the goods and Section 2A-528 governs.

(4) A subsequent buyer or lessee who buys or leases from the lessor in good faith for value as a result of a disposition under this section takes the goods free of the original lease contract and any rights of the original lessee even though the lessor fails to comply with one or more of the requirements of this Article.

(5) The lessor is not accountable to the lessee for any profit made on any disposition. A lessee who has rightfully rejected or justifiably revoked acceptance shall account to the lessor for any excess over the amount of the lessee's security interest (Section 2A-508(5)).

As amended in 1990.

§ 2A-528.   Lessor's Damages for Non-acceptance, Failure to Pay, Repudiation, or Other Default.

(1) Except as otherwise provided with respect to damages liquidated in the lease agreement (Section 2A-504) or otherwise determined pursuant to agreement of the parties (Section 1-102(3) and 2A-503), if a lessor elects to retain the goods or a lessor elects to dispose of the goods and the disposition is by lease agreement that for any reason does not qualify for treatment under Section 2A-527(2), or is by sale or otherwise, the lessor may recover from the lessee as damages for a default of the type described in Section 2A-523(1) or 2A-523(3)(a), or if agreed, for other default of the lessee, (i) accrued and unpaid rent as of the date of the default if the lessee has never taken possession of the goods, or, if the lessee has taken possession of the goods, as of the date the lessor repossesses the goods or an earlier date on which the lessee makes a tender of the goods to the lessor, (ii) the present value as of the date determined under clause (i) of the total rent for the then remaining lease term of the original lease agreement minus the present value as of the same date of the market rent as the place where the goods are located computed for the same lease term, and (iii) any incidental damages allowed under Section 2A-530, less expenses saved in consequence of the lessee's default.

(2) If the measure of damages provided in subsection (1) is inadequate to put a lessor in as good a position as performance would have, the measure of damages is the present value of the profit, including reasonable overhead, the lessor would have made from full performance by the lessee, together with any incidental damages allowed under Section 2A-530, due allowance for costs reasonably incurred and due credit for payments or proceeds of disposition.

As amended in 1990.

§ 2A–529.   Lessor's Action for the Rent.

(1) After default by the lessee under the lease contract of the type described in Section 2A–523(1) or 2A–523(3)(a) or, if agreed, after other default by the lessee, if the lessor complies with subsection (2), the lessor may recover from the lessee as damages:

(a) for goods accepted by the lessee and not repossessed by or tendered to the lessor, and for conforming goods lost or damaged within a commercially reasonable time after risk of loss passes to the lessee (Section 2A–219), (i) accrued and unpaid rent as of the date of entry of judgment in favor of the lessor (ii) the present value as of the same date of the rent for the then remaining lease term of the lease agreement, and (iii) any incidental damages allowed under Section 2A–530, less expenses saved in consequence of the lessee's default; and

(b) for goods identified to the lease contract if the lessor is unable after reasonable effort to dispose of them at a reasonable price or the circumstances reasonably indicate that effort will be unavailing, (i) accrued and unpaid rent as of the date of entry of judgment in favor of the lessor, (ii) the present value as of the same date of the rent for the then remaining lease term of the lease agreement, and (iii) any incidental damages allowed under Section 2A–530, less expenses saved in consequence of the lessee's default.

(2) Except as provided in subsection (3), the lessor shall hold for the lessee for the remaining lease term of the lease agreement any goods that have been identified to the lease contract and are in the lessor's control.

(3) The lessor may dispose of the goods at any time before collection of the judgment for damages obtained pursuant to subsection (1). If the disposition is before the end of the remaining lease term of the lease agreement, the lessor's recovery against the lessee for damages is governed by Section 2A–527 or Section 2A–528, and the lessor will cause an appropriate credit to be provided against a judgment for damages to the extent that the amount of the judgment exceeds the recovery available pursuant to Section 2A–527 or 2A–528.

(4) Payment of the judgment for damages obtained pursuant to subsection (1) entitles the lessee to the use and possession of the goods not then disposed of for the remaining lease term of and in accordance with the lease agreement.

(5) After default by the lessee under the lease contract of the type described in Section 2A–523(1) or Section 2A–523(3)(a) or, if agreed, after other default by the lessee, a lessor who is held not entitled to rent under this section must nevertheless be awarded damages for non-acceptance under Sections 2A–527 and 2A–528.

As amended in 1990.

§ 2A–530.   Lessor's Incidental Damages.

Incidental damages to an aggrieved lessor include any commercially reasonable charges, expenses, or commissions incurred in stopping delivery, in the transportation, care and custody of goods after the lessee's default, in connection with return or disposition of the goods, or otherwise resulting from the default.

§ 2A–531.   Standing to Sue Third Parties for Injury to Goods.

(1) If a third party so deals with goods that have been identified to a lease contract as to cause actionable injury to a party to the lease contract (a) the lessor has a right of action against the third party, and (b) the lessee also has a right of action against the third party if the lessee:

(i) has a security interest in the goods;

(ii) has an insurable interest in the goods; or

(iii) bears the risk of loss under the lease contract or has since the injury assumed that risk as against the lessor and the goods have been converted or destroyed.

(2) If at the time of the injury the party plaintiff did not bear the risk of loss as against the other party to the lease contract and there is no arrangement between them for disposition of the recovery, his [or her] suit or settlement, subject to his [or her] own interest, is as a fiduciary for the other party to the lease contract.

(3) Either party with the consent of the other may sue for the benefit of whom it may concern.

§ 2A–532.   Lessor's Rights to Residual Interest.

In addition to any other recovery permitted by this Article or other law, the lessor may recover from the lessee an amount that will fully compensate the lessor for any loss of or damage to the lessor's residual interest in the goods caused by the default of the lessee.

As added in 1990.

Revised Article 3
NEGOTIABLE INSTRUMENTS

Part 1   General Provisions and Definitions

§ 3–101.   Short Title.

This Article may be cited as Uniform Commercial Code–Negotiable Instruments.

§ 3–102.   Subject Matter.

(a) This Article applies to negotiable instruments. It does not apply to money, to payment orders governed by Article 4A, or to securities governed by Article 8.

(b) If there is conflict between this Article and Article 4 or 9, Articles 4 and 9 govern.

(c) Regulations of the Board of Governors of the Federal Reserve System and operating circulars of the Federal Reserve Banks supersede any inconsistent provision of this Article to the extent of the inconsistency.

§ 3–103.   Definitions.

(a) In this Article:

(1) "Acceptor" means a drawee who has accepted a draft.

(2) "Drawee" means a person ordered in a draft to make payment.

(3) "Drawer" means a person who signs or is identified in a draft as a person ordering payment.

(4) "Good faith" means honesty in fact and the observance of reasonable commercial standards of fair dealing.

(5) "Maker" means a person who signs or is identified in a note as a person undertaking to pay.

(6) "Order" means a written instruction to pay money signed by the person giving the instruction. The instruction may be addressed to any person, including the person giving the instruction, or to one or more persons jointly or in the alternative but not in succession. An authorization to pay is not an order unless the person authorized to pay is also instructed to pay.

(7) "Ordinary care" in the case of a person engaged in business means observance of reasonable commercial standards, prevailing in the area in which the person is located, with respect to the business in which the person is engaged. In the case of a bank that takes an instrument for processing for collection or payment by automated means, reasonable commercial standards do not require the bank to examine the instrument if the failure to examine does not violate the bank's prescribed procedures and the bank's procedures do not vary unreasonably from general banking usage not disapproved by this Article or Article 4.

(8) "Party" means a party to an instrument.

(9) "Promise" means a written undertaking to pay money signed by the person undertaking to pay. An acknowledgment of an obligation by the obligor is not a promise unless the obligor also undertakes to pay the obligation.

(10) "Prove" with respect to a fact means to meet the burden of establishing the fact (Section 1–201(8)).

(11) "Remitter" means a person who purchases an instrument from its issuer if the instrument is payable to an identified person other than the purchaser.

(b) [Other definitions' section references deleted.]

(c) [Other definitions' section references deleted.]

(d) In addition, Article 1 contains general definitions and principles of construction and interpretation applicable throughout this Article.

§ 3–104.   Negotiable Instrument.

(a) Except as provided in subsections (c) and (d), "negotiable instrument" means an unconditional promise or order to pay a fixed amount of money, with or without interest or other charges described in the promise or order, if it:

(1) is payable to bearer or to order at the time it is issued or first comes into possession of a holder;

(2) is payable on demand or at a definite time; and

(3) does not state any other undertaking or instruction by the person promising or ordering payment to do any act in addition to the payment of money, but the promise or order may contain (i) an undertaking or power to give, maintain, or protect collateral to secure payment, (ii) an authorization or power to the holder to confess judgment or realize on or dispose of collateral, or (iii) a waiver of the benefit of any law intended for the advantage or protection of an obligor.

(b) "Instrument" means a negotiable instrument.

(c) An order that meets all of the requirements of subsection (a), except paragraph (1), and otherwise falls within the definition of "check" in subsection (f) is a negotiable instrument and a check.

(d) A promise or order other than a check is not an instrument if, at the time it is issued or first comes into possession of a holder, it contains a conspicuous statement, however expressed, to the effect that the promise or order is not negotiable or is not an instrument governed by this Article.

(e) An instrument is a "note" if it is a promise and is a "draft" if it is an order. If an instrument falls within the definition of both "note" and "draft," a person entitled to enforce the instrument may treat it as either.

(f) "Check" means (i) a draft, other than a documentary draft, payable on demand and drawn on a bank or (ii) a cashier's check or teller's check. An instrument may be a check even though it is described on its face by another term, such as "money order."

(g) "Cashier's check" means a draft with respect to which the drawer and drawee are the same bank or branches of the same bank.

(h) "Teller's check" means a draft drawn by a bank (i) on another bank, or (ii) payable at or through a bank.

(i) "Traveler's check" means an instrument that (i) is payable on demand, (ii) is drawn on or payable at or through a bank, (iii) is designated by the term "traveler's check" or by a substantially similar term, and (iv) requires, as a condition to payment, a countersignature by a person whose specimen signature appears on the instrument.

(j) "Certificate of deposit" means an instrument containing an acknowledgment by a bank that a sum of money has been received by the bank and a promise by the bank to repay the sum of money. A certificate of deposit is a note of the bank.

§ 3–105.   Issue of Instrument.

(a) "Issue" means the first delivery of an instrument by the maker or drawer, whether to a holder or nonholder, for the purpose of giving rights on the instrument to any person.

(b) An unissued instrument, or an unissued incomplete instrument that is completed, is binding on the maker or drawer, but nonissuance is a defense. An instrument that is conditionally issued or is issued for a special purpose is binding on the maker or drawer, but failure of the condition or special purpose to be fulfilled is a defense.

(c) "Issuer" applies to issued and unissued instruments and means a maker or drawer of an instrument.

§ 3–106.   Unconditional Promise or Order.

(a) Except as provided in this section, for the purposes of Section 3–104(a), a promise or order is unconditional unless it states (i) an express condition to payment, (ii) that the promise or order is subject to or governed by another writing, or (iii) that rights or obligations with respect to the promise or order are stated in another writing. A reference to another writing does not of itself make the promise or order conditional.

(b) A promise or order is not made conditional (i) by a reference to another writing for a statement of rights with respect to collateral, prepayment, or acceleration, or (ii) because payment is limited to resort to a particular fund or source.

(c) If a promise or order requires, as a condition to payment, a countersignature by a person whose specimen signature appears on the promise or order, the condition does not make the promise or order conditional for the purposes of Section 3–104(a). If the person whose specimen signature appears on an instrument fails to countersign the instrument, the failure to countersign is a defense to the obligation of the issuer, but the failure does not prevent a transferee of the instrument from becoming a holder of the instrument.

(d) If a promise or order at the time it is issued or first comes into possession of a holder contains a statement, required by applicable statutory or administrative law, to the effect that the rights of a holder or transferee are subject to claims or defenses that the issuer could assert against the original payee, the promise or order is not thereby made conditional for the purposes of Section 3–104(a); but if the promise or order is an instrument, there cannot be a holder in due course of the instrument.

§ 3–107. Instrument Payable in Foreign Money.

Unless the instrument otherwise provides, an instrument that states the amount payable in foreign money may be paid in the foreign money or in an equivalent amount in dollars calculated by using the current bank-offered spot rate at the place of payment for the purchase of dollars on the day on which the instrument is paid.

§ 3–108. Payable on Demand or at Definite Time.

(a) A promise or order is "payable on demand" if it (i) states that it is payable on demand or at sight, or otherwise indicates that it is payable at the will of the holder, or (ii) does not state any time of payment.

(b) A promise or order is "payable at a definite time" if it is payable on elapse of a definite period of time after sight or acceptance or at a fixed date or dates or at a time or times readily ascertainable at the time the promise or order is issued, subject to rights of (i) prepayment, (ii) acceleration, (iii) extension at the option of the holder, or (iv) extension to a further definite time at the option of the maker or acceptor or automatically upon or after a specified act or event.

(c) If an instrument, payable at a fixed date, is also payable upon demand made before the fixed date, the instrument is payable on demand until the fixed date and, if demand for payment is not made before that date, becomes payable at a definite time on the fixed date.

§ 3–109. Payable to Bearer or to Order.

(a) A promise or order is payable to bearer if it:

(1) states that it is payable to bearer or to the order of bearer or otherwise indicates that the person in possession of the promise or order is entitled to payment;

(2) does not state a payee; or

(3) states that it is payable to or to the order of cash or otherwise indicates that it is not payable to an identified person.

(b) A promise or order that is not payable to bearer is payable to order if it is payable (i) to the order of an identified person or (ii) to an identified person or order. A promise or order that is payable to order is payable to the identified person.

(c) An instrument payable to bearer may become payable to an identified person if it is specially indorsed pursuant to Section 3–205(a). An instrument payable to an identified person may become payable to bearer if it is indorsed in blank pursuant to Section 3–205(b).

§ 3–110. Identification of Person to Whom Instrument Is Payable.

(a) The person to whom an instrument is initially payable is determined by the intent of the person, whether or not authorized, signing as, or in the name or behalf of, the issuer of the instrument. The instrument is payable to the person intended by the signer even if that person is identified in the instrument by a name or other identification that is not that of the intended person. If more than one person signs in the name or behalf of the issuer of an instrument and all the signers do not intend the same person as payee, the instrument is payable to any person intended by one or more of the signers.

(b) If the signature of the issuer of an instrument is made by automated means, such as a check-writing machine, the payee of the instrument is determined by the intent of the person who supplied the name or identification of the payee, whether or not authorized to do so.

(c) A person to whom an instrument is payable may be identified in any way, including by name, identifying number, office, or account number. For the purpose of determining the holder of an instrument, the following rules apply:

(1) If an instrument is payable to an account and the account is identified only by number, the instrument is payable to the person to whom the account is payable. If an instrument is payable to an account identified by number and by the name of a person, the instrument is payable to the named person, whether or not that person is the owner of the account identified by number.

(2) If an instrument is payable to:

(i) a trust, an estate, or a person described as trustee or representative of a trust or estate, the instrument is payable to the trustee, the representative, or a successor of either, whether or not the beneficiary or estate is also named;

(ii) a person described as agent or similar representative of a named or identified person, the instrument is payable to the represented person, the representative, or a successor of the representative;

(iii) a fund or organization that is not a legal entity, the instrument is payable to a representative of the members of the fund or organization; or

(iv) an office or to a person described as holding an office, the instrument is payable to the named person, the incumbent of the office, or a successor to the incumbent.

(d) If an instrument is payable to two or more persons alternatively, it is payable to any of them and may be negotiated, discharged, or enforced by any or all of them in possession of the instrument. If an instrument is payable to two or more persons not alternatively, it is payable to all of them and may be negotiated, discharged, or enforced only by all of them. If an instrument payable to two or more persons is ambiguous as to whether it is payable to the persons alternatively, the instrument is payable to the persons alternatively.

§ 3–111. Place of Payment.

Except as otherwise provided for items in Article 4, an instrument is payable at the place of payment stated in the instrument. If no place of payment is stated, an instrument is payable at the address of the drawee or maker stated in the instrument. If no address is stated, the place of payment is the place of business of the drawee or maker. If a drawee or maker has more than one place of business, the place of payment is any place of business of the drawee or maker chosen by the person entitled to enforce the instrument. If the drawee or maker has no place of business, the place of payment is the residence of the drawee or maker.

§ 3–112. Interest.

(a) Unless otherwise provided in the instrument, (i) an instrument is not payable with interest, and (ii) interest on an interest-bearing instrument is payable from the date of the instrument.

(b) Interest may be stated in an instrument as a fixed or variable amount of money or it may be expressed as a fixed or variable rate or rates. The amount or rate of interest may be stated or described in the instrument in any manner and may require reference to information not contained in the instrument. If an instrument provides for interest, but the amount of interest payable cannot be ascertained from the description, interest is payable at the judgment rate in effect at the place of payment of the instrument and at the time interest first accrues.

§ 3–113. Date of Instrument.

(a) An instrument may be antedated or postdated. The date stated determines the time of payment if the instrument is payable at a fixed period after date. Except as provided in Section 4–401(c), an instrument payable on demand is not payable before the date of the instrument.

(b) If an instrument is undated, its date is the date of its issue or, in the case of an unissued instrument, the date it first comes into possession of a holder.

§ 3–114. Contradictory Terms of Instrument.

If an instrument contains contradictory terms, typewritten terms prevail over printed terms, handwritten terms prevail over both, and words prevail over numbers.

§ 3–115. Incomplete Instrument.

(a) "Incomplete instrument" means a signed writing, whether or not issued by the signer, the contents of which show at the time of signing that it is incomplete but that the signer intended it to be completed by the addition of words or numbers.

(b) Subject to subsection (c), if an incomplete instrument is an instrument under Section 3–104, it may be enforced according to its terms if it is not completed, or according to its terms as augmented by completion. If an incomplete instrument is not an instrument under Section 3–104, but, after completion, the requirements of Section 3–104 are met, the instrument may be enforced according to its terms as augmented by completion.

(c) If words or numbers are added to an incomplete instrument without authority of the signer, there is an alteration of the incomplete instrument under Section 3–407.

(d) The burden of establishing that words or numbers were added to an incomplete instrument without authority of the signer is on the person asserting the lack of authority.

§ 3–116. Joint and Several Liability; Contribution.

(a) Except as otherwise provided in the instrument, two or more persons who have the same liability on an instrument as makers, drawers, acceptors, indorsers who indorse as joint payees, or anomalous indorsers are jointly and severally liable in the capacity in which they sign.

(b) Except as provided in Section 3–419(e) or by agreement of the affected parties, a party having joint and several liability who pays the instrument is entitled to receive from any party having the same joint and several liability contribution in accordance with applicable law.

(c) Discharge of one party having joint and several liability by a person entitled to enforce the instrument does not affect the right under subsection (b) of a party having the same joint and several liability to receive contribution from the party discharged.

§ 3–117. Other Agreements Affecting Instrument.

Subject to applicable law regarding exclusion of proof of contemporaneous or previous agreements, the obligation of a party to an instrument to pay the instrument may be modified, supplemented, or nullified by a separate agreement of the obligor and a person entitled to enforce the instrument, if the instrument is issued or the obligation is incurred in reliance on the agreement or as part of the same transaction giving rise to the agreement. To the extent an obligation is modified, supplemented, or nullified by an agreement under this section, the agreement is a defense to the obligation.

§ 3–118. Statute of Limitations.

(a) Except as provided in subsection (e), an action to enforce the obligation of a party to pay a note payable at a definite time must be commenced within six years after the due date or dates stated in the note or, if a due date is accelerated, within six years after the accelerated due date.

(b) Except as provided in subsection (d) or (e), if demand for payment is made to the maker of a note payable on demand, an action to enforce the obligation of a party to pay the note must be commenced within six years after the demand. If no demand for payment is made to the maker, an action to enforce the note is barred if neither principal nor interest on the note has been paid for a continuous period of 10 years.

(c) Except as provided in subsection (d), an action to enforce the obligation of a party to an unaccepted draft to pay the draft must be commenced within three years after dishonor of the draft or 10 years after the date of the draft, whichever period expires first.

(d) An action to enforce the obligation of the acceptor of a certified check or the issuer of a teller's check, cashier's check, or traveler's check must be commenced within three years after demand for payment is made to the acceptor or issuer, as the case may be.

(e) An action to enforce the obligation of a party to a certificate of deposit to pay the instrument must be commenced within six years after demand for payment is made to the maker, but if the instrument states a due date and the maker is not required to pay before that date, the six-year period begins when a demand for payment is in effect and the due date has passed.

(f) An action to enforce the obligation of a party to pay an accepted draft, other than a certified check, must be commenced (i) within six years after the due date or dates stated in the draft or acceptance if the obligation of the acceptor is payable at a definite time, or (ii) within six years after the date of the acceptance if the obligation of the acceptor is payable on demand.

(g) Unless governed by other law regarding claims for indemnity or contribution, an action (i) for conversion of an instrument, for money had and received, or like action based on conversion, (ii) for breach of warranty, or (iii) to enforce an obligation, duty, or right arising under this Article and not governed by this section must be commenced within three years after the [cause of action] accrues.

§ 3-119. Notice of Right to Defend Action.

In an action for breach of an obligation for which a third person is answerable over pursuant to this Article or Article 4, the defendant may give the third person written notice of the litigation, and the person notified may then give similar notice to any other person who is answerable over. If the notice states (i) that the person notified may come in and defend and (ii) that failure to do so will bind the person notified in an action later brought by the person giving the notice as to any determination of fact common to the two litigations, the person notified is so bound unless after seasonable receipt of the notice the person notified does come in and defend.

Part 2 Negotiation, Transfer, and Indorsement

§ 3-201. Negotiation.

(a) "Negotiation" means a transfer of possession, whether voluntary or involuntary, of an instrument by a person other than the issuer to a person who thereby becomes its holder.

(b) Except for negotiation by a remitter, if an instrument is payable to an identified person, negotiation requires transfer of possession of the instrument and its indorsement by the holder. If an instrument is payable to bearer, it may be negotiated by transfer of possession alone.

§ 3-202. Negotiation Subject to Rescission.

(a) Negotiation is effective even if obtained (i) from an infant, a corporation exceeding its powers, or a person without capacity, (ii) by fraud, duress, or mistake, or (iii) in breach of duty or as part of an illegal transaction.

(b) To the extent permitted by other law, negotiation may be rescinded or may be subject to other remedies, but those remedies may not be asserted against a subsequent holder in due course or a person paying the instrument in good faith and without knowledge of facts that are a basis for rescission or other remedy.

§ 3-203. Transfer of Instrument; Rights Acquired by Transfer.

(a) An instrument is transferred when it is delivered by a person other than its issuer for the purpose of giving to the person receiving delivery the right to enforce the instrument.

(b) Transfer of an instrument, whether or not the transfer is a negotiation, vests in the transferee any right of the transferor to enforce the instrument, including any right as a holder in due course, but the transferee cannot acquire rights of a holder in due course by a transfer, directly or indirectly, from a holder in due course if the transferee engaged in fraud or illegality affecting the instrument.

(c) Unless otherwise agreed, if an instrument is transferred for value and the transferee does not become a holder because of lack of indorsement by the transferor, the transferee has a specifically enforceable right to the unqualified indorsement of the transferor, but negotiation of the instrument does not occur until the indorsement is made.

(d) If a transferor purports to transfer less than the entire instrument, negotiation of the instrument does not occur. The transferee obtains no rights under this Article and has only the rights of a partial assignee.

§ 3-204. Indorsement.

(a) "Indorsement" means a signature, other than that of a signer as maker, drawer, or acceptor, that alone or accompanied by other words is made on an instrument for the purpose of (i) negotiating the instrument, (ii) restricting payment of the instrument, or (iii) incurring indorser's liability on the instrument, but regardless of the intent of the signer, a signature and its accompanying words is an indorsement unless the accompanying words, terms of the instrument, place of the signature, or other circumstances unambiguously indicate that the signature was made for a purpose other than indorsement. For the purpose of determining whether a signature is made on an instrument, a paper affixed to the instrument is a part of the instrument.

(b) "Indorser" means a person who makes an indorsement.

(c) For the purpose of determining whether the transferee of an instrument is a holder, an indorsement that transfers a security interest in the instrument is effective as an unqualified indorsement of the instrument.

(d) If an instrument is payable to a holder under a name that is not the name of the holder, indorsement may be made by the holder in the name stated in the instrument or in the holder's name or both, but signature in both names may be required by a person paying or taking the instrument for value or collection.

§ 3-205. Special Indorsement; Blank Indorsement; Anomalous Indorsement.

(a) If an indorsement is made by the holder of an instrument, whether payable to an identified person or payable to bearer, and the indorsement identifies a person to whom it makes the instrument payable, it is a "special indorsement." When specially indorsed, an instrument becomes payable to the identified person and may be negotiated only by the indorsement of that person. The principles stated in Section 3-110 apply to special indorsements.

(b) If an indorsement is made by the holder of an instrument and it is not a special indorsement, it is a "blank indorsement." When indorsed in blank, an instrument becomes payable to bearer and may be negotiated by transfer of possession alone until specially indorsed.

(c) The holder may convert a blank indorsement that consists only of a signature into a special indorsement by writing, above the signature of the indorser, words identifying the person to whom the instrument is made payable.

(d) "Anomalous indorsement" means an indorsement made by a person who is not the holder of the instrument. An anomalous indorsement does not affect the manner in which the instrument may be negotiated.

§ 3–206.   Restrictive Indorsement.

(a) An indorsement limiting payment to a particular person or otherwise prohibiting further transfer or negotiation of the instrument is not effective to prevent further transfer or negotiation of the instrument.

(b) An indorsement stating a condition to the right of the indorsee to receive payment does not affect the right of the indorsee to enforce the instrument. A person paying the instrument or taking it for value or collection may disregard the condition, and the rights and liabilities of that person are not affected by whether the condition has been fulfilled.

(c) If an instrument bears an indorsement (i) described in Section 4–201(b), or (ii) in blank or to a particular bank using the words "for deposit," "for collection," or other words indicating a purpose of having the instrument collected by a bank for the indorser or for a particular account, the following rules apply:

(1) A person, other than a bank, who purchases the instrument when so indorsed converts the instrument unless the amount paid for the instrument is received by the indorser or applied consistently with the indorsement.

(2) A depositary bank that purchases the instrument or takes it for collection when so indorsed converts the instrument unless the amount paid by the bank with respect to the instrument is received by the indorser or applied consistently with the indorsement.

(3) A payor bank that is also the depositary bank or that takes the instrument for immediate payment over the counter from a person other than a collecting bank converts the instrument unless the proceeds of the instrument are received by the indorser or applied consistently with the indorsement.

(4) Except as otherwise provided in paragraph (3), a payor bank or intermediary bank may disregard the indorsement and is not liable if the proceeds of the instrument are not received by the indorser or applied consistently with the indorsement.

(d) Except for an indorsement covered by subsection (c), if an instrument bears an indorsement using words to the effect that payment is to be made to the indorsee as agent, trustee, or other fiduciary for the benefit of the indorser or another person, the following rules apply:

(1) Unless there is notice of breach of fiduciary duty as provided in Section 3–307, a person who purchases the instrument from the indorsee or takes the instrument from the indorsee for collection or payment may pay the proceeds of payment or the value given for the instrument to the indorsee without regard to whether the indorsee violates a fiduciary duty to the indorser.

(2) A subsequent transferee of the instrument or person who pays the instrument is neither given notice nor otherwise affected by the restriction in the indorsement unless the transferee or payor knows that the fiduciary dealt with the instrument or its proceeds in breach of fiduciary duty.

(e) The presence on an instrument of an indorsement to which this section applies does not prevent a purchaser of the instrument from becoming a holder in due course of the instrument unless the purchaser is a converter under subsection (c) or has notice or knowledge of breach of fiduciary duty as stated in subsection (d).

(f) In an action to enforce the obligation of a party to pay the instrument, the obligor has a defense if payment would violate an indorsement to which this section applies and the payment is not permitted by this section.

§ 3–207.   Reacquisition.

Reacquisition of an instrument occurs if it is transferred to a former holder, by negotiation or otherwise. A former holder who reacquires the instrument may cancel indorsements made after the reacquirer first became a holder of the instrument. If the cancellation causes the instrument to be payable to the reacquirer or to bearer, the reacquirer may negotiate the instrument. An indorser whose indorsement is canceled is discharged, and the discharge is effective against any subsequent holder.

Part 3   Enforcement of Instruments

§ 3–301.   Person Entitled to Enforce Instrument.

"Person entitled to enforce" an instrument means (i) the holder of the instrument, (ii) a nonholder in possession of the instrument who has the rights of a holder, or (iii) a person not in possession of the instrument who is entitled to enforce the instrument pursuant to Section 3–309 or 3–418(d). A person may be a person entitled to enforce the instrument even though the person is not the owner of the instrument or is in wrongful possession of the instrument.

§ 3–302.   Holder in Due Course.

(a) Subject to subsection (c) and Section 3–106(d), "holder in due course" means the holder of an instrument if:

(1) the instrument when issued or negotiated to the holder does not bear such apparent evidence of forgery or alteration or is not otherwise so irregular or incomplete as to call into question its authenticity; and

(2) the holder took the instrument (i) for value, (ii) in good faith, (iii) without notice that the instrument is overdue or has been dishonored or that there is an uncured default with respect to payment of another instrument issued as part of the same series, (iv) without notice that the instrument contains an unauthorized signature or has been altered, (v) without notice of any claim to the instrument described in Section 3–306, and (vi) without notice that any party has a defense or claim in recoupment described in Section 3–305(a).

(b) Notice of discharge of a party, other than discharge in an insolvency proceeding, is not notice of a defense under subsection (a), but discharge is effective against a person who became a holder in due course with notice of the discharge. Public filing or recording of a document does not of itself constitute notice of a defense, claim in recoupment, or claim to the instrument.

(c) Except to the extent a transferor or predecessor in interest has rights as a holder in due course, a person does not acquire rights of a holder in due course of an instrument taken (i) by legal process or by purchase in an execution, bankruptcy, or creditor's sale or similar proceeding, (ii) by purchase as part of a bulk transaction not in ordinary course of business of the transferor, or (iii) as the successor in interest to an estate or other organization.

(d) If, under Section 3–303(a)(1), the promise of performance that is the consideration for an instrument has been partially performed, the holder may assert rights as a holder in due course of the instrument only to the fraction of the amount payable under the instrument equal to the value of the partial performance divided by the value of the promised performance.

(e) If (i) the person entitled to enforce an instrument has only a security interest in the instrument and (ii) the person obliged to pay the instrument has a defense, claim in recoupment, or claim to the instrument that may be asserted against the person who granted the security interest, the person entitled to enforce the instrument may assert rights as a holder in due course only to an amount payable under the instrument which, at the time of enforcement of the instrument, does not exceed the amount of the unpaid obligation secured.

(f) To be effective, notice must be received at a time and in a manner that gives a reasonable opportunity to act on it.

(g) This section is subject to any law limiting status as a holder in due course in particular classes of transactions.

§ 3–303.   Value and Consideration.

(a) An instrument is issued or transferred for value if:

(1) the instrument is issued or transferred for a promise of performance, to the extent the promise has been performed;

(2) the transferee acquires a security interest or other lien in the instrument other than a lien obtained by judicial proceeding;

(3) the instrument is issued or transferred as payment of, or as security for, an antecedent claim against any person, whether or not the claim is due;

(4) the instrument is issued or transferred in exchange for a negotiable instrument; or

(5) the instrument is issued or transferred in exchange for the incurring of an irrevocable obligation to a third party by the person taking the instrument.

(b) "Consideration" means any consideration sufficient to support a simple contract. The drawer or maker of an instrument has a defense if the instrument is issued without consideration. If an instrument is issued for a promise of performance, the issuer has a defense to the extent performance of the promise is due and the promise has not been performed. If an instrument is issued for value as stated in subsection (a), the instrument is also issued for consideration.

§ 3–304.   Overdue Instrument.

(a) An instrument payable on demand becomes overdue at the earliest of the following times:

(1) on the day after the day demand for payment is duly made;

(2) if the instrument is a check, 90 days after its date; or

(3) if the instrument is not a check, when the instrument has been outstanding for a period of time after its date which is unreasonably long under the circumstances of the particular case in light of the nature of the instrument and usage of the trade.

(b) With respect to an instrument payable at a definite time the following rules apply:

(1) If the principal is payable in installments and a due date has not been accelerated, the instrument becomes overdue upon default under the instrument for nonpayment of an installment, and the instrument remains overdue until the default is cured.

(2) If the principal is not payable in installments and the due date has not been accelerated, the instrument becomes overdue on the day after the due date.

(3) If a due date with respect to principal has been accelerated, the instrument becomes overdue on the day after the accelerated due date.

(c) Unless the due date of principal has been accelerated, an instrument does not become overdue if there is default in payment of interest but no default in payment of principal.

§ 3–305.   Defenses and Claims in Recoupment.

(a) Except as stated in subsection (b), the right to enforce the obligation of a party to pay an instrument is subject to the following:

(1) a defense of the obligor based on (i) infancy of the obligor to the extent it is a defense to a simple contract, (ii) duress, lack of legal capacity, or illegality of the transaction which, under other law, nullifies the obligation of the obligor, (iii) fraud that induced the obligor to sign the instrument with neither knowledge nor reasonable opportunity to learn of its character or its essential terms, or (iv) discharge of the obligor in insolvency proceedings;

(2) a defense of the obligor stated in another section of this Article or a defense of the obligor that would be available if the person entitled to enforce the instrument were enforcing a right to payment under a simple contract; and

(3) a claim in recoupment of the obligor against the original payee of the instrument if the claim arose from the transaction that gave rise to the instrument; but the claim of the obligor may be asserted against a transferee of the instrument only to reduce the amount owing on the instrument at the time the action is brought.

(b) The right of a holder in due course to enforce the obligation of a party to pay the instrument is subject to defenses of the obligor stated in subsection (a)(1), but is not subject to defenses of the obligor stated in subsection (a)(2) or claims in recoupment stated in subsection (a)(3) against a person other than the holder.

(c) Except as stated in subsection (d), in an action to enforce the obligation of a party to pay the instrument, the obligor may not assert against the person entitled to enforce the instrument a defense, claim in recoupment, or claim to the instrument (Section 3–306) of another person, but the other person's claim to the instrument may be asserted by the obligor if the other person is joined in the action and personally asserts the claim against the person entitled to enforce the instrument. An obligor is not obliged to pay the instrument if the person seeking enforcement of the instrument does not have rights of a holder in due course and the obligor proves that the instrument is a lost or stolen instrument.

(d) In an action to enforce the obligation of an accommodation party to pay an instrument, the accommodation party may assert against the person entitled to enforce the instrument any defense or claim in recoupment under subsection (a) that the accommodated party could assert against the person entitled to enforce the instrument, except the defenses of discharge in insolvency proceedings, infancy, and lack of legal capacity.

§ 3–306.   Claims to an Instrument.

A person taking an instrument, other than a person having rights of a holder in due course, is subject to a claim of a property or possessory right in the instrument or its proceeds, including a claim to rescind a negotiation and to recover the instrument or its proceeds. A person having rights of a holder in due course takes free of the claim to the instrument.

§ 3–307.   Notice of Breach of Fiduciary Duty.

(a) In this section:

(1) "Fiduciary" means an agent, trustee, partner, corporate officer or director, or other representative owing a fiduciary duty with respect to an instrument.

(2) "Represented person" means the principal, beneficiary, partnership, corporation, or other person to whom the duty stated in paragraph (1) is owed.

(b) If (i) an instrument is taken from a fiduciary for payment or collection or for value, (ii) the taker has knowledge of the fiduciary status of the fiduciary, and (iii) the represented person makes a claim to the instrument or its proceeds on the basis that the transaction of the fiduciary is a breach of fiduciary duty, the following rules apply:

(1) Notice of breach of fiduciary duty by the fiduciary is notice of the claim of the represented person.

(2) In the case of an instrument payable to the represented person or the fiduciary as such, the taker has notice of the breach of fiduciary duty if the instrument is (i) taken in payment of or as security for a debt known by the taker to be the personal debt of the fiduciary, (ii) taken in a transaction known by the taker to be for the personal benefit of the fiduciary, or (iii) deposited to an account other than an account of the fiduciary, as such, or an account of the represented person.

(3) If an instrument is issued by the represented person or the fiduciary as such, and made payable to the fiduciary personally, the taker does not have notice of the breach of fiduciary duty unless the taker knows of the breach of fiduciary duty.

(4) If an instrument is issued by the represented person or the fiduciary as such, to the taker as payee, the taker has notice of the breach of fiduciary duty if the instrument is (i) taken in payment of or as security for a debt known by the taker to be the personal debt of the fiduciary, (ii) taken in a transaction known by the taker to be for the personal benefit of the fiduciary, or (iii) deposited to an account other than an account of the fiduciary, as such, or an account of the represented person.

§ 3–308.   Proof of Signatures and Status as Holder in Due Course.

(a) In an action with respect to an instrument, the authenticity of, and authority to make, each signature on the instrument is admitted unless specifically denied in the pleadings. If the validity of a signature is denied in the pleadings, the burden of establishing validity is on the person claiming validity, but the signature is presumed to be authentic and authorized unless the action is to enforce the liability of the purported signer and the signer is dead or incompetent at the time of trial of the issue of validity of the signature. If an action to enforce the instrument is brought against a person as the undisclosed principal of a person who signed the instrument as a party to the instrument, the plaintiff has the burden of establishing that the defendant is liable on the instrument as a represented person under Section 3–402(a).

(b) If the validity of signatures is admitted or proved and there is compliance with subsection (a), a plaintiff producing the instrument is entitled to payment if the plaintiff proves entitlement to enforce the instrument under Section 3–301, unless the defendant proves a defense or claim in recoupment. If a defense or claim in recoupment is proved, the right to payment of the plaintiff is subject to the defense or claim, except to the extent the plaintiff proves that the plaintiff has rights of a holder in due course which are not subject to the defense or claim.

§ 3–309.   Enforcement of Lost, Destroyed, or Stolen Instrument.

(a) A person not in possession of an instrument is entitled to enforce the instrument if (i) the person was in possession of the instrument and entitled to enforce it when loss of possession occurred, (ii) the loss of possession was not the result of a transfer by the person or a lawful seizure, and (iii) the person cannot reasonably obtain possession of the instrument because the instrument was destroyed, its whereabouts cannot be determined, or it is in the wrongful possession of an unknown person or a person that cannot be found or is not amenable to service of process.

(b) A person seeking enforcement of an instrument under subsection (a) must prove the terms of the instrument and the person's right to enforce the instrument. If that proof is made, Section 3–308 applies to the case as if the person seeking enforcement had produced the instrument. The court may not enter judgment in favor of the person seeking enforcement unless it finds that the person required to pay the instrument is adequately protected against loss that might occur by reason of a claim by another person to enforce the instrument. Adequate protection may be provided by any reasonable means.

§ 3–310. Effect of Instrument on Obligation for Which Taken.

(a) Unless otherwise agreed, if a certified check, cashier's check, or teller's check is taken for an obligation, the obligation is discharged to the same extent discharge would result if an amount of money equal to the amount of the instrument were taken in payment of the obligation. Discharge of the obligation does not affect any liability that the obligor may have as an indorser of the instrument.

(b) Unless otherwise agreed and except as provided in subsection (a), if a note or an uncertified check is taken for an obligation, the obligation is suspended to the same extent the obligation would be discharged if an amount of money equal to the amount of the instrument were taken, and the following rules apply:

(1) In the case of an uncertified check, suspension of the obligation continues until dishonor of the check or until it is paid or certified. Payment or certification of the check results in discharge of the obligation to the extent of the amount of the check.

(2) In the case of a note, suspension of the obligation continues until dishonor of the note or until it is paid. Payment of the note results in discharge of the obligation to the extent of the payment.

(3) Except as provided in paragraph (4), if the check or note is dishonored and the obligee of the obligation for which the instrument was taken is the person entitled to enforce the instrument, the obligee may enforce either the instrument or the obligation. In the case of an instrument of a third person which is negotiated to the obligee by the obligor, discharge of the obligor on the instrument also discharges the obligation.

(4) If the person entitled to enforce the instrument taken for an obligation is a person other than the obligee, the obligee may not enforce the obligation to the extent the obligation is suspended. If the obligee is the person entitled to enforce the instrument but no longer has possession of it because it was lost, stolen, or destroyed, the obligation may not be enforced to the extent of the amount payable on the instrument, and to that extent the obligee's rights against the obligor are limited to enforcement of the instrument.

(c) If an instrument other than one described in subsection (a) or (b) is taken for an obligation, the effect is (i) that stated in subsection (a) if the instrument is one on which a bank is liable as maker or acceptor, or (ii) that stated in subsection (b) in any other case.

§ 3–311. Accord and Satisfaction by Use of Instrument.

(a) If a person against whom a claim is asserted proves that (i) that person in good faith tendered an instrument to the claimant as full satisfaction of the claim, (ii) the amount of the claim was unliquidated or subject to a bona fide dispute, and (iii) the claimant obtained payment of the instrument, the following subsections apply.

(b) Unless subsection (c) applies, the claim is discharged if the person against whom the claim is asserted proves that the instrument or an accompanying written communication contained a conspicuous statement to the effect that the instrument was tendered as full satisfaction of the claim.

(c) Subject to subsection (d), a claim is not discharged under subsection (b) if either of the following applies:

(1) The claimant, if an organization, proves that (i) within a reasonable time before the tender, the claimant sent a conspicuous statement to the person against whom the claim is asserted that communications concerning disputed debts, including an instrument tendered as full satisfaction of a debt, are to be sent to a designated person, office, or place, and (ii) the instrument or accompanying communication was not received by that designated person, office, or place.

(2) The claimant, whether or not an organization, proves that within 90 days after payment of the instrument, the claimant tendered repayment of the amount of the instrument to the person against whom the claim is asserted. This paragraph does not apply if the claimant is an organization that sent a statement complying with paragraph (1)(i).

(d) A claim is discharged if the person against whom the claim is asserted proves that within a reasonable time before collection of the instrument was initiated, the claimant, or an agent of the claimant having direct responsibility with respect to the disputed obligation, knew that the instrument was tendered in full satisfaction of the claim.

§ 3–312. Lost, Destroyed, or Stolen Cashier's Check, Teller's Check, or Certified Check.

(a) In this section:

(1) "Check" means a cashier's check, teller's check, or certified check.

(2) "Claimant" means a person who claims the right to receive the amount of a cashier's check, teller's check, or certified check that was lost, destroyed, or stolen.

(3) "Declaration of loss" means a written statement, made under penalty of perjury, to the effect that (i) the declarer lost possession of a check, (ii) the declarer is the drawer or payee of the check, in the case of a certified check, or the remitter or payee of the check, in the case of a cashier's check or teller's check, (iii) the loss of possession was not the result of a transfer by the declarer or a lawful seizure, and (iv) the declarer cannot reasonably obtain possession of the check because the check was destroyed, its whereabouts cannot be determined, or it is in the wrongful possession of an unknown person or a person that cannot be found or is not amenable to service of process.

(4) "Obligated bank" means the issuer of a cashier's check or teller's check or the acceptor of a certified check.

(b) A claimant may assert a claim to the amount of a check by a communication to the obligated bank describing the check with reasonable certainty and requesting payment of the amount of the check, if (i) the claimant is the drawer or payee of a certified check or the remitter or payee of a cashier's check or teller's check, (ii) the communication contains or is accompanied by a declaration of loss of the claimant with respect to the check, (iii) the communication is received at a time and in a manner affording the bank a reasonable time to act on it before the check is paid, and (iv) the claimant provides reasonable identification if requested by the obligated bank. Delivery of a declaration of loss is a warranty of the truth of the statements made in the declaration. If a claim is asserted in compliance with this subsection, the following rules apply:

(1) The claim becomes enforceable at the later of (i) the time the claim is asserted, or (ii) the 90th day following the date of the check, in the case of a cashier's check or teller's check, or the 90th day following the date of the acceptance, in the case of a certified check.

(2) Until the claim becomes enforceable, it has no legal effect and the obligated bank may pay the check or, in the case of a teller's check, may permit the drawee to pay the check. Payment to a person entitled to enforce the check discharges all liability of the obligated bank with respect to the check.

(3) If the claim becomes enforceable before the check is presented for payment, the obligated bank is not obliged to pay the check.

(4) When the claim becomes enforceable, the obligated bank becomes obliged to pay the amount of the check to the claimant if payment of the check has not been made to a person entitled to enforce the check. Subject to Section 4–302(a)(1), payment to the claimant discharges all liability of the obligated bank with respect to the check.

(c) If the obligated bank pays the amount of a check to a claimant under subsection (b)(4) and the check is presented for payment by a person having rights of a holder in due course, the claimant is obliged to (i) refund the payment to the obligated bank if the check is paid, or (ii) pay the amount of the check to the person having rights of a holder in due course if the check is dishonored.

(d) If a claimant has the right to assert a claim under subsection (b) and is also a person entitled to enforce a cashier's check, teller's check, or certified check which is lost, destroyed, or stolen, the claimant may assert rights with respect to the check either under this section or Section 3–309.

Added in 1991.

Part 4   Liability of Parties

§ 3–401.   Signature.

(a) A person is not liable on an instrument unless (i) the person signed the instrument, or (ii) the person is represented by an agent or representative who signed the instrument and the signature is binding on the represented person under Section 3–402.

(b) A signature may be made (i) manually or by means of a device or machine, and (ii) by the use of any name, including a trade or assumed name, or by a word, mark, or symbol executed or adopted by a person with present intention to authenticate a writing.

§ 3–402.   Signature by Representative.

(a) If a person acting, or purporting to act, as a representative signs an instrument by signing either the name of the represented person or the name of the signer, the represented person is bound by the signature to the same extent the represented person would be bound if the signature were on a simple contract. If the represented person is bound, the signature of the representative is the "authorized signature of the represented person" and the represented person is liable on the instrument, whether or not identified in the instrument.

(b) If a representative signs the name of the representative to an instrument and the signature is an authorized signature of the represented person, the following rules apply:

(1) If the form of the signature shows unambiguously that the signature is made on behalf of the represented person who is identified in the instrument, the representative is not liable on the instrument.

(2) Subject to subsection (c), if (i) the form of the signature does not show unambiguously that the signature is made in a representative capacity or (ii) the represented person is not identified in the instrument, the representative is liable on the instrument to a holder in due course that took the instrument without notice that the representative was not intended to be liable on the instrument. With respect to any other person, the representative is liable on the instrument unless the representative proves that the original parties did not intend the representative to be liable on the instrument.

(c) If a representative signs the name of the representative as drawer of a check without indication of the representative status and the check is payable from an account of the represented person who is identified on the check, the signer is not liable on the check if the signature is an authorized signature of the represented person.

§ 3–403.   Unauthorized Signature.

(a) Unless otherwise provided in this Article or Article 4, an unauthorized signature is ineffective except as the signature of the unauthorized signer in favor of a person who in good faith pays the instrument or takes it for value. An unauthorized signature may be ratified for all purposes of this Article.

(b) If the signature of more than one person is required to constitute the authorized signature of an organization, the signature of the organization is unauthorized if one of the required signatures is lacking.

(c) The civil or criminal liability of a person who makes an unauthorized signature is not affected by any provision of this Article which makes the unauthorized signature effective for the purposes of this Article.

§ 3–404.   Impostors; Fictitious Payees.

(a) If an impostor, by use of the mails or otherwise, induces the issuer of an instrument to issue the instrument to the impostor, or to a person acting in concert with the impostor, by impersonating the payee of the instrument or a person authorized to act for the payee, an indorsement of the instrument by any person in the name of the payee is effective as the indorsement of the payee in favor of a person who, in good faith, pays the instrument or takes it for value or for collection.

(b) If (i) a person whose intent determines to whom an instrument is payable (Section 3–110(a) or (b)) does not intend the person identified as payee to have any interest in the instrument, or (ii) the person identified as payee of an instrument is a fictitious person, the following rules apply until the instrument is negotiated by special indorsement:

(1) Any person in possession of the instrument is its holder.

(2) An indorsement by any person in the name of the payee stated in the instrument is effective as the indorsement of the payee in favor of a person who, in good faith, pays the instrument or takes it for value or for collection.

(c) Under subsection (a) or (b), an indorsement is made in the name of a payee if (i) it is made in a name substantially similar to that of the payee or (ii) the instrument, whether or not indorsed, is deposited in a depositary bank to an account in a name substantially similar to that of the payee.

(d) With respect to an instrument to which subsection (a) or (b) applies, if a person paying the instrument or taking it for value or for collection fails to exercise ordinary care in paying or taking the instrument and that failure substantially contributes to loss resulting from payment of the instrument, the person bearing the loss may recover from the person failing to exercise ordinary care to the extent the failure to exercise ordinary care contributed to the loss.

§ 3–405.   Employer's Responsibility for Fraudulent Indorsement by Employee.

(a) In this section:

(1) "Employee" includes an independent contractor and employee of an independent contractor retained by the employer.

(2) "Fraudulent indorsement" means (i) in the case of an instrument payable to the employer, a forged indorsement purporting to be that of the employer, or (ii) in the case of an instrument with respect to which the employer is the issuer, a forged indorsement purporting to be that of the person identified as payee.

(3) "Responsibility" with respect to instruments means authority (i) to sign or indorse instruments on behalf of the employer, (ii) to process instruments received by the employer for bookkeeping purposes, for deposit to an account, or for other disposition, (iii) to prepare or process instruments for issue in the name of the employer, (iv) to supply information determining the names or addresses of payees of instruments to be issued in the name of the employer, (v) to control the disposition of instruments to be issued in the name of the employer, or (vi) to act otherwise with respect to instruments in a responsible capacity. "Responsibility" does not include authority that merely allows an employee to have access to instruments or blank or incomplete instrument forms that are being stored or transported or are part of incoming or outgoing mail, or similar access.

(b) For the purpose of determining the rights and liabilities of a person who, in good faith, pays an instrument or takes it for value or for collection, if an employer entrusted an employee with responsibility with respect to the instrument and the employee or a person acting in concert with the employee makes a fraudulent indorsement of the instrument, the indorsement is effective as the indorsement of the person to whom the instrument is payable if it is made in the name of that person. If the person paying the instrument or taking it for value or for collection fails to exercise ordinary care in paying or taking the instrument and that failure substantially contributes to loss resulting from the fraud, the person bearing the loss may recover from the person failing to exercise ordinary care to the extent the failure to exercise ordinary care contributed to the loss.

(c) Under subsection (b), an indorsement is made in the name of the person to whom an instrument is payable if (i) it is made in a name substantially similar to the name of that person or (ii) the instrument, whether or not indorsed, is deposited in a depositary bank to an account in a name substantially similar to the name of that person.

§ 3–406.   Negligence Contributing to Forged Signature or Alteration of Instrument.

(a) A person whose failure to exercise ordinary care substantially contributes to an alteration of an instrument or to the making of a forged signature on an instrument is precluded from asserting the alteration or the forgery against a person who, in good faith, pays the instrument or takes it for value or for collection.

(b) Under subsection (a), if the person asserting the preclusion fails to exercise ordinary care in paying or taking the instrument and that failure substantially contributes to loss, the loss is allocated between the person precluded and the person asserting the preclusion according to the extent to which the failure of each to exercise ordinary care contributed to the loss.

(c) Under subsection (a), the burden of proving failure to exercise ordinary care is on the person asserting the preclusion. Under subsection (b), the burden of proving failure to exercise ordinary care is on the person precluded.

§ 3–407.   Alteration.

(a) "Alteration" means (i) an unauthorized change in an instrument that purports to modify in any respect the obligation of a party, or (ii) an unauthorized addition of words or numbers or other change to an incomplete instrument relating to the obligation of a party.

(b) Except as provided in subsection (c), an alteration fraudulently made discharges a party whose obligation is affected by the alteration unless that party assents or is precluded from asserting the alteration. No other alteration discharges a party, and the instrument may be enforced according to its original terms.

(c) A payor bank or drawee paying a fraudulently altered instrument or a person taking it for value, in good faith and without notice of the alteration, may enforce rights with respect to the instrument (i) according to its original terms, or (ii) in the case of an incomplete instrument altered by unauthorized completion, according to its terms as completed.

§ 3–408.   Drawee Not Liable on Unaccepted Draft.

A check or other draft does not of itself operate as an assignment of funds in the hands of the drawee available for its payment, and the drawee is not liable on the instrument until the drawee accepts it.

§ 3–409.   Acceptance of Draft; Certified Check.

(a) "Acceptance" means the drawee's signed agreement to pay a draft as presented. It must be written on the draft and may consist of the drawee's signature alone. Acceptance may be made at any time and becomes effective when notification pursuant to instructions is given or the accepted draft is delivered for the purpose of giving rights on the acceptance to any person.

(b) A draft may be accepted although it has not been signed by the drawer, is otherwise incomplete, is overdue, or has been dishonored.

(c) If a draft is payable at a fixed period after sight and the acceptor fails to date the acceptance, the holder may complete the acceptance by supplying a date in good faith.

(d) "Certified check" means a check accepted by the bank on which it is drawn. Acceptance may be made as stated in subsection (a) or by a writing on the check which indicates that the check is certified. The drawee of a check has no obligation to certify the check, and refusal to certify is not dishonor of the check.

§ 3–410.   Acceptance Varying Draft.

(a) If the terms of a drawee's acceptance vary from the terms of the draft as presented, the holder may refuse the acceptance and treat the draft as dishonored. In that case, the drawee may cancel the acceptance.

(b) The terms of a draft are not varied by an acceptance to pay at a particular bank or place in the United States, unless the acceptance states that the draft is to be paid only at that bank or place.

(c) If the holder assents to an acceptance varying the terms of a draft, the obligation of each drawer and indorser that does not expressly assent to the acceptance is discharged.

§ 3–411.   Refusal to Pay Cashier's Checks, Teller's Checks, and Certified Checks.

(a) In this section, "obligated bank" means the acceptor of a certified check or the issuer of a cashier's check or teller's check bought from the issuer.

(b) If the obligated bank wrongfully (i) refuses to pay a cashier's check or certified check, (ii) stops payment of a teller's check, or (iii) refuses to pay a dishonored teller's check, the person asserting the right to enforce the check is entitled to compensation for expenses and loss of interest resulting from the nonpayment and may recover consequential damages if the obligated bank refuses to pay after receiving notice of particular circumstances giving rise to the damages.

(c) Expenses or consequential damages under subsection (b) are not recoverable if the refusal of the obligated bank to pay occurs because (i) the bank suspends payments, (ii) the obligated bank asserts a claim or defense of the bank that it has reasonable grounds to believe is available against the person entitled to enforce the instrument, (iii) the obligated bank has a reasonable doubt whether the person demanding payment is the person entitled to enforce the instrument, or (iv) payment is prohibited by law.

§ 3–412.   Obligation of Issuer of Note or Cashier's Check.

The issuer of a note or cashier's check or other draft drawn on the drawer is obliged to pay the instrument (i) according to its terms at the time it was issued or, if not issued, at the time it first came into possession of a holder, or (ii) if the issuer signed an incomplete instrument, according to its terms when completed, to the extent stated in Sections 3–115 and 3–407. The obligation is owed to a person entitled to enforce the instrument or to an indorser who paid the instrument under Section 3–415.

§ 3–413.   Obligation of Acceptor.

(a) The acceptor of a draft is obliged to pay the draft (i) according to its terms at the time it was accepted, even though the acceptance states that the draft is payable "as originally drawn" or equivalent terms, (ii) if the acceptance varies the terms of the draft, according to the terms of the draft as varied, or (iii) if the acceptance is of a draft that is an incomplete instrument, according to its terms when completed, to the extent stated in Sections 3–115 and 3–407. The obligation is owed to a person entitled to enforce the draft or to the drawer or an indorser who paid the draft under Section 3–414 or 3–415.

(b) If the certification of a check or other acceptance of a draft states the amount certified or accepted, the obligation of the acceptor is that amount. If (i) the certification or acceptance does not state an amount, (ii) the amount of the instrument is subsequently raised, and (iii) the instrument is then negotiated to a holder in due course, the obligation of the acceptor is the amount of the instrument at the time it was taken by the holder in due course.

§ 3–414.   Obligation of Drawer.

(a) This section does not apply to cashier's checks or other drafts drawn on the drawer.

(b) If an unaccepted draft is dishonored, the drawer is obliged to pay the draft (i) according to its terms at the time it was issued or, if not issued, at the time it first came into possession of a holder, or (ii) if the drawer signed an incomplete instrument, according to its terms when completed, to the extent stated in Sections 3–115 and 3–407. The obligation is owed to a person entitled to enforce the draft or to an indorser who paid the draft under Section 3–415.

(c) If a draft is accepted by a bank, the drawer is discharged, regardless of when or by whom acceptance was obtained.

(d) If a draft is accepted and the acceptor is not a bank, the obligation of the drawer to pay the draft if the draft is dishonored by the acceptor is the same as the obligation of an indorser under Section 3–415(a) and (c).

(e) If a draft states that it is drawn "without recourse" or otherwise disclaims liability of the drawer to pay the draft, the drawer is not liable under subsection (b) to pay the draft if the draft is not a check. A disclaimer of the liability stated in subsection (b) is not effective if the draft is a check.

(f) If (i) a check is not presented for payment or given to a depositary bank for collection within 30 days after its date, (ii) the drawee suspends payments after expiration of the 30-day period without paying the check, and (iii) because of the suspension of payments, the drawer is deprived of funds maintained with the drawee to cover payment of the check, the drawer to the extent deprived of funds may discharge its obligation to pay the check by assigning to the person entitled to enforce the check the rights of the drawer against the drawee with respect to the funds.

§ 3–415.   Obligation of Indorser.

(a) Subject to subsections (b), (c), and (d) and to Section 3–419(d), if an instrument is dishonored, an indorser is obliged to pay the amount due on the instrument (i) according to the terms of the instrument at the time it was indorsed, or (ii) if the indorser indorsed an incomplete instrument, according to its terms when completed, to the extent stated in Sections 3–115 and 3–407. The obligation of the indorser is owed to a person entitled to enforce the instrument or to a subsequent indorser who paid the instrument under this section.

(b) If an indorsement states that it is made "without recourse" or otherwise disclaims liability of the indorser, the indorser is not liable under subsection (a) to pay the instrument.

(c) If notice of dishonor of an instrument is required by Section 3–503 and notice of dishonor complying with that section is not given to an indorser, the liability of the indorser under subsection (a) is discharged.

(d) If a draft is accepted by a bank after an indorsement is made, the liability of the indorser under subsection (a) is discharged.

(e) If an indorser of a check is liable under subsection (a) and the check is not presented for payment, or given to a depositary bank for collection, within 30 days after the day the indorsement was made, the liability of the indorser under subsection (a) is discharged. As amended in 1993.

§ 3–416.   Transfer Warranties.

(a) A person who transfers an instrument for consideration warrants to the transferee and, if the transfer is by indorsement, to any subsequent transferee that:

(1) the warrantor is a person entitled to enforce the instrument;

(2) all signatures on the instrument are authentic and authorized;

(3) the instrument has not been altered;

(4) the instrument is not subject to a defense or claim in recoupment of any party which can be asserted against the warrantor; and

(5) the warrantor has no knowledge of any insolvency proceeding commenced with respect to the maker or acceptor or, in the case of an unaccepted draft, the drawer.

(b) A person to whom the warranties under subsection (a) are made and who took the instrument in good faith may recover from the warrantor as damages for breach of warranty an amount equal to the loss suffered as a result of the breach, but not more than the amount of the instrument plus expenses and loss of interest incurred as a result of the breach.

(c) The warranties stated in subsection (a) cannot be disclaimed with respect to checks. Unless notice of a claim for breach of warranty is given to the warrantor within 30 days after the claimant has reason to know of the breach and the identity of the warrantor, the liability of the warrantor under subsection (b) is discharged to the extent of any loss caused by the delay in giving notice of the claim.

(d) A [cause of action] for breach of warranty under this section accrues when the claimant has reason to know of the breach.

§ 3–417.   Presentment Warranties.

(a) If an unaccepted draft is presented to the drawee for payment or acceptance and the drawee pays or accepts the draft, (i) the person obtaining payment or acceptance, at the time of presentment, and (ii) a previous transferor of the draft, at the time of transfer, warrant to the drawee making payment or accepting the draft in good faith that:

(1) the warrantor is, or was, at the time the warrantor transferred the draft, a person entitled to enforce the draft or authorized to obtain payment or acceptance of the draft on behalf of a person entitled to enforce the draft;

(2) the draft has not been altered; and

(3) the warrantor has no knowledge that the signature of the drawer of the draft is unauthorized.

(b) A drawee making payment may recover from any warrantor damages for breach of warranty equal to the amount paid by the drawee less the amount the drawee received or is entitled to receive from the drawer because of the payment. In addition, the drawee is entitled to compensation for expenses and loss of interest resulting from the breach. The right of the drawee to recover damages under this subsection is not affected by any failure of the drawee to exercise ordinary care in making payment. If the drawee accepts the draft, breach of warranty is a defense to the obligation of the acceptor. If the acceptor makes payment with respect to the draft, the acceptor is entitled to recover from any warrantor for breach of warranty the amounts stated in this subsection.

(c) If a drawee asserts a claim for breach of warranty under subsection (a) based on an unauthorized indorsement of the draft or an alteration of the draft, the warrantor may defend by proving that the indorsement is effective under Section 3–404 or 3–405 or the drawer is precluded under Section 3–406 or 4–406 from asserting against the drawee the unauthorized indorsement or alteration.

(d) If (i) a dishonored draft is presented for payment to the drawer or an indorser or (ii) any other instrument is presented for payment to a party obliged to pay the instrument, and (iii) payment is received, the following rules apply:

(1) The person obtaining payment and a prior transferor of the instrument warrant to the person making payment in good faith that the warrantor is, or was, at the time the warrantor transferred the instrument, a person entitled to enforce the instrument or authorized to obtain payment on behalf of a person entitled to enforce the instrument.

(2) The person making payment may recover from any warrantor for breach of warranty an amount equal to the amount paid plus expenses and loss of interest resulting from the breach.

(e) The warranties stated in subsections (a) and (d) cannot be disclaimed with respect to checks. Unless notice of a claim for breach of warranty is given to the warrantor within 30 days after the claimant has reason to know of the breach and the identity of the warrantor, the liability of the warrantor under subsection (b) or (d) is discharged to the extent of any loss caused by the delay in giving notice of the claim.

(f) A [cause of action] for breach of warranty under this section accrues when the claimant has reason to know of the breach.

§ 3–418.   Payment or Acceptance by Mistake.

(a) Except as provided in subsection (c), if the drawee of a draft pays or accepts the draft and the drawee acted on the mistaken belief that (i) payment of the draft had not been stopped pursuant to Section 4–403 or (ii) the signature of the drawer of the draft was authorized, the drawee may recover the amount of the draft from the person to whom or for whose benefit payment was made or, in the case of acceptance, may revoke the acceptance. Rights of the drawee under this subsection are not affected by failure of the drawee to exercise ordinary care in paying or accepting the draft.

(b) Except as provided in subsection (c), if an instrument has been paid or accepted by mistake and the case is not covered by subsection (a), the person paying or accepting may, to the extent permitted by the law governing mistake and restitution, (i) recover the payment from the person to whom or for whose benefit payment was made or (ii) in the case of acceptance, may revoke the acceptance.

(c) The remedies provided by subsection (a) or (b) may not be asserted against a person who took the instrument in good faith and for value or who in good faith changed position in reliance on the payment or acceptance. This subsection does not limit remedies provided by Section 3–417 or 4–407.

(d) Notwithstanding Section 4–215, if an instrument is paid or accepted by mistake and the payor or acceptor recovers payment or revokes acceptance under subsection (a) or (b), the instrument is deemed not to have been paid or accepted and is treated as dishonored, and the person from whom payment is recovered has rights as a person entitled to enforce the dishonored instrument.

§ 3–419.   Instruments Signed for Accommodation.

(a) If an instrument is issued for value given for the benefit of a party to the instrument ("accommodated party") and another party to the instrument ("accommodation party") signs the instrument for the purpose of incurring liability on the instrument without being a direct beneficiary of the value given for the instrument, the instrument is signed by the accommodation party "for accommodation."

(b) An accommodation party may sign the instrument as maker, drawer, acceptor, or indorser and, subject to subsection (d), is obliged to pay the instrument in the capacity in which the accommodation party signs. The obligation of an accommodation party may be enforced notwithstanding any statute of frauds and whether or not the accommodation party receives consideration for the accommodation.

(c) A person signing an instrument is presumed to be an accommodation party and there is notice that the instrument is signed for accommodation if the signature is an anomalous indorsement or is accompanied by words indicating that the signer is acting as surety or guarantor with respect to the obligation of another party to the instrument. Except as provided in Section 3–605, the obligation of an accommodation party to pay the instrument is not affected by the fact that the person enforcing the obligation had notice when the instrument was taken by that person that the accommodation party signed the instrument for accommodation.

(d) If the signature of a party to an instrument is accompanied by words indicating unambiguously that the party is guaranteeing collection rather than payment of the obligation of another party to the instrument, the signer is obliged to pay the amount due on the instrument to a person entitled to enforce the instrument only if (i) execution of judgment against the other party has been returned unsatisfied, (ii) the other party is insolvent or in an insolvency proceeding, (iii) the other party cannot be served with process, or (iv) it is otherwise apparent that payment cannot be obtained from the other party.

(e) An accommodation party who pays the instrument is entitled to reimbursement from the accommodated party and is entitled to enforce the instrument against the accommodated party. An accommodated party who pays the instrument has no right of recourse against, and is not entitled to contribution from, an accommodation party.

§ 3–420.   Conversion of Instrument.

(a) The law applicable to conversion of personal property applies to instruments. An instrument is also converted if it is taken by transfer, other than a negotiation, from a person not entitled to enforce the instrument or a bank makes or obtains payment with respect to the instrument for a person not entitled to enforce the instrument or receive payment. An action for conversion of an instrument may not be brought by (i) the issuer or acceptor of the instrument or (ii) a payee or indorsee who did not receive delivery of the instrument either directly or through delivery to an agent or a co-payee.

(b) In an action under subsection (a), the measure of liability is presumed to be the amount payable on the instrument, but recovery may not exceed the amount of the plaintiff's interest in the instrument.

(c) A representative, other than a depositary bank, who has in good faith dealt with an instrument or its proceeds on behalf of one who was not the person entitled to enforce the instrument is not liable in conversion to that person beyond the amount of any proceeds that it has not paid out.

Part 5   Dishonor

§ 3–501.   Presentment.

(a) "Presentment" means a demand made by or on behalf of a person entitled to enforce an instrument (i) to pay the instrument made to the drawee or a party obliged to pay the instrument or, in the case of a note or accepted draft payable at a bank, to the bank, or (ii) to accept a draft made to the drawee.

(b) The following rules are subject to Article 4, agreement of the parties, and clearing-house rules and the like:

(1) Presentment may be made at the place of payment of the instrument and must be made at the place of payment if the

instrument is payable at a bank in the United States; may be made by any commercially reasonable means, including an oral, written, or electronic communication; is effective when the demand for payment or acceptance is received by the person to whom presentment is made; and is effective if made to any one of two or more makers, acceptors, drawees, or other payors.

(2) Upon demand of the person to whom presentment is made, the person making presentment must (i) exhibit the instrument, (ii) give reasonable identification and, if presentment is made on behalf of another person, reasonable evidence of authority to do so, and (. . .) sign a receipt on the instrument for any payment made or surrender the instrument if full payment is made.

(3) Without dishonoring the instrument, the party to whom presentment is made may (i) return the instrument for lack of a necessary indorsement, or (ii) refuse payment or acceptance for failure of the presentment to comply with the terms of the instrument, an agreement of the parties, or other applicable law or rule.

(4) The party to whom presentment is made may treat presentment as occurring on the next business day after the day of presentment if the party to whom presentment is made has established a cut-off hour not earlier than 2 p.m. for the receipt and processing of instruments presented for payment or acceptance and presentment is made after the cut-off hour.

§ 3–502.   Dishonor.

(a) Dishonor of a note is governed by the following rules:

(1) If the note is payable on demand, the note is dishonored if presentment is duly made to the maker and the note is not paid on the day of presentment.

(2) If the note is not payable on demand and is payable at or through a bank or the terms of the note require presentment, the note is dishonored if presentment is duly made and the note is not paid on the day it becomes payable or the day of presentment, whichever is later.

(3) If the note is not payable on demand and paragraph (2) does not apply, the note is dishonored if it is not paid on the day it becomes payable.

(b) Dishonor of an unaccepted draft other than a documentary draft is governed by the following rules:

(1) If a check is duly presented for payment to the payor bank otherwise than for immediate payment over the counter, the check is dishonored if the payor bank makes timely return of the check or sends timely notice of dishonor or nonpayment under Section 4–301 or 4–302, or becomes accountable for the amount of the check under Section 4–302.

(2) If a draft is payable on demand and paragraph (1) does not apply, the draft is dishonored if presentment for payment is duly made to the drawee and the draft is not paid on the day of presentment.

(3) If a draft is payable on a date stated in the draft, the draft is dishonored if (i) presentment for payment is duly made to the drawee and payment is not made on the day the draft becomes payable or the day of presentment, whichever is later, or (ii) presentment for acceptance is duly made before the day the draft becomes payable and the draft is not accepted on the day of presentment.

(4) If a draft is payable on elapse of a period of time after sight or acceptance, the draft is dishonored if presentment for acceptance is duly made and the draft is not accepted on the day of presentment.

(c) Dishonor of an unaccepted documentary draft occurs according to the rules stated in subsection (b)(2), (3), and (4), except that payment or acceptance may be delayed without dishonor until no later than the close of the third business day of the drawee following the day on which payment or acceptance is required by those paragraphs.

(d) Dishonor of an accepted draft is governed by the following rules:

(1) If the draft is payable on demand, the draft is dishonored if presentment for payment is duly made to the acceptor and the draft is not paid on the day of presentment.

(2) If the draft is not payable on demand, the draft is dishonored if presentment for payment is duly made to the acceptor and payment is not made on the day it becomes payable or the day of presentment, whichever is later.

(e) In any case in which presentment is otherwise required for dishonor under this section and presentment is excused under Section 3–504, dishonor occurs without presentment if the instrument is not duly accepted or paid.

(f) If a draft is dishonored because timely acceptance of the draft was not made and the person entitled to demand acceptance consents to a late acceptance, from the time of acceptance the draft is treated as never having been dishonored.

§ 3–503.   Notice of Dishonor.

(a) The obligation of an indorser stated in Section 3–415(a) and the obligation of a drawer stated in Section 3–414(d) may not be enforced unless (i) the indorser or drawer is given notice of dishonor of the instrument complying with this section or (ii) notice of dishonor is excused under Section 3–504(b).

(b) Notice of dishonor may be given by any person; may be given by any commercially reasonable means, including an oral, written, or electronic communication; and is sufficient if it reasonably identifies the instrument and indicates that the instrument has been dishonored or has not been paid or accepted. Return of an instrument given to a bank for collection is sufficient notice of dishonor.

(c) Subject to Section 3–504(c), with respect to an instrument taken for collection by a collecting bank, notice of dishonor must be given (i) by the bank before midnight of the next banking day following the banking day on which the bank receives notice of dishonor of the instrument, or (ii) by any other person within 30 days following the day on which the person receives notice of dishonor. With respect to any other instrument, notice of dishonor must be given within 30 days following the day on which dishonor occurs.

§ 3–504.   Excused Presentment and Notice of Dishonor.

(a) Presentment for payment or acceptance of an instrument is excused if (i) the person entitled to present the instrument cannot with reasonable diligence make presentment, (ii) the maker or acceptor has repudiated an obligation to pay the instrument or is dead or in insolvency proceedings, (iii) by the terms of the instrument presentment is not necessary to enforce the obligation of indorsers or the drawer, (iv) the drawer or indorser whose obligation is being enforced has waived presentment or otherwise has no reason to expect or right to require that the instrument be paid or accepted, or (v) the drawer instructed the drawee not to pay or accept the draft or the drawee was not obligated to the drawer to pay the draft.

(b) Notice of dishonor is excused if (i) by the terms of the instrument notice of dishonor is not necessary to enforce the obligation of a party to pay the instrument, or (ii) the party whose obligation is being enforced waived notice of dishonor. A waiver of presentment is also a waiver of notice of dishonor.

(c) Delay in giving notice of dishonor is excused if the delay was caused by circumstances beyond the control of the person giving the notice and the person giving the notice exercised reasonable diligence after the cause of the delay ceased to operate.

§ 3–505.   Evidence of Dishonor.

(a) The following are admissible as evidence and create a presumption of dishonor and of any notice of dishonor stated:

(1) a document regular in form as provided in subsection (b) which purports to be a protest;

(2) a purported stamp or writing of the drawee, payor bank, or presenting bank on or accompanying the instrument stating that acceptance or payment has been refused unless reasons for the refusal are stated and the reasons are not consistent with dishonor;

(3) a book or record of the drawee, payor bank, or collecting bank, kept in the usual course of business which shows dishonor, even if there is no evidence of who made the entry.

(b) A protest is a certificate of dishonor made by a United States consul or vice consul, or a notary public or other person authorized to administer oaths by the law of the place where dishonor occurs. It may be made upon information satisfactory to that person. The protest must identify the instrument and certify either that presentment has been made or, if not made, the reason why it was not made, and that the instrument has been dishonored by nonacceptance or nonpayment. The protest may also certify that notice of dishonor has been given to some or all parties.

Part 6   Discharge and Payment

§ 3–601.   Discharge and Effect of Discharge.

(a) The obligation of a party to pay the instrument is discharged as stated in this Article or by an act or agreement with the party which would discharge an obligation to pay money under a simple contract.

(b) Discharge of the obligation of a party is not effective against a person acquiring rights of a holder in due course of the instrument without notice of the discharge.

§ 3–602.   Payment.

(a) Subject to subsection (b), an instrument is paid to the extent payment is made (i) by or on behalf of a party obliged to pay the instrument, and (ii) to a person entitled to enforce the instrument. To the extent of the payment, the obligation of the party obliged to pay the instrument is discharged even though payment is made with knowledge of a claim to the instrument under Section 3–306 by another person.

(b) The obligation of a party to pay the instrument is not discharged under subsection (a) if:

(1) a claim to the instrument under Section 3–306 is enforceable against the party receiving payment and (i) payment is made with knowledge by the payor that payment is prohibited by injunction or similar process of a court of competent jurisdiction, or (ii) in the case of an instrument other than a cashier's check, teller's check, or certified check, the party making payment accepted, from the person having a claim to the instrument, indemnity against loss resulting from refusal to pay the person entitled to enforce the instrument; or

(2) the person making payment knows that the instrument is a stolen instrument and pays a person it knows is in wrongful possession of the instrument.

§ 3–603.   Tender of Payment.

(a) If tender of payment of an obligation to pay an instrument is made to a person entitled to enforce the instrument, the effect of tender is governed by principles of law applicable to tender of payment under a simple contract.

(b) If tender of payment of an obligation to pay an instrument is made to a person entitled to enforce the instrument and the tender is refused, there is discharge, to the extent of the amount of the tender, of the obligation of an indorser or accommodation party having a right of recourse with respect to the obligation to which the tender relates.

(c) If tender of payment of an amount due on an instrument is made to a person entitled to enforce the instrument, the obligation of the obligor to pay interest after the due date on the amount tendered is discharged. If presentment is required with respect to an instrument and the obligor is able and ready to pay on the due date at every place of payment stated in the instrument, the obligor is deemed to have made tender of payment on the due date to the person entitled to enforce the instrument.

§ 3–604.   Discharge by Cancellation or Renunciation.

(a) A person entitled to enforce an instrument, with or without consideration, may discharge the obligation of a party to pay the instrument (i) by an intentional voluntary act, such as surrender of the instrument to the party, destruction, mutilation, or cancellation of the instrument, cancellation or striking out of the party's signature, or the addition of words to the instrument indicating discharge, or (ii) by agreeing not to sue or otherwise renouncing rights against the party by a signed writing.

(b) Cancellation or striking out of an indorsement pursuant to subsection (a) does not affect the status and rights of a party derived from the indorsement.

§ 3–605.   Discharge of Indorsers and Accommodation Parties.

(a) In this section, the term "indorser" includes a drawer having the obligation described in Section 3–414(d).

(b) Discharge, under Section 3–604, of the obligation of a party to pay an instrument does not discharge the obligation of an indorser or accommodation party having a right of recourse against the discharged party.

(c) If a person entitled to enforce an instrument agrees, with or without consideration, to an extension of the due date of the obligation of a party to pay the instrument, the extension discharges an indorser or accommodation party having a right of recourse against the party whose obligation is extended to the extent the indorser or accommodation party proves that the extension caused loss to the indorser or accommodation party with respect to the right of recourse.

(d) If a person entitled to enforce an instrument agrees, with or without consideration, to a material modification of the obligation of a party other than an extension of the due date, the modification discharges the obligation of an indorser or accommodation party having a right of recourse against the person whose obligation is modified to the extent the modification causes loss to the indorser or accommodation party with respect to the right of recourse. The loss suffered by the indorser or accommodation party as a result of the modification is equal to the amount of the right of recourse unless the person enforcing the instrument proves that no loss was caused by the modification or that the loss caused by the modification was an amount less than the amount of the right of recourse.

(e) If the obligation of a party to pay an instrument is secured by an interest in collateral and a person entitled to enforce the instrument impairs the value of the interest in collateral, the obligation of an indorser or accommodation party having a right of recourse against the obligor is discharged to the extent of the impairment. The value of an interest in collateral is impaired to the extent (i) the value of the interest is reduced to an amount less than the amount of the right of recourse of the party asserting discharge, or (ii) the reduction in value of the interest causes an increase in the amount by which the amount of the right of recourse exceeds the value of the interest. The burden of proving impairment is on the party asserting discharge.

(f) If the obligation of a party is secured by an interest in collateral not provided by an accommodation party and a person entitled to enforce the instrument impairs the value of the interest in collateral, the obligation of any party who is jointly and severally liable with respect to the secured obligation is discharged to the extent the impairment causes the party asserting discharge to pay more than that party would have been obliged to pay, taking into account rights of contribution, if impairment had not occurred. If the party asserting discharge is an accommodation party not entitled to discharge under subsection (e), the party is deemed to have a right to contribution based on joint and several liability rather than a right to reimbursement. The burden of proving impairment is on the party asserting discharge.

(g) Under subsection (e) or (f), impairing value of an interest in collateral includes (i) failure to obtain or maintain perfection or recordation of the interest in collateral, (ii) release of collateral without substitution of collateral of equal value, (iii) failure to perform a duty to preserve the value of collateral owed, under Article 9 or

other law, to a debtor or surety or other person secondarily liable, or (iv) failure to comply with applicable law in disposing of collateral.

(h) An accommodation party is not discharged under subsection (c), (d), or (e) unless the person entitled to enforce the instrument knows of the accommodation or has notice under Section 3–419(c) that the instrument was signed for accommodation.

(i) A party is not discharged under this section if (i) the party asserting discharge consents to the event or conduct that is the basis of the discharge, or (ii) the instrument or a separate agreement of the party provides for waiver of discharge under this section either specifically or by general language indicating that parties waive defenses based on suretyship or impairment of collateral.

ADDENDUM TO REVISED ARTICLE 3

Notes to Legislative Counsel

1. If revised Article 3 is adopted in your state, the reference in Section 2–511 to Section 3–802 should be changed to Section 3–310.

2. If revised Article 3 is adopted in your state and the Uniform Fiduciaries Act is also in effect in your state, you may want to consider amending Uniform Fiduciaries Act § 9 to conform to Section 3–307(b)(2)(iii) and (4)(iii). See Official Comment 3 to Section 3–307.

Revised Article 4
BANK DEPOSITS AND COLLECTIONS

Part 1   General Provisions and Definitions

§ 4–101.   Short Title.

This Article may be cited as Uniform Commercial Code—Bank Deposits and Collections.

As amended in 1990.

§ 4–102.   Applicability.

(a) To the extent that items within this Article are also within Articles 3 and 8, they are subject to those Articles. If there is conflict, this Article governs Article 3, but Article 8 governs this Article.

(b) The liability of a bank for action or non-action with respect to an item handled by it for purposes of presentment, payment, or collection is governed by the law of the place where the bank is located. In the case of action or non-action by or at a branch or separate office of a bank, its liability is governed by the law of the place where the branch or separate office is located.

§ 4–103.   Variation by Agreement; Measure
of Damages; Action Constituting Ordinary Care.

(a) The effect of the provisions of this Article may be varied by agreement, but the parties to the agreement cannot disclaim a bank's responsibility for its lack of good faith or failure to exercise ordinary care or limit the measure of damages for the lack or failure. However, the parties may determine by agreement the standards by which the bank's responsibility is to be measured if those standards are not manifestly unreasonable.

(b) Federal Reserve regulations and operating circulars, clearing-house rules, and the like have the effect of agreements under subsection (a), whether or not specifically assented to by all parties interested in items handled.

(c) Action or non-action approved by this Article or pursuant to Federal Reserve regulations or operating circulars is the exercise of ordinary care and, in the absence of special instructions, action or non-action consistent with clearing-house rules and the like or with a general banking usage not disapproved by this Article, is prima facie the exercise of ordinary care.

(d) The specification or approval of certain procedures by this Article is not disapproval of other procedures that may be reasonable under the circumstances.

(e) The measure of damages for failure to exercise ordinary care in handling an item is the amount of the item reduced by an amount that could not have been realized by the exercise of ordinary care. If there is also bad faith it includes any other damages the party suffered as a proximate consequence.

As amended in 1990.

§ 4–104.   Definitions and Index of Definitions.

(a) In this Article, unless the context otherwise requires:

(1) "Account" means any deposit or credit account with a bank, including a demand, time, savings, passbook, share draft, or like account, other than an account evidenced by a certificate of deposit;

(2) "Afternoon" means the period of a day between noon and midnight;

(3) "Banking day" means the part of a day on which a bank is open to the public for carrying on substantially all of its banking functions;

(4) "Clearing house" means an association of banks or other payors regularly clearing items;

(5) "Customer" means a person having an account with a bank or for whom a bank has agreed to collect items, including a bank that maintains an account at another bank;

(6) "Documentary draft" means a draft to be presented for acceptance or payment if specified documents, certificated securities (Section 8–102) or instructions for uncertificated securities (Section 8–102), or other certificates, statements, or the like are to be received by the drawee or other payor before acceptance or payment of the draft;

(7) "Draft" means a draft as defined in Section 3–104 or an item, other than an instrument, that is an order;

(8) "Drawee" means a person ordered in a draft to make payment;

(9) "Item" means an instrument or a promise or order to pay money handled by a bank for collection or payment. The term does not include a payment order governed by Article 4A or a credit or debit card slip;

(10) "Midnight deadline" with respect to a bank is midnight on its next banking day following the banking day on which it receives the relevant item or notice or from which the time for taking action commences to run, whichever is later;

(11) "Settle" means to pay in cash, by clearing-house settlement, in a charge or credit or by remittance, or otherwise as agreed. A settlement may be either provisional or final;

(12) "Suspends payments" with respect to a bank means that it has been closed by order of the supervisory authorities, that a public officer has been appointed to take it over, or that it ceases or refuses to make payments in the ordinary course of business.

(b) [Other definitions' section references deleted.]

(c) [Other definitions' section references deleted.]

(d) In addition, Article 1 contains general definitions and principles of construction and interpretation applicable throughout this Article.

§ 4–105.   "Bank"; "Depositary Bank"; "Payor Bank"; "Intermediary Bank"; "Collecting Bank"; "Presenting Bank".

In this Article:

(1) "Bank" means a person engaged in the business of banking, including a savings bank, savings and loan association, credit union, or trust company;

(2) "Depositary bank" means the first bank to take an item even though it is also the payor bank, unless the item is presented for immediate payment over the counter;

(3) "Payor bank" means a bank that is the drawee of a draft;

(4) "Intermediary bank" means a bank to which an item is transferred in course of collection except the depositary or payor bank;

(5) "Collecting bank" means a bank handling an item for collection except the payor bank;

(6) "Presenting bank" means a bank presenting an item except a payor bank.

§ 4–106.   Payable Through or Payable at Bank: Collecting Bank.

(a) If an item states that it is "payable through" a bank identified in the item, (i) the item designates the bank as a collecting bank and does not by itself authorize the bank to pay the item, and (ii) the item may be presented for payment only by or through the bank.

Alternative A

(b) If an item states that it is "payable at" a bank identified in the item, the item is equivalent to a draft drawn on the bank.

Alternative B

(b) If an item states that it is "payable at" a bank identified in the item, (i) the item designates the bank as a collecting bank and does not by itself authorize the bank to pay the item, and (ii) the item may be presented for payment only by or through the bank.

(c) If a draft names a nonbank drawee and it is unclear whether a bank named in the draft is a co-drawee or a collecting bank, the bank is a collecting bank.

As added in 1990.

§ 4–107.   Separate Office of Bank.

A branch or separate office of a bank is a separate bank for the purpose of computing the time within which and determining the place at or to which action may be taken or notices or orders shall be given under this Article and under Article 3.

As amended in 1962 and 1990.

§ 4–108.   Time of Receipt of Items.

(a) For the purpose of allowing time to process items, prove balances, and make the necessary entries on its books to determine its position for the day, a bank may fix an afternoon hour of 2 p.m. or later as a cutoff hour for the handling of money and items and the making of entries on its books.

(b) An item or deposit of money received on any day after a cutoff hour so fixed or after the close of the banking day may be treated as being received at the opening of the next banking day.

As amended in 1990.

§ 4–109.   Delays.

(a) Unless otherwise instructed, a collecting bank in a good faith effort to secure payment of a specific item drawn on a payor other than a bank, and with or without the approval of any person involved, may waive, modify, or extend time limits imposed or permitted by this [act] for a period not exceeding two additional banking days without discharge of drawers or indorsers or liability to its transferor or a prior party.

(b) Delay by a collecting bank or payor bank beyond time limits prescribed or permitted by this [act] or by instructions is excused if (i) the delay is caused by interruption of communication or computer facilities, suspension of payments by another bank, war, emergency conditions, failure of equipment, or other circumstances beyond the control of the bank, and (ii) the bank exercises such diligence as the circumstances require.

§ 4–110.   Electronic Presentment.

(a) "Agreement for electronic presentment" means an agreement, clearing-house rule, or Federal Reserve regulation or operating circular, providing that presentment of an item may be made by transmission of an image of an item or information describing the item ("presentment notice") rather than delivery of the item itself. The agreement may provide for procedures governing retention, presentment, payment, dishonor, and other matters concerning items subject to the agreement.

(b) Presentment of an item pursuant to an agreement for presentment is made when the presentment notice is received.

(c) If presentment is made by presentment notice, a reference to "item" or "check" in this Article means the presentment notice unless the context otherwise indicates.

As added in 1990.

§ 4–111.   Statute of Limitations.

An action to enforce an obligation, duty, or right arising under this Article must be commenced within three years after the [cause of action] accrues.

As added in 1990.

Part 2   Collection of Items:
Depositary and Collecting Banks

§ 4–201.   Status of Collecting Bank as Agent and Provisional
Status of Credits; Applicability of Article; Item Indorsed "Pay Any Bank".

(a) Unless a contrary intent clearly appears and before the time that a settlement given by a collecting bank for an item is or becomes final, the bank, with respect to an item, is an agent or subagent of the owner of the item and any settlement given for the item is provisional. This provision applies regardless of the form of indorsement or lack of indorsement and even though credit given for the item is subject to immediate withdrawal as of right or is in fact withdrawn; but the continuance of ownership of an item by its owner and any rights of the owner to proceeds of the item are subject to rights of a collecting bank, such as those resulting from outstanding advances on the item and rights of recoupment or setoff. If an item is handled by banks for purposes of presentment, payment, collection, or return, the relevant provisions of this Article apply even though action of the parties clearly establishes that a particular bank has purchased the item and is the owner of it.

(b) After an item has been indorsed with the words "pay any bank" or the like, only a bank may acquire the rights of a holder until the item has been:

(1) returned to the customer initiating collection; or

(2) specially indorsed by a bank to a person who is not a bank.

As amended in 1990.

§ 4–202.   Responsibility for Collection or Return; When Action Timely.

(a) A collecting bank must exercise ordinary care in:

(1) presenting an item or sending it for presentment;

(2) sending notice of dishonor or nonpayment or returning an item other than a documentary draft to the bank's transferor after learning that the item has not been paid or accepted, as the case may be;

(3) settling for an item when the bank receives final settlement; and

(4) notifying its transferor of any loss or delay in transit within a reasonable time after discovery thereof.

(b) A collecting bank exercises ordinary care under subsection (a) by taking proper action before its midnight deadline following receipt of an item, notice, or settlement. Taking proper action within a reasonably longer time may constitute the exercise of ordinary care, but the bank has the burden of establishing timeliness.

(c) Subject to subsection (a)(1), a bank is not liable for the insolvency, neglect, misconduct, mistake, or default of another bank or person or for loss or destruction of an item in the possession of others or in transit.

As amended in 1990.

§ 4–203.   Effect of Instructions.

Subject to Article 3 concerning conversion of instruments (Section 3–420) and restrictive indorsements (Section 3–206), only a collecting bank's transferor can give instructions that affect the bank or constitute notice to it, and a collecting bank is not liable to prior parties for any action taken pursuant to the instructions or in accordance with any agreement with its transferor.

§ 4–204.   Methods of Sending and Presenting; Sending Directly to Payor Bank.

(a) A collecting bank shall send items by a reasonably prompt method, taking into consideration relevant instructions, the nature of the item, the number of those items on hand, the cost of collection involved, and the method generally used by it or others to present those items.

(b) A collecting bank may send:

(1) an item directly to the payor bank;

(2) an item to a nonbank payor if authorized by its transferor; and

(3) an item other than documentary drafts to a nonbank payor, if authorized by Federal Reserve regulation or operating circular, clearing-house rule, or the like.

(c) Presentment may be made by a presenting bank at a place where the payor bank or other payor has requested that presentment be made.

As amended in 1990.

§ 4–205. Depositary Bank Holder of Unindorsed Item.

If a customer delivers an item to a depositary bank for collection:

(1) the depositary bank becomes a holder of the item at the time it receives the item for collection if the customer at the time of delivery was a holder of the item, whether or not the customer indorses the item, and, if the bank satisfies the other requirements of Section 3–302, it is a holder in due course; and

(2) the depositary bank warrants to collecting banks, the payor bank or other payor, and the drawer that the amount of the item was paid to the customer or deposited to the customer's account.

As amended in 1990.

§ 4–206. Transfer Between Banks.

Any agreed method that identifies the transferor bank is sufficient for the item's further transfer to another bank.

As amended in 1990.

§ 4–207. Transfer Warranties.

(a) A customer or collecting bank that transfers an item and receives a settlement or other consideration warrants to the transferee and to any subsequent collecting bank that:

(1) the warrantor is a person entitled to enforce the item;

(2) all signatures on the item are authentic and authorized;

(3) the item has not been altered;

(4) the item is not subject to a defense or claim in recoupment (Section 3–305(a)) of any party that can be asserted against the warrantor; and

(5) the warrantor has no knowledge of any insolvency proceeding commenced with respect to the maker or acceptor or, in the case of an unaccepted draft, the drawer.

(b) If an item is dishonored, a customer or collecting bank transferring the item and receiving settlement or other consideration is obliged to pay the amount due on the item (i) according to the terms of the item at the time it was transferred, or (ii) if the transfer was of an incomplete item, according to its terms when completed as stated in Sections 3–115 and 3–407. The obligation of a transferor is owed to the transferee and to any subsequent collecting bank that takes the item in good faith. A transferor cannot disclaim its obligation under this subsection by an indorsement stating that it is made "without recourse" or otherwise disclaiming liability.

(c) A person to whom the warranties under subsection (a) are made and who took the item in good faith may recover from the warrantor as damages for breach of warranty an amount equal to the loss suffered as a result of the breach, but not more than the amount of the item plus expenses and loss of interest incurred as a result of the breach.

(d) The warranties stated in subsection (a) cannot be disclaimed with respect to checks. Unless notice of a claim for breach of warranty is given to the warrantor within 30 days after the claimant has reason to know of the breach and the identity of the warrantor, the warrantor is discharged to the extent of any loss caused by the delay in giving notice of the claim.

(e) A cause of action for breach of warranty under this section accrues when the claimant has reason to know of the breach.

As amended in 1990.

§ 4–208. Presentment Warranties.

(a) If an unaccepted draft is presented to the drawee for payment or acceptance and the drawee pays or accepts the draft, (i) the person obtaining payment or acceptance, at the time of presentment, and (ii) a previous transferor of the draft, at the time of transfer, warrant to the drawee that pays or accepts the draft in good faith that:

(1) the warrantor is, or was, at the time the warrantor transferred the draft, a person entitled to enforce the draft or authorized to obtain payment or acceptance of the draft on behalf of a person entitled to enforce the draft;

(2) the draft has not been altered; and

(3) the warrantor has no knowledge that the signature of the purported drawer of the draft is unauthorized.

(b) A drawee making payment may recover from a warrantor damages for breach of warranty equal to the amount paid by the drawee less the amount the drawee received or is entitled to receive from the drawer because of the payment. In addition, the drawee is entitled to compensation for expenses and loss of interest resulting from the breach. The right of the drawee to recover damages under this subsection is not affected by any failure of the drawee to exercise ordinary care in making payment. If the drawee accepts the draft (i) breach of warranty is a defense to the obligation of the acceptor, and (ii) if the acceptor makes payment with respect to the draft, the acceptor is entitled to recover from a warrantor for breach of warranty the amounts stated in this subsection.

(c) If a drawee asserts a claim for breach of warranty under subsection (a) based on an unauthorized indorsement of the draft or an alteration of the draft, the warrantor may defend by proving that the indorsement is effective under Section 3–404 or 3–405 or the drawer is precluded under Section 3–406 or 4–406 from asserting against the drawee the unauthorized indorsement or alteration.

(d) If (i) a dishonored draft is presented for payment to the drawer or an indorser or (ii) any other item is presented for payment to a party obliged to pay the item, and the item is paid, the person obtaining payment and a prior transferor of the item warrant to the person making payment in good faith that the warrantor is, or was, at the time the warrantor transferred the item, a person entitled to enforce the item or authorized to obtain payment on behalf of a person entitled to enforce the item. The person making payment may recover from any warrantor for breach of warranty an amount equal to the amount paid plus expenses and loss of interest resulting from the breach.

(e) The warranties stated in subsections (a) and (d) cannot be disclaimed with respect to checks. Unless notice of a claim for breach of warranty is given to the warrantor within 30 days after the claimant has reason to know of the breach and the identity of the warrantor, the warrantor is discharged to the extent of any loss caused by the delay in giving notice of the claim.

(f) A cause of action for breach of warranty under this section accrues when the claimant has reason to know of the breach.

As amended in 1990.

§ 4–209.   Encoding and Retention Warranties.

(a) A person who encodes information on or with respect to an item after issue warrants to any subsequent collecting bank and to the payor bank or other payor that the information is correctly encoded. If the customer of a depositary bank encodes, that bank also makes the warranty.

(b) A person who undertakes to retain an item pursuant to an agreement for electronic presentment warrants to any subsequent collecting bank and to the payor bank or other payor that retention and presentment of the item comply with the agreement. If a customer of a depositary bank undertakes to retain an item, that bank also makes this warranty.

(c) A person to whom warranties are made under this section and who took the item in good faith may recover from the warrantor as damages for breach of warranty an amount equal to the loss suffered as a result of the breach, plus expenses and loss of interest incurred as a result of the breach.

As added in 1990.

§ 4–210.   Security Interest of Collecting Bank
in Items, Accompanying Documents and Proceeds.

(a) A collecting bank has a security interest in an item and any accompanying documents or the proceeds of either:

(1) in case of an item deposited in an account, to the extent to which credit given for the item has been withdrawn or applied;

(2) in case of an item for which it has given credit available for withdrawal as of right, to the extent of the credit given, whether or not the credit is drawn upon or there is a right of charge-back; or

(3) if it makes an advance on or against the item.

(b) If credit given for several items received at one time or pursuant to a single agreement is withdrawn or applied in part, the security interest remains upon all the items, any accompanying documents or the proceeds of either. For the purpose of this section, credits first given are first withdrawn.

(c) Receipt by a collecting bank of a final settlement for an item is a realization on its security interest in the item, accompanying documents, and proceeds. So long as the bank does not receive final settlement for the item or give up possession of the item or accompanying documents for purposes other than collection, the security interest continues to that extent and is subject to Article 9, but:

(1) no security agreement is necessary to make the security interest enforceable (Section 9–203(1)(a));

(2) no filing is required to perfect the security interest; and

(3) the security interest has priority over conflicting perfected security interests in the item, accompanying documents, or proceeds.

As amended in 1990 and 1999.

§ 4–211.   When Bank Gives Value for Purposes of Holder in Due Course.

For purposes of determining its status as a holder in due course, a bank has given value to the extent it has a security interest in an item, if the bank otherwise complies with the requirements of Section 3–302 on what constitutes a holder in due course.

As amended in 1990.

§ 4–212.   Presentment by Notice of Item
Not Payable by, Through, or at Bank; Liability of Drawer or Indorser.

(a) Unless otherwise instructed, a collecting bank may present an item not payable by, through, or at a bank by sending to the party to accept or pay a written notice that the bank holds the item for acceptance or payment. The notice must be sent in time to be received on or before the day when presentment is due and the bank must meet any requirement of the party to accept or pay under Section 3–501 by the close of the bank's next banking day after it knows of the requirement.

(b) If presentment is made by notice and payment, acceptance, or request for compliance with a requirement under Section 3–501 is not received by the close of business on the day after maturity or, in the case of demand items, by the close of business on the third banking day after notice was sent, the presenting bank may treat the item as dishonored and charge any drawer or indorser by sending it notice of the facts.

As amended in 1990.

§ 4–213.   Medium and Time of Settlement by Bank.

(a) With respect to settlement by a bank, the medium and time of settlement may be prescribed by Federal Reserve regulations or circulars, clearing-house rules, and the like, or agreement. In the absence of such prescription:

(1) the medium of settlement is cash or credit to an account in a Federal Reserve bank of or specified by the person to receive settlement; and

(2) the time of settlement is:

(i) with respect to tender of settlement by cash, a cashier's check, or teller's check, when the cash or check is sent or delivered;

(ii) with respect to tender of settlement by credit in an account in a Federal Reserve Bank, when the credit is made;

(iii) with respect to tender of settlement by a credit or debit to an account in a bank, when the credit or debit is made or, in the case of tender of settlement by authority to charge an account, when the authority is sent or delivered; or

(iv) with respect to tender of settlement by a funds transfer, when payment is made pursuant to Section 4A–406(a) to the person receiving settlement.

(b) If the tender of settlement is not by a medium authorized by subsection (a) or the time of settlement is not fixed by subsection (a), no settlement occurs until the tender of settlement is accepted by the person receiving settlement.

(c) If settlement for an item is made by cashier's check or teller's check and the person receiving settlement, before its midnight deadline:

(1) presents or forwards the check for collection, settlement is final when the check is finally paid; or

(2) fails to present or forward the check for collection, settlement is final at the midnight deadline of the person receiving settlement.

(d) If settlement for an item is made by giving authority to charge the account of the bank giving settlement in the bank receiving settlement, settlement is final when the charge is made by the bank receiving settlement if there are funds available in the account for the amount of the item.

As amended in 1990.

§ 4–214.   Right of Charge-Back or Refund; Liability of Collecting Bank: Return of Item.

(a) If a collecting bank has made provisional settlement with its customer for an item and fails by reason of dishonor, suspension of payments by a bank, or otherwise to receive settlement for the item which is or becomes final, the bank may revoke the settlement given by it, charge back the amount of any credit given for the item to its customer's account, or obtain refund from its customer, whether or not it is able to return the item, if by its midnight deadline or within a longer reasonable time after it learns the facts it returns the item or sends notification of the facts. If the return or notice is delayed beyond the bank's midnight deadline or a longer reasonable time after it learns the facts, the bank may revoke the settlement, charge back the credit, or obtain refund from its customer, but it is liable for any loss resulting from the delay. These rights to revoke, charge back, and obtain refund terminate if and when a settlement for the item received by the bank is or becomes final.

(b) A collecting bank returns an item when it is sent or delivered to the bank's customer or transferor or pursuant to its instructions.

(c) A depositary bank that is also the payor may charge back the amount of an item to its customer's account or obtain refund in accordance with the section governing return of an item received by a payor bank for credit on its books (Section 4–301).

(d) The right to charge back is not affected by:

(1) previous use of a credit given for the item; or

(2) failure by any bank to exercise ordinary care with respect to the item, but a bank so failing remains liable.

(e) A failure to charge back or claim refund does not affect other rights of the bank against the customer or any other party.

(f) If credit is given in dollars as the equivalent of the value of an item payable in foreign money, the dollar amount of any charge-back or refund must be calculated on the basis of the bank-offered spot rate for the foreign money prevailing on the day when the person entitled to the charge-back or refund learns that it will not receive payment in ordinary course.

As amended in 1990.

§ 4–215.   Final Payment of Item by Payor Bank; When Provisional Debits and Credits Become Final; When Certain Credits Become Available for Withdrawal.

(a) An item is finally paid by a payor bank when the bank has first done any of the following:

(1) paid the item in cash;

(2) settled for the item without having a right to revoke the settlement under statute, clearing-house rule, or agreement; or

(3) made a provisional settlement for the item and failed to revoke the settlement in the time and manner permitted by statute, clearing-house rule, or agreement.

(b) If provisional settlement for an item does not become final, the item is not finally paid.

(c) If provisional settlement for an item between the presenting and payor banks is made through a clearing house or by debits or credits in an account between them, then to the extent that provisional debits or credits for the item are entered in accounts between the presenting and payor banks or between the presenting and successive prior collecting banks seriatim, they become final upon final payment of the item by the payor bank.

(d) If a collecting bank receives a settlement for an item which is or becomes final, the bank is accountable to its customer for the amount of the item and any provisional credit given for the item in an account with its customer becomes final.

(e) Subject to (i) applicable law stating a time for availability of funds and (ii) any right of the bank to apply the credit to an obligation of the customer, credit given by a bank for an item in a customer's account becomes available for withdrawal as of right:

(1) if the bank has received a provisional settlement for the item, when the settlement becomes final and the bank has had a reasonable time to receive return of the item and the item has not been received within that time;

(2) if the bank is both the depositary bank and the payor bank, and the item is finally paid, at the opening of the bank's second banking day following receipt of the item.

(f) Subject to applicable law stating a time for availability of funds and any right of a bank to apply a deposit to an obligation of the depositor, a deposit of money becomes available for withdrawal as of right at the opening of the bank's next banking day after receipt of the deposit.

As amended in 1990.

§ 4–216.   Insolvency and Preference.

(a) If an item is in or comes into the possession of a payor or collecting bank that suspends payment and the item has not been finally paid, the item must be returned by the receiver, trustee, or agent in charge of the closed bank to the presenting bank or the closed bank's customer.

(b) If a payor bank finally pays an item and suspends payments without making a settlement for the item with its customer or the presenting bank which settlement is or becomes final, the owner of the item has a preferred claim against the payor bank.

(c) If a payor bank gives or a collecting bank gives or receives a provisional settlement for an item and thereafter suspends payments, the suspension does not prevent or interfere with the settlement's becoming final if the finality occurs automatically upon the lapse of certain time or the happening of certain events.

(d) If a collecting bank receives from subsequent parties settlement for an item, which settlement is or becomes final and the bank suspends payments without making a settlement for the item with its customer which settlement is or becomes final, the owner of the item has a preferred claim against the collecting bank.

As amended in 1990.

Part 3   Collection of Items: Payor Banks

§ 4–301.   Deferred Posting; Recovery of Payment
by Return of Items; Time of Dishonor; Return of Items by Payor Bank.

(a) If a payor bank settles for a demand item other than a documentary draft presented otherwise than for immediate payment over the counter before midnight of the banking day of receipt, the payor bank may revoke the settlement and recover the settlement if, before it has made final payment and before its midnight deadline, it

(1) returns the item; or

(2) sends written notice of dishonor or nonpayment if the item is unavailable for return.

(b) If a demand item is received by a payor bank for credit on its books, it may return the item or send notice of dishonor and may revoke any credit given or recover the amount thereof withdrawn by its customer, if it acts within the time limit and in the manner specified in subsection (a).

(c) Unless previous notice of dishonor has been sent, an item is dishonored at the time when for purposes of dishonor it is returned or notice sent in accordance with this section.

(d) An item is returned:

(1) as to an item presented through a clearing house, when it is delivered to the presenting or last collecting bank or to the clearing house or is sent or delivered in accordance with clearing-house rules; or

(2) in all other cases, when it is sent or delivered to the bank's customer or transferor or pursuant to instructions.

As amended in 1990.

§ 4–302.   Payor Bank's Responsibility for Late Return of Item.

(a) If an item is presented to and received by a payor bank, the bank is accountable for the amount of:

(1) a demand item, other than a documentary draft, whether properly payable or not, if the bank, in any case in which it is not also the depositary bank, retains the item beyond midnight of the banking day of receipt without settling for it or, whether or not it is also the depositary bank, does not pay or return the item or send notice of dishonor until after its midnight deadline; or

(2) any other properly payable item unless, within the time allowed for acceptance or payment of that item, the bank

either accepts or pays the item or returns it and accompanying documents.

(b) The liability of a payor bank to pay an item pursuant to subsection (a) is subject to defenses based on breach of a presentment warranty (Section 4–208) or proof that the person seeking enforcement of the liability presented or transferred the item for the purpose of defrauding the payor bank.

As amended in 1990.

§ 4–303.   When Items Subject to Notice, Stop-Payment Order,
Legal Process, or Setoff; Order in Which Items May Be Charged or Certified.

(a) Any knowledge, notice, or stop-payment order received by, legal process served upon, or setoff exercised by a payor bank comes too late to terminate, suspend, or modify the bank's right or duty to pay an item or to charge its customer's account for the item if the knowledge, notice, stop-payment order, or legal process is received or served and a reasonable time for the bank to act thereon expires or the setoff is exercised after the earliest of the following:

(1) the bank accepts or certifies the item;

(2) the bank pays the item in cash;

(3) the bank settles for the item without having a right to revoke the settlement under statute, clearing-house rule, or agreement;

(4) the bank becomes accountable for the amount of the item under Section 4–302 dealing with the payor bank's responsibility for late return of items; or

(5) with respect to checks, a cutoff hour no earlier than one hour after the opening of the next banking day after the banking day on which the bank received the check and no later than the close of that next banking day or, if no cutoff hour is fixed, the close of the next banking day after the banking day on which the bank received the check.

(b) Subject to subsection (a), items may be accepted, paid, certified, or charged to the indicated account of its customer in any order.

As amended in 1990.

Part 4   Relationship Between Payor Bank and Its Customer

§ 4–401.   When Bank May Charge Customer's Account.

(a) A bank may charge against the account of a customer an item that is properly payable from the account even though the charge creates an overdraft. An item is properly payable if it is authorized by the customer and is in accordance with any agreement between the customer and bank.

(b) A customer is not liable for the amount of an overdraft if the customer neither signed the item nor benefited from the proceeds of the item.

(c) A bank may charge against the account of a customer a check that is otherwise properly payable from the account, even though payment was made before the date of the check, unless the customer has given notice to the bank of the postdating describing the check with reasonable certainty. The notice is effective for the period stated in Section 4–403(b) for stop-payment orders, and must be received at such time and in such manner as to afford the bank a reasonable opportunity to act on it before the bank takes any action with respect to the check described in Section 4–303. If a bank charges against the account of a customer a check before the date stated in the notice of postdating, the bank is liable for damages for the loss resulting from its act. The loss may include damages for dishonor of subsequent items under Section 4–402.

(d) A bank that in good faith makes payment to a holder may charge the indicated account of its customer according to:

(1) the original terms of the altered item; or

(2) the terms of the completed item, even though the bank knows the item has been completed unless the bank has notice that the completion was improper.

As amended in 1990.

§ 4–402. Bank's Liability to Customer for Wrongful Dishonor; Time of Determining Insufficiency of Account.

(a) Except as otherwise provided in this Article, a payor bank wrongfully dishonors an item if it dishonors an item that is properly payable, but a bank may dishonor an item that would create an overdraft unless it has agreed to pay the overdraft.

(b) A payor bank is liable to its customer for damages proximately caused by the wrongful dishonor of an item. Liability is limited to actual damages proved and may include damages for an arrest or prosecution of the customer or other consequential damages. Whether any consequential damages are proximately caused by the wrongful dishonor is a question of fact to be determined in each case.

(c) A payor bank's determination of the customer's account balance on which a decision to dishonor for insufficiency of available funds is based may be made at any time between the time the item is received by the payor bank and the time that the payor bank returns the item or gives notice in lieu of return, and no more than one determination need be made. If, at the election of the payor bank, a subsequent balance determination is made for the purpose of reevaluating the bank's decision to dishonor the item, the account balance at that time is determinative of whether a dishonor for insufficiency of available funds is wrongful.

As amended in 1990.

§ 4–403. Customer's Right to Stop Payment; Burden of Proof of Loss.

(a) A customer or any person authorized to draw on the account if there is more than one person may stop payment of any item drawn on the customer's account or close the account by an order to the bank describing the item or account with reasonable certainty received at a time and in a manner that affords the bank a reasonable opportunity to act on it before any action by the bank with respect to the item described in Section 4–303. If the signature of more than one person is required to draw on an account, any of these persons may stop payment or close the account.

(b) A stop-payment order is effective for six months, but it lapses after 14 calendar days if the original order was oral and was not confirmed in writing within that period. A stop-payment order may be renewed for additional six-month periods by a writing given to the bank within a period during which the stop-payment order is effective.

(c) The burden of establishing the fact and amount of loss resulting from the payment of an item contrary to a stop-payment order or order to close an account is on the customer. The loss from payment of an item contrary to a stop-payment order may include damages for dishonor of subsequent items under Section 4–402.

As amended in 1990.

§ 4–404. Bank Not Obliged to Pay Check More Than Six Months Old.

A bank is under no obligation to a customer having a checking account to pay a check, other than a certified check, which is presented more than six months after its date, but it may charge its customer's account for a payment made thereafter in good faith.

§ 4–405. Death or Incompetence of Customer.

(a) A payor or collecting bank's authority to accept, pay, or collect an item or to account for proceeds of its collection, if otherwise effective, is not rendered ineffective by incompetence of a customer of either bank existing at the time the item is issued or its collection is undertaken if the bank does not know of an adjudication of incompetence. Neither death nor incompetence of a customer revokes the authority to accept, pay, collect, or account until the bank knows of the fact of death or of an adjudication of incompetence and has reasonable opportunity to act on it.

(b) Even with knowledge, a bank may for 10 days after the date of death pay or certify checks drawn on or before the date unless ordered to stop payment by a person claiming an interest in the account.

As amended in 1990.

§ 4–406. Customer's Duty to Discover and Report Unauthorized Signature or Alteration.

(a) A bank that sends or makes available to a customer a statement of account showing payment of items for the account shall either return or make available to the customer the items paid or provide information in the statement of account sufficient to allow the customer reasonably to identify the items paid. The statement of account provides sufficient information if the item is described by item number, amount, and date of payment.

(b) If the items are not returned to the customer, the person retaining the items shall either retain the items or, if the items are destroyed, maintain the capacity to furnish legible copies of the items until the expiration of seven years after receipt of the items. A customer may request an item from the bank that paid the item, and that bank must provide in a reasonable time either the item or, if the item has been destroyed or is not otherwise obtainable, a legible copy of the item.

(c) If a bank sends or makes available a statement of account or items pursuant to subsection (a), the customer must exercise reasonable promptness in examining the statement or the items to determine whether any payment was not authorized because of an alteration of an item or because a purported signature by or on behalf of the customer was not authorized. If, based on the statement or items provided, the customer should reasonably have discovered the unauthorized payment, the customer must promptly notify the bank of the relevant facts.

(d) If the bank proves that the customer failed, with respect to an item, to comply with the duties imposed on the customer by subsection (c), the customer is precluded from asserting against the bank:

(1) the customer's unauthorized signature or any alteration on the item, if the bank also proves that it suffered a loss by reason of the failure; and

(2) the customer's unauthorized signature or alteration by the same wrongdoer on any other item paid in good faith by the bank if the payment was made before the bank received notice from the customer of the unauthorized signature or alteration and after the customer had been afforded a reasonable period of time, not exceeding 30 days, in which to examine the item or statement of account and notify the bank.

(e) If subsection (d) applies and the customer proves that the bank failed to exercise ordinary care in paying the item and that the failure substantially contributed to loss, the loss is allocated between the customer precluded and the bank asserting the preclusion according to the extent to which the failure of the customer to comply with subsection (c) and the failure of the bank to exercise ordinary care contributed to the loss. If the customer proves that the bank did not pay the item in good faith, the preclusion under subsection (d) does not apply.

(f) Without regard to care or lack of care of either the customer or the bank, a customer who does not within one year after the statement or items are made available to the customer (subsection (a)) discover and report the customer's unauthorized signature on or any alteration on the item is precluded from asserting against the bank the unauthorized signature or alteration. If there is a preclusion under this subsection, the payor bank may not recover for breach or warranty under Section 4–208 with respect to the unauthorized signature or alteration to which the preclusion applies.

As amended in 1990.

§ 4–407.   Payor Bank's Right to Subrogation on Improper Payment.

If a payor has paid an item over the order of the drawer or maker to stop payment, or after an account has been closed, or otherwise under circumstances giving a basis for objection by the drawer or maker, to prevent unjust enrichment and only to the extent necessary to prevent loss to the bank by reason of its payment of the item, the payor bank is subrogated to the rights

(1) of any holder in due course on the item against the drawer or maker;

(2) of the payee or any other holder of the item against the drawer or maker either on the item or under the transaction out of which the item arose; and

(3) of the drawer or maker against the payee or any other holder of the item with respect to the transaction out of which the item arose.

As amended in 1990.

Part 5   Collection of Documentary Drafts

§ 4–501.   Handling of Documentary Drafts; Duty to Send for Presentment and to Notify Customer of Dishonor.

A bank that takes a documentary draft for collection shall present or send the draft and accompanying documents for presentment and, upon learning that the draft has not been paid or accepted in due course, shall seasonably notify its customer of the fact even though it may have discounted or bought the draft or extended credit available for withdrawal as of right.

As amended in 1990.

§ 4–502.   Presentment of "On Arrival" Drafts.

If a draft or the relevant instructions require presentment "on arrival", "when goods arrive" or the like, the collecting bank need not present until in its judgment a reasonable time for arrival of the goods has expired. Refusal to pay or accept because the goods have not arrived is not dishonor; the bank must notify its transferor of the refusal but need not present the draft again until it is instructed to do so or learns of the arrival of the goods.

§ 4–503.   Responsibility of Presenting Bank for Documents and Goods; Report of Reasons for Dishonor; Referee in Case of Need.

Unless otherwise instructed and except as provided in Article 5, a bank presenting a documentary draft:

(1) must deliver the documents to the drawee on acceptance of the draft if it is payable more than three days after presentment, otherwise, only on payment; and

(2) upon dishonor, either in the case of presentment for acceptance or presentment for payment, may seek and follow instructions from any referee in case of need designated in the draft or, if the presenting bank does not choose to utilize the referee's services, it must use diligence and good faith to ascertain the reason for dishonor, must notify its transferor of the dishonor and of the results of its effort to ascertain the reasons therefor, and must request instructions.

However, the presenting bank is under no obligation with respect to goods represented by the documents except to follow any reasonable instructions seasonably received; it has a right to reimbursement for any expense incurred in following instructions and to prepayment of or indemnity for those expenses.

As amended in 1990.

§ 4–504.   Privilege of Presenting Bank to Deal With Goods; Security Interest for Expenses.

(a) A presenting bank that, following the dishonor of a documentary draft, has seasonably requested instructions but does not receive them within a reasonable time may store, sell, or otherwise deal with the goods in any reasonable manner.

(b) For its reasonable expenses incurred by action under subsection (a) the presenting bank has a lien upon the goods or their proceeds, which may be foreclosed in the same manner as an unpaid seller's lien.

As amended in 1990.

Article 4A
FUNDS TRANSFERS

Part 1   Subject Matter and Definitions

§ 4A–101.   Short Title.

This Article may be cited as Uniform Commercial Code—Funds Transfers.

§ 4A–102. Subject Matter.

Except as otherwise provided in Section 4A–108, this Article applies to funds transfers defined in Section 4A–104.

§ 4A–103. Payment Order–Definitions.

(a) In this Article:

(1) "Payment order" means an instruction of a sender to a receiving bank, transmitted orally, electronically, or in writing, to pay, or to cause another bank to pay, a fixed or determinable amount of money to a beneficiary if:

(i) the instruction does not state a condition to payment to the beneficiary other than time of payment,

(ii) the receiving bank is to be reimbursed by debiting an account of, or otherwise receiving payment from, the sender, and

(iii) the instruction is transmitted by the sender directly to the receiving bank or to an agent, funds-transfer system, or communication system for transmittal to the receiving bank.

(2) "Beneficiary" means the person to be paid by the beneficiary's bank.

(3) "Beneficiary's bank" means the bank identified in a payment order in which an account of the beneficiary is to be credited pursuant to the order or which otherwise is to make payment to the beneficiary if the order does not provide for payment to an account.

(4) "Receiving bank" means the bank to which the sender's instruction is addressed.

(5) "Sender" means the person giving the instruction to the receiving bank.

(b) If an instruction complying with subsection (a)(1) is to make more than one payment to a beneficiary, the instruction is a separate payment order with respect to each payment.

(c) A payment order is issued when it is sent to the receiving bank.

§ 4A–104. Funds Transfer–Definitions.

In this Article:

(a) "Funds transfer" means the series of transactions, beginning with the originator's payment order, made for the purpose of making payment to the beneficiary of the order. The term includes any payment order issued by the originator's bank or an intermediary bank intended to carry out the originator's payment order. A funds transfer is completed by acceptance by the beneficiary's bank of a payment order for the benefit of the beneficiary of the originator's payment order.

(b) "Intermediary bank" means a receiving bank other than the originator's bank or the beneficiary's bank.

(c) "Originator" means the sender of the first payment order in a funds transfer.

(d) "Originator's bank" means (i) the receiving bank to which the payment order of the originator is issued if the originator is not a bank, or (ii) the originator if the originator is a bank.

§ 4A–105. Other Definitions.

(a) In this Article:

(1) "Authorized account" means a deposit account of a customer in a bank designated by the customer as a source of payment of payment orders issued by the customer to the bank. If a customer does not so designate an account, any account of the customer is an authorized account if payment of a payment order from that account is not inconsistent with a restriction on the use of that account.

(2) "Bank" means a person engaged in the business of banking and includes a savings bank, savings and loan association, credit union, and trust company. A branch or separate office of a bank is a separate bank for purposes of this Article.

(3) "Customer" means a person, including a bank, having an account with a bank or from whom a bank has agreed to receive payment orders.

(4) "Funds-transfer business day" of a receiving bank means the part of a day during which the receiving bank is open for the receipt, processing, and transmittal of payment orders and cancellations and amendments of payment orders.

(5) "Funds-transfer system" means a wire transfer network, automated clearing house, or other communication system of a clearing house or other association of banks through which a payment order by a bank may be transmitted to the bank to which the order is addressed.

(6) "Good faith" means honesty in fact and the observance of reasonable commercial standards of fair dealing.

(7) "Prove" with respect to a fact means to meet the burden of establishing the fact (Section 1–201(8)).

(b) Other definitions applying to this Article and the sections in which they appear are:

"Acceptance"	Section 4A–209
"Beneficiary"	Section 4A–103
"Beneficiary's bank"	Section 4A–103
"Executed"	Section 4A–301
"Execution date"	Section 4A–301
"Funds transfer"	Section 4A–104
"Funds-transfer system rule"	Section 4A–501
"Intermediary bank"	Section 4A–104
"Originator"	Section 4A–104
"Originator's bank"	Section 4A–104
"Payment by beneficiary's bank to beneficiary"	Section 4A–405
"Payment by originator to beneficiary"	Section 4A–406
"Payment by sender to receiving bank"	Section 4A–403
"Payment date"	Section 4A–401
"Payment order"	Section 4A–103
"Receiving bank"	Section 4A–103
"Security procedure"	Section 4A–201
"Sender"	Section 4A–103

(c) The following definitions in Article 4 apply to this Article:

"Clearing house" Section 4–104

"Item" Section 4–104

"Suspends payments" Section 4–104

(d) In addition, Article 1 contains general definitions and principles of construction and interpretation applicable throughout this Article.

§ 4A–106. Time Payment Order Is Received.

(a) The time of receipt of a payment order or communication cancelling or amending a payment order is determined by the rules applicable to receipt of a notice stated in Section 1–201(27). A receiving bank may fix a cut-off time or times on a funds-transfer business day for the receipt and processing of payment orders and communications cancelling or amending payment orders. Different cut-off times may apply to payment orders, cancellations, or amendments, or to different categories of payment orders, cancellations, or amendments. A cut-off time may apply to senders generally or different cut-off times may apply to different senders or categories of payment orders. If a payment order or communication cancelling or amending a payment order is received after the close of a funds-transfer business day or after the appropriate cut-off time on a funds-transfer business day, the receiving bank may treat the payment order or communication as received at the opening of the next funds-transfer business day.

(b) If this Article refers to an execution date or payment date or states a day on which a receiving bank is required to take action, and the date or day does not fall on a funds-transfer business day, the next day that is a funds-transfer business day is treated as the date or day stated, unless the contrary is stated in this Article.

§ 4A–107. Federal Reserve Regulations and Operating Circulars.

Regulations of the Board of Governors of the Federal Reserve System and operating circulars of the Federal Reserve Banks supersede any inconsistent provision of this Article to the extent of the inconsistency.

§ 4A–108. Exclusion of Consumer Transactions Governed by Federal Law.

This Article does not apply to a funds transfer any part of which is governed by the Electronic Fund Transfer Act of 1978 (Title XX, Public Law 95–630, 92 Stat. 3728, 15 U.S.C. § 1693 *et seq.*) as amended from time to time.

Part 2 Issue and Acceptance of Payment Order

§ 4A–201. Security Procedure.

"Security procedure" means a procedure established by agreement of a customer and a receiving bank for the purpose of (i) verifying that a payment order or communication amending or cancelling a payment order is that of the customer, or (ii) detecting error in the transmission or the content of the payment order or communication. A security procedure may require the use of algorithms or other codes, identifying words or numbers, encryption, callback procedures, or similar security devices. Comparison of a signature on a payment order or communication with an authorized specimen signature of the customer is not by itself a security procedure.

§ 4A–202. Authorized and Verified Payment Orders.

(a) A payment order received by the receiving bank is the authorized order of the person identified as sender if that person authorized the order or is otherwise bound by it under the law of agency.

(b) If a bank and its customer have agreed that the authenticity of payment orders issued to the bank in the name of the customer as sender will be verified pursuant to a security procedure, a payment order received by the receiving bank is effective as the order of the customer, whether or not authorized, if (i) the security procedure is a commercially reasonable method of providing security against unauthorized payment orders, and (ii) the bank proves that it accepted the payment order in good faith and in compliance with the security procedure and any written agreement or instruction of the customer restricting acceptance of payment orders issued in the name of the customer. The bank is not required to follow an instruction that violates a written agreement with the customer or notice of which is not received at a time and in a manner affording the bank a reasonable opportunity to act on it before the payment order is accepted.

(c) Commercial reasonableness of a security procedure is a question of law to be determined by considering the wishes of the customer expressed to the bank, the circumstances of the customer known to the bank, including the size, type, and frequency of payment orders normally issued by the customer to the bank, alternative security procedures offered to the customer, and security procedures in general use by customers and receiving banks similarly situated. A security procedure is deemed to be commercially reasonable if (i) the security procedure was chosen by the customer after the bank offered, and the customer refused, a security procedure that was commercially reasonable for that customer, and (ii) the customer expressly agreed in writing to be bound by any payment order, whether or not authorized, issued in its name and accepted by the bank in compliance with the security procedure chosen by the customer.

(d) The term "sender" in this Article includes the customer in whose name a payment order is issued if the order is the authorized order of the customer under subsection (a), or it is effective as the order of the customer under subsection (b).

(e) This section applies to amendments and cancellations of payment orders to the same extent it applies to payment orders.

(f) Except as provided in this section and in Section 4A–203(a)(1), rights and obligations arising under this section or Section 4A–203 may not be varied by agreement.

§ 4A–203. Unenforceability of Certain Verified Payment Orders.

(a) If an accepted payment order is not, under Section 4A–202(a), an authorized order of a customer identified as sender, but is effective as an order of the customer pursuant to Section 4A–202(b), the following rules apply:

(1) By express written agreement, the receiving bank may limit the extent to which it is entitled to enforce or retain payment of the payment order.

(2) The receiving bank is not entitled to enforce or retain payment of the payment order if the customer proves that the order was not caused, directly or indirectly, by a person

(i) entrusted at any time with duties to act for the customer with respect to payment orders or the security procedure, or (ii) who obtained access to transmitting facilities of the customer or who obtained, from a source controlled by the customer and without authority of the receiving bank, information facilitating breach of the security procedure, regardless of how the information was obtained or whether the customer was at fault. Information includes any access device, computer software, or the like.

(b) This section applies to amendments of payment orders to the same extent it applies to payment orders.

§ 4A-204. Refund of Payment and Duty of Customer to Report with Respect to Unauthorized Payment Order.

(a) If a receiving bank accepts a payment order issued in the name of its customer as sender which is (i) not authorized and not effective as the order of the customer under Section 4A-202, or (ii) not enforceable, in whole or in part, against the customer under Section 4A-203, the bank shall refund any payment of the payment order received from the customer to the extent the bank is not entitled to enforce payment and shall pay interest on the refundable amount calculated from the date the bank received payment to the date of the refund. However, the customer is not entitled to interest from the bank on the amount to be refunded if the customer fails to exercise ordinary care to determine that the order was not authorized by the customer and to notify the bank of the relevant facts within a reasonable time not exceeding 90 days after the date the customer received notification from the bank that the order was accepted or that the customer's account was debited with respect to the order. The bank is not entitled to any recovery from the customer on account of a failure by the customer to give notification as stated in this section.

(b) Reasonable time under subsection (a) may be fixed by agreement as stated in Section 1-204(1), but the obligation of a receiving bank to refund payment as stated in subsection (a) may not otherwise be varied by agreement.

§ 4A-205. Erroneous Payment Orders.

(a) If an accepted payment order was transmitted pursuant to a security procedure for the detection of error and the payment order (i) erroneously instructed payment to a beneficiary not intended by the sender, (ii) erroneously instructed payment in an amount greater than the amount intended by the sender, or (iii) was an erroneously transmitted duplicate of a payment order previously sent by the sender, the following rules apply:

(1) If the sender proves that the sender or a person acting on behalf of the sender pursuant to Section 4A-206 complied with the security procedure and that the error would have been detected if the receiving bank had also complied, the sender is not obliged to pay the order to the extent stated in paragraphs (2) and (3).

(2) If the funds transfer is completed on the basis of an erroneous payment order described in clause (i) or (iii) of subsection (a), the sender is not obliged to pay the order and the receiving bank is entitled to recover from the beneficiary any

amount paid to the beneficiary to the extent allowed by the law governing mistake and restitution.

(3) If the funds transfer is completed on the basis of a payment order described in clause (ii) of subsection (a), the sender is not obliged to pay the order to the extent the amount received by the beneficiary is greater than the amount intended by the sender. In that case, the receiving bank is entitled to recover from the beneficiary the excess amount received to the extent allowed by the law governing mistake and restitution.

(b) If (i) the sender of an erroneous payment order described in subsection (a) is not obliged to pay all or part of the order, and (ii) the sender receives notification from the receiving bank that the order was accepted by the bank or that the sender's account was debited with respect to the order, the sender has a duty to exercise ordinary care, on the basis of information available to the sender, to discover the error with respect to the order and to advise the bank of the relevant facts within a reasonable time, not exceeding 90 days, after the bank's notification was received by the sender. If the bank proves that the sender failed to perform that duty, the sender is liable to the bank for the loss the bank proves it incurred as a result of the failure, but the liability of the sender may not exceed the amount of the sender's order.

(c) This section applies to amendments to payment orders to the same extent it applies to payment orders.

§ 4A-206. Transmission of Payment Order through Funds-Transfer or Other Communication System.

(a) If a payment order addressed to a receiving bank is transmitted to a funds-transfer system or other third party communication system for transmittal to the bank, the system is deemed to be an agent of the sender for the purpose of transmitting the payment order to the bank. If there is a discrepancy between the terms of the payment order transmitted to the system and the terms of the payment order transmitted by the system to the bank, the terms of the payment order of the sender are those transmitted by the system. This section does not apply to a funds-transfer system of the Federal Reserve Banks.

(b) This section applies to cancellations and amendments to payment orders to the same extent it applies to payment orders.

§ 4A-207. Misdescription of Beneficiary.

(a) Subject to subsection (b), if, in a payment order received by the beneficiary's bank, the name, bank account number, or other identification of the beneficiary refers to a nonexistent or unidentifiable person or account, no person has rights as a beneficiary of the order and acceptance of the order cannot occur.

(b) If a payment order received by the beneficiary's bank identifies the beneficiary both by name and by an identifying or bank account number and the name and number identify different persons, the following rules apply:

(1) Except as otherwise provided in subsection (c), if the beneficiary's bank does not know that the name and number refer to different persons, it may rely on the number as the proper identification of the beneficiary of the order. The

beneficiary's bank need not determine whether the name and number refer to the same person.

(2) If the beneficiary's bank pays the person identified by name or knows that the name and number identify different persons, no person has rights as beneficiary except the person paid by the beneficiary's bank if that person was entitled to receive payment from the originator of the funds transfer. If no person has rights as beneficiary, acceptance of the order cannot occur.

(c) If (i) a payment order described in subsection (b) is accepted, (ii) the originator's payment order described the beneficiary inconsistently by name and number, and (iii) the beneficiary's bank pays the person identified by number as permitted by subsection (b)(1), the following rules apply:

(1) If the originator is a bank, the originator is obliged to pay its order.

(2) If the originator is not a bank and proves that the person identified by number was not entitled to receive payment from the originator, the originator is not obliged to pay its order unless the originator's bank proves that the originator, before acceptance of the originator's order, had notice that payment of a payment order issued by the originator might be made by the beneficiary's bank on the basis of an identifying or bank account number even if it identifies a person different from the named beneficiary. Proof of notice may be made by any admissible evidence. The originator's bank satisfies the burden of proof if it proves that the originator, before the payment order was accepted, signed a writing stating the information to which the notice relates.

(d) In a case governed by subsection (b)(1), if the beneficiary's bank rightfully pays the person identified by number and that person was not entitled to receive payment from the originator, the amount paid may be recovered from that person to the extent allowed by the law governing mistake and restitution as follows:

(1) If the originator is obliged to pay its payment order as stated in subsection (c), the originator has the right to recover.

(2) If the originator is not a bank and is not obliged to pay its payment order, the originator's bank has the right to recover.

§ 4A–208.   Misdescription of Intermediary Bank or Beneficiary's Bank.

(a) This subsection applies to a payment order identifying an intermediary bank or the beneficiary's bank only by an identifying number.

(1) The receiving bank may rely on the number as the proper identification of the intermediary or beneficiary's bank and need not determine whether the number identifies a bank.

(2) The sender is obliged to compensate the receiving bank for any loss and expenses incurred by the receiving bank as a result of its reliance on the number in executing or attempting to execute the order.

(b) This subsection applies to a payment order identifying an intermediary bank or the beneficiary's bank both by name and an identifying number if the name and number identify different persons.

(1) If the sender is a bank, the receiving bank may rely on the number as the proper identification of the intermediary or beneficiary's bank if the receiving bank, when it executes the sender's order, does not know that the name and number identify different persons. The receiving bank need not determine whether the name and number refer to the same person or whether the number refers to a bank. The sender is obliged to compensate the receiving bank for any loss and expenses incurred by the receiving bank as a result of its reliance on the number in executing or attempting to execute the order.

(2) If the sender is not a bank and the receiving bank proves that the sender, before the payment order was accepted, had notice that the receiving bank might rely on the number as the proper identification of the intermediary or beneficiary's bank even if it identifies a person different from the bank identified by name, the rights and obligations of the sender and the receiving bank are governed by subsection (b)(1), as though the sender were a bank. Proof of notice may be made by any admissible evidence. The receiving bank satisfies the burden of proof if it proves that the sender, before the payment order was accepted, signed a writing stating the information to which the notice relates.

(3) Regardless of whether the sender is a bank, the receiving bank may rely on the name as the proper identification of the intermediary or beneficiary's bank if the receiving bank, at the time it executes the sender's order, does not know that the name and number identify different persons. The receiving bank need not determine whether the name and number refer to the same person.

(4) If the receiving bank knows that the name and number identify different persons, reliance on either the name or the number in executing the sender's payment order is a breach of the obligation stated in Section 4A–302(a)(1).

§ 4A–209.   Acceptance of Payment Order.

(a) Subject to subsection (d), a receiving bank other than the beneficiary's bank accepts a payment order when it executes the order.

(b) Subject to subsections (c) and (d), a beneficiary's bank accepts a payment order at the earliest of the following times:

(1) When the bank (i) pays the beneficiary as stated in Section 4A–405(a) or 4A–405(b), or (ii) notifies the beneficiary of receipt of the order or that the account of the beneficiary has been credited with respect to the order unless the notice indicates that the bank is rejecting the order or that funds with respect to the order may not be withdrawn or used until receipt of payment from the sender of the order;

(2) When the bank receives payment of the entire amount of the sender's order pursuant to Section 4A–403(a)(1) or 4A–403(a)(2); or

(3) The opening of the next funds-transfer business day of the bank following the payment date of the order if, at that time, the amount of the sender's order is fully covered by a withdrawable credit balance in an authorized account of the sender or the bank has otherwise received full payment from

the sender, unless the order was rejected before that time or is rejected within (i) one hour after that time, or (ii) one hour after the opening of the next business day of the sender following the payment date if that time is later. If notice of rejection is received by the sender after the payment date and the authorized account of the sender does not bear interest, the bank is obliged to pay interest to the sender on the amount of the order for the number of days elapsing after the payment date to the day the sender receives notice or learns that the order was not accepted, counting that day as an elapsed day. If the withdrawable credit balance during that period falls below the amount of the order, the amount of interest payable is reduced accordingly.

(c) Acceptance of a payment order cannot occur before the order is received by the receiving bank. Acceptance does not occur under subsection (b)(2) or (b)(3) if the beneficiary of the payment order does not have an account with the receiving bank, the account has been closed, or the receiving bank is not permitted by law to receive credits for the beneficiary's account.

(d) A payment order issued to the originator's bank cannot be accepted until the payment date if the bank is the beneficiary's bank, or the execution date if the bank is not the beneficiary's bank. If the originator's bank executes the originator's payment order before the execution date or pays the beneficiary of the originator's payment order before the payment date and the payment order is subsequently cancelled pursuant to Section 4A–211(b), the bank may recover from the beneficiary any payment received to the extent allowed by the law governing mistake and restitution.

§ 4A–210.   Rejection of Payment Order.

(a) A payment order is rejected by the receiving bank by a notice of rejection transmitted to the sender orally, electronically, or in writing. A notice of rejection need not use any particular words and is sufficient if it indicates that the receiving bank is rejecting the order or will not execute or pay the order. Rejection is effective when the notice is given if transmission is by a means that is reasonable in the circumstances. If notice of rejection is given by a means that is not reasonable, rejection is effective when the notice is received. If an agreement of the sender and receiving bank establishes the means to be used to reject a payment order, (i) any means complying with the agreement is reasonable and (ii) any means not complying is not reasonable unless no significant delay in receipt of the notice resulted from the use of the noncomplying means.

(b) This subsection applies if a receiving bank other than the beneficiary's bank fails to execute a payment order despite the existence on the execution date of a withdrawable credit balance in an authorized account of the sender sufficient to cover the order. If the sender does not receive notice of rejection of the order on the execution date and the authorized account of the sender does not bear interest, the bank is obliged to pay interest to the sender on the amount of the order for the number of days elapsing after the execution date to the earlier of the day the order is cancelled pursuant to Section 4A–211(d) or the day the sender receives notice or learns that the order was not executed, counting the final day of the period as an elapsed day. If the withdrawable credit balance

during that period falls below the amount of the order, the amount of interest is reduced accordingly.

(c) If a receiving bank suspends payments, all unaccepted payment orders issued to it are are deemed rejected at the time the bank suspends payments.

(d) Acceptance of a payment order precludes a later rejection of the order. Rejection of a payment order precludes a later acceptance of the order.

§ 4A–211.   Cancellation and Amendment of Payment Order.

(a) A communication of the sender of a payment order cancelling or amending the order may be transmitted to the receiving bank orally, electronically, or in writing. If a security procedure is in effect between the sender and the receiving bank, the communication is not effective to cancel or amend the order unless the communication is verified pursuant to the security procedure or the bank agrees to the cancellation or amendment.

(b) Subject to subsection (a), a communication by the sender cancelling or amending a payment order is effective to cancel or amend the order if notice of the communication is received at a time and in a manner affording the receiving bank a reasonable opportunity to act on the communication before the bank accepts the payment order.

(c) After a payment order has been accepted, cancellation or amendment of the order is not effective unless the receiving bank agrees or a funds-transfer system rule allows cancellation or amendment without agreement of the bank.

(1) With respect to a payment order accepted by a receiving bank other than the beneficiary's bank, cancellation or amendment is not effective unless a conforming cancellation or amendment of the payment order issued by the receiving bank is also made.

(2) With respect to a payment order accepted by the beneficiary's bank, cancellation or amendment is not effective unless the order was issued in execution of an unauthorized payment order, or because of a mistake by a sender in the funds transfer which resulted in the issuance of a payment order (i) that is a duplicate of a payment order previously issued by the sender, (ii) that orders payment to a beneficiary not entitled to receive payment from the originator, or (iii) that orders payment in an amount greater than the amount the beneficiary was entitled to receive from the originator. If the payment order is cancelled or amended, the beneficiary's bank is entitled to recover from the beneficiary any amount paid to the beneficiary to the extent allowed by the law governing mistake and restitution.

(d) An unaccepted payment order is cancelled by operation of law at the close of the fifth funds-transfer business day of the receiving bank after the execution date or payment date of the order.

(e) A cancelled payment order cannot be accepted. If an accepted payment order is cancelled, the acceptance is nullified and no person has any right or obligation based on the acceptance. Amendment of a payment order is deemed to be cancellation of the original order at the time of amendment and issue of a new payment order in the amended form at the same time.

(f) Unless otherwise provided in an agreement of the parties or in a funds-transfer system rule, if the receiving bank, after accepting a payment order, agrees to cancellation or amendment of the order by the sender or is bound by a funds-transfer system rule allowing cancellation or amendment without the bank's agreement, the sender, whether or not cancellation or amendment is effective, is liable to the bank for any loss and expenses, including reasonable attorney's fees, incurred by the bank as a result of the cancellation or amendment or attempted cancellation or amendment.

(g) A payment order is not revoked by the death or legal incapacity of the sender unless the receiving bank knows of the death or of an adjudication of incapacity by a court of competent jurisdiction and has reasonable opportunity to act before acceptance of the order.

(h) A funds-transfer system rule is not effective to the extent it conflicts with subsection (c)(2).

§ 4A–212.   Liability and Duty of Receiving Bank Regarding Unaccepted Payment Order.

If a receiving bank fails to accept a payment order that it is obliged by express agreement to accept, the bank is liable for breach of the agreement to the extent provided in the agreement or in this Article, but does not otherwise have any duty to accept a payment order or, before acceptance, to take any action, or refrain from taking action, with respect to the order except as provided in this Article or by express agreement. Liability based on acceptance arises only when acceptance occurs as stated in Section 4A–209, and liability is limited to that provided in this Article. A receiving bank is not the agent of the sender or beneficiary of the payment order it accepts, or of any other party to the funds transfer, and the bank owes no duty to any party to the funds transfer except as provided in this Article or by express agreement.

Part 3   Execution of Sender's Payment Order by Receiving Bank

§ 4A–301.   Execution and Execution Date.

(a) A payment order is "executed" by the receiving bank when it issues a payment order intended to carry out the payment order received by the bank. A payment order received by the beneficiary's bank can be accepted but cannot be executed.

(b) "Execution date" of a payment order means the day on which the receiving bank may properly issue a payment order in execution of the sender's order. The execution date may be determined by instruction of the sender but cannot be earlier than the day the order is received and, unless otherwise determined, is the day the order is received. If the sender's instruction states a payment date, the execution date is the payment date or an earlier date on which execution is reasonably necessary to allow payment to the beneficiary on the payment date.

§ 4A–302.   Obligations of Receiving Bank in Execution of Payment Order.

(a) Except as provided in subsections (b) through (d), if the receiving bank accepts a payment order pursuant to Section 4A–209(a), the bank has the following obligations in executing the order:

(1) The receiving bank is obliged to issue, on the execution date, a payment order complying with the sender's order and to follow the sender's instructions concerning (i) any intermediary bank or funds-transfer system to be used in carrying out the funds transfer, or (ii) the means by which payment orders are to be transmitted in the funds transfer. If the originator's bank issues a payment order to an intermediary bank, the originator's bank is obliged to instruct the intermediary bank according to the instruction of the originator. An intermediary bank in the funds transfer is similarly bound by an instruction given to it by the sender of the payment order it accepts.

(2) If the sender's instruction states that the funds transfer is to be carried out telephonically or by wire transfer or otherwise indicates that the funds transfer is to be carried out by the most expeditious means, the receiving bank is obliged to transmit its payment order by the most expeditious available means, and to instruct any intermediary bank accordingly. If a sender's instruction states a payment date, the receiving bank is obliged to transmit its payment order at a time and by means reasonably necessary to allow payment to the beneficiary on the payment date or as soon thereafter as is feasible.

(b) Unless otherwise instructed, a receiving bank executing a payment order may (i) use any funds-transfer system if use of that system is reasonable in the circumstances, and (ii) issue a payment order to the beneficiary's bank or to an intermediary bank through which a payment order conforming to the sender's order can expeditiously be issued to the beneficiary's bank if the receiving bank exercises ordinary care in the selection of the intermediary bank. A receiving bank is not required to follow an instruction of the sender designating a funds-transfer system to be used in carrying out the funds transfer if the receiving bank, in good faith, determines that it is not feasible to follow the instruction or that following the instruction would unduly delay completion of the funds transfer.

(c) Unless subsection (a)(2) applies or the receiving bank is otherwise instructed, the bank may execute a payment order by transmitting its payment order by first class mail or by any means reasonable in the circumstances. If the receiving bank is instructed to execute the sender's order by transmitting its payment order by a particular means, the receiving bank may issue its payment order by the means stated or by any means as expeditious as the means stated.

(d) Unless instructed by the sender, (i) the receiving bank may not obtain payment of its charges for services and expenses in connection with the execution of the sender's order by issuing a payment order in an amount equal to the amount of the sender's order less the amount of the charges, and (ii) may not instruct a subsequent receiving bank to obtain payment of its charges in the same manner.

§ 4A–303.   Erroneous Execution of Payment Order.

(a) A receiving bank that (i) executes the payment order of the sender by issuing a payment order in an amount greater than the amount of the sender's order, or (ii) issues a payment order in execution of the sender's order and then issues a duplicate order, is entitled to payment of the amount of the sender's order under Section 4A–402(c) if that subsection is otherwise satisfied. The bank is entitled to recover from the beneficiary of the erroneous order the excess payment received to the extent allowed by the law governing mistake and restitution.

(b) A receiving bank that executes the payment order of the sender by issuing a payment order in an amount less than the amount of the sender's order is entitled to payment of the amount of the sender's order under Section 4A–402(c) if (i) that subsection is otherwise satisfied and (ii) the bank corrects its mistake by issuing an additional payment order for the benefit of the beneficiary of the sender's order. If the error is not corrected, the issuer of the erroneous order is entitled to receive or retain payment from the sender of the order it accepted only to the extent of the amount of the erroneous order. This subsection does not apply if the receiving bank executes the sender's payment order by issuing a payment order in an amount less than the amount of the sender's order for the purpose of obtaining payment of its charges for services and expenses pursuant to instruction of the sender.

(c) If a receiving bank executes the payment order of the sender by issuing a payment order to a beneficiary different from the beneficiary of the sender's order and the funds transfer is completed on the basis of that error, the sender of the payment order that was erroneously executed and all previous senders in the funds transfer are not obliged to pay the payment orders they issued. The issuer of the erroneous order is entitled to recover from the beneficiary of the order the payment received to the extent allowed by the law governing mistake and restitution.

§ 4A–304.   Duty of Sender to Report Erroneously Executed Payment Order.

If the sender of a payment order that is erroneously executed as stated in Section 4A–303 receives notification from the receiving bank that the order was executed or that the sender's account was debited with respect to the order, the sender has a duty to exercise ordinary care to determine, on the basis of information available to the sender, that the order was erroneously executed and to notify the bank of the relevant facts within a reasonable time not exceeding 90 days after the notification from the bank was received by the sender. If the sender fails to perform that duty, the bank is not obliged to pay interest on any amount refundable to the sender under Section 4A–402(d) for the period before the bank learns of the execution error. The bank is not entitled to any recovery from the sender on account of a failure by the sender to perform the duty stated in this section.

§ 4A–305.   Liability for Late or Improper Execution or Failure to Execute Payment Order.

(a) If a funds transfer is completed but execution of a payment order by the receiving bank in breach of Section 4A–302 results in delay in payment to the beneficiary, the bank is obliged to pay interest to either the originator or the beneficiary of the funds transfer for the period of delay caused by the improper execution. Except as provided in subsection (c), additional damages are not recoverable.

(b) If execution of a payment order by a receiving bank in breach of Section 4A–302 results in (i) noncompletion of the funds transfer,

(ii) failure to use an intermediary bank designated by the originator, or (iii) issuance of a payment order that does not comply with the terms of the payment order of the originator, the bank is liable to the originator for its expenses in the funds transfer and for incidental expenses and interest losses, to the extent not covered by subsection (a), resulting from the improper execution. Except as provided in subsection (c), additional damages are not recoverable.

(c) In addition to the amounts payable under subsections (a) and (b), damages, including consequential damages, are recoverable to the extent provided in an express written agreement of the receiving bank.

(d) If a receiving bank fails to execute a payment order it was obliged by express agreement to execute, the receiving bank is liable to the sender for its expenses in the transaction and for incidental expenses and interest losses resulting from the failure to execute. Additional damages, including consequential damages, are recoverable to the extent provided in an express written agreement of the receiving bank, but are not otherwise recoverable.

(e) Reasonable attorney's fees are recoverable if demand for compensation under subsection (a) or (b) is made and refused before an action is brought on the claim. If a claim is made for breach of an agreement under subsection (d) and the agreement does not provide for damages, reasonable attorney's fees are recoverable if demand for compensation under subsection (d) is made and refused before an action is brought on the claim.

(f) Except as stated in this section, the liability of a receiving bank under subsections (a) and (b) may not be varied by agreement.

Part 4   Payment

§ 4A–401.   Payment Date.

"Payment date" of a payment order means the day on which the amount of the order is payable to the beneficiary by the beneficiary's bank. The payment date may be determined by instruction of the sender but cannot be earlier than the day the order is received by the beneficiary's bank and, unless otherwise determined, is the day the order is received by the beneficiary's bank.

§ 4A–402.   Obligation of Sender to Pay Receiving Bank.

(a) This section is subject to Sections 4A–205 and 4A–207.

(b) With respect to a payment order issued to the beneficiary's bank, acceptance of the order by the bank obliges the sender to pay the bank the amount of the order, but payment is not due until the payment date of the order.

(c) This subsection is subject to subsection (e) and to Section 4A–303. With respect to a payment order issued to a receiving bank other than the beneficiary's bank, acceptance of the order by the receiving bank obliges the sender to pay the bank the amount of the sender's order. Payment by the sender is not due until the execution date of the sender's order. The obligation of that sender to pay its payment order is excused if the funds transfer is not completed by acceptance by the beneficiary's bank of a payment order instructing payment to the beneficiary of that sender's payment order.

(d) If the sender of a payment order pays the order and was not obliged to pay all or part of the amount paid, the bank receiving payment is obliged to refund payment to the extent the sender was not obliged to pay. Except as provided in Sections 4A–204 and 4A–304, interest is payable on the refundable amount from the date of payment.

(e) If a funds transfer is not completed as stated in subsection (c) and an intermediary bank is obliged to refund payment as stated in subsection (d) but is unable to do so because not permitted by applicable law or because the bank suspends payments, a sender in the funds transfer that executed a payment order in compliance with an instruction, as stated in Section 4A–302(a)(1), to route the funds transfer through that intermediary bank is entitled to receive or retain payment from the sender of the payment order that it accepted. The first sender in the funds transfer that issued an instruction requiring routing through that intermediary bank is subrogated to the right of the bank that paid the intermediary bank to refund as stated in subsection (d).

(f) The right of the sender of a payment order to be excused from the obligation to pay the order as stated in subsection (c) or to receive refund under subsection (d) may not be varied by agreement.

§ 4A–403.   Payment by Sender to Receiving Bank.

(a) Payment of the sender's obligation under Section 4A–402 to pay the receiving bank occurs as follows:

(1) If the sender is a bank, payment occurs when the receiving bank receives final settlement of the obligation through a Federal Reserve Bank or through a funds-transfer system.

(2) If the sender is a bank and the sender (i) credited an account of the receiving bank with the sender, or (ii) caused an account of the receiving bank in another bank to be credited, payment occurs when the credit is withdrawn or, if not withdrawn, at midnight of the day on which the credit is withdrawable and the receiving bank learns of that fact.

(3) If the receiving bank debits an account of the sender with the receiving bank, payment occurs when the debit is made to the extent the debit is covered by a withdrawable credit balance in the account.

(b) If the sender and receiving bank are members of a funds-transfer system that nets obligations multilaterally among participants, the receiving bank receives final settlement when settlement is complete in accordance with the rules of the system. The obligation of the sender to pay the amount of a payment order transmitted through the funds-transfer system may be satisfied, to the extent permitted by the rules of the system, by setting off and applying against the sender's obligation the right of the sender to receive payment from the receiving bank of the amount of any other payment order transmitted to the sender by the receiving bank through the funds-transfer system. The aggregate balance of obligations owed by each sender to each receiving bank in the funds-transfer system may be satisfied, to the extent permitted by the rules of the system, by setting off and applying against that balance the aggregate balance of obligations owed to the sender by other members of the system. The aggregate balance is determined after the right of setoff stated in the second sentence of this subsection has been exercised.

(c) If two banks transmit payment orders to each other under an agreement that settlement of the obligations of each bank to the other under Section 4A–402 will be made at the end of the day or other period, the total amount owed with respect to all orders transmitted by one bank shall be set off against the total amount owed with respect to all orders transmitted by the other bank. To the extent of the setoff, each bank has made payment to the other.

(d) In a case not covered by subsection (a), the time when payment of the sender's obligation under Section 4A–402(b) or 4A–402(c) occurs is governed by applicable principles of law that determine when an obligation is satisfied.

§ 4A–404.   Obligation of Beneficiary's Bank to Pay and Give Notice to Beneficiary.

(a) Subject to Sections 4A–211(e), 4A–405(d), and 4A–405(e), if a beneficiary's bank accepts a payment order, the bank is obliged to pay the amount of the order to the beneficiary of the order. Payment is due on the payment date of the order, but if acceptance occurs on the payment date after the close of the funds-transfer business day of the bank, payment is due on the next funds-transfer business day. If the bank refuses to pay after demand by the beneficiary and receipt of notice of particular circumstances that will give rise to consequential damages as a result of nonpayment, the beneficiary may recover damages resulting from the refusal to pay to the extent the bank had notice of the damages, unless the bank proves that it did not pay because of a reasonable doubt concerning the right of the beneficiary to payment.

(b) If a payment order accepted by the beneficiary's bank instructs payment to an account of the beneficiary, the bank is obliged to notify the beneficiary of receipt of the order before midnight of the next funds-transfer business day following the payment date. If the payment order does not instruct payment to an account of the beneficiary, the bank is required to notify the beneficiary only if notice is required by the order. Notice may be given by first class mail or any other means reasonable in the circumstances. If the bank fails to give the required notice, the bank is obliged to pay interest to the beneficiary on the amount of the payment order from the day notice should have been given until the day the beneficiary learned of receipt of the payment order by the bank. No other damages are recoverable. Reasonable attorney's fees are also recoverable if demand for interest is made and refused before an action is brought on the claim.

(c) The right of a beneficiary to receive payment and damages as stated in subsection (a) may not be varied by agreement or a funds-transfer system rule. The right of a beneficiary to be notified as stated in subsection (b) may be varied by agreement of the beneficiary or by a funds-transfer system rule if the beneficiary is notified of the rule before initiation of the funds transfer.

§ 4A–405.   Payment by Beneficiary's Bank to Beneficiary.

(a) If the beneficiary's bank credits an account of the beneficiary of a payment order, payment of the bank's obligation under Section 4A–404(a) occurs when and to the extent (i) the beneficiary is notified of the right to withdraw the credit, (ii) the bank lawfully applies the credit to a debt of the beneficiary, or (iii) funds with respect to the order are otherwise made available to the beneficiary by the bank.

(b) If the beneficiary's bank does not credit an account of the beneficiary of a payment order, the time when payment of the bank's obligation under Section 4A–404(a) occurs is governed by principles of law that determine when an obligation is satisfied.

(c) Except as stated in subsections (d) and (e), if the beneficiary's bank pays the beneficiary of a payment order under a condition to payment or agreement of the beneficiary giving the bank the right to recover payment from the beneficiary if the bank does not receive payment of the order, the condition to payment or agreement is not enforceable.

(d) A funds-transfer system rule may provide that payments made to beneficiaries of funds transfers made through the system are provisional until receipt of payment by the beneficiary's bank of the payment order it accepted. A beneficiary's bank that makes a payment that is provisional under the rule is entitled to refund from the beneficiary if (i) the rule requires that both the beneficiary and the originator be given notice of the provisional nature of the payment before the funds transfer is initiated, (ii) the beneficiary, the beneficiary's bank, and the originator's bank agreed to be bound by the rule, and (iii) the beneficiary's bank did not receive payment of the payment order that it accepted. If the beneficiary is obliged to refund payment to the beneficiary's bank, acceptance of the payment order by the beneficiary's bank is nullified and no payment by the originator of the funds transfer to the beneficiary occurs under Section 4A–406.

(e) This subsection applies to a funds transfer that includes a payment order transmitted over a funds-transfer system that (i) nets obligations multilaterally among participants, and (ii) has in effect a loss-sharing agreement among participants for the purpose of providing funds necessary to complete settlement of the obligations of one or more participants that do not meet their settlement obligations. If the beneficiary's bank in the funds transfer accepts a payment order and the system fails to complete settlement pursuant to its rules with respect to any payment order in the funds transfer, (i) the acceptance by the beneficiary's bank is nullified and no person has any right or obligation based on the acceptance, (ii) the beneficiary's bank is entitled to recover payment from the beneficiary, (iii) no payment by the originator to the beneficiary occurs under Section 4A–406, and (iv) subject to Section 4A–402(e), each sender in the funds transfer is excused from its obligation to pay its payment order under Section 4A–402(c) because the funds transfer has not been completed.

§ 4A–406. Payment by Originator to Beneficiary; Discharge of Underlying Obligation.

(a) Subject to Sections 4A–211(e), 4A–405(d), and 4A–405(e), the originator of a funds transfer pays the beneficiary of the originator's payment order (i) at the time a payment order for the benefit of the beneficiary is accepted by the beneficiary's bank in the funds transfer and (ii) in an amount equal to the amount of the order accepted by the beneficiary's bank, but not more than the amount of the originator's order.

(b) If payment under subsection (a) is made to satisfy an obligation, the obligation is discharged to the same extent discharge would result from payment to the beneficiary of the same amount in money, unless (i) the payment under subsection (a) was made by a means prohibited by the contract of the beneficiary with respect to the obligation, (ii) the beneficiary, within a reasonable time after receiving notice of receipt of the order by the beneficiary's bank, notified the originator of the beneficiary's refusal of the payment, (iii) funds with respect to the order were not withdrawn by the beneficiary or applied to a debt of the beneficiary, and (iv) the beneficiary would suffer a loss that could reasonably have been avoided if payment had been made by a means complying with the contract. If payment by the originator does not result in discharge under this section, the originator is subrogated to the rights of the beneficiary to receive payment from the beneficiary's bank under Section 4A–404(a).

(c) For the purpose of determining whether discharge of an obligation occurs under subsection (b), if the beneficiary's bank accepts a payment order in an amount equal to the amount of the originator's payment order less charges of one or more receiving banks in the funds transfer, payment to the beneficiary is deemed to be in the amount of the originator's order unless upon demand by the beneficiary the originator does not pay the beneficiary the amount of the deducted charges.

(d) Rights of the originator or of the beneficiary of a funds transfer under this section may be varied only by agreement of the originator and the beneficiary.

Part 5   Miscellaneous Provisions

§ 4A–501. Variation by Agreement and Effect of Funds-Transfer System Rule.

(a) Except as otherwise provided in this Article, the rights and obligations of a party to a funds transfer may be varied by agreement of the affected party.

(b) "Funds-transfer system rule" means a rule of an association of banks (i) governing transmission of payment orders by means of a funds-transfer system of the association or rights and obligations with respect to those orders, or (ii) to the extent the rule governs rights and obligations between banks that are parties to a funds transfer in which a Federal Reserve Bank, acting as an intermediary bank, sends a payment order to the beneficiary's bank. Except as otherwise provided in this Article, a funds-transfer system rule governing rights and obligations between participating banks using the system may be effective even if the rule conflicts with this Article and indirectly affects another party to the funds transfer who does not consent to the rule. A funds-transfer system rule may also govern rights and obligations of parties other than participating banks using the system to the extent stated in Sections 4A–404(c), 4A–405(d), and 4A–507(c).

§ 4A–502. Creditor Process Served on Receiving Bank; Setoff by Beneficiary's Bank.

(a) As used in this section, "creditor process" means levy, attachment, garnishment, notice of lien, sequestration, or similar process issued by or on behalf of a creditor or other claimant with respect to an account.

(b) This subsection applies to creditor process with respect to an authorized account of the sender of a payment order if the creditor process is served on the receiving bank. For the purpose of determining rights with respect to the creditor process, if the receiving bank accepts the payment order the balance in the authorized account is deemed to be reduced by the amount of the payment order to the extent the bank did not otherwise receive payment of the order, unless the creditor process is served at a time and in a manner affording the bank a reasonable opportunity to act on it before the bank accepts the payment order.

(c) If a beneficiary's bank has received a payment order for payment to the beneficiary's account in the bank, the following rules apply:

(1) The bank may credit the beneficiary's account. The amount credited may be set off against an obligation owed by the beneficiary to the bank or may be applied to satisfy creditor process served on the bank with respect to the account.

(2) The bank may credit the beneficiary's account and allow withdrawal of the amount credited unless creditor process with respect to the account is served at a time and in a manner affording the bank a reasonable opportunity to act to prevent withdrawal.

(3) If creditor process with respect to the beneficiary's account has been served and the bank has had a reasonable opportunity to act on it, the bank may not reject the payment order except for a reason unrelated to the service of process.

(d) Creditor process with respect to a payment by the originator to the beneficiary pursuant to a funds transfer may be served only on the beneficiary's bank with respect to the debt owed by that bank to the beneficiary. Any other bank served with the creditor process is not obliged to act with respect to the process.

§ 4A-503.   Injunction or Restraining Order with Respect to Funds Transfer.

For proper cause and in compliance with applicable law, a court may restrain (i) a person from issuing a payment order to initiate a funds transfer, (ii) an originator's bank from executing the payment order of the originator, or (iii) the beneficiary's bank from releasing funds to the beneficiary or the beneficiary from withdrawing the funds. A court may not otherwise restrain a person from issuing a payment order, paying or receiving payment of a payment order, or otherwise acting with respect to a funds transfer.

§ 4A-504.   Order in Which Items and Payment Orders May Be Charged to Account; Order of Withdrawals from Account.

(a) If a receiving bank has received more than one payment order of the sender or one or more payment orders and other items that are payable from the sender's account, the bank may charge the sender's account with respect to the various orders and items in any sequence.

(b) In determining whether a credit to an account has been withdrawn by the holder of the account or applied to a debt of the holder of the account, credits first made to the account are first withdrawn or applied.

§ 4A-505.   Preclusion of Objection to Debit of Customer's Account.

If a receiving bank has received payment from its customer with respect to a payment order issued in the name of the customer as sender and accepted by the bank, and the customer received notification reasonably identifying the order, the customer is precluded from asserting that the bank is not entitled to retain the payment unless the customer notifies the bank of the customer's objection to the payment within one year after the notification was received by the customer.

§ 4A-506.   Rate of Interest.

(a) If, under this Article, a receiving bank is obliged to pay interest with respect to a payment order issued to the bank, the amount payable may be determined (i) by agreement of the sender and receiving bank, or (ii) by a funds-transfer system rule if the payment order is transmitted through a funds-transfer system.

(b) If the amount of interest is not determined by an agreement or rule as stated in subsection (a), the amount is calculated by multiplying the applicable Federal Funds rate by the amount on which interest is payable, and then multiplying the product by the number of days for which interest is payable. The applicable Federal Funds rate is the average of the Federal Funds rates published by the Federal Reserve Bank of New York for each of the days for which interest is payable divided by 360. The Federal Funds rate for any day on which a published rate is not available is the same as the published rate for the next preceding day for which there is a published rate. If a receiving bank that accepted a payment order is required to refund payment to the sender of the order because the funds transfer was not completed, but the failure to complete was not due to any fault by the bank, the interest payable is reduced by a percentage equal to the reserve requirement on deposits of the receiving bank.

§ 4A-507.   Choice of Law.

(a) The following rules apply unless the affected parties otherwise agree or subsection (c) applies:

(1) The rights and obligations between the sender of a payment order and the receiving bank are governed by the law of the jurisdiction in which the receiving bank is located.

(2) The rights and obligations between the beneficiary's bank and the beneficiary are governed by the law of the jurisdiction in which the beneficiary's bank is located.

(3) The issue of when payment is made pursuant to a funds transfer by the originator to the beneficiary is governed by the law of the jurisdiction in which the beneficiary's bank is located.

(b) If the parties described in each paragraph of subsection (a) have made an agreement selecting the law of a particular jurisdiction to govern rights and obligations between each other, the law of that jurisdiction governs those rights and obligations, whether or not the payment order or the funds transfer bears a reasonable relation to that jurisdiction.

(c) A funds-transfer system rule may select the law of a particular jurisdiction to govern (i) rights and obligations between participating banks with respect to payment orders transmitted or processed through the system, or (ii) the rights and obligations of some or all parties to a funds transfer any part of which is carried out by means of the system. A choice of law made pursuant to clause (i) is binding on participating banks. A choice of law made pursuant to clause (ii) is binding on the originator, other sender, or a receiving bank having notice that the funds-transfer system might be used in the funds transfer and of the choice of law by the system when the originator, other sender, or receiving bank issued or accepted a payment order. The beneficiary of a funds transfer is bound by the choice of law if, when the funds transfer is initiated, the beneficiary has notice that the funds-transfer system might be used in the funds transfer and of the choice of law by the system. The law of a jurisdiction selected pursuant to this subsection may govern, whether or not that law bears a reasonable relation to the matter in issue.

(d) In the event of inconsistency between an agreement under subsection (b) and a choice-of-law rule under subsection (c), the agreement under subsection (b) prevails.

(e) If a funds transfer is made by use of more than one funds-transfer system and there is inconsistency between choice-of-law rules of the systems, the matter in issue is governed by the law of the selected jurisdiction that has the most significant relationship to the matter in issue.

* * * *

Revised Article 9
SECURED TRANSACTIONS

Part 1 General Provisions

[Subpart 1. Short Title, Definitions, and General Concepts]

§ 9–101. Short Title.

This article may be cited as Uniform Commercial Code—Secured Transactions.

§ 9–102. Definitions and Index of Definitions.

(a) In this article:

(1) "Accession" means goods that are physically united with other goods in such a manner that the identity of the original goods is not lost.

(2) "Account", except as used in "account for", means a right to payment of a monetary obligation, whether or not earned by performance, (i) for property that has been or is to be sold, leased, licensed, assigned, or otherwise disposed of, (ii) for services rendered or to be rendered, (iii) for a policy of insurance issued or to be issued, (iv) for a secondary obligation incurred or to be incurred, (v) for energy provided or to be provided, (vi) for the use or hire of a vessel under a charter or other contract, (vii) arising out of the use of a credit or charge card or information contained on or for use with the card, or (viii) as winnings in a lottery or other game of chance operated or sponsored by a State, governmental unit of a State, or person licensed or authorized to operate the game by a State or governmental unit of a State. The term includes health-care insurance receivables. The term does not include (i) rights to payment evidenced by chattel paper or an instrument, (ii) commercial tort claims, (iii) deposit accounts, (iv) investment property, (v) letter-of-credit rights or letters of credit, or (vi) rights to payment for money or funds advanced or sold, other than rights arising out of the use of a credit or charge card or information contained on or for use with the card.

(3) "Account debtor" means a person obligated on an account, chattel paper, or general intangible. The term does not include persons obligated to pay a negotiable instrument, even if the instrument constitutes part of chattel paper.

(4) "Accounting", except as used in "accounting for", means a record:

(A) authenticated by a secured party;

(B) indicating the aggregate unpaid secured obligations as of a date not more than 35 days earlier or 35 days later than the date of the record; and

(C) identifying the components of the obligations in reasonable detail.

(5) "Agricultural lien" means an interest, other than a security interest, in farm products:

(A) which secures payment or performance of an obligation for:

(i) goods or services furnished in connection with a debtor's farming operation; or

(ii) rent on real property leased by a debtor in connection with its farming operation;

(B) which is created by statute in favor of a person that:

(i) in the ordinary course of its business furnished goods or services to a debtor in connection with a debtor's farming operation; or

(ii) leased real property to a debtor in connection with the debtor's farming operation; and

(C) whose effectiveness does not depend on the person's possession of the personal property.

(6) "As-extracted collateral" means:

(A) oil, gas, or other minerals that are subject to a security interest that:

(i) is created by a debtor having an interest in the minerals before extraction; and

(ii) attaches to the minerals as extracted; or

(B) accounts arising out of the sale at the wellhead or minehead of oil, gas, or other minerals in which the debtor had an interest before extraction.

(7) "Authenticate" means:

(A) to sign; or

(B) to execute or otherwise adopt a symbol, or encrypt or similarly process a record in whole or in part, with the present intent of the authenticating person to identify the person and adopt or accept a record.

(8) "Bank" means an organization that is engaged in the business of banking. The term includes savings banks, savings and loan associations, credit unions, and trust companies.

(9) "Cash proceeds" means proceeds that are money, checks, deposit accounts, or the like.

(10) "Certificate of title" means a certificate of title with respect to which a statute provides for the security interest in question to be indicated on the certificate as a condition or result of the security interest's obtaining priority over the rights of a lien creditor with respect to the collateral.

(11) "Chattel paper" means a record or records that evidence both a monetary obligation and a security interest in specific goods, a security interest in specific goods and software used in the goods, a security interest in specific goods and license of software used in the goods, a lease of specific goods, or a lease of specific goods and license of software used in the goods. In this paragraph, "monetary obligation" means a monetary obligation secured by the goods or owed under a lease of the goods and includes a monetary obligation with respect to software used in the goods. The term does not include (i) charters or other contracts involving the use or hire of a vessel or (ii) records that evidence a right to payment arising out of the use of a credit or charge card or information contained on or for use with the card. If a transaction is evidenced by records that include an instrument or series of instruments, the group of records taken together constitutes chattel paper.

(12) "Collateral" means the property subject to a security interest or agricultural lien. The term includes:

(A) proceeds to which a security interest attaches;

(B) accounts, chattel paper, payment intangibles, and promissory notes that have been sold; and

(C) goods that are the subject of a consignment.

(13) "Commercial tort claim" means a claim arising in tort with respect to which:

(A) the claimant is an organization; or

(B) the claimant is an individual and the claim:

(i) arose in the course of the claimant's business or profession; and

(ii) does not include damages arising out of personal injury to or the death of an individual.

(14) "Commodity account" means an account maintained by a commodity intermediary in which a commodity contract is carried for a commodity customer.

(15) "Commodity contract" means a commodity futures contract, an option on a commodity futures contract, a commodity option, or another contract if the contract or option is:

(A) traded on or subject to the rules of a board of trade that has been designated as a contract market for such a contract pursuant to federal commodities laws; or

(B) traded on a foreign commodity board of trade, exchange, or market, and is carried on the books of a commodity intermediary for a commodity customer.

(16) "Commodity customer" means a person for which a commodity intermediary carries a commodity contract on its books.

(17) "Commodity intermediary" means a person that:

(A) is registered as a futures commission merchant under federal commodities law; or

(B) in the ordinary course of its business provides clearance or settlement services for a board of trade that has been designated as a contract market pursuant to federal commodities law.

(18) "Communicate" means:

(A) to send a written or other tangible record;

(B) to transmit a record by any means agreed upon by the persons sending and receiving the record; or

(C) in the case of transmission of a record to or by a filing office, to transmit a record by any means prescribed by filing-office rule.

(19) "Consignee" means a merchant to which goods are delivered in a consignment.

(20) "Consignment" means a transaction, regardless of its form, in which a person delivers goods to a merchant for the purpose of sale and:

(A) the merchant:

(i) deals in goods of that kind under a name other than the name of the person making delivery;

(ii) is not an auctioneer; and

(iii) is not generally known by its creditors to be substantially engaged in selling the goods of others;

(B) with respect to each delivery, the aggregate value of the goods is $1,000 or more at the time of delivery;

(C) the goods are not consumer goods immediately before delivery; and

(D) the transaction does not create a security interest that secures an obligation.

(21) "Consignor" means a person that delivers goods to a consignee in a consignment.

(22) "Consumer debtor" means a debtor in a consumer transaction.

(23) "Consumer goods" means goods that are used or bought for use primarily for personal, family, or household purposes.

(24) "Consumer-goods transaction" means a consumer transaction in which:

(A) an individual incurs an obligation primarily for personal, family, or household purposes; and

(B) a security interest in consumer goods secures the obligation.

(25) "Consumer obligor" means an obligor who is an individual and who incurred the obligation as part of a transaction

entered into primarily for personal, family, or household purposes.

(26) "Consumer transaction" means a transaction in which (i) an individual incurs an obligation primarily for personal, family, or household purposes, (ii) a security interest secures the obligation, and (iii) the collateral is held or acquired primarily for personal, family, or household purposes. The term includes consumer-goods transactions.

(27) "Continuation statement" means an amendment of a financing statement which:

(A) identifies, by its file number, the initial financing statement to which it relates; and

(B) indicates that it is a continuation statement for, or that it is filed to continue the effectiveness of, the identified financing statement.

(28) "Debtor" means:

(A) a person having an interest, other than a security interest or other lien, in the collateral, whether or not the person is an obligor;

(B) a seller of accounts, chattel paper, payment intangibles, or promissory notes; or

(C) a consignee.

(29) "Deposit account" means a demand, time, savings, passbook, or similar account maintained with a bank. The term does not include investment property or accounts evidenced by an instrument.

(30) "Document" means a document of title or a receipt of the type described in Section 7–201(2).

(31) "Electronic chattel paper" means chattel paper evidenced by a record or records consisting of information stored in an electronic medium.

(32) "Encumbrance" means a right, other than an ownership interest, in real property. The term includes mortgages and other liens on real property.

(33) "Equipment" means goods other than inventory, farm products, or consumer goods.

(34) "Farm products" means goods, other than standing timber, with respect to which the debtor is engaged in a farming operation and which are:

(A) crops grown, growing, or to be grown, including:

(i) crops produced on trees, vines, and bushes; and

(ii) aquatic goods produced in aquacultural operations;

(B) livestock, born or unborn, including aquatic goods produced in aquacultural operations;

(C) supplies used or produced in a farming operation; or

(D) products of crops or livestock in their unmanufactured states.

(35) "Farming operation" means raising, cultivating, propagating, fattening, grazing, or any other farming, livestock, or aquacultural operation.

(36) "File number" means the number assigned to an initial financing statement pursuant to Section 9–519(a).

(37) "Filing office" means an office designated in Section 9–501 as the place to file a financing statement.

(38) "Filing-office rule" means a rule adopted pursuant to Section 9–526.

(39) "Financing statement" means a record or records composed of an initial financing statement and any filed record relating to the initial financing statement.

(40) "Fixture filing" means the filing of a financing statement covering goods that are or are to become fixtures and satisfying Section 9–502(a) and (b). The term includes the filing of a financing statement covering goods of a transmitting utility which are or are to become fixtures.

(41) "Fixtures" means goods that have become so related to particular real property that an interest in them arises under real property law.

(42) "General intangible" means any personal property, including things in action, other than accounts, chattel paper, commercial tort claims, deposit accounts, documents, goods, instruments, investment property, letter-of-credit rights, letters of credit, money, and oil, gas, or other minerals before extraction. The term includes payment intangibles and software.

(43) "Good faith" means honesty in fact and the observance of reasonable commercial standards of fair dealing.

(44) "Goods" means all things that are movable when a security interest attaches. The term includes (i) fixtures, (ii) standing timber that is to be cut and removed under a conveyance or contract for sale, (iii) the unborn young of animals, (iv) crops grown, growing, or to be grown, even if the crops are produced on trees, vines, or bushes, and (v) manufactured homes. The term also includes a computer program embedded in goods and any supporting information provided in connection with a transaction relating to the program if (i) the program is associated with the goods in such a manner that it customarily is considered part of the goods, or (ii) by becoming the owner of the goods, a person acquires a right to use the program in connection with the goods. The term does not include a computer program embedded in goods that consist solely of the medium in which the program is embedded. The term also does not include accounts, chattel paper, commercial tort claims, deposit accounts, documents, general intangibles, instruments, investment property, letter-of-credit rights, letters of credit, money, or oil, gas, or other minerals before extraction.

(45) "Governmental unit" means a subdivision, agency, department, county, parish, municipality, or other unit of the government of the United States, a State, or a foreign country. The term includes an organization having a separate corporate existence if the organization is eligible to issue debt on which interest is exempt from income taxation under the laws of the United States.

(46) "Health-care-insurance receivable" means an interest in or claim under a policy of insurance which is a right to payment of a monetary obligation for health-care goods or services provided.

(47) "Instrument" means a negotiable instrument or any other writing that evidences a right to the payment of a monetary obligation, is not itself a security agreement or lease, and is of a type that in ordinary course of business is transferred by delivery with any necessary indorsement or assignment. The term does not include (i) investment property, (ii) letters of credit, or (iii) writings that evidence a right to payment arising out of the use of a credit or charge card or information contained on or for use with the card.

(48) "Inventory" means goods, other than farm products, which:

(A) are leased by a person as lessor;

(B) are held by a person for sale or lease or to be furnished under a contract of service;

(C) are furnished by a person under a contract of service; or

(D) consist of raw materials, work in process, or materials used or consumed in a business.

(49) "Investment property" means a security, whether certificated or uncertificated, security entitlement, securities account, commodity contract, or commodity account.

(50) "Jurisdiction of organization", with respect to a registered organization, means the jurisdiction under whose law the organization is organized.

(51) "Letter-of-credit right" means a right to payment or performance under a letter of credit, whether or not the beneficiary has demanded or is at the time entitled to demand payment or performance. The term does not include the right of a beneficiary to demand payment or performance under a letter of credit.

(52) "Lien creditor" means:

(A) a creditor that has acquired a lien on the property involved by attachment, levy, or the like;

(B) an assignee for benefit of creditors from the time of assignment;

(C) a trustee in bankruptcy from the date of the filing of the petition; or

(D) a receiver in equity from the time of appointment.

(53) "Manufactured home" means a structure, transportable in one or more sections, which, in the traveling mode, is eight body feet or more in width or 40 body feet or more in length, or, when erected on site, is 320 or more square feet, and which is built on a permanent chassis and designed to be used as a dwelling with or without a permanent foundation when connected to the required utilities, and includes the plumbing, heating, air-conditioning, and electrical systems contained therein. The term includes any structure that meets all of the requirements of this paragraph except the size requirements and with respect to which the manufacturer voluntarily files a certification required by the United States Secretary of Housing and Urban Development and complies with the standards established under Title 42 of the United States Code.

(54) "Manufactured-home transaction" means a secured transaction:

(A) that creates a purchase-money security interest in a manufactured home, other than a manufactured home held as inventory; or

(B) in which a manufactured home, other than a manufactured home held as inventory, is the primary collateral.

(55) "Mortgage" means a consensual interest in real property, including fixtures, which secures payment or performance of an obligation.

(56) "New debtor" means a person that becomes bound as debtor under Section 9–203(d) by a security agreement previously entered into by another person.

(57) "New value" means (i) money, (ii) money's worth in property, services, or new credit, or (iii) release by a transferee of an interest in property previously transferred to the transferee. The term does not include an obligation substituted for another obligation.

(58) "Noncash proceeds" means proceeds other than cash proceeds.

(59) "Obligor" means a person that, with respect to an obligation secured by a security interest in or an agricultural lien on the collateral, (i) owes payment or other performance of the obligation, (ii) has provided property other than the collateral to secure payment or other performance of the obligation, or (iii) is otherwise accountable in whole or in part for payment or other performance of the obligation. The term does not include issuers or nominated persons under a letter of credit.

(60) "Original debtor", except as used in Section 9–310(c), means a person that, as debtor, entered into a security agreement to which a new debtor has become bound under Section 9–203(d).

(61) "Payment intangible" means a general intangible under which the account debtor's principal obligation is a monetary obligation.

(62) "Person related to", with respect to an individual, means:

(A) the spouse of the individual;

(B) a brother, brother-in-law, sister, or sister-in-law of the individual;

(C) an ancestor or lineal descendant of the individual or the individual's spouse; or

(D) any other relative, by blood or marriage, of the individual or the individual's spouse who shares the same home with the individual.

(63) "Person related to", with respect to an organization, means:

(A) a person directly or indirectly controlling, controlled by, or under common control with the organization;

(B) an officer or director of, or a person performing similar functions with respect to, the organization;

(C) an officer or director of, or a person performing similar functions with respect to, a person described in subparagraph (A);

(D) the spouse of an individual described in subparagraph (A), (B), or (C); or

(E) an individual who is related by blood or marriage to an individual described in subparagraph (A), (B), (C), or (D) and shares the same home with the individual.

(64) "Proceeds", except as used in Section 9–609(b), means the following property:

(A) whatever is acquired upon the sale, lease, license, exchange, or other disposition of collateral;

(B) whatever is collected on, or distributed on account of, collateral;

(C) rights arising out of collateral;

(D) to the extent of the value of collateral, claims arising out of the loss, nonconformity, or interference with the use of, defects or infringement of rights in, or damage to, the collateral; or

(E) to the extent of the value of collateral and to the extent payable to the debtor or the secured party, insurance payable by reason of the loss or nonconformity of, defects or infringement of rights in, or damage to, the collateral.

(65) "Promissory note" means an instrument that evidences a promise to pay a monetary obligation, does not evidence an order to pay, and does not contain an acknowledgment by a bank that the bank has received for deposit a sum of money or funds.

(66) "Proposal" means a record authenticated by a secured party which includes the terms on which the secured party is willing to accept collateral in full or partial satisfaction of the obligation it secures pursuant to Sections 9–620, 9–621, and 9–622.

(67) "Public-finance transaction" means a secured transaction in connection with which:

(A) debt securities are issued;

(B) all or a portion of the securities issued have an initial stated maturity of at least 20 years; and

(C) the debtor, obligor, secured party, account debtor or other person obligated on collateral, assignor or assignee of a secured obligation, or assignor or assignee of a security interest is a State or a governmental unit of a State.

(68) "Pursuant to commitment", with respect to an advance made or other value given by a secured party, means pursuant to the secured party's obligation, whether or not a subsequent event of default or other event not within the secured party's control has relieved or may relieve the secured party from its obligation.

(69) "Record", except as used in "for record", "of record", "record or legal title", and "record owner", means information that is inscribed on a tangible medium or which is stored in an electronic or other medium and is retrievable in perceivable form.

(70) "Registered organization" means an organization organized solely under the law of a single State or the United States and as to which the State or the United States must maintain a public record showing the organization to have been organized.

(71) "Secondary obligor" means an obligor to the extent that:

(A) the obligor's obligation is secondary; or

(B) the obligor has a right of recourse with respect to an obligation secured by collateral against the debtor, another obligor, or property of either.

(72) "Secured party" means:

(A) a person in whose favor a security interest is created or provided for under a security agreement, whether or not any obligation to be secured is outstanding;

(B) a person that holds an agricultural lien;

(C) a consignor;

(D) a person to which accounts, chattel paper, payment intangibles, or promissory notes have been sold;

(E) a trustee, indenture trustee, agent, collateral agent, or other representative in whose favor a security interest or agricultural lien is created or provided for; or

(F) a person that holds a security interest arising under Section 2–401, 2–505, 2–711(3), 2A–508(5), 4–210, or 5–118.

(73) "Security agreement" means an agreement that creates or provides for a security interest.

(74) "Send", in connection with a record or notification, means:

(A) to deposit in the mail, deliver for transmission, or transmit by any other usual means of communication, with postage or cost of transmission provided for, addressed to any address reasonable under the circumstances; or

(B) to cause the record or notification to be received within the time that it would have been received if properly sent under subparagraph (A).

(75) "Software" means a computer program and any supporting information provided in connection with a transaction relating to the program. The term does not include a computer program that is included in the definition of goods.

(76) "State" means a State of the United States, the District of Columbia, Puerto Rico, the United States Virgin Islands, or any territory or insular possession subject to the jurisdiction of the United States.

(77) "Supporting obligation" means a letter-of-credit right or secondary obligation that supports the payment or performance of an account, chattel paper, a document, a general intangible, an instrument, or investment property.

(78) "Tangible chattel paper" means chattel paper evidenced by a record or records consisting of information that is inscribed on a tangible medium.

(79) "Termination statement" means an amendment of a financing statement which:

(A) identifies, by its file number, the initial financing statement to which it relates; and

(B) indicates either that it is a termination statement or that the identified financing statement is no longer effective.

(80) "Transmitting utility" means a person primarily engaged in the business of:

(A) operating a railroad, subway, street railway, or trolley bus;

(B) transmitting communications electrically, electromagnetically, or by light;

(C) transmitting goods by pipeline or sewer; or

(D) transmitting or producing and transmitting electricity, steam, gas, or water.

(b) The following definitions in other articles apply to this article:

"Applicant."	Section 5–102
"Beneficiary."	Section 5–102
"Broker."	Section 8–102
"Certificated security."	Section 8–102
"Check."	Section 3–104
"Clearing corporation."	Section 8–102
"Contract for sale."	Section 2–106
"Customer."	Section 4–104
"Entitlement holder."	Section 8–102
"Financial asset."	Section 8–102
"Holder in due course."	Section 3–302
"Issuer" (with respect to a letter of credit or letter-of-credit right).	Section 5–102
"Issuer" (with respect to a security).	Section 8–201
"Lease."	Section 2A–103
"Lease agreement."	Section 2A–103
"Lease contract."	Section 2A–103
"Leasehold interest."	Section 2A–103
"Lessee."	Section 2A–103
"Lessee in ordinary course of business."	Section 2A–103
"Lessor."	Section 2A–103
"Lessor's residual interest."	Section 2A–103
"Letter of credit."	Section 5–102
"Merchant."	Section 2–104
"Negotiable instrument."	Section 3–104
"Nominated person."	Section 5–102
"Note."	Section 3–104
"Proceeds of a letter of credit."	Section 5–114
"Prove."	Section 3–103
"Sale."	Section 2–106
"Securities account."	Section 8–501
"Securities intermediary."	Section 8–102
"Security."	Section 8–102
"Security certificate."	Section 8–102
"Security entitlement."	Section 8–102
"Uncertificated security."	Section 8–102

(c) Article 1 contains general definitions and principles of construction and interpretation applicable throughout this article.

Amended in 1999 and 2000.

§ 9–103.   Purchase-Money Security Interest; Application of Payments; Burden of Establishing.

(a) In this section:

(1) "purchase-money collateral" means goods or software that secures a purchase-money obligation incurred with respect to that collateral; and

(2) "purchase-money obligation" means an obligation of an obligor incurred as all or part of the price of the collateral or for value given to enable the debtor to acquire rights in or the use of the collateral if the value is in fact so used.

(b) A security interest in goods is a purchase-money security interest:

(1) to the extent that the goods are purchase-money collateral with respect to that security interest;

(2) if the security interest is in inventory that is or was purchase-money collateral, also to the extent that the security interest secures a purchase-money obligation incurred with respect to other inventory in which the secured party holds or held a purchase-money security interest; and

(3) also to the extent that the security interest secures a purchase-money obligation incurred with respect to software in which the secured party holds or held a purchase-money security interest.

(c) A security interest in software is a purchase-money security interest to the extent that the security interest also secures a purchase-money obligation incurred with respect to goods in which the secured party holds or held a purchase-money security interest if:

(1) the debtor acquired its interest in the software in an integrated transaction in which it acquired an interest in the goods; and

(2) the debtor acquired its interest in the software for the principal purpose of using the software in the goods.

(d) The security interest of a consignor in goods that are the subject of a consignment is a purchase-money security interest in inventory.

(e) In a transaction other than a consumer-goods transaction, if the extent to which a security interest is a purchase-money security interest depends on the application of a payment to a particular obligation, the payment must be applied:

(1) in accordance with any reasonable method of application to which the parties agree;

(2) in the absence of the parties' agreement to a reasonable method, in accordance with any intention of the obligor manifested at or before the time of payment; or

(3) in the absence of an agreement to a reasonable method and a timely manifestation of the obligor's intention, in the following order:

(A) to obligations that are not secured; and

(B) if more than one obligation is secured, to obligations secured by purchase-money security interests in the order in which those obligations were incurred.

(f) In a transaction other than a consumer-goods transaction, a purchase-money security interest does not lose its status as such, even if:

(1) the purchase-money collateral also secures an obligation that is not a purchase-money obligation;

(2) collateral that is not purchase-money collateral also secures the purchase-money obligation; or

(3) the purchase-money obligation has been renewed, refinanced, consolidated, or restructured.

(g) In a transaction other than a consumer-goods transaction, a secured party claiming a purchase-money security interest has the burden of establishing the extent to which the security interest is a purchase-money security interest.

(h) The limitation of the rules in subsections (e), (f), and (g) to transactions other than consumer-goods transactions is intended to leave to the court the determination of the proper rules in consumer-goods transactions. The court may not infer from that limitation the nature of the proper rule in consumer-goods transactions and may continue to apply established approaches.

§ 9–104.   Control of Deposit Account.

(a) A secured party has control of a deposit account if:

(1) the secured party is the bank with which the deposit account is maintained;

(2) the debtor, secured party, and bank have agreed in an authenticated record that the bank will comply with instructions originated by the secured party directing disposition of the funds in the deposit account without further consent by the debtor; or

(3) the secured party becomes the bank's customer with respect to the deposit account.

(b) A secured party that has satisfied subsection (a) has control, even if the debtor retains the right to direct the disposition of funds from the deposit account.

§ 9–105.   Control of Electronic Chattel Paper.

A secured party has control of electronic chattel paper if the record or records comprising the chattel paper are created, stored, and assigned in such a manner that:

(1) a single authoritative copy of the record or records exists which is unique, identifiable and, except as otherwise provided in paragraphs (4), (5), and (6), unalterable;

(2) the authoritative copy identifies the secured party as the assignee of the record or records;

(3) the authoritative copy is communicated to and maintained by the secured party or its designated custodian;

(4) copies or revisions that add or change an identified assignee of the authoritative copy can be made only with the participation of the secured party;

(5) each copy of the authoritative copy and any copy of a copy is readily identifiable as a copy that is not the authoritative copy; and

(6) any revision of the authoritative copy is readily identifiable as an authorized or unauthorized revision.

§ 9–106.   Control of Investment Property.

(a) A person has control of a certificated security, uncertificated security, or security entitlement as provided in Section 8–106.

(b) A secured party has control of a commodity contract if:

(1) the secured party is the commodity intermediary with which the commodity contract is carried; or

(2) the commodity customer, secured party, and commodity intermediary have agreed that the commodity intermediary will apply any value distributed on account of the commodity contract as directed by the secured party without further consent by the commodity customer.

(c) A secured party having control of all security entitlements or commodity contracts carried in a securities account or commodity account has control over the securities account or commodity account.

§ 9–107.   Control of Letter-of-Credit Right.

A secured party has control of a letter-of-credit right to the extent of any right to payment or performance by the issuer or any nominated person if the issuer or nominated person has consented to an assignment of proceeds of the letter of credit under Section 5–114(c) or otherwise applicable law or practice.

§ 9–108.   Sufficiency of Description.

(a) Except as otherwise provided in subsections (c), (d), and (e), a description of personal or real property is sufficient, whether or not it is specific, if it reasonably identifies what is described.

(b) Except as otherwise provided in subsection (d), a description of collateral reasonably identifies the collateral if it identifies the collateral by:

(1) specific listing;

(2) category;

(3) except as otherwise provided in subsection (e), a type of collateral defined in [the Uniform Commercial Code];

(4) quantity;

(5) computational or allocational formula or procedure; or

(6) except as otherwise provided in subsection (c), any other method, if the identity of the collateral is objectively determinable.

(c) A description of collateral as "all the debtor's assets" or "all the debtor's personal property" or using words of similar import does not reasonably identify the collateral.

(d) Except as otherwise provided in subsection (e), a description of a security entitlement, securities account, or commodity account is sufficient if it describes:

(1) the collateral by those terms or as investment property; or

(2) the underlying financial asset or commodity contract.

(e) A description only by type of collateral defined in [the Uniform Commercial Code] is an insufficient description of:

    (1) a commercial tort claim; or

    (2) in a consumer transaction, consumer goods, a security entitlement, a securities account, or a commodity account.

[Subpart 2. Applicability of Article]

§ 9–109.   Scope.

(a) Except as otherwise provided in subsections (c) and (d), this article applies to:

    (1) a transaction, regardless of its form, that creates a security interest in personal property or fixtures by contract;

    (2) an agricultural lien;

    (3) a sale of accounts, chattel paper, payment intangibles, or promissory notes;

    (4) a consignment;

    (5) a security interest arising under Section 2–401, 2–505, 2–711(3), or 2A–508(5), as provided in Section 9–110; and

    (6) a security interest arising under Section 4–210 or 5–118.

(b) The application of this article to a security interest in a secured obligation is not affected by the fact that the obligation is itself secured by a transaction or interest to which this article does not apply.

(c) This article does not apply to the extent that:

    (1) a statute, regulation, or treaty of the United States preempts this article;

    (2) another statute of this State expressly governs the creation, perfection, priority, or enforcement of a security interest created by this State or a governmental unit of this State;

    (3) a statute of another State, a foreign country, or a governmental unit of another State or a foreign country, other than a statute generally applicable to security interests, expressly governs creation, perfection, priority, or enforcement of a security interest created by the State, country, or governmental unit; or

    (4) the rights of a transferee beneficiary or nominated person under a letter of credit are independent and superior under Section 5–114.

(d) This article does not apply to:

    (1) a landlord's lien, other than an agricultural lien;

    (2) a lien, other than an agricultural lien, given by statute or other rule of law for services or materials, but Section 9–333 applies with respect to priority of the lien;

    (3) an assignment of a claim for wages, salary, or other compensation of an employee;

    (4) a sale of accounts, chattel paper, payment intangibles, or promissory notes as part of a sale of the business out of which they arose;

    (5) an assignment of accounts, chattel paper, payment intangibles, or promissory notes which is for the purpose of collection only;

    (6) an assignment of a right to payment under a contract to an assignee that is also obligated to perform under the contract;

    (7) an assignment of a single account, payment intangible, or promissory note to an assignee in full or partial satisfaction of a preexisting indebtedness;

    (8) a transfer of an interest in or an assignment of a claim under a policy of insurance, other than an assignment by or to a health-care provider of a health-care-insurance receivable and any subsequent assignment of the right to payment, but Sections 9–315 and 9–322 apply with respect to proceeds and priorities in proceeds;

    (9) an assignment of a right represented by a judgment, other than a judgment taken on a right to payment that was collateral;

    (10) a right of recoupment or set-off, but:

        (A) Section 9–340 applies with respect to the effectiveness of rights of recoupment or set-off against deposit accounts; and

        (B) Section 9–404 applies with respect to defenses or claims of an account debtor;

    (11) the creation or transfer of an interest in or lien on real property, including a lease or rents thereunder, except to the extent that provision is made for:

        (A) liens on real property in Sections 9–203 and 9–308;

        (B) fixtures in Section 9–334;

        (C) fixture filings in Sections 9–501, 9–502, 9–512, 9–516, and 9–519; and

        (D) security agreements covering personal and real property in Section 9–604;

    (12) an assignment of a claim arising in tort, other than a commercial tort claim, but Sections 9–315 and 9–322 apply with respect to proceeds and priorities in proceeds; or

    (13) an assignment of a deposit account in a consumer transaction, but Sections 9–315 and 9–322 apply with respect to proceeds and priorities in proceeds.

§ 9–110.   Security Interests Arising under Article 2 or 2A.

A security interest arising under Section 2–401, 2–505, 2–711(3), or 2A–508(5) is subject to this article. However, until the debtor obtains possession of the goods:

    (1) the security interest is enforceable, even if Section 9–203(b)(3) has not been satisfied;

    (2) filing is not required to perfect the security interest;

    (3) the rights of the secured party after default by the debtor are governed by Article 2 or 2A; and

    (4) the security interest has priority over a conflicting security interest created by the debtor.

Part 2   Effectiveness of Security Agreement; Attachment of Security Interest; Rights of Parties to Security Agreement

[Subpart 1. Effectiveness and Attachment]

§ 9–201.   General Effectiveness of Security Agreement.

(a) Except as otherwise provided in [the Uniform Commercial Code], a security agreement is effective according to its terms between the parties, against purchasers of the collateral, and against creditors.

(b) A transaction subject to this article is subject to any applicable rule of law which establishes a different rule for consumers and [insert reference to (i) any other statute or regulation that regulates the rates, charges, agreements, and practices for loans, credit sales, or other extensions of credit and (ii) any consumer-protection statute or regulation].

(c) In case of conflict between this article and a rule of law, statute, or regulation described in subsection (b), the rule of law, statute, or regulation controls. Failure to comply with a statute or regulation described in subsection (b) has only the effect the statute or regulation specifies.

(d) This article does not:

(1) validate any rate, charge, agreement, or practice that violates a rule of law, statute, or regulation described in subsection (b); or

(2) extend the application of the rule of law, statute, or regulation to a transaction not otherwise subject to it.

§ 9–202.   Title to Collateral Immaterial.

Except as otherwise provided with respect to consignments or sales of accounts, chattel paper, payment intangibles, or promissory notes, the provisions of this article with regard to rights and obligations apply whether title to collateral is in the secured party or the debtor.

§ 9–203.   Attachment and Enforceability of Security Interest; Proceeds; Supporting Obligations; Formal Requisites.

(a) A security interest attaches to collateral when it becomes enforceable against the debtor with respect to the collateral, unless an agreement expressly postpones the time of attachment.

(b) Except as otherwise provided in subsections (c) through (i), a security interest is enforceable against the debtor and third parties with respect to the collateral only if:

(1) value has been given;

(2) the debtor has rights in the collateral or the power to transfer rights in the collateral to a secured party; and

(3) one of the following conditions is met:

(A) the debtor has authenticated a security agreement that provides a description of the collateral and, if the security interest covers timber to be cut, a description of the land concerned;

(B) the collateral is not a certificated security and is in the possession of the secured party under Section 9–313 pursuant to the debtor's security agreement;

(C) the collateral is a certificated security in registered form and the security certificate has been delivered to the secured party under Section 8–301 pursuant to the debtor's security agreement; or

(D) the collateral is deposit accounts, electronic chattel paper, investment property, or letter-of-credit rights, and the secured party has control under Section 9–104, 9–105, 9–106, or 9–107 pursuant to the debtor's security agreement.

(c) Subsection (b) is subject to Section 4–210 on the security interest of a collecting bank, Section 5–118 on the security interest of a letter-of-credit issuer or nominated person, Section 9–110 on a security interest arising under Article 2 or 2A, and Section 9–206 on security interests in investment property.

(d) A person becomes bound as debtor by a security agreement entered into by another person if, by operation of law other than this article or by contract:

(1) the security agreement becomes effective to create a security interest in the person's property; or

(2) the person becomes generally obligated for the obligations of the other person, including the obligation secured under the security agreement, and acquires or succeeds to all or substantially all of the assets of the other person.

(e) If a new debtor becomes bound as debtor by a security agreement entered into by another person:

(1) the agreement satisfies subsection (b)(3) with respect to existing or after-acquired property of the new debtor to the extent the property is described in the agreement; and

(2) another agreement is not necessary to make a security interest in the property enforceable.

(f) The attachment of a security interest in collateral gives the secured party the rights to proceeds provided by Section 9–315 and is also attachment of a security interest in a supporting obligation for the collateral.

(g) The attachment of a security interest in a right to payment or performance secured by a security interest or other lien on personal or real property is also attachment of a security interest in the security interest, mortgage, or other lien.

(h) The attachment of a security interest in a securities account is also attachment of a security interest in the security entitlements carried in the securities account.

(i) The attachment of a security interest in a commodity account is also attachment of a security interest in the commodity contracts carried in the commodity account.

§ 9–204.   After-Acquired Property; Future Advances.

(a) Except as otherwise provided in subsection (b), a security agreement may create or provide for a security interest in after-acquired collateral.

(b) A security interest does not attach under a term constituting an after-acquired property clause to:

(1) consumer goods, other than an accession when given as additional security, unless the debtor acquires rights in them within 10 days after the secured party gives value; or

(2) a commercial tort claim.

(c) A security agreement may provide that collateral secures, or that accounts, chattel paper, payment intangibles, or promissory notes are sold in connection with, future advances or other value, whether or not the advances or value are given pursuant to commitment.

§ 9-205.   Use or Disposition of Collateral Permissible.

(a) A security interest is not invalid or fraudulent against creditors solely because:

(1) the debtor has the right or ability to:

(A) use, commingle, or dispose of all or part of the collateral, including returned or repossessed goods;

(B) collect, compromise, enforce, or otherwise deal with collateral;

(C) accept the return of collateral or make repossessions; or

(D) use, commingle, or dispose of proceeds; or

(2) the secured party fails to require the debtor to account for proceeds or replace collateral.

(b) This section does not relax the requirements of possession if attachment, perfection, or enforcement of a security interest depends upon possession of the collateral by the secured party.

§ 9-206.   Security Interest Arising in Purchase or Delivery of Financial Asset.

(a) A security interest in favor of a securities intermediary attaches to a person's security entitlement if:

(1) the person buys a financial asset through the securities intermediary in a transaction in which the person is obligated to pay the purchase price to the securities intermediary at the time of the purchase; and

(2) the securities intermediary credits the financial asset to the buyer's securities account before the buyer pays the securities intermediary.

(b) The security interest described in subsection (a) secures the person's obligation to pay for the financial asset.

(c) A security interest in favor of a person that delivers a certificated security or other financial asset represented by a writing attaches to the security or other financial asset if:

(1) the security or other financial asset:

(A) in the ordinary course of business is transferred by delivery with any necessary indorsement or assignment; and

(B) is delivered under an agreement between persons in the business of dealing with such securities or financial assets; and

(2) the agreement calls for delivery against payment.

(d) The security interest described in subsection (c) secures the obligation to make payment for the delivery.

[Subpart 2. Rights and Duties]

§ 9-207.   Rights and Duties of Secured Party Having Possession or Control of Collateral.

(a) Except as otherwise provided in subsection (d), a secured party shall use reasonable care in the custody and preservation of collateral in the secured party's possession. In the case of chattel paper or an instrument, reasonable care includes taking necessary steps to preserve rights against prior parties unless otherwise agreed.

(b) Except as otherwise provided in subsection (d), if a secured party has possession of collateral:

(1) reasonable expenses, including the cost of insurance and payment of taxes or other charges, incurred in the custody, preservation, use, or operation of the collateral are chargeable to the debtor and are secured by the collateral;

(2) the risk of accidental loss or damage is on the debtor to the extent of a deficiency in any effective insurance coverage;

(3) the secured party shall keep the collateral identifiable, but fungible collateral may be commingled; and

(4) the secured party may use or operate the collateral:

(A) for the purpose of preserving the collateral or its value;

(B) as permitted by an order of a court having competent jurisdiction; or

(C) except in the case of consumer goods, in the manner and to the extent agreed by the debtor.

(c) Except as otherwise provided in subsection (d), a secured party having possession of collateral or control of collateral under Section 9-104, 9-105, 9-106, or 9-107:

(1) may hold as additional security any proceeds, except money or funds, received from the collateral;

(2) shall apply money or funds received from the collateral to reduce the secured obligation, unless remitted to the debtor; and

(3) may create a security interest in the collateral.

(d) If the secured party is a buyer of accounts, chattel paper, payment intangibles, or promissory notes or a consignor:

(1) subsection (a) does not apply unless the secured party is entitled under an agreement:

(A) to charge back uncollected collateral; or

(B) otherwise to full or limited recourse against the debtor or a secondary obligor based on the nonpayment or other default of an account debtor or other obligor on the collateral; and

(2) subsections (b) and (c) do not apply.

§ 9-208.   Additional Duties of Secured Party Having Control of Collateral.

(a) This section applies to cases in which there is no outstanding secured obligation and the secured party is not committed to make advances, incur obligations, or otherwise give value.

(b) Within 10 days after receiving an authenticated demand by the debtor:

(1) a secured party having control of a deposit account under Section 9-104(a)(2) shall send to the bank with which the deposit account is maintained an authenticated statement that releases the bank from any further obligation to comply with instructions originated by the secured party;

(2) a secured party having control of a deposit account under Section 9-104(a)(3) shall:

(A) pay the debtor the balance on deposit in the deposit account; or

(B) transfer the balance on deposit into a deposit account in the debtor's name;

(3) a secured party, other than a buyer, having control of electronic chattel paper under Section 9–105 shall:

(A) communicate the authoritative copy of the electronic chattel paper to the debtor or its designated custodian;

(B) if the debtor designates a custodian that is the designated custodian with which the authoritative copy of the electronic chattel paper is maintained for the secured party, communicate to the custodian an authenticated record releasing the designated custodian from any further obligation to comply with instructions originated by the secured party and instructing the custodian to comply with instructions originated by the debtor; and

(C) take appropriate action to enable the debtor or its designated custodian to make copies of or revisions to the authoritative copy which add or change an identified assignee of the authoritative copy without the consent of the secured party;

(4) a secured party having control of investment property under Section 8–106(d)(2) or 9–106(b) shall send to the securities intermediary or commodity intermediary with which the security entitlement or commodity contract is maintained an authenticated record that releases the securities intermediary or commodity intermediary from any further obligation to comply with entitlement orders or directions originated by the secured party; and

(5) a secured party having control of a letter-of-credit right under Section 9–107 shall send to each person having an unfulfilled obligation to pay or deliver proceeds of the letter of credit to the secured party an authenticated release from any further obligation to pay or deliver proceeds of the letter of credit to the secured party.

§ 9–209. Duties of Secured Party If Account Debtor Has Been Notified of Assignment.

(a) Except as otherwise provided in subsection (c), this section applies if:

(1) there is no outstanding secured obligation; and

(2) the secured party is not committed to make advances, incur obligations, or otherwise give value.

(b) Within 10 days after receiving an authenticated demand by the debtor, a secured party shall send to an account debtor that has received notification of an assignment to the secured party as assignee under Section 9–406(a) an authenticated record that releases the account debtor from any further obligation to the secured party.

(c) This section does not apply to an assignment constituting the sale of an account, chattel paper, or payment intangible.

§ 9–210. Request for Accounting; Request Regarding List of Collateral or Statement of Account.

(a) In this section:

(1) "Request" means a record of a type described in paragraph (2), (3), or (4).

(2) "Request for an accounting" means a record authenticated by a debtor requesting that the recipient provide an accounting of the unpaid obligations secured by collateral and reasonably identifying the transaction or relationship that is the subject of the request.

(3) "Request regarding a list of collateral" means a record authenticated by a debtor requesting that the recipient approve or correct a list of what the debtor believes to be the collateral securing an obligation and reasonably identifying the transaction or relationship that is the subject of the request.

(4) "Request regarding a statement of account" means a record authenticated by a debtor requesting that the recipient approve or correct a statement indicating what the debtor believes to be the aggregate amount of unpaid obligations secured by collateral as of a specified date and reasonably identifying the transaction or relationship that is the subject of the request.

(b) Subject to subsections (c), (d), (e), and (f), a secured party, other than a buyer of accounts, chattel paper, payment intangibles, or promissory notes or a consignor, shall comply with a request within 14 days after receipt:

(1) in the case of a request for an accounting, by authenticating and sending to the debtor an accounting; and

(2) in the case of a request regarding a list of collateral or a request regarding a statement of account, by authenticating and sending to the debtor an approval or correction.

(c) A secured party that claims a security interest in all of a particular type of collateral owned by the debtor may comply with a request regarding a list of collateral by sending to the debtor an authenticated record including a statement to that effect within 14 days after receipt.

(d) A person that receives a request regarding a list of collateral, claims no interest in the collateral when it receives the request, and claimed an interest in the collateral at an earlier time shall comply with the request within 14 days after receipt by sending to the debtor an authenticated record:

(1) disclaiming any interest in the collateral; and

(2) if known to the recipient, providing the name and mailing address of any assignee of or successor to the recipient's interest in the collateral.

(e) A person that receives a request for an accounting or a request regarding a statement of account, claims no interest in the obligations when it receives the request, and claimed an interest in the obligations at an earlier time shall comply with the request within 14 days after receipt by sending to the debtor an authenticated record:

(1) disclaiming any interest in the obligations; and

(2) if known to the recipient, providing the name and mailing address of any assignee of or successor to the recipient's interest in the obligations.

(f) A debtor is entitled without charge to one response to a request under this section during any six-month period. The secured party may require payment of a charge not exceeding $25 for each additional response.

As amended in 1999.

Part 3   Perfection and Priority

[Subpart 1. Law Governing Perfection and Priority]

§ 9–301.   Law Governing Perfection and Priority of Security Interests.

Except as otherwise provided in Sections 9–303 through 9–306, the following rules determine the law governing perfection, the effect of perfection or nonperfection, and the priority of a security interest in collateral:

(1) Except as otherwise provided in this section, while a debtor is located in a jurisdiction, the local law of that jurisdiction governs perfection, the effect of perfection or nonperfection, and the priority of a security interest in collateral.

(2) While collateral is located in a jurisdiction, the local law of that jurisdiction governs perfection, the effect of perfection or nonperfection, and the priority of a possessory security interest in that collateral.

(3) Except as otherwise provided in paragraph (4), while negotiable documents, goods, instruments, money, or tangible chattel paper is located in a jurisdiction, the local law of that jurisdiction governs:

(A) perfection of a security interest in the goods by filing a fixture filing;

(B) perfection of a security interest in timber to be cut; and

(C) the effect of perfection or nonperfection and the priority of a nonpossessory security interest in the collateral.

(4) The local law of the jurisdiction in which the wellhead or minehead is located governs perfection, the effect of perfection or nonperfection, and the priority of a security interest in as-extracted collateral.

§ 9–302.   Law Governing Perfection and Priority of Agricultural Liens.

While farm products are located in a jurisdiction, the local law of that jurisdiction governs perfection, the effect of perfection or nonperfection, and the priority of an agricultural lien on the farm products.

§ 9–303.   Law Governing Perfection and Priority of Security Interests in Goods Covered by a Certificate of Title.

(a) This section applies to goods covered by a certificate of title, even if there is no other relationship between the jurisdiction under whose certificate of title the goods are covered and the goods or the debtor.

(b) Goods become covered by a certificate of title when a valid application for the certificate of title and the applicable fee are delivered to the appropriate authority. Goods cease to be covered by a certificate of title at the earlier of the time the certificate of title ceases to be effective under the law of the issuing jurisdiction or the time the goods become covered subsequently by a certificate of title issued by another jurisdiction.

(c) The local law of the jurisdiction under whose certificate of title the goods are covered governs perfection, the effect of perfection or nonperfection, and the priority of a security interest in goods covered by a certificate of title from the time the goods become covered by the certificate of title until the goods cease to be covered by the certificate of title.

§ 9–304.   Law Governing Perfection and Priority of Security Interests in Deposit Accounts.

(a) The local law of a bank's jurisdiction governs perfection, the effect of perfection or nonperfection, and the priority of a security interest in a deposit account maintained with that bank.

(b) The following rules determine a bank's jurisdiction for purposes of this part:

(1) If an agreement between the bank and the debtor governing the deposit account expressly provides that a particular jurisdiction is the bank's jurisdiction for purposes of this part, this article, or [the Uniform Commercial Code], that jurisdiction is the bank's jurisdiction.

(2) If paragraph (1) does not apply and an agreement between the bank and its customer governing the deposit account expressly provides that the agreement is governed by the law of a particular jurisdiction, that jurisdiction is the bank's jurisdiction.

(3) If neither paragraph (1) nor paragraph (2) applies and an agreement between the bank and its customer governing the deposit account expressly provides that the deposit account is maintained at an office in a particular jurisdiction, that jurisdiction is the bank's jurisdiction.

(4) If none of the preceding paragraphs applies, the bank's jurisdiction is the jurisdiction in which the office identified in an account statement as the office serving the customer's account is located.

(5) If none of the preceding paragraphs applies, the bank's jurisdiction is the jurisdiction in which the chief executive office of the bank is located.

§ 9–305.   Law Governing Perfection and Priority of Security Interests in Investment Property.

(a) Except as otherwise provided in subsection (c), the following rules apply:

(1) While a security certificate is located in a jurisdiction, the local law of that jurisdiction governs perfection, the effect of perfection or nonperfection, and the priority of a security interest in the certificated security represented thereby.

(2) The local law of the issuer's jurisdiction as specified in Section 8–110(d) governs perfection, the effect of perfection or nonperfection, and the priority of a security interest in an uncertificated security.

(3) The local law of the securities intermediary's jurisdiction as specified in Section 8–110(e) governs perfection, the effect of perfection or nonperfection, and the priority of a security interest in a security entitlement or securities account.

(4) The local law of the commodity intermediary's jurisdiction governs perfection, the effect of perfection or nonperfection, and the priority of a security interest in a commodity contract or commodity account.

(b) The following rules determine a commodity intermediary's jurisdiction for purposes of this part:

(1) If an agreement between the commodity intermediary and commodity customer governing the commodity account expressly provides that a particular jurisdiction is the commodity intermediary's jurisdiction for purposes of this part, this article, or [the Uniform Commercial Code], that jurisdiction is the commodity intermediary's jurisdiction.

(2) If paragraph (1) does not apply and an agreement between the commodity intermediary and commodity customer governing the commodity account expressly provides that the agreement is governed by the law of a particular jurisdiction, that jurisdiction is the commodity intermediary's jurisdiction.

(3) If neither paragraph (1) nor paragraph (2) applies and an agreement between the commodity intermediary and commodity customer governing the commodity account expressly provides that the commodity account is maintained at an office in a particular jurisdiction, that jurisdiction is the commodity intermediary's jurisdiction.

(4) If none of the preceding paragraphs applies, the commodity intermediary's jurisdiction is the jurisdiction in which the office identified in an account statement as the office serving the commodity customer's account is located.

(5) If none of the preceding paragraphs applies, the commodity intermediary's jurisdiction is the jurisdiction in which the chief executive office of the commodity intermediary is located.

(c) The local law of the jurisdiction in which the debtor is located governs:

(1) perfection of a security interest in investment property by filing;

(2) automatic perfection of a security interest in investment property created by a broker or securities intermediary; and

(3) automatic perfection of a security interest in a commodity contract or commodity account created by a commodity intermediary.

§ 9–306.   Law Governing Perfection and Priority of Security Interests in Letter-of-Credit Rights.

(a) Subject to subsection (c), the local law of the issuer's jurisdiction or a nominated person's jurisdiction governs perfection, the effect of perfection or nonperfection, and the priority of a security interest in a letter-of-credit right if the issuer's jurisdiction or nominated person's jurisdiction is a State.

(b) For purposes of this part, an issuer's jurisdiction or nominated person's jurisdiction is the jurisdiction whose law governs the liability of the issuer or nominated person with respect to the letter-of-credit right as provided in Section 5–116.

(c) This section does not apply to a security interest that is perfected only under Section 9–308(d).

§ 9–307.   Location of Debtor.

(a) In this section, "place of business" means a place where a debtor conducts its affairs.

(b) Except as otherwise provided in this section, the following rules determine a debtor's location:

(1) A debtor who is an individual is located at the individual's principal residence.

(2) A debtor that is an organization and has only one place of business is located at its place of business.

(3) A debtor that is an organization and has more than one place of business is located at its chief executive office.

(c) Subsection (b) applies only if a debtor's residence, place of business, or chief executive office, as applicable, is located in a jurisdiction whose law generally requires information concerning the existence of a nonpossessory security interest to be made generally available in a filing, recording, or registration system as a condition or result of the security interest's obtaining priority over the rights of a lien creditor with respect to the collateral. If subsection (b) does not apply, the debtor is located in the District of Columbia.

(d) A person that ceases to exist, have a residence, or have a place of business continues to be located in the jurisdiction specified by subsections (b) and (c).

(e) A registered organization that is organized under the law of a State is located in that State.

(f) Except as otherwise provided in subsection (i), a registered organization that is organized under the law of the United States and a branch or agency of a bank that is not organized under the law of the United States or a State are located:

(1) in the State that the law of the United States designates, if the law designates a State of location;

(2) in the State that the registered organization, branch, or agency designates, if the law of the United States authorizes the registered organization, branch, or agency to designate its State of location; or

(3) in the District of Columbia, if neither paragraph (1) nor paragraph (2) applies.

(g) A registered organization continues to be located in the jurisdiction specified by subsection (e) or (f) notwithstanding:

(1) the suspension, revocation, forfeiture, or lapse of the registered organization's status as such in its jurisdiction of organization; or

(2) the dissolution, winding up, or cancellation of the existence of the registered organization.

(h) The United States is located in the District of Columbia.

(i) A branch or agency of a bank that is not organized under the law of the United States or a State is located in the State in which the branch or agency is licensed, if all branches and agencies of the bank are licensed in only one State.

(j) A foreign air carrier under the Federal Aviation Act of 1958, as amended, is located at the designated office of the agent upon which service of process may be made on behalf of the carrier.

(k) This section applies only for purposes of this part.

[Subpart 2. Perfection]

§ 9–308.   When Security Interest or Agricultural Lien Is Perfected; Continuity of Perfection.

(a) Except as otherwise provided in this section and Section 9–309, a security interest is perfected if it has attached and all of the applicable requirements for perfection in Sections 9–310 through 9–316 have been satisfied. A security interest is perfected when it attaches if the applicable requirements are satisfied before the security interest attaches.

(b) An agricultural lien is perfected if it has become effective and all of the applicable requirements for perfection in Section 9–310 have been satisfied. An agricultural lien is perfected when it becomes effective if the applicable requirements are satisfied before the agricultural lien becomes effective.

(c) A security interest or agricultural lien is perfected continuously if it is originally perfected by one method under this article and is later perfected by another method under this article, without an intermediate period when it was unperfected.

(d) Perfection of a security interest in collateral also perfects a security interest in a supporting obligation for the collateral.

(e) Perfection of a security interest in a right to payment or performance also perfects a security interest in a security interest, mortgage, or other lien on personal or real property securing the right.

(f) Perfection of a security interest in a securities account also perfects a security interest in the security entitlements carried in the securities account.

(g) Perfection of a security interest in a commodity account also perfects a security interest in the commodity contracts carried in the commodity account.

Legislative Note: Any statute conflicting with subsection (e) must be made expressly subject to that subsection.

§ 9–309.   Security Interest Perfected upon Attachment.

The following security interests are perfected when they attach:

(1) a purchase-money security interest in consumer goods, except as otherwise provided in Section 9–311(b) with respect to consumer goods that are subject to a statute or treaty described in Section 9–311(a);

(2) an assignment of accounts or payment intangibles which does not by itself or in conjunction with other assignments to the same assignee transfer a significant part of the assignor's outstanding accounts or payment intangibles;

(3) a sale of a payment intangible;

(4) a sale of a promissory note;

(5) a security interest created by the assignment of a health-care-insurance receivable to the provider of the health-care goods or services;

(6) a security interest arising under Section 2–401, 2–505, 2–711(3), or 2A–508(5), until the debtor obtains possession of the collateral;

(7) a security interest of a collecting bank arising under Section 4–210;

(8) a security interest of an issuer or nominated person arising under Section 5–118;

(9) a security interest arising in the delivery of a financial asset under Section 9–206(c);

(10) a security interest in investment property created by a broker or securities intermediary;

(11) a security interest in a commodity contract or a commodity account created by a commodity intermediary;

(12) an assignment for the benefit of all creditors of the transferor and subsequent transfers by the assignee thereunder; and

(13) a security interest created by an assignment of a beneficial interest in a decedent's estate; and

(14) a sale by an individual of an account that is a right to payment of winnings in a lottery or other game of chance.

§ 9–310.   When Filing Required to Perfect Security Interest or Agricultural Lien; Security Interests and Agricultural Liens to Which Filing Provisions Do Not Apply.

(a) Except as otherwise provided in subsection (b) and Section 9–312(b), a financing statement must be filed to perfect all security interests and agricultural liens.

(b) The filing of a financing statement is not necessary to perfect a security interest:

(1) that is perfected under Section 9–308(d), (e), (f), or (g);

(2) that is perfected under Section 9–309 when it attaches;

(3) in property subject to a statute, regulation, or treaty described in Section 9–311(a);

(4) in goods in possession of a bailee which is perfected under Section 9–312(d)(1) or (2);

(5) in certificated securities, documents, goods, or instruments which is perfected without filing or possession under Section 9–312(e), (f), or (g);

(6) in collateral in the secured party's possession under Section 9–313;

(7) in a certificated security which is perfected by delivery of the security certificate to the secured party under Section 9–313;

(8) in deposit accounts, electronic chattel paper, investment property, or letter-of-credit rights which is perfected by control under Section 9–314;

(9) in proceeds which is perfected under Section 9–315; or

(10) that is perfected under Section 9–316.

(c) If a secured party assigns a perfected security interest or agricultural lien, a filing under this article is not required to continue the perfected status of the security interest against creditors of and transferees from the original debtor.

§ 9–311.   Perfection of Security Interests in Property Subject to Certain Statutes, Regulations, and Treaties.

(a) Except as otherwise provided in subsection (d), the filing of a financing statement is not necessary or effective to perfect a security interest in property subject to:

(1) a statute, regulation, or treaty of the United States whose requirements for a security interest's obtaining priority over the rights of a lien creditor with respect to the property pre-empt Section 9–310(a);

(2) [list any certificate-of-title statute covering automobiles, trailers, mobile homes, boats, farm tractors, or the like, which provides for a security interest to be indicated on the certificate as a condition or result of perfection, and any non-Uniform Commercial Code central filing statute]; or

(3) a certificate-of-title statute of another jurisdiction which provides for a security interest to be indicated on the certificate as a condition or result of the security interest's obtaining priority over the rights of a lien creditor with respect to the property.

(b) Compliance with the requirements of a statute, regulation, or treaty described in subsection (a) for obtaining priority over the rights of a lien creditor is equivalent to the filing of a financing statement under this article. Except as otherwise provided in subsection (d) and Sections 9–313 and 9–316(d) and (e) for goods covered by a certificate of title, a security interest in property subject to a statute, regulation, or treaty described in subsection (a) may be perfected only by compliance with those requirements, and a security interest so perfected remains perfected notwithstanding a change in the use or transfer of possession of the collateral.

(c) Except as otherwise provided in subsection (d) and Section 9–316(d) and (e), duration and renewal of perfection of a security interest perfected by compliance with the requirements prescribed by a statute, regulation, or treaty described in subsection (a) are governed by the statute, regulation, or treaty. In other respects, the security interest is subject to this article.

(d) During any period in which collateral subject to a statute specified in subsection (a)(2) is inventory held for sale or lease by a person or leased by that person as lessor and that person is in the business of selling goods of that kind, this section does not apply to a security interest in that collateral created by that person.

Legislative Note: This Article contemplates that perfection of a security interest in goods covered by a certificate of title occurs upon receipt by appropriate State officials of a properly tendered application for a certificate of title on which the security interest is to be indicated, without a relation back to an earlier time. States whose certificate-of-title statutes provide for perfection at a different time or contain a relation-back provision should amend the statutes accordingly.

§ 9–312.   Perfection of Security Interests in Chattel Paper, Deposit Accounts, Documents, Goods Covered by Documents, Instruments, Investment Property, Letter-of-Credit Rights, and Money; Perfection by Permissive Filing; Temporary Perfection without Filing or Transfer of Possession.

(a) A security interest in chattel paper, negotiable documents, instruments, or investment property may be perfected by filing.

(b) Except as otherwise provided in Section 9–315(c) and (d) for proceeds:

(1) a security interest in a deposit account may be perfected only by control under Section 9–314;

(2) and except as otherwise provided in Section 9–308(d), a security interest in a letter-of-credit right may be perfected only by control under Section 9–314; and

(3) a security interest in money may be perfected only by the secured party's taking possession under Section 9–313.

(c) While goods are in the possession of a bailee that has issued a negotiable document covering the goods:

(1) a security interest in the goods may be perfected by perfecting a security interest in the document; and

(2) a security interest perfected in the document has priority over any security interest that becomes perfected in the goods by another method during that time.

(d) While goods are in the possession of a bailee that has issued a nonnegotiable document covering the goods, a security interest in the goods may be perfected by:

(1) issuance of a document in the name of the secured party;

(2) the bailee's receipt of notification of the secured party's interest; or

(3) filing as to the goods.

(e) A security interest in certificated securities, negotiable documents, or instruments is perfected without filing or the taking of possession for a period of 20 days from the time it attaches to the extent that it arises for new value given under an authenticated security agreement.

(f) A perfected security interest in a negotiable document or goods in possession of a bailee, other than one that has issued a negotiable document for the goods, remains perfected for 20 days without filing if the secured party makes available to the debtor the goods or documents representing the goods for the purpose of:

(1) ultimate sale or exchange; or

(2) loading, unloading, storing, shipping, transshipping, manufacturing, processing, or otherwise dealing with them in a manner preliminary to their sale or exchange.

(g) A perfected security interest in a certificated security or instrument remains perfected for 20 days without filing if the secured party delivers the security certificate or instrument to the debtor for the purpose of:

(1) ultimate sale or exchange; or

(2) presentation, collection, enforcement, renewal, or registration of transfer.

(h) After the 20-day period specified in subsection (e), (f), or (g) expires, perfection depends upon compliance with this article.

§ 9–313.   When Possession by or Delivery to Secured Party Perfects Security Interest without Filing.

(a) Except as otherwise provided in subsection (b), a secured party may perfect a security interest in negotiable documents, goods, instruments, money, or tangible chattel paper by taking possession of the collateral. A secured party may perfect a security interest in certificated securities by taking delivery of the certificated securities under Section 8–301.

(b) With respect to goods covered by a certificate of title issued by this State, a secured party may perfect a security interest in the goods by taking possession of the goods only in the circumstances described in Section 9–316(d).

(c) With respect to collateral other than certificated securities and goods covered by a document, a secured party takes possession of collateral in the possession of a person other than the debtor, the secured party, or a lessee of the collateral from the debtor in the ordinary course of the debtor's business, when:

(1) the person in possession authenticates a record acknowledging that it holds possession of the collateral for the secured party's benefit; or

(2) the person takes possession of the collateral after having authenticated a record acknowledging that it will hold possession of collateral for the secured party's benefit.

(d) If perfection of a security interest depends upon possession of the collateral by a secured party, perfection occurs no earlier than the time the secured party takes possession and continues only while the secured party retains possession.

(e) A security interest in a certificated security in registered form is perfected by delivery when delivery of the certificated security occurs under Section 8–301 and remains perfected by delivery until the debtor obtains possession of the security certificate.

(f) A person in possession of collateral is not required to acknowledge that it holds possession for a secured party's benefit.

(g) If a person acknowledges that it holds possession for the secured party's benefit:

(1) the acknowledgment is effective under subsection (c) or Section 8–301(a), even if the acknowledgment violates the rights of a debtor; and

(2) unless the person otherwise agrees or law other than this article otherwise provides, the person does not owe any duty to the secured party and is not required to confirm the acknowledgment to another person.

(h) A secured party having possession of collateral does not relinquish possession by delivering the collateral to a person other than the debtor or a lessee of the collateral from the debtor in the ordinary course of the debtor's business if the person was instructed before the delivery or is instructed contemporaneously with the delivery:

(1) to hold possession of the collateral for the secured party's benefit; or

(2) to redeliver the collateral to the secured party.

(i) A secured party does not relinquish possession, even if a delivery under subsection (h) violates the rights of a debtor. A person to which collateral is delivered under subsection (h) does not owe any duty to the secured party and is not required to confirm the delivery to another person unless the person otherwise agrees or law other than this article otherwise provides.

§ 9–314. Perfection by Control.

(a) A security interest in investment property, deposit accounts, letter-of-credit rights, or electronic chattel paper may be perfected by control of the collateral under Section 9–104, 9–105, 9–106, or 9–107.

(b) A security interest in deposit accounts, electronic chattel paper, or letter-of-credit rights is perfected by control under Section 9–104, 9–105, or 9–107 when the secured party obtains control and remains perfected by control only while the secured party retains control.

(c) A security interest in investment property is perfected by control under Section 9–106 from the time the secured party obtains control and remains perfected by control until:

(1) the secured party does not have control; and

(2) one of the following occurs:

(A) if the collateral is a certificated security, the debtor has or acquires possession of the security certificate;

(B) if the collateral is an uncertificated security, the issuer has registered or registers the debtor as the registered owner; or

(C) if the collateral is a security entitlement, the debtor is or becomes the entitlement holder.

§ 9–315. Secured Party's Rights on Disposition of Collateral and in Proceeds.

(a) Except as otherwise provided in this article and in Section 2–403(2):

(1) a security interest or agricultural lien continues in collateral notwithstanding sale, lease, license, exchange, or other disposition thereof unless the secured party authorized the disposition free of the security interest or agricultural lien; and

(2) a security interest attaches to any identifiable proceeds of collateral.

(b) Proceeds that are commingled with other property are identifiable proceeds:

(1) if the proceeds are goods, to the extent provided by Section 9–336; and

(2) if the proceeds are not goods, to the extent that the secured party identifies the proceeds by a method of tracing, including application of equitable principles, that is permitted under law other than this article with respect to commingled property of the type involved.

(c) A security interest in proceeds is a perfected security interest if the security interest in the original collateral was perfected.

(d) A perfected security interest in proceeds becomes unperfected on the 21st day after the security interest attaches to the proceeds unless:

(1) the following conditions are satisfied:

(A) a filed financing statement covers the original collateral;

(B) the proceeds are collateral in which a security interest may be perfected by filing in the office in which the financing statement has been filed; and

(C) the proceeds are not acquired with cash proceeds;

(2) the proceeds are identifiable cash proceeds; or

(3) the security interest in the proceeds is perfected other than under subsection (c) when the security interest attaches to the proceeds or within 20 days thereafter.

(e) If a filed financing statement covers the original collateral, a security interest in proceeds which remains perfected under subsection (d)(1) becomes unperfected at the later of:

(1) when the effectiveness of the filed financing statement lapses under Section 9–515 or is terminated under Section 9–513; or

(2) the 21st day after the security interest attaches to the proceeds.

§ 9–316.   Continued Perfection of Security Interest Following Change in Governing Law.

(a) A security interest perfected pursuant to the law of the jurisdiction designated in Section 9–301(1) or 9–305(c) remains perfected until the earliest of:

(1) the time perfection would have ceased under the law of that jurisdiction;

(2) the expiration of four months after a change of the debtor's location to another jurisdiction; or

(3) the expiration of one year after a transfer of collateral to a person that thereby becomes a debtor and is located in another jurisdiction.

(b) If a security interest described in subsection (a) becomes perfected under the law of the other jurisdiction before the earliest time or event described in that subsection, it remains perfected thereafter. If the security interest does not become perfected under the law of the other jurisdiction before the earliest time or event, it becomes unperfected and is deemed never to have been perfected as against a purchaser of the collateral for value.

(c) A possessory security interest in collateral, other than goods covered by a certificate of title and as-extracted collateral consisting of goods, remains continuously perfected if:

(1) the collateral is located in one jurisdiction and subject to a security interest perfected under the law of that jurisdiction;

(2) thereafter the collateral is brought into another jurisdiction; and

(3) upon entry into the other jurisdiction, the security interest is perfected under the law of the other jurisdiction.

(d) Except as otherwise provided in subsection (e), a security interest in goods covered by a certificate of title which is perfected by any method under the law of another jurisdiction when the goods become covered by a certificate of title from this State remains perfected until the security interest would have become unperfected under the law of the other jurisdiction had the goods not become so covered.

(e) A security interest described in subsection (d) becomes unperfected as against a purchaser of the goods for value and is deemed never to have been perfected as against a purchaser of the goods for value if the applicable requirements for perfection under Section 9–311(b) or 9–313 are not satisfied before the earlier of:

(1) the time the security interest would have become unperfected under the law of the other jurisdiction had the goods not become covered by a certificate of title from this State; or

(2) the expiration of four months after the goods had become so covered.

(f) A security interest in deposit accounts, letter-of-credit rights, or investment property which is perfected under the law of the bank's jurisdiction, the issuer's jurisdiction, a nominated person's jurisdiction, the securities intermediary's jurisdiction, or the commodity intermediary's jurisdiction, as applicable, remains perfected until the earlier of:

(1) the time the security interest would have become unperfected under the law of that jurisdiction; or

(2) the expiration of four months after a change of the applicable jurisdiction to another jurisdiction.

(g) If a security interest described in subsection (f) becomes perfected under the law of the other jurisdiction before the earlier of the time or the end of the period described in that subsection, it remains perfected thereafter. If the security interest does not become perfected under the law of the other jurisdiction before the earlier of that time or the end of that period, it becomes unperfected and is deemed never to have been perfected as against a purchaser of the collateral for value.

[Subpart 3. Priority]

§ 9–317.   Interests That Take Priority over or Take Free of Security Interest or Agricultural Lien.

(a) A security interest or agricultural lien is subordinate to the rights of:

(1) a person entitled to priority under Section 9–322; and

(2) except as otherwise provided in subsection (e), a person that becomes a lien creditor before the earlier of the time:

(A) the security interest or agricultural lien is perfected; or

(B) one of the conditions specified in Section 9–203(b)(3) is met and a financing statement covering the collateral is filed.

(b) Except as otherwise provided in subsection (e), a buyer, other than a secured party, of tangible chattel paper, documents, goods, instruments, or a security certificate takes free of a security interest or agricultural lien if the buyer gives value and receives delivery of the collateral without knowledge of the security interest or agricultural lien and before it is perfected.

(c) Except as otherwise provided in subsection (e), a lessee of goods takes free of a security interest or agricultural lien if the lessee gives value and receives delivery of the collateral without knowledge of the security interest or agricultural lien and before it is perfected.

(d) A licensee of a general intangible or a buyer, other than a secured party, of accounts, electronic chattel paper, general intangibles, or investment property other than a certificated security takes free of a security interest if the licensee or buyer gives value without knowledge of the security interest and before it is perfected.

(e) Except as otherwise provided in Sections 9–320 and 9–321, if a person files a financing statement with respect to a purchase-money security interest before or within 20 days after the debtor receives delivery of the collateral, the security interest takes priority over the rights of a buyer, lessee, or lien creditor which arise between the time the security interest attaches and the time of filing.

As amended in 2000.

§ 9–318.   No Interest Retained in Right to Payment That Is Sold; Rights and Title of Seller of Account or Chattel Paper with Respect to Creditors and Purchasers.

(a) A debtor that has sold an account, chattel paper, payment intangible, or promissory note does not retain a legal or equitable interest in the collateral sold.

(b) For purposes of determining the rights of creditors of, and purchasers for value of an account or chattel paper from, a debtor that has sold an account or chattel paper, while the buyer's security interest is unperfected, the debtor is deemed to have rights and title to the account or chattel paper identical to those the debtor sold.

§ 9–319.   Rights and Title of Consignee with Respect to Creditors and Purchasers.

(a) Except as otherwise provided in subsection (b), for purposes of determining the rights of creditors of, and purchasers for value of goods from, a consignee, while the goods are in the possession of the consignee, the consignee is deemed to have rights and title to the goods identical to those the consignor had or had power to transfer.

(b) For purposes of determining the rights of a creditor of a consignee, law other than this article determines the rights and title of a consignee while goods are in the consignee's possession if, under this part, a perfected security interest held by the consignor would have priority over the rights of the creditor.

§ 9–320.   Buyer of Goods.

(a) Except as otherwise provided in subsection (e), a buyer in ordinary course of business, other than a person buying farm products from a person engaged in farming operations, takes free of a security interest created by the buyer's seller, even if the security interest is perfected and the buyer knows of its existence.

(b) Except as otherwise provided in subsection (e), a buyer of goods from a person who used or bought the goods for use primarily for personal, family, or household purposes takes free of a security interest, even if perfected, if the buyer buys:

(1) without knowledge of the security interest;

(2) for value;

(3) primarily for the buyer's personal, family, or household purposes; and

(4) before the filing of a financing statement covering the goods.

(c) To the extent that it affects the priority of a security interest over a buyer of goods under subsection (b), the period of effectiveness of a filing made in the jurisdiction in which the seller is located is governed by Section 9–316(a) and (b).

(d) A buyer in ordinary course of business buying oil, gas, or other minerals at the wellhead or minehead or after extraction takes free of an interest arising out of an encumbrance.

(e) Subsections (a) and (b) do not affect a security interest in goods in the possession of the secured party under Section 9–313.

§ 9–321.   Licensee of General Intangible and Lessee of Goods in Ordinary Course of Business.

(a) In this section, "licensee in ordinary course of business" means a person that becomes a licensee of a general intangible in good faith, without knowledge that the license violates the rights of another person in the general intangible, and in the ordinary course from a person in the business of licensing general intangibles of that kind. A person becomes a licensee in the ordinary course if the license to the person comports with the usual or customary practices in the kind of business in which the licensor is engaged or with the licensor's own usual or customary practices.

(b) A licensee in ordinary course of business takes its rights under a nonexclusive license free of a security interest in the general intangible created by the licensor, even if the security interest is perfected and the licensee knows of its existence.

(c) A lessee in ordinary course of business takes its leasehold interest free of a security interest in the goods created by the lessor, even if the security interest is perfected and the lessee knows of its existence.

§ 9–322.   Priorities among Conflicting Security Interests in and Agricultural Liens on Same Collateral.

(a) Except as otherwise provided in this section, priority among conflicting security interests and agricultural liens in the same collateral is determined according to the following rules:

(1) Conflicting perfected security interests and agricultural liens rank according to priority in time of filing or perfection. Priority dates from the earlier of the time a filing covering the collateral is first made or the security interest or agricultural lien is first perfected, if there is no period thereafter when there is neither filing nor perfection.

(2) A perfected security interest or agricultural lien has priority over a conflicting unperfected security interest or agricultural lien.

(3) The first security interest or agricultural lien to attach or become effective has priority if conflicting security interests and agricultural liens are unperfected.

(b) For the purposes of subsection (a)(1):

(1) the time of filing or perfection as to a security interest in collateral is also the time of filing or perfection as to a security interest in proceeds; and

(2) the time of filing or perfection as to a security interest in collateral supported by a supporting obligation is also the time of filing or perfection as to a security interest in the supporting obligation.

(c) Except as otherwise provided in subsection (f), a security interest in collateral which qualifies for priority over a conflicting security interest under Section 9–327, 9–328, 9–329, 9–330, or 9–331 also has priority over a conflicting security interest in:

(1) any supporting obligation for the collateral; and

(2) proceeds of the collateral if:

(A) the security interest in proceeds is perfected;

(B) the proceeds are cash proceeds or of the same type as the collateral; and

(C) in the case of proceeds that are proceeds of proceeds, all intervening proceeds are cash proceeds, proceeds of the same type as the collateral, or an account relating to the collateral.

(d) Subject to subsection (e) and except as otherwise provided in subsection (f), if a security interest in chattel paper, deposit accounts, negotiable documents, instruments, investment property, or letter-of-credit rights is perfected by a method other than filing, conflicting perfected security interests in proceeds of the collateral rank according to priority in time of filing.

(e) Subsection (d) applies only if the proceeds of the collateral are not cash proceeds, chattel paper, negotiable documents, instruments, investment property, or letter-of-credit rights.

(f) Subsections (a) through (e) are subject to:

(1) subsection (g) and the other provisions of this part;

(2) Section 4–210 with respect to a security interest of a collecting bank;

(3) Section 5–118 with respect to a security interest of an issuer or nominated person; and

(4) Section 9–110 with respect to a security interest arising under Article 2 or 2A.

(g) A perfected agricultural lien on collateral has priority over a conflicting security interest in or agricultural lien on the same collateral if the statute creating the agricultural lien so provides.

§ 9–323.   Future Advances.

(a) Except as otherwise provided in subsection (c), for purposes of determining the priority of a perfected security interest under Section 9–322(a)(1), perfection of the security interest dates from the time an advance is made to the extent that the security interest secures an advance that:

(1) is made while the security interest is perfected only:

(A) under Section 9–309 when it attaches; or

(B) temporarily under Section 9–312(e), (f), or (g); and

(2) is not made pursuant to a commitment entered into before or while the security interest is perfected by a method other than under Section 9–309 or 9–312(e), (f), or (g).

(b) Except as otherwise provided in subsection (c), a security interest is subordinate to the rights of a person that becomes a lien creditor to the extent that the security interest secures an advance made more than 45 days after the person becomes a lien creditor unless the advance is made:

(1) without knowledge of the lien; or

(2) pursuant to a commitment entered into without knowledge of the lien.

(c) Subsections (a) and (b) do not apply to a security interest held by a secured party that is a buyer of accounts, chattel paper, payment intangibles, or promissory notes or a consignor.

(d) Except as otherwise provided in subsection (e), a buyer of goods other than a buyer in ordinary course of business takes free of a security interest to the extent that it secures advances made after the earlier of:

(1) the time the secured party acquires knowledge of the buyer's purchase; or

(2) 45 days after the purchase.

(e) Subsection (d) does not apply if the advance is made pursuant to a commitment entered into without knowledge of the buyer's purchase and before the expiration of the 45-day period.

(f) Except as otherwise provided in subsection (g), a lessee of goods, other than a lessee in ordinary course of business, takes the leasehold interest free of a security interest to the extent that it secures advances made after the earlier of:

(1) the time the secured party acquires knowledge of the lease; or

(2) 45 days after the lease contract becomes enforceable.

(g) Subsection (f) does not apply if the advance is made pursuant to a commitment entered into without knowledge of the lease and before the expiration of the 45-day period.

As amended in 1999.

§ 9–324.   Priority of Purchase-Money Security Interests.

(a) Except as otherwise provided in subsection (g), a perfected purchase-money security interest in goods other than inventory or livestock has priority over a conflicting security interest in the same goods, and, except as otherwise provided in Section 9–327, a perfected security interest in its identifiable proceeds also has priority, if the purchase-money security interest is perfected when the debtor receives possession of the collateral or within 20 days thereafter.

(b) Subject to subsection (c) and except as otherwise provided in subsection (g), a perfected purchase-money security interest in inventory has priority over a conflicting security interest in the same inventory, has priority over a conflicting security interest in chattel paper or an instrument constituting proceeds of the inventory and in proceeds of the chattel paper, if so provided in Section 9–330, and, except as otherwise provided in Section 9–327, also has priority in identifiable cash proceeds of the inventory to the extent the identifiable cash proceeds are received on or before the delivery of the inventory to a buyer, if:

(1) the purchase-money security interest is perfected when the debtor receives possession of the inventory;

(2) the purchase-money secured party sends an authenticated notification to the holder of the conflicting security interest;

(3) the holder of the conflicting security interest receives the notification within five years before the debtor receives possession of the inventory; and

(4) the notification states that the person sending the notification has or expects to acquire a purchase-money security interest in inventory of the debtor and describes the inventory.

(c) Subsections (b)(2) through (4) apply only if the holder of the conflicting security interest had filed a financing statement covering the same types of inventory:

(1) if the purchase-money security interest is perfected by filing, before the date of the filing; or

(2) if the purchase-money security interest is temporarily perfected without filing or possession under Section 9–312(f), before the beginning of the 20-day period thereunder.

(d) Subject to subsection (e) and except as otherwise provided in subsection (g), a perfected purchase-money security interest in livestock that are farm products has priority over a conflicting security interest in the same livestock, and, except as otherwise provided in Section 9–327, a perfected security interest in their identifiable proceeds and identifiable products in their unmanufactured states also has priority, if:

(1) the purchase-money security interest is perfected when the debtor receives possession of the livestock;

(2) the purchase-money secured party sends an authenticated notification to the holder of the conflicting security interest;

(3) the holder of the conflicting security interest receives the notification within six months before the debtor receives possession of the livestock; and

(4) the notification states that the person sending the notification has or expects to acquire a purchase-money security interest in livestock of the debtor and describes the livestock.

(e) Subsections (d)(2) through (4) apply only if the holder of the conflicting security interest had filed a financing statement covering the same types of livestock:

(1) if the purchase-money security interest is perfected by filing, before the date of the filing; or

(2) if the purchase-money security interest is temporarily perfected without filing or possession under Section 9–312(f), before the beginning of the 20-day period thereunder.

(f) Except as otherwise provided in subsection (g), a perfected purchase-money security interest in software has priority over a conflicting security interest in the same collateral, and, except as otherwise provided in Section 9–327, a perfected security interest in its identifiable proceeds also has priority, to the extent that the purchase-money security interest in the goods in which the software was acquired for use has priority in the goods and proceeds of the goods under this section.

(g) If more than one security interest qualifies for priority in the same collateral under subsection (a), (b), (d), or (f):

(1) a security interest securing an obligation incurred as all or part of the price of the collateral has priority over a security interest securing an obligation incurred for value given to enable the debtor to acquire rights in or the use of collateral; and

(2) in all other cases, Section 9–322(a) applies to the qualifying security interests.

§ 9–325.   Priority of Security Interests in Transferred Collateral.

(a) Except as otherwise provided in subsection (b), a security interest created by a debtor is subordinate to a security interest in the same collateral created by another person if:

(1) the debtor acquired the collateral subject to the security interest created by the other person;

(2) the security interest created by the other person was perfected when the debtor acquired the collateral; and

(3) there is no period thereafter when the security interest is unperfected.

(b) Subsection (a) subordinates a security interest only if the security interest:

(1) otherwise would have priority solely under Section 9–322(a) or 9–324; or

(2) arose solely under Section 2–711(3) or 2A–508(5).

§ 9–326.   Priority of Security Interests Created by New Debtor.

(a) Subject to subsection (b), a security interest created by a new debtor which is perfected by a filed financing statement that is effective solely under Section 9–508 in collateral in which a new debtor has or acquires rights is subordinate to a security interest in the same collateral which is perfected other than by a filed financing statement that is effective solely under Section 9–508.

(b) The other provisions of this part determine the priority among conflicting security interests in the same collateral perfected by filed financing statements that are effective solely under Section 9–508. However, if the security agreements to which a new debtor became bound as debtor were not entered into by the same original debtor, the conflicting security interests rank according to priority in time of the new debtor's having become bound.

§ 9–327.   Priority of Security Interests in Deposit Account.

The following rules govern priority among conflicting security interests in the same deposit account:

(1) A security interest held by a secured party having control of the deposit account under Section 9–104 has priority over a conflicting security interest held by a secured party that does not have control.

(2) Except as otherwise provided in paragraphs (3) and (4), security interests perfected by control under Section 9–314 rank according to priority in time of obtaining control.

(3) Except as otherwise provided in paragraph (4), a security interest held by the bank with which the deposit account is maintained has priority over a conflicting security interest held by another secured party.

(4) A security interest perfected by control under Section 9–104(a)(3) has priority over a security interest held by the bank with which the deposit account is maintained.

§ 9–328.   Priority of Security Interests in Investment Property.

The following rules govern priority among conflicting security interests in the same investment property:

(1) A security interest held by a secured party having control of investment property under Section 9–106 has priority over a

security interest held by a secured party that does not have control of the investment property.

(2) Except as otherwise provided in paragraphs (3) and (4), conflicting security interests held by secured parties each of which has control under Section 9–106 rank according to priority in time of:

(A) if the collateral is a security, obtaining control;

(B) if the collateral is a security entitlement carried in a securities account and:

(i) if the secured party obtained control under Section 8–106(d)(1), the secured party's becoming the person for which the securities account is maintained;

(ii) if the secured party obtained control under Section 8–106(d)(2), the securities intermediary's agreement to comply with the secured party's entitlement orders with respect to security entitlements carried or to be carried in the securities account; or

(iii) if the secured party obtained control through another person under Section 8–106(d)(3), the time on which priority would be based under this paragraph if the other person were the secured party; or

(C) if the collateral is a commodity contract carried with a commodity intermediary, the satisfaction of the requirement for control specified in Section 9–106(b)(2) with respect to commodity contracts carried or to be carried with the commodity intermediary.

(3) A security interest held by a securities intermediary in a security entitlement or a securities account maintained with the securities intermediary has priority over a conflicting security interest held by another secured party.

(4) A security interest held by a commodity intermediary in a commodity contract or a commodity account maintained with the commodity intermediary has priority over a conflicting security interest held by another secured party.

(5) A security interest in a certificated security in registered form which is perfected by taking delivery under Section 9–313(a) and not by control under Section 9–314 has priority over a conflicting security interest perfected by a method other than control.

(6) Conflicting security interests created by a broker, securities intermediary, or commodity intermediary which are perfected without control under Section 9–106 rank equally.

(7) In all other cases, priority among conflicting security interests in investment property is governed by Sections 9–322 and 9–323.

§ 9–329.   Priority of Security Interests in Letter-of-Credit Right.

The following rules govern priority among conflicting security interests in the same letter-of-credit right:

(1) A security interest held by a secured party having control of the letter-of-credit right under Section 9–107 has priority to the extent of its control over a conflicting security interest held by a secured party that does not have control.

(2) Security interests perfected by control under Section 9–314 rank according to priority in time of obtaining control.

§ 9–330.   Priority of Purchaser of Chattel Paper or Instrument.

(a) A purchaser of chattel paper has priority over a security interest in the chattel paper which is claimed merely as proceeds of inventory subject to a security interest if:

(1) in good faith and in the ordinary course of the purchaser's business, the purchaser gives new value and takes possession of the chattel paper or obtains control of the chattel paper under Section 9–105; and

(2) the chattel paper does not indicate that it has been assigned to an identified assignee other than the purchaser.

(b) A purchaser of chattel paper has priority over a security interest in the chattel paper which is claimed other than merely as proceeds of inventory subject to a security interest if the purchaser gives new value and takes possession of the chattel paper or obtains control of the chattel paper under Section 9–105 in good faith, in the ordinary course of the purchaser's business, and without knowledge that the purchase violates the rights of the secured party.

(c) Except as otherwise provided in Section 9–327, a purchaser having priority in chattel paper under subsection (a) or (b) also has priority in proceeds of the chattel paper to the extent that:

(1) Section 9–322 provides for priority in the proceeds; or

(2) the proceeds consist of the specific goods covered by the chattel paper or cash proceeds of the specific goods, even if the purchaser's security interest in the proceeds is unperfected.

(d) Except as otherwise provided in Section 9–331(a), a purchaser of an instrument has priority over a security interest in the instrument perfected by a method other than possession if the purchaser gives value and takes possession of the instrument in good faith and without knowledge that the purchase violates the rights of the secured party.

(e) For purposes of subsections (a) and (b), the holder of a purchase-money security interest in inventory gives new value for chattel paper constituting proceeds of the inventory.

(f) For purposes of subsections (b) and (d), if chattel paper or an instrument indicates that it has been assigned to an identified secured party other than the purchaser, a purchaser of the chattel paper or instrument has knowledge that the purchase violates the rights of the secured party.

§ 9–331.   Priority of Rights of Purchasers of Instruments, Documents, and Securities under Other Articles; Priority of Interests in Financial Assets and Security Entitlements under Article 8.

(a) This article does not limit the rights of a holder in due course of a negotiable instrument, a holder to which a negotiable document of title has been duly negotiated, or a protected purchaser of a security. These holders or purchasers take priority over an earlier security interest, even if perfected, to the extent provided in Articles 3, 7, and 8.

(b) This article does not limit the rights of or impose liability on a person to the extent that the person is protected against the assertion of a claim under Article 8.

(c) Filing under this article does not constitute notice of a claim or defense to the holders, or purchasers, or persons described in subsections (a) and (b).

§ 9–332.   Transfer of Money; Transfer of Funds from Deposit Account.

(a) A transferee of money takes the money free of a security interest unless the transferee acts in collusion with the debtor in violating the rights of the secured party.

(b) A transferee of funds from a deposit account takes the funds free of a security interest in the deposit account unless the transferee acts in collusion with the debtor in violating the rights of the secured party.

§ 9–333.   Priority of Certain Liens Arising by Operation of Law.

(a) In this section, "possessory lien" means an interest, other than a security interest or an agricultural lien:

(1) which secures payment or performance of an obligation for services or materials furnished with respect to goods by a person in the ordinary course of the person's business;

(2) which is created by statute or rule of law in favor of the person; and

(3) whose effectiveness depends on the person's possession of the goods.

(b) A possessory lien on goods has priority over a security interest in the goods unless the lien is created by a statute that expressly provides otherwise.

§ 9–334.   Priority of Security Interests in Fixtures and Crops.

(a) A security interest under this article may be created in goods that are fixtures or may continue in goods that become fixtures. A security interest does not exist under this article in ordinary building materials incorporated into an improvement on land.

(b) This article does not prevent creation of an encumbrance upon fixtures under real property law.

(c) In cases not governed by subsections (d) through (h), a security interest in fixtures is subordinate to a conflicting interest of an encumbrancer or owner of the related real property other than the debtor.

(d) Except as otherwise provided in subsection (h), a perfected security interest in fixtures has priority over a conflicting interest of an encumbrancer or owner of the real property if the debtor has an interest of record in or is in possession of the real property and:

(1) the security interest is a purchase-money security interest;

(2) the interest of the encumbrancer or owner arises before the goods become fixtures; and

(3) the security interest is perfected by a fixture filing before the goods become fixtures or within 20 days thereafter.

(e) A perfected security interest in fixtures has priority over a conflicting interest of an encumbrancer or owner of the real property if:

(1) the debtor has an interest of record in the real property or is in possession of the real property and the security interest:

(A) is perfected by a fixture filing before the interest of the encumbrancer or owner is of record; and

(B) has priority over any conflicting interest of a predecessor in title of the encumbrancer or owner;

(2) before the goods become fixtures, the security interest is perfected by any method permitted by this article and the fixtures are readily removable:

(A) factory or office machines;

(B) equipment that is not primarily used or leased for use in the operation of the real property; or

(C) replacements of domestic appliances that are consumer goods;

(3) the conflicting interest is a lien on the real property obtained by legal or equitable proceedings after the security interest was perfected by any method permitted by this article; or

(4) the security interest is:

(A) created in a manufactured home in a manufactured-home transaction; and

(B) perfected pursuant to a statute described in Section 9–311(a)(2).

(f) A security interest in fixtures, whether or not perfected, has priority over a conflicting interest of an encumbrancer or owner of the real property if:

(1) the encumbrancer or owner has, in an authenticated record, consented to the security interest or disclaimed an interest in the goods as fixtures; or

(2) the debtor has a right to remove the goods as against the encumbrancer or owner.

(g) The priority of the security interest under paragraph (f)(2) continues for a reasonable time if the debtor's right to remove the goods as against the encumbrancer or owner terminates.

(h) A mortgage is a construction mortgage to the extent that it secures an obligation incurred for the construction of an improvement on land, including the acquisition cost of the land, if a recorded record of the mortgage so indicates. Except as otherwise provided in subsections (e) and (f), a security interest in fixtures is subordinate to a construction mortgage if a record of the mortgage is recorded before the goods become fixtures and the goods become fixtures before the completion of the construction. A mortgage has this priority to the same extent as a construction mortgage to the extent that it is given to refinance a construction mortgage.

(i) A perfected security interest in crops growing on real property has priority over a conflicting interest of an encumbrancer or owner of the real property if the debtor has an interest of record in or is in possession of the real property.

(j) Subsection (i) prevails over any inconsistent provisions of the following statutes:

[List here any statutes containing provisions inconsistent with subsection (i).]

Legislative Note: States that amend statutes to remove provisions inconsistent with subsection (i) need not enact subsection (j).

§ 9–335.   Accessions.

(a) A security interest may be created in an accession and continues in collateral that becomes an accession.

(b) If a security interest is perfected when the collateral becomes an accession, the security interest remains perfected in the collateral.

(c) Except as otherwise provided in subsection (d), the other provisions of this part determine the priority of a security interest in an accession.

(d) A security interest in an accession is subordinate to a security interest in the whole which is perfected by compliance with the requirements of a certificate-of-title statute under Section 9–311(b).

(e) After default, subject to Part 6, a secured party may remove an accession from other goods if the security interest in the accession has priority over the claims of every person having an interest in the whole.

(f) A secured party that removes an accession from other goods under subsection (e) shall promptly reimburse any holder of a security interest or other lien on, or owner of, the whole or of the other goods, other than the debtor, for the cost of repair of any physical injury to the whole or the other goods. The secured party need not reimburse the holder or owner for any diminution in value of the whole or the other goods caused by the absence of the accession removed or by any necessity for replacing it. A person entitled to reimbursement may refuse permission to remove until the secured party gives adequate assurance for the performance of the obligation to reimburse.

§ 9–336.   Commingled Goods.

(a) In this section, "commingled goods" means goods that are physically united with other goods in such a manner that their identity is lost in a product or mass.

(b) A security interest does not exist in commingled goods as such. However, a security interest may attach to a product or mass that results when goods become commingled goods.

(c) If collateral becomes commingled goods, a security interest attaches to the product or mass.

(d) If a security interest in collateral is perfected before the collateral becomes commingled goods, the security interest that attaches to the product or mass under subsection (c) is perfected.

(e) Except as otherwise provided in subsection (f), the other provisions of this part determine the priority of a security interest that attaches to the product or mass under subsection (c).

(f) If more than one security interest attaches to the product or mass under subsection (c), the following rules determine priority:

(1) A security interest that is perfected under subsection (d) has priority over a security interest that is unperfected at the time the collateral becomes commingled goods.

(2) If more than one security interest is perfected under subsection (d), the security interests rank equally in proportion to the value of the collateral at the time it became commingled goods.

§ 9–337.   Priority of Security Interests in Goods Covered by Certificate of Title.

If, while a security interest in goods is perfected by any method under the law of another jurisdiction, this State issues a certificate of title that does not show that the goods are subject to the security interest or contain a statement that they may be subject to security interests not shown on the certificate:

(1) a buyer of the goods, other than a person in the business of selling goods of that kind, takes free of the security interest if the buyer gives value and receives delivery of the goods after issuance of the certificate and without knowledge of the security interest; and

(2) the security interest is subordinate to a conflicting security interest in the goods that attaches, and is perfected under Section 9–311(b), after issuance of the certificate and without the conflicting secured party's knowledge of the security interest.

§ 9–338.   Priority of Security Interest or Agricultural Lien Perfected by Filed Financing Statement Providing Certain Incorrect Information.

If a security interest or agricultural lien is perfected by a filed financing statement providing information described in Section 9–516(b)(5) which is incorrect at the time the financing statement is filed:

(1) the security interest or agricultural lien is subordinate to a conflicting perfected security interest in the collateral to the extent that the holder of the conflicting security interest gives value in reasonable reliance upon the incorrect information; and

(2) a purchaser, other than a secured party, of the collateral takes free of the security interest or agricultural lien to the extent that, in reasonable reliance upon the incorrect information, the purchaser gives value and, in the case of chattel paper, documents, goods, instruments, or a security certificate, receives delivery of the collateral.

§ 9–339.   Priority Subject to Subordination.

This article does not preclude subordination by agreement by a person entitled to priority.

[Subpart 4. Rights of Bank]

§ 9–340.   Effectiveness of Right of Recoupment or Set-Off against Deposit Account.

(a) Except as otherwise provided in subsection (c), a bank with which a deposit account is maintained may exercise any right of recoupment or set-off against a secured party that holds a security interest in the deposit account.

(b) Except as otherwise provided in subsection (c), the application of this article to a security interest in a deposit account does not affect a right of recoupment or set-off of the secured party as to a deposit account maintained with the secured party.

(c) The exercise by a bank of a set-off against a deposit account is ineffective against a secured party that holds a security interest in the deposit account which is perfected by control under Section 9–104(a)(3), if the set-off is based on a claim against the debtor.

§ 9–341.   Bank's Rights and Duties with Respect to Deposit Account.

Except as otherwise provided in Section 9–340(c), and unless the bank otherwise agrees in an authenticated record, a bank's rights and duties with respect to a deposit account maintained with the bank are not terminated, suspended, or modified by:

(1) the creation, attachment, or perfection of a security interest in the deposit account;

(2) the bank's knowledge of the security interest; or

(3) the bank's receipt of instructions from the secured party.

§ 9–342.   Bank's Right to Refuse to Enter into or Disclose Existence of Control Agreement.

This article does not require a bank to enter into an agreement of the kind described in Section 9–104(a)(2), even if its customer so requests or directs. A bank that has entered into such an agreement is not required to confirm the existence of the agreement to another person unless requested to do so by its customer.

Part 4   Rights of Third Parties

§ 9–401.   Alienability of Debtor's Rights.

(a) Except as otherwise provided in subsection (b) and Sections 9–406, 9–407, 9–408, and 9–409, whether a debtor's rights in collateral may be voluntarily or involuntarily transferred is governed by law other than this article.

(b) An agreement between the debtor and secured party which prohibits a transfer of the debtor's rights in collateral or makes the transfer a default does not prevent the transfer from taking effect.

§ 9–402.   Secured Party Not Obligated on Contract of Debtor or in Tort.

The existence of a security interest, agricultural lien, or authority given to a debtor to dispose of or use collateral, without more, does not subject a secured party to liability in contract or tort for the debtor's acts or omissions.

§ 9–403.   Agreement Not to Assert Defenses against Assignee.

(a) In this section, "value" has the meaning provided in Section 3–303(a).

(b) Except as otherwise provided in this section, an agreement between an account debtor and an assignor not to assert against an assignee any claim or defense that the account debtor may have against the assignor is enforceable by an assignee that takes an assignment:

(1) for value;

(2) in good faith;

(3) without notice of a claim of a property or possessory right to the property assigned; and

(4) without notice of a defense or claim in recoupment of the type that may be asserted against a person entitled to enforce a negotiable instrument under Section 3–305(a).

(c) Subsection (b) does not apply to defenses of a type that may be asserted against a holder in due course of a negotiable instrument under Section 3–305(b).

(d) In a consumer transaction, if a record evidences the account debtor's obligation, law other than this article requires that the record include a statement to the effect that the rights of an assignee are subject to claims or defenses that the account debtor could assert against the original obligee, and the record does not include such a statement:

(1) the record has the same effect as if the record included such a statement; and

(2) the account debtor may assert against an assignee those claims and defenses that would have been available if the record included such a statement.

(e) This section is subject to law other than this article which establishes a different rule for an account debtor who is an individual and who incurred the obligation primarily for personal, family, or household purposes.

(f) Except as otherwise provided in subsection (d), this section does not displace law other than this article which gives effect to an agreement by an account debtor not to assert a claim or defense against an assignee.

§ 9–404.   Rights Acquired by Assignee; Claims and Defenses against Assignee.

(a) Unless an account debtor has made an enforceable agreement not to assert defenses or claims, and subject to subsections (b) through (e), the rights of an assignee are subject to:

(1) all terms of the agreement between the account debtor and assignor and any defense or claim in recoupment arising from the transaction that gave rise to the contract; and

(2) any other defense or claim of the account debtor against the assignor which accrues before the account debtor receives a notification of the assignment authenticated by the assignor or the assignee.

(b) Subject to subsection (c) and except as otherwise provided in subsection (d), the claim of an account debtor against an assignor may be asserted against an assignee under subsection (a) only to reduce the amount the account debtor owes.

(c) This section is subject to law other than this article which establishes a different rule for an account debtor who is an individual and who incurred the obligation primarily for personal, family, or household purposes.

(d) In a consumer transaction, if a record evidences the account debtor's obligation, law other than this article requires that the record include a statement to the effect that the account debtor's recovery against an assignee with respect to claims and defenses against the assignor may not exceed amounts paid by the account debtor under the record, and the record does not include such a statement, the extent to which a claim of an account debtor against the assignor may be asserted against an assignee is determined as if the record included such a statement.

(e) This section does not apply to an assignment of a health-care-insurance receivable.

§ 9–405.   Modification of Assigned Contract.

(a) A modification of or substitution for an assigned contract is effective against an assignee if made in good faith. The assignee acquires corresponding rights under the modified or substituted contract. The assignment may provide that the modification or substitution is a breach of contract by the assignor. This subsection is subject to subsections (b) through (d).

(b) Subsection (a) applies to the extent that:

(1) the right to payment or a part thereof under an assigned contract has not been fully earned by performance; or

(2) the right to payment or a part thereof has been fully earned by performance and the account debtor has not received notification of the assignment under Section 9–406(a).

(c) This section is subject to law other than this article which establishes a different rule for an account debtor who is an individual and who incurred the obligation primarily for personal, family, or household purposes.

(d) This section does not apply to an assignment of a health-care-insurance receivable.

§ 9–406.   Discharge of Account Debtor; Notification of Assignment; Identification and Proof of Assignment; Restrictions on Assignment of Accounts, Chattel Paper, Payment Intangibles, and Promissory Notes Ineffective.

(a) Subject to subsections (b) through (i), an account debtor on an account, chattel paper, or a payment intangible may discharge its obligation by paying the assignor until, but not after, the account debtor receives a notification, authenticated by the assignor or the assignee, that the amount due or to become due has been assigned and that payment is to be made to the assignee. After receipt of the notification, the account debtor may discharge its obligation by paying the assignee and may not discharge the obligation by paying the assignor.

(b) Subject to subsection (h), notification is ineffective under subsection (a):

(1) if it does not reasonably identify the rights assigned;

(2) to the extent that an agreement between an account debtor and a seller of a payment intangible limits the account debtor's duty to pay a person other than the seller and the limitation is effective under law other than this article; or

(3) at the option of an account debtor, if the notification notifies the account debtor to make less than the full amount of any installment or other periodic payment to the assignee, even if:

(A) only a portion of the account, chattel paper, or payment intangible has been assigned to that assignee;

(B) a portion has been assigned to another assignee; or

(C) the account debtor knows that the assignment to that assignee is limited.

(c) Subject to subsection (h), if requested by the account debtor, an assignee shall seasonably furnish reasonable proof that the assignment has been made. Unless the assignee complies, the account debtor may discharge its obligation by paying the assignor, even if the account debtor has received a notification under subsection (a).

(d) Except as otherwise provided in subsection (e) and Sections 2A–303 and 9–407, and subject to subsection (h), a term in an agreement between an account debtor and an assignor or in a promissory note is ineffective to the extent that it:

(1) prohibits, restricts, or requires the consent of the account debtor or person obligated on the promissory note to the assignment or transfer of, or the creation, attachment, perfection, or enforcement of a security interest in, the account, chattel paper, payment intangible, or promissory note; or

(2) provides that the assignment or transfer or the creation, attachment, perfection, or enforcement of the security interest may give rise to a default, breach, right of recoupment, claim, defense, termination, right of termination, or remedy under the account, chattel paper, payment intangible, or promissory note.

(e) Subsection (d) does not apply to the sale of a payment intangible or promissory note.

(f) Except as otherwise provided in Sections 2A–303 and 9–407 and subject to subsections (h) and (i), a rule of law, statute, or regulation that prohibits, restricts, or requires the consent of a government, governmental body or official, or account debtor to the assignment or transfer of, or creation of a security interest in, an account or chattel paper is ineffective to the extent that the rule of law, statute, or regulation:

(1) prohibits, restricts, or requires the consent of the government, governmental body or official, or account debtor to the assignment or transfer of, or the creation, attachment, perfection, or enforcement of a security interest in the account or chattel paper; or

(2) provides that the assignment or transfer or the creation, attachment, perfection, or enforcement of the security interest may give rise to a default, breach, right of recoupment, claim, defense, termination, right of termination, or remedy under the account or chattel paper.

(g) Subject to subsection (h), an account debtor may not waive or vary its option under subsection (b)(3).

(h) This section is subject to law other than this article which establishes a different rule for an account debtor who is an individual and who incurred the obligation primarily for personal, family, or household purposes.

(i) This section does not apply to an assignment of a health-care-insurance receivable.

(j) This section prevails over any inconsistent provisions of the following statutes, rules, and regulations:

[List here any statutes, rules, and regulations containing provisions inconsistent with this section.]

Legislative Note: States that amend statutes, rules, and regulations to remove provisions inconsistent with this section need not enact subsection (j).

As amended in 1999 and 2000.

§ 9–407.   Restrictions on Creation or Enforcement of Security Interest in Leasehold Interest or in Lessor's Residual Interest.

(a) Except as otherwise provided in subsection (b), a term in a lease agreement is ineffective to the extent that it:

(1) prohibits, restricts, or requires the consent of a party to the lease to the assignment or transfer of, or the creation, attachment, perfection, or enforcement of a security interest

in an interest of a party under the lease contract or in the lessor's residual interest in the goods; or

(2) provides that the assignment or transfer or the creation, attachment, perfection, or enforcement of the security interest may give rise to a default, breach, right of recoupment, claim, defense, termination, right of termination, or remedy under the lease.

(b) Except as otherwise provided in Section 2A–303(7), a term described in subsection (a)(2) is effective to the extent that there is:

(1) a transfer by the lessee of the lessee's right of possession or use of the goods in violation of the term; or

(2) a delegation of a material performance of either party to the lease contract in violation of the term.

(c) The creation, attachment, perfection, or enforcement of a security interest in the lessor's interest under the lease contract or the lessor's residual interest in the goods is not a transfer that materially impairs the lessee's prospect of obtaining return performance or materially changes the duty of or materially increases the burden or risk imposed on the lessee within the purview of Section 2A–303(4) unless, and then only to the extent that, enforcement actually results in a delegation of material performance of the lessor.

As amended in 1999.

§ 9–408.   Restrictions on Assignment of Promissory Notes, Health-Care-Insurance Receivables, and Certain General Intangibles Ineffective.

(a) Except as otherwise provided in subsection (b), a term in a promissory note or in an agreement between an account debtor and a debtor which relates to a health-care-insurance receivable or a general intangible, including a contract, permit, license, or franchise, and which term prohibits, restricts, or requires the consent of the person obligated on the promissory note or the account debtor to, the assignment or transfer of, or creation, attachment, or perfection of a security interest in, the promissory note, health-care-insurance receivable, or general intangible, is ineffective to the extent that the term:

(1) would impair the creation, attachment, or perfection of a security interest; or

(2) provides that the assignment or transfer or the creation, attachment, or perfection of the security interest may give rise to a default, breach, right of recoupment, claim, defense, termination, right of termination, or remedy under the promissory note, health-care-insurance receivable, or general intangible.

(b) Subsection (a) applies to a security interest in a payment intangible or promissory note only if the security interest arises out of a sale of the payment intangible or promissory note.

(c) A rule of law, statute, or regulation that prohibits, restricts, or requires the consent of a government, governmental body or official, person obligated on a promissory note, or account debtor to the assignment or transfer of, or creation of a security interest in, a promissory note, health-care-insurance receivable, or general intangible, including a contract, permit, license, or franchise between an account debtor and a debtor, is ineffective to the extent that the rule of law, statute, or regulation:

(1) would impair the creation, attachment, or perfection of a security interest; or

(2) provides that the assignment or transfer or the creation, attachment, or perfection of the security interest may give rise to a default, breach, right of recoupment, claim, defense, termination, right of termination, or remedy under the promissory note, health-care-insurance receivable, or general intangible.

(d) To the extent that a term in a promissory note or in an agreement between an account debtor and a debtor which relates to a health-care-insurance receivable or general intangible or a rule of law, statute, or regulation described in subsection (c) would be effective under law other than this article but is ineffective under subsection (a) or (c), the creation, attachment, or perfection of a security interest in the promissory note, health-care-insurance receivable, or general intangible:

(1) is not enforceable against the person obligated on the promissory note or the account debtor;

(2) does not impose a duty or obligation on the person obligated on the promissory note or the account debtor;

(3) does not require the person obligated on the promissory note or the account debtor to recognize the security interest, pay or render performance to the secured party, or accept payment or performance from the secured party;

(4) does not entitle the secured party to use or assign the debtor's rights under the promissory note, health-care-insurance receivable, or general intangible, including any related information or materials furnished to the debtor in the transaction giving rise to the promissory note, health-care-insurance receivable, or general intangible;

(5) does not entitle the secured party to use, assign, possess, or have access to any trade secrets or confidential information of the person obligated on the promissory note or the account debtor; and

(6) does not entitle the secured party to enforce the security interest in the promissory note, health-care-insurance receivable, or general intangible.

(e) This section prevails over any inconsistent provisions of the following statutes, rules, and regulations:

[List here any statutes, rules, and regulations containing provisions inconsistent with this section.]

Legislative Note: States that amend statutes, rules, and regulations to remove provisions inconsistent with this section need not enact subsection (e).

As amended in 1999.

§ 9–409.   Restrictions on Assignment of Letter-of-Credit Rights Ineffective.

(a) A term in a letter of credit or a rule of law, statute, regulation, custom, or practice applicable to the letter of credit which prohibits, restricts, or requires the consent of an applicant, issuer, or nominated person to a beneficiary's assignment of or creation of a security interest in a letter-of-credit right is ineffective to the extent that the term or rule of law, statute, regulation, custom, or practice:

(1) would impair the creation, attachment, or perfection of a security interest in the letter-of-credit right; or

(2) provides that the assignment or the creation, attachment, or perfection of the security interest may give rise to a default, breach, right of recoupment, claim, defense, termination, right of termination, or remedy under the letter-of-credit right.

(b) To the extent that a term in a letter of credit is ineffective under subsection (a) but would be effective under law other than this article or a custom or practice applicable to the letter of credit, to the transfer of a right to draw or otherwise demand performance under the letter of credit, or to the assignment of a right to proceeds of the letter of credit, the creation, attachment, or perfection of a security interest in the letter-of-credit right:

(1) is not enforceable against the applicant, issuer, nominated person, or transferee beneficiary;

(2) imposes no duties or obligations on the applicant, issuer, nominated person, or transferee beneficiary; and

(3) does not require the applicant, issuer, nominated person, or transferee beneficiary to recognize the security interest, pay or render performance to the secured party, or accept payment or other performance from the secured party.

As amended in 1999.

Part 5   Filing

[Subpart 1. Filing Office; Contents and Effectiveness of Financing Statement]

§ 9–501.   Filing Office.

(a) Except as otherwise provided in subsection (b), if the local law of this State governs perfection of a security interest or agricultural lien, the office in which to file a financing statement to perfect the security interest or agricultural lien is:

(1) the office designated for the filing or recording of a record of a mortgage on the related real property, if:

(A) the collateral is as-extracted collateral or timber to be cut; or

(B) the financing statement is filed as a fixture filing and the collateral is goods that are or are to become fixtures; or

(2) the office of [ ] [or any office duly authorized by [ ]], in all other cases, including a case in which the collateral is goods that are or are to become fixtures and the financing statement is not filed as a fixture filing.

(b) The office in which to file a financing statement to perfect a security interest in collateral, including fixtures, of a transmitting utility is the office of [ ]. The financing statement also constitutes a fixture filing as to the collateral indicated in the financing statement which is or is to become fixtures.

Legislative Note: The State should designate the filing office where the brackets appear. The filing office may be that of a governmental official (e.g., the Secretary of State) or a private party that maintains the State's filing system.

§ 9–502.   Contents of Financing Statement; Record of Mortgage as Financing Statement; Time of Filing Financing Statement.

(a) Subject to subsection (b), a financing statement is sufficient only if it:

(1) provides the name of the debtor;

(2) provides the name of the secured party or a representative of the secured party; and

(3) indicates the collateral covered by the financing statement.

(b) Except as otherwise provided in Section 9–501(b), to be sufficient, a financing statement that covers as-extracted collateral or timber to be cut, or which is filed as a fixture filing and covers goods that are or are to become fixtures, must satisfy subsection (a) and also:

(1) indicate that it covers this type of collateral;

(2) indicate that it is to be filed [for record] in the real property records;

(3) provide a description of the real property to which the collateral is related [sufficient to give constructive notice of a mortgage under the law of this State if the description were contained in a record of the mortgage of the real property]; and

(4) if the debtor does not have an interest of record in the real property, provide the name of a record owner.

(c) A record of a mortgage is effective, from the date of recording, as a financing statement filed as a fixture filing or as a financing statement covering as-extracted collateral or timber to be cut only if:

(1) the record indicates the goods or accounts that it covers;

(2) the goods are or are to become fixtures related to the real property described in the record or the collateral is related to the real property described in the record and is as-extracted collateral or timber to be cut;

(3) the record satisfies the requirements for a financing statement in this section other than an indication that it is to be filed in the real property records; and

(4) the record is [duly] recorded.

(d) A financing statement may be filed before a security agreement is made or a security interest otherwise attaches.

Legislative Note: Language in brackets is optional. Where the State has any special recording system for real property other than the usual grantor-grantee index (as, for instance, a tract system or a title registration or Torrens system) local adaptations of subsection (b) and Section 9–519(d) and (e) may be necessary. See, e.g., Mass. Gen. Laws Chapter 106, Section 9–410.

§ 9–503.   Name of Debtor and Secured Party.

(a) A financing statement sufficiently provides the name of the debtor:

(1) if the debtor is a registered organization, only if the financing statement provides the name of the debtor indicated on the public record of the debtor's jurisdiction of organization which shows the debtor to have been organized;

(2) if the debtor is a decedent's estate, only if the financing statement provides the name of the decedent and indicates that the debtor is an estate;

(3) if the debtor is a trust or a trustee acting with respect to property held in trust, only if the financing statement:

(A) provides the name specified for the trust in its organic documents or, if no name is specified, provides the name of the settlor and additional information sufficient to distinguish the debtor from other trusts having one or more of the same settlors; and

(B) indicates, in the debtor's name or otherwise, that the debtor is a trust or is a trustee acting with respect to property held in trust; and

(4) in other cases:

(A) if the debtor has a name, only if it provides the individual or organizational name of the debtor; and

(B) if the debtor does not have a name, only if it provides the names of the partners, members, associates, or other persons comprising the debtor.

(b) A financing statement that provides the name of the debtor in accordance with subsection (a) is not rendered ineffective by the absence of:

(1) a trade name or other name of the debtor; or

(2) unless required under subsection (a)(4)(B), names of partners, members, associates, or other persons comprising the debtor.

(c) A financing statement that provides only the debtor's trade name does not sufficiently provide the name of the debtor.

(d) Failure to indicate the representative capacity of a secured party or representative of a secured party does not affect the sufficiency of a financing statement.

(e) A financing statement may provide the name of more than one debtor and the name of more than one secured party.

§ 9–504. Indication of Collateral.

A financing statement sufficiently indicates the collateral that it covers if the financing statement provides:

(1) a description of the collateral pursuant to Section 9–108; or

(2) an indication that the financing statement covers all assets or all personal property.

As amended in 1999.

§ 9–505. Filing and Compliance with Other Statutes and Treaties for Consignments, Leases, Other Bailments, and Other Transactions.

(a) A consignor, lessor, or other bailor of goods, a licensor, or a buyer of a payment intangible or promissory note may file a financing statement, or may comply with a statute or treaty described in Section 9–311(a), using the terms "consignor", "consignee", "lessor", "lessee", "bailor", "bailee", "licensor", "licensee", "owner", "registered owner", "buyer", "seller", or words of similar import, instead of the terms "secured party" and "debtor".

(b) This part applies to the filing of a financing statement under subsection (a) and, as appropriate, to compliance that is equivalent to filing a financing statement under Section 9–311(b), but the filing or compliance is not of itself a factor in determining whether the collateral secures an obligation. If it is determined for another reason that the collateral secures an obligation, a security interest held by the consignor, lessor, bailor, licensor, owner, or buyer which attaches to the collateral is perfected by the filing or compliance.

§ 9–506. Effect of Errors or Omissions.

(a) A financing statement substantially satisfying the requirements of this part is effective, even if it has minor errors or omissions, unless the errors or omissions make the financing statement seriously misleading.

(b) Except as otherwise provided in subsection (c), a financing statement that fails sufficiently to provide the name of the debtor in accordance with Section 9–503(a) is seriously misleading.

(c) If a search of the records of the filing office under the debtor's correct name, using the filing office's standard search logic, if any, would disclose a financing statement that fails sufficiently to provide the name of the debtor in accordance with Section 9–503(a), the name provided does not make the financing statement seriously misleading.

(d) For purposes of Section 9–508(b), the "debtor's correct name" in subsection (c) means the correct name of the new debtor.

§ 9–507. Effect of Certain Events on Effectiveness of Financing Statement.

(a) A filed financing statement remains effective with respect to collateral that is sold, exchanged, leased, licensed, or otherwise disposed of and in which a security interest or agricultural lien continues, even if the secured party knows of or consents to the disposition.

(b) Except as otherwise provided in subsection (c) and Section 9–508, a financing statement is not rendered ineffective if, after the financing statement is filed, the information provided in the financing statement becomes seriously misleading under Section 9–506.

(c) If a debtor so changes its name that a filed financing statement becomes seriously misleading under Section 9–506:

(1) the financing statement is effective to perfect a security interest in collateral acquired by the debtor before, or within four months after, the change; and

(2) the financing statement is not effective to perfect a security interest in collateral acquired by the debtor more than four months after the change, unless an amendment to the financing statement which renders the financing statement not seriously misleading is filed within four months after the change.

§ 9–508. Effectiveness of Financing Statement If New Debtor Becomes Bound by Security Agreement.

(a) Except as otherwise provided in this section, a filed financing statement naming an original debtor is effective to perfect a security interest in collateral in which a new debtor has or acquires rights to the extent that the financing statement would have been effective had the original debtor acquired rights in the collateral.

(b) If the difference between the name of the original debtor and that of the new debtor causes a filed financing statement that is effective under subsection (a) to be seriously misleading under Section 9–506:

(1) the financing statement is effective to perfect a security interest in collateral acquired by the new debtor before, and within four months after, the new debtor becomes bound under Section 9B–203(d); and

(2) the financing statement is not effective to perfect a security interest in collateral acquired by the new debtor more than four months after the new debtor becomes bound under Section 9–203(d) unless an initial financing statement providing the name of the new debtor is filed before the expiration of that time.

(c) This section does not apply to collateral as to which a filed financing statement remains effective against the new debtor under Section 9–507(a).

§ 9–509.   Persons Entitled to File a Record.

(a) A person may file an initial financing statement, amendment that adds collateral covered by a financing statement, or amendment that adds a debtor to a financing statement only if:

(1) the debtor authorizes the filing in an authenticated record or pursuant to subsection (b) or (c); or

(2) the person holds an agricultural lien that has become effective at the time of filing and the financing statement covers only collateral in which the person holds an agricultural lien.

(b) By authenticating or becoming bound as debtor by a security agreement, a debtor or new debtor authorizes the filing of an initial financing statement, and an amendment, covering:

(1) the collateral described in the security agreement; and

(2) property that becomes collateral under Section 9–315(a)(2), whether or not the security agreement expressly covers proceeds.

(c) By acquiring collateral in which a security interest or agricultural lien continues under Section 9–315(a)(1), a debtor authorizes the filing of an initial financing statement, and an amendment, covering the collateral and property that becomes collateral under Section 9–315(a)(2).

(d) A person may file an amendment other than an amendment that adds collateral covered by a financing statement or an amendment that adds a debtor to a financing statement only if:

(1) the secured party of record authorizes the filing; or

(2) the amendment is a termination statement for a financing statement as to which the secured party of record has failed to file or send a termination statement as required by Section 9–513(a) or (c), the debtor authorizes the filing, and the termination statement indicates that the debtor authorized it to be filed.

(e) If there is more than one secured party of record for a financing statement, each secured party of record may authorize the filing of an amendment under subsection (d).

As amended in 2000.

§ 9–510.   Effectiveness of Filed Record.

(a) A filed record is effective only to the extent that it was filed by a person that may file it under Section 9–509.

(b) A record authorized by one secured party of record does not affect the financing statement with respect to another secured party of record.

(c) A continuation statement that is not filed within the six-month period prescribed by Section 9–515(d) is ineffective.

§ 9–511.   Secured Party of Record.

(a) A secured party of record with respect to a financing statement is a person whose name is provided as the name of the secured party or a representative of the secured party in an initial financing statement that has been filed. If an initial financing statement is filed under Section 9–514(a), the assignee named in the initial financing statement is the secured party of record with respect to the financing statement.

(b) If an amendment of a financing statement which provides the name of a person as a secured party or a representative of a secured party is filed, the person named in the amendment is a secured party of record. If an amendment is filed under Section 9–514(b), the assignee named in the amendment is a secured party of record.

(c) A person remains a secured party of record until the filing of an amendment of the financing statement which deletes the person.

§ 9–512.   Amendment of Financing Statement.

[Alternative A]

(a) Subject to Section 9–509, a person may add or delete collateral covered by, continue or terminate the effectiveness of, or, subject to subsection (e), otherwise amend the information provided in, a financing statement by filing an amendment that:

(1) identifies, by its file number, the initial financing statement to which the amendment relates; and

(2) if the amendment relates to an initial financing statement filed [or recorded] in a filing office described in Section 9–501(a)(1), provides the information specified in Section 9–502(b).

[Alternative B]

(a) Subject to Section 9–509, a person may add or delete collateral covered by, continue or terminate the effectiveness of, or, subject to subsection (e), otherwise amend the information provided in, a financing statement by filing an amendment that:

(1) identifies, by its file number, the initial financing statement to which the amendment relates; and

(2) if the amendment relates to an initial financing statement filed [or recorded] in a filing office described in Section 9–501(a)(1), provides the date [and time] that the initial financing statement was filed [or recorded] and the information specified in Section 9–502(b).

[End of Alternatives]

(b) Except as otherwise provided in Section 9–515, the filing of an amendment does not extend the period of effectiveness of the financing statement.

(c) A financing statement that is amended by an amendment that adds collateral is effective as to the added collateral only from the date of the filing of the amendment.

(d) A financing statement that is amended by an amendment that adds a debtor is effective as to the added debtor only from the date of the filing of the amendment.

(e) An amendment is ineffective to the extent it:

(1) purports to delete all debtors and fails to provide the name of a debtor to be covered by the financing statement; or

(2) purports to delete all secured parties of record and fails to provide the name of a new secured party of record.

Legislative Note: States whose real-estate filing offices require additional information in amendments and cannot search their records by both the name of the debtor and the file number should enact Alternative B to Sections 9–512(a), 9–518(b), 9–519(f), and 9–522(a).

§ 9–513.   Termination Statement.

(a) A secured party shall cause the secured party of record for a financing statement to file a termination statement for the financing statement if the financing statement covers consumer goods and:

(1) there is no obligation secured by the collateral covered by the financing statement and no commitment to make an advance, incur an obligation, or otherwise give value; or

(2) the debtor did not authorize the filing of the initial financing statement.

(b) To comply with subsection (a), a secured party shall cause the secured party of record to file the termination statement:

(1) within one month after there is no obligation secured by the collateral covered by the financing statement and no commitment to make an advance, incur an obligation, or otherwise give value; or

(2) if earlier, within 20 days after the secured party receives an authenticated demand from a debtor.

(c) In cases not governed by subsection (a), within 20 days after a secured party receives an authenticated demand from a debtor, the secured party shall cause the secured party of record for a financing statement to send to the debtor a termination statement for the financing statement or file the termination statement in the filing office if:

(1) except in the case of a financing statement covering accounts or chattel paper that has been sold or goods that are the subject of a consignment, there is no obligation secured by the collateral covered by the financing statement and no commitment to make an advance, incur an obligation, or otherwise give value;

(2) the financing statement covers accounts or chattel paper that has been sold but as to which the account debtor or other person obligated has discharged its obligation;

(3) the financing statement covers goods that were the subject of a consignment to the debtor but are not in the debtor's possession; or

(4) the debtor did not authorize the filing of the initial financing statement.

(d) Except as otherwise provided in Section 9–510, upon the filing of a termination statement with the filing office, the financing statement to which the termination statement relates ceases to be effective. Except as otherwise provided in Section 9–510, for purposes of Sections 9–519(g), 9–522(a), and 9–523(c), the filing with the filing office of a termination statement relating to a financing statement that indicates that the debtor is a transmitting utility also causes the effectiveness of the financing statement to lapse.
As amended in 2000.

§ 9–514.   Assignment of Powers of Secured Party of Record.

(a) Except as otherwise provided in subsection (c), an initial financing statement may reflect an assignment of all of the secured party's power to authorize an amendment to the financing statement by providing the name and mailing address of the assignee as the name and address of the secured party.

(b) Except as otherwise provided in subsection (c), a secured party of record may assign of record all or part of its power to authorize an amendment to a financing statement by filing in the filing office an amendment of the financing statement which:

(1) identifies, by its file number, the initial financing statement to which it relates;

(2) provides the name of the assignor; and

(3) provides the name and mailing address of the assignee.

(c) An assignment of record of a security interest in a fixture covered by a record of a mortgage which is effective as a financing statement filed as a fixture filing under Section 9–502(c) may be made only by an assignment of record of the mortgage in the manner provided by law of this State other than [the Uniform Commercial Code].

§ 9–515.   Duration and Effectiveness of Financing Statement; Effect of Lapsed Financing Statement.

(a) Except as otherwise provided in subsections (b), (e), (f), and (g), a filed financing statement is effective for a period of five years after the date of filing.

(b) Except as otherwise provided in subsections (e), (f), and (g), an initial financing statement filed in connection with a public-finance transaction or manufactured-home transaction is effective for a period of 30 years after the date of filing if it indicates that it is filed in connection with a public-finance transaction or manufactured-home transaction.

(c) The effectiveness of a filed financing statement lapses on the expiration of the period of its effectiveness unless before the lapse a continuation statement is filed pursuant to subsection (d). Upon lapse, a financing statement ceases to be effective and any security interest or agricultural lien that was perfected by the financing statement becomes unperfected, unless the security interest is perfected otherwise. If the security interest or agricultural lien becomes unperfected upon lapse, it is deemed never to have been perfected as against a purchaser of the collateral for value.

(d) A continuation statement may be filed only within six months before the expiration of the five-year period specified in subsection

(a) or the 30-year period specified in subsection (b), whichever is applicable.

(e) Except as otherwise provided in Section 9–510, upon timely filing of a continuation statement, the effectiveness of the initial financing statement continues for a period of five years commencing on the day on which the financing statement would have become ineffective in the absence of the filing. Upon the expiration of the five-year period, the financing statement lapses in the same manner as provided in subsection (c), unless, before the lapse, another continuation statement is filed pursuant to subsection (d). Succeeding continuation statements may be filed in the same manner to continue the effectiveness of the initial financing statement.

(f) If a debtor is a transmitting utility and a filed financing statement so indicates, the financing statement is effective until a termination statement is filed.

(g) A record of a mortgage that is effective as a financing statement filed as a fixture filing under Section 9–502(c) remains effective as a financing statement filed as a fixture filing until the mortgage is released or satisfied of record or its effectiveness otherwise terminates as to the real property.

§ 9–516.   What Constitutes Filing; Effectiveness of Filing.

(a) Except as otherwise provided in subsection (b), communication of a record to a filing office and tender of the filing fee or acceptance of the record by the filing office constitutes filing.

(b) Filing does not occur with respect to a record that a filing office refuses to accept because:

(1) the record is not communicated by a method or medium of communication authorized by the filing office;

(2) an amount equal to or greater than the applicable filing fee is not tendered;

(3) the filing office is unable to index the record because:

(A) in the case of an initial financing statement, the record does not provide a name for the debtor;

(B) in the case of an amendment or correction statement, the record:

(i) does not identify the initial financing statement as required by Section 9–512 or 9–518, as applicable; or

(ii) identifies an initial financing statement whose effectiveness has lapsed under Section 9–515;

(C) in the case of an initial financing statement that provides the name of a debtor identified as an individual or an amendment that provides a name of a debtor identified as an individual which was not previously provided in the financing statement to which the record relates, the record does not identify the debtor's last name; or

(D) in the case of a record filed [or recorded] in the filing office described in Section 9–501(a)(1), the record does not provide a sufficient description of the real property to which it relates;

(4) in the case of an initial financing statement or an amendment that adds a secured party of record, the record does not provide a name and mailing address for the secured party of record;

(5) in the case of an initial financing statement or an amendment that provides a name of a debtor which was not previously provided in the financing statement to which the amendment relates, the record does not:

(A) provide a mailing address for the debtor;

(B) indicate whether the debtor is an individual or an organization; or

(C) if the financing statement indicates that the debtor is an organization, provide:

(i) a type of organization for the debtor;

(ii) a jurisdiction of organization for the debtor; or

(iii) an organizational identification number for the debtor or indicate that the debtor has none;

(6) in the case of an assignment reflected in an initial financing statement under Section 9–514(a) or an amendment filed under Section 9–514(b), the record does not provide a name and mailing address for the assignee; or

(7) in the case of a continuation statement, the record is not filed within the six-month period prescribed by Section 9–515(d).

(c) For purposes of subsection (b):

(1) a record does not provide information if the filing office is unable to read or decipher the information; and

(2) a record that does not indicate that it is an amendment or identify an initial financing statement to which it relates, as required by Section 9–512, 9–514, or 9–518, is an initial financing statement.

(d) A record that is communicated to the filing office with tender of the filing fee, but which the filing office refuses to accept for a reason other than one set forth in subsection (b), is effective as a filed record except as against a purchaser of the collateral which gives value in reasonable reliance upon the absence of the record from the files.

§ 9–517.   Effect of Indexing Errors.

The failure of the filing office to index a record correctly does not affect the effectiveness of the filed record.

§ 9–518.   Claim Concerning Inaccurate or Wrongfully Filed Record.

(a) A person may file in the filing office a correction statement with respect to a record indexed there under the person's name if the person believes that the record is inaccurate or was wrongfully filed.

[Alternative A]

(b) A correction statement must:

(1) identify the record to which it relates by the file number assigned to the initial financing statement to which the record relates;

(2) indicate that it is a correction statement; and

(3) provide the basis for the person's belief that the record is inaccurate and indicate the manner in which the person believes the record should be amended to cure any inaccuracy or provide the basis for the person's belief that the record was wrongfully filed.

[Alternative B]

(b) A correction statement must:

(1) identify the record to which it relates by:

(A) the file number assigned to the initial financing statement to which the record relates; and

(B) if the correction statement relates to a record filed [or recorded] in a filing office described in Section 9–501(a)(1), the date [and time] that the initial financing statement was filed [or recorded] and the information specified in Section 9–502(b);

(2) indicate that it is a correction statement; and

(3) provide the basis for the person's belief that the record is inaccurate and indicate the manner in which the person believes the record should be amended to cure any inaccuracy or provide the basis for the person's belief that the record was wrongfully filed.

[End of Alternatives]

(c) The filing of a correction statement does not affect the effectiveness of an initial financing statement or other filed record.

Legislative Note: States whose real-estate filing offices require additional information in amendments and cannot search their records by both the name of the debtor and the file number should enact Alternative B to Sections 9–512(a), 9–518(b), 9–519(f), and 9–522(a).

[Subpart 2.   Duties and Operation of Filing Office]

§ 9–519.   Numbering, Maintaining, and Indexing Records; Communicating Information Provided in Records.

(a) For each record filed in a filing office, the filing office shall:

(1) assign a unique number to the filed record;

(2) create a record that bears the number assigned to the filed record and the date and time of filing;

(3) maintain the filed record for public inspection; and

(4) index the filed record in accordance with subsections (c), (d), and (e).

(b) A file number [assigned after January 1, 2002,] must include a digit that:

(1) is mathematically derived from or related to the other digits of the file number; and

(2) aids the filing office in determining whether a number communicated as the file number includes a single-digit or transpositional error.

(c) Except as otherwise provided in subsections (d) and (e), the filing office shall:

(1) index an initial financing statement according to the name of the debtor and index all filed records relating to the initial financing statement in a manner that associates with one another an initial financing statement and all filed records relating to the initial financing statement; and

(2) index a record that provides a name of a debtor which was not previously provided in the financing statement to which the record relates also according to the name that was not previously provided.

(d) If a financing statement is filed as a fixture filing or covers as-extracted collateral or timber to be cut, [it must be filed for record and] the filing office shall index it:

(1) under the names of the debtor and of each owner of record shown on the financing statement as if they were the mortgagors under a mortgage of the real property described; and

(2) to the extent that the law of this State provides for indexing of records of mortgages under the name of the mortgagee, under the name of the secured party as if the secured party were the mortgagee thereunder, or, if indexing is by description, as if the financing statement were a record of a mortgage of the real property described.

(e) If a financing statement is filed as a fixture filing or covers as-extracted collateral or timber to be cut, the filing office shall index an assignment filed under Section 9–514(a) or an amendment filed under Section 9–514(b):

(1) under the name of the assignor as grantor; and

(2) to the extent that the law of this State provides for indexing a record of the assignment of a mortgage under the name of the assignee, under the name of the assignee.

[Alternative A]

(f) The filing office shall maintain a capability:

(1) to retrieve a record by the name of the debtor and by the file number assigned to the initial financing statement to which the record relates; and

(2) to associate and retrieve with one another an initial financing statement and each filed record relating to the initial financing statement.

[Alternative B]

(f) The filing office shall maintain a capability:

(1) to retrieve a record by the name of the debtor and:

(A) if the filing office is described in Section 9–501(a)(1), by the file number assigned to the initial financing statement to which the record relates and the date [and time] that the record was filed [or recorded]; or

(B) if the filing office is described in Section 9–501(a)(2), by the file number assigned to the initial financing statement to which the record relates; and

(2) to associate and retrieve with one another an initial financing statement and each filed record relating to the initial financing statement.

[End of Alternatives]

(g) The filing office may not remove a debtor's name from the index until one year after the effectiveness of a financing statement naming the debtor lapses under Section 9–515 with respect to all secured parties of record.

(h) The filing office shall perform the acts required by subsections (a) through (e) at the time and in the manner prescribed by filing-office rule, but not later than two business days after the filing office receives the record in question.

[(i) Subsection[s] [(b)] [and] [(h)] do[es] not apply to a filing office described in Section 9–501(a)(1).]

Legislative Notes:

1. States whose filing offices currently assign file numbers that include a verification number, commonly known as a "check digit," or can implement this requirement before the effective date of this Article should omit the bracketed language in subsection (b).

2. In States in which writings will not appear in the real property records and indices unless actually recorded the bracketed language in subsection (d) should be used.

3. States whose real-estate filing offices require additional information in amendments and cannot search their records by both the name of the debtor and the file number should enact Alternative B to Sections 9–512(a), 9–518(b), 9–519(f), and 9–522(a).

4. A State that elects not to require real-estate filing offices to comply with either or both of subsections (b) and (h) may adopt an applicable variation of subsection (i) and add "Except as otherwise provided in subsection (i)," to the appropriate subsection or subsections.

§ 9–520.   Acceptance and Refusal to Accept Record.

(a) A filing office shall refuse to accept a record for filing for a reason set forth in Section 9–516(b) and may refuse to accept a record for filing only for a reason set forth in Section 9–516(b).

(b) If a filing office refuses to accept a record for filing, it shall communicate to the person that presented the record the fact of and reason for the refusal and the date and time the record would have been filed had the filing office accepted it. The communication must be made at the time and in the manner prescribed by filing-office rule but [, in the case of a filing office described in Section 9–501(a)(2),] in no event more than two business days after the filing office receives the record.

(c) A filed financing statement satisfying Section 9–502(a) and (b) is effective, even if the filing office is required to refuse to accept it for filing under subsection (a). However, Section 9–338 applies to a filed financing statement providing information described in Section 9–516(b)(5) which is incorrect at the time the financing statement is filed.

(d) If a record communicated to a filing office provides information that relates to more than one debtor, this part applies as to each debtor separately.

Legislative Note: A State that elects not to require real-property filing offices to comply with subsection (b) should include the bracketed language.

§ 9–521.   Uniform Form of Written Financing Statement and Amendment.

(a) A filing office that accepts written records may not refuse to accept a written initial financing statement in the following form and format except for a reason set forth in Section 9–516(b):

[NATIONAL UCC FINANCING STATEMENT (FORM UCC1) (REV. 7/29/98)]

[NATIONAL UCC FINANCING STATEMENT ADDENDUM (FORM UCC1Ad) (REV. 07/29/98)]

(b) A filing office that accepts written records may not refuse to accept a written record in the following form and format except for a reason set forth in Section 9–516(b):

[NATIONAL UCC FINANCING STATEMENT AMENDMENT (FORM UCC3) (REV. 07/29/98)]

[NATIONAL UCC FINANCING STATEMENT AMENDMENT ADDENDUM (FORM UCC3Ad) (REV. 07/29/98)]

§ 9–522.   Maintenance and Destruction of Records.

[Alternative A]

(a) The filing office shall maintain a record of the information provided in a filed financing statement for at least one year after the effectiveness of the financing statement has lapsed under Section 9–515 with respect to all secured parties of record. The record must be retrievable by using the name of the debtor and by using the file number assigned to the initial financing statement to which the record relates.

[Alternative B]

(a) The filing office shall maintain a record of the information provided in a filed financing statement for at least one year after the effectiveness of the financing statement has lapsed under Section 9–515 with respect to all secured parties of record. The record must be retrievable by using the name of the debtor and:

(1) if the record was filed [or recorded] in the filing office described in Section 9–501(a)(1), by using the file number assigned to the initial financing statement to which the record relates and the date [and time] that the record was filed [or recorded]; or

(2) if the record was filed in the filing office described in Section 9–501(a)(2), by using the file number assigned to the initial financing statement to which the record relates.

[End of Alternatives]

(b) Except to the extent that a statute governing disposition of public records provides otherwise, the filing office immediately may destroy any written record evidencing a financing statement. However, if the filing office destroys a written record, it shall maintain another record of the financing statement which complies with subsection (a).

Legislative Note: States whose real-estate filing offices require additional information in amendments and cannot search their records by both the name of the debtor and the file number should enact Alternative B to Sections 9–512(a), 9–518(b), 9–519(f), and 9–522(a).

§ 9–523.   Information from Filing Office; Sale or License of Records.

(a) If a person that files a written record requests an acknowledgment of the filing, the filing office shall send to the person an image of the record showing the number assigned to the record pursuant to Section 9–519(a)(1) and the date and time of the filing of the record. However, if the person furnishes a copy of the record to the filing office, the filing office may instead:

(1) note upon the copy the number assigned to the record pursuant to Section 9–519(a)(1) and the date and time of the filing of the record; and

(2) send the copy to the person.

(b) If a person files a record other than a written record, the filing office shall communicate to the person an acknowledgment that provides:

(1) the information in the record;

(2) the number assigned to the record pursuant to Section 9–519(a)(1); and

(3) the date and time of the filing of the record.

(c) The filing office shall communicate or otherwise make available in a record the following information to any person that requests it:

(1) whether there is on file on a date and time specified by the filing office, but not a date earlier than three business days before the filing office receives the request, any financing statement that:

(A) designates a particular debtor [or, if the request so states, designates a particular debtor at the address specified in the request];

(B) has not lapsed under Section 9–515 with respect to all secured parties of record; and

(C) if the request so states, has lapsed under Section 9–515 and a record of which is maintained by the filing office under Section 9–522(a);

(2) the date and time of filing of each financing statement; and

(3) the information provided in each financing statement.

(d) In complying with its duty under subsection (c), the filing office may communicate information in any medium. However, if requested, the filing office shall communicate information by issuing [its written certificate] [a record that can be admitted into evidence in the courts of this State without extrinsic evidence of its authenticity].

(e) The filing office shall perform the acts required by subsections (a) through (d) at the time and in the manner prescribed by filing-office rule, but not later than two business days after the filing office receives the request.

(f) At least weekly, the [insert appropriate official or governmental agency] [filing office] shall offer to sell or license to the public on a nonexclusive basis, in bulk, copies of all records filed in it under this part, in every medium from time to time available to the filing office.

Legislative Notes:

1. States whose filing office does not offer the additional service of responding to search requests limited to a particular address should omit the bracketed language in subsection (c)(1)(A).

2. A State that elects not to require real-estate filing offices to comply with either or both of subsections (e) and (f) should specify in the appropriate subsection(s) only the filing office described in Section 9–501(a)(2).

§ 9–524.   Delay by Filing Office.

Delay by the filing office beyond a time limit prescribed by this part is excused if:

(1) the delay is caused by interruption of communication or computer facilities, war, emergency conditions, failure of equipment, or other circumstances beyond control of the filing office; and

(2) the filing office exercises reasonable diligence under the circumstances.

§ 9–525.   Fees.

(a) Except as otherwise provided in subsection (e), the fee for filing and indexing a record under this part, other than an initial financing statement of the kind described in subsection (b), is [the amount specified in subsection (c), if applicable, plus]:

(1) $[X] if the record is communicated in writing and consists of one or two pages;

(2) $[2X] if the record is communicated in writing and consists of more than two pages; and

(3) $[½X] if the record is communicated by another medium authorized by filing-office rule.

(b) Except as otherwise provided in subsection (e), the fee for filing and indexing an initial financing statement of the following kind is [the amount specified in subsection (c), if applicable, plus]:

(1) $_____ if the financing statement indicates that it is filed in connection with a public-finance transaction;

(2) $_____ if the financing statement indicates that it is filed in connection with a manufactured-home transaction.

[Alternative A]

(c) The number of names required to be indexed does not affect the amount of the fee in subsections (a) and (b).

[Alternative B]

(c) Except as otherwise provided in subsection (e), if a record is communicated in writing, the fee for each name more than two required to be indexed is $_____.

[End of Alternatives]

(d) The fee for responding to a request for information from the filing office, including for [issuing a certificate showing] [communicating] whether there is on file any financing statement naming a particular debtor, is:

(1) $_____ if the request is communicated in writing; and

(2) $_____ if the request is communicated by another medium authorized by filing-office rule.

(e) This section does not require a fee with respect to a record of a mortgage which is effective as a financing statement filed as a fixture filing or as a financing statement covering as-extracted collateral or timber to be cut under Section 9–502(c). However, the recording and satisfaction fees that otherwise would be applicable to the record of the mortgage apply.

Legislative Notes:

1. To preserve uniformity, a State that places the provisions of this section together with statutes setting fees for other services should do so without modification.

2. A State should enact subsection (c), Alternative A, and omit the bracketed language in subsections (a) and (b) unless its indexing system entails a substantial additional cost when indexing additional names.

As amended in 2000.

§ 9–526. Filing-Office Rules.

(a) The [insert appropriate governmental official or agency] shall adopt and publish rules to implement this article. The filing-office rules must be[:

(1)] consistent with this article[; and

(2) adopted and published in accordance with the [insert any applicable state administrative procedure act]].

(b) To keep the filing-office rules and practices of the filing office in harmony with the rules and practices of filing offices in other jurisdictions that enact substantially this part, and to keep the technology used by the filing office compatible with the technology used by filing offices in other jurisdictions that enact substantially this part, the [insert appropriate governmental official or agency], so far as is consistent with the purposes, policies, and provisions of this article, in adopting, amending, and repealing filing-office rules, shall:

(1) consult with filing offices in other jurisdictions that enact substantially this part; and

(2) consult the most recent version of the Model Rules promulgated by the International Association of Corporate Administrators or any successor organization; and

(3) take into consideration the rules and practices of, and the technology used by, filing offices in other jurisdictions that enact substantially this part.

§ 9–527. Duty to Report.

The [insert appropriate governmental official or agency] shall report [annually on or before _____] to the [Governor and Legislature] on the operation of the filing office. The report must contain a statement of the extent to which:

(1) the filing-office rules are not in harmony with the rules of filing offices in other jurisdictions that enact substantially this part and the reasons for these variations; and

(2) the filing-office rules are not in harmony with the most recent version of the Model Rules promulgated by the International Association of Corporate Administrators, or any successor organization, and the reasons for these variations.

Part 6   Default

[Subpart 1.   Default and Enforcement of Security Interest]

§ 9–601.   Rights after Default; Judicial Enforcement; Consignor or Buyer of Accounts, Chattel Paper, Payment Intangibles, or Promissory Notes.

(a) After default, a secured party has the rights provided in this part and, except as otherwise provided in Section 9–602, those provided by agreement of the parties. A secured party:

(1) may reduce a claim to judgment, foreclose, or otherwise enforce the claim, security interest, or agricultural lien by any available judicial procedure; and

(2) if the collateral is documents, may proceed either as to the documents or as to the goods they cover.

(b) A secured party in possession of collateral or control of collateral under Section 9–104, 9–105, 9–106, or 9–107 has the rights and duties provided in Section 9–207.

(c) The rights under subsections (a) and (b) are cumulative and may be exercised simultaneously.

(d) Except as otherwise provided in subsection (g) and Section 9–605, after default, a debtor and an obligor have the rights provided in this part and by agreement of the parties.

(e) If a secured party has reduced its claim to judgment, the lien of any levy that may be made upon the collateral by virtue of an execution based upon the judgment relates back to the earliest of:

(1) the date of perfection of the security interest or agricultural lien in the collateral;

(2) the date of filing a financing statement covering the collateral; or

(3) any date specified in a statute under which the agricultural lien was created.

(f) A sale pursuant to an execution is a foreclosure of the security interest or agricultural lien by judicial procedure within the meaning of this section. A secured party may purchase at the sale and thereafter hold the collateral free of any other requirements of this article.

(g) Except as otherwise provided in Section 9–607(c), this part imposes no duties upon a secured party that is a consignor or is a buyer of accounts, chattel paper, payment intangibles, or promissory notes.

§ 9–602.   Waiver and Variance of Rights and Duties.

Except as otherwise provided in Section 9–624, to the extent that they give rights to a debtor or obligor and impose duties on a secured party, the debtor or obligor may not waive or vary the rules stated in the following listed sections:

(1) Section 9–207(b)(4)(C), which deals with use and operation of the collateral by the secured party;

(2) Section 9–210, which deals with requests for an accounting and requests concerning a list of collateral and statement of account;

(3) Section 9–607(c), which deals with collection and enforcement of collateral;

(4) Sections 9–608(a) and 9–615(c) to the extent that they deal with application or payment of noncash proceeds of collection, enforcement, or disposition;

(5) Sections 9–608(a) and 9–615(d) to the extent that they require accounting for or payment of surplus proceeds of collateral;

(6) Section 9–609 to the extent that it imposes upon a secured party that takes possession of collateral without judicial process the duty to do so without breach of the peace;

(7) Sections 9–610(b), 9–611, 9–613, and 9–614, which deal with disposition of collateral;

(8) Section 9–615(f), which deals with calculation of a deficiency or surplus when a disposition is made to the secured party, a person related to the secured party, or a secondary obligor;

(9) Section 9–616, which deals with explanation of the calculation of a surplus or deficiency;

(10) Sections 9–620, 9–621, and 9–622, which deal with acceptance of collateral in satisfaction of obligation;

(11) Section 9–623, which deals with redemption of collateral;

(12) Section 9–624, which deals with permissible waivers; and

(13) Sections 9–625 and 9–626, which deal with the secured party's liability for failure to comply with this article.

§ 9–603.   Agreement on Standards Concerning Rights and Duties.

(a) The parties may determine by agreement the standards measuring the fulfillment of the rights of a debtor or obligor and the duties of a secured party under a rule stated in Section 9–602 if the standards are not manifestly unreasonable.

(b) Subsection (a) does not apply to the duty under Section 9–609 to refrain from breaching the peace.

§ 9–604.   Procedure If Security Agreement Covers Real Property or Fixtures.

(a) If a security agreement covers both personal and real property, a secured party may proceed:

(1) under this part as to the personal property without prejudicing any rights with respect to the real property; or

(2) as to both the personal property and the real property in accordance with the rights with respect to the real property, in which case the other provisions of this part do not apply.

(b) Subject to subsection (c), if a security agreement covers goods that are or become fixtures, a secured party may proceed:

(1) under this part; or

(2) in accordance with the rights with respect to real property, in which case the other provisions of this part do not apply.

(c) Subject to the other provisions of this part, if a secured party holding a security interest in fixtures has priority over all owners and encumbrancers of the real property, the secured party, after default, may remove the collateral from the real property.

(d) A secured party that removes collateral shall promptly reimburse any encumbrancer or owner of the real property, other than the debtor, for the cost of repair of any physical injury caused by the removal. The secured party need not reimburse the encumbrancer or owner for any diminution in value of the real property caused by the absence of the goods removed or by any necessity of replacing them. A person entitled to reimbursement may refuse permission to remove until the secured party gives adequate assurance for the performance of the obligation to reimburse.

§ 9–605.   Unknown Debtor or Secondary Obligor.

A secured party does not owe a duty based on its status as secured party:

(1) to a person that is a debtor or obligor, unless the secured party knows:

(A) that the person is a debtor or obligor;

(B) the identity of the person; and

(C) how to communicate with the person; or

(2) to a secured party or lienholder that has filed a financing statement against a person, unless the secured party knows:

(A) that the person is a debtor; and

(B) the identity of the person.

§ 9–606.   Time of Default for Agricultural Lien.

For purposes of this part, a default occurs in connection with an agricultural lien at the time the secured party becomes entitled to enforce the lien in accordance with the statute under which it was created.

§ 9–607.   Collection and Enforcement by Secured Party.

(a) If so agreed, and in any event after default, a secured party:

(1) may notify an account debtor or other person obligated on collateral to make payment or otherwise render performance to or for the benefit of the secured party;

(2) may take any proceeds to which the secured party is entitled under Section 9–315;

(3) may enforce the obligations of an account debtor or other person obligated on collateral and exercise the rights of the debtor with respect to the obligation of the account debtor or other person obligated on collateral to make payment or otherwise render performance to the debtor, and with respect to any property that secures the obligations of the account debtor or other person obligated on the collateral;

(4) if it holds a security interest in a deposit account perfected by control under Section 9–104(a)(1), may apply the balance of the deposit account to the obligation secured by the deposit account; and

(5) if it holds a security interest in a deposit account perfected by control under Section 9–104(a)(2) or (3), may instruct the bank to pay the balance of the deposit account to or for the benefit of the secured party.

(b) If necessary to enable a secured party to exercise under subsection (a)(3) the right of a debtor to enforce a mortgage nonjudicially, the secured party may record in the office in which a record of the mortgage is recorded:

(1) a copy of the security agreement that creates or provides for a security interest in the obligation secured by the mortgage; and

(2) the secured party's sworn affidavit in recordable form stating that:

(A) a default has occurred; and

(B) the secured party is entitled to enforce the mortgage nonjudicially.

(c) A secured party shall proceed in a commercially reasonable manner if the secured party:

(1) undertakes to collect from or enforce an obligation of an account debtor or other person obligated on collateral; and

(2) is entitled to charge back uncollected collateral or otherwise to full or limited recourse against the debtor or a secondary obligor.

(d) A secured party may deduct from the collections made pursuant to subsection (c) reasonable expenses of collection and enforcement, including reasonable attorney's fees and legal expenses incurred by the secured party.

(e) This section does not determine whether an account debtor, bank, or other person obligated on collateral owes a duty to a secured party.

As amended in 2000.

§ 9–608. Application of Proceeds of Collection or Enforcement; Liability for Deficiency and Right to Surplus.

(a) If a security interest or agricultural lien secures payment or performance of an obligation, the following rules apply:

(1) A secured party shall apply or pay over for application the cash proceeds of collection or enforcement under Section 9–607 in the following order to:

(A) the reasonable expenses of collection and enforcement and, to the extent provided for by agreement and not prohibited by law, reasonable attorney's fees and legal expenses incurred by the secured party;

(B) the satisfaction of obligations secured by the security interest or agricultural lien under which the collection or enforcement is made; and

(C) the satisfaction of obligations secured by any subordinate security interest in or other lien on the collateral subject to the security interest or agricultural lien under which the collection or enforcement is made if the secured party receives an authenticated demand for proceeds before distribution of the proceeds is completed.

(2) If requested by a secured party, a holder of a subordinate security interest or other lien shall furnish reasonable proof of the interest or lien within a reasonable time. Unless the holder complies, the secured party need not comply with the holder's demand under paragraph (1)(C).

(3) A secured party need not apply or pay over for application noncash proceeds of collection and enforcement under Section 9–607 unless the failure to do so would be commercially unreasonable. A secured party that applies or pays over for application noncash proceeds shall do so in a commercially reasonable manner.

(4) A secured party shall account to and pay a debtor for any surplus, and the obligor is liable for any deficiency.

(b) If the underlying transaction is a sale of accounts, chattel paper, payment intangibles, or promissory notes, the debtor is not entitled to any surplus, and the obligor is not liable for any deficiency.

As amended in 2000.

§ 9–609. Secured Party's Right to Take Possession after Default.

(a) After default, a secured party:

(1) may take possession of the collateral; and

(2) without removal, may render equipment unusable and dispose of collateral on a debtor's premises under Section 9–610.

(b) A secured party may proceed under subsection (a):

(1) pursuant to judicial process; or

(2) without judicial process, if it proceeds without breach of the peace.

(c) If so agreed, and in any event after default, a secured party may require the debtor to assemble the collateral and make it available to the secured party at a place to be designated by the secured party which is reasonably convenient to both parties.

§ 9–610. Disposition of Collateral after Default.

(a) After default, a secured party may sell, lease, license, or otherwise dispose of any or all of the collateral in its present condition or following any commercially reasonable preparation or processing.

(b) Every aspect of a disposition of collateral, including the method, manner, time, place, and other terms, must be commercially reasonable. If commercially reasonable, a secured party may dispose of collateral by public or private proceedings, by one or more contracts, as a unit or in parcels, and at any time and place and on any terms.

(c) A secured party may purchase collateral:

(1) at a public disposition; or

(2) at a private disposition only if the collateral is of a kind that is customarily sold on a recognized market or the subject of widely distributed standard price quotations.

(d) A contract for sale, lease, license, or other disposition includes the warranties relating to title, possession, quiet enjoyment, and the like which by operation of law accompany a voluntary disposition of property of the kind subject to the contract.

(e) A secured party may disclaim or modify warranties under subsection (d):

(1) in a manner that would be effective to disclaim or modify the warranties in a voluntary disposition of property of the kind subject to the contract of disposition; or

(2) by communicating to the purchaser a record evidencing the contract for disposition and including an express disclaimer or modification of the warranties.

(f) A record is sufficient to disclaim warranties under subsection (e) if it indicates "There is no warranty relating to title, possession, quiet enjoyment, or the like in this disposition" or uses words of similar import.

§ 9–611. Notification before Disposition of Collateral.

(a) In this section, "notification date" means the earlier of the date on which:

(1) a secured party sends to the debtor and any secondary obligor an authenticated notification of disposition; or

(2) the debtor and any secondary obligor waive the right to notification.

(b) Except as otherwise provided in subsection (d), a secured party that disposes of collateral under Section 9–610 shall send to the persons specified in subsection (c) a reasonable authenticated notification of disposition.

(c) To comply with subsection (b), the secured party shall send an authenticated notification of disposition to:

(1) the debtor;

(2) any secondary obligor; and

(3) if the collateral is other than consumer goods:

(A) any other person from which the secured party has received, before the notification date, an authenticated notification of a claim of an interest in the collateral;

(B) any other secured party or lienholder that, 10 days before the notification date, held a security interest in or other lien on the collateral perfected by the filing of a financing statement that:

(i) identified the collateral;

(ii) was indexed under the debtor's name as of that date; and

(iii) was filed in the office in which to file a financing statement against the debtor covering the collateral as of that date; and

(C) any other secured party that, 10 days before the notification date, held a security interest in the collateral perfected by compliance with a statute, regulation, or treaty described in Section 9–311(a).

(d) Subsection (b) does not apply if the collateral is perishable or threatens to decline speedily in value or is of a type customarily sold on a recognized market.

(e) A secured party complies with the requirement for notification prescribed by subsection (c)(3)(B) if:

(1) not later than 20 days or earlier than 30 days before the notification date, the secured party requests, in a commercially reasonable manner, information concerning financing statements indexed under the debtor's name in the office indicated in subsection (c)(3)(B); and

(2) before the notification date, the secured party:

(A) did not receive a response to the request for information; or

(B) received a response to the request for information and sent an authenticated notification of disposition to each secured party or other lienholder named in that response whose financing statement covered the collateral.

§ 9–612.   Timeliness of Notification before Disposition of Collateral.

(a) Except as otherwise provided in subsection (b), whether a notification is sent within a reasonable time is a question of fact.

(b) In a transaction other than a consumer transaction, a notification of disposition sent after default and 10 days or more before the earliest time of disposition set forth in the notification is sent within a reasonable time before the disposition.

§ 9–613.   Contents and Form of Notification before Disposition of Collateral: General.

Except in a consumer-goods transaction, the following rules apply:

(1) The contents of a notification of disposition are sufficient if the notification:

(A) describes the debtor and the secured party;

(B) describes the collateral that is the subject of the intended disposition;

(C) states the method of intended disposition;

(D) states that the debtor is entitled to an accounting of the unpaid indebtedness and states the charge, if any, for an accounting; and

(E) states the time and place of a public disposition or the time after which any other disposition is to be made.

(2) Whether the contents of a notification that lacks any of the information specified in paragraph (1) are nevertheless sufficient is a question of fact.

(3) The contents of a notification providing substantially the information specified in paragraph (1) are sufficient, even if the notification includes:

(A) information not specified by that paragraph; or

(B) minor errors that are not seriously misleading.

(4) A particular phrasing of the notification is not required.

(5) The following form of notification and the form appearing in Section 9–614(3), when completed, each provides sufficient information:

NOTIFICATION OF DISPOSITION OF COLLATERAL

To: [*Name of debtor, obligor, or other person to which the notification is sent*]

From: [*Name, address, and telephone number of secured party*]

Name of Debtor(s): [*Include only if debtor(s) are not an addressee*]

[*For a public disposition:*]

We will sell [*or lease or license, as applicable*] the [*describe collateral*] [*to the highest qualified bidder*] in public as follows:

Day and Date: _____

Time: _____

Place: _____

[*For a private disposition:*]

We will sell [*or lease or license, as applicable*] the [*describe collateral*] privately sometime after [*day and date*].

You are entitled to an accounting of the unpaid indebtedness secured by the property that we intend to sell [*or lease or license, as applicable*] [for a charge of $_____]. You may request an accounting by calling us at [*telephone number*].

[End of Form]

As amended in 2000.

§ 9–614.   Contents and Form of Notification before Disposition of Collateral: Consumer-Goods Transaction.

In a consumer-goods transaction, the following rules apply:

(1) A notification of disposition must provide the following information:

(A) the information specified in Section 9–613(1);

(B) a description of any liability for a deficiency of the person to which the notification is sent;

(C) a telephone number from which the amount that must be paid to the secured party to redeem the collateral under Section 9–623 is available; and

(D) a telephone number or mailing address from which additional information concerning the disposition and the obligation secured is available.

(2) A particular phrasing of the notification is not required.

(3) The following form of notification, when completed, provides sufficient information:

[*Name and address of secured party*]

[*Date*]

NOTICE OF OUR PLAN TO SELL PROPERTY

[*Name and address of any obligor who is also a debtor*]

Subject: [*Identification of Transaction*]

We have your [*describe collateral*], because you broke promises in our agreement.

[*For a public disposition:*]

We will sell [*describe collateral*] at public sale. A sale could include a lease or license. The sale will be held as follows:

Date: _____

Time: _____

Place: _____

You may attend the sale and bring bidders if you want.

[*For a private disposition:*]

We will sell [*describe collateral*] at private sale sometime after [*date*]. A sale could include a lease or license.

The money that we get from the sale (after paying our costs) will reduce the amount you owe. If we get less money than you owe, you [*will or will not, as applicable*] still owe us the difference. If we get more money than you owe, you will get the extra money, unless we must pay it to someone else.

You can get the property back at any time before we sell it by paying us the full amount you owe (not just the past due payments), including our expenses. To learn the exact amount you must pay, call us at [*telephone number*].

If you want us to explain to you in writing how we have figured the amount that you owe us, you may call us at [telephone number] [or write us at [*secured party's address*]] and request a written explanation. [We will charge you $_____ for the explanation if we sent you another written explanation of the amount you owe us within the last six months.]

If you need more information about the sale call us at [*telephone number*] [or write us at [secured party's address]].

We are sending this notice to the following other people who have an interest in [*describe collateral*] or who owe money under your agreement:

[*Names of all other debtors and obligors, if any*]

[End of Form]

(4) A notification in the form of paragraph (3) is sufficient, even if additional information appears at the end of the form.

(5) A notification in the form of paragraph (3) is sufficient, even if it includes errors in information not required by paragraph (1), unless the error is misleading with respect to rights arising under this article.

(6) If a notification under this section is not in the form of paragraph (3), law other than this article determines the effect of including information not required by paragraph (1).

§ 9–615.   Application of Proceeds of Disposition; Liability for Deficiency and Right to Surplus.

(a) A secured party shall apply or pay over for application the cash proceeds of disposition under Section 9–610 in the following order to:

(1) the reasonable expenses of retaking, holding, preparing for disposition, processing, and disposing, and, to the extent provided for by agreement and not prohibited by law, reasonable attorney's fees and legal expenses incurred by the secured party;

(2) the satisfaction of obligations secured by the security interest or agricultural lien under which the disposition is made;

(3) the satisfaction of obligations secured by any subordinate security interest in or other subordinate lien on the collateral if:

(A) the secured party receives from the holder of the subordinate security interest or other lien an authenticated demand for proceeds before distribution of the proceeds is completed; and

(B) in a case in which a consignor has an interest in the collateral, the subordinate security interest or other lien is senior to the interest of the consignor; and

(4) a secured party that is a consignor of the collateral if the secured party receives from the consignor an authenticated demand for proceeds before distribution of the proceeds is completed.

(b) If requested by a secured party, a holder of a subordinate security interest or other lien shall furnish reasonable proof of the interest or lien within a reasonable time. Unless the holder does so, the secured party need not comply with the holder's demand under subsection (a)(3).

(c) A secured party need not apply or pay over for application noncash proceeds of disposition under Section 9–610 unless the failure to do so would be commercially unreasonable. A secured party that applies or pays over for application noncash proceeds shall do so in a commercially reasonable manner.

(d) If the security interest under which a disposition is made secures payment or performance of an obligation, after making the payments and applications required by subsection (a) and permitted by subsection (c):

(1) unless subsection (a)(4) requires the secured party to apply or pay over cash proceeds to a consignor, the secured party shall account to and pay a debtor for any surplus; and

(2) the obligor is liable for any deficiency.

(e) If the underlying transaction is a sale of accounts, chattel paper, payment intangibles, or promissory notes:

(1) the debtor is not entitled to any surplus; and

(2) the obligor is not liable for any deficiency.

(f) The surplus or deficiency following a disposition is calculated based on the amount of proceeds that would have been realized in a disposition complying with this part to a transferee other than the secured party, a person related to the secured party, or a secondary obligor if:

(1) the transferee in the disposition is the secured party, a person related to the secured party, or a secondary obligor; and

(2) the amount of proceeds of the disposition is significantly below the range of proceeds that a complying disposition to a person other than the secured party, a person related to the secured party, or a secondary obligor would have brought.

(g) A secured party that receives cash proceeds of a disposition in good faith and without knowledge that the receipt violates the rights of the holder of a security interest or other lien that is not subordinate to the security interest or agricultural lien under which the disposition is made:

(1) takes the cash proceeds free of the security interest or other lien;

(2) is not obligated to apply the proceeds of the disposition to the satisfaction of obligations secured by the security interest or other lien; and

(3) is not obligated to account to or pay the holder of the security interest or other lien for any surplus.

As amended in 2000.

§ 9–616. Explanation of Calculation of Surplus or Deficiency.

(a) In this section:

(1) "Explanation" means a writing that:

(A) states the amount of the surplus or deficiency;

(B) provides an explanation in accordance with subsection (c) of how the secured party calculated the surplus or deficiency;

(C) states, if applicable, that future debits, credits, charges, including additional credit service charges or interest, rebates, and expenses may affect the amount of the surplus or deficiency; and

(D) provides a telephone number or mailing address from which additional information concerning the transaction is available.

(2) "Request" means a record:

(A) authenticated by a debtor or consumer obligor;

(B) requesting that the recipient provide an explanation; and

(C) sent after disposition of the collateral under Section 9–610.

(b) In a consumer-goods transaction in which the debtor is entitled to a surplus or a consumer obligor is liable for a deficiency under Section 9–615, the secured party shall:

(1) send an explanation to the debtor or consumer obligor, as applicable, after the disposition and:

(A) before or when the secured party accounts to the debtor and pays any surplus or first makes written demand on the consumer obligor after the disposition for payment of the deficiency; and

(B) within 14 days after receipt of a request; or

(2) in the case of a consumer obligor who is liable for a deficiency, within 14 days after receipt of a request, send to the consumer obligor a record waiving the secured party's right to a deficiency.

(c) To comply with subsection (a)(1)(B), a writing must provide the following information in the following order:

(1) the aggregate amount of obligations secured by the security interest under which the disposition was made, and, if the amount reflects a rebate of unearned interest or credit service charge, an indication of that fact, calculated as of a specified date:

(A) if the secured party takes or receives possession of the collateral after default, not more than 35 days before the secured party takes or receives possession; or

(B) if the secured party takes or receives possession of the collateral before default or does not take possession of the collateral, not more than 35 days before the disposition;

(2) the amount of proceeds of the disposition;

(3) the aggregate amount of the obligations after deducting the amount of proceeds;

(4) the amount, in the aggregate or by type, and types of expenses, including expenses of retaking, holding, preparing for disposition, processing, and disposing of the collateral, and attorney's fees secured by the collateral which are known to the secured party and relate to the current disposition;

(5) the amount, in the aggregate or by type, and types of credits, including rebates of interest or credit service charges, to which the obligor is known to be entitled and which are not reflected in the amount in paragraph (1); and

(6) the amount of the surplus or deficiency.

(d) A particular phrasing of the explanation is not required. An explanation complying substantially with the requirements of subsection (a) is sufficient, even if it includes minor errors that are not seriously misleading.

(e) A debtor or consumer obligor is entitled without charge to one response to a request under this section during any six-month period in which the secured party did not send to the debtor or consumer obligor an explanation pursuant to subsection (b)(1). The secured party may require payment of a charge not exceeding $25 for each additional response.

§ 9–617. Rights of Transferee of Collateral.

(a) A secured party's disposition of collateral after default:

(1) transfers to a transferee for value all of the debtor's rights in the collateral;

(2) discharges the security interest under which the disposition is made; and

(3) discharges any subordinate security interest or other subordinate lien [other than liens created under [cite acts

or statutes providing for liens, if any, that are not to be discharged]].

(b) A transferee that acts in good faith takes free of the rights and interests described in subsection (a), even if the secured party fails to comply with this article or the requirements of any judicial proceeding.

(c) If a transferee does not take free of the rights and interests described in subsection (a), the transferee takes the collateral subject to:

(1) the debtor's rights in the collateral;

(2) the security interest or agricultural lien under which the disposition is made; and

(3) any other security interest or other lien.

§ 9–618.   Rights and Duties of Certain Secondary Obligors.

(a) A secondary obligor acquires the rights and becomes obligated to perform the duties of the secured party after the secondary obligor:

(1) receives an assignment of a secured obligation from the secured party;

(2) receives a transfer of collateral from the secured party and agrees to accept the rights and assume the duties of the secured party; or

(3) is subrogated to the rights of a secured party with respect to collateral.

(b) An assignment, transfer, or subrogation described in subsection (a):

(1) is not a disposition of collateral under Section 9–610; and

(2) relieves the secured party of further duties under this article.

§ 9–619.   Transfer of Record or Legal Title.

(a) In this section, "transfer statement" means a record authenticated by a secured party stating:

(1) that the debtor has defaulted in connection with an obligation secured by specified collateral;

(2) that the secured party has exercised its post-default remedies with respect to the collateral;

(3) that, by reason of the exercise, a transferee has acquired the rights of the debtor in the collateral; and

(4) the name and mailing address of the secured party, debtor, and transferee.

(b) A transfer statement entitles the transferee to the transfer of record of all rights of the debtor in the collateral specified in the statement in any official filing, recording, registration, or certificate-of-title system covering the collateral. If a transfer statement is presented with the applicable fee and request form to the official or office responsible for maintaining the system, the official or office shall:

(1) accept the transfer statement;

(2) promptly amend its records to reflect the transfer; and

(3) if applicable, issue a new appropriate certificate of title in the name of the transferee.

(c) A transfer of the record or legal title to collateral to a secured party under subsection (b) or otherwise is not of itself a disposition of collateral under this article and does not of itself relieve the secured party of its duties under this article.

§ 9–620.   Acceptance of Collateral in Full or Partial Satisfaction of Obligation; Compulsory Disposition of Collateral.

(a) Except as otherwise provided in subsection (g), a secured party may accept collateral in full or partial satisfaction of the obligation it secures only if:

(1) the debtor consents to the acceptance under subsection (c);

(2) the secured party does not receive, within the time set forth in subsection (d), a notification of objection to the proposal authenticated by:

(A) a person to which the secured party was required to send a proposal under Section 9–621; or

(B) any other person, other than the debtor, holding an interest in the collateral subordinate to the security interest that is the subject of the proposal;

(3) if the collateral is consumer goods, the collateral is not in the possession of the debtor when the debtor consents to the acceptance; and

(4) subsection (e) does not require the secured party to dispose of the collateral or the debtor waives the requirement pursuant to Section 9–624.

(b) A purported or apparent acceptance of collateral under this section is ineffective unless:

(1) the secured party consents to the acceptance in an authenticated record or sends a proposal to the debtor; and

(2) the conditions of subsection (a) are met.

(c) For purposes of this section:

(1) a debtor consents to an acceptance of collateral in partial satisfaction of the obligation it secures only if the debtor agrees to the terms of the acceptance in a record authenticated after default; and

(2) a debtor consents to an acceptance of collateral in full satisfaction of the obligation it secures only if the debtor agrees to the terms of the acceptance in a record authenticated after default or the secured party:

(A) sends to the debtor after default a proposal that is unconditional or subject only to a condition that collateral not in the possession of the secured party be preserved or maintained;

(B) in the proposal, proposes to accept collateral in full satisfaction of the obligation it secures; and

(C) does not receive a notification of objection authenticated by the debtor within 20 days after the proposal is sent.

(d) To be effective under subsection (a)(2), a notification of objection must be received by the secured party:

(1) in the case of a person to which the proposal was sent pursuant to Section 9–621, within 20 days after notification was sent to that person; and

(2) in other cases:

(A) within 20 days after the last notification was sent pursuant to Section 9–621; or

(B) if a notification was not sent, before the debtor consents to the acceptance under subsection (c).

(e) A secured party that has taken possession of collateral shall dispose of the collateral pursuant to Section 9–610 within the time specified in subsection (f) if:

(1) 60 percent of the cash price has been paid in the case of a purchase-money security interest in consumer goods; or

(2) 60 percent of the principal amount of the obligation secured has been paid in the case of a non-purchase-money security interest in consumer goods.

(f) To comply with subsection (e), the secured party shall dispose of the collateral:

(1) within 90 days after taking possession; or

(2) within any longer period to which the debtor and all secondary obligors have agreed in an agreement to that effect entered into and authenticated after default.

(g) In a consumer transaction, a secured party may not accept collateral in partial satisfaction of the obligation it secures.

§ 9–621. Notification of Proposal to Accept Collateral.

(a) A secured party that desires to accept collateral in full or partial satisfaction of the obligation it secures shall send its proposal to:

(1) any person from which the secured party has received, before the debtor consented to the acceptance, an authenticated notification of a claim of an interest in the collateral;

(2) any other secured party or lienholder that, 10 days before the debtor consented to the acceptance, held a security interest in or other lien on the collateral perfected by the filing of a financing statement that:

(A) identified the collateral;

(B) was indexed under the debtor's name as of that date; and

(C) was filed in the office or offices in which to file a financing statement against the debtor covering the collateral as of that date; and

(3) any other secured party that, 10 days before the debtor consented to the acceptance, held a security interest in the collateral perfected by compliance with a statute, regulation, or treaty described in Section 9–311(a).

(b) A secured party that desires to accept collateral in partial satisfaction of the obligation it secures shall send its proposal to any secondary obligor in addition to the persons described in subsection (a).

§ 9–622. Effect of Acceptance of Collateral.

(a) A secured party's acceptance of collateral in full or partial satisfaction of the obligation it secures:

(1) discharges the obligation to the extent consented to by the debtor;

(2) transfers to the secured party all of a debtor's rights in the collateral;

(3) discharges the security interest or agricultural lien that is the subject of the debtor's consent and any subordinate security interest or other subordinate lien; and

(4) terminates any other subordinate interest.

(b) A subordinate interest is discharged or terminated under subsection (a), even if the secured party fails to comply with this article.

§ 9–623. Right to Redeem Collateral.

(a) A debtor, any secondary obligor, or any other secured party or lienholder may redeem collateral.

(b) To redeem collateral, a person shall tender:

(1) fulfillment of all obligations secured by the collateral; and

(2) the reasonable expenses and attorney's fees described in Section 9–615(a)(1).

(c) A redemption may occur at any time before a secured party:

(1) has collected collateral under Section 9–607;

(2) has disposed of collateral or entered into a contract for its disposition under Section 9–610; or

(3) has accepted collateral in full or partial satisfaction of the obligation it secures under Section 9–622.

§ 9–624. Waiver.

(a) A debtor or secondary obligor may waive the right to notification of disposition of collateral under Section 9–611 only by an agreement to that effect entered into and authenticated after default.

(b) A debtor may waive the right to require disposition of collateral under Section 9–620(e) only by an agreement to that effect entered into and authenticated after default.

(c) Except in a consumer-goods transaction, a debtor or secondary obligor may waive the right to redeem collateral under Section 9–623 only by an agreement to that effect entered into and authenticated after default.

[Subpart 2. Noncompliance with Article]

§ 9–625. Remedies for Secured Party's Failure to Comply with Article.

(a) If it is established that a secured party is not proceeding in accordance with this article, a court may order or restrain collection, enforcement, or disposition of collateral on appropriate terms and conditions.

(b) Subject to subsections (c), (d), and (f), a person is liable for damages in the amount of any loss caused by a failure to comply with this article. Loss caused by a failure to comply may include loss resulting from the debtor's inability to obtain, or increased costs of, alternative financing.

(c) Except as otherwise provided in Section 9–628:

(1) a person that, at the time of the failure, was a debtor, was an obligor, or held a security interest in or other lien on the collateral may recover damages under subsection (b) for its loss; and

(2) if the collateral is consumer goods, a person that was a debtor or a secondary obligor at the time a secured party failed to comply with this part may recover for that failure in

any event an amount not less than the credit service charge plus 10 percent of the principal amount of the obligation or the time-price differential plus 10 percent of the cash price.

(d) A debtor whose deficiency is eliminated under Section 9–626 may recover damages for the loss of any surplus. However, a debtor or secondary obligor whose deficiency is eliminated or reduced under Section 9–626 may not otherwise recover under subsection (b) for noncompliance with the provisions of this part relating to collection, enforcement, disposition, or acceptance.

(e) In addition to any damages recoverable under subsection (b), the debtor, consumer obligor, or person named as a debtor in a filed record, as applicable, may recover $500 in each case from a person that:

(1) fails to comply with Section 9–208;

(2) fails to comply with Section 9–209;

(3) files a record that the person is not entitled to file under Section 9–509(a);

(4) fails to cause the secured party of record to file or send a termination statement as required by Section 9–513(a) or (c);

(5) fails to comply with Section 9–616(b)(1) and whose failure is part of a pattern, or consistent with a practice, of noncompliance; or

(6) fails to comply with Section 9–616(b)(2).

(f) A debtor or consumer obligor may recover damages under subsection (b) and, in addition, $500 in each case from a person that, without reasonable cause, fails to comply with a request under Section 9–210. A recipient of a request under Section 9–210 which never claimed an interest in the collateral or obligations that are the subject of a request under that section has a reasonable excuse for failure to comply with the request within the meaning of this subsection.

(g) If a secured party fails to comply with a request regarding a list of collateral or a statement of account under Section 9–210, the secured party may claim a security interest only as shown in the list or statement included in the request as against a person that is reasonably misled by the failure.

As amended in 2000.

§ 9–626.   Action in Which Deficiency or Surplus Is in Issue.

(a) In an action arising from a transaction, other than a consumer transaction, in which the amount of a deficiency or surplus is in issue, the following rules apply:

(1) A secured party need not prove compliance with the provisions of this part relating to collection, enforcement, disposition, or acceptance unless the debtor or a secondary obligor places the secured party's compliance in issue.

(2) If the secured party's compliance is placed in issue, the secured party has the burden of establishing that the collection, enforcement, disposition, or acceptance was conducted in accordance with this part.

(3) Except as otherwise provided in Section 9–628, if a secured party fails to prove that the collection, enforcement, disposition, or acceptance was conducted in accordance with the provisions of this part relating to collection, enforcement, disposition, or acceptance, the liability of a debtor or

a secondary obligor for a deficiency is limited to an amount by which the sum of the secured obligation, expenses, and attorney's fees exceeds the greater of:

(A) the proceeds of the collection, enforcement, disposition, or acceptance; or

(B) the amount of proceeds that would have been realized had the noncomplying secured party proceeded in accordance with the provisions of this part relating to collection, enforcement, disposition, or acceptance.

(4) For purposes of paragraph (3)(B), the amount of proceeds that would have been realized is equal to the sum of the secured obligation, expenses, and attorney's fees unless the secured party proves that the amount is less than that sum.

(5) If a deficiency or surplus is calculated under Section 9–615(f), the debtor or obligor has the burden of establishing that the amount of proceeds of the disposition is significantly below the range of prices that a complying disposition to a person other than the secured party, a person related to the secured party, or a secondary obligor would have brought.

(b) The limitation of the rules in subsection (a) to transactions other than consumer transactions is intended to leave to the court the determination of the proper rules in consumer transactions. The court may not infer from that limitation the nature of the proper rule in consumer transactions and may continue to apply established approaches.

§ 9–627.   Determination of Whether Conduct Was Commercially Reasonable.

(a) The fact that a greater amount could have been obtained by a collection, enforcement, disposition, or acceptance at a different time or in a different method from that selected by the secured party is not of itself sufficient to preclude the secured party from establishing that the collection, enforcement, disposition, or acceptance was made in a commercially reasonable manner.

(b) A disposition of collateral is made in a commercially reasonable manner if the disposition is made:

(1) in the usual manner on any recognized market;

(2) at the price current in any recognized market at the time of the disposition; or

(3) otherwise in conformity with reasonable commercial practices among dealers in the type of property that was the subject of the disposition.

(c) A collection, enforcement, disposition, or acceptance is commercially reasonable if it has been approved:

(1) in a judicial proceeding;

(2) by a bona fide creditors' committee;

(3) by a representative of creditors; or

(4) by an assignee for the benefit of creditors.

(d) Approval under subsection (c) need not be obtained, and lack of approval does not mean that the collection, enforcement, disposition, or acceptance is not commercially reasonable.

§ 9–628.   Nonliability and Limitation on Liability of Secured Party; Liability of Secondary Obligor.

(a) Unless a secured party knows that a person is a debtor or obligor, knows the identity of the person, and knows how to communicate with the person:

(1) the secured party is not liable to the person, or to a secured party or lienholder that has filed a financing statement against the person, for failure to comply with this article; and

(2) the secured party's failure to comply with this article does not affect the liability of the person for a deficiency.

(b) A secured party is not liable because of its status as secured party:

(1) to a person that is a debtor or obligor, unless the secured party knows:

(A) that the person is a debtor or obligor;

(B) the identity of the person; and

(C) how to communicate with the person; or

(2) to a secured party or lienholder that has filed a financing statement against a person, unless the secured party knows:

(A) that the person is a debtor; and

(B) the identity of the person.

(c) A secured party is not liable to any person, and a person's liability for a deficiency is not affected, because of any act or omission arising out of the secured party's reasonable belief that a transaction is not a consumer-goods transaction or a consumer transaction or that goods are not consumer goods, if the secured party's belief is based on its reasonable reliance on:

(1) a debtor's representation concerning the purpose for which collateral was to be used, acquired, or held; or

(2) an obligor's representation concerning the purpose for which a secured obligation was incurred.

(d) A secured party is not liable to any person under Section 9–625(c)(2) for its failure to comply with Section 9–616.

(e) A secured party is not liable under Section 9–625(c)(2) more than once with respect to any one secured obligation.

Part 7   Transition

§ 9–701.   Effective Date.

This [Act] takes effect on July 1, 2001.

§ 9–702.   Savings Clause.

(a) Except as otherwise provided in this part, this [Act] applies to a transaction or lien within its scope, even if the transaction or lien was entered into or created before this [Act] takes effect.

(b) Except as otherwise provided in subsection (c) and Sections 9–703 through 9–709:

(1) transactions and liens that were not governed by [former Article 9], were validly entered into or created before this [Act] takes effect, and would be subject to this [Act] if they had been entered into or created after this [Act] takes effect, and the rights, duties, and interests flowing from those transactions and liens remain valid after this [Act] takes effect; and

(2) the transactions and liens may be terminated, completed, consummated, and enforced as required or permitted by this [Act] or by the law that otherwise would apply if this [Act] had not taken effect.

(c) This [Act] does not affect an action, case, or proceeding commenced before this [Act] takes effect.

As amended in 2000.

§ 9–703.   Security Interest Perfected before Effective Date.

(a) A security interest that is enforceable immediately before this [Act] takes effect and would have priority over the rights of a person that becomes a lien creditor at that time is a perfected security interest under this [Act] if, when this [Act] takes effect, the applicable requirements for enforceability and perfection under this [Act] are satisfied without further action.

(b) Except as otherwise provided in Section 9–705, if, immediately before this [Act] takes effect, a security interest is enforceable and would have priority over the rights of a person that becomes a lien creditor at that time, but the applicable requirements for enforceability or perfection under this [Act] are not satisfied when this [Act] takes effect, the security interest:

(1) is a perfected security interest for one year after this [Act] takes effect;

(2) remains enforceable thereafter only if the security interest becomes enforceable under Section 9–203 before the year expires; and

(3) remains perfected thereafter only if the applicable requirements for perfection under this [Act] are satisfied before the year expires.

§ 9–704.   Security Interest Unperfected before Effective Date.

A security interest that is enforceable immediately before this [Act] takes effect but which would be subordinate to the rights of a person that becomes a lien creditor at that time:

(1) remains an enforceable security interest for one year after this [Act] takes effect;

(2) remains enforceable thereafter if the security interest becomes enforceable under Section 9–203 when this [Act] takes effect or within one year thereafter; and

(3) becomes perfected:

(A) without further action, when this [Act] takes effect if the applicable requirements for perfection under this [Act] are satisfied before or at that time; or

(B) when the applicable requirements for perfection are satisfied if the requirements are satisfied after that time.

§ 9–705.   Effectiveness of Action Taken before Effective Date.

(a) If action, other than the filing of a financing statement, is taken before this [Act] takes effect and the action would have resulted in priority of a security interest over the rights of a person that becomes a lien creditor had the security interest become enforceable before this [Act] takes effect, the action is effective to perfect a security interest that attaches under this [Act] within one year after this [Act] takes effect. An attached security interest becomes unperfected one year after this [Act] takes effect unless the security interest becomes a perfected security interest under this [Act] before the expiration of that period.

(b) The filing of a financing statement before this [Act] takes effect is effective to perfect a security interest to the extent the filing would satisfy the applicable requirements for perfection under this [Act].

(c) This [Act] does not render ineffective an effective financing statement that, before this [Act] takes effect, is filed and satisfies the applicable requirements for perfection under the law of the jurisdiction governing perfection as provided in [former Section 9–103]. However, except as otherwise provided in subsections (d) and (e) and Section 9–706, the financing statement ceases to be effective at the earlier of:

(1) the time the financing statement would have ceased to be effective under the law of the jurisdiction in which it is filed; or

(2) June 30, 2006.

(d) The filing of a continuation statement after this [Act] takes effect does not continue the effectiveness of the financing statement filed before this [Act] takes effect. However, upon the timely filing of a continuation statement after this [Act] takes effect and in accordance with the law of the jurisdiction governing perfection as provided in Part 3, the effectiveness of a financing statement filed in the same office in that jurisdiction before this [Act] takes effect continues for the period provided by the law of that jurisdiction.

(e) Subsection (c)(2) applies to a financing statement that, before this [Act] takes effect, is filed against a transmitting utility and satisfies the applicable requirements for perfection under the law of the jurisdiction governing perfection as provided in [former Section 9–103] only to the extent that Part 3 provides that the law of a jurisdiction other than the jurisdiction in which the financing statement is filed governs perfection of a security interest in collateral covered by the financing statement.

(f) A financing statement that includes a financing statement filed before this [Act] takes effect and a continuation statement filed after this [Act] takes effect is effective only to the extent that it satisfies the requirements of Part 5 for an initial financing statement.

§ 9–706.   When Initial Financing Statement Suffices to Continue Effectiveness of Financing Statement.

(a) The filing of an initial financing statement in the office specified in Section 9–501 continues the effectiveness of a financing statement filed before this [Act] takes effect if:

(1) the filing of an initial financing statement in that office would be effective to perfect a security interest under this [Act];

(2) the pre-effective-date financing statement was filed in an office in another State or another office in this State; and

(3) the initial financing statement satisfies subsection (c).

(b) The filing of an initial financing statement under subsection (a) continues the effectiveness of the pre-effective-date financing statement:

(1) if the initial financing statement is filed before this [Act] takes effect, for the period provided in [former Section 9–403] with respect to a financing statement; and

(2) if the initial financing statement is filed after this [Act] takes effect, for the period provided in Section 9–515 with respect to an initial financing statement.

(c) To be effective for purposes of subsection (a), an initial financing statement must:

(1) satisfy the requirements of Part 5 for an initial financing statement;

(2) identify the pre-effective-date financing statement by indicating the office in which the financing statement was filed and providing the dates of filing and file numbers, if any, of the financing statement and of the most recent continuation statement filed with respect to the financing statement; and

(3) indicate that the pre-effective-date financing statement remains effective.

§ 9–707.   Amendment of Pre-Effective-Date Financing Statement.

(a) In this section, "Pre-effective-date financing statement" means a financing statement filed before this [Act] takes effect.

(b) After this [Act] takes effect, a person may add or delete collateral covered by, continue or terminate the effectiveness of, or otherwise amend the information provided in, a pre-effective-date financing statement only in accordance with the law of the jurisdiction governing perfection as provided in Part 3. However, the effectiveness of a pre-effective-date financing statement also may be terminated in accordance with the law of the jurisdiction in which the financing statement is filed.

(c) Except as otherwise provided in subsection (d), if the law of this State governs perfection of a security interest, the information in a pre-effective-date financing statement may be amended after this [Act] takes effect only if:

(1) the pre-effective-date financing statement and an amendment are filed in the office specified in Section 9–501;

(2) an amendment is filed in the office specified in Section 9–501 concurrently with, or after the filing in that office of, an initial financing statement that satisfies Section 9–706(c); or

(3) an initial financing statement that provides the information as amended and satisfies Section 9–706(c) is filed in the office specified in Section 9–501.

(d) If the law of this State governs perfection of a security interest, the effectiveness of a pre-effective-date financing statement may be continued only under Section 9–705(d) and (f) or 9–706.

(e) Whether or not the law of this State governs perfection of a security interest, the effectiveness of a pre-effective-date financing statement filed in this State may be terminated after this [Act] takes effect by filing a termination statement in the office in which the pre-effective-date financing statement is filed, unless an initial financing statement that satisfies Section 9–706(c) has been filed in the office specified by the law of the jurisdiction governing perfection as provided in Part 3 as the office in which to file a financing statement.

As amended in 2000.

§ 9–708.   Persons Entitled to File Initial Financing Statement or Continuation Statement.

A person may file an initial financing statement or a continuation statement under this part if:

(1) the secured party of record authorizes the filing; and

(2) the filing is necessary under this part:

(A) to continue the effectiveness of a financing statement filed before this [Act] takes effect; or

(B) to perfect or continue the perfection of a security interest.

As amended in 2000.

§ 9–709.   Priority.

(a) This [Act] determines the priority of conflicting claims to collateral. However, if the relative priorities of the claims were established before this [Act] takes effect, [former Article 9] determines priority.

(b) For purposes of Section 9–322(a), the priority of a security interest that becomes enforceable under Section 9–203 of this [Act] dates from the time this [Act] takes effect if the security interest is perfected under this [Act] by the filing of a financing statement before this [Act] takes effect which would not have been effective to perfect the security interest under [former Article 9]. This subsection does not apply to conflicting security interests each of which is perfected by the filing of such a financing statement.

As amended in 2000.

* * * *

Appendix D

Answers to *Issue Spotters*

Chapter 1

1. No. The U.S. Constitution is the supreme law of the land and applies to all jurisdictions. A law in violation of the Constitution (in this question, the First Amendment to the Constitution) will be declared unconstitutional.

2. Yes. Administrative rulemaking starts with the publication of a notice of the rulemaking in the *Federal Register*. Among other details, this notice states where and when the proceedings, such as a public hearing, will be held. Proponents and opponents can offer their comments and concerns regarding the pending rule. After reviewing all the comments from the proceedings, the agency's decision makers consider what was presented and draft the final rule.

Chapter 2

1. No. Even if commercial speech is not related to illegal activities or misleading, it may be restricted if a state has a substantial government interest that cannot be achieved by less restrictive means. In this case, the interest in energy conservation is substantial, but it could be achieved by less restrictive means. That would be the utilities' defense against the enforcement of this state law.

2. Yes. The tax would limit the liberty of some persons, such as out-of-state businesses, so it is subject to a review under the equal protection clause. Protecting local businesses from out-of-state competition is not a legitimate government objective. Thus, such a tax would violate the equal protection clause.

Chapter 3

1. Tom could file a motion for a directed verdict. This motion asks the judge to direct a verdict for Tom on the ground that Sue presented no evidence that would justify granting her relief. The judge grants the motion if there is insufficient evidence to raise an issue of fact.

2. Yes. Submission of the dispute to mediation or nonbinding arbitration is mandatory, but compliance with the decision of the mediator or arbitrator is voluntary.

Chapter 4

1. Probably. To recover on the basis of negligence, the injured party as a plaintiff must show that the truck's owner owed the plaintiff a duty of care, that the owner breached that duty, that the plaintiff was injured, and that the breach caused the injury. In this problem, the owner's actions breached the duty of reasonable care. The billboard falling on the plaintiff was the direct cause of the injury, not the plaintiff's own negligence. Thus, liability turns on whether the plaintiff can connect the breach of duty to the injury. This involves the test of proximate cause—the question of foreseeability. The consequences to the injured party must have been a foreseeable result of the owner's carelessness.

2. The company might defend against this electrician's claim by asserting that the electrician should have known of the risk and, therefore, the company had no duty to warn. According to the problem, the danger is common knowledge in the electrician's field and should have been apparent to this electrician, given his years of training and experience. In other words, the company most likely had no need to warn the electrician of the risk.

The firm could also raise comparative negligence. Both parties' negligence, if any, could be weighed and the liability distributed proportionately. The defendant could furthermore assert assumption of risk, claiming that the electrician voluntarily entered into a dangerous situation, knowing the risk involved.

Chapter 5

1. Yes. The manufacturer is liable for the injuries to the user of the product. A manufacturer is liable for its failure to exercise due care to any person who sustains an injury proximately caused by a negligently made (defective) product. In this scenario, the failure to inspect is a failure to use due care. Thus, Rim Corporation is liable to the injured buyer, Uri. Of course, the maker of the component part may also be liable.

2. Bensing can assert the defense of preemption. An injured party may not be able to sue the manufacturer of defective products that are subject to comprehensive federal regulatory schemes (such as medical devices and vaccinations). In this situation, it is likely that a court would conclude that the federal regulations pertaining to drug labeling preempt Ohio's common law rules. Therefore, Bensing would not be liable to Rothfus for defective labeling if it complied with federal law.

Chapter 6

1. Yes, Roslyn has committed theft of trade secrets. Lists of suppliers and customers cannot be patented, copyrighted, or trademarked, but the information they contain is protected against appropriation by others as trade secrets. And most likely, Roslyn signed a contract, agreeing not to use this information outside her employment by Organic. But even without this contract, Organic could have made a convincing case against its ex-employee for a theft of trade secrets.

2. This is patent infringement. A software maker in this situation might best protect its product, save litigation costs, and profit from its patent by the use of a license. In the context of this problem, a license would grant permission to sell a patented item. (A license can be limited to certain purposes and to the licensee only.)

Chapter 7

1. Karl may have committed trademark infringement. Search engines compile their results by looking through Web sites' keyword fields. Key words, or meta tags, increase the likelihood that a site will be included in search engine results, even if the words have no connection to the site.

A site that appropriates the key words of other sites with more frequent hits will appear in the same search engine results as the more popular sites. But using another's trademark as a key word without the owner's permission normally constitutes trademark infringement. Of course, some uses of another's trademark as a meta tag may be permissible if the use is reasonably necessary and does not suggest that the owner authorized or sponsored the use.

2. Yes. This may be an instance of trademark dilution. Dilution occurs when a trademark is used, without permission, in a way that diminishes the distinctive quality of the mark. Dilution does not require proof that consumers are likely to be confused by the use of the unauthorized mark. The products involved do not have to be similar. Dilution does require, however, that a mark be famous when the dilution occurs.

Chapter 8

1. Yes. With respect to the gas station, Daisy has obtained goods by false pretenses. She might also be charged with the crimes of larceny and forgery, and most states have special statutes covering illegal use of credit cards.

2. Yes. The Counterfeit Access Device and Computer Fraud and Abuse Act provides that a person who accesses a computer online, without permission, to obtain classified data—such as consumer credit files in a credit agency's database—is subject to criminal prosecution. The crime has two elements: accessing the computer without permission and taking data. It is a felony if done for private financial gain. Penalties include fines and imprisonment for up to twenty years. The victim of the theft can also bring a civil suit against the criminal to obtain damages and other relief.

Chapter 9

1. When a corporation decides to respond to what it sees as a moral obligation to correct for past discrimination by adjusting pay differences among its employees, an ethical conflict is raised between the firm and its employees and between the firm and its shareholders. This dilemma arises directly out of the effect such a decision has on the firm's profits. If satisfying this obligation increases profitability, then the dilemma is easily resolved in favor of "doing the right thing."

2. Maybe. On the one hand, it is not the company's "fault" when a product is misused. Also, keeping the product on the market is not a violation of the law, and stopping sales would hurt profits. On the other hand, suspending sales could reduce suffering and could prevent negative publicity that might occur if sales continued.

Chapter 10

1. Under the objective theory of contracts, if a reasonable person would have thought that Joli had accepted Kerin's offer when she signed and returned the letter, then a contract was made, and Joli is obligated to buy the book. This depends, in part, on what was said in the letter and what was said in response. For instance, did the letter contain a valid offer, and did the response constitute a valid acceptance? Under any circumstances, the issue is not whether either party subjectively believed that they did, or did not, have a contract.

2. No. This contract, although not fully executed, is for an illegal purpose and therefore is void. A void contract gives rise to no legal obligation on the part of any party. A contract that is void is no contract. There is nothing to enforce.

Chapter 11

1. No. Revocation of an offer may be implied by conduct inconsistent with the offer. When Fidelity Corporation rehired Monica, and Ron learned of the hiring, the offer was revoked. His acceptance was too late.

2. First, it might be noted that the Uniform Electronic Transactions Act (UETA) does not apply unless the parties to a contract agree to use e-commerce in their transaction. In this deal, of course, the parties used e-commerce. The UETA removes barriers to e-commerce by giving the same legal effect to e-records and e-signatures as to paper documents and signatures. The UETA itself does not include rules for e-commerce transactions, however.

Chapter 12

1. Yes. The original contract was executory—that is, not yet performed by both parties. The parties rescinded the original contract and agreed to a new contract.

2. No. Generally, an exculpatory clause (a clause attempting to absolve a party of negligence or other wrongs) is not enforced if the party seeking its enforcement is involved in a business that is important to the public as a matter of practical necessity, such as an airline. Because of the essential nature of such services, the party would have an advantage in bargaining strength and could insist that anyone contracting for its services agree not to hold it liable.

Chapter 13

1. Yes. Rescission may be granted on the basis of fraudulent misrepresentation. The elements of fraudulent misrepresentation include intent to deceive, or *scienter*. *Scienter* exists if a party makes a statement recklessly, without regard to whether it is true or false, or if a party says or implies that a statement is made on some basis such as personal knowledge or personal investigation when it is not.

2. No. This memo is not a sufficient writing to enforce the contract against Nu! Sales, because it does not include Nu!'s signature. If My-T had been the party refusing to complete the deal, however, the memo would be considered a sufficient writing to enforce the contract against it. Letterhead stationery can constitute a signature. If the memo names the parties, the subject matter, the consideration, and the quantity involved in the transaction, it may be sufficient to be enforced against the party whose letterhead appears on it.

Chapter 14

1. Yes. Generally, if a contract clearly states that a right is not assignable, no assignment will be effective, but there are exceptions. Assignment of the right to receive monetary payment cannot be prohibited.

2. Contracts that are executory on both sides—contracts on which neither party has performed—can be rescinded solely by agreement. Contracts that are executed on one side—contracts on which one party has performed—can be rescinded only if the party who has performed receives consideration for the promise to call off the deal.

Chapter 15

1. A nonbreaching party is entitled to her or his benefit of the bargain under the contract. Here, the innocent party is entitled to be put in the position she would have been in if the contract had been fully performed. The measure of the benefit is the cost to complete the work ($500). These are compensatory damages.

2. No. To recover damages that flow from the consequences of a breach but that are caused by circumstances beyond the contract (consequential damages), the breaching party must know, or have reason to know, that special circumstances will cause the nonbreaching party to suffer the additional loss. That was not the circumstance in this problem.

Chapter 16

1. Under the principle of comity, a U.S court would defer and give effect to foreign laws and judicial decrees that are consistent with U.S. law and public policy.

2. The practice described in this problem is known as dumping, which is regarded as an unfair international trade practice. Dumping is the sale of imported goods at "less than fair value." Based on the price of those goods in the exporting country, an extra tariff—known as an antidumping duty—can be imposed on the imports.

Chapter 17

1. A shipment of nonconforming goods constitutes an acceptance and a breach, unless the seller seasonably notifies the buyer that the nonconforming shipment does not constitute an acceptance and is offered only as an accommodation. Thus, since there was no notification in this problem, the shipment was both an acceptance and a breach.

2. Yes. In a transaction between merchants, the requirement of a writing is satisfied if one of them sends to the other a signed written confirmation that indicates the terms of the agreement, and the merchant receiving it has reason to know of its contents. If the merchant who receives the confirmation does not object in writing within ten days after receipt, the writing will be enforceable against him or her even though he or she has not signed anything.

Chapter 18

1. Yes. A seller is obligated to deliver goods in conformity with a contract in every detail. This is the perfect tender rule. The exception of the seller's right to cure does not apply here because the seller delivered too little too late to take advantage of this exception.

2. Yes. When anticipatory repudiation occurs, a buyer (or lessee) can resort to any remedy for breach even if the buyer tells the seller (the repudiating party in this problem) that the buyer will wait for the seller's performance.

Chapter 19

1. A statement that "I.O.U." money (or anything else) or an instruction to a bank stating, "I wish you would pay," would render any instrument nonnegotiable. To be negotiable, an instrument must contain an express promise to pay. An I.O.U. is only an acknowledgment of indebtedness. An order stating, "I wish you would pay," is not sufficiently precise.

2. No. When a drawer's employee provides the drawer with the name of a fictitious payee (a payee whom the drawer does not actually intend to have any interest in an instrument), a forgery of the payee's name is effective to pass good title to subsequent transferees.

Chapter 20

1. Yes, to both questions. In a civil suit, a drawer (Lyn) is liable to a payee (Nan) or to a holder of a check that is not honored. If intent to defraud can be proved, the drawer (Lyn) can also be subject to criminal prosecution for writing a bad check.

2. The drawer is entitled to $6,300—the amount to which the check was altered ($7,000) less the amount that the drawer ordered the bank to pay ($700). The bank may recover this amount from the party who presented the altered check for payment.

Chapter 21

1. When collateral consists of consumer goods, and the debtor has paid less than 60 percent of the debt or the purchase price, the creditor has the option of disposing of the collateral in a commercially reasonable manner. This generally requires notice to the debtor of the place, time, and manner of sale. A debtor can waive the right to notice, but only after default. Before the disposal, a debtor can redeem the collateral by tendering performance of all of the obligations secured by the collateral and by paying the creditor's reasonable expenses in retaking and maintaining the collateral.

2. Each of the parties can place a mechanic's lien on the debtor's property. If the debtor does not pay what is owed, the property can be sold to satisfy the debt. The only requirements are that the lien be filed within a specific time from the time of the work, depending on the state statute, and that notice of the foreclosure and sale be given to the debtor in advance.

Chapter 22

1. No. Besides the claims listed in this problem, the debts that cannot be discharged in bankruptcy include amounts borrowed to pay back taxes, goods obtained by fraud, debts that were not listed in the petition, domestic support obligations, certain cash advances, and others.

2. Yes. A debtor's payment to a creditor made for a preexisting debt, within ninety days (one year in the case of an insider or fraud) of a bankruptcy filing, can be recovered if it gives a creditor more than he or she would have received in the bankruptcy proceedings. A trustee can recover this preference using his or her specific avoidance powers.

Chapter 23

1. No. Nadine, as an agent, is prohibited from taking advantage of the agency relationship to obtain property that the principal

(Dimka Corporation) wants to purchase. This is the *duty of loyalty* that arises with every agency relationship.

2. Yes. A principal has a duty to indemnify (reimburse) an agent for liabilities incurred because of authorized and lawful acts and transactions and for losses suffered because of the principal's failure to perform his or her duties.

Chapter 24

1. Workers' compensation laws establish a procedure for compensating workers who are injured on the job. Instead of suing to collect benefits, an injured worker notifies the employer of the injury and files a claim with the appropriate state agency. The right to recover is normally determined without regard to negligence or fault, but intentionally inflicted injuries are not covered. Unlike the potential for recovery in a lawsuit based on negligence or fault, recovery under a workers' compensation statute is limited to the specific amount designated in the statute for the employee's injury.

2. No. A closed shop (a company that requires union membership as a condition of employment) is illegal. A union shop (a company that does not require union membership as a condition of employment but requires workers to join the union after a certain time on the job) is illegal in a state with a right-to-work law, which makes it illegal to require union membership for continued employment.

Chapter 25

1. Yes. One type of sexual harassment occurs when a request for sexual favors is a condition of employment, and the person making the request is a supervisor or acts with the authority of the employer. A tangible employment action, such as continued employment, may also lead to the employer's liability for the supervisor's conduct. That the injured employee is a male and the supervisor a female, instead of the other way around, would not affect the outcome. Same-gender harassment is also actionable.

2. Yes, Koko could succeed in a discrimination suit if she can show that she was not hired solely because of her disability. The other elements for a discrimination suit based on a disability are that the plaintiff (1) has a disability and (2) is otherwise qualified for the job. Both of these elements appear to be satisfied in this scenario.

Chapter 26

1. When a business is relatively small and is not diversified, employs relatively few people, has modest profits, and is not likely to expand significantly or require extensive financing in the immediate future, the most appropriate form for doing business may be a sole proprietorship.

2. Yes. Failing to meet a specified sales quota can constitute a breach of a franchise agreement. If the franchisor is acting in good faith, "cause" may also include the death or disability of the franchisee, the insolvency of the franchisee, and a breach of another term of the franchise agreement.

Chapter 27

1. No. A widow (or widower) has no right to take a dead partner's place. A partner's death causes dissociation after which the partnership must purchase the dissociated partner's partnership interest. Therefore, the surviving partners must pay the decedent's estate (for his widow) the value of the deceased partner's interest in the partnership.

2. No. Under the partners' fiduciary duty, a partner must account to the partnership for any personal profits or benefits derived without the consent of all the partners in connection with the use of any partnership property. Here, the leasing partner may not keep the funds.

Chapter 28

1. The members of a limited liability company (LLC) may designate a group to run their firm. In that situation, the firm would be a manager-managed LLC. The group may include only members, only nonmembers, or members and nonmembers. If, instead, all members participate in management, the firm would be a member-managed LLC. In fact, unless the members agree otherwise, all members are considered to participate in the management of the firm.

2. Although there are differences, all of these forms of business organizations resemble corporations. A joint stock company, for example, features ownership by shares of stock, it is managed by directors and officers, and it has perpetual existence. A business trust, like a corporation, distributes profits to persons who are not personally responsible for the debts of the organization, and management of the business is in the hands of trustees, just as the management of a corporation is in the hands of directors and officers. An incorporated cooperative, which is subject to state laws covering nonprofit corporations, distributes profits to its owners.

Chapter 29

1. Yes. Small businesses that meet certain requirements can qualify as S corporations, created specifically to permit small businesses to avoid double taxation. The six requirements of an S corporation are (1) the firm must be a domestic corporation; (2) the firm must not be a member of an affiliated group of corporations; (3) the firm must have fewer than a certain number of shareholders; (4) the shareholders must be individuals, estates, or qualified trusts (or corporations in some cases); (5) there can be only one class of stock; and (6) no shareholder can be a nonresident alien.

2. Yes. A shareholder can bring a derivative suit on behalf of a corporation if some wrong is done to the corporation. Normally, any damages recovered go into the corporate treasury.

Chapter 30

1. The average investor is not concerned with minor inaccuracies but with facts that if disclosed would tend to deter him or her from buying the securities. These would include material facts that have an important bearing on the condition of the issuer and its business—such as liabilities, loans to officers and directors, customer delinquencies, and pending lawsuits.

2. No. The Securities Exchange Act of 1934 extends liability to officers and directors in their personal transactions for taking advantage of inside information when they know it is unavailable to the persons with whom they are dealing.

Chapter 31

1. Size alone does not determine whether a firm is a monopoly—size in relation to the market is what matters. A small store in a small, isolated town is a monopolist if it is the only store serving that market. Monopoly involves the power to affect prices and output. If a firm has sufficient market power to control prices and exclude competition, that firm has monopoly power. Monopoly power in itself is not a violation of Section 2 of the Sherman Act. The offense also requires an intent to acquire or maintain that power through anticompetitive means.

2. This agreement is a tying arrangement. The legality of a tying arrangement depends on the purpose of the agreement, the agreement's likely effect on competition in the relevant markets (the market for the tying product and the market for the tied product), and other factors. Tying arrangements for commodities are subject to Section 3 of the Clayton Act. Tying arrangements for services can be agreements in restraint of trade in violation of Section 1 of the Sherman Act.

Chapter 32

1. Under an extensive set of procedures established by the U.S. Food and Drug Administration, which administers the federal Food, Drug, and Cosmetic Act, drugs must be shown to be effective as well as safe before they may be marketed to the public. In general, manufacturers are responsible for ensuring that the drugs they offer for sale are free of any substances that could injure consumers.

2. The Comprehensive Environmental Response, Compensation, and Liability Act (CERCLA) regulates the cleanup of hazardous waste disposal sites. Any potentially responsible party can be charged with the entire cost of cleaning up a site. Potentially responsible parties include the person that generated the waste (ChemCorp), the person that transported the waste to the site (Disposal), the person that owned or operated the site at the time of the disposal (Eliminators), and the current owner or operator of the site (Fluid). A party held responsible for the entire cost may be able to recoup some of it in a lawsuit against other potentially responsible parties.

Chapter 33

1. Yes. In these circumstances, when the accountant knows that the bank will use the statement, the bank is a foreseeable user. A foreseeable user is a third party within the class of parties to whom an accountant may be liable for negligence.

2. No. In the circumstances described, the accountant will not be held liable to a purchaser of the securities. Although an accountant may be liable under securities laws for including untrue statements or omitting material facts from financial statements, due diligence is a defense to liability. Due diligence requires an accountant to conduct a reasonable investigation and have reason to believe that the financial statements were true at the time. The facts say that the misstatement of material fact in Omega's financial statement was not attributable to any fraud or negligence on Nora's part. Therefore, Nora can show that she used due diligence and will not be held liable to Pat.

Chapter 34

1. The ring is classified as lost property because it was discovered under circumstances indicating that the owner had not placed the property there voluntarily. The general rule is that the finder of the lost property has the right to possession (and eventual title) over all others *except* the true owner of the lost property. Therefore, Martin, as the true owner of the ring, is entitled to repossess the ring from Hunter.

2. Rosa de la Mar Corporation, the shipper, suffers the loss. A common carrier is liable for damage caused by the willful acts of third persons or by an accident. Other losses must be borne by the shipper (or the recipient, depending on the terms of their contract). In this situation, this shipment was lost due to an act of God.

Chapter 35

1. This is a breach of the warranty deed's covenant of quiet enjoyment. Consuela can sue Bernie and recover the purchase price of the house, plus any damages.

2. Yes. An owner of a fee simple has the most rights possible—he or she can give the property away, sell it, transfer it by will, use it for almost any purpose, possess it to the exclusion of all the world, or, as in this case, transfer possession for any period of time. The party to whom possession is transferred can also transfer her or his interest (usually only with the owner's permission) for any lesser period of time.

Chapter 36

1. No. To have testamentary capacity, a testator must be of legal age and sound mind *at the time the will is made*. Generally, the testator must (1) know the nature of the act, (2) comprehend and remember the "natural objects of his or her bounty," (3) know the nature and extent of her or his property, and (4) understand the distribution of assets called for by the will. In this situation, Sheila had testamentary capacity at the time she made the will. The fact that she was ruled mentally incompetent two years after making the will does not provide sufficient grounds to revoke it.

2. The estate will pass according to the state's intestacy laws. Intestacy laws set out how property is distributed when a person dies without a will. Their purpose is to carry out the likely intent of the decedent. The laws determine which of the deceased's natural heirs (including, in this order, the surviving spouse, lineal descendants, parents, and collateral heirs) inherit his or her property.

Appendix E

<table>
<tr><td>

Answers to Even-Numbered *Learning Objectives Check* Questions

</td></tr>
</table>

Chapter 1

2. What is the common law tradition?

Because of our colonial heritage, much of American law is based on the English legal system. After the Norman Conquest of England in 1066, the king's courts sought to establish a uniform set of rules for the entire country. What evolved in these courts was the common law—a body of general legal principles that applied throughout the entire English realm. Courts developed the common law rules from the principles underlying judges' decisions in actual legal controversies.

4. What is the difference between remedies at law and remedies in equity?

An award of compensation in either money or property, including land, is a remedy at law. Remedies in equity include the following:

1. A decree for specific performance—that is, an order to perform what was promised.

2. An injunction, which is an order directing a party to do or refrain from doing a particular act.

3. A rescission, or cancellation, of a contract and a return of the parties to the positions that they held before the contract's formation.

As a rule, courts will grant an equitable remedy only when the remedy at law (monetary damages) is inadequate. Remedies in equity on the whole are more flexible than remedies at law.

Chapter 2

2. What constitutional clause gives the federal government the power to regulate commercial activities among the various states?

To prevent states from establishing laws and regulations that would interfere with trade and commerce among the states, the Constitution expressly delegated to the national government the power to regulate interstate commerce. The commerce clause—Article I, Section 8, of the U.S. Constitution—expressly permits Congress "to regulate Commerce with foreign Nations, and among the several States, and with the Indian Tribes."

4. What is the Bill of Rights? What freedoms does the First Amendment guarantee?

The Bill of Rights consists of the first ten amendments to the U.S. Constitution. Adopted in 1791, the Bill of Rights embodies protections for individuals against interference by the federal government. Some of the protections also apply to business entities. The First Amendment guarantees the freedoms of religion, speech, and the press, and the rights to assemble peaceably and to petition the government.

Chapter 3

2. How are the courts applying traditional jurisdictional concepts to cases involving Internet transactions?

To hear a case, a court must have jurisdiction over the person against whom the suit is brought or over the property involved in the suit. The court must also have jurisdiction over the subject matter. Generally, courts apply a "sliding-scale" standard to determine when it is proper to exercise jurisdiction over a defendant whose only connection with the jurisdiction is the Internet.

4. What is discovery, and how does electronic discovery differ from traditional discovery?

Discovery is the process of obtaining information and evidence about a case from the other party or third parties. Discovery entails gaining access to witnesses, documents, records, and other types of evidence. Electronic discovery differs in its subject—that is, e-media, such as e-mail or text messages, rather than traditional sources of information, such as paper documents.

Chapter 4

2. What are two basic categories of torts?

Generally, the purpose of tort law is to provide remedies for the invasion of legally recognized and protected interests, such as personal safety, freedom of movement, property, and some intangibles, including privacy and reputation. The two broad categories of torts are intentional and unintentional.

4. Identify the four elements of negligence.

The four elements of negligence are as follows:

1. A duty of care owed by the defendant to the plaintiff.

2. The defendant's breach of that duty.

3. The plaintiff's suffering a legally recognizable injury.

4. The in-fact and proximate cause of that injury by the defendant's breach.

Chapter 5

2. What public policy assumptions underlie strict product liability?

The law imposes strict product liability as a matter of public policy. This public policy rests on the threefold assumption that:

1. Consumers should be protected against unsafe products.

2. Manufacturers and distributors should not escape liability for faulty products simply because they are not in privity of contract with the ultimate user of those products.

3. Manufacturers, sellers, and lessors of products are generally in a better position than consumers to bear the costs associated with injuries caused by their products—costs that they can ultimately pass on to all consumers in the form of higher prices.

4. What are three types of product defects?

The three types of product defects traditionally recognized in product liability law are manufacturing defects, design defects, and defective (inadequate) warnings.

A manufacturing defect is a departure from a product unit's design specifications that results in products that are physically flawed, damaged, or incorrectly assembled.

A product with a design defect is made in conformity with the manufacturer's design specifications, but it nevertheless results in injury to the user because the design itself is flawed.

A product may also be deemed defective because of inadequate instructions or warnings about foreseeable risks. The seller or other distributor must include comprehensible warnings if the product will not be reasonably safe without them. The seller must also warn consumers about foreseeable misuses of the product.

Chapter 6

2. Why is the protection of trademarks important?

Article I, Section 8, of the U.S. Constitution authorizes Congress "to promote the Progress of Science and useful Arts, by securing for limited Times to Authors and Inventors the exclusive Right to their respective Writings and Discoveries." Laws protecting trademarks—and patents and copyrights as well—are designed to protect and reward inventive and artistic creativity.

4. What laws protect authors' rights in the works they create?

Copyright law protects the rights of the authors of certain literary or artistic productions. The Copyright Act of 1976, as amended, covers these rights.

Chapter 7

2. What steps have been taken to protect intellectual property rights in the digital age?

The steps that have been taken to protect intellectual property in today's digital age include the application of traditional and existing law in the cyber context. For example, the passage of such federal laws as the Digital Millennium Copyright Act and the drafting of such state laws as the Uniform Electronic Transactions Act (UETA) are major steps in protecting intellectual property rights. Additionally, the signing of such treaties as the Trade-Related Aspects of Intellectual Property Rights (TRIPS) agreement and the World Intellectual Property Organization (WIPO) Copyright Treaty add protection on a global level.

4. What law governs whether Internet service providers are liable for online defamatory statements made by users?

The Communications Decency Act (CDA) sets out the liability of Internet service providers (ISPs) for online defamatory statements made by users.

Under the CDA, "No provider or user of an interactive computer service shall be treated as the publisher or speaker of any information provided by another information content provider." Thus, an ISP is usually not liable for the publication of a user's defamatory statement. This is a broad shield, and some courts have established some limits. For example, an ISP that prompts its users to make such statements would likely not be permitted to avoid liability for the statements.

Chapter 8

2. What are five broad categories of crimes? What is white-collar crime?

Traditionally, crimes have been grouped into the following categories: violent crime (crimes against persons), property crime, public order crime, white-collar crime, and organized crime.

White-collar crime is an illegal act or series of acts committed by an individual or business entity using some nonviolent means, usually in the course of a legitimate occupation.

4. What constitutional safeguards exist to protect persons accused of crimes?

Under the Fourth Amendment, before searching or seizing private property, law enforcement officers must obtain a search warrant, which requires probable cause.

Under the Fifth Amendment, no one can be deprived of "life, liberty, or property without due process of law." The Fifth Amendment also protects persons against double jeopardy and self-incrimination.

The Sixth Amendment guarantees the right to a speedy trial, the right to a jury trial, the right to a public trial, the right to confront witnesses, and the right to counsel. Individuals who are arrested must be informed of certain constitutional rights, including their Fifth Amendment right to remain silent and their Sixth Amendment right to counsel. All evidence obtained in violation of the Fourth, Fifth, and Sixth Amendments, as well as all evidence derived from the illegally obtained evidence, must be excluded from the trial.

The Eighth Amendment prohibits excessive bail and fines, and cruel and unusual punishment.

Chapter 9

2. How do duty-based ethical standards differ from outcome-based ethical standards?

Duty-based ethical standards are derived from religious precepts or philosophical principles. Outcome-based ethics focus on the consequences of an action, not on the nature of the action or on a set of pre-established moral values or religious beliefs.

4. How can business leaders encourage their companies to act ethically?

Ethical leadership is important to create and maintain an ethical workplace. Managers can set standards and then apply those standards to themselves and their firm's employees.

Chapter 10

2. What are the four basic elements necessary to the formation of a valid contract?

The basic elements for the formation of a valid contract are an agreement, consideration, contractual capacity, and legality.

4. How does a void contract differ from a voidable contract? What is an unenforceable contract?

A void contract is not a valid contract—it is not a contract at all. A voidable contract is a valid contract, but one that can be avoided at the option of one or both of the parties.

An unenforceable contract is one that cannot be enforced because of certain legal defenses against it.

Chapter 11

2. In what circumstances will an offer be irrevocable?

An offeror may not effectively revoke an offer if the offeree has changed position in justifiable reliance on the offer. Also, an option contract takes away the offeror's power to revoke an offer for the period of time specified in the option (or, if unspecified, for a reasonable time).

4. How do shrink-wrap and click-on agreements differ from other contracts? How have traditional laws been applied to these agreements?

With a shrink-wrap agreement, the terms are expressed inside the box in which the goods are packaged. A click-on agreement arises when a buyer, completing a transaction on a computer, is required to indicate assent to the terms by clicking on a button that says, for example, "I agree."

Generally, courts have enforced the terms of these agreements the same as the terms of other contracts, applying the traditional common law of contracts. Article 2 of the Uniform Commercial Code provides that acceptance can be made by conduct. The *Restatement (Second) of Contracts* has a similar provision. Under these provisions, a binding contract can be created by conduct, including conduct accepting the terms in a shrink-wrap or click-on agreement.

Chapter 12

2. In what circumstances might a promise be enforced despite a lack of consideration?

Under the doctrine of promissory estoppel (or detrimental reliance), a promisor (the offeror) is estopped, or prevented, from revoking a promise even in the absence of consideration. There are three required elements:

1. A clear and definite promise.
2. The promisee's justifiable reliance on the promise.
3. Reliance of a substantial and definite character.

4. Under what circumstances will a covenant not to compete be enforced? When will such covenants not be enforced?

A covenant not to compete can be enforced:

1. If it is ancillary (secondary) to an agreement to sell an ongoing business, thus enabling the seller to sell, and the purchaser to buy, the goodwill and reputation of the business.
2. If it is contained in an employment contract and is reasonable in terms of time and geographic area.

A covenant not to compete will be unenforceable if it does not protect a legitimate business interest or is broader than necessary to protect a legitimate interest. This is because such a covenant would unreasonably restrain trade and be contrary to public policy.

Chapter 13

2. What is the difference between a unilateral mistake and a bilateral mistake?

A unilateral mistake occurs when only one party is mistaken as to a material fact underlying the contract. Normally, the contract is enforceable even if one party made a mistake, unless an exception applies. A bilateral, or mutual, mistake occurs when both parties are mistaken about the same material fact. When the mistake is mutual, the contract can be rescinded, or canceled, by either party.

4. What contracts must be in writing to be enforceable?

Contracts that are normally required to be in writing or evidenced by a written memorandum include:

- Contracts involving interests in land.
- Contracts that cannot by their terms be performed within one year from the day after the date of formation.
- Collateral contracts, such as promises to answer for the debt or duty of another.

- Promises made in consideration of marriage.
- Contracts for the sale of goods priced at $500 or more.

Chapter 14

2. In what situations is the delegation of duties prohibited?

Delegation of duties is prohibited in the following situations:

1. When the performance depends on the personal skill or talents of the obligor.
2. When special trust has been placed in the obligor.
3. When performance by a third party will vary materially from that expected by the obligee under the contract.
4. When the contract expressly prohibits delegation.

4. How are most contracts discharged?

The most common way to discharge, or terminate, a contract is by the performance of contractual duties.

Chapter 15

2. What is the difference between compensatory damages and consequential damages? What are nominal damages, and when do courts award nominal damages?

Compensatory damages compensate an injured party for injuries or damages. Foreseeable damages that result from a party's breach of contract are consequential damages. Consequential damages differ from compensatory damages in that they are caused by special circumstances beyond the contract.

Nominal damages are awarded to an innocent party when no actual damage has been suffered. Nominal damages might be awarded as a matter of principle to establish fault or wrongful behavior.

4. When do courts grant specific performance as a remedy?

Specific performance might be granted as a remedy when damages offer an inadequate remedy and the subject matter of the contract is unique.

Chapter 16

2. What is the act of state doctrine? In what circumstances is this doctrine applied?

The act of state doctrine is a judicially created doctrine that provides that the judicial branch of one country will not examine the validity of public acts committed by a recognized foreign government within its own territory. This doctrine is often employed in cases involving expropriation or confiscation.

4. What are some clauses commonly included in international business contracts?

Choice-of-language, forum-selection, choice-of-law, and *force majeure* clauses are commonly used in international business contracts.

Chapter 17

2. In a sales contract, if an offeree includes additional or different terms in an acceptance, will a contract result? If so, what happens to these terms?

Under the Uniform Commercial Code, a contract can be formed even if the offeree's acceptance includes additional or different terms. If one of the parties is a nonmerchant, the contract does not include the additional terms. If both parties are merchants, the additional terms automatically become part of the contract unless one of the following occurs:

1. The original offer expressly limits acceptance to the terms of the offer.
2. The new or changed terms materially alter the contract.
3. The offeror objects to the new or changed terms within a reasonable period of time.

(If the additional terms expressly require the offeror's assent, the offeree's response is not an acceptance, but a counteroffer.) Under some circumstances, a court might strike the additional terms.

4. Risk of loss does not necessarily pass with title. If the parties to a contract do not expressly agree when risk passes and the goods are to be delivered without movement by the seller, when does risk pass?

If the seller holds the goods and is a merchant, the risk of loss passes to the buyer when the buyer takes physical possession of the goods. If the seller holds the goods and is not a merchant, the risk of loss passes to the buyer on tender of delivery. When a bailee is holding the goods, the risk of loss passes to the buyer when (1) the buyer receives a negotiable document of title for the goods, (2) the bailee acknowledges the buyer's right to possess the goods, or (3) the buyer receives a nonnegotiable document of title and has had a reasonable time to present the document to the bailee and demand the goods.

Chapter 18

2. What is the perfect tender rule? What are some important exceptions to this rule that apply to sales and lease contracts?

Under the perfect tender rule, the seller or lessor has an obligation to ship or tender conforming goods. If the goods or tender of delivery fails in any respect, the buyer or lessee has the right to accept the goods, reject the entire shipment, or accept part and reject part. Exceptions to the rule may be established by agreement.

When goods are rejected because they are nonconforming and the time for performance has not expired, the seller or lessor can notify the buyer or lessee promptly of the intention to cure and then do so within the contract time for performance. If the time for performance has expired, the seller or lessor can still cure within a reasonable time if, at the time of delivery, he or she had reasonable grounds to believe that the nonconforming tender would be acceptable. When an agreed-on manner of delivery becomes impracticable or unavailable through no fault of either party, a seller may choose a commercially reasonable substitute.

4. What remedies are available to a seller or lessor when the buyer or lessee breaches the contract?

Depending on the circumstances at the time of a buyer's or lessee's breach, a seller or lessor may have the right to cancel the contract, withhold delivery, or resell or dispose of the goods subject to the contract. In addition, a seller or lessor may have the right to recover the purchase price (or lease payments), recover damages, stop delivery in transit, or reclaim the goods.

Chapter 19

2. What is the advantage of transferring an instrument by negotiation? How does the negotiation of order instruments differ from the negotiation of bearer instruments?

Negotiation is the only way to transfer an instrument that allows the party receiving the instrument to obtain the rights of a holder. Unlike a transfer by assignment, a transfer by negotiation can make it possible for a holder to receive more rights in the instrument than the prior possessor had [UCC 3–202(b), 3–305, 3–306].

Negotiating order instruments requires both delivery and indorsement. In contrast, negotiating bearer instruments is accomplished by delivery alone (without the need for indorsement).

4. What is the difference between signature liability and warranty liability?

The key to liability on a negotiable instrument is a signature. Every party, except a qualified indorser, who signs a negotiable instrument is primarily or secondarily liable for payment of that instrument when it comes due.

Signature liability arises from indorsing an instrument. Warranty liability arises from transferring an instrument, whether or not the transferor also indorses it.

Chapter 20

2. When may a bank properly dishonor a customer's check without being liable to the customer?

A bank may dishonor a customer's check without liability to the customer when the customer's account contains insufficient funds to pay the check, providing the bank did not agree to cover overdrafts. A bank may also properly dishonor a stale check, a timely check subject to a valid stop-payment order, a check drawn after the customer's death, and forged or altered checks.

4. What is electronic check presentment, and how does it differ from the traditional check-clearing process?

With electronic check presentment, items are encoded with information (such as the amount of the check) that is read and processed by other banks' computers. A check may sometimes be retained at its place of deposit, and then only its image or description is presented for payment. A bank that encodes information on an item warrants to any subsequent bank or payor that the encoded information is correct.

This differs from the traditional check-clearing process because employees of each bank in the collection chain no longer have to physically handle each check that passes through the bank for collection or payment. Therefore, obtaining payment is much quicker. Whereas manual check processing can take days, electronic check presentment can be done on the day of deposit.

Chapter 21

2. How is a purchase-money security interest in consumer goods created and perfected?

A purchase-money security interest (PMSI) in consumer goods is created when a person buys goods and the seller or lender agrees to extend credit for part or all of the purchase price of the goods. The entity that extends the credit and obtains the PMSI can be either the seller (a store, for example) or a financial institution that lends the buyer the funds with which to purchase the goods [UCC 9–102(a)(2)].

A PMSI in consumer goods is perfected automatically at the time of a credit sale—that is, at the time the PMSI is created. The seller in this situation does not need to do anything more to perfect her or his interest.

4. How does a mechanic's lien assist creditors?

When a creditor follows the individual state's procedure to create a mechanic's lien, the debtor's real estate becomes security for the debt. If the debtor continues not to pay the underlying debt, the creditor can foreclose on the debtor's real property to collect the amount due.

Chapter 22

2. In a Chapter 7 bankruptcy, what happens if a court finds that there was "substantial abuse"? How is the means test used?

If a court concludes there was substantial abuse, the court can dismiss a petition or convert it from a Chapter 7 to a Chapter 11 or Chapter 13 case. In the means test, the debtor's average monthly income in recent months is compared with the median income in the geographic area in which the person lives. If the debtor's income is below the median income, the debtor usually is allowed to file for Chapter 7 bankruptcy. If the debtor's income is above the median income, then further calculations are necessary to determine if there is substantial abuse. The goal is to determine whether the person will have sufficient disposable income in the future to repay at least some of his or her unsecured debts.

4. In a Chapter 11 reorganization, what is the role of the debtor in possession?

Under Chapter 11, a debtor in possession (DIP) is allowed to continue to operate his or her business while the bankruptcy proceeds. The DIP's role is similar to that of a trustee in a liquidation, or Chapter 7, proceeding. Like a trustee, the DIP has certain powers and can avoid preferential transfers and cancel unperformed contracts and unexpired leases.

Chapter 23

2. How do agency relationships arise?

Agency relationships normally are consensual—that is, they arise by voluntary consent and agreement between the parties.

4. When is a principal liable for the agent's actions with respect to third parties? When is the agent liable?

A disclosed or partially disclosed principal is liable to a third party for a contract made by an agent who was acting within the scope of her or his authority. If the agent exceeds the scope of authority and the principal fails to ratify the contract, the agent may be liable (and the principal may not).

When neither the fact of agency nor the identity of the principal is disclosed, the agent is liable, and if the agent has acted within the scope of his or her authority, the undisclosed principal is also liable. Each party is liable for his or her own torts and crimes. A principal may also be liable for an agent's torts committed within the course or scope of employment. A principal is liable for an agent's crime if the principal participated by conspiracy or other action.

Chapter 24

2. What federal statute governs working hours and wages?

The Fair Labor Standards Act is the most significant federal statute governing working hours and wages.

4. What are the two most important federal statutes governing immigration and employment today?

The most important federal statutes governing immigration and the employment of noncitizens are the Immigration Reform and Control Act (IRCA) and the Immigration Act.

Chapter 25

2. What must an employer do to avoid liability for religious discrimination?

Employers cannot treat their employees more or less favorably based on their religious beliefs or practices. Employers also cannot require employees to participate in any religious activity (or forbid them from participating in one). An employer must reasonably accommodate the religious practices of its employees, unless to do so would cause undue hardship to the employer's business.

4. What federal act prohibits discrimination based on age?

The Age Discrimination in Employment Act prohibits discrimination on the basis of age.

Chapter 26

2. What are the most common types of franchises?

The majority of franchises are distributorships, chain-style business operations, or manufacturing or processing-plant arrangements.

4. How are franchises normally terminated? When will a court decide that a franchisor has wrongfully terminated a franchise?

Franchise agreements are usually terminated through provisions in the franchise contract, which often specify that the termination must be "for cause." Cause might include, for instance, the death or disability of the franchisee, insolvency of the franchisee, breach of the franchise agreement, or failure to meet specified sales quotas.

Usually, notice of the termination must be given to the franchisee. The franchisee may be given a chance to cure a breach of the contract within a specific period of time.

If a franchisor has acted arbitrarily or unfairly terminated a franchise (i.e., not in good faith) a court may decide that the termination was wrongful and provide a remedy to the franchisee. Courts look at the good faith and fair dealing of the parties in the franchise relationship when deciding whether the termination was wrongful.

Chapter 27

2. What are the rights and duties of partners in an ordinary partnership?

The rights and duties of partners may be whatever the partners declare them to be. In the absence of partners' agreements to the contrary, the law imposes certain rights and duties. These include:

- A sharing of profits and losses in equal measure.
- The ability to assign a partnership interest.
- Equal rights in managing the firm (subject to majority rule).
- Access to all of the firm's books and records.
- An accounting of assets and profits.
- A sharing of the firm's property.

The duties include fiduciary duties, being bound to third parties through contracts entered into with other partners, and liability for the firm's debts and liabilities.

4. What advantages do limited liability partnerships offer to businesspersons that are not offered by general partnerships?

An advantage of a limited liability partnership over a general partnership is that, depending on the applicable state statute, the liability of the partners for partnership and partners' debts and torts can be limited to the amount of the partners' investments. Another advantage is that partners in a limited liability partnership generally are not liable for other partners' malpractice.

Chapter 28

2. What advantages do limited liability companies offer to businesspersons that are not offered by sole proprietorships or partnerships?

An important advantage of limited liability companies (LLCs) is that the liability of the members is limited to the amount of their investments. Another advantage of LLCs is the flexibility they offer in regard to taxation and management.

4. What is a joint venture? How is it similar to a partnership? How is it different?

A joint venture is an enterprise in which two or more persons or business entities combine their efforts or their property for a single transaction or project, or a related series of transactions or projects.

Generally, partnership law applies to joint ventures, although joint venturers have less implied and apparent authority than partners because they have less power to bind the members of their organization.

Chapter 29

2. What four steps are involved in bringing a corporation into existence?

The four basic steps to bring a corporation into existence include (1) selecting the state of incorporation, (2) securing the corporate name, (3) preparing the articles of incorporation, and (4) filing those articles with the state.

4. What are the duties of corporate directors and officers?

Directors and officers are fiduciaries of the corporation. The fiduciary duties of the directors and officers include the duty of care and the duty of loyalty.

Chapter 30

2. What are the two major statutes regulating the securities industry?

The major statutes regulating the securities industry are the Securities Act of 1933 and the Securities Exchange Act of 1934, which created the Securities and Exchange Commission.

4. What are some of the features of state securities laws?

Typically, state laws have disclosure requirements and antifraud provisions patterned after Section 10(b) of the Securities Exchange Act of 1934 and SEC Rule 10b-5. State laws provide for the registration or qualification of securities offered or issued for sale within the state with the appropriate state official. Also, most state securities laws regulate securities brokers and dealers.

Chapter 31

2. What rule do courts apply to price-fixing agreements, and why?

Courts apply the *per se* rule to price-fixing agreements. Because agreements to fix prices are so blatantly and substantially anticompetitive, they are deemed *per se* illegal. That is, even if the parties had good reasons for entering the agreement, if the agreement restricts output or artificially fixes prices, it violates Section 1 of the Sherman Act.

4. What are the four major provisions of the Clayton Act, and what types of activities do these provisions prohibit?

Section 2 of the Clayton Act prohibits price discrimination. Section 3 prohibits two types of vertical agreements involving exclusionary practices: exclusive-dealing contracts and tying arrangements. Section 7 prohibits mergers or acquisitions that result in monopoly power or a substantial lessening of competition in the marketplace. Section 8 prohibits a person from being a director in two or more competing corporations at the same time if either of the corporations has capital, surplus, or undivided profits aggregating more than a specified amount or competitive sales of a certain amount or more (the dollar limits are changed periodically by Congress).

Chapter 32

2. What law protects consumers against contaminated and misbranded foods and drugs?

The Federal Food, Drug, and Cosmetic Act (FDCA) protects consumers against adulterated and misbranded foods and drugs. The FDCA establishes food standards, specifies safe levels of potentially hazardous food additives, and provides classifications of foods and food advertising.

4. What is contained in an environmental impact statement, and who must file one?

An environmental impact statement (EIS) analyzes the following:

1. The impact on the environment that an action will have.

2. Any adverse effects on the environment and alternative actions that might be taken.

3. Irreversible effects the action might generate.

An EIS must be prepared for every major federal action that significantly affects the quality of the environment. An action is "major" if it involves a substantial commitment of resources (monetary or otherwise). An action is "federal" if a federal agency has the power to control it.

Chapter 33

2. What are the rules concerning an auditor's liability to third parties?

An auditor may be liable to a third party on the ground of negligence, when the auditor knew or should have known that the third party would benefit from the auditor's work. Depending on the jurisdiction, liability may be imposed only if one of the following occurs:

1. The auditor is in privity, or near privity, with the third party.

2. The third party's reliance on the auditor's work was foreseen, or the third party was within a class of known or foreseeable users.

3. The third party's use of the auditor's work was reasonably foreseeable.

4. What crimes might an accountant commit under the Internal Revenue Code?

Crimes under the Internal Revenue Code include the following:

1. Aiding or assisting in the preparation of a false tax return.

2. Aiding or abetting an individual's understatement of tax liability.

3. Negligently or willfully understating a client's tax liability, or recklessly or intentionally disregarding Internal Revenue Code rules or regulations.

4. Failing to provide a taxpayer with a copy of a tax return, failing to sign the return, or failing to furnish the appropriate tax identification numbers.

Chapter 34

2. What are the three necessary elements for an effective gift?

To make an effective gift, the donor must intend to make the gift, the gift must be delivered to the donee, and the donee must accept the gift.

4. What are the basic duties of a bailee?

The bailee has two basic responsibilities: (1) to take appropriate care of the property and (2) to surrender the property at the end of the bailment. The appropriate degree of care required for the bailor's property depends on whether the bailment is for the benefit of the bailor, the benefit of the bailee, or for their mutual benefit.

Chapter 35

2. What is the difference between a joint tenancy and a tenancy in common?

A tenancy in common is a form of co-ownership in which each of two or more persons owns an undivided interest in the whole property. On the death of a tenant in common, that tenant's interest passes to his or her heirs. In a joint tenancy, each of two or more persons owns an undivided interest in the property, and a deceased joint tenant's interest passes to the surviving joint tenant or tenants. This right distinguishes the joint tenancy from the tenancy in common.

4. What are the requirements for acquiring property by adverse possession?

The adverse possessor's possession must be (1) actual and exclusive, (2) open, visible, and notorious, not secret or clandestine, (3) continuous and peaceable for the statutory period of time, and (4) hostile and adverse.

Chapter 36

2. How do courts interpret ambiguities in an insurance policy?

The courts will interpret the words used in an insurance contract according to their ordinary meanings in light of the nature of the coverage involved. When there is an ambiguity in the policy, the provision generally is interpreted *against the insurance company*.

4. What is the difference between a *per stirpes* distribution and a *per capita* distribution of an estate to the grandchildren of the deceased?

Per stirpes distribution dictates that grandchildren share the part of the estate that their deceased parent (and descendant of the deceased grandparent) would have been entitled to inherit.

Per capita distribution dictates that each grandchild takes an equal share of the estate.

Appendix F

Sample Answers for *Business Case Problems with Sample Answer*

1–6. Sample Answer—Law around the World.

The common law system spread throughout medieval England after the Norman Conquest in 1066. Courts developed the common law rules from the principles behind the decisions in actual legal controversies. Judges attempted to be consistent. When possible, they based their decisions on the principles suggested by earlier cases. They sought to decide similar cases in a similar way and considered new cases with care because they knew that their decisions would make new law. Each interpretation became part of the law on the subject and served as a legal precedent. Later cases that involved similar legal principles or facts could be decided with reference to that precedent.

The practice of deciding new cases with reference to former decisions, or precedents, eventually became a cornerstone of the English and American judicial systems. It forms a doctrine called stare decisis. Under this doctrine, judges are obligated to follow the precedents established within their jurisdictions. Generally, those countries that were once colonies of Great Britain retained their English common law heritage after they achieved their independence. Today, common law systems exist in Australia, Canada, India, Ireland, and New Zealand, as well as the United States.

Most of the other European nations base their legal systems on Roman civil law. Civil law is codified law—an ordered grouping of legal principles enacted into law by a legislature or governing body. In a civil law system, the primary source of law is a statutory code, and case precedents are not judicially binding as they are in a common law system. Nonetheless, judges in such systems commonly refer to previous decisions as sources of legal guidance. The difference is that judges in a civil law system are not bound by precedent—in other words, the doctrine of *stare decisis* does not apply.

2–3. Sample Answer—Establishment Clause.

The establishment clause prohibits the government from passing laws or taking actions that promote religion or show a preference for one religion over another. In assessing a government action, the courts look at the predominant purpose for the action and ask whether the action has the effect of endorsing religion.

Although DeWeese claimed to have a nonreligious purpose for displaying the poster of the Ten Commandments in a courtroom, his own statements showed a religious purpose. These statements reflected his views about "warring" legal philosophies and his belief that "our legal system is based on moral absolutes from divine law handed down by God through the Ten Commandments." This plainly constitutes a religious purpose that violates the establishment clause because it has the effect of endorsing Judaism or Christianity over other religions. In the case on which this problem is based, the court ruled in favor of the American Civil Liberties Union.

3–6. Sample Answer—Discovery.

Yes, the items that were deleted from a Facebook page can be recovered. Normally, a party must hire an expert to recover material in an electronic format, and this can be time consuming and expensive.

Electronic evidence, or e-evidence, consists of all computer-generated or electronically recorded information, such as posts on Facebook and other social media sites. The effect that e-evidence can have in a case depends on its relevance and what it reveals. In the facts presented in this problem, Isaiah should be sanctioned—he should be required to cover Allied's cost to hire the recovery expert and attorney's fees to confront the misconduct. In a jury trial, the court might also instruct the jury to presume that any missing items are harmful to Isaiah's case. If all of the material is retrieved and presented at the trial, any prejudice (disadvantage) to Allied's case might thereby be mitigated (lessened). If not, of course, the court might go so far as to order a new trial.

In the actual case on which this problem is based, Allied hired an expert, who determined that Isaiah had in fact removed some photos and other items from his Facebook page. After the expert testified about the missing material, Isaiah provided Allied with all of it, including the photos that he had deleted. Allied sought a retrial, but the court instead reduced the amount of Isaiah's damages by the amount that it cost Allied to address his "misconduct."

4–5. Sample Answer—Negligence.

Negligence requires proof that (a) the defendant owed a duty of care to the plaintiff, (b) the defendant breached that duty, (c) the defendant's breach caused the plaintiff's injury, and (d) the plaintiff suffered a legally recognizable injury. With respect to the duty of care, a business owner has a duty to use reasonable care to protect business invitees. This duty includes an obligation to discover and correct or warn of unreasonably dangerous conditions that the owner of the premises should reasonably foresee might endanger an invitee. Some risks are so obvious that an owner need not warn of them. But even if a risk is obvious, a business owner may not be excused from the duty to protect the business's customers from foreseeable harm.

Because Lucario was the Weatherford's business invitee, the hotel owed her a duty of reasonable care to make its premises safe for her use. The balcony ran nearly the entire width of the window in Lucario's room. She could have reasonably believed that the window was a means of access to the balcony. The window/balcony configuration was dangerous, however, because the window opened wide enough for an adult to climb out, but the twelve-inch gap between one side of the window and the balcony was unprotected. This unprotected gap opened to a drop of more than three stories to a concrete surface below.

Should the hotel have anticipated the potential harm to a guest opening the window in Room 59 and attempting to access the balcony? The hotel encouraged guests to "step out onto the balcony" to smoke. The dangerous window/balcony configuration could have been remedied at a minimal cost. These circumstances could be perceived as creating an "unreasonably dangerous" condition. And it could be concluded that the hotel created or knew of the condition and failed to take reasonable steps to warn of it or correct it. Of course, the Weatherford might argue that the window/balcony configuration was so obvious that the hotel was not liable for Lucario's fall.

In the actual case on which this problem is based, the court concluded that the Weatherford did not breach its duty of care to Lucario. On McMurtry's appeal, a state intermediate appellate court held that this conclusion was in error, vacated the lower court's judgment in favor of the hotel on this issue, and remanded the case.

5-7. Sample Answer—Product Liability.

The accident in this case was caused by Jett's inattention, not by the texting device in the cab of his truck. In a product-liability case based on a design defect, the plaintiff has to prove that the product was defective at the time it left the hands of the seller or lessor. The plaintiff must also show that this defective condition made it "unreasonably dangerous" to the user or consumer. If the product was delivered in a safe condition and subsequent mishandling made it harmful to the user, the seller or lessor normally is not liable. To successfully assert a design defect, a plaintiff has to show that a reasonable alternative design was available and that the defendant failed to use it.

The plaintiffs could argue that the defendant manufacturer of the texting device owed them a duty of care because injuries to vehicle drivers, passengers, and others on the roads were reasonably foreseeable. They could claim that the product's design (1) required the driver to divert his eyes from the road to view an incoming text, and (2) permitted the receipt of texts while the vehicle was moving.

But manufacturers are not required to design a product incapable of distracting a driver. The duty owed by a manufacturer to the user or consumer of a product does not require guarding against hazards that are commonly known or obvious. Nor does a manufacturer's duty extend to protecting against injuries that result from a user's careless conduct, such as Jett's carelessness in this situation.

6-6. Sample Answer—Patents.

One ground on which the denial of the patent application in this problem could be reversed on appeal is that the design of Raymond Gianelli's "Rowing Machine" is *not obvious* in light of the design of the "Chest Press Apparatus for Exercising Regions of the Upper Body."

To obtain a patent, an applicant must demonstrate to the satisfaction of the U.S. Patent and Trademark Office (PTO) that the invention, discovery, process, or design is novel, useful, and not obvious in light of current technology. In this problem, the PTO denied Gianelli's application for a patent for his "Rowing Machine"—an exercise machine on which a user *pulls* on handles to perform a rowing motion against a selected resistance to strengthen the back muscles. The PTO considered the device obvious in light of a patented "Chest Press Apparatus for Exercising Regions of the Upper Body"—a chest press exercise machine on which a user *pushes* on handles to overcome a selected resistance. But it can be easily argued that it is *not* obvious to modify a machine with handles designed to be *pushed* into one with handles designed to be *pulled*. In fact, anyone who has used exercise machines knows that a way to cause injury is to use a machine in a manner not intended by the manufacturer.

In the actual case on which this problem is based, the U.S. Court of Appeals for the Federal Circuit reversed the PTO's denial of Gianelli's application for a patent, based on the reasoning stated above.

7-5. Sample Answer—Privacy.

No, Rolfe did not have a privacy interest in the information obtained by the subpoenas issued to Midcontinent Communications. The courts have held that the right to privacy is guaranteed by the U.S. Constitution's Bill of Rights, and some state constitutions contain an explicit guarantee of the right. A person must have a reasonable expectation of privacy, though, to maintain a suit or to assert a successful defense for an invasion of privacy.

People clearly have a reasonable expectation of privacy when they enter their personal banking or credit-card information online. They also have a reasonable expectation that online companies will follow their own privacy policies. But people do not have a reasonable expectation of privacy in statements made on Twitter and other data that they publicly disseminate. In other words, there is no violation of a subscriber's right to privacy when a third party Internet service provider receives a subpoena and discloses the subscriber's information.

Here, Rolfe supplied his e-mail address and other personal information, including his Internet protocol address, to Midcontinent. In other words, Rolfe publicly disseminated this information. Law enforcement officers obtained this information from Midcontinent through the subpoenas issued by the South Dakota state court. Rolfe provided his information to Midcontinent—he has no legitimate expectation of privacy in that information.

In the actual case on which this problem is based, Rolfe was charged with, and convicted of, possessing, manufacturing, and distributing child pornography, as well as other crimes. As part of the proceedings, the court found that Rolfe had no expectation of privacy in the information that he made available to Midcontinent. On appeal, the South Dakota Supreme Court upheld the conviction.

8–5. Sample Answer—Criminal Liability.

Yes, Green exhibited the required mental state to establish criminal liability. A wrongful mental state (*mens rea*) is one of the elements typically required to establish criminal liability. The required mental state, or intent, is indicated in an applicable statute or law. For example, for murder, the required mental state is the intent to take another's life. A court can also find that the required mental state is present when a defendant's acts are reckless or criminally negligent. A defendant is criminally reckless if he or she consciously disregards a substantial and unjustifiable risk.

In this problem, Green was clearly aware of the danger to which he was exposing people on the street below, but he did not indicate that he specifically intended to harm anyone. The risk of death created by his conduct, however, was obvious. He must have known what was likely to happen if a bottle or plate thrown from the height of twenty-six stories hit a pedestrian or the windshield of an occupied motor vehicle on the street below. Despite his claim that he was intoxicated, he was sufficiently aware to stop throwing things from the balcony when he saw police in the area, and he later recalled what he had done and what had happened.

In the actual case on which this problem is based, after a jury trial, Green was convicted of reckless endangerment. On appeal, a state intermediate appellate court affirmed the conviction, based in part on the reasoning just stated.

9–4. Sample Answer—Online Privacy.

Facebook created a program that makes decisions for users. Many believe that privacy is an extremely important right that should be fiercely protected. Thus, using duty-based ethics, any program that has a default setting of giving out information is unethical. Facebook should create the program as an opt-in program.

In addition, under the Kantian categorical imperative, if every company used opt-out programs that allowed the disclosure of potentially personal information, privacy might become merely theoretical. If privacy were reduced or eliminated, the world might not be a better place. From a utilitarian or outcome-based approach, an opt-out program might offer the benefits of being easy to created and start, as well as making it easy to recruit partner programs. On the negative side, the program would eliminate users' ability to chose whether to disclose information about themselves. An opt-in program would maintain that user control but might entail higher start-up costs because it would require more marketing to users up front to persuade them to opt in.

10–6. Sample Answer—Quasi Contract.

Gutkowski does not have a valid claim for payment, nor should he recover on the basis of a quasi contract. Quasi contracts are imposed by courts on parties in the interest of fairness and justice. Usually, a quasi contract is imposed to avoid the unjust enrichment of one party at the expense of another. Gutkowski was compensated as a consultant. For him to establish a claim that he is due more compensation based on unjust enrichment, he must have proof. As it is, he has only his claim that there were discussions

about him being a part owner of YES. Discussions and negotiations are not a basis for recovery on a quasi contract.

In the actual case on which this problem is based, the court dismissed Gutkowski's claim for payment.

11–4. Sample Answer—Online Acceptances.

No. A shrink-wrap agreement is an agreement whose terms are expressed inside the box in which the goods are packaged. The party who opens the box may be informed that he or she agrees to the terms by keeping whatever is in the box. In many cases, the courts have enforced the terms of shrink-wrap agreements just as they enforce the terms of other contracts.

But not all of the terms presented in shrink-wrap agreements have been enforced by the courts. One important consideration is whether the buyer had adequate notice of the terms. A click-on agreement is formed when a buyer, completing a transaction on a computer, is required to indicate his or her assent to be bound by the terms of an offer by clicking on a button that says, for example, "I agree."

In Reasonover's situation, the confirmation e-mail sent by Clearwire was not adequate notice of its "Terms of Service" (TOS). The e-mail did not contain a direct link to the terms—accessing them required clicks on further links through the firm's homepage. The written, shrink-wrap materials accompanying the modem did not provide adequate notice of the TOS. There was only a reference to Clearwire's Web site in small print at the bottom of one page.

Similarly, Reasonover's access to an "I accept terms" box did not establish notice of the terms. She did not click on the box but quit the page. Even if any of these references were sufficient notice, Reasonover kept the modem only because Clearwire told her that she could not return it. In the actual case on which this problem is based, the court refused to compel arbitration on the basis of the clause in Clearwire's TOS.

12–3. Sample Answer—Unconscionable Contracts or Clauses.

In this case, the agreement that restricted the buyer's options for resolution of a dispute to arbitration and limited the amount of damages was both procedurally and substantively unconscionable. Procedural unconscionability concerns the manner in which the parties enter into a contract. Substantive unconscionability can occur when a contract leaves one party to the agreement without a remedy for the nonperformance of the other.

Here, GeoEx told customers that the arbitration terms in its release form were nonnegotiable and that climbers would encounter the same requirements with any other travel company. This amounted to procedural unconscionability, underscoring the customers' lack of bargaining power. The imbalance resulted in oppressive terms, with no real negotiation and an absence of meaningful choice. Furthermore, the restriction on forum (San Francisco) and the limitation on damages (the cost of the trip)—with no limitation on GeoEx's damages—amounted to substantive unconscionability.

In the actual case on which this problem is based, the court ruled that the agreement was unconscionable.

13–7. Sample Answer—Fraudulent Misrepresentation.

Yes, the facts in this problem evidence fraud. There are three elements to fraud: (1) the misrepresentation of a material fact, (2) an intent to deceive, and (3) an innocent party's justifiable reliance on the misrepresentation. To collect damages, the innocent party must suffer an injury.

Here, Pervis represented to Pauley that no further commission would be paid by Osbrink. This representation was false—despite Pervis's statement to the contrary, Osbrink continued to send payments to Pervis. Pervis knew the representation was false, as shown by the fact that she made it more than once during the time that she was continuing to receive payments from Osbrink. Each time Pauley asked about commissions, Pervis replied that she was not receiving any. Pauley's reliance on her business associate's statements was justified and reasonable. And for the purpose of recovering damages, Pauley suffered an injury in the amount of her share of the commissions that Pervis received as a result of the fraud.

In the actual case on which this problem is based, Pauley filed a suit in a Georgia state court against Pervis, who filed for bankruptcy in a federal bankruptcy court to stay the state action. The federal court held Pervis liable on the ground of fraud for the amount of the commissions that were not paid to Pauley, and denied Pervis a discharge of the debt.

14–5. Sample Answer—Material Breach.

Yes, STR breached the contract with NTI. A breach of contract is the nonperformance of a contractual duty. A breach is *material* when performance is not at least substantial. On a material breach, the nonbreaching party is excused from performance. If a breach is *minor,* the nonbreaching party's duty to perform can sometimes be suspended until the breach has been remedied, but the duty to perform is not entirely excused. Once a minor breach has been cured, the nonbreaching party must resume performance. Any breach—material or minor—entitles the nonbreaching party to sue for damages.

In this problem, NTI had to redo its work constantly because STR permitted its employees and the employees of other subcontractors to walk over and damage the newly installed tile. Furthermore, despite NTI's requests for payment, STR remitted only half the amount due under their contract. Thus, NTI was deprived of at least half of the money it was owed under the contract. And STR terminated the contract, apparently wrongfully and without cause. The tile work would have been completed satisfactorily if STR had not allowed other workers to trample the newly installed tile before it had cured.

In the actual case on which this problem is based, when STR refused to pay NTI and then terminated their contract, the subcontractor filed a suit in a Texas state court to recover. From a jury verdict in NTI's favor, STR appealed. A state intermediate appellate court affirmed. "The evidence presented was legally sufficient for the jury to conclude that STR materially breached the contract."

15–6. Sample Answer—Consequential Damages.

Simard is liable only for the losses and expenses related to the first resale. Simard could reasonably anticipate that his breach would require another sale and that the sales price might be less than what he agreed to pay. Therefore, he should be liable for the difference between his sales price and the first resale price ($29,000), plus any expenses arising from the first resale.

Simard is not liable, however, for any expenses and losses related to the second resale. After all, Simard did not cause the second purchaser's default, and he could not reasonably foresee that default as a probable result of his breach.

16–6. Sample Answer—Import Controls.

Yes, an antidumping duty can be assessed retrospectively (retroactively). But it does not seem likely that such a duty should be assessed here.

In this problem, the Wind Tower Trade Coalition (an association of domestic manufacturers of utility scale wind towers) filed a suit in the U.S. Court of International Trade against the U.S. Department of Commerce. Wind Tower challenged the Commerce Department's decision to impose only *prospective* antidumping duties on imports of utility scale wind towers from China and Vietnam. The Commerce Department had found that the domestic industry had not suffered any "material injury" or "threat of material injury," and that it would be protected by a prospective assessment. Because there was no previously cognizable injury—and any retrospective duties collected would not be payable to the members of the domestic industry—it does not seem likely that retroactive duties should be imposed.

In the actual case on which this problem is based, the court denied the plaintiff's request for an injunction. On appeal, the U.S. Court of Appeals for the Federal Circuit affirmed the denial, holding that the lower court acted within its discretion in determining that retrospective duties were not appropriate.

17–3. Sample Answer—Passage of Title.

Altieri held title to the car that she was driving at the time of the accident in which Godfrey was injured. Once goods exist and are identified, title can be determined. Under the UCC, any explicit understanding between the buyer and the seller determines when title passes. If there is no such agreement, title passes to the buyer at the time and place that the seller physically delivers the goods.

In lease contracts, title to the goods is retained by the lessor-owner of the goods. The UCC's provisions relating to passage to title do not apply to leased goods. Here, Altieri originally leased the car from G.E. Capital Auto Lease, Inc., but by the time of the accident she had bought it. Even though she had not fully paid for the car or completed the transfer-of-title paperwork, she owned it. Title to the car passed to Altieri when she bought it and took delivery of it. Thus, Altieri, not G.E., was the owner of the car at the time of the accident.

In the actual case on which this problem is based, the court concluded that G.E. was not the owner of the vehicle when Godfrey was injured.

18–5. Sample Answer—Nonconforming Goods.

Padma notified Universal Exports about its breach, so Padma has two ways to recover even though it accepted the goods. Padma's first option is to argue that it revoked its acceptance, giving it the right to reject the goods. To revoke acceptance, Padma would have to show that:

1. The nonconformity substantially impaired the value of the shipment.

2. It predicated its acceptance on a reasonable assumption that Universal Exports would cure the nonconformity.

3. Universal Exports did not cure the nonconformity within a reasonable time.

Padma's second option is to keep the goods and recover for the damages caused by Universal Exports' breach. Under this option, Padma could recover at least the difference between the value of the goods as promised and their value as accepted.

19–5. Sample Answer—Negotiation.

A negotiable instrument can be transferred by assignment or by negotiation. An assignment is a transfer of rights by contract. A transfer by assignment to an assignee gives the assignee only those rights that the assignor possessed. Any defenses that can be raised against the assignor can be raised against the assignee. When an instrument is transferred by negotiation, the transferee becomes a holder. A holder receives at least the rights of the previous possessor.

Unlike an assignment, a transfer by negotiation can make it possible for the holder to receive more rights in the instrument than the prior possessor had. A holder who receives greater rights is a holder in due course (HDC) and takes the instrument free of any claims to it and defenses against its payment. Negotiating order instruments requires delivery and indorsement. If a party to whom a negotiable note is made payable signs it and delivers it to a bank, the transfer is a negotiation, and the bank becomes a holder. If the party does not sign it, however, the transfer would be treated as an assignment, and the bank would become an assignee instead of a holder.

In this problem, Argent was the payee of the note and its holder. Argent transferred the note to Wells Fargo without an indorsement. Thus, the transfer was not a negotiation but an assignment. Wells Fargo did not then become a holder of the note but an assignee. As an assignee, the bank acquired only those rights that the lender possessed before the assignment. And any defenses—including fraud in connection with the note—that Ford could assert against the lender could also be asserted by the borrower against the bank. If Argent indorsed the note to Wells Fargo now, after the defendant's response to the complaint, the bank could become a holder of the note, but it could not become an HDC. One of the requirements for HDC status is that a holder must take an instrument without notice of defenses against payment. The bank could not do this, because it is now aware of the borrower's defenses.

In the actual case on which this problem is based, the court issued a judgment in Wells Fargo's favor, and Ford appealed. A state intermediate appellate court reversed the judgment and remanded the case for trial, finding that the bank had failed to prove that it was a holder, an assignee, or even a transferee of the note.

20–4. Sample Answer—Honoring Checks.

Wells Fargo is liable to W Financial for the amount of the check. A bank that pays a customer's check bearing a forged indorsement must recredit the customer's account or be liable to the customer-drawer for breach of contract. The bank must recredit the account because it failed to carry out the drawer's order to pay to the order of the named party. Eventually, the loss falls on the first party to take the instrument bearing the forged indorsement because a forged indorsement does not transfer title. Thus, whoever takes an instrument with a forged indorsement cannot become a holder.

Under these rules, Wells Fargo is liable to W Financial for the amount of the check. The bank had an obligation to ensure that the check was properly indorsed. The bank did not pay the check to the order of Lateef, the named payee, but accepted the check for deposit into the account of CA Houston without Lateef's indorsement. The bank did not obtain title to the instrument and could not become a holder, nor was it entitled to enforce the instrument on behalf of any other party who was entitled to enforce it.

In the actual case on which this problem is based, the court held the bank liable to pay the amount of the check to W Financial.

21–4. Sample Answer—Perfecting a Security Interest.

Yes, these financing statements were sufficient to perfect the bank's security interests in Tille's equipment. In most situations, perfection is accomplished by filing a financing statement with the appropriate official. To effectively perfect a security interest, a financing statement must contain (1) the debtor's signature, (2) the debtor's and creditor's addresses, and (3) a description of the collateral by type or item.

In this case, all of Union's financing statements were sufficient to perfect security interests. They each provided the name and address of the debtor (Tille), the name and address of the secured party (Union Bank), and a description of the collateral covered by the financing statement. One loan covered all of Tille's equipment, including after-acquired property; another loan covered the truck crane; and the third loan was for a Bobcat mini excavator. These descriptions were clearly sufficient to put a prospective creditor on notice that the collateral was the subject of a security interest.

In the actual case on which this problem is based, the court concluded that all of the statements created perfected security interests.

22–4. Sample Answer—Automatic Stay.

Gholston can recover damages because EZ Auto willfully violated the automatic stay. EZ Auto repossessed the car even though it received notice of the automatic stay from the bankruptcy court. Moreover, EZ Auto retained the car even after it was reminded of the stay by Gholston's attorney. Thus, EZ Auto knew about the automatic stay and violated it intentionally. Because Gholston suffered direct damages as a result, she can recover from EZ Auto.

23–7. Sample Answer—Determining Employee Status.

No, Cox is not liable to Cayer for the injuries or damage that she sustained in the accident with Ovalles. Generally, an employer is not liable for physical harm caused to a third person by the negligent act of an independent contractor in the performance of a contract. This is because the employer does not have the right to control the details of the performance. In determining whether a worker has the status of an independent contractor, how much control the employer can exercise over the details of the work is the most important factor weighed by the courts.

In this problem, Ovalles worked as a cable installer for Cox under an agreement with M&M. The agreement disavowed any employer-employee relationship between Cox and M&M's installers. Ovalles was required to designate his affiliation with Cox on his van, clothing, and an I.D. badge. But Cox had minimal contact with Ovalles and limited power to control the manner in which he performed his work. Cox supplied cable wire and other equipment, but these items were delivered to M&M, not Ovalles. These facts indicate that Ovalles was an independent contractor, not an employee. Thus, Cox was not liable to Cayer for the harm caused to her by Ovalles when his van rear-ended Cayer's car.

In the actual case on which this problem is based, the court issued a judgment in Cox's favor. The Rhode Island Supreme Court affirmed, applying the principles stated above to arrive at the same conclusion.

24–7. Sample Answer—Unemployment Compensation.

Yes, Ramirez qualifies for unemployment compensation. Generally, to be eligible for unemployment compensation, a worker must be willing and able to work. Workers who have been fired for misconduct or who have voluntarily left their jobs are not eligible for benefits. In the facts of this problem, the applicable state statute disqualifies an employee from receiving benefits if he or she voluntarily leaves work without "good cause."

The issue is whether Ramirez left her job for "good cause." When her father in the Dominican Republic had a stroke, she asked her employer for time off to be with him. Her employer refused the request. But Ramirez left to be with her father and called to inform her employer. It seems likely that this family emergency would constitute "good cause," and Ramirez's call and return to work after her father's death indicated that she did not disregard her employer's interests.

In the actual case on which this problem is based, the state of Florida denied Ramirez unemployment compensation. On Ramirez's appeal, a state intermediate appellate court reversed, on the reasoning stated above.

25–7. Sample Answer—Age Discrimination.

No, Sanofi-Aventis U.S. LLC (S-A) does not appear to have engaged in age discrimination. The Age Discrimination in Employment Act (ADEA) prohibits employment discrimination on the basis of age against individuals forty years of age or older. For the act to apply, an employer must have twenty or more employees, and the employer's business activities must affect interstate commerce.

To establish a *prima facie* case, a plaintiff must show that he or she was (1) a member of the protected age group, (2) qualified for the position from which he or she was discharged, and (3) discharged because of age discrimination. If the employer offers a legitimate reason for its action, the plaintiff must show that the stated reason is only a pretext.

In this problem, Rangel was over forty years old. But he also had negative sales performance reviews for more than two years before he was terminated as part of S-A's nationwide reduction in force of all sales professionals who had not met the "Expectations" guidelines, including younger workers. The facts do not indicate that a person younger than Rangel replaced him or that S-A intended to discriminate against him on the basis of age. Based on these facts, Rangel could not establish a *prima facie* case of age discrimination on the part of S-A.

In the actual case on which this problem is based, in Rangel's suit against S-A under the ADEA, alleging age discrimination, a federal district court issued a judgment in S-A's favor. On Rangel's appeal, the U.S. Court of Appeals for the Tenth Circuit affirmed, according to the reasoning stated above.

26–5. Sample Answer—Wrongful Termination of a Franchise.

Oshana and GTO have stated a claim for wrongful termination of their franchise. A franchisor must act in good faith when terminating a franchise agreement. If the termination is arbitrary or unfair, a franchisee may have a claim for wrongful termination.

In this case, Oshana and GTO have alleged that Buchanan acted in bad faith. Their failure to pay rent would ordinarily be a valid basis for termination, but not if it was entirely precipitated by Buchanan. Thus, Oshana and GTO may recover if they can prove that their allegations are true.

27–6. Sample Answer—Partnerships.

Yes, Sacco is entitled to 50 percent of the profits of Pierce Paxton Collections, PPDS, and KPD. The requirements for establishing a partnership are (1) a sharing of profits and losses, (2) a joint ownership of the business, and (3) an equal right to be involved in the management of the business.

The effort and time that Sacco expended in the business constituted a sharing of losses. His proprietary interest in the assets of the partnership consisted of his share of the profits, which he had expressly left in the business to "grow the company" and "build sweat equity" for the future. He was involved in every aspect of the business. Although he was not paid a salary, he was reimbursed for business expenses charged to his personal credit card, which Paxton also used. These facts arguably meet the requirements for establishing a partnership.

In the actual case on which this problem is based, Sacco filed a suit in a Louisiana state court against Paxton, and the court awarded Sacco 50 percent of the profits. A state intermediate appellate court affirmed, based generally on the reasoning stated above.

28–6. Sample Answer—LLC Operation.

No. One Bluewater member could not unilaterally "fire" another member without providing a reason. Part of the attractiveness of an LLC as a form of business enterprise is its flexibility. The members can decide how to operate the business through an operating agreement. For example, the agreement can set forth procedures for choosing or removing members or managers.

Here, the Bluewater operating agreement provided for a "super majority" vote to remove a member under circumstances that would jeopardize the firm's contractor status. Thus, one Bluewater member could not unilaterally "fire" another member without providing a reason. In fact, a majority of the members could not terminate the other's interest in the firm without providing a reason. Moreover, the only acceptable reason would be a circumstance that undercut the firm's status as a contractor.

The flexibility of the LLC business form relates to its framework, not to its members' capacity to violate its operating agreement. In the actual case on which this problem is based, Smith attempted to "fire" Williford without providing a reason. In Williford's suit, the court issued a judgment in his favor.

29-6. Sample Answer—Duty of Loyalty.

Dweck breached the fiduciary duty of loyalty that a director and officer owes to his or her corporation—in this case, Kids. The essence of the duty of loyalty is the subordination of self-interest to the interest of the entity to which the duty is owed. The duty presumes constant loyalty to the corporation on the part of the directors and officers. The duty prohibits directors from using corporate funds or confidential corporate information for their personal advantage.

Here, Dweck breached her duty of loyalty to Kids by establishing a competing company that usurped Kids' business opportunities and converted Kids' resources—employees, office space, credit, and customer relationships—to conduct the competing firm's operations. The "administrative fee" was most likely insufficient compensation. Dweck would be liable to Kids for the damages caused by this breach of duty.

In the actual case on which this problem is based, the court held that Dweck breached her duty of loyalty to Kids and awarded as damages the lost profits that Kids would have generated from the business diverted to Success.

30-3. Sample Answer—Violations of the 1934 Act.

An omission or misrepresentation of a material fact in connection with the purchase or sale of a security may violate Section 10(b) of the Securities Exchange Act of 1934 and SEC Rule 10b-5. The key question is whether the omitted or misrepresented information is material. A fact, by itself, is not automatically material. A fact will be regarded as material only if it is significant enough that it would likely affect an investor's decision as to whether to buy or sell the company's securities. For example, a company's potential liability in a product liability suit and the financial consequences to the firm are material facts that must be disclosed because they are significant enough to affect an investor's decision as to whether to buy stock in the company.

In this case, the plaintiffs' claim should not be dismissed. To prevail on their claim that the defendants made material omissions in violation of Section 10(b) and SEC Rule 10-5, the plaintiffs must prove that the omission was material. Their complaint alleged the omission of information linking Zicam and anosmia (a loss of the sense of smell) and plausibly suggested that reasonable investors would have viewed this information as material. Zicam products account for 70 percent of Matrixx's sales. Matrixx received reports of consumers who suffered anosia after using Zicam Cold Remedy.

In public statements discussing revenues and product safety, Matrixx did not disclose this information. But the information was significant enough to likely affect a consumer's decision to use the product, and this would affect revenue and ultimately the commercial viability of the product. The information was therefore significant enough to likely affect an investor's decision whether to buy or sell Matrixx's stock, and this would affect the stock price.

Thus, the plaintiffs' allegations were sufficient. Contrary to the defendants' assertion, statistical sampling is not required to show materiality—reasonable investors could view reports of adverse events as material even if the reports did not provide statistically significant evidence.

31-5. Sample Answer—Price Discrimination.

Spa Steel satisfies most of the requirements for a price discrimination claim under Section 2 of the Clayton Act. Dayton Superior is engaged in interstate commerce, and it sells goods of like grade and quality to at least three purchasers. Moreover, Spa Steel can show that, because it sells Dayton Superior's products at a higher price, it lost business and thus suffered an injury. To recover, however, Spa Steel will also need to prove that Dayton Superior charged Spa Steel's competitors a lower price for the same product. Spa Steel cannot recover if its prices were higher for reasons related to its own business, such as having higher overhead or seeking a larger profit.

32-4. Sample Answer—Fair Debt Collection Practices.

Engler may recover under the Fair Debt Collection Practices Act (FDCPA). Atlantic is subject to the FDCPA because it is a debt-collection agency and it was attempting to collect a debt on behalf of Bank of America. Atlantic also used offensive tactics to collect from Engler. After all, Atlantic gave Engler's employer the false impression that Engler was a criminal, had a pending case, and was about to be arrested. Finally, Engler suffered harm because he experienced discomfort, embarrassment, and distress as a result of Atlantic's abusive conduct. Engler may recover actual damages, statutory damages, and attorneys' fees from Atlantic.

33-7. Sample Answer—Potential Liability to Third Parties.

KPMG is potentially liable to the hedge funds' partners under the *Restatement (Third) of Torts*. Under Section 552 of the *Restatement*, an auditor owes a duty to "persons for whose benefit and guidance the accountant intends to supply . . . information."

In this case, KPMG prepared annual reports on the hedge funds and addressed them to the funds' "Partners." Additionally, KPMG knew who the partners were because it prepared individual tax forms for them each year. Thus, KPMG's annual reports were for the partners' benefit and guidance. The partners relied on the reports, including their representations that they complied with generally accepted accounting principles.

As a result, they lost millions of dollars, which exposes KPMG to possible liability under Section 552.

34-6. Sample Answer—Bailment Obligation.

Moreland should be awarded damages, and Gray should take nothing. The bailee must exercise reasonable care in preserving the bailed property. What constitutes reasonable care in a bailment situation normally depends on the nature and specific circumstances of the bailment. If the bailed property has been lost or is returned damaged, a court will presume that the bailee was negligent.

In the circumstances of this problem, when the bailor (Moreland, the owner of the aircraft) entrusted the plane to the bailee's (Gray's) repair shop for painting, the work was not properly performed. This violated the bailee's duty to exercise reasonable care and breached the bailment contract. Because the plane was returned damaged, this may also constitute negligence. In the event of a breach, the bailor may sue for damages. The measure of damages is the difference between the value of the bailed property in its present condition and what it would have been worth if the work had been properly performed.

Thus, Gray is liable to Moreland for failing to properly paint the plane. In the actual case on which this problem is based, the court upheld a jury award to Moreland of damages and attorneys' fees.

35–5. Sample Answer—Adverse Possession.

The McKeags satisfied the first three requirements for adverse possession:

1. Their possession was actual and exclusive because they used the beach and prevented others from doing so, including the Finleys.

2. Their possession was open, visible, and notorious because they made improvements to the beach and regularly kept their belongings there.

3. Their possession was continuous and peaceable for the required ten years. They possessed the property for more than four decades, and they even kept a large float there during the winter months.

Nevertheless, the McKeags' possession was *not* hostile and adverse, which is the fourth requirement. The Finleys had substantial evidence that they gave the McKeags permission to use the beach. Rather than reject the Finleys' permission as unnecessary, the McKeags sometimes said nothing and other times seemingly affirmed that the property belonged to the Finleys. Thus, because the McKeags did not satisfy all four requirements, they cannot establish adverse possession.

36–5. Sample Answer—Undue Influence.

No, undue influence does not appear to have occurred in this problem. To invalidate a will on the basis of undue influence, a plaintiff must show that the decedent's plan of distribution was the result of improper pressure brought by another person. Undue influence may be inferred if the testator ignores blood relatives and names as a beneficiary a nonrelative who is in constant close contact and in a position to influence the making of the will.

In this problem, although Tommy's ex-wife lived with Susie Walker and was thus in a position to influence Susie's will, she was not a beneficiary under it, so there is no inference of undue influence. Moreover, neither of the wills that Walker executed left any property to her son, so there was no indication that she had been influenced to change her mind regarding the distribution of her estate. Additionally, she expressly disinherited her son, and several witnesses testified that she was mentally competent at the time she made the will.

In the actual case on which this problem is based, the court presumed that Walker's will was valid.

Appendix G

Case Excerpts for *Case Analysis Questions*

Case No. 1 for Chapter 6

Winstead v. Jackson
United States Court of Appeals, Third Circuit, 2013 WL 139622 (2013).

PER CURIAM. [By the Whole Court]
* * * *

* * * Winstead filed his * * * complaint in the United States District Court for the District of New Jersey, claiming that Jackson's album/CD and film derived their contents from, and infringed the copyright of, his book.
* * * *

* * * The District Court dismissed Winstead's * * * complaint * * * , concluding that Jackson * * * did not improperly copy protected aspects of Winstead's book.
* * * *

Winstead appeals.
* * * *

Here, it is not disputed that Winstead is the owner of the copyrighted property * * *. However, *not all copying is copyright infringement, so even if actual copying is proven, the court must decide, by comparing the allegedly infringing work with the original work, whether the copying was unlawful. Copying may be proved inferentially by showing that the allegedly infringing work is substantially similar to the copyrighted work.* A court compares the allegedly infringing work with the original work, and considers whether a "lay-observer" would believe that the copying was of protectable aspects of the copyrighted work. The inquiry involves distinguishing between the author's expression and the idea or theme that he or she seeks to convey or explore, because the former is protected and the latter is not. The court must determine whether the allegedly infringing work is similar because it appropriates the unique expressions of the original work, or merely because it contains elements that would be expected when two works express the same idea or explore the same theme. [Emphasis added.]

* * * A lay observer would not believe that Jackson's album/CD and film copied protectable aspects of Winstead's book. Jackson's album/CD is comprised of 16 individual songs, which explore drug-dealing, guns and money, vengeance, and other similar clichés of hip hop gangsterism. Jackson's fictional film is the story of a young man who turns to violence when his mother is killed in a

drive-by shooting. The young man takes revenge by killing the man who killed his mother, and then gets rich by becoming an "enforcer" for a powerful criminal. He takes up with a woman who eventually betrays him, and is shot to death by her boyfriend, who has just been released from prison. The movie ends with his younger brother vowing to seek vengeance. Winstead's book purports to be autobiographical and tells the story of a young man whose beloved father was a Bishop in the church. The protagonist was angry as a child because his stepmother abused him, but he found acceptance and self-esteem on the streets of Newark because he was physically powerful. He earned money robbing and beating people, went to jail, returned to crime upon his release, and then made even more money. The protagonist discusses his time at Rahway State Prison in great and compelling detail. The story ends when the protagonist learns that his father has passed away; he conveys his belief that this tragedy has led to his redemption, and he hopes that others might learn from his mistakes.

* * * Although Winstead's book and Jackson's works share similar themes and setting, the story of an angry and wronged protagonist who turns to a life of violence and crime has long been a part of the public domain [and is therefore not protected by copyright law]. Winstead argues * * * that a protagonist asking for God's help when his father dies, cutting drugs with mixing agents to maximize profits, and complaining about relatives who are addicts and steal the product, are protectable, but these things are not unique. To the extent that Jackson's works contain these elements, they are to be expected when two works express the same idea about "the streets" or explore the same theme. Winstead argues that not every protagonist whose story concerns guns, drugs, and violence in an urban setting winds up in prison or loses a parent, but this argument only serves to illustrate an important difference between his book and Jackson's film. Jackson's protagonist never spends any time in prison, whereas Winstead's protagonist devotes a considerable part of his story to his incarcerations.

In addition, Winstead's book and Jackson's works are different with respect to character, plot, mood, and sequence of events. Winstead's protagonist embarks on a life of crime at a very young age, but is redeemed by the death of his beloved father. Jackson's protagonist turns to crime when he is much older and only after his mother is murdered. He winds up dead at a young age, unredeemed. Winstead's book is hopeful; Jackson's film is characterized * * * by moral apathy. It is true that both works involve the loss of a parent and the protagonist's recognition of the parent's importance in his life, but nowhere does Jackson appropriate anything unique about Winstead's expression of this generic topic.

Winstead contends that direct phrases from his book appear in Jackson's film. * * * He emphasizes these phrases: "Yo, where is my money at," "I would never have done no shit like that to you," "my father, my strength was gone," "he was everything to me," and "I did not know what to do," but, like the phrases "putting the work in," "get the dope, cut the dope," "let's keep it popping," and "the strong take from the weak but the smart take from everybody," they are either common in general or common with respect to hip hop culture, and do not enjoy copyright protection. *The average person reading or listening to these phrases in the context of an overall story or song would not regard them as unique and protectable.* Moreover, words and short phrases do not enjoy copyright protection. The similarity between Winstead's book and the lyrics to Jackson's songs on the album/CD is even more tenuous. "Stretching the dope" and "bloodshot red eyes" are common phrases that do not enjoy copyright protection. *A side-by-side comparison of Winstead's book and the lyrics from Jackson's album/CD do not support a claim of copyright infringement.* [Emphasis added.]

For the foregoing reasons, we will affirm the order of the District Court dismissing [Winstead's] complaint.

Case No. 2 for Chapter 11

Gyabaah v. Rivlab Transportation Corp.
New York Supreme Court, Appellate Division, First Department, 102 A.D.3d 451, 958 N.Y.S.2d 109 (2013).

TOM, J.P. [Judge Presiding], *ANDRIAS, RENWICK, DEGRASSE, ABDUS-SALAAM*, JJ. [Judges]

* * * *

[Adwoa Gyabaah was hit by a bus owned by Rivlab Transportation Corporation. She retained attorney Jeffrey Aronsky to represent her in negotiations with Rivlab, its insurer National Casualty Company, and their attorneys. Gyabaah agreed to pay Aronsky a contingency fee of one-third of the amount of her recovery. Aronsky] commenced this personal injury action on plaintiff's behalf on August 25, 2010 [against Rivlab]. By letter to Aronsky dated October 1, 2010, defendant's carrier tendered its $1 million policy limits for purposes of settlement. Aronsky explained the proposal to plaintiff who, at that time, chose to accept the settlement. Accordingly, plaintiff executed a general release on October 5, 2010 * * *. Aronsky advised plaintiff that he would hold the release pending receipt of * * * advice from plaintiff as to whether she preferred to have the settlement structured [paid over a period of time rather than in one lump sum].

By December 9, 2010, plaintiff had retained new counsel, Kenneth A. Wilhelm, Esq. [Esquire, or lawyer]. On that date, Wilhelm advised Aronsky that plaintiff did not wish to settle the case or have the release sent to defendant. Aronsky moved the court below for an order enforcing what he contended was a $1 million settlement and setting his firm's contingency fee at one-third of the recovery pursuant to plaintiff's retainer agreement. In making

his motion, Aronsky did not allege that acceptance of the offer was ever communicated to defendant or its carrier. This omission is fatal to Aronsky's claim of a settlement for reasons that follow. Aronsky maintained that "plaintiff's signing of the General Release constituted a binding legal contract." The court denied the motion and vacated the release in what it perceived to be the interest of justice.

* * * The application of contract law * * * required the denial of Aronsky's motion. A general release is governed by principles of contract law. * * * *It is essential in any bilateral contract that the fact of acceptance be communicated to the offeror. Therefore, this action was not settled because the executed release was never forwarded to defendant nor was acceptance of the offer otherwise communicated to defendant or its carrier.* This record does not contain a single affidavit by anyone asserting that either occurred. * * * We do not share the * * * view that an October 6, 2010 letter from defendant's counsel to Aronsky "evidenced" an agreement to settle. Defense counsel's statement in the letter that he was "advised" of a settlement does not suffice as evidence that such a settlement was effected. * * * Because there has been no settlement, the amount of Aronsky's fee should be determined upon the disposition of this action [as a percentage of the fee recovered by the Wilhelm firm based on the *pro rata* share of the work the two attorneys performed in obtaining the recovery]. [Emphasis added.]

* * * We see no need for a hearing to determine whether Aronsky was discharged for cause. The record discloses that plaintiff has not made a *prima facie* showing of any cause for Aronsky's discharge. Plaintiff stated in her affidavit that she signed the release * * * because she felt "pressured" to do so. Plaintiff made no mention of what the pressure consisted of or, more importantly, what professional misconduct, if any, brought it about. To be sure, a hearing was not warranted by plaintiff's untenable [indefensible] argument that Aronsky disobeyed her instructions by making the instant motion albeit [although] after he had already been discharged as her attorney.

[The order of the lower court denying Aronsky's motion insofar as it sought to enforce a purported settlement and set Aronsky's fee accordingly is affirmed.]

Case No. 3 for Chapter 19

Mills v. Chauvin
Supreme Court of New York, Appellate Division, Third Department, 103 A.D.3d 1041, 962 N.Y.S.2d 412 (2013).

PER CURIAM. [By the Whole Court]

* * * *

Plaintiff, Gregory Mills, and defendant, Robert Chauvin, are two experienced attorneys who shared both a friendship and a professional/business relationship. Those longstanding relationships deteriorated and gave rise to this action.

* * * *

* * * The parties formed a partnership and took ownership of a commercial office building located on Crescent Road in the Town of Clifton Park, Saratoga County. * * * After Chauvin decided, for a

variety of reasons, that he no longer wished to maintain his ownership of the Crescent Road property, the parties agreed that Mills would purchase Chauvin's one-half interest in such property and they executed a purchase and sale agreement establishing a purchase price of $261,176.67 and a closing date.

* * * *

Chauvin was an investor in the Amelia Village [real estate development] project [in Virginia]. Over a course of time, Mills made multiple monetary payments to Chauvin—totaling $395,750—which Chauvin claims were investments in the project and Mills claims were loans. Ultimately, Mills requested that Chauvin return the payments he had advanced. In connection therewith, Chauvin executed a promissory note * * * that obligated him to pay Mills $395,750. However, Chauvin later challenged the validity of the promissory note and claimed that Mills was not entitled to a return of his investments.

* * * *

Mills subsequently filed [a] complaint [in a New York state court against Chauvin] to recover the payments Mills had made with respect to the Amelia Village project, based upon claims of breach of contract and unjust enrichment, respectively.

* * * *

The action proceeded to a nonjury trial * * *. At the conclusion thereof, Supreme Court [the trial court] found * * * that the promissory note was valid and enforceable and that Mills was entitled to recover pursuant to its terms. Chauvin now appeals from the judgment entered upon that decision.

* * * *

* * * Initially, we reject Chauvin's claim that Supreme Court erred in concluding that the * * * promissory note was enforceable. Chauvin does not dispute that Mills had previously paid him $395,750 in connection with the Amelia Village project, that he signed the promissory note promising to repay that amount to Mills, or that he tendered the note to Mills for the purpose of providing documentation to Mills' lending institution in support of Mills' application for financing of the purchase of the Crescent Road property. Instead, Chauvin claims that the promissory note was not enforceable because it was not given to secure a debt and, therefore, lacked consideration.

In this regard, Mills testified that * * * the parties * * * agreed that Chauvin would repay Mills all of the money that Mills had contributed to the Amelia Village project and that the promissory note confirmed their agreement. On the other hand, Chauvin claims that the payments that Mills made to the Amelia Village project were investments that could not be returned when Mills withdrew from that project, and that the promissory note was not intended to be a promise of repayment.

* * * *

The record amply supports Supreme Court's finding that the consideration for the promissory note was the $395,750 that Mills had provided to Chauvin in connection with the Amelia Village project and that the promissory note represented security for Chauvin's antecedent obligation to repay such funds. *The note itself—which was drafted by Chauvin, signed by him, notarized and transmitted to Mills clearly states that it was executed in return for a loan received by Chauvin and contained an unconditional promise*

or order to pay a sum certain in money. In addition, Mills took the note as a holder in due course. Based upon our independent evaluation of the evidence and, giving due deference to the trial court's credibility determinations concerning witnesses, we conclude that Supreme Court's determination that Chauvin failed to establish a bona fide defense of lack of consideration is supported by the record. [Emphasis added.]

* * * *

ORDERED that the order and judgments are affirmed, with costs to plaintiff.

Case No. 4 for Chapter 25

Dees v. United Rentals North America, Inc.
United States Court of Appeals, Ninth Circuit, 505 Fed.Appx. 302 (2013).

PER CURIAM:

* * * *

In * * * 2006 [Ellis Dees, an African American, applied] to United Rentals for employment at its Gulfport, Mississippi location, and was offered a service technician position in St. Rose, Louisiana. Branch Manager Mike Sauve made the decision to make the offer, which Dees accepted.

Although the first two years of Dees' employment in St. Rose went smoothly, United Rentals contends that his attitude and work performance deteriorated beginning in 2009. Specifically, it alleges that he began, with increasing frequency, to mark equipment as fit to be rented even though it was not in working order. Dees' managers—Sauve and Lee Vincent—coached him when these incidents occurred, and noted them in his 2009 mid-year and full-year performance reviews. Dees was also given written warnings in August 2009, October 2009, February 2010, and March 2010. Dees was given a "final written warning" on March 4, 2010, advising him that "the next incident will result in immediate termination." Following a further incident six days later, Sauve and Vincent told Dees that he was fired. Dees was sixty-two years old at the time.

Dees filed a charge with the Equal Employment Opportunity Commission, alleging employment discrimination based on his race and age [in violation of Title VII of the Civil Rights Act and the Age Discrimination in Employment Act (ADEA)]. After receiving a "right to sue" notice, he filed suit in [a federal district court]. United Rentals filed a motion for summary judgment, which the district court granted * * *. Dees timely appealed.

* * * *

* * * [Under Title VII or the ADEA] Dees first must make a *prima facie* case of discrimination based on age or race. To establish a *prima facie* case, Dees must show that he: (1) was a member of a protected group; (2) qualified for the position in question; (3) was subjected to an adverse employment action; and (4) received less favorable treatment due to his membership in the protected class than did other similarly situated employees who were not members of the protected class, under nearly identical circumstances.

If Dees makes a prima facie *case, the burden then shifts to United Rentals to articulate a legitimate, non-discriminatory reason for firing him.* If it does so, Dees must, as to his Title VII claim, offer sufficient evidence to create a genuine issue of material fact either (1) that United Rentals' reason is not true, but is instead a pretext for discrimination * * *; or (2) that United Rentals' reason, while true, is only one of the reasons for its conduct, and another motivating factor is Dees' protected characteristic. [Emphasis added.]

* * * *

The district court assumed, without deciding, that Dees established a *prima facie* case of discrimination under Title VII and the ADEA. The district court * * * determined that United Rentals had provided extensive evidence of a legitimate, non-discriminatory reason for Dees' termination—namely, unsatisfactory job performance. * * * The burden shifted back to Dees to produce evidence that United Rentals' reason was a pretext for discrimination. The district court concluded that Dees had only made conclusory [conclusive] allegations that he was discriminated against.

* * * *

His termination notice states that he was terminated for failing to follow United Rentals' policy of ensuring that the batteries in rental equipment were in good working order prior to delivery of the equipment.

* * * Dees has presented nothing to tie United Rentals' final termination decision to a discriminatory motive. * * * Dees himself describes United Rentals as motivated by an "I ain't missing no rents" philosophy that encouraged renting out equipment regardless of its readiness. No evidence shows that United Rentals' philosophy also included discriminating against African Americans or senior workers. Similarly, no evidence demonstrates that United Rentals' decision to discharge Dees was motivated by his race or age. * * * Dees' subjective belief that United Rentals discriminated against him is clearly insufficient to demonstrate pretext.

* * * *

For the reasons set forth above, we AFFIRM the district court's grant of summary judgment in United Rentals' favor.

Case No. 5 for Chapter 30

City of Livonia Employees' Retirement System and Local 295/Local 851 v. Boeing Co.
United States Court of Appeals, Seventh Circuit, 711 F.3d 754 (2013).

POSNER, Circuit Judge.

* * * *

* * * On April 21 [2009] Boeing [Company] performed a stress test on the wings of its new 787-8 Dreamliner, a plane that had not yet flown. The wings failed the test * * *. Yet Boeing announced on May 3 that "all structural tests required on the static airframe prior to first flight are complete" and that "the initial results of the test are positive" * * *. The implication was that the plane was on track for its "First Flight," which had been scheduled for June 30.

In mid-May, after making some changes in the design * * *, Boeing conducted another test. Although the plane failed that test too, [Boeing's chief executive officer James] McNerney stated publicly that he thought the plane would fly in June. Later [the head of Boeing's commercial aircraft division Scott] Carson told [the media] that the Dreamliner "definitely will fly" this month (June).

* * * Yet on June 23, * * * Boeing announced that the First Flight of the Dreamliner had been canceled because, Carson explained, of an "anomaly" revealed by the * * * tests. He said that Boeing had hoped to be able to solve the problem in time for a First Flight in June, but had been unable to do so. In fact the First Flight did not take place until December 2009.

When Boeing announced the cancellation of the First Flight, it also announced that the cancellation would cause a delay of unspecified length in the delivery of the Dreamliner, which many airlines had already ordered. In the two days after these announcements, Boeing's stock price dropped by more than 10 percent. * * * Persons who bought Boeing stock between the tests and the announcements of the cancellation and of the delay in delivery and who therefore lost money when the price dropped [filed a suit in a federal district court against Boeing and its officers, alleging violations of Section 10(b) and Rule 10b-5].

The district judge dismissed the * * * complaint. [The plaintiffs appealed.]

There is no securities fraud by hindsight. The law does not require public disclosure of mere risks of failure. No prediction—even a prediction that the sun will rise tomorrow—has a 100 percent probability of being correct. The future is shrouded in uncertainty. If a mistaken prediction is deemed a fraud, there will be few predictions, including ones that are well grounded, as no one wants to be held hostage to an unknown future. [Emphasis added.]

Any sophisticated purchaser of a product that is still on the drawing boards knows, moreover, that its market debut may be delayed, or indeed that the project may be abandoned before it yields salable product. The purchasers of the Dreamliner protected themselves against the possibility of delay in delivery by reserving the right to cancel their orders; there are no allegations regarding cancellation penalties, or for that matter penalties imposed on Boeing for delivery delays. And therefore * * * the defendants * * * had, so far as appears, little incentive to delay the announcement of the postponement.

Without a motive to commit securities fraud, businessmen are unlikely to commit it. A more plausible inference than that of fraud is that the defendants, unsure whether they could fix the problem by the end of June, were reluctant to tell the world "we have a problem and maybe it will cause us to delay the First Flight and maybe not, but we're working on the problem and we hope we can fix it in time to prevent any significant delay, but we can't be sure, so stay tuned." There is a difference * * * between a duty of truthfulness and a duty of candor, or between a lie and reticence [uncommunicativeness]. There is no duty of total corporate transparency—no rule that every hitch or glitch, every pratfall [embarrassing mistake], in a company's operations must be disclosed in real time, forming a running commentary, a baring of the corporate innards, day and night. [Emphasis added.]

* * * *

* * * The * * * complaint alleged [that] what McNerney and Carson knew about the likely postponement of the First Flight * * * was confirmed by "internal e-mails" of Boeing. The reference to internal e-mails implied that someone inside Boeing was aiding the plaintiffs. But as no such person was identified, the judge could not determine whether such e-mails * * * existed.

Allegations * * * merely implying unnamed confidential sources of damaging information require a heavy discount. The sources may be ill-informed, may be acting from spite rather than knowledge, may be misrepresented, may even be nonexistent * * *. The district judge therefore rightly refused to give any weight to the "internal e-mails" to which the complaint referred.

* * * *

The judgment dismissing the suit is affirmed.

Case No. 6 for Chapter 31

Leegin Creative Leather Products, Inc. v. PSKS, Inc.
Supreme Court of the United States, 551 U.S. 877, 127 S.Ct. 2705, 168 L.Ed.2d 623 (2007).

Justice *KENNEDY* delivered the opinion of the Court.

* * * *

Petitioner, Leegin Creative Leather Products, Inc. (Leegin), designs, manufactures, and distributes leather goods and accessories. In 1991, Leegin began to sell [products] under the brand name "Brighton."

Respondent, PSKS, Inc. (PSKS), operates Kay's Kloset, a women's apparel store in Lewisville, Texas. * * * It first started purchasing Brighton goods from Leegin in 1995.

* * * *

In December 2002, Leegin discovered Kay's Kloset had been marking down Brighton's entire line by 20 percent. * * * Leegin stopped selling [Brighton products] to the store.

PSKS sued Leegin in the United States District Court for the Eastern District of Texas. It alleged, among other claims, that Leegin had violated the antitrust laws by "enter[ing] into agreements with retailers to charge only those prices fixed by Leegin." * * * [The court] entered judgment against Leegin in the amount of $3,975,000.80.

The [U.S.] Court of Appeals for the Fifth Circuit affirmed. * * * We granted *certiorari* * * *.

* * * *

The rule of reason is the accepted standard for testing whether a practice restrains trade in violation of [Section] 1 [of the Sherman Act].

* * * *

Resort to per se *rules is confined to restraints * * * that would always or almost always tend to restrict competition and decrease output. To justify a* per se *prohibition a restraint must have manifestly anticompetitive effects, and lack * * * any redeeming virtue.* [Emphasis added.]

As a consequence, the *per se* rule is appropriate only after courts have had considerable experience with the type of restraint at issue, and only if courts can predict with confidence that it would be invalidated in all or almost all instances under the rule of reason.

* * * *

The reasoning of the Court's more recent jurisprudence has rejected the rationales on which [the application of the *per se* rule to minimum resale price maintenance agreements] was based. * * * [These rationales were] based on formalistic legal doctrine rather than demonstrable economic effect. * * *

* * * Furthermore [the Court] treated vertical agreements a manufacturer makes with its distributors as analogous to a horizontal combination among competing distributors. * * * Our recent cases formulate antitrust principles in accordance with the appreciated differences in economic effect between vertical and horizontal agreements * * *.

* * * *

The justifications for vertical price restraints are similar to those for other vertical restraints. *Minimum resale price maintenance can stimulate interbrand competition * * * by reducing intrabrand competition * * *.* The promotion of interbrand competition is important because the primary purpose of the antitrust laws is to protect this type of competition. * * * *Resale price maintenance also has the potential to give consumers more options so that they can choose among low-price, low-service brands; high-price, high-service brands; and brands that fall in between.* [Emphasis added.]

* * * *

While vertical agreements setting minimum resale prices can have procompetitive justifications, they may have anticompetitive effects in other cases; and unlawful price fixing, designed solely to obtain monopoly profits, is an ever present temptation.

* * * *

Notwithstanding the risks of unlawful conduct, it cannot be stated with any degree of confidence that resale price maintenance always or almost always tends to restrict competition and decrease output. Vertical agreements establishing minimum resale prices can have either procompetitive or anticompetitive effects, depending upon the circumstances in which they are formed. * * * As the [per se] rule would proscribe a significant amount of procompetitive conduct, these agreements appear ill suited for *per se* condemnation.

* * * *

The judgment of the Court of Appeals is reversed, and the case is remanded for proceedings consistent with this opinion.

Case No. 7 for Chapter 35

Town of Midland v. Morris
Court of Appeals of North Carolina, 704 S.E.2d 329 (2011).

STEPHENS, Judge.

The Transcontinental Pipeline transports and distributes natural gas from the Gulf of Mexico to the northeastern United States. In April 2002, the City of Monroe, North Carolina, decided to supply the citizens of Monroe and the surrounding area with natural gas by a direct connection between its natural gas distribution system and the Transcontinental Pipeline. To directly connect to the Transcontinental Pipeline, Monroe needed to acquire the rights to property through which to run a pipeline along the forty-two miles between Monroe and the direct connection on the Transcontinental Pipeline located in Iredell County.

To facilitate the acquisition of land for the construction of the new pipeline ("Pipeline"), Monroe, located in Union County, entered into interlocal agreements with the Town of Mooresville, located in Iredell County, and the Town of Midland, located in Cabarrus County.

The relevant terms of the interlocal agreement between Midland and Monroe * * * provide as follows:

4. Midland shall be responsible for obtaining either by acquisition or by the power of eminent domain and holding in its name for the benefit of the parties and this Interlocal Agreement all easements (both permanent and temporary construction), rights of way, and real property required for the project in Cabarrus County.

* * * *

20. * * * Midland shall retain a perpetual right to locate and install one (1) tap in the pipeline within the corporate limits of Midland from which to operate and supply its own natural gas distribution utility for the benefit of Midland's utility customers in Cabarrus County only. The one tap for Midland's use shall be subject to a right of first refusal granted to a private natural gas provider to serve customers that would otherwise be served by Midland. . . .

* * * *

In 2008 Midland began the process of acquiring the property necessary for the construction of the Pipeline. When negotiations for voluntary acquisitions for the rights of way failed, Midland exercised its eminent domain authority to condemn the needed property.

The present controversy stems from fifteen condemnation actions filed by the Town of Midland in Cabarrus County Superior Court. In those fifteen actions, the opposing parties (hereinafter "Property Owners") filed defenses and counterclaims, challenging Midland's power to condemn the properties in question * * *.

* * * *

Property Owners first argue that because Midland neither currently provides natural gas services to its citizens, nor currently has any plans to provide natural gas to its citizens in the future, the condemnations were undertaken in violation of the statutes governing eminent domain. We disagree.

* * * *

* * * *We find it manifest [obvious] that Midland may acquire property by condemnation to establish a gas transmission and distribution system, even in the absence of a concrete, immediate plan to furnish gas services to its citizens.* [Emphasis added.]

While we acknowledge the existence of the requirement that the public enterprise be established and conducted for the city and its citizens, we conclude that this requirement is satisfied by Midland's placement of a tap on the Pipeline and by Midland's acquisition of the right to low-cost natural gas. Further, * * * *there is nothing in the record to indicate that Midland will never offer natural gas services to its citizens. In fact, Midland's contracted-for right to install a tap on the Pipeline "from which to operate and supply its own natural gas distribution utility for the benefit of Midland's utility customers" indicates just the opposite*: that Midland will, eventually, furnish natural gas services to its citizens. [Emphasis added.]

* * * *

Property Owners further argue that Midland's condemnations violate [the state's statute] because the condemnations are not "for the public use or benefit."

* * * *

It is clear from the statutory language that establishing a gas transmission and distribution system is an appropriate purpose for the condemnation of property under [the relevant provisions].

Despite the disjunctive language of this statutory requirement, our courts have determined the propriety of a condemnation under [the statute] based on the condemnation's satisfaction of both a "public use test" and a "public benefit test."

The first approach—the public use test—asks whether the public has a right to a definite use of the condemned property. The second approach—the public benefit test—asks whether some benefit accrues to the public as a result of the desired condemnation.

Under the public use test, "the principal and dispositive determination is whether the general public has a right to a definite use of the property sought to be condemned." * * * Applying this test to the present case in the appropriate context, there is nothing to indicate that gas services—were they to be provided by Midland—would be available to anything less than the entire population. Accordingly, there can be no doubt that the Midland condemnations would pass the public use test * * *.

* * * *

Under the public benefit test, *"a given condemnor's desired use of the condemned property in question is for 'the public use or benefit' if that use would contribute to the general welfare and prosperity of the public at large."* In this case, we must take care in defining Midland's "desired use" of the property. Midland is condemning the property to run the Pipeline and to control a tap on the Pipeline, not to immediately provide gas to the citizens of Midland. Accordingly, it is the *availability* of natural gas that must contribute to the general welfare and prosperity of the public at large. [Emphasis added.]

As noted by our Courts, the construction and extension of public utilities, and especially the concomitant commercial and residential growth, provide a clear public benefit to local citizens. * * * Midland's tap on the Pipeline, and its potential to provide natural gas service, likely will spur growth, as well as provide Midland with an advantage in industrial recruitment. These opportunities must be seen as public benefits accruing to the citizens of Midland, such that Midland's condemnations are for the public benefit.

* * * *

Accordingly, we conclude that the Midland condemnations were not undertaken to provide a solely private benefit.

* * * *

We hold that Midland lawfully exercised its eminent domain power.

Glossary

A

Abandoned Property Property that has been discarded by the owner, who has no intention of reclaiming it.

Acceleration Clause A clause that allows a payee or other holder of a time instrument to demand payment of the entire amount due, with interest, if a certain event occurs, such as a default in the payment of an installment when due.

Acceptance The act of voluntarily agreeing, through words or conduct, to the terms of an offer, thereby creating a contract. In negotiable instruments law, a drawee's signed agreement to pay a draft when it is presented.

Acceptor A drawee that accepts, or promises to pay, an instrument when it is presented later for payment.

Accession The addition of value to personal property by the use of labor or materials.

Accord and Satisfaction A common means of settling a disputed claim, whereby a debtor offers to pay a lesser amount than the creditor purports to be owed.

Accredited Investor In the context of securities offerings, sophisticated investors, such as banks, insurance companies, investment companies, the issuer's executive officers and directors, and persons whose income or net worth exceeds certain limits.

Act of State Doctrine A doctrine providing that the judicial branch of one country will not examine the validity of public acts committed by a recognized foreign government within its own territory.

Actionable Capable of serving as the basis of a lawsuit. An actionable claim can be pursued in a lawsuit or other court action.

Actual Malice The deliberate intent to cause harm that exists when a person makes a statement with either knowledge of its falsity or reckless disregard of the truth. Actual malice is required to establish defamation against public figures.

Actus Reus A guilty (prohibited) act; one of the two essential elements required to establish criminal liability.

Adhesion Contract A standard-form contract in which the stronger party dictates the terms.

Adjudicate To render a judicial decision. Adjudication is the trial-like proceeding in which an administrative law judge hears and resolves disputes involving an administrative agency's regulations.

Administrative Agency A federal or state government agency created by the legislature to perform a specific function, such as to make and enforce rules pertaining to the environment.

Administrative Law The body of law created by administrative agencies in order to carry out their duties and responsibilities.

Administrative Law Judge (ALJ) One who presides over an administrative agency hearing and has the power to administer oaths, take testimony, rule on questions of evidence, and make determinations of fact.

Administrative Process The procedure used by administrative agencies in administering the law.

Administrator One who is appointed by a court to administer a person's estate if the decedent died without a valid will or if the executor named in the will cannot serve.

Adverse Possession The acquisition of title to real property through open occupation, without the consent of the owner, for a period of time specified by a state statute. The occupation must be actual, exclusive, open, continuous, and in opposition to all others, including the owner.

Affirmative Action Job-hiring policies that give special consideration to members of protected classes in an effort to overcome present effects of past discrimination.

After-Acquired Property Property that is acquired by the debtor after the execution of a security agreement.

Age of Majority The age (eighteen in most states) at which a person, formerly a minor, is recognized by law as an adult and is legally responsible for his or her actions.

Agency A relationship between two parties in which one party (the agent) agrees to represent or act for the other (the principal).

Agency Coupled with an Interest An agency, created for the benefit of the agent, in which the agent has some legal right (interest) in the property that is the subject of the agency.

Agreement A mutual understanding or meeting of the minds between two or more individuals regarding the terms of a contract.

Alien Corporation A corporation formed in another country but doing business in the United States.

Alienation The transfer of title to real property (which "alienates" the real property from the former owner).

Alternative Dispute Resolution (ADR) The resolution of disputes in ways other than those involved in the traditional judicial process, such as negotiation, mediation, and arbitration.

Answer Procedurally, a defendant's response to the plaintiff's complaint.

Anticipatory Repudiation An assertion or action by a party indicating that he or she will not perform a contractual obligation.

Antitrust Law Laws protecting commerce from unlawful restraints and anticompetitive practices.

Apparent Authority Authority that is only apparent, not real. An agent's apparent authority arises when the principal causes a third party to believe that the agent has authority, even though she or he does not.

Appropriation In tort law, the use by one person of another person's name, likeness, or other identifying characteristic without permission and for the benefit of the user.

Arbitration The settling of a dispute by submitting it to a disinterested third party (other than a court), who renders a decision.

Arbitration Clause A clause in a contract that provides that, in the event of a dispute, the parties will submit the dispute to arbitration rather than litigate the dispute in court.

Arson The intentional burning of a building.

Articles of Incorporation The document that is filed with the appropriate state official, usually the secretary of state, when a business is incorporated and that contains basic information about the corporation

Articles of Organization The document filed with a designated state official by which a limited liability company is formed.

Articles of Partnership A written agreement that sets forth each partner's rights and obligations with respect to the partnership.

Artisan's Lien A possessory lien held by a party who has made improvements and added value to the personal property of another party as security for payment for services performed.

Assault Any word or action intended to make another person fearful of immediate physical harm—a reasonably believable threat.

Assignee A party to whom the rights under a contract are transferred, or assigned.

Assignment The transfer to another of all or part of one's rights arising under a contract.

Assignor A party who transfers (assigns) his or her rights under a contract to another party (the *assignee*).

Assumption of Risk A defense to negligence that bars a plaintiff from recovering for injuries or damage suffered as a result of risks he or she knew of and voluntarily assumed.

Attachment In a secured transaction, the process by which a secured creditor's interest "attaches" to the collateral and the creditor's security interest becomes enforceable. In the context of judicial liens, a court-ordered seizure of property before a judgment is secured for a past-due debt.

Attempted Monopolization An action by a firm that involves anticompetitive conduct, the intent to gain monopoly power, and a "dangerous probability" of success in achieving monopoly power.

Auditor An accountant qualified to perform audits (systematic inspections) of a business's financial records.

Authorization Card A card signed by an employee that gives a union permission to act on his or her behalf in negotiations with management.

Automatic Stay In bankruptcy proceedings, the suspension of almost all litigation and other action by creditors against the debtor or the debtor's property. The stay is effective the moment the debtor files a petition in bankruptcy.

Award The monetary compensation given to a party at the end of a trial or other proceeding.

B

Bailee One to whom goods are entrusted by a bailor.

Bailee's Lien A possessory (artisan's) lien that a bailee entitled to compensation can place on the bailed property to ensure that he or she will be paid for the services provided.

Bailment A situation in which the personal property of one person (a bailor) is entrusted to another (a bailee), who is obligated to return the bailed property to the bailor or dispose of it as directed.

Bailor One who entrusts goods to a bailee.

Bait-and-Switch Advertising Advertising a product at an attractive price and then telling the consumer that the advertised product is not available or is of poor quality and encouraging her or him to purchase a more expensive item.

Bankruptcy Court A federal court of limited jurisdiction that handles only bankruptcy proceedings, which are governed by federal bankruptcy law.

Bankruptcy Trustee A person appointed by the court to manage the debtor's funds.

Battery Physical contact with another that is unexcused, harmful or offensive, and intentionally performed.

Bearer A person in possession of an instrument payable to bearer or indorsed in blank.

Bearer Instrument Any instrument that is not payable to a specific person, including instruments payable to the bearer or to "cash."

Benefit Corporation A for-profit corporation that seeks to have a material positive impact on society and the environment. It is available by statute in a number of states.

Bequest A gift of personal property by will (from the verb *to bequeath*).

Beyond a Reasonable Doubt The standard of proof used in criminal cases.

Bilateral Contract A type of contract that arises when a promise is given in exchange for a return promise.

Bilateral Mistake A mistake that occurs when both parties to a contract are mistaken about the same material fact.

Bill of Rights The first ten amendments to the U.S. Constitution.

Binder A written, temporary insurance policy.

Binding Authority Any source of law that a court *must* follow when deciding a case.

Blank Indorsement An indorsement on an instrument that specifies no indorsee. An order instrument that is indorsed in blank becomes a bearer instrument.

Bona Fide Occupational Qualification (BFOQ) An identifiable characteristic reasonably necessary to the normal operation of a particular business. Such characteristics can include gender, national origin, and religion, but not race.

Bond A security that evidences a corporate (or government) debt.

Botnet A network of compromised computers connected to the Internet that can be used to generate spam, relay viruses, or cause servers to fail.

Breach of Contract The failure, without legal excuse, of a promisor to perform the obligations of a contract.

Brief A written summary or statement prepared by one side in a lawsuit to explain its case to the judge.

Browse-Wrap Term A term or condition of use that is presented when an online buyer downloads a product but to which the buyer does not have to agree before installing or using the product.

Burglary The unlawful entry or breaking into a building with the intent to commit a felony.

Business Ethics The application of moral and ethical principles in a business context.

Business Invitee A person, such as a customer or a client, who is invited onto business premises by the owner of those premises for business purposes.

Business Judgment Rule A rule under which courts will not hold corporate officers and directors liable for honest mistakes of judgment and bad business decisions that were made in good faith.

Business Necessity A defense to an allegation of employment discrimination in which the employer demonstrates that an employment practice that discriminates against members of a protected class is related to job performance.

Business Tort Wrongful interference with another's business rights and relationships.

Business Trust A form of business organization, created by a written trust agreement, that resembles a corporation. Legal ownership and management of the trust's property stay with the trustees, and the profits are distributed to the beneficiaries, who have limited liability.

Buyer in the Ordinary Course of Business A buyer who, in good faith and without knowledge that the sale violates the ownership rights or security interest of a third party in the goods, purchases goods in the ordinary course of business from a person in the business of selling goods of that kind.

Buyout Price The amount payable to a partner on his or her dissociation from a partnership, based on the amount distributable to that partner if the firm were wound up on that date, and offset by any damages for wrongful dissociation.

Bylaws The internal rules of management adopted by a corporation at its first organizational meeting.

C

Case Law The rules of law announced in court decisions. Case law interprets statutes, regulations, constitutional provisions, and other case law.

Cashier's Check A check drawn by a bank on itself.

Categorical Imperative An ethical guideline developed by Immanuel Kant under which an action is evaluated in terms of what would happen if everybody else in the same situation, or category, acted the same way.

Causation in Fact An act or omission without which an event would not have occurred.

Cease-and-Desist Order An administrative or judicial order prohibiting a person or business firm from conducting activities that an agency or court has deemed illegal.

Certificate of Deposit (CD) A note issued by a bank in which the bank acknowledges the receipt of funds from a party and promises to repay that amount, with interest, to the party on a certain date.

Certificate of Limited Partnership The document that must be filed with a designated state official to form a limited partnership.

Certification Mark A mark used by one or more persons, other than the owner, to certify the region, materials, mode of manufacture, quality, or other characteristic of specific goods or services.

Certified Check A check that has been accepted in writing by the bank on which it is drawn. By certifying (accepting) the check, the bank promises to pay the check at the time it is presented.

Charging Order In partnership law, an order granted by a court to a judgment creditor that entitles the creditor to attach a partner's interest in the partnership.

Charitable Trust A trust in which the property held by the trustee must be used for a charitable purpose, such as the advancement of health, education, or religion.

Chattel Personal property.

Check A draft drawn by a drawer ordering the drawee bank or financial institution to pay a certain amount of funds to the payee on demand.

Checks and Balances The principle under which the powers of the national government are divided among three separate branches—the executive, legislative, and judicial branches—each of which exercises a check on the actions of the others.

Choice-of-Language Clause A clause in a contract designating the official language by which the contract will be interpreted in the event of a disagreement over the contract's terms.

Choice-of-Law Clause A clause in a contract designating the law (such as the law of a particular state or nation) that will govern the contract.

Citation A reference to a publication in which a legal authority—such as a statute or a court decision—or other source can be found.

Civil Law The branch of law dealing with the definition and enforcement of all private or public rights, as opposed to criminal matters.

Civil Law System A system of law derived from Roman law that is based on codified laws (rather than on case precedents).

Clearinghouse A system or place where banks exchange checks and drafts drawn on each other and settle daily balances.

Click-On Agreement An agreement that arises when an online buyer clicks on "I agree" or otherwise indicates her or his assent to be bound by the terms of an offer.

Close Corporation A corporation whose shareholders are limited to a small group of persons, often family members.

Closed Shop A firm that requires union membership by its workers as a condition of employment.

Cloud Computing The delivery to users of on-demand services from third-party servers over a network.

Codicil A written supplement or modification to a will. A codicil must be executed with the same formalities as a will.

Collateral Under Article 9 of the UCC, the property subject to a security interest.

Collateral Promise A secondary promise to a primary transaction, such as a promise made by one person to pay the debts of another if the latter fails to perform. A collateral promise normally must be in writing to be enforceable.

Collecting Bank Any bank handling an item for collection, except the payor bank.

Collective Bargaining The process by which labor and management negotiate the terms and conditions of employment, including working hours and workplace conditions.

Collective Mark A mark used by members of a cooperative, association, union, or other organization to certify the region, materials, mode of manufacture, quality, or other characteristic of specific goods or services.

Comity The principle by which one nation defers to and gives effect to the laws and judicial decrees of another nation. This recognition is based primarily on respect.

Commerce Clause The provision in Article I, Section 8, of the U.S. Constitution that gives Congress the power to regulate interstate commerce.

Commercial Impracticability A doctrine that may excuse the duty to perform a contract when performance becomes much more difficult or costly due to forces that neither party could control or foresee at the time the contract was formed.

Commingle To put funds or goods together into one mass so that they are mixed to such

a degree that they no longer have separate identities.

Common Law The body of law developed from custom or judicial decisions in English and U.S. courts, not attributable to a legislature.

Common Stock Shares of ownership in a corporation that give the owner a proportionate interest in the corporation with regard to control, earnings, and net assets. Common stock is lowest in priority with respect to payment of dividends and distribution of the corporation's assets on dissolution.

Community Property A form of concurrent property ownership in which each spouse owns an undivided one-half interest in property acquired during the marriage.

Comparative Negligence A rule in tort law, used in the majority of states, that reduces the plaintiff's recovery in proportion to the plaintiff's degree of fault, rather than barring recovery completely.

Compelling Government Interest A test of constitutionality that requires the government to have convincing reasons for passing any law that restricts fundamental rights, such as free speech, or distinguishes between people based on a suspect trait.

Compensatory Damages A monetary award equivalent to the actual value of injuries or damage sustained by the aggrieved party.

Complaint The pleading made by a plaintiff alleging wrongdoing on the part of the defendant. When filed with a court, the complaint initiates a lawsuit.

Computer Crime Any violation of criminal law that involves knowledge of computer technology for its perpetration, investigation, or prosecution.

Concentrated Industry An industry in which a single firm or a small number of firms control a large percentage of market sales.

Concurrent Conditions Conditions that must occur or be performed at the same time—they are mutually dependent. No obligations arise until these conditions are simultaneously performed.

Concurrent Jurisdiction Jurisdiction that exists when two different courts have the power to hear a case.

Concurrent Ownership Joint ownership.

Concurring Opinion A court opinion by one or more judges or justices who agree with the majority but want to make or emphasize a point that was not made or emphasized in the majority's opinion.

Condemnation Proceedings The judicial procedure by which the government exercises its power of eminent domain. It generally involves two phases: a taking and a determination of fair value.

Condition A qualification, provision, or clause in a contractual agreement, the occurrence or nonoccurrence of which creates, suspends, or terminates the obligations of the contracting parties.

Condition Precedent A condition in a contract that must be met before a party's promise becomes absolute.

Condition Subsequent A condition in a contract that, if it occurs, operates to terminate a party's absolute promise to perform.

Confiscation A government's taking of a privately owned business or personal property without a proper public purpose or an award of just compensation.

Conforming Goods Goods that conform to contract specifications.

Confusion The mixing together of goods belonging to two or more owners to such an extent that the separately owned goods cannot be identified.

Consequential Damages Foreseeable damages that result from a party's breach of contract but are caused by special circumstances beyond the contract itself.

Consideration The value given in return for a promise or performance in a contractual agreement.

Constitutional Law The body of law derived from the U.S. Constitution and the constitutions of the various states.

Constructive Delivery A symbolic delivery of property that cannot be physically delivered.

Constructive Discharge A termination of employment brought about by making the employee's working conditions so intolerable that the employee reasonably feels compelled to leave.

Constructive Eviction A form of eviction that occurs when a landlord fails to perform adequately any of the duties required by the lease, thereby making the tenant's further use and enjoyment of the property exceedingly difficult or impossible.

Constructive Fraud Conduct that is treated as fraud under the law even when there is no proof of intent to defraud, usually because of the existence of a special relationship or fiduciary duty.

Constructive Trust An equitable trust that is imposed in the interests of fairness and justice when someone wrongfully holds legal title to property.

Consumer-Debtor One whose debts result primarily from the purchases of goods for personal, family, or household use.

Continuation Statement A statement that, if filed within six months prior to the expiration date of the original financing statement, continues the perfection of the security interest for another five years.

Contract A set of promises constituting an agreement between parties, giving each a

legal duty to the other and the right to seek a remedy for the breach of the promises or duties.

Contractual Capacity The capacity required by the law for a party who enters into a contract to be bound by that contract.

Contributory Negligence A rule in tort law, used in only a few states, that completely bars the plaintiff from recovering any damages if the damage suffered is partly the plaintiff's own fault.

Conversion Wrongfully taking or retaining possession of an individual's personal property and placing it in the service of another.

Conveyance The transfer of title to real property from one person to another by deed or other document.

Cookie A small file sent from a Web site and stored in a user's Web browser to track the user's Web browsing activities.

"Cooling-Off" Laws Laws that allow buyers of goods sold in certain transactions to cancel their contracts within three business days.

Cooperative An association, which may or may not be incorporated, that is organized to provide an economic service to its members. Unincorporated cooperatives are often treated like partnerships for tax and other legal purposes.

Copyright The exclusive right of an author or originator of a literary or artistic production to publish, print, sell, or otherwise use that production for a statutory period of time.

Corporate Governance A set of policies specifying the rights and responsibilities of the various participants in a corporation and spelling out the rules and procedures for making corporate decisions.

Corporate Social Responsibility (CSR) The idea that corporations can and should act ethically and be accountable to society for their actions.

Corporation A legal entity formed in compliance with statutory requirements that is distinct from its shareholder-owners.

Correspondent Bank A bank that acts on behalf of another bank for the purpose of facilitating fund transfers.

Cost-Benefit Analysis A decision-making technique that involves weighing the costs of a given action against the benefits of that action.

Co-Surety A joint surety; a party who assumes liability jointly with another surety for the payment of a debtor's obligation under a suretyship arrangement.

Counteradvertising New advertising that is undertaken to correct earlier false claims that were made about a product.

Counterclaim A claim made by a defendant in a civil lawsuit against the plaintiff. In effect, the defendant is suing the plaintiff.

Counteroffer An offeree's response to an offer in which the offeree rejects the original offer and at the same time makes a new offer.

Course of Dealing Prior conduct between the parties to a contract that establishes a common basis for their understanding.

Course of Performance The conduct that occurs under the terms of a particular agreement, which indicates what the parties to that agreement intended the agreement to mean.

Covenant Not to Compete A contractual promise of one party to refrain from conducting business similar to that of another party for a certain period of time and within a specified geographical area.

Covenant Not to Sue An agreement to substitute a contractual obligation for some other type of legal action based on a valid claim.

Cover A remedy that allows the buyer or lessee, on the seller's or lessor's breach, to obtain substitute goods from another seller or lessor.

Cram-Down Provision A provision of the Bankruptcy Code that allows a court to confirm a debtor's Chapter 11 reorganization plan even though only one class of creditors has accepted it.

Creditors' Composition Agreement A contract between a debtor and his or her creditors in which the creditors agree to discharge the debts on the debtor's payment of a sum less than the amount actually owed.

Crime A wrong against society proclaimed in a statute and, if committed, punishable by society through fines, imprisonment, or death.

Criminal Law The branch of law that defines and punishes wrongful actions committed against the public.

Cross-Collateralization The use of an asset that is not the subject of a loan to collateralize that loan.

Crowdfunding A cooperative activity in which people network and pool funds and other resources via the Internet to assist a cause (such as disaster relief) or invest in a venture (business).

Cure The right of a party who tenders nonconforming performance to correct his or her performance within the contract period.

Cyber Crime A crime that occurs in the online environment.

Cyber Fraud Any misrepresentation knowingly made over the Internet with the intention of deceiving another for the purpose of obtaining property or funds.

Cyberlaw An informal term used to refer to all laws governing electronic communications and transactions, particularly those conducted via the Internet.

Cybersquatting The act of registering a domain name that is the same as, or confusingly similar to, the trademark of another and then offering to sell that domain name back to the trademark owner.

Cyber Tort A tort committed via the Internet.

D

Damages A monetary award sought as a remedy for a breach of contract or a tortious action.

Debtor Under Article 9 of the UCC, any party who owes payment or performance of a secured obligation.

Debtor in Possession (DIP) In Chapter 11 bankruptcy proceedings, a debtor who is allowed to continue in possession of the estate in property (the business) and to continue business operations.

Deceptive Advertising Advertising that misleads consumers, either by making unjustified claims about a product's performance or by omitting a material fact concerning the product's composition or performance.

Deed A document by which title to real property is passed.

Defalcation Embezzlement or misappropriation of funds.

Defamation Anything published or publicly spoken that causes injury to another's good name, reputation, or character.

Default Failure to pay a debt when it is due.

Default Judgment A judgment entered by a court against a defendant who has failed to appear in court to answer or defend against the plaintiff's claim.

Defendant One against whom a lawsuit is brought or the accused person in a criminal proceeding.

Defense A reason offered by a defendant in an action or lawsuit as to why the plaintiff should not recover or establish what she or he seeks.

Deficiency Judgment A judgment against a debtor for the amount of a debt remaining unpaid after the collateral has been repossessed and sold.

Delegatee A party to whom contractual obligations are transferred, or delegated.

Delegation of Duties The transfer to another of a contractual duty.

Delegator A party who transfers (delegates) her or his obligations under a contract to another party (the *delegatee*).

Depositary Bank The first bank to receive a check for payment.

Deposition The testimony of a party to a lawsuit or a witness taken under oath before a trial.

Destination Contract A contract for the sale of goods in which the seller is required or authorized to ship the goods by carrier and tender delivery of the goods at a particular destination. The seller assumes liability for any losses or damage to the goods until they are tendered at the destination specified in the contract.

Devise A gift of real property by will, or the act of giving real property by will.

Devisee One designated in a will to receive a gift of real property.

Digital Cash Prepaid funds stored on microchips in laptops, smartphones, tablets, and other devices.

Disaffirmance The legal avoidance, or setting aside, of a contractual obligation.

Discharge The termination of an obligation, such as occurs when the parties to a contract have fully performed their contractual obligations. The termination of a bankruptcy debtor's obligation to pay debts.

Disclosed Principal A principal whose identity is known to a third party at the time the agent makes a contract with the third party.

Discovery A method by which the opposing parties obtain information from each other to prepare for trial.

Dishonor To refuse to pay or to accept a negotiable instrument that has been presented in a timely and proper manner.

Disparagement of Property An economically injurious falsehood about another's product or property.

Disparate-Impact Discrimination Discrimination that results from certain employer practices or procedures that, although not discriminatory on their face, have a discriminatory effect.

Disparate-Treatment Discrimination A form of employment discrimination that results when an employer intentionally discriminates against employees who are members of protected classes.

Dissenting Opinion A court opinion that presents the views of one or more judges or justices who disagree with the majority's decision.

Dissociation The severance of the relationship between a partner and a partnership.

Dissolution The formal disbanding of a partnership or a corporation. Partnerships can be dissolved by acts of the partners, by operation of law, or by judicial decree.

Distributed Network A network that can be used by persons located (distributed) around the country or the globe to share computer files.

Distribution Agreement A contract between a seller and a distributor of the seller's products setting out the terms and conditions of the distributorship.

Diversity of Citizenship A basis for federal court jurisdiction over a lawsuit between citizens of different states or a lawsuit involving a U.S. citizen and a citizen of a different country.

Divestiture A company's sale of one or more of its divisions' operating functions under court order as part of the enforcement of the antitrust laws.

Dividend A distribution of corporate profits to the corporation's shareholders in proportion to the number of shares held.

Docket The list of cases entered on a court's calendar and thus scheduled to be heard by the court.

Document of Title A paper exchanged in the regular course of business that evidences the right to possession of goods (for example, a bill of lading or a warehouse receipt).

Domain Name Part of an Internet address, such as "cengage.com." The series of letters and symbols used to identify a site operator on the Internet; an Internet "address."

Domestic Corporation In a given state, a corporation that is organized under the law of that state.

Dominion Ownership rights in property, including the right to possess and control the property.

Double Jeopardy The Fifth Amendment requirement that prohibits a person from being tried twice for the same criminal offense.

Down Payment An initial cash payment made when an expensive item, such as a house, is purchased. The payment represents a percentage of the purchase price, and the remainder is financed.

Draft Any instrument drawn on a drawee that orders the drawee to pay a certain amount of funds, usually to a third party (the payee), on demand or at a definite future time.

Dram Shop Act A state statute that imposes liability on the owners of bars and taverns, as well as those who serve alcoholic drinks to the public, for injuries resulting from accidents caused by intoxicated persons when the sellers or servers of alcoholic drinks contributed to the intoxication.

Drawee The party that is ordered to pay a draft or check. With a check, a bank or a financial institution is always the drawee.

Drawer The party that initiates a draft (such as a check), thereby ordering the drawee to pay.

Due Diligence A required standard of care that certain professionals, such as accountants, must meet to avoid liability for securities violations.

Due Process Clause The provisions in the Fifth and Fourteenth Amendments that guarantee that no person shall be deprived of life, liberty, or property without due process of law. State constitutions often include similar clauses.

Dumping The sale of goods in a foreign country at a price below the price charged for the same goods in the domestic market.

Duress Unlawful pressure brought to bear on a person, causing the person to perform an act that she or he would not otherwise perform.

Duty-based Ethics An ethical philosophy rooted in the idea that every person has certain duties to others, including both humans and the planet. Those duties may be derived from religious principles or from other philosophical reasoning.

Duty of Care The duty of all persons, as established by tort law, to exercise a reasonable amount of care in their dealings with others. Failure to exercise due care, which is normally determined by the reasonable person standard, constitutes the tort of negligence.

E

Easement A nonpossessory right, established by express or implied agreement, to make limited use of another's property without removing anything from the property.

E-Contract A contract that is formed electronically.

E-Evidence A type of evidence that consists of computer-generated or electronically recorded information.

Electronic Fund Transfer (EFT) A transfer of funds through the use of an electronic terminal, a telephone, a computer, or magnetic tape.

Emancipation In regard to minors, the act of being freed from parental control.

Embezzlement The fraudulent appropriation of funds or other property by a person who was entrusted with the funds or property.

Eminent Domain The power of a government to take land from private citizens for public use on the payment of just compensation.

E-Money Prepaid funds stored on microchips in laptops, smartphones, tablets, and other devices.

Employment at Will A common law doctrine under which either party may terminate an employment relationship at any time for any reason, unless a contract specifies otherwise.

Employment Contract A contract between an employer and an employee in which the terms and conditions of employment are stated.

Enabling Legislation A statute enacted by Congress that authorizes the creation of an administrative agency and specifies the name, composition, purpose, and powers of the agency being created.

Entrapment A defense in which a defendant claims that he or she was induced by a public official to commit a crime that he or she would otherwise not have committed.

Entrepreneur One who initiates and assumes the financial risk of a new business enterprise and undertakes to provide or control its management.

Entrustment Rule The rule that entrusting goods to a merchant who deals in goods of that kind gives that merchant the power to transfer those goods and all rights to them to a buyer in the ordinary course of business.

Environmental Impact Statement (EIS) A formal analysis required for any major federal action that will significantly affect the quality of the environment to determine the action's impact and explore alternatives.

Equal Dignity Rule A rule requiring that an agent's authority be in writing if the contract to be made on behalf of the principal must be in writing.

Equal Protection Clause The provision in the Fourteenth Amendment that requires state governments to treat similarly situated individuals in a similar manner.

Equitable Principles and Maxims General propositions or principles of law that have to do with fairness (equity).

Equitable Right of Redemption The right of a mortgagor who has breached the mortgage agreement to redeem or purchase the mortgaged property prior to foreclosure proceedings.

E-Signature An electronic sound, symbol, or process attached to or logically associated with a record and adopted by a person with the intent to sign the record.

Establishment Clause The provision in the First Amendment that prohibits the government from establishing any state-sponsored religion or enacting any law that promotes religion or favors one religion over another.

Estate in Bankruptcy All of the property owned by a person, including real estate and personal property.

Estopped Barred, impeded, or precluded.

Estray Statute A statute defining finders' rights in property when the true owners are unknown.

Ethical Reasoning A reasoning process in which an individual links his or her moral convictions or ethical standards to the situation at hand.

Ethics Moral principles and values applied to social behavior.

Eviction A landlord's act of depriving a tenant of possession of the leased premises.

Exclusionary Rule A rule that prevents evidence that is obtained illegally or without a proper search warrant from being admissible in court.

Exclusive-Dealing Contract An agreement under which a seller forbids a buyer to purchase products from the seller's competitors.

Exclusive Jurisdiction Jurisdiction that exists when a case can be heard only in a particular court or type of court.

Exculpatory Clause A clause that releases a contractual party from liability in the event of monetary or physical injury, no matter who is at fault.

Executed Contract A contract that has been fully performed by both parties.

Execution The implementation of a court's decree or judgment.

Executor A person appointed by a testator in a will to administer her or his estate.

Executory Contract A contract that has not yet been fully performed.

Export The sale of goods and services by domestic firms to buyers located in other countries.

Express Contract A contract in which the terms of the agreement are stated in words, oral or written.

Express Warranty A seller's or lessor's promise as to the quality, condition, description, or performance of the goods being sold or leased.

Expropriation A government's seizure of a privately owned business or personal property for a proper public purpose and with just compensation.

Extension Clause A clause in a time instrument that allows the instrument's date of maturity to be extended into the future.

Extrinsic Evidence Any evidence not contained in the contract itself, which may include the testimony of the parties, additional agreements or communications, or other information relevant to determining the parties' intent.

F

Federal Form of Government A system of government in which the states form a union and the sovereign power is divided between the central government and the member states.

Federal Question A question that pertains to the U.S. Constitution, an act of Congress, or a treaty and provides a basis for federal jurisdiction in a case.

Federal Reserve System A network of twelve district banks and related branches located around the country and headed by the

Federal Reserve Board of Governors. Most banks in the United States have Federal Reserve accounts.

Fee Simple An ownership interest in land in which the owner has the greatest possible aggregation of rights, privileges, and power.

Felony A crime—such as arson, murder, rape, or robbery—that carries the most severe sanctions, ranging from more than one year in a state or federal prison to the death penalty.

Fictitious Payee A payee on a negotiable instrument whom the maker or drawer did not intend to have an interest in the instrument. Indorsements by fictitious payees are treated as authorized indorsements under UCC Article 3.

Fiduciary As a noun, a person having a duty created by his or her undertaking to act primarily for another's benefit in matters connected with the undertaking. As an adjective, a relationship founded on trust and confidence.

Filtering Software A computer program that is designed to block access to certain Web sites, based on their content. The software blocks the retrieval of a site whose URL or key words are on a list within the program.

Financing Statement A document filed by a secured creditor with the appropriate official to give notice to the public of the creditor's security interest in collateral belonging to the debtor named in the statement.

Firm Offer An offer (by a merchant) that is irrevocable without the necessity of consideration for a stated period of time or, if no definite period is stated, for a reasonable time (neither period to exceed three months).

Fixed-Term Tenancy A type of tenancy under which property is leased for a specified period of time, such as a month, a year, or a period of years; also called a *tenancy for years*.

Fixture An item of personal property that has become so closely associated with real property that it is legally regarded as part of that real property.

Floating Lien A security interest in proceeds, after-acquired property, or collateral subject to future advances by the secured party (or all three). The security interest is retained even when the collateral changes in character, classification, or location.

Forbearance A postponement of part or all of the payments on a loan for a limited time. The act of refraining from an action that one has a legal right to undertake.

***Force Majeure* Clause** A provision in a contract stipulating that certain unforeseen events—such as war, political upheavals, or acts of God—will excuse a party from liability for nonperformance of contractual obligations.

Foreclosure The legal process by which a lender repossesses and disposes of property that has secured a loan.

Foreign Corporation In a given state, a corporation that does business in that state but is not incorporated there.

Foreign Exchange Market A worldwide system in which foreign currencies are bought and sold.

Forgery The fraudulent making or altering of any writing in a way that changes the legal rights and liabilities of another.

Formal Contract An agreement that by law requires a specific form for its validity.

Forum-Selection Clause A provision in a contract designating the court, jurisdiction, or tribunal that will decide any disputes arising under the contract.

Franchise Any arrangement in which the owner of a trademark, trade name, or copyright licenses another to use that trademark, trade name, or copyright in the selling of goods or services.

Franchisee One receiving a license to use another's (the franchisor's) trademark, trade name, or copyright in the sale of goods and services.

Franchisor One licensing another (the franchisee) to use the owner's trademark, trade name, or copyright in the selling of goods or services.

Fraudulent Misrepresentation Any misrepresentation, either by misstatement or by omission of a material fact, knowingly made with the intention of deceiving another and on which a reasonable person would and does rely to his or her detriment.

Free Exercise Clause The provision in the First Amendment that prohibits the government from interfering with people's religious practices or forms of worship.

Free-Writing Prospectus A written, electronic, or graphic communication associated with the offer to sell a security and used during the waiting period to supplement other information about the security.

Frustration of Purpose A court-created doctrine under which a party to a contract will be relieved of her or his duty to perform when the objective purpose for performance no longer exists due to reasons beyond that party's control.

Fungible Goods Goods that are alike by physical nature, agreement, or trade usage.

G

Garnishment A legal process whereby a creditor collects a debt by seizing property of the debtor that is in the hands of a third party.

General Damages In a tort case, an amount awarded to compensate individuals for the nonmonetary aspects of the harm suffered, such as pain and suffering. Not available to companies.

Generally Accepted Accounting Principles (GAAP) The conventions, rules, and procedures developed by the Financial Accounting Standards Board to define accepted accounting practices at a particular time.

Generally Accepted Auditing Standards (GAAS) Standards established by the American Institute of Certified Public Accountants to define the professional qualities and judgment that should be exercised by an auditor in performing an audit.

General Partner In a limited partnership, a partner who assumes responsibility for the management of the partnership and has full liability for all partnership debts.

Gift A voluntary transfer of property made without consideration, past or present.

Gift *Causa Mortis* A gift made in contemplation of imminent death. The gift is revoked if the donor does not die as contemplated.

Gift *Inter Vivos* A gift made during one's lifetime and not in contemplation of imminent death, in contrast to a gift *causa mortis*.

Good Faith Purchaser A purchaser who buys without notice of any circumstance that would cause a person of ordinary prudence to inquire as to whether the seller has valid title to the goods being sold.

Good Samaritan Statute A state statute stipulating that persons who provide emergency services to, or rescue, someone in peril cannot be sued for negligence unless they act recklessly and cause further harm.

Goodwill In the business context, the valuable reputation of a business viewed as an intangible asset.

Grand Jury A group of citizens who decide, after hearing the state's evidence, whether a reasonable basis (probable cause) exists for believing that a crime has been committed and that a trial ought to be held.

Group Boycott An agreement by two or more sellers to refuse to deal with a particular person or firm.

Guarantor A third party who promises to be responsible for a debtor's obligation under a guaranty arrangement.

H

Hacker A person who uses computers to gain unauthorized access to data.

Historical School A school of legal thought that looks to the past to determine what the principles of contemporary law should be.

Holder Any person in possession of an instrument drawn, issued, or indorsed to him or her, to his or her order, to bearer, or in blank.

Holder in Due Course (HDC) A holder who acquires a negotiable instrument for value, in good faith, and without notice that the instrument is defective.

Holographic Will A will written entirely in the testator's handwriting.

Homeowner's Insurance A form of property insurance that protects the holder against damage or loss to the holder's home.

Homestead Exemption A law permitting a debtor to retain the family home, either in its entirety or up to a specified dollar amount, free from the claims of unsecured creditors or trustees in bankruptcy.

Horizontal Merger A merger between two firms that are competing in the same market.

Horizontal Restraint Any agreement that restrains competition between rival firms competing in the same market.

Hot-Cargo Agreement An illegal agreement in which employers voluntarily agree with unions not to handle, use, or deal in the nonunion-produced goods of other employers.

I

I-551 Alien Registration Receipt A document, known as a "green card," that shows that a foreign-born individual can legally work in the United States.

I-9 Verification The process of verifying the employment eligibility and identity of a new worker. It must be completed within three days after the worker commences employment.

Identification In a sale of goods, the express designation of the goods provided for in the contract.

Identity Theft The illegal use of someone else's personal information to access the victim's financial resources.

Implied Contract A contract formed in whole or in part from the conduct of the parties.

Implied Warranty A warranty that arises by law because of the circumstances of a sale and not from the seller's express promise.

Implied Warranty of Fitness for a Particular Purpose A warranty that goods sold or leased are fit for the particular purpose for which the buyer or lessee will use the goods.

Implied Warranty of Habitability An implied promise by a seller of a new house that the house is fit for human habitation. Also, the implied promise by a landlord that rented residential premises are habitable.

Implied Warranty of Merchantability A warranty that goods being sold or leased are reasonably fit for the general purpose for which they are sold or leased, are properly packaged and labeled, and are of proper quality.

Impossibility of Performance A doctrine under which a party to a contract is relieved of his or her duty to perform when performance becomes objectively impossible or totally impracticable.

Imposter One who induces a maker or drawer to issue a negotiable instrument in the name of an impersonated payee. Indorsements by imposters are treated as authorized indorsements under UCC Article 3.

Incidental Beneficiary A third party who benefits from a contract even though the contract was not formed for that purpose. An incidental beneficiary has no rights in the contract and cannot sue to have it enforced.

Incidental Damages Damages that compensate for expenses directly incurred because of a breach of contract, such as those incurred to obtain performance from another source.

Incontestability Clause A clause in a policy for life or health insurance stating that after the policy has been in force for a specified length of time (usually two or three years), the insurer cannot contest statements made in the policyholder's application.

Independent Contractor One who works for, and receives payment from, an employer but whose working conditions and methods are not controlled by the employer. An independent contractor is not an employee but may be an agent.

Indictment A formal charge by a grand jury that there is probable cause to believe that a named person has committed a crime.

Indorsement A signature placed on an instrument for the purpose of transferring ownership rights in the instrument.

Informal Contract A contract that does not require a specific form or method of creation to be valid.

Information A formal accusation or complaint (without an indictment) issued in certain types of actions (usually criminal actions involving lesser crimes) by a government prosecutor.

Information Return A tax return submitted by a partnership that reports the business's income and losses. The partnership itself does not pay taxes on the income, but each partner's share of the profit (whether distributed or not) is taxed as individual income to that partner.

Innocent Misrepresentation A misrepresentation that occurs when a person makes a false statement of fact that he or she believes is true.

Inside Director A person on the board of directors who is also an officer of the corporation.

Insider Trading The purchase or sale of securities on the basis of information that has not been made available to the public.

Insolvent A condition in which a person cannot pay his or her debts as they become due or ceases to pay debts in the ordinary course of business.

Installment Contract A contract that requires or authorizes delivery in two or more separate lots to be accepted and paid for separately.

Insurable Interest A property interest in goods being sold or leased that is sufficiently substantial to permit a party to insure against damage to the goods. An interest that exists when a person benefits from the preservation of the health or life of the insured or the property to be insured.

Insurance A contract by which the insurer promises to reimburse the insured or a beneficiary in the event that the insured is injured, dies, or sustains damage to property as a result of particular, stated contingencies.

Intangible Property Property that cannot be seen or touched but exists only conceptually, such as corporate stocks. Such property is not governed by Article 2 of the UCC.

Integrated Contract A written contract that constitutes the final expression of the parties' agreement. Evidence extraneous to the contract that contradicts or alters the meaning of the contract in any way is inadmissible.

Intellectual Property Property resulting from intellectual and creative processes.

Intended Beneficiary A third party for whose benefit a contract is formed. An intended beneficiary can sue the promisor if the contract is breached.

Intentional Tort A wrongful act knowingly committed.

Intermediary Bank Any bank to which an item is transferred in the course of collection, except the depositary or payor bank.

International Financial Reporting Standards (IFRS) A set of global accounting standards that are being phased in by companies in the United States.

International Law The law that governs relations among nations.

International Organization An organization composed mainly of member nations and usually established by treaty—for example, the United Nations. More broadly, the term also includes nongovernmental organizations (NGOs) such as the Red Cross.

Internet Service Provider (ISP) A business or organization that offers users access to the Internet and related services.

Interpretive Rule A nonbinding rule or policy statement issued by an administrative agency that explains how it interprets and intends to apply the statutes it enforces.

Interrogatories A series of written questions for which written answers are prepared by a party to a lawsuit, usually with the assistance of the party's attorney, and then signed under oath.

Intestacy Laws State statutes that specify how property will be distributed when a person dies intestate (without a valid will).

Intestate As a noun, one who has died without having created a valid will. As an adjective, the state of having died without a will.

Investment Company A company that acts on the behalf of many smaller shareholders-owners by buying a large portfolio of securities and professionally managing that portfolio.

Investment Contract In securities law, a transaction in which a person invests in a common enterprise reasonably expecting profits that are derived primarily from the efforts of others.

J

Joint and Several Liability In partnership law, a doctrine under which a plaintiff may sue, and collect a judgment from, all of the partners together (jointly) or one or more of the partners separately (severally, or individually). A partner can be held liable even if she or he did not participate in, ratify, or know about the conduct that gave rise to the lawsuit.

Joint Liability In partnership law, the partners' shared liability for partnership obligations and debts. A third party must sue all of the partners as a group, but each partner can be held liable for the full amount.

Joint Stock Company A hybrid form of business organization that combines characteristics of a corporation and a partnership. Usually, a joint stock company is regarded as a partnership for tax and other legal purposes.

Joint Tenancy Joint ownership of property by two or more co-owners in which each co-owner owns an undivided portion of the property. On the death of one of the joint tenants, his or her interest automatically passes to the surviving joint tenant(s).

Joint Venture A joint undertaking by two or more persons or business entities to combine their efforts or their property for a single transaction or project or for a related series of transactions or projects. A joint venture is generally treated like a partnership for tax and other legal purposes.

Judicial Review The process by which a court decides on the constitutionality of legislative enactments and actions of the executive branch.

Jurisdiction The authority of a court to hear and decide a specific case.

Jurisprudence The science or philosophy of law.

Justiciable Controversy A controversy that is not hypothetical or academic but real and substantial; a requirement that must be satisfied before a court will hear a case.

L

Larceny The wrongful taking and carrying away of another person's personal property with the intent to permanently deprive the owner of the property.

Latent Defect A defect that is not obvious or cannot readily be ascertained.

Law A body of enforceable rules governing relationships among individuals and between individuals and their society.

Lease Under Article 2A of the UCC, a transfer of the right to possess and use goods for a period of time in exchange for payment.

Lease Agreement An agreement in which one person (the lessor) agrees to transfer the right to the possession and use of property to another person (the lessee) in exchange for rental payments.

Leasehold Estate An interest in real property that gives a tenant a qualified right to possess and/or use the property for a limited time under a lease.

Legacy A gift of personal property under a will.

Legal Positivism A school of legal thought centered on the assumption that there is no law higher than the laws created by a national government. Laws must be obeyed, even if they are unjust, to prevent anarchy.

Legal Realism A school of legal thought that holds that the law is only one factor to be considered when deciding cases and that social and economic circumstances should also be taken into account.

Legatee One designated in a will to receive a gift of personal property.

Legislative Rule An administrative agency rule that carries the same weight as a congressionally enacted statute.

Lessee A person who acquires the right to the possession and use of another's goods in exchange for rental payments.

Lessor A person who transfers the right to the possession and use of goods to another in exchange for rental payments.

Letter of Credit A written document in which the issuer (usually a bank) promises to honor drafts or other demands for payment by third persons in accordance with the terms of the instrument.

Levy The legal process of obtaining funds through the seizure and sale of nonexempt property, usually done after a writ of execution has been issued.

Liability The state of being legally responsible (liable) for something, such as a debt or obligation.

Libel Defamation in writing or another permanent form (such as a digital recording).

License An agreement by the owner of intellectual property to permit another to use a trademark, copyright, patent, or trade secret for certain limited purposes. In the context of real property, a revocable right or privilege to enter onto another person's land.

Lien An encumbrance on a property to satisfy a debt or protect a claim for payment of a debt.

Life Estate An interest in land that exists only for the duration of the life of a specified individual, usually the holder of the estate.

Limited Liability Company (LLC) A hybrid form of business enterprise that offers the limited liability of a corporation and the tax advantages of a partnership.

Limited Liability Partnership (LLP) A hybrid form of business organization that is used mainly by professionals who normally do business in a partnership. An LLP is a pass-through entity for tax purposes, but a partner's personal liability for the malpractice of other partners is limited.

Limited Partner In a limited partnership, a partner who contributes capital to the partnership but has no right to participate in its management and has no liability for partnership debts beyond the amount of her or his investment.

Limited Partnership (LP) A partnership consisting of one or more general partners and one or more limited partners.

Liquidated Damages An amount, stipulated in a contract, that the parties to the contract believe to be a reasonable estimation of the damages that will occur in the event of a breach.

Liquidated Debt A debt whose amount has been ascertained, fixed, agreed on, settled, or exactly determined.

Liquidation The sale of the nonexempt assets of a debtor and the distribution of the funds received to creditors.

Litigation The process of resolving a dispute through the court system.

Living (*Inter Vivos*) Trust A trust created by the grantor (settlor) and effective during his or her lifetime.

Lockout An action in which an employer shuts down to prevent employees from working, typically because it cannot reach a collective bargaining agreement with the employees' union.

Long Arm Statute A state statute that permits a state to exercise jurisdiction over nonresident defendants.

Lost Property Property that the owner has involuntarily by the owner.

M

Mailbox Rule A common law rule that acceptance takes effect, and thus completes formation of the contract, at the time the offeree sends or delivers the acceptance via the communication mode expressly or impliedly authorized by the offeror.

Majority Opinion A court opinion that represents the views of the majority (more than half) of the judges or justices deciding the case.

Maker One who promises to pay a fixed amount of funds to the holder of a promissory note or a certificate of deposit (CD).

Malpractice Professional misconduct or the lack of the requisite degree of skill as a professional. Professional negligence, or failure to exercise reasonable care and professional judgment, that results in injury, loss, or damage to those relying on the professional.

Malware Malicious software programs, such as viruses and worms, that are designed to cause harm to a computer, network, or other device.

Market Concentration The degree to which a small number of firms control a large percentage of a relevant market.

Market Power The power of a firm to control the market price of its product. A monopoly has the greatest degree of market power.

Market-Share Liability A theory under which liability is shared among all firms that manufactured and distributed a particular product during a certain period of time. This form of liability sharing is used only when the specific source of the harmful product is unidentifiable.

Mechanic's Lien A nonpossessory, filed lien on an owner's real estate for labor, services, or materials furnished for making improvements on the realty.

Mediation A method of settling disputes outside the courts by using the services of a neutral third party, who acts as a communicating agent between the parties and assists them in negotiating a settlement.

Member A person who has an ownership interest in a limited liability company.

Mens Rea A wrongful mental state ("guilty mind"), or intent; one of the two essential elements required to establish criminal liability.

Merchant Under the UCC, a person who deals in goods of the kind involved in the sales contract or who holds herself or himself out as having skill or knowledge peculiar to the practices or goods being purchased or sold.

Metadata Data that are automatically recorded by electronic devices and provide information about who created a file and when, and who accessed, modified, or transmitted the file on their hard drives. Can be described as data about data.

Meta Tag A key word in a document that can serve as an index reference to the document. On the Web, search engines return results based, in part, on the tags in Web documents.

Minimum Wage The lowest wage, either by government regulation or union contract, that an employer may pay an hourly worker.

Mirror Image Rule A common law rule that requires that the terms of the offeree's acceptance adhere exactly to the terms of the offeror's offer for a valid contract to be formed.

Misdemeanor A lesser crime than a felony, punishable by a fine or incarceration in jail for up to one year.

Mislaid Property Property that the owner has voluntarily parted with and then has inadvertently forgotten.

Mitigation of Damages The requirement that a plaintiff do whatever is reasonable to minimize the damages caused by the defendant's breach of contract.

Money Laundering Engaging in financial transactions to conceal the identity, source, or destination of illegally gained funds.

Monopolization The possession of monopoly power in the relevant market and the willful acquisition or maintenance of that power, as distinguished from growth or development as a consequence of a superior product, business acumen, or historic accident.

Monopoly A market in which there is a single seller or a very limited number of sellers.

Monopoly Power The ability of a monopoly to dictate what takes place in a given market.

Moral Minimum The minimum level of ethical behavior expected by society, which is usually defined as compliance with the law.

Mortgage A written instrument that gives a creditor an interest in, or lien on, a debtor's real property as security for a debt.

Motion for a Directed Verdict A motion for the judge to take the decision out of the hands of the jury and to direct a verdict for the party making the motion on the ground that the other party has not produced sufficient evidence to support her or his claim.

Motion for a New Trial A motion asserting that the trial was so fundamentally flawed (because of error, newly discovered evidence, prejudice, or another reason) that a new trial is necessary to prevent a miscarriage of justice.

Motion for Judgment *n.o.v.* A motion requesting the court to grant judgment in favor of the party making the motion on the ground that the jury's verdict against him or her was unreasonable and erroneous.

Motion for Judgment on the Pleadings A motion by either party to a lawsuit at the close of the pleadings requesting the court to decide the issue solely on the pleadings without proceeding to trial. The motion will be granted only if no facts are in dispute.

Motion for Summary Judgment A motion requesting the court to enter a judgment without proceeding to trial. The motion can be based on evidence outside the pleadings and will be granted only if no facts are in dispute.

Motion to Dismiss A pleading in which a defendant admits the facts as alleged by the plaintiff but asserts that the plaintiff's claim to state a cause of action has no basis in law.

Multiple Product Order An order requiring a firm that has engaged in deceptive advertising to cease and desist from false advertising in regard to all the firm's products.

Mutual Fund A specific type of investment company that continually buys or sells to investors shares of ownership in a portfolio.

N

National Law Law that pertains to a particular nation (as opposed to international law).

Natural Law The oldest school of legal thought, based on the belief that the legal system should reflect universal ("higher") moral and ethical principles that are inherent in human nature.

Necessaries Necessities required for life, such as food, shelter, clothing, and medical attention.

Negligence The failure to exercise the standard of care that a reasonable person would exercise in similar circumstances.

Negligence *Per Se* An action or failure to act in violation of a statutory requirement.

Negligent Misrepresentation A misrepresentation that occurs when a person makes a false statement of fact because he or she did not exercise reasonable care or use the skill and competence required by her or his business or profession.

Negotiable Instrument A signed writing (record) that contains an unconditional promise or order to pay an exact sum on demand or at a specified future time to a specific person or order, or to bearer.

Negotiation A process in which parties attempt to settle their dispute informally, with or without attorneys to represent them. In the context of negotiable instruments, the transfer of an instrument in such form that the transferee (the person to whom the instrument is transferred) becomes a holder.

Nominal Damages A small monetary award (often one dollar) granted to a plaintiff when no actual damage was suffered.

Nonpossessory Interest In the context of real property, an interest that involves the right to use land but not the right to possess it.

Normal Trade Relations (NTR) Status A legal trade status granted to member countries of the World Trade Organization.

Notary Public A public official authorized to attest to the authenticity of signatures.

Novation The substitution, by agreement, of a new contract for an old one, with the rights under the old one being terminated.

Nuisance A common law doctrine under which persons may be held liable for using their property in a manner that unreasonably interferes with others' rights to use or enjoy their own property.

Nuncupative Will An oral will (often called a *deathbed will*) made before witnesses. Usually, such wills are limited to transfers of personal property.

O

Objective Theory of Contracts The view that contracting parties shall only be bound by terms that can be objectively inferred from promises made.

Obligee One to whom an obligation is owed.

Obligor One who owes an obligation to another.

Offer A promise or commitment to perform or refrain from performing some specified act in the future.

Offeree A person to whom an offer is made.

Offeror A person who makes an offer.

Online Dispute Resolution (ODR) The resolution of disputes with the assistance of organizations that offer dispute-resolution services via the Internet.

Operating Agreement An agreement in which the members of a limited liability company set forth the details of how the business will be managed and operated.

Option Contract A contract under which the offeror cannot revoke the offer for a stipulated time period (because the offeree has given consideration for the offer to remain open).

Order for Relief A court's grant of assistance to a complainant. In bankruptcy proceedings, the order relieves the debtor of the immediate obligation to pay the debts listed in the bankruptcy petition.

Order Instrument A negotiable instrument that is payable "to the order of an identified person" or "to an identified person or order."

Ordinance A regulation enacted by a city or county legislative body that becomes part of that state's statutory law.

Outcome-based Ethics An ethical philosophy that focuses on the impacts of a decision on society or on key stakeholders.

Output Contract An agreement in which a seller agrees to sell and a buyer agrees to buy all or up to a stated amount of what the seller produces.

Outside Director A person on the board of directors who does not hold a management position at the corporation.

Overdraft A check that is paid by a bank when the checking account on which the check is written contains insufficient funds to cover the check.

P

Parol Evidence Rule A rule of contracts under which a court will not receive into evidence prior or contemporaneous external agreements that contradict the terms of the parties' written contract.

Partially Disclosed Principal A principal whose identity is unknown by a third party, but the third party knows that the agent is or may be acting for a principal at the time the agent and the third party form a contract.

Partnering Agreement An agreement between a seller and a buyer who frequently do business with each other concerning the terms and conditions that will apply to all subsequently formed electronic contracts.

Partnership An agreement by two or more persons to carry on, as co-owners, a business for profit.

Partnership by Estoppel A partnership imposed by a court when nonpartners have held themselves out to be partners, or have allowed themselves to be held out as partners, and others have detrimentally relied on their misrepresentations.

Pass-Through Entity A business entity that has no tax liability. The entity's income is passed through to the owners, and they pay taxes on the income.

Past Consideration An act that takes place before a contract is made and that ordinarily, by itself, cannot later be consideration with respect to that contract.

Patent A property right granted by the federal government that gives an inventor an exclusive right to make, use, sell, or offer to sell an invention in the United States for a limited time.

Payee A person to whom an instrument is made payable.

Payor Bank The bank on which a check is drawn (the drawee bank).

Peer-to-Peer (P2P) Networking The sharing of resources (such as files, hard drives, and processing styles) among multiple computers without the requirement of a central network server.

Penalty A contract clause that specifies a certain amount to be paid in the event of a default or breach of contract but is unenforceable because it is designed to punish the breaching party rather than to provide a reasonable estimate of damages.

Per Capita A method of distributing an intestate's estate so that each heir in a certain class (such as grandchildren) receives an equal share.

Per Curiam **Opinion** A court opinion that does not indicate which judge or justice authored the opinion.

Perfection The legal process by which secured parties protect themselves against the claims of third parties who may wish to have their debts satisfied out of the same collateral. It is usually accomplished by filing a financing statement with the appropriate government official.

Performance The fulfillment of one's duties under a contract—the normal way of discharging one's contractual obligations.

Periodic Tenancy A lease interest in land for an indefinite period involving payment of rent at fixed intervals, such as week to week, month to month, or year to year.

Per Se **Violation** A restraint of trade that is so anticompetitive that it is deemed inherently (*per se*) illegal.

Personal Defense A defense that can be used to avoid payment to an ordinary holder of a negotiable instrument but not a holder in due course (HDC) or a holder with the rights of an HDC.

Personal Property Property that is movable. Any property that is not real property.

Per Stirpes A method of distributing an intestate's estate so that each heir in a certain class (such as grandchildren) takes the share to which her or his deceased ancestor (such as a mother or father) would have been entitled.

Persuasive Authority Any legal authority or source of law that a court may look to for guidance but need not follow when making its decision.

Petition in Bankruptcy The document that is filed with a bankruptcy court to initiate bankruptcy proceedings.

Petty Offense The least serious kind of criminal offense, such as a traffic or building-code violation.

Phishing A form of identity theft in which the perpetrator sends e-mails purporting to be from legitimate businesses to induce recipients to reveal their personal financial data, passwords, or other information.

Piercing the Corporate Veil The action of a court to disregard the corporate entity and hold the shareholders personally liable for corporate debts and obligations.

Plaintiff One who initiates a lawsuit.

Plea Bargaining The process by which a criminal defendant and the prosecutor work out an agreement to dispose of the criminal case, subject to court approval.

Pleadings Statements by the plaintiff and the defendant that detail the facts, charges, and defenses of a case.

Pledge A security device in which personal property is transferred into the possession of the creditor as security for the payment of a debt and retained by the creditor until the debt is paid.

Plurality Opinion A court opinion that is joined by the largest number of the judges or justices hearing the case, but less than half of the total number.

Police Powers Powers possessed by the states as part of their inherent sovereignty. These powers may be exercised to protect or promote the public order, health, safety, morals, and general welfare.

Policy In insurance law, the contract between the insurer and the insured.

Potentially Responsible Party (PRP) A party liable for the costs of cleaning up a hazardous waste disposal site under the Comprehensive Environmental Response, Compensation, and Liability Act.

Power of Attorney Authorization for another to act as one's agent or attorney either in specified circumstances (special) or in all situations (general).

Precedent A court decision that furnishes an example or authority for deciding subsequent cases involving identical or similar facts.

Predatory Pricing The pricing of a product below cost with the intent to drive competitors out of the market.

Predominant-Factor Test A test courts use to determine whether a contract is primarily for the sale of goods or for the sale of services.

Preemption A doctrine under which certain federal laws preempt, or take precedence over, conflicting state or local laws.

Preemptive Rights The right of a shareholder in a corporation to have the first opportunity to purchase a new issue of that corporation's stock in proportion to the amount of stock already owned by the shareholder.

Preference In bankruptcy proceedings, a property transfer or payment made by the debtor that favors one creditor over others.

Preferred Creditor In the context of bankruptcy, a creditor who has received a preferential transfer from a debtor.

Preferred Stock Stock that has priority over common stock as to payment of dividends and distribution of assets on the corporation's dissolution.

Premium In insurance law, the price paid by the insured for insurance protection for a specified period of time.

Prenuptial Agreement An agreement made before marriage that defines each partner's ownership rights in the other partner's property. Prenuptial agreements must be in writing to be enforceable.

Prepayment Penalty Clause A mortgage provision requiring the borrower to pay a penalty if the mortgage is repaid in full within a certain period.

Presentment The act of presenting an instrument to the party liable on the instrument in order to collect payment. Presentment also occurs when a person presents an instrument to a drawee for a required acceptance.

Presentment Warranty A person who presents an instrument for payment or acceptance impliedly makes three warranties relating to good title, no alterations, and no unauthorized signatures.

Price Discrimination A seller's act of charging competing buyers different prices for identical products or services.

Price-Fixing Agreement An agreement between competitors to fix the prices of products or services at a certain level.

Prima Facie Case A case in which the plaintiff has produced sufficient evidence of his or her claim that the case will be decided for the plaintiff unless the defendant produces no evidence to rebut it.

Primary Source of Law A document that establishes the law on a particular issue, such as a constitution, a statute, an administrative rule, or a court decision.

Principle of Rights The belief that human beings have certain fundamental rights. Whether an action or decision is ethical depends on how it affects the rights of various groups, such as owners, employees, consumers, suppliers, the community, and society.

Private Equity Capital Funds invested by a private equity firm in an existing corporation, usually to purchase and reorganize it.

Privilege A special right, advantage, or immunity that enables a person or a class of persons to avoid liability for defamation.

Privity of Contract The relationship that exists between the promisor and the promisee of a contract.

Probable Cause Reasonable grounds for believing that a search should be conducted or that a person should be arrested.

Probate The process of proving and validating a will and settling all matters pertaining to an estate.

Probate Court A state court of limited jurisdiction that conducts proceedings relating to the settlement of a deceased person's estate.

Procedural Law Law that establishes the methods of enforcing the rights established by substantive law.

Proceeds Under Article 9 of the UCC, whatever is received when collateral is sold or disposed of in some other way.

Product Liability The legal liability of manufacturers, sellers, and lessors of goods for injuries or damage caused by the goods to consumers, users, or bystanders.

Profit In real property law, the right to enter onto another's property and remove something of value from that property.

Promise A declaration that binds a person who makes it (the promisor) to do or not to do a certain act.

Promisee A person to whom a promise is made.

Promisor A person who makes a promise.

Promissory Estoppel A doctrine that can be used to enforce a promise when the promisee has justifiably relied on the promise and when justice will be better served by enforcing the promise.

Promissory Note A written promise made by one person (the maker) to pay a fixed amount of funds to another person (the payee or a subsequent holder) on demand or on a specified date.

Prospectus A written document required by securities laws when a security is being sold. The prospectus describes the security, the financial operations of the issuing corporation, and the risk attaching to the security.

Protected Class A group of persons protected by specific laws because of the group's defining characteristics, including race, color, religion, national origin, gender, age, and disability.

Proximate Cause Legal cause. It exists when the connection between an act and an injury is strong enough to justify imposing liability.

Proxy When a shareholder formally authorizes another to serve as his or her agent and vote his or her shares in a certain manner.

Publicly Held Corporation A corporation whose shares are publicly traded in securities markets, such as the New York Stock Exchange or the NASDAQ.

Puffery A salesperson's exaggerated claims concerning the quality of property offered for sale. Such claims involve opinions rather than facts and are not legally binding promises or warranties.

Punitive Damages Monetary damages that may be awarded to a plaintiff to punish the defendant and deter similar conduct in the future.

Purchase-Money Security Interest (PMSI) A security interest that arises when a seller or lender extends credit for part or all of the purchase price of goods purchased by a buyer.

Q

Qualified Indorsement An indorsement on a negotiable instrument in which the indorser disclaims any contract liability on the instrument. The notation "without recourse" is commonly used to create a qualified indorsement.

Quantum Meruit A Latin phrase meaning "as much as he or she deserves." The expression describes the extent of compensation owed under a quasi contract.

Quasi Contract An obligation or contract imposed by law (a court), in the absence of an agreement, to prevent the unjust enrichment of one party.

Question of Fact In a lawsuit, an issue that involves only disputed facts, and not what the law is on a given point.

Question of Law In a lawsuit, an issue involving the application or interpretation of a law.

Quitclaim Deed A deed that conveys only whatever interest the grantor had in the property and therefore offers the least amount of protection against defects of title.

Quorum The number of members of a decision-making body that must be present before business may be transacted.

Quota A set limit on the amount of goods that can be imported.

R

Ratification The acceptance or confirmation of an act or agreement that gives legal force to an obligation that previously was not enforceable.

Reaffirmation Agreement An agreement between a debtor and a creditor in which the debtor voluntarily agrees to pay a debt dischargeable in bankruptcy.

Real Property Land and everything attached to it, such as trees and buildings.

Reasonable Person Standard The standard of behavior expected of a hypothetical "reasonable person." It is the standard against which negligence is measured and that must be observed to avoid liability for negligence.

Receiver In a corporate dissolution, a court-appointed person who winds up corporate affairs and liquidates corporate assets.

Record Information that is either inscribed on a tangible medium or stored in an electronic or other medium and is retrievable.

Recording Statute A statute that allow deeds, mortgages, and other real property transactions to be recorded so as to provide notice to future purchasers or creditors of an existing claim on the property.

Reformation A court-ordered correction of a written contract so that it reflects the true intentions of the parties.

Regulation E A set of rules issued by the Federal Reserve System's Board of Governors to protect users of electronic fund transfer systems.

Regulation Z A set of rules issued by the Federal Reserve Board of Governors to implement the provisions of the Truth-in-Lending Act.

Release An agreement in which one party gives up the right to pursue a legal claim against another party.

Remedy The relief given to an innocent party to enforce a right or compensate for the violation of a right.

Replevin An action that can be used by a buyer or lessee to recover identified goods from a third party, such as a bailee, who is wrongfully withholding them.

Reply Procedurally, a plaintiff's response to a defendant's answer.

Requirements Contract An agreement in which a buyer agrees to purchase and the seller agrees to sell all or up to a stated amount of what the buyer needs or requires.

Resale Price Maintenance Agreement An agreement between a manufacturer and a retailer in which the manufacturer specifies what the retail prices of its products must be.

Rescission A remedy whereby a contract is canceled and the parties are returned to the positions they occupied before the contract was made.

Res Ipsa Loquitur A doctrine under which negligence may be inferred simply because an event occurred, if it is the type of event that would not occur in the absence of negligence. Literally, the term means "the facts speak for themselves."

Respondeat Superior A doctrine under which a principal or an employer is held liable for the wrongful acts committed by agents or employees while acting within the course and scope of their agency or employment.

Restitution An equitable remedy under which a person is restored to his or her original position prior to loss or injury, or placed in the position he or she would have been in had the breach not occurred.

Restrictive Indorsement An indorsement on a negotiable instrument that requires the indorsee to comply with certain instructions regarding the funds involved.

Resulting Trust An implied trust that arises when one party holds the legal title to another's property only for that other's benefit.

Retained Earnings The portion of a corporation's profits that has not been paid out as dividends to shareholders.

Revocation The withdrawal of a contract offer by the offeror. Unless an offer is irrevocable, it can be revoked at any time prior to acceptance without liability.

Right of Contribution The right of a co-surety who pays more than his or her proportionate share on a debtor's default to recover the excess paid from other co-sureties.

Right of Reimbursement The right of a party to be repaid for costs, expenses, or losses incurred on behalf of another.

Right of Subrogation The right of a party to stand in the place of another, giving the substituted party the same legal rights that the original party had.

Right-to-Work Law A state law providing that employees may not be required to join a union as a condition of retaining employment.

Risk A prediction concerning potential loss based on known and unknown factors.

Risk Management In the context of insurance, the transfer of certain risks from the insured to the insurance company by contractual agreement.

Robbery The act of forcefully and unlawfully taking personal property of any value from another.

Rulemaking The process by which an administrative agency formally adopts a new regulation or amends an old one.

Rule of Four A rule of the United States Supreme Court under which the Court will not issue a writ of *certiorari* unless at least four justices approve of the decision to issue the writ.

Rule of Reason A test used to determine whether an anticompetitive agreement constitutes a reasonable restraint on trade. Courts consider such factors as the purpose of the agreement, its effect on competition, and whether less restrictive means could have been used.

S

Sale The passing of title to property from the seller to the buyer for a price.

Sales Contract A contract for the sale of goods.

Scienter Knowledge on the part of a misrepresenting party that material facts have been falsely represented or omitted with an intent to deceive.

S Corporation A close business corporation that has most corporate attributes, including limited liability, but qualifies under the Internal Revenue Code to be taxed as a partnership.

Search Warrant An order granted by a public authority, such as a judge, that authorizes law enforcement personnel to search particular premises or property.

Seasonably Within a specified time period or, if no period is specified, within a reasonable time.

Secondary Source of Law A publication that summarizes or interprets the law, such as a legal encyclopedia, a legal treatise, or an article in a law review.

SEC Rule 10b-5 A rule of the Securities and Exchange Commission that prohibits the commission of fraud in connection with the purchase or sale of any security.

Secured Party A creditor who has a security interest in the debtor's collateral, including a seller, lender, cosigner, or buyer of accounts or chattel paper.

Secured Transaction Any transaction in which the payment of a debt is guaranteed, or secured, by personal property owned by the debtor or in which the debtor has a legal interest.

Securities Generally, stocks, bonds, or other items that represent an ownership interest in a corporation or a promise of repayment of debt by a corporation.

Security Agreement An agreement that creates or provides for a security interest between the debtor and a secured party.

Security Interest Any interest in personal property or fixtures that secures payment or performance of an obligation.

Self-Defense The legally recognized privilege to do what is reasonably necessary to protect oneself, one's property, or someone else against injury by another.

Self-Incrimination Giving testimony in a trial or other legal proceeding that could expose the person testifying to criminal prosecution.

Seniority System A system in which those who have worked longest for an employer are first in line for promotions, salary increases, and other benefits, and are last to be laid off if the workforce must be reduced.

Service Mark A trademark that is used to distinguish the services (rather than the products) of one person or company from those of another.

Service of Process The delivery of the complaint and summons to a defendant.

Sexual Harassment The demanding of sexual favors in return for job promotions or other benefits, or language or conduct that is so sexually offensive that it creates a hostile working environment.

Shareholder's Derivative Suit A suit brought by a shareholder to enforce a corporate cause of action against a third person.

Shelter Principle The principle that the holder of a negotiable instrument who cannot qualify as a holder in due course (HDC), but who derives his or her title through an HDC, acquires the rights of an HDC.

Shipment Contract A contract for the sale of goods in which the seller is required or authorized to ship the goods by carrier. The seller assumes liability for any losses or damage to the goods until they are delivered to the carrier.

Short Sale A sale of mortgaged property for less than the balance due on the mortgage loan.

Short-Swing Profits Profits earned by a purchase and sale, or sale and purchase, of the same security within a six-month period.

Shrink-Wrap Agreement An agreement whose terms are expressed in a document located inside a box in which goods (usually software) are packaged.

Slander Defamation in oral form.

Slander of Quality (Trade Libel) The publication of false information about another's product, alleging that it is not what its seller claims.

Slander of Title The publication of a statement that denies or casts doubt on another's legal ownership of property, causing financial loss to that property's owner.

Small Claims Court A special court in which parties can litigate small claims without an attorney.

Smart Card A card containing a microprocessor and typically used for financial transactions, personal identification, and other purposes.

Social Media Forms of communication through which users create and share information, ideas, messages, and other content via the Internet.

Sole Proprietorship The simplest form of business organization, in which the owner is the business. The owner reports business income on his or her personal income tax return and is legally responsible for all debts and obligations incurred by the business.

Sovereign Immunity A doctrine that immunizes foreign nations from the jurisdiction of U.S. courts when certain conditions are satisfied.

Spam Bulk, unsolicited (junk) e-mail.

Special Damages In a tort case, an amount awarded to compensate the plaintiff for quantifiable monetary losses, such as medical expenses, property damage, and lost wages and benefits (now and in the future).

Special Indorsement An indorsement on an instrument that identifies the specific person to whom the indorser intends to make the instrument payable.

Special Warranty Deed A deed that warrants only that the grantor held good title during his or her ownership of the property and does not warrant that there were no defects of title when the property was held by previous owners.

Specific Performance An equitable remedy in which a court orders the parties to perform as promised in the contract. This remedy normally is granted only when the legal remedy (monetary damages) is inadequate.

Spendthrift Trust A trust created to protect the beneficiary from spending all the funds to which she or he is entitled. Only a certain portion of the total amount is given to the beneficiary at any one time, and most states prohibit creditors from attaching assets of the trust.

Stakeholders Groups that are affected by corporate decisions. Stakeholders include employees, customers, creditors, suppliers, and the community in which the corporation operates.

Stale Check A check, other than a certified check, that is presented for payment more than six months after its date.

Standing to Sue The legal requirement that an individual must have a sufficient stake in a controversy before he or she can bring a lawsuit.

Stare Decisis A common law doctrine under which judges are obligated to follow the precedents established in prior decisions.

Statute of Frauds A state statute that requires certain types of contracts to be in writing to be enforceable.

Statute of Repose A statute that places outer time limits on product liability actions. Such statutes cut off absolutely the right to bring an action after a specified period of time following some event (often the product's manufacture or purchase) other than the occurrence of an injury.

Statutory Law The body of law enacted by legislative bodies (as opposed to constitutional law, administrative law, or case law).

Statutory Right of Redemption A right provided by statute in some states under which mortgagors can redeem or purchase their property after a judicial foreclosure for a limited time period, such as one year.

Stock An ownership (equity) interest in a corporation, measured in units of shares.

Stock Certificate A certificate issued by a corporation evidencing the ownership of a specified number of shares in the corporation.

Stock Option A right to buy a given number of shares of stock at a set price, usually within a specified time period.

Stop-Payment Order An order by a bank customer to his or her bank not to pay or certify a certain check.

Stored-Value Card A card bearing a magnetic strip that holds magnetically encoded data providing access to stored funds.

Strict Liability Liability regardless of fault, which is imposed on those engaged in abnormally dangerous activities, on persons who keep dangerous animals, and on manufacturers or sellers that introduce into commerce defective and unreasonably dangerous goods.

Strike An action undertaken by unionized workers when collective bargaining fails. The workers leave their jobs, refuse to work, and (typically) picket the employer's workplace.

Sublease A tenant's transfer of all or part of the leased premises to a third person for a period shorter than the lease term.

Substantive Law Law that defines, describes, regulates, and creates legal rights and obligations.

Summary Jury Trial (SJT) A method of settling disputes by holding a trial in which the jury's verdict is not binding but instead guides the parties toward reaching an agreement during the mandatory negotiations that immediately follow.

Summons A document informing a defendant that a legal action has been commenced against her or him and that the defendant must appear in court on a certain date to answer the plaintiff's complaint.

Supremacy Clause The provision in Article VI of the U.S. Constitution that the Constitution, laws, and treaties of the United States are "the supreme Law of the Land."

Surety A third party who promises to be responsible for a debtor's obligation under a suretyship arrangement.

Suretyship A promise made by a third party to be responsible for a debtor's obligation.

Symbolic Speech Nonverbal expressions of beliefs. Symbolic speech, which includes gestures, movements, and articles of clothing, is given substantial protection by the courts.

Syndicate A group of individuals or firms that join together to finance a project. A syndicate is also called an *investment group*.

T

Taking The taking of private property by the government for public use through the power of eminent domain.

Tangible Employment Action A significant change in employment status or benefits, such as occurs when an employee is fired, refused a promotion, or reassigned to a lesser position.

Tangible Property Property that has physical existence and can be distinguished by the senses of touch and sight.

Tariff A tax on imported goods.

Tenancy at Sufferance A tenancy that arises when a tenant wrongfully continues to occupy leased property after the lease has terminated.

Tenancy at Will A type of tenancy that either the landlord or the tenant can terminate without notice.

Tenancy by the Entirety Joint ownership of property by a married couple in which neither spouse can transfer his or her interest in the property without the consent of the other.

Tenancy in Common Joint ownership of property in which each party owns an undivided interest that passes to his or her heirs at death.

Tender An unconditional offer to perform an obligation by a person who is ready, willing, and able to do so.

Tender of Delivery A seller's or lessor's act of placing conforming goods at the disposal of the buyer or lessee and providing whatever notification is reasonably necessary to enable the buyer or lessee to take delivery.

Testamentary Trust A trust that is created by will and therefore does not take effect until the death of the testator.

Testate Having left a will at death.

Testator One who makes and executes a will.

Third Party Beneficiary One who is not a party to the contract but who stands to benefit from the contract's performance.

Tippee A person who receives inside information.

Tolling Temporary suspension of the running of a prescribed time period, such as a statute of limitations.

Tort A wrongful act (other than a breach of contract) that results in harm or injury to another and leads to civil liability.

Tortfeasor One who commits a tort.

Totten Trust A trust created when a person deposits funds in his or her own name for a specific beneficiary, who will receive the funds on the depositor's death. The trust is revocable at will until the depositor dies or completes the gift.

Toxic Tort A civil wrong arising from exposure to a toxic substance, such as asbestos, radiation, or hazardous waste.

Trade Dress The image and overall appearance of a product.

Trademark A distinctive word, symbol, or design that identifies the manufacturer as the source of particular goods and distinguishes its products from those made or sold by others.

Trademark Dilution The unauthorized use of a distinctive and famous mark in a way that impairs the mark's distinctiveness or harms its reputation.

Trade Name A name that a business uses to identify itself and its brand. A trade name is directly related to a business's reputation and goodwill and is protected under trademark law.

Trade Secret A formula, device, idea, process, or other information used in a business that gives the owner a competitive advantage in the marketplace.

Transferred Intent A legal principle under which a person who intends to harm one individual, but unintentionally harms a different individual, can be liable to the second victim for an intentional tort.

Transfer Warranty A person who transfers an instrument for consideration impliedly makes five warranties—relating to good title, authentic signatures, no alterations, defenses, or insolvencies—to all subsequent transferees.

Traveler's Check A check that is payable on demand, drawn on or payable through a financial institution, and designated as a traveler's check.

Treaty A formal international agreement negotiated between two nations or among several nations.

Treble Damages Damages that, by statute, are three times the amount of actual damages suffered.

Trespass to Land Entry onto, above, or below the surface of land owned by another without the owner's permission or legal authorization.

Trespass to Personal Property Wrongfully taking or harming the personal property of another or otherwise interfering with the lawful owner's possession of personal property.

Triple Bottom Line A measure that includes a corporation's profits, its impact on people, and its impact on the planet.

Trust An arrangement in which title to property is held by one person (a trustee) for the benefit of another (a beneficiary).

Trust Indorsement An indorsement to a person who is to hold or use funds for the benefit of the indorser or a third person. It is also known as an *agency indorsement*.

Tying Arrangement A seller's act of conditioning the sale of a product or service on the buyer's agreement to purchase another product or service from the seller.

Typosquatting A form of cybersquatting that relies on mistakes, such as typographical errors, made by Internet users when inputting information into a Web browser.

U

Ultra Vires **Acts** Acts of a corporation that are beyond its express and implied powers to undertake (the Latin phrase means "beyond the powers").

Unconscionable (Contract or Clause) A contract or clause that is void on the basis of public policy because one party was forced to accept terms that are unfairly burdensome and that unfairly benefit the other party.

Underwriter In insurance law, the insurer, or the one assuming a risk in return for the payment of a premium.

Undisclosed Principal A principal whose identity is unknown by a third party, and that person has no knowledge that the agent is acting for a principal at the time the agent and the third party form a contract.

Undue Influence Persuasion that is less than actual force but more than advice and that induces a person to act according to the will or purposes of the dominating party.

Unenforceable Contract A valid contract rendered unenforceable by some statute or law.

Uniform Law A model law developed by the National Conference of Commissioners on Uniform State Laws for the states to consider enacting into statute.

Unilateral Contract A type of contract that results when an offer can be accepted only by the offeree's performance.

Unilateral Mistake A mistake that occurs when one party to a contract is mistaken as to a material fact.

Union Shop A firm that requires all workers, once employed, to become union members within a specified period of time as a condition of their continued employment.

Universal Defense A defense that can be used to avoid payment to all holders of a negotiable instrument, including a holder in due course (HDC) or a holder with the rights of an HDC. Also called a *real defense*.

Unliquidated Debt A debt that is uncertain in amount.

Unreasonably Dangerous Product A product that is so defective that it is dangerous beyond the expectation of an ordinary consumer or a product for which a less dangerous alternative was feasible but the manufacturer failed to produce it.

Usage of Trade Any practice or method of dealing that is so regularly observed in a place, vocation, or trade that parties justifiably expect it will be observed in their transaction.

Usury Charging an illegal rate of interest.

Utilitarianism An approach to ethical reasoning in which an action is evaluated in terms of its consequences for those whom it will affect. A "good" action is one that results in the greatest good for the greatest number of people.

V

Valid Contract A contract that results when the elements necessary for contract formation (agreement, consideration, capacity, and legality) are present.

Venture Capital Financing provided by professional, outside investors (venture capitalists) to new business ventures.

Venue The geographic district in which a legal action is tried and from which the jury is selected.

Vertically Integrated Firm A firm that carries out two or more functional phases (manufacturing, distribution, and retailing, for example) of the chain of production.

Vertical Merger The acquisition by a company at one stage of production of a company at a higher or lower stage of production (such as a company merging with one of its suppliers or retailers).

Vertical Restraint A restraint of trade created by an agreement between firms at different levels in the manufacturing and distribution process.

Vesting The creation of an absolute or unconditional right or power.

Vicarious Liability Indirect liability imposed on a supervisory party (such as an employer) for the actions of a subordinate (such as an employee) because of the relationship between the two parties.

Virus A software program that can replicate itself over a network and spread from one device to another, altering files and interfering with normal operations.

Voidable Contract A contract that may be legally avoided at the option of one or both of the parties.

Void Contract A contract having no legal force or binding effect.

Voir Dire An important part of the jury selection process in which the attorneys question prospective jurors about their backgrounds, attitudes, and biases to ascertain whether they can be impartial jurors.

W

Warranty Deed A deed that provides the greatest amount of protection for the grantee. The grantor promises that she or he has title to the property conveyed in the deed, that there are no undisclosed encumbrances on the property, and that the grantee will enjoy quiet possession of the property.

Waste The use of real property in a manner that damages or destroys its value.

Whistleblowing An employee's disclosure to government authorities, upper-level managers, or the media that the employer is engaged in unsafe or illegal activities.

White-Collar Crime Nonviolent crime committed by individuals or corporations to obtain a personal or business advantage.

Will An instrument made by a testator directing what is to be done with her or his property after death.

Will Substitutes Various instruments, such as living trusts and life insurance plans, that may be used to avoid the formal probate process.

Winding Up The second of two stages in the termination of a partnership or corporation, in which the firm's assets are collected, liquidated, and distributed, and liabilities are discharged.

Workers' Compensation Laws State statutes that establish an administrative process for compensating workers for injuries that arise in the course of their employment, regardless of fault.

Working Papers The documents used and developed by an accountant during an audit, such as notes, computations, and memoranda.

Workout Agreement A contract that describes the respective rights and responsibilities of a borrower and a lender as they try to resolve the borrower's default.

Worm A software program that automatically replicates itself over a network but does not alter files and is usually invisible to the user until it has consumed system resources.

Writ of Attachment A court order to seize a debtor's nonexempt property prior to a court's final determination of a creditor's rights to the property.

Writ of *Certiorari* A writ from a higher court asking a lower court for the record of a case.

Writ of Execution A court order directing the sheriff to seize (levy) and sell a debtor's nonexempt real or personal property to satisfy a court's judgment in the creditor's favor.

Wrongful Discharge An employer's termination of an employee's employment in violation of the law or an employment contract.

Table of Cases

For your convenience and reference, here is a list of all the cases mentioned in this text, including those within the footnotes, features, and case problems. The summarized cases in the chapters of this text are given special emphasis by having their titles appear in **boldface**.

Index